IN · THE
MIND'S
EYE

IN · THE
MIND'S
EYE

CREATIVE VISUAL THINKERS, GIFTED DYSLEXICS, AND THE RISE OF VISUAL TECHNOLOGIES

THOMAS G. WEST

Prometheus Books

Guilford, Connecticut

Prometheus Books

An imprint of The Rowman & Littlefield Publishing Group, Inc.
4501 Forbes Blvd., Ste. 200
Lanham, MD 20706
www.rowman.com

Distributed by NATIONAL BOOK NETWORK

British Library Cataloguing in Publication Information Available

Library of Congress Cataloging-in-Publication Data

West, Thomas G. 1943–
    In the mind's eye: creative visual thinkers, gifted dyslexics, and the rise of visual technologies / by Thomas G. West. — Second edition.
        p. cm.
    Includes bibliographical references and index.
    ISBN 978-1-59102-700-3 (cloth : alk. paper)
    ISBN 978-1-63388-642-1 (pbk. : alk. paper)
    1. Genius. 2. Imagery (Psychology). 3. Creative ability. 4. Learning disabilities. 5. Trait intercorrelations. 6. Gifted persons—Case studies. 7. Computer graphics—Psychological aspects. 8. Neuropsychology. I. Title.
    HB501.B636 2009
    330.12'2—dc22

                                                                            2009024994

∞™ The paper used in this publication meets the minimum requirements of American National Standard for Information Sciences—Permanence of Paper for Printed Library Materials, ANSI/NISO Z39.48-1992

In memory of

A NNE W ARNER W EST

who taught by example
that we must always
follow our talents

CONTENTS

8 CONTENTS

Faraday, in his mind's eye, saw lines of force traversing all space where the mathematicians saw centres of force attracting at a distance: Faraday saw a medium where they saw nothing but distance: Faraday sought the seat of the phenomena in real actions going on in the medium, they were satisfied that they had found it in a power of action at a distance impressed on the electric fluids.

—James Clerk Maxwell, *A Treatise on Electricity and Magnetism*

In examining the influences of gravitation on light, he declared, making another breach in Newtonian physics, that a light ray undergoes a deviation in proportion to the gravitation, so that it acquires the shape of a parabola. He wrote this from his desk—perhaps he looked up at an exceptionally bright night sky as he did so, perhaps his eyes remained fixed on his paper, but it wouldn't have mattered: there was a picture of the star studded sky in his mind's eye. By thought alone . . . he established the laws that govern this inaccessible world.

—Antonina Vallentin, *The Drama of Albert Einstein*

We think that the same mind's eye that can justly survey and appraise and prescribe beforehand the values of a truly great picture in one all-embracing regard, in one flash of simultaneous and homogeneous comprehension, would also . . . be able to pronounce with sureness upon any other high activity of the human intellect.

—Winston Churchill, "Painting as a Pastime,"
in *Thoughts and Adventures*

In the mind's eye, a fractal is a way of seeing infinity.
—James Gleick, *Chaos: Making a New Science*

FOREWORD TO THE SECOND EDITION
Oliver Sacks, M.D.

Although, as a neurologist, I sometimes see cases of alexia—the loss of a previously existing ability to read, usually caused by a stroke in the visual areas of the brain—congenital difficulties in reading, dyslexias, are not something I often encounter, especially with a mostly geriatric practice such as my own. Thus I have been particularly fascinated—sometimes astonished—by the wide range of considerations that Thomas G. West has brought together in this seminal investigation of dyslexia, *In the Mind's Eye.*

People with dyslexia are often regarded as defective, as missing something—a facility in reading or linguistic thinking—which the rest of us have. But those of us who are predominantly verbal or "lexical" thinkers could just as well be thought of as "avisuals." There may indeed be a sort of reciprocity between lexical and visual powers, and West makes a convincing argument that a substantial section of the population, often highly intelligent, may combine reading problems with heightened visual powers, and are often adept at compensating for their problems in one way or another—even though they may suffer greatly at school, where so much is based on reading. Some of our greatest scientists and artists would probably be diagnosed today as dyslexic, as West shows in his profiles of Einstein, Edison, da Vinci, Yeats, and others. West himself is dyslexic—this, no doubt, has strongly influenced his life and research interests, but it also gives him a uniquely sympathetic understanding of dyslexia from the inside as well as the outside.

My own experience seems to be in the opposite camp—I learned to read very early, and my own thinking is largely in terms of concepts and words. I am rather deficient in visual imagery, and have a great deal of difficulty recognizing places and even people. When I met Temple Grandin, the autistic animal psychologist who is clearly a visual thinker (one of her books is titled *Thinking in Pictures*), she was taken aback when I said I could hardly visualize anything: "How *do* you think?" she asked. Grandin herself has very heightened spatial and visual imagination, and thinks in very concrete images.

The idea of compensation for various neurological "deficits" is well supported by neuroscientific studies, which have shown, for instance, that people blind from birth have heightened tactile, auditory, and musical powers, or that congenitally deaf people who use sign language have heightened visual and spatial capacities, and perhaps a special attunement to facial expression. People with dyslexia, similarly, may develop various strategies to compensate for difficulties in reading. They are often very highly skilled at auditory comprehension or memorization, at pattern recognition, complex spatial reasoning, or visual imagination. Such visual thinkers, indeed, may be especially gifted and vital to many fields; among them may well be the next generation of creative geniuses in computer modeling and graphics.

In the Mind's Eye brings out not only the special problems of people with dyslexia but also their strengths, which are so often overlooked. Its accent is not so much on pathology as on how much human minds vary. It stands alongside Howard Gardner's *Frames of Mind* as a testament to the range of human talent and possibility.

PREFACE TO THE SECOND EDITION

With this second edition of *In the Mind's Eye*, I continue to be amazed and somewhat puzzled at the staying power of this book. When I started this project, I really did not know where it would lead, but I did feel strongly that there was a story to be told and a point of view to be explained that were not being provided by others. It is a source of considerable gratification that readers (and listeners) have responded to my story and perspective over these many years. Indeed, I feel privileged to be in a position to have provided something that seems to be of special interest and value to so many. However, I suspect that mainly I had chanced upon a topic, or set of interrelated topics, whose time had come. As our technology, economy, and society are transformed at ever greater rates, while our institutions hold fast ever more tightly to outmoded ideas, perhaps it is time for some really fresh thinking—especially from a quarter where it might have been least expected. The old measurement scales do not quite fit anymore, as some have long suspected, in spite of what they had been taught to believe. And many have suffered for no good reason as a consequence.

I am especially pleased that this edition includes a foreword from Dr. Oliver Sacks, who has done so much to help a wide audience understand the diversity of human experience and how even things that seem only to be problems can confer unexpected advantages and offer deep insights. Dr. Sacks's observations are all the more supportive since, as he himself notes, he comes from the nonvisual or "avisual" camp, being among those who think more readily in words than images. I hope that his interest will help to build a wider audience for these stories and perspectives.

Over the years, it has become increasingly clear that conventional academic measures and practices have been built on an enormously constricted conception of human intelligence and capability. Our ancestors, with little or no higher education, were quite capable of great accomplishments in technological innovation, entrepreneurial business, political practicality, and scientific discovery. There is no reason other than habit, really, to link intelligence with book learning alone.

There has been much talk and writing about the modern "knowledge" society or economy. However, I would argue that there always had to be high levels of specialist knowledge, but in the distant past this specialist knowledge came mostly from learning by doing and observing rather than from the reading and memorizing that is so often the case with us today. It is a remarkable irony that those who have had the greatest difficulties with bookish technologies seem to be those now best suited to lead the larger population back once again to a world of vision and thoughtful observation—one that is consistent with both the old hands-on ways of learning and the newest computer information visualization modes of learning and understanding.

We now seem to be at the edge of a new era when real diversity can be properly appreciated and usefully employed—if we can teach ourselves that there are forms of smartness that have little to do with school grades or test scores. Both da Vinci and Galileo encountered steep resistance to their use of the newest technologies and their own powers of careful observation, as opposed to quoting classical texts as was done by the scholars, schoolmen, and professors of their day. Since many of our institutions today are run by those who had the best grades and highest test scores, it may be that we are much closer to these ancient practices than we might think. Accordingly, it may be all the more important that the visual thinkers and dyslexic visionaries seem now to be in the ascendancy, ready to use the newest technologies of their era to regain a genuine new rebirth of learning and understanding—a new renaissance, perhaps, based on visual thinkers, dyslexic visionaries, and new visual, "fat pipe" technologies.

Although this is a second edition, remarkably few changes have been necessary in the main text. We have corrected the errors that inevitably turn up. But mostly I have found, to my surprise and delight, that the text does not date quickly. This doubtless shows the advantage of dealing with a lot of historical information via primary sources and discussing technical issues on a fairly high level of generality. The details may change, but the main ideas, concepts, and trends endure—that is, if you are basically on the right track. Of course, it is also a big help to choose intellectual mentors whose work has been shown to be consistently ahead of their times. For this, Dr. Norman Geschwind and Dr. Samuel Torrey Orton are well placed. Not all their speculations and hypotheses have been supported over time. But the general trend of their thought has stood the test of time remarkably well. Needless to say, most of the individuals profiled in the book, famous and not so famous, continue to hold our interest because their accomplishments seem unusual in their persistent value.

For a book that is already seen as too long by some—especially for those in my readership who do not take lightly to reading any book—I have chosen to provide an epilogue which is suggestive rather than comprehensive. It deals with aspects that I find personally interesting—snapshots of some recent developments—rather than those things that may be regarded as most important by specialists in one group or another. Over the past few years, so much has been learned in these fields—from computer science to neuroscience to giftedness to learning difficulties—that it would take another book or two to provide a proper survey. The same approach has been used for the updated bibliography and sources of information. The intention has been to give a sampling of newer items and classics (including films and DVDs) not listed previously that can serve as starting points for those who want to learn more about the diverse topics that fan out in many directions. I believe this approach is especially appropriate in an era when Web sites on the Internet have rapidly become the preferred way of posting and gaining information on virtually any topic. Also, I have attempted to provide a mix of references that would not likely turn up in conventional searches.

I have used the epilogue to briefly introduce to a wider audience materials that have been used previously in different forms in a mix of talks, articles, chapters, and columns for various groups and diverse publications—dealing with a range of topics from visual literacy, computer graphics, and information visualization to creativity, giftedness, and learning difficulties to innovation in business, education, and scientific research. I have hoped to carry forward in a slightly more enduring form some of the more interesting materials and observations that have previously been presented to diverse audiences.

The way *In the Mind's Eye* has been received may justify its somewhat unusual approach. The book was written in the assumption that sometimes a broader view can be taken in the hope that we will make up in a clearer perspective on larger patterns what we necessarily lose in detail at lower levels. As in the short film *Powers of Ten* and the Imax film *Cosmic Voyage*, patterns and varieties of structures emerge and disappear as we shift through level upon level of magnitude—zooming in for a close view, then backing off farther and farther away.

I hope it will suffice that the basic ideas are set forth in ordinary language and illustrated in a number of stories without extensive elaboration. I also hope that it will continue to appeal to a diverse general audience, including some who are not particularly fond of reading long books. With this in mind, this book has been organized in a kind of treelike structure: the first chapter contains most of the main ideas and arguments, while the subsequent chapters branch out in various directions from these main ideas, amplifying, reiterating, and further illustrating different aspects, while new related ideas are also introduced. Thus, once the main ideas are presented in the initial overview chapter, the subsequent chapters are intended to be read (or skipped over) in any desired order. (In recent years, I have suggested that some readers—especially dyslexic readers—go immediately to the stories and profiles in the middle of the book where the main ideas arise naturally out of the life experiences described. Then I suggest, perhaps, they read on through the last chapters—before coming back to the initial overview chapter as a summary in large.)

Many of us have been trained to take a limited subject and give it exhaustive treatment. In this book, I have taken the opposite strategy—giving a brief tour of a large territory, hoping that less detailed information will have a greater clarity and impact—hoping that readers will be sufficiently interested to look further elsewhere and to reconsider their own personal experience from this new perspective. Some readers will doubtless find in these pages a vindication of ideas they have long held, although they are aware that these ideas run counter to conventional belief. Others will find some of the basic ideas familiar but may be surprised at where their fuller development leads. Still others may find a fresh new way of looking at their world.

This book is intended to be a short tour of a large area. It is meant to provide a view of the whole, like a remote, unmapped archipelago made up of dots too small to be seen from a great height. Some investigations of depth here and there will show the richness of possibility, but most will be left for later discovery. As from the air, we will view the graceful curve of an island chain, green lands surrounded by white reefs, the rolling surf, the bright beaches, the lush green of the volcanic mountain sides, and the misty valleys. From time to time we will stop to look at the shape of a tree, or taste a fruit, or watch a bird pecking for tiny seeds, or see an insect racing across our path, or we will dive into the calm lagoon to see the flashing fish among the shallow reefs.

Much will be seen, yet we will hardly be able to suggest the vastness beneath that awaits our search—the massive undersea mountains that lie below, whose weathered peaks are our fragile sunlit islands; or the varieties of creatures, great and small, who teem in the dark ocean space between these darker masses; or the fiery furnaces that lie asleep within for which these great mountains are merely capricious periodic ventings; or the much vaster world beneath, with slow flowing magma, to which these tall mountains and deep oceans are but a thin film of surface skin.

Thomas G. West
Washington, D.C.
March 2009

PREFACE TO THE
FIRST EDITION

Several years ago, I was intrigued to learn that some neurologists were coming to believe that certain forms of early brain growth have beneficial effects at the same time that they produce notable difficulties in brain function. As I had considered the lives of a number of especially creative historical persons, I was impressed by the frequency with which they had curious deficiencies mixed with the more obvious gifts and special talents. I thought it was worth looking into these connections a little deeper in light of this new research to see what could be learned.

In addition, I had long thought that there was a different way of looking at these things, one that was not receiving appropriate consideration. I knew that some people have a strong tendency to convert almost everything into pictures in their minds, and felt that this propensity had greater significance than was usually appreciated. I was gratified to find ample evidence of this tendency and its great power in the extraordinarily creative persons profiled here.

While carrying out this research I began, tangentially, to consider the possible implications of this perspective in connection with several recent technological and scientific developments. Some new technologies, such as increasingly powerful and inexpensive personal computers, are making the usual problem areas less and less important.

Common areas of weakness, such as spelling and calculation, can now be dealt with easily by these machines.

In a marvelous coincidence of historical change new opportunities are currently unfolding that may require special talents and abilities in just those areas where many individuals with learning difficulties often have their greatest strengths, such as in the visualization of scientific concepts and the analysis and manipulation of complex, three-dimensional information graphically displayed on these same personal computers (or more powerful personal workstations). As these new opportunities continue to unfold, it is not hard to imagine that skill with the manipulation of images may become more important, in some unexpected areas, than skill with words and numbers.

It is possible, therefore, that conditions are reversing themselves in a way that is especially favorable to some who are strong visual thinkers but who may have had serious difficulties in conventional academic settings. With further technological development, we may see striking new opportunities for these creative, visual-thinking persons. We may soon see them crossing over from the arts, their traditional stronghold, to the scientific and technical fields that have long been largely closed to them. We are accustomed to hearing of mathematicians, scientists, and computer programmers who are also talented musicians. Perhaps in the future we might see the solution of difficult problems in statistics, molecular biology, materials development, or higher mathematics coming from people who are graphic artists, sculptors, craftsmen, film makers, or designers of animated computer graphics. Different kinds of problems and different kinds of tools may require different talents and favor different kinds of brains.

Thomas G. West
Washington, D.C.

1

SLOW WORDS, QUICK IMAGES

An Overview

In the summer of 1841 Michael Faraday, the self-educated black-smith's son who came to be recognized as one of the leading scientific minds of Queen Victoria's Britain, was on holiday in Switzerland. He had journeyed from Interlaken to the falls of the Giessbach, on the lake of Brientz. As he watched the cataract shoot down a series of precipices, Faraday noted his impressions in his journal. At the base of each cataract, the water was shattered into foam and then tossed into "water-dust" in the air.

> August 12th, 1841.—To-day every fall was foaming from the abundance of water, and the current of wind brought down by it was in some places too strong to stand against. The sun shone brightly, and rainbows seen from various points were very beautiful. One at the bottom of a fine but furious fall was very pleasant,—there it remained motionless, whilst the gusts and clouds of spray swept furiously across its place and were dashed against the rock. It looked like a spirit strong in faith and steadfast in the midst of the storm of passions sweeping across it, and though it might fade and revive, still it held on to the rock as in hope and giving hope. And the very drops, which in the whirlwind of their fury seemed as if they would carry all away, were made to revive it and give it greater beauty.[1]

These were brief notes jotted down by Faraday in his personal journal on an afternoon's excursion during a restful summer holiday. Faraday had no serious intent. He wrote for himself and perhaps a friend or two. It was a habit of journal-keeping developed to provide detailed records of his extensive experiments and to compensate for an especially unreliable memory.

Yet these few lines provide us with a small window into the mind and way of seeing of a great and curious visual thinker who lies close to the center of the story that will unfold in the chapters that follow. In Faraday's description, the major image is the rainbow, a form that, while brilliant and strikingly beautiful, is not really there. A form without substance, it consists of the refracted light bouncing off the tiny water droplets, perceived in a broad, arcing pattern. But the pattern is formed by the light and the perspective of the observer—for there is no pattern, no arc, no rainbow, in the random motion of the droplets that fill the space. Without the light and the observer, the pattern is not there. Yet, it is a stable and enduring form that moves as the observer moves, strangely seeming to draw strength from the ferocity of the spray from which it is made and which allows it to be seen.

It is this paradox to which Faraday draws our attention. The more wild and furious the spray, the more bright and clear and well-defined and beautiful is the form that is seen. It is the wildness and the chaotic confusion that provide the clearest image of the form and at the same time teach us seemingly contradictory things—that our clear view of the form relies upon the fury and the wildness—and that a form without substance can be strong, steadfast, and enduring. When the fury and wildness are gone, the clear image of the form disappears as well. Yet the more the fury and the wildness threaten to tear the form to pieces, the stronger the form becomes and the more brightly it shows forth, "steadfast in the midst of the storm . . . as in hope."

Faraday was one of the greatest scientists of his age, perhaps of any age, yet this description and the mode of thought it shows is more like that of a poet. As in the best poetry, the simple metaphorical image illuminates, in a fresh way, a larger and apparently unrelated truth. Whether in the countryside or the laboratory, Faraday used his unusually powerful visual imagination to take the stuff of experience and experiment and form fresh, original models of reality in his mind, in his mind's eye—unconcerned that these models did not correspond to any of the accepted scientific ideas of his day. Yet it is just these same models of reality—especially the idea of the electromagnetic field—that provided the essential basis for the later theories of James Clerk Maxwell and Albert Einstein.

One of the central perspectives of this book is that a powerful visual imagination such as Faraday's seems sometimes to come at a cost. Sometimes (but not always) great proficiencies in some areas can involve surprising and unexpected deficiencies in other areas. This is not seen as a cruel trick of fate, but rather a basic quality of design: what is optimized (deliberately or inadvertently) for one function may involve fundamental elements that make it unsuited for another function; a special proficiency in one area sometimes involves a corresponding deficiency in some other area.

It is the intent of this book to indicate something of what is being learned of how this process works and to indicate what an understanding of this process can mean for the way we view ourselves and those around us.

The story we will be telling provides evidence that, historically, some of the most original thinkers in fields ranging from physical science and mathematics to politics and poetry have relied heavily on visual modes of thought. Some of these same thinkers, however, have shown evidence of a striking range of difficulties in their early schooling, including problems with reading, speaking, spelling, calculation, and memory. Irony and paradox are recurring elements of the general pattern. For example, even those who are known for their great verbal gifts may have surprising difficulties in certain specific verbal skills. Those known for their talents at higher mathematics may have curious difficulties with simple arithmetic.

Recently, studies of the microscopic structure of the brain and of early neurological growth patterns have provided the beginnings of solid evidence for a view of the brain different from that which has long been accepted. It is a view that emphasizes the great diversity of brain structure and capability rather than its presumed "blank slate" homogeneity. From this new perspective, it is becoming apparent that early growth processes can sometimes produce substantial diversity among different brains and that this diversity frequently has great benefit for the larger society over time, promoting forms and magnitudes of creativity and originality that might not otherwise have been possible. Those who learn with great difficulty in one setting may learn with surprising ease in another.

This fresh perspective suggests that we should be more concerned with results than with trying to get everyone to learn things in the same way, especially if we are more interested in creating new knowledge than in merely absorbing and passing on old knowledge. In some cases, the conventional educational system may eliminate many of those who have the greatest high-level talents, especially when these talents are predominantly visual rather than verbal.

The unfortunate losses occur because of wide-spread misconceptions about what visual talents are capable of doing and where they are required. Teachers and professionals at all levels understand, of course, that visual talents are important for the visual arts, graphic design, architecture, photography, film-making, and the like. But few of those who are teaching the basic courses or designing the basic tests may fully appreciate that these same visual and spatial talents are, in some important cases, indispensable for the highest levels of original work in certain areas of science, engineering, medicine, and mathematics—even in areas not usually thought to be highly visual. Consequently, some of those with the highest visual talents—those who may have the best opportunity to produce really original work in certain areas—may be barred from just those areas where they might otherwise have made the greatest contributions.

This view may seem improbable until we look closely at the early experience of some of those profiled here. Then, we can see how close some came to being eliminated themselves. Then, we may imagine how many others, with similar patterns of mixed talents and academic difficulties, were successfully eliminated and were never able to find a way to make their contribution.

Some people are so deeply accustomed to a linear view of intelligence and potential that they find it almost impossible to believe that certain persons may find advanced subject matter quite easy while they find some elementary subject matter quite difficult. Yet, among some of the most brilliant and creative minds, this general pattern is precisely what we do find. It is hoped that a better understanding of this paradoxical pattern of mixed capabilities would lead to better development and use of a wide range of special talents throughout the population. Indeed, it is becoming increasingly evident that the ability to recognize and accommodate this pattern of mixed capabilities may come to be especially important for future changes in education and work.

In the near future, creative visual thinkers with some learning difficulties might very well find themselves far better adapted to certain fundamental changes. They may have had difficulty memorizing formulas and learning the mechanical operations of mathematics, but as computer visualization techniques are increasingly employed to analyze vast and complex systems they may find themselves far better adapted to seeing new patterns than those with greater academic skills but weaker visual capabilities.

They may have had difficulty learning from books and lectures, but with future changes they may find themselves far better adapted to learning from simulations of reality as education and testing programs begin to emphasize interactive computer simulation over the verbal description of reality traditionally provided in books and lectures.

And, as an essential element in the ironic pattern, for these people it may be easier to create new knowledge than to learn and retain old knowledge. For these people, it is sometimes far easier to learn firsthand from nature than it is to learn secondhand from books.

The creative process is a continuing mystery. In our technological culture, this process is almost universally acknowledged as the source of all we are most proud of in science, technology, and art, yet a satisfactory explanation of the process has remained elusive. While an extensive body of literature on creativity has been produced over the years, only comparatively recently have new insights been brought together, from a wide variety of sources, that seem to provide an increasingly coherent picture of the process and its modes of operation.[2]

One of the fertile sources of new insights into the creative process seems now to be the growing body of research defining the modes of thought generally believed to be associated with the two hemispheres of the brain. Many are now familiar with the experiments of R.W. Sperry and others in the 1950s and 1960s. These studies indicated that, in general, the right and left hemispheres are relatively specialized in their functions, operating in two different but complementary modes. The greatly oversimplified versions of Sperry's work that passed rapidly into popular culture during the 1970s and early 1980s created a loose shorthand in popular psychology that has led to the superficial categorization of "right-brained" people and "left-brained" people. Despite such popular oversimplifications, the idea of different but complementary modes of operation for the two hemispheres is now widely accepted and continues to be a major consideration in current research in neurology and psychology.

While the work of Sperry and others has been widely reported, far less attention has been paid to the work of Norman Geschwind and other neurologists whose research into nonsymmetrical development of the two hemispheres has suggested promising new perspectives. This research has indicated that, while in most people the left hemisphere is dominant for many functions, some people have relatively symmetrical brains—and that this unusual symmetry may lead to notable differences in both special abilities and special areas of difficulty.

This body of research also suggests a variety of possible interrelationships between highly diverse elements, such as unusual patterns of early neurological development, special talents, learning disorders, hormonal effects, handedness, delayed maturation, allergies, the operation of the immune system and various developmental diseases. Some aspects of the interrelated nature of these apparently highly diverse elements will be discussed as our story unfolds, but it may be sufficient here to point out that the same fundamental processes that influence early neurological growth and development can also have widespread effects on the early development of many other, seemingly unrelated, body systems.[3]

TWO HEMISPHERES, TWO MODES

The view of the two hemispheres now commonly accepted is that certain skills and abilities are specialized in one hemisphere while other skills and abilities are specialized in the other. However, there is often complex interaction between the two hemispheres on any given task. Abilities such as logic, language, orderliness, sequential time, and arithmetic are seen to be largely specialized in the left hemisphere whereas the processing of visual images, spatial relationships, face and pattern recognition, gesture, and proportion are seen to be specialized in the right hemisphere.[4] In general, one might say that the left thinks in words and numbers, while the right thinks visually, in pictures and images in three-dimensional space.

While these descriptions are useful in a general way, the actual functions are far more complex. For example, some more recent studies suggest that in certain persons the roles of the hemispheres may be reversed, and in other persons the two hemispheres may be less fully specialized—having, for example, relatively sophisticated language ability on both sides.[5] Other studies indicate that although the left hemisphere is generally regarded as the seat of language, the right hemisphere may serve certain specialized linguistic functions. For example, evidence has been found for greater right hemisphere sensitivity to non literal aspects of language, such as the connotations of words.[6] Also, the right hemisphere appears to have a greater role in controlling the hand gestures and tone of voice that accompany and embellish verbal language.[7]

It is becoming increasingly clear that most activities involve both hemispheres to one degree or another, as well as various combinations of structures within each hemisphere. What is most important for our purposes, however, is that there is evidence for two very different but complementary modes of thought, each generally associated with one of the hemispheres of the brain. We are more interested in the interplay between these two modes of thought than we are in their exclusive physical domains.[8]

Curiously, one of the important developments that arose from research on the functions of the two hemispheres is the idea that the right hemisphere is actually thinking at all, that is, the clear demonstration that consciousness and thought are, indeed, possible without words. Sperry and his associates showed that in patients where communications between the two hemispheres had been cut, the (generally) nonverbal right hemisphere could reliably identify (by only touching with the fingers) a range of small articles (such as pencils), although it could not say the names of the articles.

It might be asked how it is that we have so little awareness of this other half of ourselves. One answer is that many functions of the right hemisphere are so fundamental that they are easily taken for granted.[9] Another answer is that the overt concerns of modern culture appear to be almost entirely dominated by the modes of thought most compatible with the left hemisphere, that our view of the world, our educational system, our system of rewards, our aspirations, and our value systems are all effectively focused on reinforcing the operation of the left hemisphere (while the more basic contributions of the right are largely ignored or seen as primitive).

Research into the possible connection between creativity and the functions of the two hemispheres has shown that some creative individuals have an ability to balance, and alternate between, the right and left hemispheres (and the corresponding dissimilar modes of thought). As we will see, the alternation between two modes of consciousness is rather clearly shown in descriptions of the creative process by Albert Einstein and others. A similar alternation has also been documented in studies of gifted children.[10]

These findings suggest that this balance entails a facility with the right hemisphere that is relatively uncommon, not, perhaps, because it has been unusual for mankind throughout a long history, but because our culture has encouraged such a strong and enduring left shift. The ability to think in two different modes may be as important as it is rare.

A strong predisposition toward one mode of thought can sometimes lead to difficulties with respect to the other. Clearly, the predominant contemporary world view tends to favor the specific and the particular—the world view of the specialist, who may have difficulty seeing the whole. In contrast, most of the individuals we will focus on in this book seem to have held a world view preoccupied with the general and the whole, although they may have occasionally muddled some of the parts.

DYSLEXIA AND LEARNING DIFFICULTIES: PATTERNS OF MIXED CAPABILITIES

The possible relationship between creativity and visual-spatial or right-hemisphere modes of thought becomes more interesting when we begin to consider the varied complex of traits usually associated with the terms "dyslexia," "learning disabilities," or "learning difficulties." These terms are a matter of continuing discussion and controversy. "Dyslexia" is a term used chiefly by medical professionals. "Learning disabilities" is a term used chiefly by educators and educational administrators. Each group seems to be uncomfortable with the terminology, definitions, and usage of the other group. While in some circumstances the differences in definition can be enormously important (particularly in legal cases), it is argued here that, for our purposes, the similarities between the terms are more important than the differences.

"Dyslexia" refers most specifically to the condition of children of average or superior intelligence who are either unable to read or find reading extraordinarily difficult.[11] Common usage and many dictionary definitions refer primarily or exclusively to this aspect of dyslexia—great difficulty in learning to read.

However, some neurologists and others find it more useful to employ the term in a broader sense, one that corresponds more closely to the complex and interrelated manner in which different forms of language are processed in the brain. Thus, they would use the term in a broader but more literal sense—that is, "dys-" for "difficulty" and "-lexia" for "words."[12] Simply, difficulty or trouble with words. This usage of the term would include difficulty with decoding written symbols into spoken sounds or verbal meaning, but would also include other related problems, such as difficulty recalling names, remembering lines of text, finding the right word, or hesitant or stuttering speech. This usage of the term may carry with it some administrative and practical difficulties, since it cuts across a number of separate professional and therapeutic specialties. The reading tutor and the speech pathologist are normally trained separately and work separately to different goals. Yet the perspective of the neurologist emphasizes the complex interrelatedness of these varied functions and difficulties.

The term "learning disabilities" is somewhat more general in its application, referring to similar patterns of unusual learning problems, but the emphasis is on performance in an educational setting rather than on neurological function. In one current official definition, "learning disabilities" refers to "a heterogeneous group of disorders" indicated by "significant difficulties in the acquisition and use of listening, speaking, reading, writing, reasoning or mathematical abilities." These difficulties may involve other problems, such as difficulty with the perception of social cues, but such problems in themselves are not seen as constituting a learning disability as such.[13]

The term "learning difficulties" is more a lay person's description than a professional diagnostic term, although it is used by some professional groups to include the full range of unusual difficulties with reading, arithmetic, writing, memory, and other skill areas. For example, one Canadian provincial education ministry uses "the general title of learning difficulties" to refer to that "heterogeneous" group of students that includes those covered by the terms "perceptual difficulties, dyslexia, dyscalculia [special difficulty with calculation], dysorthography [special difficulty with spelling], speech diffaculties . . . etc."[14]

The three terms, "dyslexia," "learning disabilities," and "learning difficulties" will be used throughout this book as related but distinct terms, referring to different aspects of a more general pattern. The latter term, "learning difficulties" will be used as the most general and generic term, providing broad coverage without consideration of distinctions between subgroups of the larger pattern. These distinctions are important in some contexts but may be misleading in others.

In addition, since the term "learning difficulties" is a comparatively neutral description, it avoids the emotional overtones and resulting resistance that other terms sometimes carry with them. For our purposes, it is considered more useful to focus on the presence or absence of a number of specific traits and reduce emphasis on various definitions and labels. The definitions and labels may change over time, but the traits remain.

In summary, while combinations of these traits vary widely from person to person, particular individuals may exhibit one or several of the following: difficulty with handwriting, a general lack of organization (although compensation may eventually result in extreme orderliness), indifference to schedules (a poorly developed sense of time), excessive daydreaming, difficulties with arithmetic (but sometimes not geometry, statistics, or higher mathematics), difficulty with speech (delayed speech development, hesitation, or, occasionally, stuttering), ineptness or lack of tact in social situations (but in some cases showing exceptional powers of social perceptiveness), poor coordination and lack of athletic ability (but in some cases having superior athletic abilities), special difficulty in memorizing assigned information by rote (but often having surprising powers of memory for selected types of information), difficulty with retaining certain kinds of data (such as the multiplication tables), difficulty with learning foreign languages, especially in classroom settings (but sometimes developing unusual facility with one's native language), being overactive, easily distracted, inattentive, and "in their own world"—in short, a whole complex of problems that can be paradoxical and apparently unrelated and usually seem inconsistent with the apparent high abilities and intelligence of the particular child or adult.[15]

As more and more children are identified as having some combination of these traits and are tutored to address their difficulties, it is becoming apparent that the condition affects a significant number of children, to one degree or another, and is seen in one or both parents or other family members as well. It is no longer unusual for some parents to realize, after their children are diagnosed, that they themselves have long suffered silently with some form of learning disability.

These difficulties can, of course, often lead to major educational and vocational problems. But, curiously, many affected parents appear to be among the most successful in their fields, having worked out elaborate strategies to capitalize on strengths and to disguise or discount areas of weakness. In some cases, evidence of a pattern of mixed talents and difficulties can be traced back through generations. Anecdotal evidence, suggesting some form of the general pattern, is often considered interesting or amusing material for family stories and is passed down as family lore from one generation to the next. Such patterns can be traced in a number of the most prominent and best-documented families.

In recognition of this wider awareness, schools that in the past have dealt only with children with learning disabilities have more recently begun to work with adults. Apparently, one may learn to compensate for the condition, and even become extremely adept at hiding it, but rarely does one eradicate all symptoms.

LEARNING DIFFICULTIES AMONG THE FAMOUS: LARGER PATTERNS

In an effort to comfort parents and children, it is often pointed out that a number of famous people—artists, writers, scientists and others—were able to achieve a great deal despite of having had, apparently, some form of dyslexia or learning disability, or, at the very least, some substantial form of learning difficulty. Hans Christian Andersen, Albert Einstein, Thomas Edison, Gustave Flaubert, Harvey

Cushing, Auguste Rodin, Leonardo da Vinci, George Patton, William James, King Karl XI of Sweden, Woodrow Wilson, Nelson Rockefeller, William Butler Yeats and others have been identified by various writers as having had some form of dyslexia or learning disability.[16]

In recent years there has been a growing awareness of the existence of these traits among some contemporary public figures as well. Several organizations concerned with learning disabilities have begun to extend recognition to contemporary figures who have achieved notable success in varied fields despite extraordinary difficulties in reading, writing, memory, speaking, calculation, and other areas. Candidates are usually tested to verify the existence of the disabilities, but despite considerable career success, sometimes these public figures are surprised at their own deep reluctance to acknowledge their long-standing difficulties. A selection of those recognized in recent years shows a wide range of talent and accomplishment: an experimental psychologist, a Grand Prix racing car driver, a Nobel laureate immunologist, an explorer, a government agency director, an inventor, an artist, actors and actresses, business men and women, and Olympic gold medal athletes.[17]

Considering the variety and extent of the problems experienced by these historical and contemporary figures, it is perhaps not surprising that similar difficulties are often found among the children of talented professionals, architects, artists, photographers, actors, musicians, film makers, sculptors, athletes, engineers, scientists, radiologists, lawyers, and mathematicians.[18]

SOME UNEXPECTED ADVANTAGES: A "PATHOLOGY OF SUPERIORITY"

A major hypothesis of this book is that many of these individuals may have achieved success or even greatness not in spite of but because of their apparent disabilities. They may have been so much in touch with their visual-spatial, nonverbal, right-hemisphere modes of thought that they have had difficulty in doing orderly, sequential, verbal-mathematical, left-hemisphere tasks in a culture where left-hemisphere capabilities are so highly valued.

This does not mean that these individuals accomplished extraordinary things because they compensated for their handicaps. We are arguing, rather, that they succeeded because they could not fully compensate. Ironically, if they had been able to compensate fully, they might not have been able to do anything out of the ordinary. Also, we do not mean that their handicap molded their character, strengthening their ambition to accomplish extraordinary things. A handicap of one sort or another may intensify motivation, mold characters, or help one to learn many things, but it would appear to be wholly insufficient to explain the most towering and unexpected achievements, such as Einstein's theories or Edison's inventions. On the contrary, what is being suggested here is that for a certain group of people the handicap itself may be fundamentally and essentially associated with a gift. For some the handicap and the gift may be two aspects of the same thing. How we perceive it depends entirely on the context.[19] In other words, the complex of traits referred to as "learning difficulties" or "dyslexia" may be in part the outward manifestation of the relative strength of a different mode of thought, one that is available to everyone to one degree or another, but one that a few children (and adults) find it difficult to suppress. Too often, the gift is not recognized and is regarded only as a problem.

Some recent trends in neurological research seem increasingly to support this hypothesis. These trends are most evident in the work of Norman Geschwind. In investigating dyslexia at the neurological level, Geschwind focused both on the advantages and the disadvantages of the condition. In an address to the Orton Dyslexia Society in 1982, he observed,

> I had the experience recently of raising this issue [the advantages of the predisposition to dyslexia] at a meeting on the genetics of speech and language disorders only to find that this suggestion was greeted with incredulity by many of the other attendants, who could not conceive what possible advantage dyslexia might confer on its bearer.[20]

Geschwind goes on to explain that such apparent paradoxes are not rare in medicine and frequently reveal new areas of understanding.

> One of the most important lessons to be learned from the genetic study of many diseases in recent years has been that the paradoxi-

cally high frequency of certain conditions is explained by the fact that the important advantages conferred on those who carry the predisposition to these conditions may outweigh the obvious dramatic disadvantages.

To explain this point, Geschwind indicates the way some genetic diseases (such as anemias) may serve to protect carriers from other more threatening diseases (such as malaria). But he points out that unlike these conditions, the prevention of dyslexia may be more problematical because it appears that the disadvantages of the condition may be fundamentally linked to the advantages.

> It has become increasingly clear in recent years that *dyslexics themselves are frequently endowed with high talents in many areas.* . . . I need only point out the names of Thomas Edison and Albert Einstein to make it clear that dyslexics do not merely succeed in making a marginal adjustment in some instances, but that they rank high among those who have created the very fabric of our modern world. I would suggest to you that this is no accident. There have been in recent years an increasing number of studies that have pointed out that many dyslexics have superior talents in certain areas of non-verbal skill, such as art, architecture, engineering, and athletics. The immediate naive presumption is that success in these fields is simply the result of compensatory achievement in non-verbal fields on the part of those who do not succeed in readily acquiring reading. I believe that this explanation must convey at best a very small fraction of the truth.

The compensation theory seems less compelling when it is realized that dyslexics can be identified when very young—not by early indication of problems but rather by early indication of unusual talents and gifts. Geschwind points out that three-year-olds who show "unusual skill in drawing, or doing mechanical puzzles, or building models" may be identified as likely dyslexics by experienced observers, prior to any reading education, primarily because of the positive traits that they share with other dyslexics but do not share with nondyslexics.

The "special ability" hypothesis concerning dyslexia is further supported by its prevalence, according to Geschwind. If certain special abilities and dyslexia tend to come together, then in preliterate societies only the advantages would be apparent, not the disadvantages. And, because these conditions have prevailed through most of human history, it is not surprising that dyslexia should be relatively common and would not be evident as a problem until secondary and higher education (with their great degree of verbal orientation) is required for very large proportions of the society. Thus Geschwind observes,

> If certain changes on the left side of the brain lead to superiority of other regions, particularly on the right side of the brain, then there would be little disadvantage to the carrier of such changes in an illiterate society; their talents would make them highly successful citizens. It is thus not surprising that this type of brain organization should occur with such high frequency. Only when literacy becomes an important goal is it discovered that a significant fraction of these highly talented individuals suffer from some disadvantage. We are thus brought to the apparently paradoxical notion that the very same anomalies on the left side of the brain that have led to the disability of dyslexia in certain literate societies also determine superiority in some brains. We can, thus, speak of a "pathology of superiority" without fear of being contradictory!

In this way, a relatively stable set of biological traits may be perceived as an advantage in one context or time period and then as a disadvantage in another.

VISUAL THINKING, PATTERN RECOGNITION, AND CREATIVITY

Let us carry this approach further, introducing a second major hypothesis. One might argue that a number of conventionally observed right hemisphere traits are, in reality, merely varied manifestations of a single mode of thought. That is, one might see visual thinking, spatial ability, pattern recognition, problem solving, and related forms of creativity as linked together in a continuum.

We may consider "visual thinking" as that form of thought in which images are generated or recalled in the mind and are manipulated, overlaid, translated, associated with other similar forms (as with a metaphor), rotated, increased or reduced in size, distorted, or otherwise transformed gradually from one familiar image into another. These images may be visual representations of material things or they may be nonphysical, abstract concepts manipulated in the same way as visual forms. It may be noted in passing that these visual forms need not be actually derived from vision. A blind person may build up a mental image of a room through movement, touch and sound. Indeed, some scientists and mathematicians have been observed to have greater freedom and depth of imaginative conception because they are blind.[21]

Our second term, "spatial ability," is closely related to visual thinking but emphasizes those elements of three-dimensional space evident in the work of the architect, mechanic, sculptor, or athlete, areas where the two dimensional image is filled out into weighty masses or empty volumes, providing a sense of proportion as well as distance, momentum, leverage, balance, and the like.

Our third term, "pattern recognition," has been a major concern in artificial intelligence research and has proved to be quite complex. It has turned out to be one of those things which is very difficult for computers but easy for most human beings. This fact may provide a clue to the importance of the other mode of thought we are investigating. For our purposes, we will consider pattern recognition to be the ability to discern similarities of form among two or more things, whether these be textile designs, facial resemblance of family members, graphs of repeating biological growth cycles, or similarities between historical epochs. This description, of course, does not address questions about the nature of the similarities discerned, nor does it address which aspects are considered similar or how these similarities are immediately perceived by many people without special prompting. These questions will probably continue to be mysteries for a while longer. However, pattern recognition is familiar to us all in daily life, even if we do not yet understand how it works.

From pattern recognition it is but a short step to "problem solving," since, at least for its more common aspects, problem solving generally involves the recognition of a developing or repeating pattern and the carrying out of actions to obtain desired results based on one's understanding of this pattern.

Finally, problem solving may be considered nearly synonymous with some of the most important forms of creativity. An original and effective solution to a problem is usually considered creative.

Consequently, we may be justified in treating these linked and overlapping capabilities as several manifestations of visual thinking, each different but closely related. One may suspect, perhaps, that once the neurological mechanisms that serve the most elementary functions are understood, then we may also see that slight modifications of these basic functions will yield this string of related capabilities. This view would be consistent with the observation that "mechanisms of importance in higher animals often embody processes found in very primitive forms."[22] Thus, we might argue that this group of right-hemisphere traits may be merely the varied manifestations of a single elemental mode of thought: visual thinking, spatial ability, pattern recognition, problem solving, and related forms of creativity.

MIXED DYSLEXIC TRAITS AND SOCIAL BENEFIT

If this second major hypothesis were to be confirmed, then the same set of traits may be perceived very differently, depending upon the survival needs of individuals, groups, or the society at large at particular stages in human history. In preliterate societies, these traits would be essential for finding game and shelter in jungles and forests (without maps and signposts). In literate societies, the same set of traits would be a major disadvantage, since its problematical aspects would be more apparent and would lead to major barriers to making meaningful contributions to the society.

However, one might carry the same reasoning further into our current historical situation. That is, our factual understanding of ourselves and our world grows at an ever increasing rate, yet solutions to problems of great complexity and seriousness seem elusive. Could it be then, that mankind might be entering a third stage, one in which this same set of traits might come once again to the fore, perhaps providing truly new and creative solutions to complex and apparently insoluble problems?

If this approach is correct, then Geschwind's further comments on the possible prevention of dyslexia take on an extra dimension of significance. He points out that, since the same unusual neurological formations that lead to dyslexia may also promote superior abilities, then "the dilemma . . . becomes obvious. Not only do many dyslexics carry remarkable talents that benefit their society enormously, but the same talents exist in unusually high frequency among their unaffected relatives. If we could somehow prevent these brain changes, and thus prevent the appearance of dyslexia, might we not find that we have deprived the society of an important and irreplaceable group of individuals endowed with remarkable talents?"

In spite of this, Geschwind is hopeful that the advantages and disadvantages are not necessarily connected. This hope is based on evidence that there are many nondyslexic "individuals among the relatives of dyslexics who are left-handed and possessed of remarkable spatial talents. . . . We know that especially frequently the sisters of dyslexics are likely to share the talents without the disadvantages of dyslexia. Once we gain intimate information as to the mechanisms of formation of the anomalies that lead to the superior talents, we should be able to retain the advantages while avoiding the disadvantages."

Geschwind hopes to have one without the other. We too may well hope for this, but we need also to consider the possibility, as he suggested previously, that it may not always be possible. We may need to consider that it may be an essential part of the nature of things that, in a significant number of cases, one cannot have one without the other.[23]

Is it possible that our brains have such design constraints? Is it possible that unusual proficiency in one area will often mean a significant lack of proficiency in another? Or, conversely, is it possible that a deficiency in one area may indicate the likelihood of special abilities in other areas? Recent neurological evidence suggests that this may in fact be so. One of Geschwind's associates, Albert Galaburda, has been carrying out micro-anatomical studies of the brains of dyslexics. After detailed examination of several cases, Galaburda describes the role of microscopic lesions (areas of damage or diminished growth) and the unusual symmetry of certain formations (the "planum temporale") that had been observed in all dyslexic brains up to that time. Although the cases have been few in number, the results are seen as highly significant, because the probability of such consistent results would be very low.

Galaburda observes that the lesions may be capable of suppressing the development of some areas, but he suggests a role for them in actually increasing the development of other areas. This research suggests a biological basis for the frequent paradoxical coexistence of special abilities and disabilities in the same individual. "We all know that these lesions may in fact be capable of reorganizing the brain. But they don't always reorganize the brain to produce dyslexics. I am sure that similar mechanisms are used to reorganize the brain to produce geniuses too, and sometimes both of them occur in the same person."[24]

THE WORLD OF THE CHILD EXTENDED, TWO MODES OF THOUGHT

Now let us turn from the researches of Geschwind and Galaburda to examine more closely the possible direct relationships between learning difficulties and the creative process, especially with respect to the modes of thought now associated with visual processing in the right hemisphere. It is often observed that one of the essential characteristics of creativity is a "childlike" view of the world, full of freshness and flexibility. As they grow older, most children gradually lose this view. They appear to shift their thinking to a more rigid left-hemisphere dominance at a certain age, as is expected. But it seems that some children cannot shift to the usual one-sided dominance so readily; they are delayed in the maturing process. They grow up using both sides of their brain or mature with a greater facility with the right hemisphere than is usual. This may lead to some degree of confusion, ambivalence, and awkwardness, but the intellectual resource may be profoundly richer thereby, and that makes all the difference.

Maturity is a key concept here. Maturity suggests responsibility, conventional education, having children, understanding the adult world, and finding a place in it—making one's way or doing one's duty. A child cares little for these things. He or she is too busy discovering the world, examining things closely, seeing how they behave, trying to figure out how things work, how people respond when you do different things, and investigating touch, sounds, smells, tastes, and images. All of this starts well before words or numbers. All of this is play—learning and discovering.

While maturity is, of course, necessary to make one's way in the adult world, we are aware that it is good to preserve something of the child, especially if we desire the freshness of view that seems to promote creativity. This much is generally known and understood. What is not generally known is that it may be a good thing when the maturing process takes a little longer than usual. Parents are usually pleased when their children mature quickly, becoming more independent, more organized, and more self-directed in advance of their peers. What is not generally known is that late maturation can be useful, although it seems to contradict conventional belief. The neurological evidence indicates that the onset of puberty stops neurological development. "The studies show that on the average . . . quick development means you sort of 'gel' earlier and you don't develop as fully. It is not just true for brain development; it is true for growth also. People who grow slowly tend to grow taller."[25]

Accordingly, it is possible that early developers may be good at what they can do, but they may be able to do less than those who have developed over a longer period. Thus, later maturity may be seen as desirable in at least three ways: First, the plastic, absorbent world of the child may be experienced longer, giving the adolescent a deeper store of real seeing and feeling experience of the world to draw on—and to build intuition on—before the adult world of fixed, literate, learned knowledge takes over. Second, there is a real possibility of significantly increased neurological capacity, at least in some cases and in certain areas, which may more than compensate for earlier awkwardness and some lingering areas of relative disability. And third, the late developer may be able to retain some aspects of the child's view throughout life, such as a sense of wonder, or, a comparative freshness and lack of preconception, making the expression of creativity much more probable. Although the clock of maturation follows its own beat, it is good to know that a slower pace may have, under the right circumstances, notable advantages.

With respect to creativity, the freshness of the child's view is not to be underestimated. When the world of the child is properly understood, then perhaps it is no surprise that Einstein said he was led to his discoveries by asking questions that "only children ask." This view of himself is clearly evident in the following curious passage: "I sometimes ask myself . . . how did it come that I was the one to develop the theory of relativity. The reason, I think, is that a normal adult never stops to think about problems of space and time. These are things he has thought of as a child. But my intellectual development was retarded, as a result of which I began to wonder about space and time only when I had already grown up. Naturally, I could go deeper into the problem than a child with normal abilities."[26]

If delayed development is acknowledged as one major factor, then the childlike playfulness of this strong visual thinker may have been another. Einstein sometimes referred to the source of his ideas as "playing" with "images." When he described the process in his own words, the childlike approach and the interplay of the two hemispheres seems clearly evident.

> The words or the language, as they are written or spoken, do not seem to play any role in my mechanism of thought. The psychical entities which seem to serve as elements in thought are certain signs and more or less clear images which can be "voluntarily" reproduced and combined.
>
> There is, of course, a certain connection between those elements and relevant logical concepts. It is also clear that the desire to arrive finally at logically connected concepts is the emotional basis of this rather vague play with the above mentioned elements. But taken from a psychological viewpoint, this combinatory play seems to be the essential feature in productive thought—before there is any connection with logical construction in words or other kinds of signs which can be communicated to others.
>
> The above mentioned elements are, in my case, of visual and some of muscular type. Conventional words or other signs have to be sought for laboriously only in a secondary stage, when the mentioned associative play is sufficiently established and can be reproduced at will.[27]

It is of no small significance that Einstein's words clearly describe a two-mode process that corresponds closely to the findings of those who have been investigating the roles of the two hemispheres. He first "plays" with "images" in the visual right hemisphere, the apparent source of new ideas or perceptions of order, possibly relatively independently of conventional thought, current scientific understanding, and education. He plays until he arrives at the desired result. And then, "only in a secondary stage" does he have to seek "laboriously" for the right words and mathematical symbols to express the ideas in terms of the verbal left hemisphere, in terms of the world, in terms that fit within the structure of scientific thinking, in terms that can be "communicated to others."

It should be pointed out that these observations are not entirely unusual, nor should they be expected to be. Such observations as Einstein's occur frequently in the literature of creativity.[28] The concept of two modes of consciousness has been cropping up in the medical literature for at least a hundred years, particularly with reference to artists, musicians, and composers.[29] What is new is that research on the two hemispheres of the brain has yielded such substantial evidence that serious investigators have been forced to reverse a major trend in scientific thought (behaviorism) and not only recognize, once again, the concept of consciousness, but also entertain the concept that there are not one but two major modes of consciousness, each fundamentally different from the other—one that we know a little about, the other that we know almost nothing about.[30]

VERBAL SLIP TWO FORMS OF INFORMATION STORAGE

Let us return to our main consideration. How might the difficulties experienced by the dyslexic be related to the creative process? Einstein's description of his own thinking process clearly shows the central role of image and visual imagination. If our second hypothesis is correct (that these nonverbal, primarily visual and spatial thought elements are manifestations of a single major mode of thought, which also includes pattern recognition and creative problem solving), then we may be able to make a direct connection to at least one of the traits frequently associated with dyslexia.

In her autobiography, *Reversals*, psychologist and novelist Eileen Simpson, who is dyslexic, describes her youthful chagrin at saying words like "leaf" when she meant to say "feather." As she was growing up, and before she knew anything about dyslexia, she would be upset by this embarrassing tendency. Fortunately, she learned early to cover up by pretending that her slips were intentional jokes, so that her young friends would see her as a clown rather than somehow strange.[31] The tendency to make certain verbal slips is one of the varied manifestations of dyslexia and is generally seen solely as an undesirable variation in the way information is processed in the brain. In some studies this tendency to substitute words is called "paralexia," the unintentional substitution of a related word for the appropriate one.[32] This tendency might not reflect a truly abnormal process at all, but might instead bejust an awkward manifestation of a normal, desirable, and critically important process.

Paralexia may be seen as indicating the operation of an alternative method of information storage in the brain. The basic concept may be explained by a metaphor. Suppose that the usual mode of word storage is extraordinarily neat and orderly, like post office boxes arranged in rows and columns. Each time a word is sought, it is selected by a precise address within the row and column matrix, and the intended word is unfailingly delivered. This is the steady and orderly mode of operation that has come to be associated with the left hemisphere. This is the mode of operation that is taught and most highly praised by our schools and universities, emphasizing speed, precision, and reliability in learning and recall. But we might conceive of a second (right hemisphere) mode made up of fluid-filled cylinders, each containing many related words or concepts. Whereas the first mode uses specific, distinct locations for each word, the second mode groups words together according to some basis of general association. A leaf and a feather are similar in that they are both flat, pointed, broad, tapered and thin, either moved by air or moving air. In this second mode, the similarities are the predominant considerations in sorting; the differences are only secondary. Thus, perhaps, when selecting a word, one may select the proper cylinder but may occasionally come up with the wrong word from among its contents.[33] The one mode assures the maintenance of distinctions, while the other assures the recognition of similarities.[34] Both modes are useful or necessary. We must be able to perceive both similarities and differences.

Each mode has built-in strengths and weaknesses. The first mode might serve to keep different words and concepts well separated but would, at the same time, frequently fail to recognize important similarities. On the other hand, the second (more fluid or associative) mode would have exactly complementary strengths and weaknesses. That is, it would be extraordinarily effective in recognizing similarities, but might often fail to consider distinctions that would be important in other contexts.[35]

SPATIAL INTELLIGENCE THINKING IN VISUAL IMAGES

Visual metaphors are linguistically evident everywhere in ordinary speech, for example, terms such as "imagination," "visionary," "reflection," "insight," and "perspective." However, when one confines one's attention to the greatest and most original in the arts and sciences, rather than the merely learned, eminent, or successful, one is struck by the frequent references to visual modes of thought. Investigators of the creative process have often made reference to the central role of visual modes of thought, although this emphasis has varied over time. However, in comparatively recent times this mode of thought has been given increased attention by professional students of the mind. In his book *Frames of Mind*, Howard Gardner focuses on visual and spatial ways of thinking as one of several identifiable human capacities. Gardner draws together material from a broad range of disciplines to propose a theory of multiple intelligences—one that recognizes six distinct forms: linguistic, musical, logical-mathematical, spatial, bodily-kinesthetic, and personal. His treatment of "spatial intelligence" (or the visual mode of thought) includes observations especially pertinent to the approach set forth here. According to Gardner, "spatial intelligence entails a number of loosely related capacities: the ability to recognize instances of the same element; the ability to transform or to recognize a transformation of one element into another; the capacity to conjure up mental imagery and then to transform that imagery; the capacity to produce a graphic likeness of spatial information; and the like." Although these capacities can be applied to a vast array of tangible situations, Gardner observes that there are other uses of spatial intelligence that are more "abstract and elusive." One involves "sensitivity to the various lines of force that enter into a visual or spatial display. I refer here to the feelings of tension, balance, and composition that characterize a painting, a work of sculpture, and many natural elements (like a fire or a waterfall) as well. These facets, which contribute to the power of a display, occupy the attention of artists and viewers of the arts."[36] Gardner does not elaborate on this observation, but this "sensitivity" to "lines of force" would appear to be precisely the same capacity that seems pivotal in several of the most original scientific thinkers.

FARADAY, MAXWELL, AND LINES OF FORCE IN THE MIND'S EYE

The idea of "lines of force" immediately brings to mind Michael Faraday, the self-educated scientist of the early nineteenth century we met at the beginning of this chapter. A tireless worker, Faraday was responsible for a great many fundamental discoveries in chemistry and physics, although he hated these specialist terms. He preferred to call himself a "philosopher."

Among many achievements, his greatest was that he originated the concept of subtle electromagnetic "lines of force," as well as the associated concept of the nonvisible electromagnetic "field." (These are the same lines as those produced by the effect of a strong magnet on iron filings spread on a piece of paper.) So sensitive was Faraday to these "lines of force" that for him they were "as real as matter."[37] His powerful visual conception of these ideas provided the basis for James Clerk Maxwell's famous mathematical equations which, in turn, provided the foundation for modern physics by defining the relationship between light, electricity, and magnetism. The ideas set forth by these men have been remarkably enduring—they have remained virtually unchanged up to the present time.

Both Faraday and Maxwell are extraordinarily important in the history of modern physics, and yet, unlike Einstein, who greatly respected their work, neither is well known to the lay public. The enduring position of these scientists, as well as the nature of their contributions, is summarized in Isaac Asimov's *History of Physics*. "Faraday . . . perhaps the greatest electrical innovator of all, was completely innocent of mathematics, and he developed his notion of lines of force in a remarkably unsophisticated way, picturing them almost like rubber bands." Asimov is somewhat uneasy about the foregoing description of Faraday's "unsophisticated" pictures, and he comments in a footnote, "This is not meant as a sneer at Faraday, who was certainly one of the greatest scientists of all time. His intuition was that of a first-class genius. Although his views were built up without the aid of a carefully worked out mathematical analysis, they were solid. When the mathematics was finally supplied, the essence of Faraday's notions was shown to be correct"

This ambivalence toward Faraday is repeated over and over again by scientific writers, showing their difficulty in taking seriously a scientist who was not a mathematician, no matter how original, productive, or prescient the scientist may have been. Asimov continues,

> In the 1860s, Maxwell, a great admirer of Faraday, set about supplying the mathematical analysis of the interrelationship of electricity and magnetism in order to round out Faraday's non-mathematical treatment. . . . In 1864, Maxwell devised a set of four comparatively simple equations, known ever since as "Maxwell's equations." From these, it proved possible to deduce the nature of the interrelationships of electricity and magnetism under all possible conditions. . . . Maxwell's equations were more successful than Newton's laws. The latter were shown to be but approximations that held for low velocities and short distances. They required the modification of Einstein's broader relativistic viewpoint if they were to be made to apply with complete generality. Maxwell's equations, on the other hand, survived all the changes introduced by relativity and the quantum theory; they are as valid in the light of present knowledge as they were when they were first introduced a century ago.[38]

The long-term consequences of Faraday's ideas recast in Maxwell's mathematical formulations have been extraordinarily broad and pervasive down to the present time. One of Maxwell's biographers pointed out that, "There is hardly an area of modern technology and physics in which Maxwell's theory has not contributed something of importance—from electrical power generation and transmission to communication systems or the monster accelerators of modern physics. The scientific, practical, and engineering consequences of Maxwell's equations have been seminal, all-pervasive and quite impossible to list. Maxwell's theory, however, was more than a synthesis or a source of future technologies. It involved a radical change in our conception of reality, a fundamental shift in point of view—it was . . . a *scientific revolution.*"[39]

The full significance of Maxwell's achievements and of Faraday's ideas, on which they are based, is little known to the nonprofessional. Richard Feynman, a Nobel Prize–winning physicist and author, declared that, "From a long view of the history of mankind—seen from, say, ten thousand years from now—there can be little doubt that the most significant event of the nineteenth century will be judged as Maxwell's discovery of the laws of electrodynamics. The American Civil War will pale into provincial insignificance in comparison with this important scientific event of the same decade."[40]

Although Maxwell was one of the foremost mathematicians of his time, he did not consider Faraday's total ignorance of formal mathematics a reason to take his ideas less seriously. On the contrary, he found the precision and logic of Faraday's conceptions so compelling that he termed them "mathematical." Indeed, Maxwell explicitly stated that the development of his own equations was merely a translation of Faraday's ideas into conventional mathematical form. In the preface to *A Treatise on Electricity and Magnetism*, his major work, first published in 1873, Maxwell explained,

> Before I began the study of electricity I resolved to read no mathematics on the subject till I had first read through Faraday's *Experimental Researches in Electricity*. I was aware that there was supposed to be a difference between Faraday's way of conceiving phenomena and that of the mathematicians, so that neither he nor they were satisfied with each other's language. I had also the conviction that the discrepancy did not arise from either party being wrong. . . . As I proceeded with the study of Faraday, I perceived that his method of conceiving the phenomena was also a mathematical one, though not exhibited in the conventional form of symbols. I also found that these methods were capable of being expressed in the ordinary mathematical forms, and thus compared with those of the professed mathematicians.[41]

Maxwell also provided a particularly illuminating description of Faraday's thought in comparison with that of the mathematicians of the time. An extended quotation shows the contrast in their approaches and ways of thinking.

> For instance, Faraday, in his mind's eye, saw lines of force traversing all space where the mathematicians saw centres of force attracting at

a distance: Faraday saw a medium where they saw nothing but distance: Faraday sought the seat of the phenomena in real actions going on in the medium, they were satisfied that they had found it in a power of action at a distance impressed on the electric fluids.

When I had translated what I considered to be Faraday's ideas into a mathematical form, I found that in general the results of the two methods coincided . . . but that Faraday's methods resembled those in which we begin with the whole and arrive at the parts by analysis, while the ordinary mathematical methods were founded on the principle of beginning with the parts and building up the whole by synthesis.

I also found that several of the most fertile methods of research discovered by the mathematicians could be expressed much better in terms of ideas derived from Faraday than in their original form.

The whole theory, for instance, of the potential, considered as a quantity which satisfies a certain partial differential equation, belongs essentially to the method which I have called that of Faraday. . . . Hence many of the mathematical discoveries of Laplace, Poisson, Green and Gauss find their proper place in this treatise, and their appropriate expressions in terms of conceptions mainly derived from Faraday.[42]

One does not have to be a scientist or a mathematician to see the sincere admiration Maxwell had for Faraday's ideas and his deep appreciation of the complete originality of Faraday's approach. He saw that Faraday's conception was as capable of explaining the same phenomena as that of the professional mathematicians, but his approach involved a clearer vision of the whole and provided a "much better" way of expressing some of the "most fertile" ideas.

Maxwell's ready acknowledgment of his intellectual debt to Faraday is admirable. What seems more remarkable is the ease with which Maxwell absorbed and translated Faraday's relatively unfashionable ideas and the vigor with which he defended the uneducated originator of these ideas. There seemed to be an unusual correspondence in modes of thought between the two men concerning concepts that were apparently unintelligible to other scientists of their time. One scientific historian noted, "An important characteristic feature in their reasoning, which Faraday and Maxwell shared, was the habit of thinking in terms of physical pictures. Although an accomplished mathematician, Maxwell, as has been remarked by many, relied more on diagrams and geometrical notions than on symbols.[43] This factor might also help to explain the general incomprehensibility of their work to their contemporaries, who presumably had relatively less extensive visual-spatial capacities.[44]

Although neither Maxwell nor Faraday appeared to have had significant reading or writing difficulties, both exhibited traits that do fit within the broader definition of learning difficulties. Maxwell was known for an unusually lucid writing style. However, he was often surprisingly obscure when he had to speak suddenly, a particular pattern that is often observed in certain groups of children with learning disabilities. Maxwell also had difficulty with stuttering throughout his life. Faraday seems to have had some lesser difficulties with speech, but appears to have had major problems with mathematics and a poor memory. It is often assumed that his difficulties with mathematics were entirely due to his lack of appropriate education. However, there is evidence that his difficulties might have resulted from special problems with certain kinds of symbol systems. These difficulties, together with the positive traits associated with their unusually vivid and creative visual imaginations, suggest a special role for Maxwell and Faraday among those we are considering.[45]

In the earlier stages of the formulation of his theory, Maxwell developed elaborate, almost mechanical, models of his own, based on Faraday's visual-spatial concepts, but these were abandoned once they had served to bring him to the mathematical formulations. "Once he had arrived at his . . . general equations, Maxwell kicked away the scaffolding from under him—the physical model of vortices in the ether—and thus inaugurated the post-Newtonian era in physics, with its renunciation of all models and representations in terms of sensory experience."[46] Although Maxwell is still considered a master of mathematical formulation, he was very much aware of the value of having two different ways of approaching nature, the one mathematical, the other through physical or visual analogies (as, at least, aids to thought). It is, perhaps, an open question as to the price that has been paid by modern physics in adhering to the former while rejecting the latter. One might wonder whether the time for this mode of thought has entirely passed, or whether there is much of value to be gained by returning to it to deal with some difficult contemporary problems.

A partial answer to this question might be obtained by reminding ourselves that "sensitivity" to "lines of force" also seems partly to characterize the thought of Albert Einstein. Einstein's "productive" thought was intensely visual in nature. Indeed some have suggested that Einstein may have been less creative and productive in later life because he shifted emphasis away from the visual toward the conventional mathematical. It is especially notable that the first paragraph of Einstein's famous 1905 paper on special relativity begins with reference to the behavior of the lines of force in Faraday's experiments and an apparent incongruity ("asymmetry") that arises from Maxwell's equations describing this behavior.[47] Thus, not only does Einstein appear to share their propensity for visual modes of thought, but his earliest work picks up where they had left off some thirty to sixty years before.

The predisposition to thinking in pictures appears to span the ages and produces a special affinity between those who have it, not because they were physicists or mathematicians or musicians (for there are many forms of each), but because of the special correspondence in their ways of thinking. In his study in Princeton, Einstein had pictures of three scientists on the wall: Newton, Faraday, and Maxwell. It was the work of Faraday and Maxwell that most interested Einstein when he was a student, despite the fact that they were largely ignored by Einstein's professors. Indeed, Einstein's knowledge of Faraday's and Maxwell's work was so great that it impressed Einstein's future employer and got him his first job at the Swiss Patent Office, after his long, unsuccessful search for a secure position.[48] To a friend who had given him a book about Faraday, Einstein wrote, "You have given me great joy with the little book about Faraday. This man loved mysterious Nature as a lover loves his distant beloved. In his day, there did not yet exist the dull specialization that stares with self-conceit through hornrimmed glasses and destroys poetry."[49]

In his *Autobiographical Notes*, Einstein breaks abruptly into a passage describing the development of his scientific thought to address Isaac Newton (as if he were alive and in the room), explaining that his own work does not refute Newton's, rather that his work extends Newton's into realms that Newton did not deal with.[50] Other instances of this special affinity can be cited, but it is sufficient to point out that the visual mode of thought may lead to immediate recognition of an extraordinary rapport, regardless of time, place, or area of knowledge.

Let us return to the second of Gardner's "more abstract and elusive" spatial capabilities: "A final facet of spatial intelligence grows out of the resemblances that may exist across two seemingly disparate forms, or, for that matter, across two seemingly remote domains of experience. In my view, that metaphoric ability to discern similarities across diverse domains derives in many instances from a manifestation of spatial intelligence."

Here Gardner proposes that the truly original thinker, the one capable of making unconventional but apt associations in the manner of metaphor and analogy, may be relying primarily upon the visual-spatial mode of thought, whether he is an artist, poet, political leader, or scientist. It is significant that Gardner chooses physicians and scientists to illustrate his view.

> When the gifted essayist Lewis Thomas draws analogies between microorganisms and an organized human society, depicts the sky as a membrane, or describes mankind as a heap of earth, he is capturing in words a kind of resemblance that may well have occurred to him initially in spatial form. Indeed, underlying many scientific theories are "images" of wide scope: Darwin's vision of the "tree of life," Freud's notion of the unconscious as submerged like an iceberg, John Dalton's view of the atom as a tiny solar system, are the productive figures that give rise to, and help to embody, key scientific conceptions. It is possible that such mental models or images also play a role in more mundane forms of problem solving.[51]

VISUAL IMAGES, STATISTICS, AND MATHEMATICS

The power of the visual image to embody major concepts and to reveal repeating patterns in apparently unrelated things is clearly evident in the early development of the science of statistics. The usefulness of the visual or graphic or "geometric" (or right hemisphere) approach is most apparent in the work of Karl Pearson and that of his son, E. S. Pearson. Karl Pearson is credited with being the first man, in the latter part of the nineteenth century, to apply statistics systematically to biological phenomena. He placed great store in the visual or graphic method (as opposed to merely numerical or algebraic expression). He wrote in his lecture notes, "Contest of geometry and arithmetic as scientific tools in dealing with physical and social phenomena. Erroneous opinion that geometry is only a means of popular representation; it is a fundamental method of investigating and analyzing statistical material."[52]

The same perspective was set forth by E. S. Pearson, writing in the 1950s. "A visual survey of the 'pattern' of his data provides the statistician . . . with the quickest method of checking whether the model he proposes to use is likely to be appropriate or not. That understanding can be achieved through visual aids may be regarded as a proposition so obvious that it needs no restatement by me; yet there is much evidence that the average mathematically trained student who forms today the raw material of our classes in mathematical statistics is not too well endowed with visual imagination."[53]

In this way, E. S. Pearson showed how a profession that presumably was created largely by one mode of thought may become gradually filled with those who rely primarily on the other mode of thought. In defense of the one mode, he pointed out that the visual presentation could help the statistician in "understanding the meaning of his mathematical results; in avoiding mistakes through lack of fit of his models; in saving time; and in . . . making clear his methods of analysis to the non-statistician. But the prestige of mathematical procedures based on algebraic formulae is deeply entrenched in our lecture courses and our text-books, so that few mathematical statisticians will use to the full their visual faculties unless they are trained to do so." This situation is especially regrettable because E. S. Pearson had learned from personal experience that "the intellectual stimulus which can come from use of the visual imagination may be very great." After giving two specific examples of how visual presentation made complex mathematical problems "beautifully simple" to him, E. S. Pearson observed, "I am told that I have been fortunately endowed with an extra amount of visual imagination, and that it is unfair for me to expect others of my staff or students to be helped by statistical geometry."[54]

Thus, it would appear that E. S. Pearson was aware that much of value had been lost in the transition from visual to exclusively mathematical analysis. It is as if one mode of thought created the discipline, but that another (relatively antithetical) mode of thought took over the discipline and cut all ligatures of connection with its origins. Since one would expect the university system to select for those most proficient in verbal-logical-mathematical modes of thought and against those proficient mainly in visual-spatial modes of thought, it is not surprising that the younger Pearson found himself surrounded, eventually, by relatively alien souls.

Presumably, E. S. Pearson had inherited from his father some of the visual-spatial mind-set that originally seized upon the unconventional connections and he retained a profound respect for the power of this same mind-set to create new connections in the future. But as the unconventional became conventional, the new practitioners and professors regarded the origins as primitive and therefore regressive. This attitude is underscored by the fact that the old mind-set—the visual-spatial approach—often allows sophisticated concepts to be understood by ordinary people. Thus we see two of the major figures in the development of statistics arguing with conviction for greater use of the visual-spatial mode of thought—although there were and still are powerful pressures to diminish its use.

There are, however, encouraging signs that visual modes of thought are once again being given serious attention by some scientists and statisticians, partly because of the growing capabilities of powerful new computers and partly because of the great difficulty of dealing effectively with the masses of information that these machines have produced. Some years ago reports began to appear that computer-generated multidimensional graphic displays helped scientists to detect relationships in data that would never have been detected by conventional methods.

> Scientists at Stanford's Linear Accelerator Center, and at Harvard University, for example, are seeing patterns in data that never would have been picked up with standard statistical techniques. The aim of data analysis is to discover patterns, to find non-random clusters of data points. Traditionally, this is done by using mathematical formulas. But, with the advent of computer motion graphics, it has become possible to look at three dimensional projections of the data and to make use of the uniquely human ability to recognize meaningful patterns in the data.[55]

INCREASINGLY, "GRAPHIC IMAGES ARE THE KEY"

The increasing importance of the visual image as a primary focus of analysis is seen in the recent development of the new science known as "chaos." Chaos is a loosely associated family of new analytical approaches in mathematics and science. Books and articles on chaos for the layman have begun to appear in recent years, but its associated theories have been developing for several decades.[56] According to James Gleick, the author of a recent book on the subject, *Chaos: Making a New Science*, its theory and techniques may apply equally to the historical prices of cotton, the turbulence of water, the beating of a human heart, or the behavior of clusters of stars. The development of this new discipline is of particular interest here because it has involved a clear shift of emphasis toward visual modes of thought and analysis.

There are many different definitions of chaos, but there are distinct underlying similarities. For some, chaos is the study of mathematical patterns (hidden under apparent randomness) that can be found, especially at high levels of energy, in large and complex and rapidly changing systems, such as global weather. For others, chaos is the remarkable ability of surprisingly simple processes (and mathematical formulas) to generate, through massive repetition systems (and corresponding graphic images) of great complexity. And for others, chaos is the curious "sensitivity to initial conditions" that allows identical processes to generate extremely different end results because of extremely small differences in the starting points of the processes. And for still others, chaos is mainly characterized by self-similarity of mathematical (and graphical) patterns at different scales and magnitudes. The colored images of these strikingly beautiful patterns have been reproduced widely in popular and professional scientific magazines over the last few years: the skewered snowman or the many-tongues-of-fire, paisleylike "fractal" images. These images are, in fact, just different aspects or different views of the same pattern at different magnifications.

Chaos is not seen as serving every need, even by its strongest adherents. Different forms of analysis are needed for different purposes. Practitioners of the new approaches want it to be clearly understood that the old ways are not being abandoned. However, the old ways have limits and the new ways are producing answers and solutions that were thought impossible only a short time ago. These developments are exciting in themselves, as they appear to slowly peel away, in a most unexpected and surprising manner, another whole layer of reality. But they are of interest to us mainly because of the way they shift emphasis to primarily visual modes of analysis and thought. The developments associated with chaos suggest the beginning of a major trend away from traditional mathematical analysis and toward the analysis of visual images of the kinds we have been discussing. As Gleick observes,

> Chaos has become not just theory but also method, not just a canon of beliefs but also a way of doing science. Chaos has created its own technique of using computers, a technique that does not require the vast speed of Crays and Cybers but instead favors modest terminals that allow flexible ping interaction. To chaos researchers, mathematics has become an experimental science, with the computer replacing laboratories full of test tubes and microscopes. Graphic images are the key. "It's masochism for a mathematician to do without pictures," one chaos specialist would say. "How can they see the relationship between that motion and this? How can they develop intuition?" Some carry out their work explicitly denying that it is a revolution; others deliberately use [the] language of paradigm shifts to describe the changes they witness.[57]

It is almost uncanny that these new developments should result in views so closely parallel to the observations of the two Pearsons. The Pearsons knew they were seeing the relationships in the data primarily through their own unusual ability to visualize these data in their imaginations, sometimes in the form of extremely simple graphics. In contrast, their colleagues and students pretty much kept to the mathematical symbols alone—the algebraic approach—and left the graphics to popular presentations. Presumably, as E. S. Pearson observed, these colleagues were more comfortable with the disciplined logic and order of the symbolic system and had less well-developed visual imaginations. Now, however, about a hundred years after the elder Pearson's work, the tables may be turning once again, and those working with the new tools and concepts may be those more comfortable with computer images occasionally translated into mathematical formulas than with formulas occasionally translated into computer or other graphical images.

The Pearsons' colleagues, in the late nineteenth and early twentieth centuries, did not understand their intense interest in pictures. The chaos researcher, in the late twentieth century, cannot see how anyone can understand the relationships without pictures, especially the moving and responsive pictures produced on demand on one's personal computer—powerful aids to the imagination. It is a complete reversal in the making.

Several trends converge. The new science of chaos has provided new mathematical tools and new ways of looking at problems that were either ignored or thought insoluble before. Whole classes of phenomena had not been dealt with previously because the mathematical tools were not available to do the job. This has changed.

But presumably these new tools will increasingly require new skills and talents. With the further development of smaller, cheaper, but more powerful computers having sophisticated visual-projection capabilities, we might expect a new trend to be emerging in which visual proficiencies could play an increasingly important role in areas that have been almost exclusively dominated in the past by those most proficient in verbal-logical-mathematical modes of thought. Increasingly, graphic images are the key.

SPATIAL INTELLIGENCE AND A SENSE OF THE WHOLE

Returning to Gardner's perspective, we find that he argues for the special status of visual-spatial intelligence generally. "In the view of many, spatial intelligence is the 'other intelligence'—the one that should be arrayed against, and be considered equal in importance to, 'linguistic intelligence.'" Although he does not subscribe to the idea of the dichotomization of intelligence into separate hemispheres, Gardner says, "Still, I would admit that, for most of the tasks used by experimental psychologists, linguistic and spatial intelligences provide the principle sources of storage and solution."[58]

The special status Gardner accords this mode of thought is underlined by his concluding observations about it. Gardner indicates that there is evidence that this particular mode has greater longevity in individuals, and may be associated in a fundamental way with what we know as wisdom. Here, once again, is the preoccupation with wholes, rather than parts, with patterns rather than pieces, with similarities rather than differences.

> My own view is that each form of intelligence has a natural life course: while logical-mathematical thought proves fragile later in life, across all individuals . . . at least certain aspects of visual and spatial knowledge prove robust, especially in individuals who have practiced them regularly throughout their lives. There is a sense of the whole, a "gestalt" sensitivity, which is central in spatial intelligence, and which seems to be a reward for aging—a continuing or perhaps even an enhanced capacity to appreciate the whole, to discern patterns even when certain details or fine points may be lost. Perhaps wisdom draws on this sensitivity to patterns, forms, and whole.

This "sensitivity to patterns, forms, and whole" does indeed appear to be a recurrent theme among the visual thinkers we are considering. It is a habit of mind that seems to bring with it certain considerable advantages and possibly some disadvantages. We have already noted Maxwell's observations about Faraday's approach—starting from the whole and working to the parts, in contrast to that of the mathematicians. A similar predisposition, on several levels, has been observed about Maxwell himself. One biographer said his own approach to Maxwell's life has necessarily "laid stress on Maxwell's *wholeness*—the remarkable way in which from an early age, his life, his work, and his philosophy were always interwoven."[60]

In a somewhat different way, Einstein was observed to have an uncanny sense of the whole in the scientific problems on which he was working. One biographer pointed out that, although Einstein had a reputation for making frequent small errors, he was able to arrive at correct results in very complex calculations where even small errors could easily have thrown him off the scent.[61] Aware of this special ability, Einstein joked that he had a good "nose" for such things. Curiously, this sense of the whole also is often seen to characterize the thought of dyslexic and learning-disabled children. They are quite often described as being "global" thinkers who have a heightened sense of the whole but make frequent errors in details.

If Gardner's observations are correct—that the visual-spatial mode may not only yield unexpected solutions but also may be strongly associated with real wisdom—then the presumed relationship between spatial intelligence and dyslexia gains significantly in importance. For, if so, then it would appear that the capacity that can promote both innovation and wisdom may be relatively undeveloped or underrepresented in our conventional leaders, whether in the sciences, politics, or other areas. Or, alternatively, it could be that many of those people most able to comprehend and provide enduring solutions to some of the most complex problems may be the same ones usually excluded from positions of authority or excluded from the community of discourse that informs and advises those in authority.

What is needed is balance in individuals and in groups. The tendency of the educational system to be preoccupied with quick verbal responses and vast amounts of testable "facts" may have had the regrettable, long term effect of influencing individual development in a one-sided way.[62] Thus, the same system could serve a dual function—molding some individuals in one-sided, limited ways, while at the same time excluding those who would not or could not be molded. Such a system would award credentials to only one sort of person, where many sorts are needed.

Only rarely, perhaps, does a thinker such as Einstein slip through the net of exclusion because of a series of improbable circumstances. And more rarely still is the apparent connection observed between an unusually effectual mode of thought and certain disabilities.

> An apparent defect in a particular person may merely indicate an imbalance of our normal expectations. A noted deficiency should alert us to look for a proficiency of a different kind in the exceptional person. The late use of language in childhood, the difficulty in learning foreign languages . . . may indicate a polarization or displacement in some of the skill from the verbal to another area. That other, enhanced area is without a doubt, in Einstein's case, an extraordinary kind of visual imagery that penetrates his very thought processes.[63]

These observations by Gerald Holton, a physicist and a historian of science, seem surprisingly close to those of the neurologists Geschwind and Galaburda. The basis and extent of the presumed association of visual thinking, creativity, and certain linguistic or mathematical disabilities are still far from clear. However, this convergence of evidence from various disciplines indicates that an unexpected new line of development may be emerging.

PRELIMINARY OBSERVATIONS

The foregoing discussion suggests that the conventional beliefs on which our educational system and major institutions are based may be fundamentally flawed. The idea is in opposition to common belief, yet it seems that it may very well be true: there may exist, in some cases, an essential and necessary link between some extraordinary abilities (especially those associated with creative, visual-spatial thinking) and dyslexia or some forms of learning difficulties (however varied in type or severity). Should we expect, then, that the person with unusual creative abilities may not be able to write, or to read, or to add, or to remember, or to speak as quickly or as well as others do? Or, conversely, should we expect that one who does all these things early and well is thereby more limited? Although the evidence supporting this new perspective may be inconclusive, it is clear that we should be asking some new questions. The implications in at least three areas seem especially important.

Assessment. Perhaps we should be assessing children (and adults) not for ten or twelve skills in order to try to measure intelligence and ability, but rather for scores or hundreds of skills. Each skill might be considered separately, with the understanding that low ability in some areas might be an indicator of extraordinarily high abilities in other areas, perhaps not yet discovered because they are rarely measured. Through the use of modern graphics and gesture-based personal computers and related devices (possibly with sophisticated sound and motion-simulation capabilities), it may be possible to measure, at a comparatively modest cost, a vastly increased range of visual-spatial and other socially valued skills that have not previously lent themselves to conventional paper-and-pencil methods of assessment. An excessive focus on "normal" abilities may have obscured an understanding of the high degree of variation within populations, masking many forms of giftedness which may often go undetected. One of the common indicators of bright dyslexics and others like them is a distinctive peak-

and-valley pattern in intelligence tests and other measures of ability.[64] In many places these extreme scores are averaged together to produce an overall score in the middle range that completely obscures the realities of these people's minds—a mix of unusual talents and disabilities. In time, modest increases in assessment testing might have major benefits in avoiding wasted effort, frustration, and rebellion as well as self-destructive and antisocial behavior.

Education. Our educational system, in focusing on remediation of certain disabilities, may be dealing with only half a condition, and the least interesting half. Somehow, a way needs to be found to deal with a very broad range of skill levels to address both unusual abilities and special difficulties in the same individuals. With far more comprehensive forms of assessment, educational efforts could be focused on developing areas of unusual strength (even in less conventional areas), avoiding the common practices of either streaming students based on an average across a limited set of conventional indicators or placing them in remedial groups based almost exclusively on areas of unusual weakness. If the view set forth here is correct, the main emphasis should be on cultivating these individuals for their varied and unusual gifts and abilities rather than mainly remediating them for their special difficulties. These abilities have little to do with the range and variety of skills needed in the past, those that have shaped our traditional categories and conventional indicators. One anthropologist has observed, "We Americans are oriented toward the sensorily homogenized masses—men and women without any particular talent, or if they have talent, that is what is *not* studied. Consequently, our psychology has not contributed much to man's knowledge of the range of capabilities of the human species as it should. This is a mistake. Our Einsteins not only lead the way but set things up so that less gifted people can follow."[65]

Much changes if we consider that there are broad areas that we have hardly begun to understand. In one major area, a careful study of the journals and papers (especially the drawings, sketches, mechanical models, and sculptured surfaces) of exceptional visual thinkers such as Faraday, Maxwell, Einstein, and Edison might provide profound new insights concerning the operation of the visual mode and ways to improve its development and application in those with similar talents. Also, it is apparent that visual spatial modes of thought need far more attention in the educational process, especially at higher levels. While visual approaches have received greater attention at lower grade levels for some time, higher education is slow to change and still relies heavily on traditional academic methods—books and lectures. Systematic experimentation with a range of emerging, visually oriented tools and processes might prove to be especially fruitful for many different kinds of students with different talents and different brains. Recent efforts toward visualizing scientific and mathematical concepts using animated computer graphics are a major step in this direction, already yielding substantial educational and research benefits. Another major step is the increasing use of computer-based simulators to teach and test professionals ranging from airline pilots and military personnel to medical students.[66] Today many are concerned with those who have low reading abilities and those who have difficulty absorbing large quantities of written material. If our perspective is correct, it may not be very long before we are equally concerned with those who have low visualization abilities and those who have great difficulty applying specialized knowledge to simulated reality.

Organizations. Whether corporations, universities, research centers, or government agencies, organizations could be adapted to make far better use of persons with uneven abilities, recognizing that some of the most gifted may often have great difficulty with things that are easy for others.[67] Our diverse, specialized, pluralistic society should provide a wealth of opportunities for the best fit of individuals to a variety of institutional settings, especially when valuable unused talents may provide original and effective solutions for enduring problems. The range of opportunities should be expected to grow rapidly as we see successive waves of inexpensive, "smart" electronic devices whose capabilities are nicely matched to many conventional areas of difficulty. Indeed, in some cases, these machines may come to be used as extensions and amplifiers of the imagination, permitting gifted visual-spatial thinkers to work in a visual-spatial language on fast and powerful graphics-oriented computers, developing and effectively communicating their ideas in novel ways.[68] During a time of greatly increased international competition, a variety of organizations may be able to tolerate, and substantially benefit from (in ways rarely possible before), great diversity in capabilities and talents.

In the past there have been many examples of the success of exceptional creative skills applied to pressing organizational and institutional needs. But, if we look carefully, these successes have often been achieved in spite of, rather than because of, conventional education and selection criteria. Creative people with high levels of traditional academic skills may be as rare today as creative people with noble blood were centuries ago. Perhaps, in the future, we can start to do by design and intention what has heretofore occurred mostly by accident.[69]

A better understanding of dyslexia and other learning difficulties might shed light on normal but poorly understood human capabilities—modes of thought that may be essential to finding truly effective creative solutions to the complex problems affecting our society. It is not unusual, in the history of medicine or science, to pursue the investigation of what was first thought to be a relatively minor question—merely a puzzling loose end—and end up with a surprising new understanding that at once not only answers the original question but also entirely transforms the former perspective of the whole.

2

DYSLEXIA AND LEARNING DIFFICULTIES FROM THE INSIDE

A rticles on dyslexia and learning disabilities have been appearing in the popular press off and on for a number of years. However, first-person accounts of the experience of dyslexics have been quite rare until comparatively recently. Among the earliest book-length personal accounts was Eileen Simpson's *Reversals*, published in 1979. Earlier accounts were few and short. As Simpson observes in the preface to her book, "The autobiographical accounts one does find are brief . . . anonymous or pseudonymous. Even nowadays, when the confessional mode is in style, and people talk candidly about what used to be called their private lives, the inhibition against revealing intellectual failures and limitations is strong. The old shame and fear of ridicule remain forever lively."[1]

Accordingly, we should not be surprised to find that one of the earliest and most common responses of the dyslexic to his or her condition is to hide it, often going to great lengths to maintain an elaborate pretense. It should also be no surprise, consequently, that dyslexics, whether children or adults, are rarely willing to remove a cover they have built with much care over many years (especially if the intellectual milieu of the time provides no clear rationale for benefiting themselves or others through such revelations). Fortunately, this has begun to change.

Although the inability to read printed words had come to be recognized in the medical literature as a specific problem as early as the 1890s, it was most often seen as merely an indicator of low intellectual ability.[2] However, attitudes slowly began to change. Among those who came in contact with Dr. Samuel T. Orton and his associates in the 1920s and 1930s dyslexia came to be seen as primarily neurological in origin and as a condition that was not inconsistent with high intelligence. But for a long time it was a comparatively small group that viewed the problem this way, one made up of a few committed physicians, psychologists, teachers, tutors, and parents. The time was not right, and unsympathetic psychological and psychoanalytic explanations for learning difficulties dominated, a situation that continued for the next four or five decades.

It was only in the 1970s and 1980s that the gradual increase of knowledge and a shift of attitudes, together with official recognition and legislation, has spread the contemporary view of dyslexia as a relatively stigma-free condition that is not uncommon among persons of normal or superior intelligence, a condition that may cause a good deal of difficulty and heartache but one that usually responds to treatment by those with the proper training. Indeed, in more recent years, the diagnosis of dyslexia seems to have become a source of comfort to many parents with children having unusual difficulty with academic work.

During recent years, more and more prominent people have been revealing that they are dyslexics and that, in spite of their substantial success in varied career fields, they continue to have difficulties with many of the problems that have bothered them since their youth. As dyslexia and learning disabilities have become more clearly identified with persons of high intelligence and ability, these conditions seem less frightening and people are less reluctant to admit the problem and seek appropriate help. Lately, a substantial number of personal accounts of dyslexia had appeared, providing a clear impression of what dyslexia really looks like, and feels like, from the inside.

DWAYNE

One of the earlier accounts that deal at some length with the life of a dyslexic (rather than the usual brief clinical profile) is the story of

Dwayne. This story, published in 1968 in a booklet of twenty-three pages, deals extensively with the wide life effects experienced by an adult dyslexic. The account shows the notable lack of public awareness about dyslexia, even among the educational and mental-health professionals of the time to whom the publication is addressed. Dwayne is described as

> a young man [who] paints pictures in his spare time, writes song lyrics, plays the guitar, and engages his friends in discussions of everything from the findings of Galileo to subtle points of physics or the writings of . . . Plato. None of this would seem too remarkable except for one fact. Dwayne, 32, can neither read nor write. He is a victim of dyslexia . . . although until very recent years he simply thought of himself as either damaged or stupid. Nothing in his looks reveals his problem. A large man, he resembles a college football player. He dresses neatly, speaks well. His clear blue eyes look directly at one, and his dimples show often. His face is pleasant, bearing no evidence of the ravages of a disability which he has been struggling all of his life to conceal.[3]

A number of the points mentioned here are often observed with respect to dyslexics and those with learning disabilities—talent in the visual arts and verse writing, interest in philosophical and scientific thought, skill in music. The pattern is quite distinctive: the paradoxically wide intellectual interests coupled with special abilities in art and music are often seen in combination with major difficulties in reading and writing. Sometimes (but not always) these are also seen in combination with difficulties in speaking and certain forms of mathematical computation.

Dwayne's story, like many earlier case histories, is retold by another person. It is only in more recent years that we are seeing autobiographies. Interestingly, most of the early autobiographical accounts were given by women. One psychologist experienced in the field has observed that the rarity of early reports by men may be attributed to the greater reserve men seem to have in admitting to any form of weakness, whether physical or intellectual.[4]

SHOCK OF RECOGNITION

In recent years, there seems to have been a greater acceptance of the wide range of normal variation, so that not all differences are treated as deviations from an artificial mass standard. However, the existence and the prevalence of dyslexia and learning disabilities continue to be matters of considerable debate. Nonetheless, while teachers, parents, psychologists, and school administrators may argue about definitions, standard deviations, and cutoff scores, the children know, in their bones, from the beginning, that something they experience is very different from what their classmates experience. According to Eileen Simpson,

> There was something wrong with my brain. What had previously been a shadowy suspicion that hovered on the edge of consciousness became certain knowledge the year I was nine and entered fourth grade. I seemed to be like other children, but I was not like them: I could not learn to read or spell. Had my present friends, acquaintances, colleagues, and I grown up together, there would have been an abyss between them and me. The books they were then reading, I did not read. Their compositions merited gold stars, won prizes; mine were unacceptable. They were at the top of their classes; I was at the bottom. Throughout my childhood and youth the nature of my disorder remained mysterious to me and those in my milieu. When I was twenty-two it was diagnosed—not by a psychologist but by a poet: I was dyslexic.[5]

Fourth grade was also a watershed of realization for Dwayne.

> Although Dwayne was able to get through the first three grades with adequate report cards and no gross difficulties, he knew that something was wrong with him. When he stood up to recite in class, the children laughed at his expressions. He feigned sore throats, did everything he knew to keep from going to school—painful school where he had to try and try and try and never quite succeed in being like the other children. He soon learned that if his mother read an assignment to him, he could begin to memorize it and recite it in class. The coping mechanisms started to work.[6]

For dyslexics, the third and fourth grades can be a time of crisis and intense emotional turmoil. But, for some, the full recognition of the problem may not come until adolescence or well into adult life. The early traumas, especially when they are deeply suppressed and surrounded with self-denial, might not come to the surface until much later, when some crucial experience forces a self-confrontation. Then the deep and powerful emotions become fully evident.

One man, seeing a film on dyslexia, became violently ill while observing the painful attempts at oral reading of a dyslexic third grader, bringing back in a flash his own early difficulties and humiliations. Powerful and long-standing self-denial frequently makes it difficult for affected parents to recognize and accept clear evidence of the problem in their own children. Another father, on learning of the likelihood of dyslexia in his young son, began to tremble and shiver uncontrollably—not realizing until much later that the cause was not a sudden change in the temperature of the room. One young woman, on learning in college of the basis of the problems that had tortured her during her early educational experience, wept for weeks.[7]

Apparently, some dyslexics can hide the problem from themselves as well as from others, but the powerful emotions remain. Often it is only a matter of time before it all comes flooding back. But then the problem can be addressed squarely, permitting the exploration of many alternative solutions. It is difficult to devise effective solutions until the problem is first fully acknowledged. This acknowledgment can also lead to a clearer picture of strengths, and may ultimately serve to promote greater self confidence and a greater willingness to risk developing areas of special strength even though this may involve a departure from formerly cautious patterns of behavior.

GETTING BY: COMPENSATION AND DECEIT

As we have noted, many dyslexics learn from the start that the best strategy (if they don't have understanding people around them) is to hide their disabilities as much as possible. There are no rewards for revelation, and the penalties can take the most humiliating forms. One psychiatrist familiar with the experience of dyslexics has observed that, "Because of the great rewards in being considered normal, almost all persons who are in the position to pass as being fluent readers, even though they really are not, will do so. This puts one who 'passes' in jeopardy, for he is constantly liable to the threat of exposure . . . These people live in a world that teeters on the verge of collapse at any moment. They are constantly liable to being exposed and thus being discredited. The chronic anxiety that this provokes is a variant of the phobic state."[8]

These observations are confirmed in Dwayne's experience. In his classes he would try to hide behind the other students so the teacher would not call on him. When these maneuvers failed and he was called on, he would recite some other part of the book that he had memorized beforehand—then the teacher would think he was reading from the wrong page, not that he could not read at all. "I lived a big lie," Dwayne said. "I would devour funny books because I could get the story. I adored mechanical jobs. I drew whenever I could, but I never let anyone know that I really couldn't read, couldn't make sense out of a written page."[9] Dwayne would try to do things he was good at and would compensate where possible by absorbing information in other forms, but mostly, as the pressure began to build, he had to fall back on evasion, cheating, and deceit. "All my time was spent in learning how to 'get by,'" Dwayne explained. "I would study the teachers to learn their methods of giving tests and of grading. I fought as if every day were a new battle which had to be survived. I learned to put down answers in my own kind of understandable shorthand on pencils, inside of socks, on my fingers, anywhere. I systematically changed my way of cheating and worked at the project constantly."[10]

In this passage we see not only how hard Dwayne worked to avoid detection, but also how inventive and sophisticated he could be, presumably using resources that far surpassed those that would ordinarily have been needed to do the set assignments as required—if, indeed, it had been possible for him to do them as assigned. It is notable that one instance of his inventiveness was the creation of his own shorthand, one that was understandable to him alone.

This special interest in learning a shorthand or creating some other unconventional symbolic system occurs repeatedly among those we are considering. For example, Susan Hampshire, the dyslexic English actress, devised a personal system of pictures, symbols, and other cues to help her read and absorb the scripts for her stage and film roles. Conventional shorthand, however, remained mysterious to her.[11] Among the various learning disability traits shown by Woodrow Wilson was a curious and passionate interest in stenographic shorthand, which he taught himself and used extensively.[12] It is noteworthy that even Leonardo da Vinci, whose extraordinary visual abilities were mixed with language difficulties, often used symbols akin to stenographic shorthand in his notebooks.[13] If one has special difficulty with conventional written language, one may devise one's own written language. Often it takes a form based on pictures (like Chinese ideographs or ancient Egyptian hieroglyphs) or on forms that can be written quickly and read as wholes (like stenographic shorthand). Both forms presumably avoid some of the problems of syntax, sequencing, and confusing idiosyncrasies of spelling common to English and other languages. The precise form of Dwayne's shorthand is not described, although it would not be surprising to find it based on some comparable form of symbolic system.[14]

Dwayne's capacity for inventive deception led to clever strategies in adult life.

> His coping skills were needed in job applications. When he was handed an application to fill out, he suddenly looked at his watch and said, "I didn't realize it was so late. I have a doctor's appointment. May I bring this back tomorrow?" Or, "My father is circling the block in all this traffic. Suppose I take this home and return it later." Then at home, his mother would fill out the application and give it to him to return.[15]

It is not at all difficult to imagine how this habit of deceit could eventually lead to serious trouble, as in fact it sometimes does. But it was clear that for Dwayne it was a source of pride to achieve goals honestly whenever possible. It was a way of proving himself to himself. Much later he had an opportunity to cheat on a test to get a job he wanted. But he refused to cheat because it was so important to him to prove himself in a truthful way and because he was concerned that other people's well-being might be affected by his disability.[16]

UNRULY WORDS, ELUSIVE LETTERS

For some dyslexics, difficulties with handwriting can be as severe as those with reading. A particularly vivid description of how unruly words can be is given by one severely affected individual in his description of the use of personal computers as remedial writing tools:

> I'm thirty-one years old, dyslexic and dysgraphic. As many dyslexic people who have struggled with writing know, hard work alone doesn't eliminate the problem. Spelling, organization and logic problems, coupled with dyslexia-caused mistakes, are always present to undermine our writing and our morale. But there are tools that can help us compensate. The newest ones—microcomputers and word processing programs—have completely changed the part of the writing process that has made writing so hard and inaccessible for many people with learning disabilities. I read a line and as I get to the end of it I start to lose the beginning. I go back and reread the beginning and lose the end. This is assuming that what I am seeing is what's on the page. I may be reversing letters within words, changing their meaning, or reversing words within the sentence, changing its meaning. I type a first draft, then go back and read it. I type a second draft to correct the mistakes I found. In reading the second draft, I find a new set of mistakes. Not only are there new clerical mistakes which anyone might make, but there are words misspelled which I spelled correctly on the first draft! When this is compounded with the initial problem of holding whole sentence chunks in my head at one time I wonder how I can read and write at all.[17]

REVEALING PARTY GAMES

The early school years tend to emphasize the most common areas of weakness for many dyslexics. It is virtually a matter of definition that this should be so—most dyslexics are identified primarily because they have difficulties in just these areas. In later adult life many of these same problem areas can often be avoided with relative ease. For the dyslexic, early schooling is not the only hazardous time, however. In certain groups, friendly dinner parties and harmless parlor games can be just as dangerous. Simpson explains how joining her husband in an academic environment would have made life especially difficult if an accident of history had not saved her, for a time, from repeated exposure and humiliation. "One might expect that it would have been more difficult for me to pass in academic society, especially at Harvard, than with my New York friends. And so it might have been but for the war which had greatly curtailed entertaining. There were none of those little dinner parties, such as I would go to later, where the guests behave as if they are examiners at Ph.D. orals ('What do you think of . . . ?' 'Have you read . . . ?'), where one is expected to shine, compete, perform."[18]

Simpson also recalls an occasion when resistance to a spelling game and then her obstinate refusal to read parts of a play during an informal summer vacation entertainment created an embarrassing situation impossible for her husband and friends to understand. Simpson describes one of the penalties for passing as if one is like those unaffected. "Spelling and now reading aloud! What were amusements for others, who had learned to read precociously and had been the stars of their classes, was torture for me. There could have been no more brutal reminder that I was far from cured. . . . To be asked to take a part set off the trembling again. Trying to keep the terror out of my voice, I declined."[19]

Thomas Edison's poor memory for words and names was also once revealed during a summer vacation parlor game. But unlike many, Edison was, at the time, already recognized and successful as an inventor so that he apparently had no reservations about recording the incident, without further comment, in his brief diary of the time.

ALTERNATE WAYS OF LEARNING

Dramatic changes during the past few years with respect to dyslexia have not been restricted to changes in attitudes. There has also been an explosion of alternative channels for learning. Books on audio tapes, videotaped films, and educational television have made a vast range of information available in inexpensive, varied, and easily accessible forms ideally suited to dyslexics. Dwayne's experience provides an especially poignant example of the great value of these materials:

> Finally the breakthrough came one evening when he was in his early twenties. He returned home from his job and saw a program on educational television. The program was on Zen Buddhism. Dwayne sat down in front of the set and was instantly absorbed in the discussion.

The vocabulary exceeded his ability to comprehend, but he knew that he was grasping the essence of the subject. Soon Dwayne was following the educational programs on television. He heard a Scandinavian physicist and scientist. . . . He . . . grew excited with the understanding. . . . The black cloth of nonlearning was lifted from his eyes, and he saw and felt and remembered and understood.[20]

COMPENSATING TALENTS, SKIPPING OVER THE BASICS

It is often observed that dyslexics, like those with other handicaps, naturally learn to compensate by focusing on other areas where there are greater strengths. In some cases, this seems to be so. In other cases, not. Occasionally, however, the difficulty itself can provide an occasion for learning a useful skill that might otherwise never have been acquired. Simpson provides a particularly vivid sketch of how she converted some of her awkward dyslexic traits from liabilities into assets.

Quite by chance I made an invaluable discovery. If, when I made a slip of the tongue, I put on a droll expression, or if, when I made an awkward gesture, I gave it a Chaplinesque flourish, my audience ceased mocking and began applauding. This act was not easy to bring off. It required alertness (for which I was not famous), as well as timing and practice. Above all, it was essential to suppress the sense of shock I felt at each fresh bit of evidence that my skull housed an unruly brain.

Instead of being astonished to have said, "The birds are losing their leaves" (when what 1 meant, of course, was that they were losing their feathers), I had to catch the cue from my interlocutors' expression that what I had said was ludicrous and pretend to have said it on purpose. Instead of blushing with confusion to have extended my left instead of my right to shake hands, I had to make my left hand describe an amusing arabesque in the air as if it had been a mere preparation for presenting the right. The first time I brought it off Aunt Lucy said, "You are a sketch!" To be a sketch was greatly preferable to being the family idiot.

Encouraged, I tried out my act in school. What had made Aunt Lucy smile ruefully made my classmates, always greedy for a diversion, explode with laughter. The same boys and girls who the previous year had laughed at the freak were now laughing with the jester. The teacher clapped her hands and said, "Class! Class!" calling it to order, but she was laughing too. It wasn't long before I was acknowledged to be the class clown.

A side effect of my clowning, as agreeable as it was unpredictable, was that I became popular. . . . At P.S. 52, to be popular was very, very important. It gave one more status than having a good character, being pretty, rich, athletic, or even intelligent.[21]

Sometimes the passage of time is enough to remove some of the most difficult tasks for dyslexics. As we have observed before, while the material studied becomes more demanding in the upper grades, paradoxically it sometimes becomes easier for bright dyslexics who thrive on the advanced content and benefit greatly when elementary tasks, which are especially difficult for them, are dropped from the curriculum. Simpson notes, "To my great relief, to my great joy, oral reading disappeared from the syllabus in fifth grade. And with its disappearance my reading grade rose from a failure to a 65: passing, but only just. My new teacher seemed to be much more interested in her students' conduct than in their intellectual performance."[22]

EMPLOYMENT PANIC

For many dyslexics, the experience of school is difficult, painful, and often humiliating. But the prospect of real work in the world of adults is a cause for despair and even terror. For those to whom education has meant progressing from strength to strength, adult work is seen as an opportunity to confidently display acknowledged talents. For those to whom education has meant a string of defeats in nearly all areas, from academics to athletics, the prospect of adult work can be threatening in the extreme.

Of course, this need not be so, if the right choices are made. Adult life provides a vast range of opportunities rarely met with in schools where many dyslexics can succeed and gain recognition, perhaps for the first time in their lives. But after being battered by eleven or twelve years of repeated failure, many dyslexics see only imminent disaster and have little thought of opportunities. Others are more fortunate and are merely anxious and frightened.

Susan Hampshire is an actress who has become known in Britain and America through her roles in films, plays, and popular television series based on the novels of Anthony Trollope, William Thackeray, and others. Her book *Susan's Story* was published in 1981. Its subtitle was "An Autobiographical Account of My Struggle with Words." Since the publication of her book, she has been active in informing the British public about dyslexia through television interviews and other media. In *Susan's Story*, Hampshire describes her great concern about the narrow work options apparently open to her when she finished school. She had been educated in a school run by her mother which, fortunately, allowed her to focus on areas of strength. But her severe academic weaknesses remained. Thus, although many higher education and professional career opportunities for young women were beginning to open in the 1950s, Hampshire's reading ability and academic skills were so weak that almost all attractive options seemed to be closed.

> The universities, medical schools, hospitals and law schools were taking a small percentage of women. . . . But what were the options open to me? My two sisters had worked for a short time in the theater and now taught in the school. This, of course, I could not do. I still had not mastered the alphabet. I didn't get any "O" levels, except Art, as I couldn't read the questions. . . . What path could possibly be open to a girl with my remarkable lack of achievement? Mother's help? Cook? Children's nanny? Gardener? Swimming-pool attendant? I couldn't even become a chauffeuse—I didn't know right from left—or a telephonist, since I couldn't remember numbers in sequence. I couldn't become a nurse as Latin "O" level was obligatory, nor a secretary since I couldn't spell and shorthand was even more mysterious to me than plain English.

The only answer seemed to be marriage. But that meant the loss of freedom. For Hampshire, "freedom was a very high priority." In the end, she remembered her successes acting in school plays and decided to try the stage. With the help of a friend, she wrote letters "to all the repertory companies in England. I got one reply, with the offer of a job."[23]

LEARNING WITHOUT BOOKS

Hampshire's job was with a small theater group and it made many demands on her—making sets, mending costumes, as well as acting in a variety of roles. It proved, however, to be an immensely positive factor in her early development. She was able to learn by doing, producing each day real products needed by her group. (As we will see, Winston Churchill explained that he would have preferred some similar alternative route for himself, avoiding the traditional academic preparation altogether or at least delaying it until a later time, when he would have gotten more out of it.) Hampshire could develop at her own speed while she did useful work, receiving pay for this work (however small), and not having to deal with her virtually non-existent academic skills. Neither her mother's school nor this work experience trained her to think of herself as defective. Indeed, her coworkers throughout her early career had no idea that she had such severe trouble with reading and other academic skills. While it is good that special remedial help is now available for those with learning disabilities, we ought not to forget the great advantage of being able to work and to pay one's own way using one's strengths, while one is slowly dealing with areas of weakness and difficulty.

It may be possible that dyslexia and other learning disabilities have come to be seen as important and widespread problems only in those societies that have almost totally eliminated any form of the apprenticeship system and have almost universally replaced it with an academic approach to nearly all learning. In a time when even manual and vocational skills are often taught largely in classroom settings, we may wonder to what extent Hampshire's successful development as an actress had to do with the fact that she was able to take another route to her career, avoiding the emotional pounding that an academic route, however caring and humane, would have necessarily entailed. Surely, it must make a lot of difference whether one's daily efforts are devoted to fixing one's own extensive deficiencies or to doing things well, producing things that are needed and valued by others, using one's special strengths.

When rare, the typewritten letter used to carry special weight; now, it is said, the handwritten note commands the most attention. Similarly, as the wheel turns once again, in the future we might possibly find, as the increasingly diluted academic approach has spread nearly everywhere, and as a new economy demands some very different skills, that new forms of apprenticeship (ones that can allow to flower those with trouble in traditional academic settings) could become the most desirable and effective routes to some of the most sought-after and productive positions.

Our great-great-grandfathers (whether farmers, merchants, or craftsmen) learned mostly from doing, from helping and imitating, and from making mistakes, relying more on hand and eye than on word and phrase. Our grandfathers and our mothers and fathers learned primarily from books; in most cases they were not allowed into the world of real work until quite late and rarely received further education afterward.

Before long, however, we may see another major reversal in the culture of education and work. Our sons and daughters may learn mostly from experience once again, actively, using all their senses, but this time using visual and kinesthetic computer simulations of reality as much as reality itself. And in this reversed new world, where education would alternate with real work throughout life, the creative dyslexics and imaginative experimenters may find themselves, once again, better adapted to changed circumstances than those who are (only) best at reading, retaining, and accurately recalling millions and millions of words.

PEER DENIAL AND DISBELIEF

It is of great importance for dyslexics to receive confirmation that their academic problems do in fact result from real difficulties not experienced by others. They need to know that the problems that they experience are real and not imagined. To have extreme difficulty with things that are easy for one's peers is painful. To be told that one's problems result merely from laziness or lack of motivation is difficult to bear. To have others believe that one is playing the fool and courting humiliation repeatedly and voluntarily is intolerable. The relief and sense of personal vindication that comes from a positive diagnosis based on a professional evaluation should not be underestimated, whether for children or adults, especially for adults. When one has struggled so long without recognition, it is a great comfort to have something like objective confirmation of what one has always known but few others believed or understood.

This confirmation is valuable not as an excuse to avoid performing but as an aid in finding alternative ways to real accomplishment. (Indeed, if we are correct, then often—but not always—more rather than less should be expected of dyslexics and those like them compared with those having "ordinary" brains.) It is also an important validation of one's perception of personal reality and a verification of the reality of one's struggle—one which may often have been a cause for considerable personal uncertainty and confusion. Once testing and evaluation has confirmed one's suspicions, often one may still be confronted with the fixed idea, even among those experienced in the field, that dyslexia and other learning disabilities are incompatible with high intelligence, ability, or professional competence.

Drawing on her experience as a clinical psychologist, Simpson provides a striking example of this fixed idea in a professional setting. When Simpson was completing a two-year assistantship at a reading center for dyslexics in Rutgers, New Jersey, intending to go into private practice, she realized that the director of the center, a Dr. Starr, had forgotten Simpson's plan and was instead grooming her to take over the center when she retired. Although Simpson felt quite pleased with her own development as a psychotherapist, she found that her own history of dyslexia caused her to be "insufficiently objective with the pupils at the center to be useful, much less happy, working with them." She points out in passing, however, that other dyslexics, who do not feel as she does, often are among the best remedial teachers.

When Starr attempted to persuade Simpson to stay at the center at the end of her assistantship, Simpson tried to explain her feelings about working at the center. During the conversation she provided a brief account of her own personal history of dyslexia. Starr's reaction was immediate: "She was incredulous. What nonsense! I could never have been like the children at the Center. To pretend that I had been was 'self-dramatization.' Perhaps I had been a little slower in reading than in other subjects . . . but dyslexic? Impossible."

Clearly, Starr was one among the numbers of professionals in education and psychology who saw a vast gulf between persons of high intelligence and dyslexics. One group is made up of those like oneself, the capable ones, one's peer group, those always at the top of the class. The other group is made up of the dependent ones, those who need one's help, those always at the bottom.

Part of the reason this fixed idea could persist is that those dyslexics with high intelligence have often developed such successful coping strategies that they can anticipate and control situations that might reveal weaknesses. As Simpson points out,

> Dr. Starr, who never saw adult dyslexics, or rather, didn't recognize them because they passed so cunningly, underestimated what they are capable of, even without remedial training. . . . One way or another, intelligent dyslexics do learn to read—inefficiently, painfully, slowly. What proper teaching spares those who receive it is the inefficiency, a good deal of the pain, and the terrible waste of years.[24]

Simpson highlights a frequent point of confusion, shared among professionals and laypeople alike. Dyslexics do not necessarily avoid reading. Some writers have observed that those dyslexics who read extensively and are interested in books are probably misdiagnosed and are not dyslexic at all.[25] But this is one of the many illuminating paradoxes of dyslexia. Dyslexics are as interested as anyone in the content of books, even though the process of reading may be extraordinarily difficult for them. Of course, much depends upon their level of curiosity, their intelligence, and their range of interests, as with anyone else. Those books that are read are read for their content, not because the process of reading is easy. As Simpson notes, dyslexics do learn to read, but much later, with much more effort, and more slowly than others. If the interest is great, then dyslexics can go to extraordinary lengths to decipher the material, even if they need to proceed at a speed more appropriate for deciphering an ancient and alien script. This is why it is so important to use adult materials in adult literacy programs. Even if the vocabulary is considered difficult, the serious interest and sense of genuine accomplishment may easily outweigh the additional difficulties. Dwayne was described as laboring for hours over a single page because he was so intensely interested in the content of what he was trying to read. At a recent conference, a father told the story of his dyslexic daughter. His daughter's friends found reading easy, but rarely read very much, while his daughter, for whom reading was so difficult, was "reading all the time."[26]

"RELAPSE"

One of the recurring observations of dyslexics is that as they get older, learn more survival strategies, and become successful in demanding fields, they come to believe, mistakenly, that they are cured, that they are just like everyone else. Some of the worst panics, then, may come in the middle of successful careers, when they discover, to their horror, that this is not true. Simpson describes an event of this kind that happened to her after she had been living in Europe for a while with her husband. An idea for a short story had begun to take shape.

> There followed a period of bad days as severe as any I'd suffered. . . . Superimposed upon the predictable difficulties that assail me when I ever try anything new and ambitious was the confusion caused by my recent immersion in the French language. The new language had loosened my slippery grip on the old one. French idioms crowded out American usage. Verb tenses, which I had heretofore used by ear rather than by rule, were now governed by the French sequence of tenses. My spelling became a jumble of French and English, the English its usual mixture of American and British usage. The strain of trying to write brought on a relapse. If I couldn't produce a single declarative sentence, and there were days when I couldn't, how would I ever manage ten pages of fiction?

Writing on one's own may be bad enough. Reading for a video-taping or live radio broadcast can be infinitely worse. Full of confidence, Simpson once agreed to appear on a radio program to discuss her first novel, which would involve only an amiable discussion with an old friend and reading a section of the book on the air. Her reaction was immediate and profound. "No sooner had I hung up than I began to tremble violently. 'Read a section . . .' he had said. . . . Every day for the two weeks before the program, I was at the point of calling [the interviewer] to beg off. What if I froze, as I had done at the freshman assembly in high school?" Simpson finally made it through the interview, although she had gone to the radio station "as to [her] doom." "The truth is that I paid such a heavy price for my effort in exhaustion the next day I wondered if it had been worth it. Was there no end to the struggle?"[27]

For Hampshire, the experienced and highly successful actress, the panic was caused when she agreed to read a children's story for a BBC television taping session. She had tried to learn the story by heart, as she usually did. But she was so exhausted from other work at the time that she could not do it.

> Eventually, the day for taping the show loomed up and I felt so impotent that it was like being back at school. I had already asked my agent to ring the BBC to see if there was any way in which I could postpone the job, but the reply had simply been, "Tell her not to worry. There's a teleprompter. She can use that. Everyone else does." It seemed that the fact that I could not read from a teleprompter was impossible for the BBC to comprehend. . . . Once inside the studio, the feeling of emptiness in my head that I had had as a child returned. I looked at the book and couldn't see it. The more I panicked the less I could see. . . . By the time I was sitting in front of the camera with the book on my lap, ready for me to read, I thought that my head had finally turned into a ball of string, and that I had gone blind. . . . It is well known that dyslexics are at their worst under pressure and I was no exception. Sweat poured from me, my breathing became erratic and my head felt like a block of wood. Why hadn't I been strong and said beforehand, "This is a job I *cannot* do. *I cannot read*"? The truth was that I still could not admit it. It was still half a secret."[28]

MARCIA

When learning difficulties are experienced by someone with notable intellectual gifts, it inevitably leads to some confusion and ambivalence. These feelings are evident in the case of a young woman who struggled to become a medical doctor, eventually working her way into a position as an anatomical pathologist. Her mixture of abilities and disabilities follows a familiar pattern.

Marcia first heard of learning disabilities during a lecture on the subject as part of her medical school training. During her early education, she knew nothing of the problem, but she was aware something was wrong. She could not really read at all until she was about fourteen years old. However, because of an an exceptional auditory memory, she was able to retain easily everything that she heard in class and she was able to largely bluff her way through elementary school and high school without reading. From early on, she was keenly aware of the disparity between her high abilities in some areas and her notable disabilities in others. Marcia's keen awareness of these paradoxical abilities led to confused feelings. "I have never seen myself as an exceptional person. Much of my life I have struggled with feelings of failure; I couldn't cope with the idea of being a failure. And, somehow I knew I was not really a failure—I knew I was smart, not dumb, because I could understand; I just couldn't express it."[29]

In medical school, Marcia rarely read textbooks, relying primarily on lectures.[30] She found that she could cope by limiting her reading to short passages in order to memorize selected material for examinations. While in training (as well as later professional life), she was also helped by an extraordinary visual memory for certain things, such as tissue slides. In one instance, she did 100 autopsies, took only brief notes, but remembered details of them for years, despite never writing up any reports of her examinations.[31]

This remarkable long-term memory for anatomical and visual information is accompanied, however, by a treacherous memory for numerical data, even in the short term. This especially poor memory for numbers and a predisposition to confuse sequences are two areas described as major continuing problems. "Numbers, especially memory of the sequence, remains her biggest problem in her work, so she has other staff members record those data."[32]

An especially energetic person, Marcia developed her medical practice while raising two small children. But, later, she completed her pathology residency, eventually establishing and directing the clinical laboratories for two small hospitals. In addition to these responsibilities, she prepared lectures for teaching, started and managed a health club, and took care of a number of animals on the small farm where she lived with her lawyer husband. Given this range of activity, it is surprising to learn that Marcia felt that she had always been most handicapped by her poor organizational skills. "As a young person she had difficulty even organizing her clothes to figure out what to wear together. She seems to feel totally inept in keeping personal possessions organized in her home, saying 'I don't like distractions, noise, and clutter, but I can't control it in my home!'"

Even as an adult professional, Marcia continues to have difficulty with reading and writing. Writing and lectures require extensive preparation time. With respect to reading, the particular details of the continuing difficulties are worth noting: She is unable to read if there are distractions nearby, such as the sounds of children playing. However, given a quiet environment, she can "enjoy reading almost any book now, except novels, but she still reads in short periods and relies heavily on context clues for comprehension. She does not read newspapers, except the front page and the commodities/stock market listing to check the price of animals for the farm."

Marcia's areas of special strength are noteworthy. In addition to her remarkable auditory memory, she sees her ability to improvise and adapt to new situations as one of her greatest strengths. Other notable areas of strength are the ease with which she could learn to play a variety of musical instruments for a school band and the ease with which she is able to do a range of mechanical jobs around the house (like the classic mechanically inclined male stereotype). It is not very surprising that Marcia also sees as areas of special strength her exceptional creative abilities and capacity to solve problems in an innovative manner.

However, what may be most interesting and important for the arguments developed in this book is what is described as Marcia's favorite form of relaxation.

> She says her recreation is "weird daydreams" in which she manipulates scientific facts to come up with scientific answers to problems and needs. Marcia believes that living in the quiet, isolated environment of a self-sufficient farm would allow her to let her imagination go, experiment in her private laboratory, and fulfill her potential as an innovative scientist.[33]

The theme indicated here by Marcia's favorite recreation is to be repeated again and again as we profile a remarkable group of scientists, inventors, and poets. As we will see (most obviously in Faraday, Einstein, Tesla, and Yeats), it seems that for some the life of the really imaginative mind (not to be confused with "the life of the mind" associated with intellectuals and scholars) is so rich in imagery and possibility—creating and recreating models of reality in the mind's eye—that it is itself a sufficient workplace and laboratory for truly original insights and productions—that is, when conditions permit sustained reflection, for a time, without interruption and the pressure of outside responsibilities. In this, we may begin to see one key aspect of the double-blind of a certain kind of mind: an imagination that is so powerful and so rich that it can produce the most original and profound conceptions, in science and art, but which may be so enticing (especially in youth) that it is extremely difficult for the affected person to focus on an assigned task or on tumbling symbols on a lifeless page.

FAMILY HISTORY

Family history can often be a major factor in the lives of dyslexics and others with learning difficulties. Once dyslexia is identified in a child, it is quite common for some evidence of dyslexia or other learning disability to be recognized in parents and other near relatives. Often parents will discover, only after their children are diagnosed, that they themselves have some form of significant learning problem. Of course, these parents usually have long been very much aware of the ways in which their weaknesses (and strengths) differ from those of their peers, but they often are not aware that it is part of an identifiable pattern shared by many others. Sometimes family mysteries make sense for the first time, and understanding finally displaces long-repeated, erroneous explanations. Some paradoxical or puzzling behavior may suddenly make sense. When he was so good at the subject, why was his degree never finished? Why did she set up situations to avoid introducing people, so she would not have to recall so many names on demand? Or why did she often drop her voice when giving the name of someone in an introduction? Why did he always slur over the vowels in his handwriting? Why was her handwriting so bad and her letters so messy when she could draw and paint so well? Why did he speak so well but write so little and always use short words when he did? When he is so bright, why couldn't he remember the spelling of simple words?

Hampshire observes that dyslexia is unlikely to be confined to one individual in a single generation. Her mother "started her school for me when I was about five, and for ten years I remained in her, and my sisters', good care. Every morning of those ten years my mother called out the school register, and every morning she read out almost every name incorrectly."[34]

This recurring family pattern is also apparent in the life of the dyslexic immunologist Baruj Benacerraf, a Nobel laureate. As a child he had a reading deficiency that required him to focus on one word at a time. He also had poor handwriting and "absolutely dreadful" spelling. But, in time, he became a prize-winning immunologist and a Harvard University scholar as well as president of the Dana-Farber Cancer Institute in Boston. "It was not until he recognized the same difficulties in his daughter, and then in his grandson—'a mirror image of my own problems'—that he realized that his difficulties were not unique."[35] When Benacerraf was growing up in the 1920s, his learning disabilities were unrecognized. He found a way of dealing with his problems through "hard work" and "a lot of will power." Eventually, the use of a computer helped to alleviate his handwriting and spelling problems. It is not surprising, perhaps, that Benacerraf also observes that compared to others he has "a much greater perception of space and time" and that he can readily "visualize in three dimensions," special abilities he has found of particular advantage in his scientific research.

One of the traits commonly associated with dyslexia and learning difficulties is hyperactivity, or hyperkinesia (although some neurologists argue that this is a distinct group that should be considered separately from other dyslexia types). In his autobiography, *An Uncommon Gift*, James Evans explains that, "My hyperkinesias . . . was a novelty to most people, and was accepted by my parents as healthy. . . . My parents assumed that I would grow out of my energetic stage, just as my father had done. I think he too must have been hyperkinetic, but not to the degree I am." Once, when Evans was still quite young, he was playing with his visiting grandfather in an overly energetic fashion by attacking the grandfather's constantly moving legs. After receiving repeated blows to his legs from the child, the grandfather asked the father what was wrong with the boy. The father replied, "There's nothing wrong with him, Dad. He's just like you, that's all."

I've been told that after that encounter Grandpa and I developed a very special relationship, which lasted until his death shortly after my twenty-second birthday. Like me, Grandpa found it almost impossible to sit absolutely still. I used to find it consoling when I caught myself kicking my legs back and forth under my grandparents' dinner table and peeked under the table to find both my father's and my grandfather's legs moving back and forth in the same nervous pattern.[36]

In some cases, these traits are the basis of something shared across the generations. There may be the awareness of a special rapport or basis of understanding which may have as much to do with a common mode of thought as with a shared area of difficulty. It is a comfort, especially if the affected family members seem to have done well enough or, even better, if they have done quite well. (This can be a supportive chain that is broken, unfortunately, whenever a child is adopted; adopted children are much more likely to have learning disabilities than non-adopted children.[37]) Often these affected and sympathetic family members can be especially valued for their patience and tolerance as well as their roles as guides in ways that others generally would not really understand. It's important to be close to someone who knows something of what it is like, even if they never really knew what it was.

MIRRORED MINDS

When people first hear of the reversals and mirror-imaging so often associated with dyslexia or other learning difficulties, it is not uncommon for them to be immediately reminded of Leonardo da Vinci and especially the mirror writing he almost always used in his journals, notebooks, and manuscripts.[38] This pattern of reversals is sometimes called the "Leonardo Syndrome," generally referring to those who are able to write with some facility in a completely reversed fashion (in contrast to a few reversals of single letters here and there), or, indeed, those with a strong preference for reading and writing totally reversed script. While the occurrence of a few reversals of letters and numbers is quite common among those with some form of learning disability (as well as with very small children), total mirror-image reading and writing is still comparatively rare and some question its general relevance to the study of learning disabilities.

However, as Margaret Rawson, a long-time researcher in the field, has observed, laterality (or sidedness and left-right confusion) is one of the themes that recurs repeatedly in the study of learning disabilities. Rawson argues that sometimes much can be learned about things from the more exaggerated examples of them. "In trying to understand nature, including human nature, we learn much about its common, expected forms by studying extremes."[39] One such case is that of the young dyslexic woman known by the pseudonym "Louise Baker." According to Rawson,

> Louise's childhood held the all too common experiences of the severely dyslexic, perhaps neurologically impaired, youngster. . . . She describes herself as having been a hyperactive, impulsive, difficult little girl, always in trouble and not understanding why. She was unhappy, frustrated, failing; knowing that she caused pain, exasperation and anger, not wanting to be like that but unable to change herself or her situation. There was only a loving grandfather to sense her need and stand by her, even though he, also, was baffled by her inadequacies and her simultaneous drive and eagerness to find out about everything. Adolescence was in some ways worse, for she could read almost nothing, wrote illegibly and spelled in as bizarrely "dyslexic" a way as any of us has ever seen. She had plenty that was informed and well-worded to say; two good friends helped her to get some of it on paper and meet minimally, or evade, academic demands. She had a tremendous interest, and apparently some aptitude, in science, along a trail of splintered laboratory glassware. . . .[40]

The portrait is a variation on the themes we see repeated over and over again—the high energy, the unintended troublesomeness, the paradoxical academic ineptitude linked with a passionate desire for knowledge (especially in science), the reliance on helpful friends, the academic deceptions, the bewildered sympathy of a supportive near relative. With so many severe difficulties, it is surprising that Baker was not properly tested and diagnosed until she had finished high school, still unable to "read, tell time, say the alphabet, or tell left from right."[41] Knowing of her dyslexia at first "joggled" her mind, but then "liberated her from shame and fired her determination to go to college, however long and hard the way."[42] With some special help and resolute effort, Baker started attending community college and gradually showed great improvement in many academic problem areas.

However, she continued to have trouble with mirror writing. She found it difficult to know whether she was writing from left to right or whether she was writing backward, from right to left. Most of her mirror writing "just happens" and she was often not conscious of what was taking place:

> When I get tired I often lapse into "mirror writing." When it happens it is much easier to write that way. Sometimes I know and sometimes I don't know when I do it. I do it left handed, I guess. Most of my writing is left handed, although sometimes I write right handed. When I realize I am writing backwards it seems much more natural and easier. . . . It is a relief.[43]

In another passage, Baker provides a description of mirror writing that is quite striking and may be a help in understanding why Leonardo da Vinci wrote so often in this fashion. Indeed, Baker's explanation may well provide more help in understanding da Vinci than hundreds of years of speculation by scholars and specialists. "In my college work I write most of my notes in a mirror image. That prevents other students from copying my notes and also if I lose my notes people know right off whose they are. Although when I start writing backwards on purpose I can't always stop it at will. Afterwards (almost all the time anyway) I can't tell if I'm writing in the acceptable way or not."

One letter from Baker to Rawson contains an especially interesting incident. Writing on legal paper, Baker wrote properly on the front of the sheet. But when she turned the sheet over to continue, the margin was ruled on the right, not the left. Apparently, this difference was enough to flip her perspective and transform her writing into mirror writing.

In a sense, what Baker did in this instance is quite logical. On the front of the sheet, she started writing each line toward the right, starting from the ruled margin on the left. So, in a way, it is logical to start once again at the margin, in spite of the fact that the margin on the back of the sheet happens to be on the right instead of the left. Thus, on the back side she writes from right to left in mirror fashion— once again writing across the page away from the margin. Baker wrote Rawson later, "You said in a letter I wrote to you in Feb. 24th [that] the second page was mirrored. No, that wasn't done on purpose. In all my correspondence I try my best to write the right way."[44]

And in the same letter, we are shown the extraordinary difficulty Baker sometimes had reading ordinary script. Surprisingly, these difficulties are diminished by holding the conventional writing in a mirror so she can read it more easily reversed. "You said it takes effort on your part to write backwards. It takes much strenuous effort for me to write from left to right. . . . I do not have to rely on my husband to read my mail to me. I'm getting so I can handle most reading. Yet, as I had to do with your letter. I had to hold it up in the bathroom mirror in order to read it."[45]

A more pervasive example of reversed perspective is provided by Delos Smith, whose life experience is described in an article titled, "Odyssey of a 'Mirrored' Personality."[46] As a child, Smith's experience of the world was so decidedly mirrored that he started writing and even speaking backwards. "A multi-syllabled word such as 'detective' became 'tive-tec-de.' The result was a gibberish even his parents could not understand. At four, Delos was decidedly left-handed and wrote in a reversed pattern when he first began to write his name."

Fortunately, his difficulties were diagnosed early by Dr. Samuel Orton. In 1943, Delos began training under him with a "very structured, phonic, multisensory method that treated reading, writing, and spelling in a holistic, unified way. . . . In the third grade, Delos continued remedial work. . . . His progress was remarkable and by June, nine months later, he was reading on a fifth grade level."

Smith's progress through high school and college was faltering and erratic, but he finally completed his college degree and started work as a statistician and then became a public finance economist. With many active interests outside his work he thought himself successful, and he "probably would have remained in the 'closet' which hides so many dyslexic adults, had it not been for his great love of music and his interest in studying it."

In spite of this love of music, Smith had failed in almost everything musical since kindergarten. He could not carry a tune and had no sense of pitch or rhythm. When he was older he took singing and piano lessons, but was discouraged by teachers who were dismayed by his apparent total lack of all natural musical talent. Nonetheless, he continued to try to master the subject, and, in the paradoxical pattern we see repeated over and over again, when he came to the more sophisticated and difficult study of harmony and counterpoint, he did extraordinarily well, despite all his prior failures with the more elementary studies. But it was during these more sophisticated studies that Smith came to an even more surprising and powerful realization. "It was during the study of Bach's inventions and his use of retrograde (reverse order) that Delos came to the startling realization that he had never overcome his basic natural mirror tendencies but had simply made an adjustment, in the area of language, to the world around him. With the new retrograde variation, that of playing music backwards, he developed a musical feeling and an awareness of an individualized rhythm he had never before experienced."[47]

Smith's singing and piano teachers had been baffled, especially when they realized that Smith perceived ascending scales to be descending scales, and vice versa. But, as Smith explains, in spite of his teachers' puzzlement, "in music theory, I proved to be an instant success. Harmony and counterpoint lines poured out of me and my teachers were amazed because I never could play them. I wrote the lines because I could visualize them."[48]

Smith's unexpected success with music theory was still less revealing than the striking change that occurred quite suddenly when he first tried *playing* music backwards. He had been studying piano with little success for seven years. Yet when he tried playing backwards one night when he was already tired, he found the change in himself to be sudden and dramatic. "I played song after song. I played Bach. I played Mozart. I felt no fatigue. I was on an adrenalin high. Euphoria had a new meaning. Of course, I played everything backwards, but I was really playing music." With this experience came a deeper understanding of something about the nature of music as well.

As I went on, I realized that there was true laterality in music, just as there was in language. There is left-handed music and right-handed music. . . . Left-handed music is that in which the melody and power are in the left hand, and the right merely accompanies the left. Most music has the left hand supporting the right hand. . . . The whole structure of the piece is for the right hand. A well-known left-hand piece was composed by Ravel for a concert pianist, a friend who had become incapacitated in his right hand. Bach was well known for his balanced left-right whole-brained music.[49]

After this experience, Smith decided that he would stop trying to imitate the right-handed world around him and became an "open and unashamed 'mirror.'" He found that he could not only play music infinitely better, but he could (reminding us of da Vinci) compose language much better when writing backwards. "When I write from left to right, there will be a whole wastebasket full because I can't get it to go. When I write from right to left, in mirrored script, thought flows and the words follow. I have become more prolific since I began mirror writing."[50]

As Rawson pointed out, the experience of Baker and Smith is somewhere at the edge of what we can usually expect from those with dyslexia and other forms of learning disabilities. Yet we should probably give them more attention rather than less, for experiences such as theirs may well point the way to a deeper understanding of these difficulties as well as to a deeper sense of humility (and greater reservation) in making generalizations about the possibilities inherent in the human brain and mind.

ALTERNATIVE PATTERNS

Among the most important factors in dealing successfully with dyslexia is the realization that there are a variety of desirable alternative patterns, that one does not have to be limited to remedial performance or to merely trying to bring oneself up to something like ordinary standards. Simpson tells of a dyslexic she met whose experience was very different from her own.

I reminded myself that there are dyslexics who take a more rational attitude toward reading aloud. A poet and teacher, whom I had heard read verse in class, I had spotted as a dyslexic. Yes, he was one, he admitted, when I asked. His history was different from mine.

His parents had him tested when he was a child, and found that he had superior intelligence, and decided to ignore his inability to read, convinced that he would begin to do so when he was ready. They enlisted his teachers' cooperation so that he was never asked to read aloud and was never ridiculed for his poor spelling.

The attitudes of those around the dyslexic are critical. It is not a major problem if it is not seen as a major problem. It makes a big difference if they are able to focus on the strengths and patiently wait for their full expression. Even remediation is probably best done when it is done with a light touch.

Eventually he did learn, and by the time I met him he was an unusually penetrating and gifted reader not only of verse but also of philosophical and scientific writing. When I asked how he felt about reading aloud in class, he said it didn't trouble him in the least. He had long since accepted that he would make errors, as he had accepted that he would make errors in spelling, and thought it was of little importance. In no way did it affect his view of himself as a teacher or writer.[51]

THE EASY IS HARD AND THE HARD IS EASY

One of the more puzzling of the recurrent patterns seen in the life of dyslexics is the tendency, sometimes, for the "easy" things to be hard and the "hard" things to be easy. For the bright, creative dyslexics able to survive in the academic world at all, however imperfectly, this paradoxical reversal is almost a definition of their plight. If they can make it through the "easy" and "elementary" and "basic" materials, then they often can begin to shine in areas that are considered "hard" and "sophisticated" and "advanced." This tendency is exaggerated by the older student's greater freedom, in the upper grades and in college, to concentrate in areas of strength while avoiding areas of weakness. Simpson's experience, once again, is especially instructive. "In my junior year, when for courses in logic, philosophy, and economic theory an ability to deal with abstractions was more important than knowledge based on previous education, my index rose sharply, and I enjoyed my classes. I even imagined that I was learning in the way good students learned because I earned good grades."[52] Although she did well in these courses, Simpson still had great difficulty with training herself to study properly for long-term retention of the material. However, we might consider that the most important elements here may not be her problems (poor memory and study skills) but her special talents: that she found "hard" courses like logic, philosophy, and economic theory so "easy."

This kind of observation is not uncommon and should probably receive more attention. Perhaps dyslexics like Simpson, after some reasonable effort in areas of special difficulty, should not be so hard on themselves and should allow themselves to quickly focus instead on areas where they have major strengths. Perhaps they should learn to give themselves more credit for their ability to understand and use sophisticated concepts. And perhaps they should learn to be less concerned about their inability to rapidly review and accurately recall vast quantities of factual information (which, after all, a machine can do quite easily).

The dilemma is not theirs alone. Some non-dyslexics working in quite demanding fields find that they have little need for a good factual memory compared to their great need for an ability to handle sophisticated concepts. An anecdote told at a seminar on creativity provides a particularly instructive example. A young mathematician was working on loan with a group of molecular biologists at the National Institutes of Health. After working with them for several weeks, the mathematician expressed his hope that he could complete his duties quickly so that he could return to his normal work. When asked why, his reply was that he had found his work in the world of biology especially difficult and tiring because there was simply so much to remember. In mathematics, he explained, you didn't have to learn a lot of facts; you simply needed to learn the basic concepts. All the rest could be worked out from them.[53]

Learning facts is not only a skill but also a talent. As we shall see, some of those in our profiles had surprisingly poor memories for certain types of facts while others had extraordinarily good memories. In any case, dyslexics and non-dyslexics alike need to be aware that there are some "advanced" and "hard" fields where abilities other than memory and study skills turn out to be far more important. All need to be aware that some of those who are best at creating new knowledge may have imperfect abilities assimilating and retaining old knowledge.

MATURE ACCEPTANCE

Since there is no "cure" for dyslexia, its symptoms may be diminished over the years but never fully disappear. Dyslexics may find that the old problems are usually well under control, but may reoccur from time to time with greater or lesser severity. Simpson thinks in terms of good days and bad days.

On good days I spell reasonably well. Words I'm uncertain about I can find in the dictionary without difficulty. . . . I have not advanced so far that I would think of playing a word game, such as Scrabble . . . for pleasure. Spelling remains hard work. . . .

When I speak there is no trace of the early confusion I sought to cover up by clowning. I say precisely what I mean to say.

My sense of direction is adequate for everyday use if I depend on feel rather than left/right, east/west. . . . As a reader of maps, I leave much to be desired.

My memory, which has always been excellent in some areas, serves me well even where it is weakest: in the recall of proper names.

Employing digits . . . I make errors caused by transpositions less than a quarter of the time.

As for reading, it is one of my greatest pleasures. . . . Even today, I occasionally look up from a page suffused with joy and wonderment and say to myself, *I'm reading!*

. . . I have never learned to read and eat at the same time, as during a solitary meal I've wished I could do. Nor can I attend to two competing sounds—a voice and a radio, two people talking to me simultaneously—even on good days.[54]

But the bad days, which Simpson finds come two or three together every couple of months or so, are quite different.

On bad days, which are brought on by fatigue, strong preoccupations, illness, and what else I don't know because I sometimes can't pinpoint the cause, I have little confidence in my ability to spell. The

dictionary is useless because I can't think of the opening letter or syl-
lable that will help me find the word I want. . . .

In conversation I say one thing when I mean to say another—
"The car they sold him was a melon." "You can't pull the wool over
my ears"—that sort of thing, and I am usually unaware of having
done so. . . .

My memory for proper names is so treacherous I have an acute
awareness of what it must be like, at least in this regard, to be senile.

Numbers become scrambled so that I mis-dial, mis-address, and
mis-calculate three quarters of the time. In conversation, I might say
that Columbus discovered America in 1942, and wonder why
people are amused.

In reading I have the old trouble with scudding. This morning
when I was going through the motions of reading an article in the
newspaper, I was actually planning how I would write this paragraph when I got to the typewriter, as I realized when I reached the
end of the article and hadn't the slightest idea what had preceded
it. . . .

Far and away the most disconcerting and vexing symptoms
nowadays are the lapses of memory and of speech. These are the
ones that take me by surprise and endanger my passing, because I
have learned no defense for dealing with them. I suppose these failures give me the startled and perplexed look I've seen my dyslexic
grandnephew, Billy, wear when he's telling me about an athlete
whose career he's following closely, whose name is . . . ? He frowns
in puzzlement, snaps his fingers. How could he have lost this name
he knows so well?[55]

Dyslexia is never cured, but things do get better, with or without
special help. For many reasons, knowledgeable special help is, of
course, clearly preferable, but perhaps it is best not to have too much
of it. In either case, the dyslexic needs to learn how to deal with the
ebb and flow of the old difficulties, but also, hopefully, the dyslexic
begins to learn, however slowly, of the powerful strengths and special
abilities that often accompany these difficulties.

3
CONSTELLATIONS OF TRAITS, SOME NEUROLOGICAL PERSPECTIVES

Reflections on any conceivable subject succeed one another in his racing brain. The plight of mankind, he muses, is "all the fault of the human mind being made in two lobes, only one of which does any thinking, so we are all right-handed or left-handed; whereas, if we were properly constructed, we should use our right and left hands with equal force and skill according to circumstances. As it is, those who can win a war well can rarely make a good peace, and those who could make a good peace never win."

Winston Churchill, *The Last Lion, Alone, 1932–1940*

JAMES HINSHELWOOD AND THE LANGUAGE TEACHER

In August of 1894 a patient came to see Dr. James Hinshelwood at the Glasgow Eye Infirmary. Hinshelwood observed that the patient was a man of education and intelligence, a teacher of French and German. In spite of his extensive language abilities, the patient had discovered, to his great alarm, that he had suddenly become entirely unable to read. As Hinshelwood reported,

About one month previously he was greatly startled to find that one morning in his own house he could not read the French exercise which a pupil gave him to correct. On the previous day he had read and corrected the exercises just as usual. Greatly puzzled, he went into an adjoining room, and having summoned his wife, he asked her if she could read the exercise. She read it without the slightest difficulty. He then took up a printed book to see if he could read it, and found that he could not read a single word. He remained in that condition until I saw him.[1]

Hinshelwood's examination found that there was nothing wrong with the man's vision. Nonetheless, he could not read letters of any size. Consequently, Hinshelwood concluded,

His inability to read was thus manifestly not due to any failure of visual power, but to a loss of the visual memory for words and letters. The page of a printed book appeared to him exactly as it appears to a person who has never learned to read. He saw each individual character distinctly enough, but the character was no longer a visual symbol, as he no longer remembered the special significance attached to it.

To put it briefly, he had lost the visual memory of all the printed and written characters with which he was previously familiar. . . . He had lost in a night the visual memories of the words and letters which he had acquired after years of training and education.[2]

Hinshelwood observed that the circumstances were the same whether Latin or Gothic letters were used. He considered checking the reading of musical notes as well, until he discovered the patient was entirely ignorant of music. Hinshelwood did, however, observe some perplexing additional characteristics in his patient. Although he had no success with reading any form of letters or words, he had no difficulty reading and working with numbers. Also, and even more remarkable, while the patient could not read, he was able to "write with fluency and ease to dictation, although afterwards he could not read what he had himself written."[3]

This last observation is remarkable and shows us the care needed to properly understand the minute and specific capabilities of different parts of the brain. Neurologists are accustomed to cases such as this, but to lay people, such a case seems difficult to believe or understand. On the surface, it would seem impossible for a man to take dictation, correctly converting spoken language into proper written language, yet have no idea whatsoever of the meaning of the words he had just written down.

Such a case underlines the extraordinary specialization and modularity of various skills and abilities. In such cases, most necessary components might be functioning quite well. But if just one small, essential component is damaged, as through a sudden stroke, the result may be the failure of a whole group of related components, or curious and surprising partial abilities where one part of a task can be done quite well while another part cannot be done at all.

Hinshelwood's original account of the patient with "acquired word blindness" was published in December 1895 in the British medical journal *The Lancet*.[4] Within a short time, this article was read by another British physician, W. Pringle Morgan, who noticed similar symptoms in a boy he had for a patient. Since Morgan's patient could not read but was otherwise quite intelligent, Morgan suspected that the child suffered from a congenital form of the condition that came suddenly in Hinshelwood's patient. By November 1896, Morgan had published a brief description of his case in *The British Medical Journal*.

> Percy F.—a well-grown lad, aged 14—is the eldest son of intelligent parents, the second son of a family of seven. He has always been a bright and intelligent boy, quick at games, and in no way inferior to others of his age.
>
> His great difficulty has been—and is now—his inability to learn to read. This inability is so remarkable, and so pronounced, that I have no doubt it is due to some congenital defect.
>
> He has been at school or under tutors since he was about 7 years old, and the greatest efforts have been made to teach him to read, but, in spite of his laborious and persistent training, he can only with difficulty spell out words of one syllable.[5]

Morgan noted that the boy, like Hinshelwood's language teacher, had no difficulty with reading and working with numbers. Morgan believed that word blindness was a rare and unusual condition.

> Cases of word blindness are always interesting, and this case is, I think, particularly so. It is unique, so far as I know, in that it follows

upon no injury or illness, but is evidently congenital, and due most probably to defective development of that region of the brain, disease of which in adults produces practically the same symptoms—that is, the left angular gyrus.[6]

The schoolmaster who has taught him for some years says that he would be the smartest lad in the school if the instruction were entirely oral.[7]

Hinshelwood agreed with Morgan's observations and continued to study congenital word blindness for many years, eventually publishing a collection of his articles in book form in 1917.[8]

SAMUEL ORTON AND PATIENT "M.P."

Some time later, in the United States, this thread was picked up by Samuel Torrey Orton. After years of study and work in Boston and Philadelphia, by 1919 Orton had taken on a new position which involved building and directing the new Iowa State Psychopathic Hospital. He was also to head the department of psychiatry in the medical school of the State University of Iowa. At this time there was little indication of Orton's lifelong fascination with reading difficulties and related problems.

At a meeting of his associates in 1924, Orton presented a paper entitled, "A Mobile Psychiatric Unit as the Most Feasible Method of Meeting Iowa's Mental Hygiene Needs." Four months after presenting the paper, Orton was working in a rural county in such a unit, consulting with local doctors, welfare agencies and school authorities. He had asked to see, among others, those children who were "considered defective or who were retarded or failing in their school work."[9] Among the 142 pupils referred to the clinic, Orton found one who could not to learn to read at all. As reported by Orton's wife, June Lyday Orton, "Thus the stage was set for the entrance of 'M.P.,' the sixteen-year-old youth from a rural school who was referred because 'he seemed bright but couldn't learn to read,' the prototype of the hundreds of other 'word blind' children to whom Dr. Orton was to devote the next twenty years, indeed the rest of his life."[10]

In a now-classic article published in November 1925, Orton

described his first observations. Some were similar to those of Hinshelwood; others were rather different.

> In addition to a practically complete inability to read . . . [M.P.] had submitted some extremely curious [mirror image] productions as written exercises in school. During the clinic, M.P. was tested by the Stanford-Binet method and showed the following rating: Age, 16 years, 2 months; mental age, 11 years, 4 months; intelligence quotient, 71. During the psychiatric examination which followed, however, I was strongly impressed with the feeling that this estimate did not do justice to the boy's mental equipment, and that the low rating was to be explained by the fact that the test is inadequate to gauge the equipment in a case of such a special disability."[11]

Not only was the test misleading, but the patient had some major strengths that were not immediately apparent using conventional means of measurement.

> Further, it was easily seen that while he was unable to recall the visual impressions of words clearly enough to recognize them in print, he did make facile use of visual imagery of objects of rather complex type. I asked him, for example, questions concerning the adjustment of bearings in the V type automobile engine, which required a good visualizing power for answer, and his replies were prompt and keen.[12]

It is, perhaps, no small matter that Orton immediately suspected the serious inappropriateness of the testing method for properly assessing his patient's capabilities. It is also notable that he was willing to offer another kind of test, one which drew on important, but vastly different, abilities, especially since it was one that dealt primarily with visual-spatial skills rather than verbal skills, one that required "good visualizing power" for a proper answer to be given.

Orton's selection of this form of test might possibly also tell us something about his own visual-spatial skills. He himself was known for having rather strong visual-spatial and mechanical abilities.[13] Perhaps a physician who is strongly visual himself is more likely to be able to recognize and appreciate these qualities in his patients and others, allowing him to discount certain obvious verbal difficulties.

On the other hand, professionals who are highly verbal but not very visual themselves might be more likely to believe, then as now, that a low score on a verbally oriented testing instrument is probably correct, that the measured poor verbal abilities simply indicate low intelligence and nothing more.[14]

Because of these inconsistent findings, Orton decided to use a wider range of standardized tests with M.P. A second test of intelligence, using oral rather than written questions wherever possible, yielded a fifteen point increase in IQ. "He still gave the impression, however, to one who had learned to estimate mental defect before the widespread use of mental tests, of a much better equipment than even this second rating indicated."[15]

So Orton tried a variety of nonverbal tests and found quite different results. On one performance test, he found that M.P.'s score was satisfactory for adults, earning the highest possible scores in twelve of twenty-two items. On a picture completion test, the score was 90 out of 100, superior even for adults. On a mechanical assembly test, M.P. scored 82, placing him on the par with the "highest 1 per cent of unselected army draft recruits." Tests with a mechanical puzzle box also yielded superior performance. Finally, using a test that especially interested Orton, "His capacity to read in a mirror was tested, and it was found that this reversed presentation made no difference in his ease of reading."[16] The patterns evident in M.P. were to be repeated, with variations, in many cases to follow.

Orton's view was essentially similar to those of Hinshelwood and Morgan some thirty years before. He believed he was dealing with a set of conditions caused primarily by neurological factors. During Orton's time, however, the rapid spread of psychoanalytic theory in America and elsewhere tended to overwhelm alternative theoretical perspectives. Under the influence of the psychoanalytic theory of the time, many came to hold that the difficulties experienced by dyslexics originated primarily from emotional problems rather than neurological factors, and that once the emotional problems were successfully dealt with, the reading difficulties, speech difficulties, and other problems would disappear.

Orton and his associates, however, saw it the other way around. They believed that in most cases these difficulties were neurologically based, although they might often have emotional consequences. They believed that one might have emotional problems because one could not read or write or keep up with one's peers, not the other way around.[17] Their experience indicated that as the academic difficulties were addressed with training, following the neurological model, and as the reading problems gradually improved, the emotional difficulties often began to disappear. Thus, Orton's basic approach was quite different from the dominant trend in professional thought from the 1920s to the 1940s. He was primarily interested in how "organic" or "structural" elements in the brain contributed to conditions such as dyslexia. One of Orton's students observed that he was "an organist, plain and simple." That is, Orton typically looked first to the functioning of the organ itself in his effort to explain what was going on. Other aspects were to be considered, but only after the neurological aspects were dealt with.

Speaking in 1942, Orton lamented what he saw as the excessive swing away from structural considerations during this period. "While recognizing the importance of the emphasis placed on the enormous part played in our behavior by our instincts and emotions, I think it may be fairly said that the swing went to the extreme and gave us a whole generation of psychiatrists who had not even a nodding acquaintance with the structure of man's brain."[18] Forty years later Orton's views are now widely accepted, but his approach still meets with resistance among a number of professionals.[19]

PATTERNS OF VARIATIONS

As one surveys the visual thinkers, creative dyslexics, and others with learning difficulties that we have been considering, one is increasingly persuaded that there is an underlying pattern, while at the same time one is bewildered by the variety of traits exhibited in even a small group. This is so until one begins to realize that, possibly, the essential pattern is the seemingly limitless variety itself. Some investigators of creativity have been dismayed by the great variety among highly creative persons and have despaired of finding a pattern, despaired of grouping them all into logical and stable categories. This despair may be unwarranted, however. The variety itself may not be the problem, but rather, the answer—the sought-after pattern. In the end, it may be that the most important and salient characteristic of the pattern is that each creative person is substantially different from the norm, the ordinary, but is also substantially different from other creative persons as well.

Continuous and unpredictable variation. Viruses seem to survive so well because they can change so much, so fast. How can our own immune systems or our medical researchers and practitioners keep up with them?[20] Perhaps human beings have done so well, for so long, not so much because of appositional thumbs or spoken languages or relative brain size or any other physical or social trait, but rather more because of our ability to generate a vast range of original conceptions and newly discovered knowledge—a range which may depend, in an important way, upon the variety of structures and interconnections possible among the great networks of neurons within human skulls.

We have long been aware of the great range of the human intellect and imagination. We are only slowly becoming aware that some of the brain's capacity may depend upon variations in brain growth and development that can lead, in turn, to a vastly greater range in what the human mind can imagine and work for.

When one takes very seriously the perspective proposed by Norman Geschwind and others—that certain early developmental processes can generate great neurological diversity, the same processes sometimes producing both notable strengths and notable weaknesses—then one begins to construct a very different view of the extent and role of neurological variation with respect to humanity as a whole. Perhaps the truth is that there are really a great many very different kinds of brains out there and that the appearance of similarity is really just a useful and even necessary illusion—an illusion that facilitates communication and concerted group activity but obscures the reality and essential power of enormous diversity.[21] It follows that educational and employment systems that are based more on an illusion of essential uniformity than the reality of essential diversity could have a great potential to be wasteful as well as destructive.

CONSTELLATIONS OF TERMS

In this chapter and those that follow we will be taking a closer look at this diversity and at the ways this diversity appears to be expressed in a number of exceedingly interesting individuals. However, first we need to give some additional brief attention to our terminology. As noted previously, the term "dyslexia" is being used here in its most inclusive sense. For the public at large, the term is usually restricted to reading difficulties. However, to the neurologist, the reading problem is only one symptom of deeper processes that may manifest themselves in a number of different ways.[22] The term "learning disabilities" is more inclusive than the term "dyslexia."[23] In practice, there is a great deal of overlap between the two terms, since in each case several different traits often occur in combination. Thus, at this stage, it may be most useful to keep the definition broad. There are good precedents for this. Geschwind and other neurologists have pointed out that while they appreciate the need for educators and psychologists to make finer clinical and administrative distinctions, neurologists are compelled to take a less restrictive approach, at least until their work suggests categories based on neurological structures and tissue types together with their relationship to performance and behavior.[24]

Some will doubtless object to this deliberately loose usage of the terms, but we may defend this position by pointing out that precision is not always good and that generality is not always bad. It depends upon what you are trying to do. Sometimes if you focus in too closely, too early, you run the risk of losing sight of a larger pattern, one that is only visible by stepping back a distance, to get a view of several variations on a theme, a view of the pattern of the larger whole.

At a level separate from the usual definitional discussions, however, we should point out that in the view developed in this book, we are not really talking exclusively about "learning disabilities," or even what some, with greater specificity, call "academic disabilities." These terms seem to be useful within the milieu of education and social services, but they are not really precisely what we are talking about. Nor are we only talking about "learning" alone, because we are also talking about those who have problems with presentation and performance quite apart from any problems they may or may not have with "learning." In one sense, therefore, what we are really talking about is, possibly, "neurological" disability, not just "learning" disability, because the problems cover more than just learning.[25] Perhaps a more neutral term would be "neurological variation," but variation of a special kind and, presumably, not really within the range of what we would think of as normal or "ordinary" variation.[26] To make our definitional problem still more difficult, we are not always talking about "disabilities." We are just as interested, or perhaps even more interested, in the special talents and abilities that may (or may not) come, directly or indirectly, from the same early developmental processes or from the form of the giftedness itself.

What we are talking about, then, is significant variation in both abilities and disabilities, notably mixed strengths and weaknesses manifested in a constellation of traits. As yet, however, there does not seem to be a properly neutral and fully descriptive term covering all these considerations. Nearly all the terms that have been in and out of fashion during the past one hundred years or so, from "word blindness" to "minimal brain damage," refer almost exclusively to the negative, to some deficiency or abnormality.[27]

TUMBLING SYMBOLS

It is noteworthy, however, that in at least one case, relatively neutral terminology has been proposed. In his 1925 article, Orton proposed the term "strephosymbolia."[28] Orton's term is based on the Greek words meaning "to turn" or "to twist" and "sign" or "symbol"—referring, as he said, to the "turning or reversals" or "transposition of phrases, words, or letters or of any symbols, especially in reading."[29] Orton clearly saw that it was this free floating transformation of symbol orientation, association, and sequence that was so central to what most of his patients were experiencing.[30]

The term is cumbersome and it never really did catch on, even among Orton's followers (although a few early patients referred to themselves as "strephs"). However, "strephosymbolia" is worth looking at closely. In contrast to nearly all other terms it does not refer primarily to a deficiency, abnormality, or disability; rather, it refers to a comparatively neutral and matter-of-fact description of what is actually perceived by the affected person. It simply describes a salient characteristic of the condition, which might, conceivably, be viewed as either positive or negative, depending on the circumstances.

Although it is not clear whether Orton intended it, the term he proposed also suggests something of the double-edged quality that we are most interested in, a quality of which Orton was clearly aware. On the negative side of the double edge, we see letters and symbols that may be twisted, turned, reversed, or transposed, leading to the familiar "b" for "d" or "saw" for "was" or "1948" for "1984." These reversals make reading slow and difficult and greatly promote errors of all kinds. But, if we look deeper, there is a positive side of sorts. As we have noted, Orton observed that many dyslexics could read upside down or backward or in a mirror as easily (or as haltingly) as they could with the conventional orientation. Under certain circumstances, this can be very useful. For example, when the text of a newspaper or a book was set in type on the old kind of presses, the raised letters of the printer's metal plate appeared in mirror image. It used to be of considerable value for printers (at least in small print shops) to be able to read blocks of type directly, without running a galley proof on paper, once they were set on the presses. This skill was considered special and desirable, especially by those who could not do it. However, with the coming of photo-offset printing and the almost universal abandonment of movable metal type, it is doubtful that this skill is seen as valuable in this setting any longer, although it may be in other settings. The point is that the perceived value of any given trait is greatly dependent on a continually changing social and economic context—in indeed, in the end, a changing biological context as well.

Let us take this slight ability of mirror reading (in some, apparently so closely linked with the primary disability) one step further. Let us imagine, for a moment, three-dimensional solid objects in space. They look different depending upon how you look at them—or from what point of view you look at them.

For example, a pyramid is triangular when viewed from the side, but square when viewed from the bottom (using, of course, the usual point up orientation). In the same way, a cone is triangular when viewed from the side, but circular when viewed from the bottom. Alternatively, a column or cylinder may be square or rectangular when viewed from the side, but circular when viewed from the bottom. This is the sort of thing that has long bedeviled researchers in artificial intelligence. Usually the computer will see, obtusely, each different view of a three-dimensional form as an entirely different object.[31] Human beings ordinarily have little difficulty with this kind of task, except when it comes to reading. In reading, curiously, this obtuseness is of value and is cultivated. In reading, an alternative orientation of the same thing is seen as a different thing. Thus, one might consider a "p" carved out of a solid block of wood or other material and imagine it tossed in the air, tumbling side to side and end over end, as it falls to the floor. When it lands, an observer would not be able to determine whether the original was intended to be a "p" or a "q" or a "b" or a "d." Barring certain minor idiosyncrasies of typeface design, the four letters are identical in every respect, except orientation in space.

As suggested in our earlier metaphor of mailboxes and cylinders, some minds may be far better at seeing the similarities—the fundamental identity of these shapes—than in attaching a different meaning and value to an apparently arbitrary change of orientation, no matter how conventional or important. In time, this natural tendency to ignore orientation (or treat it as unimportant) may be mitigated through special training, but (possibly) it is always there in the background.

This may very well be a good thing. We may expect, sometimes, that this sort of person, like Orton's M.P., would find it especially easy, to visualize the "adjustment of bearings in the V type automobile engine"; or, like James Clerk Maxwell, find it easy to construct elaborate mechanical models in his mind's eye from which to devise mathematical statements to shape twentieth-century physics and electronics; or, like the surgeon Harvey Cushing, find it easy to visualize, in three dimensions, the delicate, convoluted layers and microscopic structures of the human brain, and in the process shape twentieth-century neurosurgery;[32] or, like the molecular biologist of today, find it easy to visualize long, chaining clusters of precisely angled atoms in her head, using them to shape twenty-first-century chemistry, biology, and medicine.[33]

One may not have to have the disability in order to have the gift. But when the gift is there, the disability should not be allowed to prevent its recognition or development, especially when those with the greatest gifts may also have some of the greatest difficulties.

CASTING THE NET, A MATTER OF RELATIVE VALUE

We are at the stage, then, when we may need to cast our net broadly, with a fairly fine mesh, to catch all the varying forms—as in the first culling, the first level of triage. The subgroups can be distinguished and subdivided later. And the non-relevant forms and types can be sorted out later still. At this time it may be best to use our definition as a net wide enough and fine enough to catch all the traits that are related to dyslexia and other learning disabilities in their many forms—as they are also related to visual thinking and creativity—but not to catch so many traits as to lose sight of the common elements in our diverse larger grouping.

As we have seen, the preliminary research suggests that we are probably dealing with a biological process that effectively produces significant variety in brain tissue, interconnection, and structure. If we are, in fact, dealing with such a generator of variety in structure and function, then it would seem quite likely that once our group is set apart from the rest of the population, we should find substantial variation among its members.[34] And we should also not be surprised to find a great variety with respect to both "positive" and "negative" characteristics, since these may be relatively unrelated and independent outcomes of partly arbitrary growth and development patterns in the brain. In this connection, it is important to reemphasize that the extent to which traits are considered positive or negative is sometimes very much a function of a particular historical era and cultural or economic setting.

In the remote past (or in distant, hidden corners of the world today), a genetic makeup that promoted a natural facility with reading, but not, say, with hunting or finding one's way easily in the wilderness, would have been a considerable disadvantage, as Geschwind suggested. In some circumstances, such a spatial disability might have been so important that many of those with poor spatial sense would, in time, have been selected out of the population, rarely surviving to adulthood and procreation. Indeed, in some early cultures, it is not hard to imagine that formally established initiation rites, requiring survival in the wilderness alone for some period of time, would have probably exaggerated this natural tendency, over time amplifying the disadvantages of, say, being a natural reader in comparison with the advantages of being a natural hunter. The hunter-gatherer needs a good sense of direction and an alertness to the subtle signs of nature. These are predominantly visual-spatial skills and would have little verbal content. In such a culture, a propensity toward reading skill would be relatively unimportant. It would almost never be measured or valued within the context of the dominant hunter-gatherer culture. A few shamans, storytellers or priests with good verbal memory and special skill in reading runes, knot patterns, glyphs, or ideograms might prosper—but only as a contrasting, and proportionately small, feature in the dominant culture.

In a predominantly literate culture, on the other hand, where a good memory of verbal content is so highly prized, the lack of a good sense of direction and an insensitivity to subtle natural signs would generally be seen as something of little consequence. Most of the positions of high status and reward would be reserved for those who could read quickly and efficiently, memorize easily, recall accurately, and write and speak with speed and fluency.[35] In this society, all the directions are sign-posted and the natural signs are well documented in handbooks for weekend hobbyists.

The value of particular traits are relative to time and place. Traits and skills essential for survival in one era of human history are seen as wholesome but trivial recreations in another.

A POSSIBLE REVERSAL: POST-LITERATE SOCIETY

Very long ago, hunting was all important and reading (in whatever form) was a pursuit of marginal value. In the modern era, reading is all important and hunting is a pursuit of marginal value. We might imagine, however, the beginning of another era, a third phase of development—a post-literate society where the most highly valued combination of traits is reversed once again. This paradoxical pattern involves going forward by going backward, change through repetition. The coil of a spiraling helix curves forward and overlaps the same points crossed one full revolution before, but this time it is much farther along its lengthening path. Sometimes, in order to move ahead we have to cross once again the territory that we thought we had left behind long before.

In such an imagined, post-literate society, a factor of increasing importance may be computer "artificial intelligence" and "expert systems." Such systems were the basis of extremely high expectations in the early 1980s, but then fell into disfavor when these expectations were not immediately fulfilled. In the early days the performance of many expert systems was rather disappointing, partly because of incompatible systems, languages, and software, but, on a deeper level, often because of the machine's lack of common sense and common knowledge, not because of difficulties with the "expert" knowledge.[36]

More recently, however, there has been less exaggerated publicity and these systems are now quietly finding their place as a tool in some professional specialties and in some "mission critical" positions in major corporations. In some recent instances, especially in those disciplines with highly controlled concepts and vocabulary (such as medical specialties), expert systems have performed quite well.[37] American Express is currently using such systems to check in thirteen databases information on card holders and retail stores in order to make credit decisions within ninety seconds.[38] In other corporations such systems are being used to control chemical processing or product development. Given slow but steady growth and favorable trends in hardware and software, we might expect that this process may very well come to be an increasingly important factor.[39] With continued significant improvements in power and cost, it seems that it is only a matter of time before such systems are assigned many routine administrative and management functions. And as certain thresholds in power and size and availability are reached (along with the resolution of issues in hardware and software compatibility), we might have reason to expect that "expert systems" and other similar computer systems, with inexpensive and massive memory resources, would, despite uneven beginnings, increasingly work their way into secure positions throughout the economy.

However, to the extent that these systems proliferate and come to be depended upon, to the extent they show themselves to be useful and reliable, these systems might gradually begin to displace and devalue an increasingly significant proportion of the functions and knowledge painfully gained though years of training by many professionals—physicians, engineers, attorneys, administrators, scientists, and others.[40] Indeed, an ironic aspect of these developments is that these systems may be most useful, and then most threatening, mainly in those disciplines that are the most highly systematized. In such cases, evolution might appear, once again, to move backward. The earliest computers were easily programmed to do some kinds of higher mathematics, but even now the most advanced computers have great difficulty doing things that small children can easily do, like telling a cat from a dog.[41] According to long-time observers, "The first programs in artificial intelligence could do college-level calculus. . . . But when programmers tackled high-school algebra they found to their surprise that it was much *harder* to do on a machine. Grade-school mathematics—the concept of numbers—proved an even greater challenge. And exploring the child's world of blocks was almost insurmountable, except within very narrow limitations."[42]

Consequently, we might expect that the more formalized, organized, and consistent the knowledge of a particular discipline, the more easily it could be gradually taken over by machine. Whereas, on the other hand, the less formalized and the more intuitive the knowledge of a particular discipline, the less easily it could be taken over by machine. In time, it may be that much of the established professional knowledge and conventional wisdom (the "prevailing standards and practices," as the professionals would say) would come to be available primarily (and most effectively, reliably, and cheaply) through these machines, along with their operators, interpreters, managers, and owners.

In time, it is possible that many different markets for various services will begin to be "creamed" by this higher-level intellectual "automation." Considering the possible pace of such changes, we may not need to be reminded that some changes that would have in the past taken many decades to accomplish can now take place, in certain specific sectors of the economy, within years or possibly even months. Gradually, the more obvious and routine intellectual tasks might be taken over by these expert systems (and those who own them and know how to use them). Gradually, in many places, all that would be left for those with conventional training (even professional training) and abilities would be at the opposite ends of the work spectrum—at the top, the jobs that are too complex and too varied for the expert systems, and at the bottom, the jobs that are too awkward and too unprofitable for the expert systems.

If all this were to happen, or, one might say, given the extent to which this does happen, greater value may come to be attached to the more distinctly "human" skills and traits, when they are properly developed and used. It is in just these areas that creative, visual-thinking dyslexics and others with academic learning difficulties often (but not always) seem to have special talents and abilities. Many in this group seem to have a highly developed sense of the larger whole, a flair for the "lucky" hunch and intuitive judgment or a heightened sense of fitness, balance, and proportion—a sense of how to avoid getting lost among the details. Similarly, some others may have a highly developed sensitivity to subtle signs. Sometimes this is manifested in a remarkable ability to judge and even motivate other people.[43] Or, if we can guess the direction of some future trends in mathematics, technology, and scientific research, in the near future some of this group may be far more able than others to perceive new and unexpected patterns in the shapes of moving three-dimensional computer images accurately modeling systems of vast complexity.

Of course, we should not need to be reminded that many of these traits have always been considered to be of the greatest importance by wise administrators, managers, and leaders, even when academic and professional qualifications were thought, officially, to be sufficient. Some of the changes we are talking about may be seen as not really new. Rather, some of these changes may merely bring to the fore considerations that have always been important to wise and experienced leaders, although they may have long been hidden.

Such technological changes, if they were to occur in the way described, should be expected to have surprising and broad effects at all levels of society. Just as muscle power was taken over by machines in the last century, and no one could make a living wage in competition with the new machines, so, increasingly, in the future, those with clerical skills or even those with pedestrian academic, managerial, or professional skills may find it increasingly difficult to find buyers for their services in the marketplace. As machines have replaced assembly line workers and bank tellers, we may not be surprised to see an erosion of opportunities for those with certain manual or clerical skills, but many of us may not be ready to see that there may be great changes in managerial and professional roles as well. One of the fathers of computing and control systems, Norbert Weiner, saw it coming from the first. Writing in 1947, he explained,

> The first industrial revolution . . . was the devaluation of the human
> arm by the competition of machinery. . . . The modern industrial

revolution is similarly bound to devalue the human brain, at least in its simpler and more routine decisions. Of course, just as the skilled carpenter, the skilled mechanic, the skilled dressmaker have in some degree survived the first industrial revolution, so the skilled scientist and the skilled administrator may survive the second. However, taking the second revolution as accomplished, the average human being of mediocre attainments or less has nothing to sell that is worth anyone's money to buy.[44]

After more than sixty years, this is still a sobering view.

Much has come about that was unexpected since Weiner's cool appraisal, but the basic form and direction of this trend has remained unchanged. It has become increasingly clear that not only clerical and other "low level" functions are subject to threat, but also, in time, many functions formerly thought to require high intelligence and advanced degrees. As more and more information (as opposed to mere data) is organized for effective use by many such systems, we might increasingly find that voluminous reading and absorption of masses of factual material will become less and less important. What will come to be far more important is an ability to find information when it is needed, and to know how to use that information effectively once it is obtained. Indeed, some have begun to argue that beyond a certain level, much information—as in "just-in-time" manufacturing processes—should not be handled at all until the moment it is needed.[45]

If this perspective is correct, it may be that years and years of highly specialized training along traditional lines will be seen, increasingly, as simply a waste of time. Why should a man or woman try to compete directly with a machine? Or, alternatively, how would it be possible for them to compete with a professional whose work is amplified by the effective use of such intelligent systems? On the other hand, traditional educational practices, such as massive memorization of formulas and factual material, may be long retained in some fields. Sometimes they will be retained because one cannot really deal with the field effectively without mastering such material. In other cases, it may become more and more clear that these practices are retained mainly as a barrier to widespread professional status, much like the knowledge of Latin in an earlier time, that is, primarily to control the numbers admitted into a profession and, secondarily, to sustain the authority and legitimacy of the profession.

In time, however, it may be seen that the most useful forms of education are those that focus on the larger perspectives, the larger patterns, within fields and across fields, interspersed by investigations of depth here and there. Such an approach implies an ability to quickly access and correctly assess the implications of pertinent specialist information, but actually committing such information to memory would not be a high priority. As such trends continue, some unexpected things might happen. For example, it may be likely that certain forces would increasingly select against those who are primarily skilled at acquiring and retaining masses of factual information while these same forces might increasingly select in favor of those who have the less tangible intuitive abilities that yield results. In time, perhaps, many traditional academic skills may be as obsolete and devalued as John Henry's strong arms and steel hammer were with the advent of the steam drill.

Accordingly, then, it would seem that in this new, post-literate world, the expert systems may provide increasingly easy, fast, cheap, and reliable methods for the massive accumulation and logical application of the "hard facts" and of the "established and accepted" professional procedures. The continued, increasingly rapid, growth of information alone may make these changes nearly inevitable—that is, if the whole system does not collapse instead. As the flood of information mounts, with too many facts for any one mind or group to absorb or use effectively, new ways will be sought to navigate through the mass of data. Full knowledge will have been long since seen as unattainable. And ever more intensive specialization will come to be seen as an increasingly unworkable strategy. The specialties, sub-specialties and sub-sub-specialties will have already proliferated to such a fine fringe of twigs at the edge of the tree's branching that few will be able to keep up with the literature and understand the totality of their own narrow fields, to say nothing of adjacent or distant disciplines, or, worse, those relevant disciplines that are poles apart.

As in the biblical story of the Tower of Babel, the architects will no longer know how to speak to the engineers; the stonemasons will no longer understand the carpenters; the laborers will no longer be able to call the water carriers. Excessive specialization seems to bear the seeds of its own destruction. It seems reasonable to expect, sooner or later, the gradual development of a very different way of doing things, one in which the ready recognition of larger patterns, intuition, a sense of proportion, the imaginative vision, the original and unexpected approach, and the apt connection between apparently unrelated things are the salient abilities.

The prospect of great change is almost always enormously difficult to take seriously from the perspective of any given present. In early-nineteenth-century America, when over 95 percent of the population was directly involved in agriculture, not many farmers of the time would have believed that in a century or so only 2 to 3 percent of the population would provide food for the whole nation and supply the needs of many other parts of the world as well. Not many cold warriors of the 1950s and 1960s would have thought possible the enormous changes in the USSR and Eastern Europe that took place virtually overnight. Similarly, during that same period (in the late 1980s and early 1990s)—when all the most able college students continued to compete (1950s-style) with ever-increasing energy and passion for positions in management, law, and other professions—not many might have believed that the marketplace value of their hard-earned skills could be threatened by mere machines, however fast, however knowledgeable, however bright, however cheap, however small.

Trends such as these, of course, cannot be predicted in a way that even approaches certainty. Factors other than the ones mentioned here may prove to be more important. Or these factors may have very different effects. Speculation about artificial intelligence in its varied forms has long been the venue of fuzzy thinking and of exaggerated fears and expectations. We should not let ourselves be carried away. Yet, when we look at the historical developments over the past century or so, we can see clearly that our lives have been fundamentally transformed by such developments, as Weiner says, first by the machine replacing muscle power. Now, just as clearly, the machine is gradually replacing some forms of brain power.

Whatever the shape of future developments, however, it is worth pointing out, as we have done here, that such changes may yield results very different from those we might have expected. Thus we are led to view possible future developments not as hostile to the visual thinkers and creative dyslexics we have been discussing, but rather as, on the whole, much more congenial to their particular mix of strengths and weaknesses than those of prior periods. And these possibilities might engage our attention mainly because they are exactly the opposite of what nearly everyone has come to believe and expect.

Consequently, before very long, the new market for ability and skills might increasingly devalue the conventional literate accomplishments that have carried such high prestige for hundreds of years. And, although it may be difficult to believe, before very long, this new market may gradually begin to reward, instead, the creative, visual-thinking dyslexics and others like them who have had such a difficult time in literate society for so long—reward these people for the talents and strengths they have always exhibited but not penalize them or exclude them because of weaknesses that will have come to be seen as increasingly inconsequential.

CONSTELLATIONS OF TRAITS: DYSLEXIA AS DIVERSITY[46]

A brief list of traits was provided in chapter 1 as a kind of quick sketch of the pattern we are considering. Here, a more comprehensive list is provided to fill in more completely the further boundaries of the larger pattern. In a number of cases, questions of definition and terminology have been subject to debate. No effort will be made here, however, to resolve such debates. Here it is considered more important to provide a sense of the kinds of things that have been looked at than to attempt to sift through the debates of various investigators and clinicians.[47]

Although there are many approaches and variations in the description of dyslexia and other learning difficulties, there are large areas of agreement and there has been substantial continuity of focus over time. Among those whose visions have been shown to be most enduring is Samuel Orton. Norman Geschwind pointed out that a great many of the observations made by Orton as early as 1925 have largely stood the test of time. Geschwind gave a paper before the Orton Society in 1982 in which he listed a number of major points on which Orton has come to be seen as being correct from the beginning. It is still a pleasure to read of the unreserved admiration Geschwind showed for the work of Orton (reminding one of Maxwell's great admiration for Faraday). Thus, Geschwind felt that

> It is remarkable in retrospect to realize how many times in that very first year he had come to choose with remarkable accuracy those aspects of dyslexia that would continue to be important and had taken a stand that has, in almost every instance, turned out to be correct.[48]

According to Geschwind, Orton was correct on nearly a dozen major points. Orton observed that,

- His patients, while having normal eyesight and visual perception, read poorly and often showed an ability to read as easily or more easily when the text was held upside down or seen in a mirror.
- Dyslexia is often associated with stuttering, or, more generally, with difficulties in other areas, such as speech, and that these conditions ought not to be studied or dealt with in isolation (Geschwind notes that this aspect is often neglected).[50]
- Dyslexia is frequently associated with ambidexterity.
- There is a high frequency of left-handedness among dyslexics and their families.
- There is often "slowness in the acquisition of speech in dyslexic children." (Here Orton provides the foundation, according to Geschwind, for the more general concept of delay in the development of the entire language system.)
- Dyslexics are frequently clumsy (although, Geschwind observes, many clumsy children paradoxically go on to success in areas that require high degrees of manual dexterity).
- There are "children in whom difficulties in learning to read had never been present, yet who spelled extremely badly."
- Some emotional problems could come from brain changes as well as from the stress and failure experienced by dyslexics.
- Other disturbances (in eye movements, in dysfunction of the vestibular system, etc.) may be present but should be seen as associated results rather than causal factors.
- There is a genetic predisposition and a high rate of similar disorders in the families of dyslexics.
- Upon proper examination, damage or other anatomical change could be expected to be found in areas of the brains of dyslexics having to do with reading and language.[51]

Several of Orton's observations are especially notable. He went beyond reading difficulties to focus on associated delays in speech acquisition; he felt that stuttering should receive greater attention in this connection; he pointed out that one ought to consider unusual spelling difficulties even when there was no apparent reading problem; he emphasized the frequency of clumsiness; and finally, he focused on the ease of mirror reading together with its association to left-handedness and ambidexterity. All of these traits have come to be recognized as important factors in the years since Orton made his observations. And, as we shall see, each of these traits plays a special role in the lives of the creative persons we will profile.

Some of the more conventionally identified traits, including some of those noted in chapter 1, include:

- Great difficulty in reading orally.
- Unusually persistent difficulty with learning and applying the conventions of punctuation and capitalization.
- Unusual difficulty with handwriting.
- Disorganization and unusual messiness.
- Poor sense of time, scheduling, and time management.[52]
- Poor arithmetic skills, especially persistently poor retention of multiplication tables and other "math facts" (in spite of much effort).
- Excessive daydreaming or especially active imagination.
- Left/right confusion or confusion in spatial orientation.
- Difficulty carrying out complex oral instructions.
- Late maturation in behavior or appearance.
- Unusual difficulty learning and speaking foreign languages.
- Unusual difficulty with rote memorization tasks.

These traits are the "hard signs" of dyslexia or learning disabilities, those most readily identified through the basic activities that dominate the primary and secondary school years. In a secondary position are the so-called "soft signs." According to one listing, the "soft signs" include:

- The persistence of some primitive reflexes of the central nervous system, which should no longer be present after certain ages.

- Susceptibility to distraction or inability to concentrate; hyperactivity (or hyperkinesis).
- Impulsiveness.
- Perseveration (difficulty in shifting to a new subject or task).
- Inconsistency.
- Irritability.
- Excessive talkativeness (sometimes seen as a device to avoid questions to be answered on demand; occasionally seen together with some measure of insensitivity to audience responsiveness).
- An inability to moderate responses (such as an unusually loud laugh).
- Lack of fluency in one's native language.
- Social immaturity (including an insensitivity to the complexities and subtle cues of social interaction).[53]

Some consider certain traits, such as hyperactivity and left-right confusion, as primary indicators, while others consider them secondary. For many purposes, however, these distinctions may really not be as important as they might seem. In most cases it is better to look at the full list and try to recognize the elements of an overall pattern. Of course, a proper diagnosis and recommended treatment program for any specific individual should be left to professionals. Lay persons are best advised to consider the larger pattern and focus primarily on the positive possibilities suggested by the pattern rather than considering only the problems and difficulties.

Several other traits are listed less often but should be mentioned here:

- A propensity for being disoriented in large, enclosed spaces.
- Difficulty distinguishing sounds.
- Difficulty distinguishing main figure and background (with respect to either visual images or sounds).
- Auditory lag (delay in hearing and understanding).
- Avoidance of touching (because of some difficulty with or high sensitivity to touch).
- Difficulty with visual and auditory sequencing.
- Difficulty with analogy or abstraction.

- Difficulty with short- or long-term memory (especially with recalling names or numbers, or comments already formed in the mind, on demand).
- Difficulty speaking and answering questions on demand.

Several physical characteristics or family occupational traits are sometimes seen as associated:

- Especially large head (this trait has also been noted in recent anatomical studies).
- Early graying of the hair.
- Close family members who are are mathematicians, artists, sculptors, actors, musicians.
- Notable good looks.[54]

Several other traits and attributes are generally considered positive but are seen by some as being associated with learning difficulties, as well as with creativity and visual thinking:

- High talents in spatial, mechanical, and related right-hemisphere skills, with early development of sophistication in these skills.[55]
- Love of construction toys, models, and craft work.
- Love of and great skill at drawing (although the same person may have poor handwriting).
- An especially good "musical ear."
- An especially good ability to visualize and manipulate images in the mind (this may or may not be linked to good drawing skills; alternately, this might be associated with a propensity to develop a visual analog of things that others do not think of in visual terms).

The list of associated traits and attributes is long and growing. Some may see the length and heterogeneity of the list as a sign of essential weakness in the whole field of learning difficulties. How could so many diverse and sometimes self-contradictory traits be indicators of a coherent condition or syndrome? When a definition includes so many diverse and apparently unrelated characteristics, is this not evidence of some basic sloppy-mindedness? Indeed, some professionals in the field argue that the definitions must be carefully restricted or the field will not be credible and its practitioners will not be taken seriously.[56] However, if the hypothesis concerning the generation of diversity advanced by Geschwind and other neurologists turns out to be valid, then it would appear that a long list of heterogeneous indicators is not a problem or an embarrassment at all. If the hypothesis is correct, we should not be surprised to see seemingly endless variation in talents and difficulties, all different from each other and all different from the ordinary. Moreover, if it is correct that dyslexia and other learning difficulties are, in a real sense, the signs of deep generators of fundamental diversity, then, perhaps, this list can be expected to continue to grow indefinitely, until eventually it includes nearly all recognized and recognizable human capabilities, since, in each identifiable set of traits, we might well expect notable weaknesses and talents, as well as ordinary abilities.

The various listings of associated traits may be long and varied, but through this complexity it is hoped that a sensible, though roughly defined, pattern can be discerned. Perhaps it is not so much the specific traits shown as it is the pattern of significant differences that we should note—the unusual mixture of talents and difficulties.

HYPERLEXIA

In order to better understand dyslexia and related learning difficulties, it is useful to consider an apparent opposite: "hyperlexia." By definition, "hyperlexia" is a condition characterized by an ability to read with great ease, often combined with special skill at word-calling and reading out loud. The hyperlexic is very good at producing spoken words from the symbols written on the page. The symbol-to-sound translation process works very well. However, although hyperlexics read easily, they have comparatively shallow understanding of what they are reading. One might compare the hyperlexic to the skilled technical musician who performs very well but knows nothing about composition and may have little feeling for the music. Both are especially good (almost machine-like) in reproducing what is written on the page.

In such cases we are forced to be quite clear in our distinctions in order to gain a clear understanding of what we are actually dealing with. For example, one might expect the hyperlexic to make an especially good radio or television announcer but a poor news analyst or commentator. Or, alternatively, one might expect the hyperlexic to be very adept at reading and speaking foreign languages or to be superior at accurately transcribing a regional dialect into the international phonetic alphabet. But this same hyperlexic may not be very good at writing a story in the foreign language or at explaining the meaning of that story.

Despite superficial appearances to the contrary, some educational writers contend that hyperlexics and dyslexics are not really at opposite ends of the reading continuum. These writers consider the term "hyperlexic" unfortunate and misleading because it focuses exclusively on a relatively less important trait and diverts attention from the problem of poor reading comprehension and its eventual role in school failure.[57] The dyslexic may have a great deal of difficulty reading out loud and may read extremely slowly, but the bright dyslexic can be expected to gain a full appreciation of the significance of what has been read. The hyperlexic, on the other hand, may read out loud quite well and may read extremely quickly, but when it comes to understanding the full content and implications of what has been read, the hyperlexic may be found to have notably limited abilities.

The two different difficulties appear to be mirror images of each other.[58] However, perhaps they are not so much at opposite poles of reading ability as they are two opposite points of a triangle—unlike each other, but both unlike the good reader who can both read rapidly and comprehend well.

LATE BLOOMERS: SLOW DEVELOPMENT AND EXCEPTIONAL ABILITIES

In chapter 1, we indicated briefly how in some cases slow development or delayed maturation in some neurological systems may ultimately be seen as an advantage because those who experience such delays may eventually come to have greater capabilities in some areas than those who mature earlier. This concept has major implications on several levels, some of which warrant further consideration here.

An indication of the possible effects of delayed maturation is provided by a study conducted by neurologist Martha Denckla. In some cases, delayed development in certain skills may prevent, initially, the proper performance in a range of related skills. Using a test called "map walking," however, Denckla shows that, with time, surprisingly high performance may suddenly appear in the individuals who had performed so poorly a short while before. The reason for the change is that initially some component of the skill was not fully functioning. But once that one component began to function, the capabilities of all the related components could come to be applied to the task as well.

In the test situation described by Denckla, a grid of dots is placed on the floor. This grid corresponds to a grid of dots on a piece of cardboard held in the subject's hand. A pattern is sketched on the cardboard grid and the subject is asked to follow this same pattern along the grid on the floor. The study results showed a surprising reversal of relative performance of different groups over time. In a dramatic illustration of this variation on the "late blooming" pattern, those who did the worst eventually did the best, once a certain maturational threshold had been crossed.

> The younger dyslexic children, that is, children below the age of ten years (and therefore prepubertal) had the worst performance of the three groups, as measured by walking these routes correctly. A startling "late blooming" effect, however, shone forth in the data on children over ten years old. The teenaged dyslexic group, and in particular the familial dyslexic adolescents, demonstrated superior performance on this test.[59]

And in another passage, Denckla puts the study into perspective:

> Some of the previously presented data . . . on the shift during the second decade of life from poor map walking to good map walking and from poor copying of design to adequate copying of design, as well as the anecdotal accounts of late blooming in dyslexics, may be related to maturation to some adequate threshold level by some critical system within the left hemisphere. Such a maturation would then allow the superior capabilities of the right side of the brain to be allied with the now-adequate motor analyzer or motor programmer within the left hemisphere. . . . Thus, what had been

"money in the bank" can now be usefully withdrawn and displayed.[60]

As we can see in this case of "map walking," sometimes late-developing dyslexics can do certain tasks better than all others, once, finally, the several necessary components of both hemispheres have reached maturity and have finally started to work together.

The pattern of delayed maturation is an important trait of all human beings compared with other animals. Biologists explain that it is a dominant human trait to mature much later than other animals. Human infants must be protected longer by their parents and society.[61] During this helpless early period, the human infant is still building brain structures and connections in the same way it was while in the uterus. The rate of growth for the brains of primates and other mammals diminishes greatly soon after they are born. However, for periods of up to a year after birth, human infants show the same rate of brain growth and development as in the womb.[62] It is as if nature had chanced upon this strategy as a way of extending gestation well beyond the limits of what a normal birth canal would allow—permitting extended development of the brain in size and complexity well beyond what would have been possible otherwise.

But how might this extended maturation relate to late-maturing dyslexics and other late bloomers? If delayed maturation gives human beings a major advantage over other animals, then to what extent, and under what circumstances, would the additional delayed maturation among dyslexics (and others like them) provide a long-term advantage over more ordinary human beings? Could it be said that some of these late-maturing individuals are but a further extension of the same distinctly human pattern, perhaps even a major further survival strategy? Could they not be seen as merely a far extension of the same process, the far tail of the normal distribution, perhaps? Could they not be seen as a group of people neurologically awkward longer than others largely because they are continuing to build neurological complexity and specialized capacity long after their contemporaries have ceased further development—that is, long after the neurological potential for the others has been largely frozen in place?

We may not, yet, be ready to answer these questions, but the questions themselves provide a basis for a very different way of looking at the "problem" of dyslexia and learning "disability" in general. For those who are affected, considerations such as these ought to have a profound effect on self-images and the view of eventual possibilities for special contribution and creative accomplishment.

A DIFFERENT WIRING DIAGRAM, A WAY AROUND

Some of the possible mechanisms promoting such special contribution and creative accomplishment are currently being considered by researchers in neuroanatomy. Anatomical studies conducted by Albert Galaburda and his associates have indicated that "normal" or "ordinary" brains, whether in humans or animals, tend to be asymmetrical in certain important ways. Certain structures are generally larger in the left hemisphere than in the right hemisphere. However, the brains of dyslexics have been found to be more symmetrical. Ordinary brains have a left hemisphere that is larger than the right—while the dyslexic brains have two hemispheres that are approximately equal in size. There is an additional important difference. Early development in the normal brain involves the production of an excess of neurons and an excess of connections between neurons. As development proceeds, these neurons and connections tend to die off in large numbers, in a kind of internal natural selection process. Where connections are made to other neurons, the original neuron and the connecting fibers survive. Where no connection has been made, the neuron dies. This is the normal and usual process, somewhat analogous to that of the growth of bones. Bones grow along lines of stress that are defined by use.[63] To some extent, likewise, the pathways of the brain grow along lines of use. Thus, for evident reasons, both systems are well adapted and are responsive to the needs of the specific conditions experienced by the organism at a particular time.

Discussing the implications of his group's research, Galaburda indicates that studies with animals have shown that symmetrical brains, similar to those of dyslexics, have certain significant differences with respect to the numbers and density of neurons and neural projections. According to Galaburda,

> Preliminary findings suggest that there is something very peculiar
> about the symmetrical brains. . . . They fail to lose as many neurons

as they should. . . . They also fail to prune down the number of connections so that their pattern of collosal connections [connections between hemispheres] is different—which means that we can no longer think of doing language with the left hemisphere or the right hemisphere or somewhere in between.[64]

With the symmetrical brains there are more neurons than usual. Not only are there more neurons but also more connections between the two hemispheres. There may be fewer connections within areas of the same hemisphere, but this has not been studied as yet. Also, the pattern of connections between the hemispheres is different. All of this tends to produce a view of a different kind of brain. "When you have a symmetrical brain, it works together differently. The two hemispheres communicate differently." But these differences have important implications. If these brains are, in fact, different in certain important ways, then they might be expected to have different ways of functioning as well.

> You have a different wiring diagram, which raises the question that now I ask psychologists: If they have a different pattern of organization, do they solve problems differently? Are we talking about the possibility that left handers and right handers do not just differ on the basis of how good they are at particular things—but what strategies, cognitive strategies, they use to solve problems?
>   That's a very crucial question when it comes to dyslexia because it may turn out . . . —[and] we have some evidence for [this]—that certain kinds of processes require fairly rigid strategies, particularly those involving logic [while others do not].

In other words, for dyslexics, more than others, there may be a very big difference between those tasks that require the knowledge of rules and those tasks that require the development of creative solutions. In general, dyslexics may do poorly in areas involving conventions and rules while they may do quite well in those areas that require innovation and creativity. With the rule-based processes

> there is no room for creativity. Grammar by and large is one of those processes. There are phonological rules; there are syntactical rules. You can't, just because you want to, change the way, for instance, the word "promise" relates to the subject as compared with the

word "told." "John told Paul to do the dishes" relates to the subject very differently from "John promised Paul to do the dishes." . . . It's a logical property. . . . Two plus two is four and no matter how creative you are you can't get away with saying three—because it is built into the logic of the system.

Apparently, many dyslexics have difficulty with such logical systems. However, they can feel comparatively comfortable when they have to devise new solutions to problems on the spot. According to Galaburda, "If you have a brain like this . . . then you are no longer able to solve certain logical . . . tasks the same way, so you get the wrong answer—whereas certain other parts of the task that could accept some creativity are done pretty well."

Indeed, creativity may not be incidental at all. To the contrary, it may be fundamental. According to Galaburda,

> That is what I think is the way dyslexia really works. In fact, that's exactly the way dyslexics get better. When a young child is learning to read, it has to learn the formal rules. It has to learn that "ps" sounds, such as in "psychology," are pronounced very differently from "sp" sounds, such as in the word "spell." . . . But when they get older, they don't have to know them that well in order to solve the problem. Because it doesn't really matter very much whether you can read the word "sympathy" or "symphony." When you are sixteen years old and you are reading the *Boston Globe* and there is [a photo of] Seiji Ozawa holding his baton . . . you still can't read the difference between "symphony" and "sympathy" but you can guess much better.

Thus, if one has great difficulty learning or retaining the rules of translating letter combinations into sounds, one might learn to rely on a range of contextual cues to get the right answer. This approach, of course, would probably lead to many correct guesses, but could also lead to a recognizable pattern of errors.

> Now, it seems to me that it is possible . . . that what you can see in the asymmetrical to symmetrical change is the production of new machinery which may be very capable of doing a lot of things but may lose the capability of solving certain logical problems. By the same token, they may acquire the possibility of solving logical problems in a different system. Of course, what I am referring to is the

fact that we know that some dyslexics . . . are able to solve problems in higher level mathematics or three-dimensional designs that the average ordinary brain can not solve.

There is the additional possibility that if you have a [symmetrical] brain . . . and you are trying to go the logical way but you just don't have the machinery to do it, [then] you have to side step and go around to try to solve it some other way—relying more on other cues, rather than, let's say, grammatical cues; you may then see a completely new problem emerge because you side stepped and saw something else. . . . When you wanted to go over the hill, you couldn't go over the hill so you went around the hill and discovered for the first time that there was a river there. . . .

[This] may be an explanation not only for the unusual answers you might get from dyslexic children for questions that someone else with an ordinary brain might answer in a split second, but you may also get a clue as to why creativity emerges in these particular brains.

Galaburda observes that if we wish to try to explain this kind of thing in terms of human evolution and adaptive functions,

one would say that we have dyslexia not because [some people] have difficulty with some aspects of . . . English grammar, but because it forces the brain to solve problems in different ways; it increases genetic heterogeneity in the population and the possibility of solving problems that could never be solved if everybody had the same kind of brain. . . .

There is a price to be paid by variability. When you go from [a] very specialized system to [a] less specialized system, you lose the ability to do something quickly, right away, but you gain the possibility of doing other things, perhaps.

These are, of course, issues that have to be tested empirically, but it is the kind of constraint on behavioral hypotheses that might . . . come out of analyzing differences like this.

If what Galaburda suggests turns out to be true, then we ought to begin to pay less attention to getting everyone over the same hill using the same path. We may wish to encourage some to take different routes to the same end. Then we might see good reasons for paying careful attention to their descriptions of what they have found. We may wish to follow them someday.

4

PROFILES, PART 1

Faraday, Maxwell, and Einstein

In this chapter and the two that follow, we profile eleven remarkable people: three physicists, two mathematicians, two inventors, an artist, a political leader, a military leader, and a poet. Most are well known. Others are not so well known outside of their specialist areas, but nonetheless are considered to be of similar stature because of the originality and magnitude of their contributions. Several profiles describe these persons in some depth. Other profiles are quite brief, simply focusing on one or two traits of special interest.

Each of the eleven is quite different from the others. All are seen as highly creative, although the nature of their creativity varies substantially. Most are strong visual thinkers, but others are less so. All but one show some form of the pattern of learning difficulties we have been discussing, although these are varied and range widely in severity. The profile of inventor Nikola Tesla has been included as a kind of counterpoint, primarily because of his extraordinary visualization abilities, although he appears to be almost entirely free of the more classic pattern of traits. This example also indicates that one need not always have the classic pattern of traits to have special gifts.

While it is believed that most of those portrayed in these profiles exhibit individual patterns of talents and weaknesses that are consistent with the general pattern, we are not interested in checking off and weighing the severity of each and every trait to develop individual scores—this may be helpful in identification and classification but does not seem to be helpful in providing insight into the curious way that special talents work together with areas of weakness to shape the lives and work of these remarkable people. Instead, we are interested in sketching a series of portraits through the accumulation of selected detail—to reveal the lives and work of these diverse and original thinkers in a highly concrete and memorable manner, while suggesting something of the patterns of thought that may have contributed to their special accomplishments. Where possible, these portraits are sketched using their own words or the words of friends, associates, or family members. Sometimes these individuals seem to understand the paradoxical nature of their abilities more clearly than those who write about them. These individuals seem to recognize that in their own experience extraordinary accomplishments have been achieved as much because of, as in spite of, distinctive combinations of difficulties and disabilities, disabilities that are themselves sometimes the obverse of special talents.

MICHAEL FARADAY

Michael Faraday did not appear to have particular reading or writing difficulties. Yet he seems to have exhibited several traits that generally fit within the broader definition of learning difficulties. Among these were early problems with speech and some notable deficiencies in spelling, punctuation, and capitalization. His greatest difficulties, however, were problems with mathematics and an unreliable memory.[1] On the other hand, Faraday also showed several of the traits we have mentioned that can be considered as neutral or positive: a distinctly visual way of thinking; a powerful imagination that allowed him to develop original models of the physical world in his mind's eye; slow early development as a youth followed by a pattern of increasingly important original contributions even at an advanced age; a strong predisposition to look at the whole rather than the parts; a fierce originality of thought and approach, which sometimes made it difficult to communicate with and be accepted by other scientists of his time.

Michael Faraday was the son of a blacksmith recently come from the English north country, one of four children growing up in the poverty caused by the economic "distress" of 1801. A child of the streets in pre-Dickens London, public assistance allowed him one loaf of bread per week. He was a primary-school dropout, a delivery boy for rented newspapers, an unenthusiastic but steady bookbinder's apprentice, and an untrained laboratory assistant with near-janitor status. It was not a very auspicious start for a scientist who set the stage for the principal scientific and technological revolutions of the nineteenth century and whose work is still seen as surprisingly relevant to some of the chief concerns of modern physical science, more than two hundred years after his birth on September 22, 1791.

Faraday's ideas have stood the test of time. According to Joseph Agassi, a physicist and historian of science, Faraday's vision has been remarkably enduring, although it is not always fully appreciated even by modern professionals.

By now most of Faraday's ideas are commonplace in physics; he has achieved his aim, even though posthumously. Yet most of his ideas are still not attributed to him. Most scientists who happen to take any interest in history think of him as one whose researches are closely linked with intuitive models of the aether; they are very surprised to hear that so very early in the history of electromagnetism, in the late 1830s indeed, Faraday denied that the aether exists. In the present study I shall show in detail how most of his discoveries are related to his idea of matter as fields of forces and of fields of forces as polarizations of empty space. There are many reasons to consider all this outlandish. Thinkers from Euclid to Newton had viewed space as homogeneous . . . having no preferred locations and no preferred directions. This was well in accord with all factual evidence, as much as writing with all philosophy and logic: that nothing has no properties; to view matter as a property of empty space sounds absurd. There was no evidence to support Faraday's fantasy . . . hence science should ignore Faraday's fantasy. . . . [During his lifetime, in spite of extensive recognition in many areas, in this regard] Faraday's speculations were . . . ignored, and at times even rudely ignored. . . . When he died, there was still no decision on the question, had he been successful in drawing his colleagues' attention to his speculations or not? . . . Spectacular success came soon after.[2]

According to another modern admirer of Faraday's work, William Berkson, the author of *Fields of Force: The Development of a World View from Faraday to Einstein*, "Faraday's idea of material substance is different from and in some ways superior to, those of Newton, Maxwell, and Einstein."[3] Indeed, Faraday's ideas seem still to stir admiration and wonder through all the transformations, revolutions, and convulsions of twentieth-century physical science. His vision has endured.

The beginning was not auspicious, however. In a convention-ridden time, he belonged to a strict, little-known, nonconformist Protestant sect, the Sandemanians.[4] In a class-ridden society, he was the son of a workman who was in ill health and often had to be off work. "In addition to his poverty and unpopular faith, Michael Faraday was seriously handicapped with an annoying speech impediment. He could not pronounce the letter 'r'."[5]

It may be imagined that the poorest street children of today are not very much worse off than Michael Faraday was during his early life. However, he was from a stable and deeply religious family. And, more important, he was one of the original self-improvement fanatics. He had very little early schooling, but as a boy he was a devoted reader of certain inspirational self-improvement books, such as *The Improvement of the Mind* by Isaac Watt. He wrote letters to friends to practice his writing skills. From his tiny earnings as an apprentice bookbinder (and from his elder brother's small gifts), he paid to attend public lectures on scientific subjects and bought bits of metal and wire and chemicals to devise small batteries and other primitive experiments he described in letters to his friends.

He carefully recopied and bound the notes he had taken at the public lectures as a gift for his hero, the scientist-lecturer director of the Royal Institution, Sir Humphrey Davy (whose name is widely known today for the early miner's safety lamp, still called the "Davy" lamp). It is a credit to Davy that he paid any attention to the boy at all. At first, Davy discouraged Faraday from the uncertain business of science, but eventually hired him in a junior position as laboratory assistant. A friend had said Davy should "put him to wash bottles" to test the seriousness of his interest. "No, no," Davy is said to have replied, "We must try him for something better than that."[6]

At the Royal Institution, Faraday rose gradually from laboratory assistant to director. (One modern scholar used the title: "Faraday—

Servant to Savant."[7]) Early on, he traveled to the continent as Davy's assistant, apparently learning some French along the way. He formed a small public speaking group among East London young men to improve their accent and diction. In later life, he was known to be extremely conscientious about making preparations for his popular Christmastime public science lectures and demonstrations, even though they were largely addressed to amateurs and children. He worked continuously and passionately to educate and improve himself.

Faraday's family was poor and his religion austere and confining. His church was so strict, in fact, that in later life he was excluded from the fellowship of church members for a time because he was considered to have strayed from the strict, simple life by having dinner with Queen Victoria. However, the close-knit family and strict religious upbringing may have provided needed structure and support for one whose original work developed slowly but continued to improve throughout his life, in spite of recurring nervous disorders. It was not until he was twenty that Faraday completed his eight-year apprenticeship in bookbinding and began searching seriously for some way of pursuing his increasingly passionate scientific interests. After he had secured his position with Davy, Faraday's development was gradual but increasingly more productive and his results more profound.

> He was thirty when he discovered electromagnetic rotations, 40 when he discovered induction and 54 when he discovered the magneto-optical effect and diamagnetism. The latter allowed him, in his late fifties, to articulate and defend his "field" conception of forces. Not many scientists have begun their creative lives so late or continued for so long.[8]

It is often observed that many creative people have their best ideas in their youth, usually, it is thought, before they are twenty. It appears, however, that we ought to give serious consideration to an additional, contrasting, pattern, a category for Faraday and those like him, that involves a late or very late start with continuous and increasingly valuable work throughout a lifetime. This is, of course, an extreme case of the "late bloomer." It is the exact opposite, perhaps, of the early developer, the child prodigy (such as Lord Kelvin, as we shall see), where the works of advancing years are often merely further (and sometimes quite obvious) developments of old ideas or the stubborn defense of old positions.

Perhaps Faraday retained throughout his life a fluidity and freshness of mind and liveliness of imagination that one usually associates with youth. Perhaps this fluidity of mind could be related in part to neurological attributes that can contribute to various difficulties as well as to positive qualities. Both Galaburda and Denckla pointed out that delayed maturation and certain dyslexic traits may be associated, eventually, with the later development of extraordinary proficiencies in certain areas. Gardner pointed out that visual-spatial skills sometimes seem to improve with age while logical-mathematical abilities tend to diminish with age.

It is important to note that Faraday's special ability for forming the unseen and unreal in his mind's eye, in his powerful imagination, was such that he experienced it first not as a gift but as a difficulty. His imagination was so lively that he found that he needed experimentation as a way of testing and directing this powerful imagination. In a letter to a friend, he said,

> Do not suppose that I was a very deep thinker, or was marked as a precocious person. I was a very lively imaginative person, and could believe in the "Arabian Nights" as easily as in the "Encyclopaedia." But facts were important to me, and saved me. I could trust a fact, and always cross-examined an assertion. So when . . . [experiments proved] true to the facts . . . I felt that I had got hold of an anchor . . . and clung fast to it.[9]

This openness and fluidity of Faraday's thought (balanced by a need for verification through experiment) continued to be evident throughout his life in his journals and diaries and was observed by others, as we will see.

Faraday was not a "gentleman scientist" with an ample and steady income. He is apt to be confused with the many well-bred, well-educated, and well-off scientists of the later Victorian Age, such as Raleigh, Darwin, and Galton. Faraday's income from his position with the Royal Institution, even when he eventually became its director, was very small, with rare and modest increases. To earn additional income, he was continually taking on all manner of practical consulting jobs for the growing industries of Britain. He also did a good deal of additional work for the government at no extra charge. He dealt with the many problems brought up by the intensely experimental early industrial revolution, whether traveling to the mines of Wales to find ways of avoiding underground explosions or journeying to the coastal lighthouses of Britain to devise reliable and efficient means of keeping the lights burning brightly. Faraday's consulting work was only discontinued much later, and at considerable financial sacrifice, so that he could devote his full efforts to the passionate experimentation of his later life, his inquiries into the nature of electricity, magnetism, and light.

Many of Faraday's intuitions were right, but he could never prove them. We now know, well over a century later, that he was basically correct and that his experiments were on the right track, but there is no way that he could have confirmed this with the equipment available in his day. It was far too crude.[10] Joseph Agassi points out that, toward the end of Faraday's life, with his faculties failing,

> It is not at all surprising that he invested ever decreasing amounts of work; what is surprising is that the significance of his work increased up to the very end. . . . His last series of experiments was on the connection between gravity and electricity; here he had no shred of success; Einstein had some, in Eddington's observations of 1917; but electrogravity constitutes, even now, the greatest and most difficult problem in physics.[11]

Faraday was a highly successful self-teacher, as we have seen. He taught himself, or learned on the job, nearly everything he knew, whether writing, speaking, experimental design, a vast store of scientific and technological information, even, to some extent, a foreign language. But Faraday never taught himself mathematics. Why not? In his case, it does not seem sufficient to argue that, to be a good mathematician, one must have rigorous, competent, and consistent training over many years by the most talented teachers. This may be the case for many, but there are other cases of special minds learning a good deal of mathematics in the same way that they learn other things, that is, virtually on their own. Then why not Faraday? Why could he teach himself almost anything, but not mathematics?

Perhaps the simplest, most obvious, and most straightforward answer is that he couldn't—at least he could not learn that part of mathematics that deals with symbols and rules and long chains of rearrangements and inevitable consequences based on these symbols, their fixed meanings, the fixed rules, and the fixed relationships between the parts of equations. Perhaps, it is another one of those apparent paradoxes—the curious, sometimes almost unbelievable existence of surprising ineptitude linked closely with extraordinary talent.

Mathematics is partly conceptual clarity and logical process. Faraday must have had these qualities, since they are essential for research design and practice and for drawing conclusions from experimentation that hold up under unsympathetic scrutiny by other scientists. James Clerk Maxwell was quite definite in characterizing Faraday's conceptions as essentially mathematical. How then can we explain the source of Faraday's difficulty?

Let us recall the dyslexic writer in chapter 2, who liked the new personal computers and word processing programs because they helped him to gain control over the alphabetical symbols that swarmed uncontrollably in his mind. Let us also consider the student who thought of numbers as his "friends," primarily because they stayed put and behaved in his mind as letters and words would not.[12] Considering these cases, it is not difficult to imagine a contrasting case in which the numbers swarm while the letters remain steady.

Let us also consider the many references in the literature to Faraday's vivid imagination, the fluidity of his mental processes, and the unreliability of his memory. When we consider these, then perhaps we can understand better what Faraday may have had to put up with when dealing with mathematical symbols, why he hated them so much, and why he was unable to teach himself mathematics as he had so much else. In his middle years, after one of his nervous breakdowns, Faraday wrote to a friend of his increasingly poor memory and his particular difficulty with mathematical symbols, a condition that we may suppose (because of continual earlier complaints of poor memory) was not new but only worse than before.

Such papers as yours make me feel more than ever the loss of memory I have sustained, for there is no reading them, or at least retaining the argument, under such deficiency. Mathematical formulae more than anything require quickness and surety in receiving and retaining the true value of the symbols used, and when one has to look back at every moment to the beginning of a paper, to see what H or A or B mean, there is no making way. Still, though I cannot hold the whole train of reasoning in my mind at once, I am able fully to appreciate the value of the results you arrive at.[13]

Admittedly, the case is not watertight. However, it would appear that Faraday could easily have suffered from that companion form of learning disability in which numbers and formulas are as unruly as letters and words are in the more classic forms of dyslexia. Sometimes this condition is referred to as "dyscalculia," although some medical practitioners would prefer this term to be reserved for only the most severe cases of this form of neurological disability.

Faraday never seemed to have any apparent difficulty with reading, but he did show other traits commonly associated with dyslexia. Many dyslexic children, even when they finally gain some mastery—over written language, retain a striking blindness to punctuation and capitalization that is comparable only to their continuing difficulty with spelling simple words. (The longer words are often easier to visualize and spell phonetically.) Even as these children master more demanding tasks, the simple ones continue to plague them. The meticulous, self-taught Faraday seems to have had similar difficulties. His collected letters to his good friend Christian Friedrich Schönbein were published in 1899. The editors of this volume point out in the preface that they held to the principle of almost absolute fidelity to the original letters. However, with Faraday they made exceptions with respect to his punctuation. "As regards punctuation, however, we have made bold to introduce some emendations. Faraday was not given to introducing these signs: dashes and commas are sometimes, but rarely, met with, full stops never."[14]

Some seventy years later, another editor of Faraday's letters shows similar exasperation. "The insoluble problem was Faraday's punctuation. Faraday followed no system whatsoever. In many letters, he omits all use of a final period in all sentences; in others, he mingles periods with dashes; in others, periods appear in the most unlikely places. The confusion is compounded by the fact that Faraday does not always begin new sentences with a capital letter."[15]

Some examples of Faraday's spelling errors come from a letter to a friend dated July 12, 1847: "Fillaments . . . toutching . . . appologize."[16] Although Faraday's spelling was not as bad as that of some others, his difficulties were so great as to be commented on by a number of writers. Joseph Agassi playfully suggests that Faraday's frequent spelling errors may be given a Freudian interpretation (never suggesting that certain learning disabilities may have been a more plausible cause): "Incidentally, the psychoanalytically minded reader may find it relevant that Faraday had difficulties in the spelling of the words 'withhold,' 'wearies,' 'successful.'"[17]

While there is no evidence that Faraday ever had any special difficulty with reading, it does seem clear that he had to go beyond the words to understand or really retain anything that was the least bit demanding. "I could not imagine much progress by reading only. . . . I was never able to make a fact my own without seeing it."[18] Clearly, the words alone were of little help. Faraday had to see the thing in reality or in his imagination. Apparently he had to reach the stage where he could process images rather than words, perhaps with input from other senses. Multisensory learning is a mainstay of special teaching methods for dyslexics. It may be no small matter that we will find that William Butler Yeats and others have made similar statements, using words almost identical to Faraday's. Apparently even a superficial facility with reading may hide a deeper difficulty with learning anything of consequence from verbal material alone. Or, alternatively, the process of visual perception may be so rich with information that the verbal description, however detailed, is but a pale shadow of what is possible, and consequently is of comparatively little value.

Another characteristic often observed among children and adults with dyslexia or learning disabilities is a fluidity of thought that is bewildering to those who expect greater structure and logical flow. Some modern writers are quite aware of their own tendency to have "scattered thoughts" and they go to a good deal of trouble to impose a degree of order, at least for the benefit of their readers.[19] This tendency is apparent in Faraday's diaries and journals. These were kept for his own use, partly because of his extremely unreliable memory. Indeed, Faraday had to devise elaborate cross-reference systems to compensate for his poor memory, lest some important information or relationship be missed. Faraday's propensity for "scattered thoughts" elicited real shock in a modern scientist who examined the raw, primary materials for the first time.

> The *Diary* entries have the familiar and irritating form of ideas jotted down, repeated and forgotten. There are only brief episodes of reasoning, and not all of these are in the same line of thought. I realized that this *lack of pattern* was not an irritating failure to be ordered, but was *itself the evidence of how Faraday thought.* . . . The prejudice which had prevented my understanding was the idea that Faraday's thinking must have had a single coherent framework. It did not. Faraday thought about and worked at various notions of "lateral action" without elevating any idea to the status of "framework." This clarification took place, *not by rational analysis of any prior thoughts*, but by a quite different mode of thinking, *a selection of thought*. From the morass of articulated and unarticulated principles, concepts, observations and physical facts, Faraday suspended the need to understand and simply acknowledged the thoughts which came into his head. The coherence of ideas was not imposed by any prior framework, but was allowed to emerge from the chaos of thoughts he experienced.[20]

There is a steadiness and logic to the structure of established scientific knowledge. The process by which this knowledge is come by, however, may be shockingly different from its final form. One component of this process was elevated to the status of a deliberate method by some of Faraday's followers, making the central use of the imagination respectable, where it had not been formerly.

> [Faraday's] views of science . . . became increasingly heretic. Slowly he developed new ideas about science, which were very modern— more modern than those of all his disciples, for example—up to, and excluding, Einstein. Today we all agree that scientists employ their imagination—that Newton, for example, was highly imaginative. Yet, we know, Newton did not like to speak of his own imagination, nor did his biographers prior to Sir David Brewster (1831).
>
> Faraday stressed the fact that he tried to employ his power of imagination, and even systematically. This was noticed by most of his followers. His main pupil, Tyndall, wrote essays on the "Use and Limit of Imagination in Science." Today we take it naturally; then it

was a revolution. . . . Science was freed, once and for all, from its inductive basis. From then on, experiment took a new place, as a check on the imagination, not as a substitute for it. Faraday's major contribution to scientific method is this: it does not matter where you start—if you have an opinion, try to test it, and proceed in this way. . . .

Faraday's contribution is double. First, he spread his idea, through writings of his own and of his disciples. Second, and more impressive, he practiced it systematically—which is more than many scientists do even today.[21]

Faraday's views are clearly expressed in a brief letter he wrote to a young man who had written him with some of his ideas about a new theory of matter:

Royal Institution, 16th June, 1834.

Sir,

I have no hesitation in advising you to experiment in support of your views, because, whether you confirm them or confute them, good must come from your exertions.

With regard to the views themselves, I can say nothing about them, except that they are useful in exciting the mind to inquiry. A very brief consideration of the progress of experimental philosophy will show you that it is a great disturber of pre-formed theories.

I have thought long and closely about the theories of attraction and of particles and atoms of matter, and the more I think (in association with experiment) the less distinct does my idea of an atom or particle of matter become.

I am, Sir, your etc.[22]

Others found Faraday's originality with concepts and terminology to be a great source of difficulty. "Tyndall called him a prophet although not entirely in a complimentary way. He was referring to the 'entangled' meaning of Faraday's language which he found untranslatable into the scientific idiom of the time."[23] Faraday's intuitive sense was such that one is reminded of Einstein's references to his own good "nose" for tracking down the solutions to problems.

[Faraday] . . . the crowned king of experimentalists, not only found all his facts by being led by hypotheses, but more than that, his interest was never in mere facts. . . . All believers in induction, from Bacon to Keyes, accept facts "as they are." Faraday's approach was completely different. If he had a theory, he was as stubborn as a mule about it. . . . Most of his experiments were carried out again and again for years, in spite of failures as clear as any experiment can ever be. . . . Yet he could always reinterpret failure in order to elicit from it a new sign of hope. It is only a wonder that he more often got the desired "yes" than the persistent "no." There is no explanation for this. Kohlrausch said: "He smells the truth." Bence Jones speaks of his unfailing intuition and Helmholtz of his inconceivable instinct. His technique, however, was to . . . *interpret* facts in light of [his] theories: he was a master of reinterpretation.[24]

It is often observed that some dyslexics have certain heightened abilities with respect to acting, performing, or lively speech full of hand gestures and animated facial expression. All these are usually acknowledged as strong right-hemisphere traits. Dyslexics who do not show these traits may have close relatives who do, some of whom may be professional actors or performers. Of course, it is not always necessary to be a performer in the conventional sense. The special ability to give a moving performance may, of course, contribute to success in many other fields: the argument of a case in the courtroom, the rhetoric of the politician, the presentation of the master salesman, the sermon of the minister. A number of contemporary observers commented on Faraday's special talents in this respect.

Success in the lecture theater was until the last quarter of the nineteenth century a necessity for any scientist. . . . From the 1830s he drew large audiences, and by the 1840s was regarded as one of the finest of London's scientific speakers. . . . It was commonplace to contrast Faraday's use of plain language with Davy's more flowery eloquence. . . . Many commentators remarked upon Faraday's passion, and his vivacity of facial expression. This suggests a man so consumed by belief and passion for his subject that his whole body was physically animated by it. Cornelia Crosse commented on "that wonderful mobility of countenance so peculiar to him," while Juliet Pollock spoke of his gleaming eyes . . . his moving hands and irresistible eloquence.

Lectures such as these were a communal experience, not just an individual one—as Juliet Pollock said, "His audience took fire with him, and every face was flushed."[25]

It is not clear whether Faraday's slight speech impediment disappeared when he was older or whether he, like some actors and performers, was remarkably able to speak with great clarity when giving a carefully prepared talk before a large audience.

While Faraday did not have many of the more classic signs of dyslexia, it seems clear that he had a number of related traits that are now recognized as learning disabilities. As with many of those we are interested in, it seems that many of these traits contributed, at the same time, to notable difficulties as well as to many remarkable achievements. Faraday was known as the master experimenter, yet his constant experimentation was only a way of informing, testing, and verifying the products of his imagination—one of the most powerful imaginations of his age. Faraday was never a mathematician, but he provided a set of utterly original mathematical concepts which, with the help of Maxwell, brought mathematics to the center of a new kind of physics in the next century. He had certain deficiencies and difficulties that may have had more to do with his learning style and learning disabilities than they did with his almost total lack of formal schooling. Yet, while he had not had much formal education, Faraday was nature's attentive pupil all his life.

JAMES CLERK MAXWELL

While we have argued that James Clerk Maxwell shared much with Michael Faraday, it is clear that in many respects the men were very different. Both were very visual in their preferred modes of thought. In effect, they collaborated on the theory of electromagnetic fields and light that was at the same time the most important accomplishment in each of their careers and the most important scientific accomplishment of their century. Because of his famous equations, Maxwell's name is familiar to most persons having any form of scientific training. However, the full extent of his work is insufficiently known among professionals and lay persons. According to one recent biographer, C. W. F. Everitt, Maxwell made a second contribution of almost comparable importance to the electromagnetic theory of light—the systematic application of statistical methods in physics. According to Everitt, "To have been the central figure in the two greatest theoretical achievements of one's age would be enough for most scientists. Maxwell did more. His other discoveries, though smaller by comparison, would have secured the reputations of half a dozen lesser men."[26]

Maxwell began the scientific study of color and projected the first color photograph in 1860. He applied original statistical methods to explain the nature of Saturn's rings. He developed a method for the analysis of stresses in bridge structures. He wrote the first important paper on cybernetic and control theory so central to modern computers (it was an analysis of the common spinning-ball governor). He analyzed certain basic relationships between thermodynamic quantities. He made important contributions to the geometry of optics. And he developed certain important mathematical terms and coined terminology related to the study of vectors (arrows used to represent the direction and magnitude of a force).[27] Again, according to Everitt,

> Such a range of activity in a man who died at 48 suggests a most unusual personality, and Maxwell, though at a distance he sometimes appeared as a "quiet and rather silent man" . . . impressed those who came closer as someone entirely out of the ordinary.[28]

Maxwell's early life and education in the country were idyllic. An only child to older parents, his antics were the center of attention for his parents and household servants. Maxwell's earliest recollection as a child was recounted by one of his friends: "I distinctly remember his telling me, during his early manhood, that his first recollection was that of lying on the grassbefore his father's house, and looking at the sun, and *wondering*."[29]

His earliest education was from his mother, but she died of cancer when he was eight. He had a disastrous experience with one private tutor whose methods consisted largely of rough drill and hard discipline. Some biographers have regarded his experience with the tutor as so traumatic that they argue that it is the likely cause of his lifelong stuttering. (In contrast, we would suggest that this condition might have had a good deal more to do with deep neurological development processes than an unsavory tutor who used methods quite common for the time.)

The young Maxwell finally left the family country home and went to live with his aunts in Edinburgh so that he could attend the new Edinburgh Academy. He started school weeks after the term began, however, and arrived dressed in clothes designed by his father, speaking with a strong country accent. The accent and strange clothes immediately made him the object of ridicule and abuse from the city boys. (These circumstances may say as much about the naiveté of Maxwell's widower father in children's social matters as it does about the difficulties Maxwell had in dealing with early school life and difficult classmates). "For the next two years his school life was a misery. He was harassed in the Academy yard and did badly in class because of his awkwardness and hesitancy of speech."[30]

But life in later school years and at university was quite different. Maxwell gradually earned the respect of the boys and, in time, students and teachers increasingly appreciated his formidable strengths and paid less attention to his remaining difficulties and eccentricities. A telling portrait of the young man was given by his early biographers, Campbell and Garnett, in 1882. Their description is of the period from 1847 to 1850, when Maxwell was between the ages of sixteen and nineteen.

> When he entered the University of Edinburgh, James Clerk Maxwell still occasioned some concern to the more conventional amongst his friends by the originality and simplicity of his ways. His replies in ordinary conversation were indirect and enigmatical, often uttered with hesitation and in a monotonous key.

Here Campbell and Garnett explain in a note at the bottom of the page, "This entirely disappeared afterwards, except when ironically assumed. It was accompanied with a certain huskiness of voice, which was observed also in later years." The description continues:

> While extremely neat in his person, he had a rooted objection to the vanities of starch and gloves. He had a pious horror of destroying anything—even a scrap of writing paper. He preferred travelling by the third class in railway journeys, saying he liked a hard seat. When

at table he often seemed abstracted from what was going on, being absorbed in observing the effects of refracted light in the finger-glasses, or in trying some experiment with his eyes—seeing round a corner, making invisible stereoscopes, and the like. Miss Cay [his aunt, the sister of his late mother] used to call attention by crying, "Jamsie, you're in a prop" [a mathematical proposition]. He never tasted wine; and he spoke to gentle and simple in exactly the same tone. On the other hand, his teachers . . . had formed the highest opinion of his intellectual originality and force.[31]

Some of the traits we are seeking are clearly evident here. Maxwell cared little for convention and was noted for the "originality and simplicity of his ways." His conversation was often hesitant and unclear, a vivid contrast with the lucidity of his written expression. A basic love of simplicity would appear to be consistent with his preference for third-class railway accommodation, his equal dealings with upper- and lower-class people, and his distaste for "the vanities of starch and gloves"—a distaste that recalls Einstein's distaste for the conventions he came to ignore: tailed coats, starched collars, and socks.

Children with dyslexia or other learning disabilities are sometimes observed to be tactless, inept, or naive in social situations. Apparently, these children are, to some extent, blind to some of the many dimensions of social interaction—the subtle cues, the many levels of meaning, the signs of interest or disinterest, the hierarchical and power relationships, the consequences of speaking one's mind without considering the probable effects. But blindness in one area may help to promote needed focus and concentration in another. For some, a certain blindness or insensitivity to the complexity and subtlety of social convention and interaction may serve as a bulwark against distractions from one's principal concerns. It may be that the simplicity shared by Maxwell and Einstein could be closely related to some degree of social blindness—one that might have promoted the arresting honesty and absence of guile for which both were known.

The brief description of Maxwell at the dinner table is particularly telling in establishing his relative disinterest in conventional table conversation and his persistent preoccupation with observing the operation of light and other natural phenomena, whatever the situation. It is notable that all the examples mentioned are of a visual nature ("trying some experiment with his eyes—seeing around a corner, making invisible stereoscopes"). These examples lend themselves to building mental models of optical interaction and spatial relationships, which are, in turn, closely related to the mathematics of area, field, line, and force.

Maxwell relied heavily upon visual, mechanical, and geometric approaches in his mathematical and scientific work. As Everitt observed, "Maxwell's starting point in mathematics was Euclidean geometry. Euclid is now so out of fashion that few people know the excitement of his intellectual rigor. . . . With Maxwell the love of geometry stayed. . . . The love of geometry also helped interest Maxwell in Faraday's ideas about lines of force."[32]

The common thread throughout the great variety of Maxwell's accomplishments is the interplay of force and substance in a largely visual-spatial arena. The visual-spatial dominated his work. However, from the stories of his daily life we might also infer that he was thinking in geometric terms much of the time, wherever he was and whatever he was doing. An important illustration of the operation of Maxwell's visual-spatial thinking is his early appreciation of the work of the American physicist J. Willard Gibbs, one of the major figures in the development of the study of thermodynamics. In the 1870s, Gibbs published a series of papers addressing the complex thermodynamic behavior of water and other fluids using an unusual and innovative "graphical method," as he called it. The method involved a three-dimensional mental model comparable to what we would now call a "surface plot," a kind of three-dimensional graph that shows a number of points covering an undulating surface with rises and depressions like small mountains and valleys. As any point (representing a particular temperature, volume, and pressure) moves over the surface plot, the conditions change in certain predictable ways, giving a deep understanding of the behavior of the system.

Gibbs wrote about his new method and described it mathematically, but he made no effort to make a diagram of what he saw in his own mind's eye. Because he was introducing a new method and due to the difficulty of visualizing such complex material, Gibbs's ideas received little attention from his scientific collegues, especially in America. But when Maxwell read Gibbs's material he immediately saw the power and the potential of the method. Indeed, so great was his interest that "he spent an entire winter" constructing a clay model of a surface using Gibbs's data.[33] "I have just finished a clay model of a fancy surface showing the solid, liquid, and gaseous states, and the continuity of the liquid and gaseous states," Maxwell explained in a letter to a scientist friend.[34]

What Maxwell had done, in effect, was a kind of sculpture. He patiently calculated the approximate position of each point in space and then adjusted the shape of the clay surface to correspond to the array of points in different positions (just as a sculptor or stone cutter would check his own work with a series of measurements from an original). Maxwell sent a plaster cast of the clay model to Gibbs and kept another in his own laboratory at Cambridge University. Gibbs's copy is still on display outside the Yale University Physics Department, and Maxwell's copy is still on display at the Cavendish Laboratory at Cambridge.

What is most important for our discussion, then, is the way the visually oriented Maxwell immediately seized upon Gibbs's unusual but apt visual-spatial approach, eventually moving a whole generation of American and European scientists to appreciate the value of Gibbs's work. However, while Gibbs's method and approach came to be fully appreciated, the mental-spatial model on which the method was based has been almost completely ignored until very recently. As explained by Iowa State University chemistry professor Kenneth R. Jolls,

> For those who could not follow the elaborate verbal manipulation of lines and planes in space that permeates [Gibbs's] writings, the physical meaning and the artistic beauty of these brilliant analogies were lost. Indeed, the interesting connections between thermodynamics and geometry, which were the essence of Gibbs's theoretical development, have all but vanished from the literature.

Recently, however, with the development of computer-generated three dimensional graphics, all this has begun to change. Jolls and one of his graduate students, Daniel Coy, have developed a means of doing what Maxwell had done—but this time rapidly on a powerful graphics computer rather than over several months in modeling clay. According to Jolls, "There can be no doubt in the mind of any serious thermodynamicist" that images like those being produced on their computer screen "were vividly in Gibbs's mind as he wrote his famous trilogy in the mid-1870s."[35]

The reference to the art of sculpture is especially apt in Maxwell's case. As we have noted, a strong family connection is often observed between those with some form of dyslexia or learning disability and strong talents in the visual or performing arts. Historically some inventors have been artists or closely related to artists. This connection is of particular interest to Everitt as he attempts to gain a better understanding of Maxwell's extraordinary abilities. "The persistence of the artistic gift in a family so practical in outlook is a striking fact, one that must be born in mind in analyzing Maxwell's genius. Each generation threw up clever artists, among whom not the least able was Maxwell's cousin Jemima . . . whose brilliant water-color paintings of Maxwell's childhood are a perpetual delight to Maxwell scholars."[36]

Maxwell's writing and research show an unusual flexibility of mind, although it was rather unlike Faraday's. Whereas Faraday seemed to have had a remarkable tolerance for lack of structure, Maxwell could move from one structure to another, quite different structure with relative ease, retaining underlying similarities of approach. "Maxwell . . . was continually changing his outlook. His five leading papers on electromagnetic theory written between 1855 and 1868 each presented a complete view of the subject, and each viewed it from a different angle. It is this variety that makes Maxwell's writings . . . a kind of enchanted fairyland: one never knows what to expect next."[37]

Although the significance is not altogether clear, Maxwell puzzled his university friends with his considerable interest in religion and metaphysical philosophy in spite of his deep interest in science and mathematics. This was especially puzzling to his contemporary biographer, Campbell, who assumed that a clear scientific and mathematical mind would spurn such concerns. Indeed, it is interesting that Faraday, Maxwell, and Einstein all had serious (although highly individual and different) religious interests and thus would not fit the conventional modern image of the secular scientist. That the lives of these men spanned the nineteenth and early twentieth centuries does not seem sufficient to explain their serious religious interests, a strong contrast to the thread of atheism or agnosticism that developed during this period, especially among the well educated and scientifically trained.

A related attitude of these three men was their deep reverence, in varying degrees, for what they were studying, along with a relative disinterest in the fame or practical results that might come from their discoveries.

Maxwell was a professional scientist, but he was able to see well beyond the conventional science of his day. He was as fully at home in the intuitive and visual world of Faraday as he was in the world of the "professed mathematicians." He knew mathematics, but did not think in the same way as the conventional mathematicians of his time. He knew their ways but was not restricted by them. He approached physical phenomena with complex mechanical models, but when he was finished, all such analogies were made impossible (at least for a time). The consequences of his work were so extensive and profound that they set the research agenda for the next half century, yet he never received, during his lifetime, the recognition given his contemporaries of lesser stature. Maxwell was well educated, but his career was only modestly successful. His speech difficulties limited his professional advancement throughout his life. Although he was eventually appointed head of the new Cavendish Laboratory at Cambridge University, it was only after two other preferred candidates declined the position. Maxwell died too young to elaborate his work fully or to gain full recognition for his accomplishments. But in the physical sciences his work was the most important product of his century, as everyone gradually began to see. Maxwell never was able to lecture well, but he taught generations.

ALBERT EINSTEIN

Much concerning Albert Einstein's youth is already a part of popular mythology and has long been a source of comfort to many who have had some sort of difficulty in school. Some writers and researchers have considered Einstein to have been dyslexic. Others deny that this was so, strictly speaking. Several writers have emphasized Einstein's slow early development. We have already noted Gerald Holton's references to Einstein's late use of language and his difficulties with foreign languages. Of these earliest years, one biographer, Banesh Hoffmann, wrote in 1972, "Did his grandparents ever despairingly think, as his parents at one time thought, that the beloved Albert Einstein was a dullard? They had good reason to think so, and the thought must have been agonizing. . . . Considering that little Albert was to become none other than Einstein, his start was hardly auspicious."[38]

More recently, some writers have partly challenged this view and emphasized Einstein's brilliance even as a young student. One wrote in 1982, "The widespread belief that he was a poor pupil is unfounded."[39] It seems that the same evidence can be construed in very different ways by different authors. How can this be so? Perhaps the conflicting evidence itself can be instructive. In one aspect, it is mainly a matter of definition. If one is using the more restrictive definition of dyslexia (referring mainly to reading difficulties), then one is more likely to conclude that someone like Einstein was not dyslexic. But if one is using the less restrictive definition used by many neurologists (referring to varied verbal difficulties, often accompanied by special right-hemisphere talents), then one is more likely to conclude that someone like Einstein was dyslexic.[40]

A mixture of great strengths and surprising weaknesses can be confusing but can itself be the best evidence of the pattern we are interested in. If the record is mixed, then some evidence can be found to support either side of the debate. However, it would seem that Einstein's early school experience can be described as inconsistent at best. Einstein himself acknowledged this mixed pattern. He observed in a letter to an inquirer in 1955, "As a pupil I was neither particularly good nor bad. My principal weakness was a poor memory and especially a poor memory for words and texts." It was during these years that his teacher of Greek told him, in the oft-quoted statement, "You will never amount to anything."[41] Nonetheless, Einstein was able to advance rapidly in some areas where he followed his own interests. "Only in mathematics and physics was I, through self study, far beyond the school curriculum, and also with regard to philosophy."[42]

Wherever there is such mixed evidence, we need to be especially attentive to fine details and subtle indicators, as recorded by close and sensitive observers. If our approach is correct, we should expect to find no clear evidence for one side or the other, but rather curiously mixed evidence. And wherever possible, it is best to rely mainly on primary sources to avoid conflicting interpretations. Fortunately, a highly detailed sketch of Einstein's early life has been provided by his sister, Maja Winteler-Einstein, recently published in German and in English translation in the first volumes of the *Collected Papers*.[43]

From Winteler-Einstein's account, there is little doubt that a concern with Albert's rate of development was a cause for real concern in the Einstein family. "Normal childhood development proceeded slowly, and he had such difficulty with language that those around him feared that he would never learn to speak. . . . Every sentence he uttered, no matter how routine, he repeated to himself softly, moving his lips. This habit persisted until his seventh year."

From the beginning Einstein showed that his interests and abilities were somewhat different from those of his peers, and in some important cases, more advanced. "Albert refrained from joining . . . boisterous games and occupied himself with quieter things. When he occasionally did take part, he was regarded as the obvious arbiter in all disputes. Since children usually still have a very keen and unspoiled instinct for the exercise of justice, the general recognition of his authority indicates that his ability to think objectively developed early."

Einstein's earliest schooling was at home, but he did not get along with his teacher. His difficulties with the teacher suggest that he did not easily accommodate himself to the student role even at a very young age.

> At the age of five he received his first instruction at home from a woman. . . . The small, usually calm boy had inherited from grandfather Koch a tendency toward violent temper tantrums. At such moments his face would turn completely yellow, the tip of his nose snow-white, and he was no longer in control of himself. On one such occasion he grabbed a chair and struck at his teacher, who was so frightened that she ran away terrified and was never seen again. This violent temper disappeared during his early school years.[44]

A lack of sensitivity to some of the subtleties of language and social distinction seems to have been as characteristic of Einstein as it was of Maxwell. Winteler-Einstein noted young Albert's comparative social innocence, in a formal and rank-conscious society, in mixing familiar and formal forms of address: "There was . . . something impertinent, but also something naive and humorous in little Albert's way of addressing his music teacher: 'Du, Herr Schmied.' "Einstein's musical interests and abilities are well known and were evident early. It played a central role in his creative life. "His musical ability seems to have come from the Koch branch of the family, the mathematical and logical from the Einstein side. Incidentally, it is not uncommon, as far apart as these two fields seem to lie, for mathematical and musical talent to be joined in one person."[45]

In his middle teens, with the encouragement of a medical student who boarded with the Einstein family, Einstein became heavily involved with science, philosophy, and mathematics.

> Music served as his only distraction. . . . He could already play Mozart and Beethoven sonatas on the violin. . . . He would also sit at the piano and, mainly in arpeggios full of tender feeling, constantly search for new harmonies and transitions of his own invention. And yet it is really incorrect to say that these musical reveries served as a distraction. Rather, they put him in a peaceful state of mind, which facilitated his reflection. For later on, when great problems preoccupied him, he often suddenly stood up and declared: "There, now I've got it." A solution had suddenly appeared to him.[46]

In another area, we can see, as a young man, evidence of Einstein's tendency toward disorganization, along with his solution to the problem. "You know the ghastly disorder that reigns among my worldly goods & it is really lucky that I don't have much."[47]

Einstein's talents in mathematics and other subjects were not always appreciated by his teachers or reflected in his grades. In mathematics, his sister explains, the general emphasis was on rapid, reflex responses rather than thoughtful replies. Albert

> entered the public primary school at the age of seven. There he had a rather strict teacher whose methods included teaching children arithmetic, and especially the multiplication tables, with the help of whacks on the hands, so-called "Tatzen" (knuckle raps); a style of teaching that was not unusual at the time, and that prepared the children early for their future role as citizens.

The boy, self-assured and thorough in thought, was considered only moderately talented, precisely because he needed time to mull things over and didn't respond immediately with the reflex answer desired by the teacher. Nothing of his special aptitude for mathematics was noticeable at the time; he wasn't even good at arithmetic in the sense of being quick and accurate, though he was reliable and persevering. Also, he always confidently found the way to solve difficult word problems, even though he easily made errors in calculation.[48]

So, according to his sister, Einstein never was much good at the "easy" part of mathematics. To shine, he had to move on to the "hard" part. In adult life, his mathematical intuition was recognized as extraordinary and he could handle deftly the most difficult tensor calculus, but it appears that arithmetic calculation continued to be an area of comparative weakness.[49]

Teachers of today may not use "knuckle raps," but arithmetic proficiency, with speed and accuracy of calculation and response, is still widely considered to be a major early indicator of mathematical aptitude, whether in the classroom or work group, or in achieving high scores on standardized aptitude tests. In all these settings the main concern is getting the largest number of right answers in a given time, even if nearly devious methods are sometimes used to do so. The inadequacy of such teaching and testing methods to recognize deep mathematical ability beneath superficial difficulties cannot be overemphasized. Fortunately, this approach has begun to change with recent reform movements in mathematics education.[50]

Even in the initial development of his most creative early work on the special theory of relativity, we see evidence of continuing difficulties with errors of simple calculation. In 1901, Einstein wrote to his future wife, "I am now working very eagerly on an electrodynamics of moving bodies, which promises to become a capital paper. I wrote to you that I doubted the correctness of the ideas about relative motion. But my doubts were based solely on a simple mathematical error. Now I believe in it more than ever."[51]

Although Einstein did become more sophisticated in higher mathematics in his later career, some argue that this increased sophistication may have been more a hindrance than a help in his subsequent work. One mathematician of the period, David Hilbert, who came close to some of the early basic insights of general relativity, was a great admirer of Einstein's work. Hilbert claimed no share of the credit for Einstein's accomplishment, but made clear, with some exaggeration, that his accomplishment came from elsewhere than through his mathematical skill. "Every boy in the streets of Gottingen understands more about four-dimensional geometry than Einstein. Yet, in spite of that, Einstein did the work and not the mathematicians."[52]

Indeed, Abraham Pais, the author of a recent scientific biography of Einstein, notes that Einstein's increasing reliance on mathematics in later life also entailed a reduced reliance on the visual and intuitive methods used so heavily and so productively in his earlier work. It is suggested that this change in approach may have contributed to his reduced productivity in his later years. Pais observes, "It is true that the theoretical physicist who has no sense of mathematical elegance, beauty, and simplicity is lost in some essential way. At the same time it is dangerous and can be fatal to rely exclusively on formal arguments. It is a danger from which Einstein himself did not escape in his later years. The emphasis on mathematics is so different from the way the young Einstein used to proceed."[53]

When Albert was fifteen, his family moved from Germany to Italy so that his father could start a new business near Milan. It was planned that Albert should remain behind in Munich to complete the school year. However, his hatred of the German high school was so intense that finally he left school, becoming, according to one biographer, essentially a dropout. However, Einstein was sufficiently prudent to take the precaution of obtaining a medical certificate (indicating that a change of climate was needed for health reasons) before joining his family in Italy. In a letter written in 1940, he explained his reasons for dropping out of the school.

> I was summoned by my home-room teacher who expressed the wish that I leave the school. To my remark that I had done nothing amiss he replied only "your mere presence spoils the respect of the class for me."
>
> I myself, to be sure, wanted to leave school and follow my parents to Italy. But the main reason for me was the dull, mechanized method of teaching. Because of my poor memory for words, this presented me with great difficulties that it seemed senseless for me to overcome. I preferred, therefore, to endure all sorts of punishments rather than learn to gabble by rote.[54]

If one considers Einstein's words carefully, it seems clear that the main cause of his school problems was not so much his willful opposition to authoritarian instruction as it was his especially poor verbal memory.[55] The "main reason" he wanted to leave Germany was the "dull, mechanized method of teaching" which presented him with "great difficulties" because of his "poor memory for words." Like so many others with some form of significant learning difficulty, it may be that he preferred others to believe that he wouldn't do what, in fact, he couldn't do (or could do only relatively poorly and with great difficulty). As with many gifted students who have academic difficulties, it is better to appear obstinate than to appear dull-witted.

He promised his parents that he would prepare himself for university entrance examinations through self-study at home (while he also roamed the Italian countryside). When he did take the examinations, a year and a half before the usual age, he did well in mathematics and physics, but he failed. "It was a painful blow, even though half expected." But we should not be surprised to learn that "Rote subjects like languages and botany had been his undoing."[56]

Einstein's weakness in foreign languages continued into his time at the progressive Swiss Cantonal school in Aarau, his most positive school experience—and one that gave him his second chance to prepare himself for the university entrance examinations. While at Aarau, Einstein lived with the family of one of his teachers, Jost Winteler (whose son eventually married Einstein's sister Maja). During this time, Einstein's father wrote to Winteler, "Since Albert still lags far behind in the modern languages, I am taking the liberty of asking you to spur him to the utmost diligence in that direction and to arrange help through private lessons if necessary."[57]

There is evidence that Einstein's particular difficulties with foreign languages remained with him for all of his life. For example, when he visited Palestine in 1923, despite his new-found enthusiasm for Zionism, he indicated that he believed that the study of Hebrew would probably be unprofitable in his case. According to the diary of one of the officials who received Einstein after his arrival in Palestine, "He made . . . a little speech explaining the nature of his brain which he said was such that he was afraid it would be unproductive work for him to attempt to learn Hebrew."[58]

In short, Einstein did well in some subject areas and poorly in others. In a letter to Winteler, Einstein's father summed up the continuing pattern of mixed results: "I am taking the liberty of returning the enclosed school report; to be sure, not all its parts fulfill my wishes and expectations, but with Albert I got used a long time ago to finding not-so-good grades along with very good ones, and I am therefore not disconsolate about them."[59]

Once in university, Einstein continued to be an erratic student. He often skipped class, using a good friend's thorough notes to cram for exams. "As for lectures, they were for him an intrusion. He attended them only fitfully, and for the most part with little enthusiasm. . . . His classmate, Marcel Grossmann . . . gladly let Einstein study [his] notes, and without them to cram from, Einstein might well have failed the examinations."[60]

Einstein sometimes neglected his laboratory work and assigned reading, but he spent a great deal of time reading books of special interest to him, such as the works of Maxwell, which had not yet been accepted into the regular curriculum. Of his physics professor, "Einstein . . . was not impressed. . . . He did not care much for [Weber's] introduction to theoretical physics because he was disappointed not to learn anything new about Maxwell's theory. . . . As a typical representative of classical physics, [Weber] simply ignored everything which came after Helmholtz."[61]

As we saw with Faraday, and will see with others throughout these profiles, unusual difficulty with spelling is a common though not universal problem. With Faraday and others, we look to the editors of their letters and papers. With Einstein, his translator provides noteworthy evidence. "Misspelled names of persons and places (quite frequent, particularly in Einstein's letters and even his scientific notes and papers) are routinely corrected [in these translations] without comment."[62]

Even as an adult, Einstein betrayed a disinterest in mere factual information, perhaps because of his clear preference for larger concepts, broader truths, underlying patterns. In the early days, while walking to his Berlin University office one afternoon, Einstein explained to a young physicist, "I'm not much with people. . . . I want my peace. I want to know how God created this world. I am not interested in this or that phenomenon, in the spectrum of this or that element. I want to know His thoughts, the rest are details."[63]

We may wonder whether this disinterest may have been promoted in part by Einstein's relatively poor memory for these facts, being not too different, perhaps, from his poor memory for words, texts, botanical names, and foreign languages—or, conversely, we may wonder whether his poor memory for these things came partly from his clear disinterest in them. Either way, the results are probably similar.

During his first visit to America in 1921, Einstein "was given a questionnaire covering all the intellectual equipment a student was supposed to carry with him through life, once his university studies ended. To one question as to the speed of sound, Einstein replied: 'I don't know. I don't crowd my memory with facts that I can easily find in an encyclopedia.'"[64] Thus we might wish to consider not so much whether an individual's memory is good or bad, but what kinds of things his or her mind is good at remembering—the big patterns or the comparatively unimportant details. "Einstein said he 'couldn't really understand how anybody could know so much and understand so little!' Einstein always emphasized that you could know too many facts and get lost among them."[65]

In his *Autobiographical Notes*, Einstein explained that one of the main reasons he went into physics instead of mathematics was that he had a stronger intuitive sense in physics. "My intuition was not strong enough in the field of mathematics to differentiate clearly the fundamentally important, that which is really basic, from the rest of the more or less dispensable erudition." Things were different in the world of physics.

> True enough, physics also was divided into separate fields, each of which was capable of devouring a short lifetime of work without having satisfied the hunger for deeper knowledge. The mass of insufficiently connected experimental data was overwhelming here also. In this field, however, I soon learned to scent out that which might lead to fundamentals and to turn aside from everything else, from the multitude of things that clutter up the mind and divert it from the essentials.[66]

One of the more distinctive and frightening elements of the experience shared by those with dyslexia or other forms of learning difficulties is the intensification of the crisis period experienced by many in late adolescence and early adulthood. This critical time is difficult for many without special learning problems, but it can be more so for those we are considering. Especially when there is no overt recognition of the paradoxical pattern of high talents and substantial disabilities, the sufferer is confronted with internal and external conflict along with confusion on all sides. This condition may be especially intensified with the most highly gifted. They feel the wrenching conflict of knowing they are really brilliant, at least in some areas, while their ability and measured performance in other areas may be decidedly poor. They feel they have something to give but have not yet found a way to have their work accepted. Too often, the special talents may be almost totally obscured by the deficiencies and the inexplicable difficulties. And throughout, their teachers and parents can see the confusing pattern only as stupidity, laziness, or willful contrariness.

As they approach the responsibilities of adulthood, the highly gifted with learning problems see that their time is running out. Their education is coming to an end, but they see their dreams and prospects fading before their eyes. They have failed examinations or barely passed them. They are confused by the clarity of their own perceptions and the disapproval of their professors, parents, and peers. They may have glimpsed the heights, but their confidence has been shaken repeatedly. Their academic record is mixed, at best, their references, lukewarm. Their fierce honesty and impatience with conventional views, coupled with their lack of tact and social grace, may have caused them to make enemies they can ill afford to have. Employment prospects are not good. The dark clouds of depression descend. How many are lost at this stage, we might well wonder.

It is hard to appreciate fully how low Einstein sank at this critical juncture in his own life. It is sobering to realize that someone who had so much to give to the world had so little support and recognition for so long during this important phase. It is easy to gloss too quickly over this period. It seems too small in comparison with the magnificent achievements and the universal recognition of the later years. In retrospect, it does seem hard to believe, but it should not be simply explained away with a romantic notion of unrecognized genius. Not even Einstein was sure of what he was going to accomplish.

After graduation in 1900, Einstein was largely unemployed for a year. A second year passed before he found steady employment. At the Zurich Polytechnic, his extreme independence of mind had alienated many of his professors, even those, like Heinrich Weber, who had initially been his supporters. In fact, Einstein believed that Weber had organized a campaign to prevent him from getting an assistantship or other teaching position.[67] He sought unsuccessfully for a teaching job at any level. He gave private lessons for three francs an hour. In time, he found through his tutoring a few friends with whom he could discuss the early development of his wonderful ideas, but he lived so carefully and ate so little that some thought his health suffered.[68]

Einstein's father's business and health were failing again and he was of little help to his son. In return, the son felt guilty that he was of so little help to his father and his family. Even while he was still a student, his father's troubles had caused him great concern, even despair.

> If things had gone my way, Papa would have looked for employment already 2 years ago, and he and we would have been spared the worst. . . . What depresses me most is, of course, the misfortune of my poor parents who have not had a happy moment for so many years. What further hurts me deeply is that as an adult man, I have to look on without being able to do anything. After all, I am nothing but a burden to my family. . . . It would indeed be better if I were not alive at all. Only the thought that I have always done whatever lay within my modest powers, and that year in, year out I do not permit myself a single pleasure, a distraction save that which my studies offer me, sustains me and must sometimes protect me from despair.[69]

But Einstein's father helped as well as he could. After nearly a year had passed without a position for his son he wrote a desperate letter to a professor he hoped could help:

> I beg you to excuse a father who dares to approach you, dear Professor, in the interests of his son. . . .
>
> My son is profoundly unhappy about his present joblessness, and every day the idea becomes more firmly implanted in him that he is a failure in his career and will not be able to find the way back again. And on top of this he is depressed by the thought that he is a burden on us since we are not very well-to-do people. . . .
>
> I permit myself to apply to you with the plea that you will read his article published in the *Annalen der Physik* and, hopefully, that

you will write him a few lines of encouragement so that he may regain his joy in his life and his work.

If, in addition, it should be possible to obtain for him a position as assistant, now or in the fall, my gratitude would be boundless.

I beg again your forgiveness for my audacity in sending you this letter and I want to add that my son has no idea of this extraordinary step of mine.[70]

Nothing came of the letter. Time dragged on. "Einstein could still find consolation and escape in his music. And, more important, exciting scientific ideas and speculations once more came crowding into his mind. Yet even as his mind soared, he felt himself sinking helplessly in the quagmire of a world that had no place for him."

Then, in the spring of 1901, things began to improve slightly. Einstein found a temporary position and became a substitute teacher for two months at a technical school in Winterthur. During this time, he completed a research article on thermodynamics. Later he submitted it as a doctoral dissertation to the University of Zurich. The article was finally accepted for publication by the *Annalen der Physik*, but it was rejected as a Ph.D. thesis.[71]

It was probably during his time at Winterthur that Einstein learned that his student sweetheart and future wife, Mileva Maric, was pregnant. He tried to reassure her concerning his prospects. He would find something. He consulted friends of friends in a frantic effort to find work. He was desperate. Almost anything would do. He tried to find a position at an insurance firm, then at a secondary school. Finally, he found another temporary position—a job as tutor at a private school for the 1901–1902 academic year.[72]

In the end, in June 1902, came a job at the Patent Office. The job provided a small income and some stability, allowing him to marry and support a wife and children while providing enough spare time to slowly formulate the master-stroke papers eventually published three years later. Einstein was forever grateful to his student friend Marcel Grossmann (the same one who had lent him the lecture notes), who stuck by him through his worst days and who, through his own father's connections, helped him receive consideration for the job. After Grossmann's death in 1936, Einstein wrote a letter of condolence to his widow.

Our student days together come back to me. He a model student; I untidy and a daydreamer. He on excellent terms with the teachers and grasping everything easily; I aloof and discontented, not very popular. But we were good friends and our conversations over iced coffee at the Metropol every few weeks belong among my nicest memories. Then the end of the studies . . . I suddenly abandoned by everyone, facing life not knowing which way to turn. But he stood by me and through him and his father I came to Haller in the Patent Office a few years later. In a way, this saved my life; not that I would have died without it, but I would have been intellectually stunted."[73]

Einstein is probably the best-known scientist of any century and in any field. In popular mythology, his name is virtually a synonym for genius. As a high school student, he began a series of experiments in his mind's eye that would eventually transform our view of fundamental physical reality. He had nothing of conventional ambition and he loved simplicity, yet he became the most famous and respected scientist of the twentieth century, becoming the only modern scientist to achieve worldwide recognition and media stardom despite his innate simplicity and reserve. In the decades since his death, Einstein's pictures and quotations seem to grow ever more common, from computer advertisements to college dormitory posters and silk-screened t-shirts.

Einstein's school and university experience was a remarkable blend of recognized superiority and examination failure, brilliant performances and rejected theses, notable accomplishment along with evasion and avoidance of conventional curricula. In many ways, Einstein's academic record and early professional career were decidedly undistinguished, as he himself recognized. One historian described Einstein's early career as a "catastrophe." Einstein himself termed it a "comedy."[74] His early days were so difficult that he vowed he would always help gifted young men whenever it was in his power to do so.[75] Yet, in time, Einstein revolutionized physics and became teacher to all his professors, making the lectures he did not attend outdated, and the books he did not study obsolete.

A junior clerk with the Swiss Patent Office, probationary "Technical Expert, Third Class," as he wrote his early, seminal papers, Einstein soon was offered his pick of university professorships and the top positions in the most prestigious research organizations. The basic soundness of his theories was recognized early in the century, but it has been only in the last decade or so that experimental physics has reached the stage where his work has had widespread practical application and daily verification.[76]

Einstein used the most sophisticated mathematics to develop his theories, but often his sums would not come out right. He was a daydreamer who played fancifully with images in his mind, but in the process he created an objective image of the universe that transformed forever our view of physical reality. Einstein had trouble learning and remembering facts, words, and texts, but he was teacher to the world. He was slow to speak, but, in time, the world listened.

5
PROFILES, PART 2
Dodgson, Poincaré, Edison, Tesla, and da Vinci

THE FORGETFUL MATHEMATICIAN: LEWIS CARROLL

Some experts reserve the diagnosis of dyslexia or learning disability to those who have, say, some twelve or fifteen traits out of a list of some thirty-five indicators.[1] Others will find alternative definitions and points of demarcation useful. But such criteria, which may be so important in legal and administrative determinations, are, for our purposes, relatively unimportant and can be quite misleading. We may hesitate to apply the term "dyslexic" or even "learning disabled" to someone with only one or two or three of these traits, especially if they are present only in mild form. Yet these same traits may be tremendously important in a given individual case when they contribute in a significant way, positively or negatively, to a person's major abilities or accomplishments.

Thus, certain persons may not have trouble reading or speaking or even calculating, but we would find it of great interest if they had major difficulty remembering numbers or dates, especially if they were well known as mathematicians, and more so if they used special mental dexterity (in certain related but different areas) to devise ways of dealing with the problem. Such a case is that of the quiet Oxford don and lecturer in mathematics, the Rev. C. L Dodgson, better known as Lewis Carroll.

In the biographical memoir prepared by Dodgson's nephew, Dodgson is said to have had "a wonderfully good memory, except for faces and dates. . . . To help himself to remember dates, he devised a system of mnemonics, which he circulated among his friends."

It is instructive to briefly describe the elements of his system, which he called his "Memoria Technica," to give some indication of the trouble he was willing to go to in order to deal with the problem. In this system, Dodgson devised a table in which each digit corresponded to two consonants, which could be used interchangeably. Certain associations helped cement the linkages between numbers and letters. Accordingly, the digit "2" was represented by "d" from "duo" and "w" from "two." Then, in an example provided by Dodgson, the date of Columbus's discovery of America would be rendered "492" or "fnd," (dropping the initial "1" as obvious). Once this was done, he would add vowels, as convenient, and devise a line or two of verse such as

Columbus sailed the world around,
Until America was FOUND[2]

Dodgson often surprised the many visitors he entertained at Oxford University with his keen memory for the dates associated with the various colleges. They never guessed the difficulty he had with dates or the very complex means he used to memorize them.

Dodgson's difficulty remembering faces is, perhaps, even more remarkable because in addition to being the well-known author of a form of pithy fantasy much beloved by children, logicians, and mathematicians alike, he was also a serious amateur in sketching and photographing people, including child friends and many of the famous persons of his day, such as Alfred Lord Tennyson, John Ruskin, and even Michael Faraday, one of Dodgson's first subjects.

In spite of these interests and proficiencies, Dodgson's difficulty with remembering faces was well known. According to his nephew, faces

were always a stumbling-block to him, and people used to say (most unjustly) that he was intentionally short-sighted. One night he went up to London to dine with a friend, whom he had only recently met. The next morning a gentleman greeted him as he was walking. "I beg your pardon" said Mr. Dodgson, "but you have the advantage of me. I have no remembrance of having ever seen you before this moment." "That is very strange," the other replied, "for I was your host last night!" Such little incidents as this happened more than once.[3]

In addition to having trouble with remembering dates and faces, Dodgson had several other traits often directly or indirectly associated with that larger pattern we have been discussing. He was fascinated with problems of left-right reversal. This is repeatedly evident, of course, in *Alice in Wonderland* and *Through the Looking-Glass*, but also in his occasional use of mirror writing to amuse child friends with a "looking-glass letter."[4]

Like Maxwell, Dodgson was a life-long stutterer. The problem caused him considerable difficulty in his university lectures and occasional sermons.[5] Indeed, the tendency to stutter seems to have been a strong trait of many of the members of his immediate family. One biographer reports that seven of Dodgson's ten siblings were stutterers. In addition, some have suggested that Dodgson may have been a changed left hander. These factors, taken together, suggest to some observers that Dodgson may have been what they call weakly lateralized, or, to put it another way, he may have had a comparatively symmetrical brain, like those described by Galaburda.[6]

Dodgson appears to have had a mix of traits which seem to be on the one hand strongly associated with his special accomplishments but on the other paradoxically inconsistent with his professional training. He was a logician who became famous for his fantasies. He was a photographer who could not remember faces. He was a mathematician who had great difficulty remembering numbers.

GENIUS WITH MIXED ABILITIES: HENRI POINCARÉ

Henri Poincaré is acknowledged as one of the most extraordinary mathematical thinkers of the late nineteeth and early twentieth centuries. Professional mathematicians know him as the last man who, like Gauss, was a genuine mathematical universalist, one who was able to make important contributions to all major areas of mathematics, including arithmetic, algebra, geometry, and analysis, as well as to related areas such as astronomy and mathematical physics.[7] According to one historian of mathematics, Poincaré was as productive as he was original.

> Poincaré's creative period opened with [his] thesis of 1878 and closed with his death in 1912—when he was at the apex of his powers. Into this comparatively brief span of thirty-four years he crowded a mass of work that is sheerly incredible when we consider the difficulty of most of it. His record is nearly five hundred papers on *new* mathematics, many of them extensive memoirs, and more than thirty books covering practically all branches of mathematical physics, theoretical physics, and theoretical astronomy. . . . This leaves out of account his classics on the philosophy of science and his popular essays.[8]

Poincaré seemed to have a knack for seeing what new developments were going to have enduring consequences. He was an early supporter of the young Einstein, although his attitude toward Einstein was unclear in later life and may have involved some rivalry.[9] Poincaré's praise for Einstein and his unconventional methods is preserved in a passage originally prepared as a letter of reference. It is also a general statement of an approach to doing science, one that seems especially characteristic of many of those we are discussing.

> M. Einstein is one of the most original thinkers I have ever met. Despite his youth he has already achieved a most honorable place among the leading scientists of his time. What we must particularly admire in him is the facility with which he adapts himself to new concepts and knows how to draw from them every conclusion. He does not remain attached to classical principles, and when presented with a problem in physics he quickly envisages all its possibilities. This leads immediately in his mind to the prediction of new phenomena which may one day be verified by experiment. I do not mean to say that all these predictions will meet the test of experiment when such tests become possible. Since he seeks in all directions, one must, on the contrary, expect the majority of the paths on which he embarks to be blind alleys. But one must hope at the same time that one of these directions . . . may be the right one, and that is enough. This is exactly how one should proceed. The role of mathematical physics is to ask questions and only experiment can answer them.[10]

Poincaré was deeply interested in creativity in mathematics and delivered a major early lecture on the subject that was the original impetus behind the book on the same subject by Jacques Hadamard.[11] Poincaré was known for a memory that was truly amazing in some respects while it was markedly unreliable in others. He had no difficulty reading and he clearly had a great many very special talents. However, these talents were mixed with a number of curious difficulties and disabilities. The mixed pattern was evident from the beginning.

> Poincaré's mental development as a child was extremely rapid. He learned to talk very early, but also very badly at first because he thought more rapidly than he could get the words out. From infancy his motor coordination was poor. When he learned to write it was discovered that he was ambidextrous and that he could write or draw as badly with his left hand as with his right. Poincaré never outgrew his physical awkwardness.[12]

It is notable that the early speech problem is seen not as a difficulty in itself but as a mismatch between the speed of thought and speech. As we will see, Poincaré's drawing was notoriously poor. We might presume his handwriting was poor as well, at least in his early years. It is notable, however, that facsimiles of his writing in later life show an apparently satisfactory hand and also a marked propensity to doodle, especially when bored, such as during oral examination sessions.[13]

Even more notable was Poincaré's unexpected performance on a new intelligence test, originally intended to be a method of predicting children's performance in school. "As an item of some interest in this connection it may be recalled that when Poincaré was acknowledged as the foremost mathematician and leading popularizer of science of his time he submitted to the Binet tests and made such a disgraceful showing that, had he been judged as a child instead of as the famous mathematician he was, he would have been rated—by the tests—as an imbecile."[14]

Gifted dyslexic and learning-disabled children are often observed to have unusually varied scores on the successors to the Binet test, the standard "IQ" tests. They may do much more poorly than the norm on some parts of the test while, on other parts, they may have an array of top scores rarely seen. In these cases, since the unusual differences between the high and low subtest scores is the critical factor, the common practice of averaging the several subtests together is, of course, extremely misleading. The averaging obscures the very pattern that is most revealing.

For Poincaré, a childhood illness and temporary disability needs also to be considered, both as a difficulty and possibly as a factor in promoting the emergence of several of his very special gifts.

> At the age of five Henri suffered a bad setback from diphtheria which left him for nine months with a paralyzed larynx. This misfortune made him for long delicate and timid, but it also turned him back on his own resources as he was forced to shun the rougher games of children his own age. His principle diversion was reading, where his unusual talents first showed up. A book once read—at incredible speed—became a permanent possession, and he could always state the page and line where a particular thing occurred. He retained this powerful memory all his life. This rare faculty, which Poincaré shared with Euler, who had it to a lesser degree, might be called visual or spatial memory. In temporal memory—the ability to recall with uncanny precision a sequence of events long passed—he was also unusually strong. Yet he unblushingly describes his memory as "bad." His poor eyesight perhaps contributed to a third peculiarity of his memory. The majority of mathematicians appear to remember theorems and formulas mostly by eye; with Poincaré it was almost wholly by ear. Unable to see the board distinctly when he became a student of advanced mathematics, he sat back and listened, following and remembering perfectly without taking notes— an easy feat for him, but one incomprehensible to most mathematicians. Yet he must have had a vivid memory of the "inner eye" as well, for much of his work, like a good deal of Riemann's, was of the kind that goes with facile space-intuition and acute visualization. His inability to use his fingers skillfully of course handicapped him in laboratory exercises. . . . Had Poincaré been as strong in practical science as he was in theoretical he might have made a fourth with the incomparable three, Archimedes, Newton, and Gauss.[15]

With dyslexia and learning disabilities there are many paradoxes. Sometimes these paradoxes serve mainly to highlight the concepts and terrain that need to be more refined and focused. For example, the term "fine motor coordination" may not really be very useful in describing a person whose handwriting is quite poor but whose skill at drawing is quite advanced. Sometimes we have to subdivide our terms and refocus our thinking once again to begin to comprehend two activities which seem identical on one level but are apparently quite different on another. Similarly, while we are told that Poincaré was awkward in almost all physical activities, we are also told that in his youth he became an "indefatigable dancer."

In other respects, Poincaré fit some of the more common stereotypes, even in his youth. "Even at this early stage of his career Poincaré exhibited some of the more suspicious features of his mature 'absentmindedness': he frequently forgot his meals and almost never remembered whether or not he had breakfasted."

Poincaré's way of doing mathematics reminds us of two others with extraordinary memory—Mozart composing music and Tesla (as we shall see) doing mechanical and electrical design.

> The passion for mathematics seized him at adolescence or shortly before (when he was about fifteen). From the first he exhibited a lifelong peculiarity: his mathematics was done in his head as he paced restlessly about, and was committed to paper only when all had been thought through. Talking or other noise never disturbed him while he was working. In later life he wrote his mathematical memoirs at one dash without looking back to see what he had written and limiting himself to but a few erasures as he wrote.

In spite of his brilliance as a student, Poincaré at times had notable difficulties with school examinations.

> Following the usual French custom Poincaré took the examinations for his first degrees (bachelor of letters, and of science) before specializing. These he passed in 1871 at the age of seventeen—after almost failing in mathematics! He had arrived late and flustered at the examination and had fallen down on the extremely simple proof of the formula giving the sum of a convergent geometrical progression. But his fame preceded him. "Any student other than Poincaré would have been plucked," the head examiner declared.

As Poincaré became older, his remarkable mathematical skills became more evident. "He astonished his companions by capturing the first prize in mathematics without having bothered to take any lecture notes." He was also known for the incredible speed of his responses. Once, when he was questioned on particularly difficult problems by unimpressed upperclassmen, "Without apparent thought, Poincaré gave the solution immediately and walked off, leaving his crestfallen baiters asking 'How does be do it?' Others were to ask the same question all through Poincaré's career. He never seemed to think when a mathematical difficulty was submitted to him by his colleagues: 'The reply came like an arrow.'"

For all his special talents, Poincaré, again like Tesla, had such difficulty with drawing that it threatened his early academic placement and prospects.

> At the Polytechnique Poincaré was distinguished for his brilliance in mathematics, his superb incompetence in all physical exercises . . . and his utter inability to make drawings that resembled anything on heaven or earth. The last was more than a joke; his score of zero in the entrance examination in drawing had almost kept him out of the school. This had greatly embarrassed his examiners.[16]

Poincaré showed no signs of reading difficulties or other more commonly recognized learning disabilities. However, he did show evidence of highly varied strengths and weaknesses, forming a pattern comparable to the model we have seen emerging from current neurological research. Poincaré may have had great difficulty managing his body in space or portraying visual space with his pen, but he had no difficulty using his powerful visual-spatial imagination to conceive the most original mathematical relationships and the most subtle mathematical patterns.

ANALOGIES AND PERPETUAL MOTION:
THOMAS ALVA EDISON

Thomas Edison is one of the best-known personalities in the American pantheon of individualism and technological progress. Most Americans know at least something of his humble origins and incomplete schooling, his early days as an itinerant telegraph operator, his busy Menlo Park laboratory, his unusual sleeping habits, his many inventions and patents, his phonograph, his light bulb, his moving pictures, his performances for the press, his deafness, his rough, joking manner and white hair. His products have been so fully assimilated that we hardly notice them. Indeed, Edison's light bulb has become the cartoon symbol for any bright new idea.

It matters little that others may have developed this or that component in some form before Edison. He made the idea work and delivered the product to market, at least most of the time. Despite all of this, however, partly through excessive familiarity, we might be inclined to underestimate the extent of Edison's accomplishments. We are so accustomed to the world created by his inventions that it all seems to have been somehow inevitable. But this should not be the case. For all their familiarity, his inventions should nonetheless be seen as formidable.

Edison is thought by many as having been dyslexic, or at least as having had some learning disabilities, although this is debated.[17] A few examples, however, are helpful in suggesting elements of a familiar pattern. A newspaper story quoted by one biographer indicates that Edison's father and even Edison himself were concerned about his early abilities. "My father thought I was stupid, and I almost decided I must be a dunce."[18] A description of Edison's early school experiences from another biographer provides evidence of several familiar traits.

> In the fall of 1854, Alva was enrolled in the school of the Reverend and Mrs. G. B. Engle. . . . The minister, of course, taught by rote, a method from which Alva was inclined to disassociate himself. He alternated between letting his mind travel to distant places and putting his body in perpetual motion in his seat. The Reverend Engle, finding him inattentive and unruly, swished his cane. Alva, afraid and out of place, held up a few weeks, then ran away from the school.
>
> It was midwinter, a time when Alva frequently came down with colds, earaches, bronchitis, and other pulmonary ailments. Nancy [his mother], having lost three children, was especially protective of Alva. She decided to keep him home and teach him herself.[19]

Much later, a diary entry from the adult Edison recounts a parlor game which highlights Edison's poor memory for names in sequence and, incidentally, displays his idiosyncratic use of capitalization and punctuation. In the handwritten entry, dated July 18, 1885, Edison says that, after a nap, he

> Went out yachting = I was delightfully unhot, Ladies played game called memory—Scheme No 1 calls out name of prominent author No 2 Repeats this name and adds another & so on. soon one has to remember a dozen names all of which must be repeated in the order given—result Miss Daisy had the best & I the poorest memory—[20]

The evidence that Edison had reading problems is less clear. Some sources indicate that in school he had trouble with rote learning, spelling, grammar, syntax, arithmetic, and overall classroom performance ("always at the foot of the class").[21] In his *Diary*, Edison recounts a story about having read "the library" in Detroit when a boy, although some recent biographers question this claim.[22] He claimed that he saw his deafness as at least partly a blessing in disguise because it led him to books and shielded him from distractions.[23] Yet, in the same passage, he suggests that his mode of reading occasionally involved a lot of skipping and skimming, as when he was reading, or perhaps looking through, Isaac Newton's *Principia.* "Amidst a wilderness of mathematics there were intervals of ordinary English literature of the better kind."[24]

It is sometimes difficult to separate fact from the "good stories" and "tall tales" Edison was wont to tell. However, his numerous references to other writers and books suggests that he did read rather widely as an adult. In the diary he kept briefly during the summer of 1885 he makes references to German metaphysics, Galton, Hawthorne, Dickens, Charlotte Brontë, DeQuincy, and others. Edison also read about authors and others in magazines and newspapers, so it is sometimes difficult to tell whether he had actually read their books.[25] Even if he had not read as much as he would have had us believe, he had apparently read widely enough to be familiar with many writers and to delight in jokes about them.

But as we have already noted, many dyslexics do read widely. They read because of their interest in the content, not because the process is easy. In fact, one might expect that generally dyslexics might be more discerning in their reading, because the process is too laborious to waste their time and effort on books that are of little consequence. Indeed, Edison remarks, "I could enjoy good literature, and had found that there was virtually no enjoyment in trash."[26]

This approach may be contrasted with those who read long, light novels with great speed and in great numbers. One would expect that dyslexics and others who read with difficulty would never do this. They would not find it enjoyable and they would never squander their resources in this way—the effort would be too great and the return too small. Those dyslexics who make the effort are driven on by the content, in spite of the difficulties, and would not be expected to find "escape" in "light reading" as others do.

While it is not clear whether or not Edison had difficulty with reading, it seems clear that he did read, even as a child. Yet, there are many ways to be mislead. For example, one article that questions Edison's dyslexia cites his reading, at age nine, Parker's *School Compendium of Natural and Experimental Philosophy* as evidence of his advanced reading skill at this age.[27]

However, when one looks carefully at Parker's *Compendium* (a school textbook that was reprinted frequently and used widely all over America during the mid-nineteeth century) one sees that it is a book filled with pictures of mechanical devices and simple electrical apparatus, and with comparatively short sections of text, largely commenting on the abundant illustrations. Consequently, the book that Edison read so early and loved so much (and was so pleased with that in adulthood he gave a copy to Henry Ford to be preserved in his museum)[28] is not the imposing tome of dry scholarship that the title suggests to the modern reader, but is, in large measure, a picture book of mechanical and electrical devices—just the kind of book that would be devoured by almost any visual-thinking boy with strong mechanical and experimental inclinations—whether or not he fitted into a narrow definition of dyslexia.[29]

Edison may not have fitted the profile of a classic dyslexic or person with learning disabilities in every respect, but it seems that there is a preponderance of evidence that suggests that he largely followed a variation of the pattern in difficulties as well as in special talents, inclinations, and abilities.

It is to Edison's special abilities that we should now turn to obtain a clearer picture of the kind of mind we are dealing with. In the course of our discussion so far, we have referred repeatedly to a set of related traits—that is, the ability to easily make analogies, associations, and connections between distant and apparently unrelated entities. We have also made reference to the high mechanical and visualization skills evident in some children, even when small. These can indicate, to an informed observer, a predisposition to dyslexia well before it is time to learn to read. These traits are strongly evident in Edison's modes of thought and work.

In recent years, evidence emerging from a long-term study of the vast collection of Edison's business and personal papers has begun to indicate that Edison's inventiveness may be traced largely to his "powerful ability—never fully recognized until now—to reason through analogy. It was perhaps this trait more than any flashes of brilliance . . . that accounts for his great inventiveness. It is now thought that this hidden ability is what transformed one successful invention into another, eventually producing the phonograph, the incandescent light bulb, systems of electric power generation and motion pictures."[30]

When Edison died in 1931, he left behind more than three million pages of notebooks and letters. Much of this material documents the development of the stream of inventions that resulted in his 1,093 patents, more than were produced by any other inventor. Such extensive documentation permits the tracing of the development of many concepts, step by step. This development is apparent not only from notebooks and sketches, but also from a kind of preliminary patent, called a "caveat," that Edison used to protect his ideas as they evolved into fmished products. According to project researchers,

> Edison's inventions were often more closely related in their origins than anyone ever suspected. . . . For example, early drawings of his kinetoscope, a prototype of the motion-picture machine, reveal that it evolved from Edison's already successful phonograph. . . . Surprisingly, the very first caveat looked nothing like the finished machine but instead showed a cylinder covered with a spiral of images meant to be viewed through an eyepiece. The resemblance to Edison's first phonograph, made a decade earlier, was striking. Each of the two inventions had an axle and a cylinder. And each had an instrument (stylus or eyepiece) that deciphered a spiral of information (grooves for sound, images for pictures).

It is also clear from Edison's written commentary that he was very much aware that the second invention proceeded by analogy from the first. On the first page of his motion picture caveat, Edison wrote, "I am experimenting upon an instrument which does for the eye what the phonograph does for the ear. . . . The invention consists in photographing continuously a series of pictures . . . in a continuous spiral on a cylinder or plate in the same manner as sound is recorded on the phonograph."[31]

The use of analogy and metaphor for the manipulation and transformation of images in the mind is clearly a powerful tool, whether used by poet, physicist, mathematician, or inventor. Edison's analogies are so direct and straightforward that one wonders why they were not conceived before.

MODELS IN THE MIND: NIKOLA TESLA

Nikola Tesla is still relatively unknown among lay people, but among professional electrical engineers and others who know the electric power industry, he is regarded as the man who almost single-handedly developed the concept behind the electric power systems used throughout the world today. These included alternating current, great hydroelectric generators, simple and efficient motors, high-voltage transformers, and long-distance transmission lines. It was Tesla's ideas that were sold to Westinghouse and led eventually to the great war between alternating-current power systems and Edison's direct-current systems. The final victory of alternating current systems was assumed after the great success of the 15,000-horsepower Niagara Falls power plant in 1895. The Tesla-Westinghouse system was selected by a seventeen-man commission headed by British scientist and engineer Lord Kelvin.[32]

Tesla was a lonely man with many odd habits and strong compulsions. For example, he had to calculate the cubic area of each bite of food before eating it, and he had to finish reading whatever he started, even when it ran into many volumes, and whether or not he had decided that he was getting minimal return for his effort. Tesla was nonetheless highly productive and he was responsible for an extraordinary number of innovative inventions and experiments: electrical coils of very high voltages, high frequency currents, X-rays, diathermy, discharge lightning, radio-controlled robotic devices, high-speed, bladeless turbine engines, and high speed radio transmission, among others. Many years after the fact, a U.S. court ruled that Tesla, not Marconi, should be credited with the basic development of the radio. Indeed, Tesla's output was so prodigious and some of his concepts so ahead of his time that for some he is almost a cult figure.

Tesla is of special interest for us primarily because of his especially vivid visual imagination. He does not appear to have been dyslexic or learning disabled in any of the usual ways. He could read easily, spoke many languages, had an extraordinary verbal memory, and could do calculations in his head as easily as on paper. Indeed, his verbal memory was so good (and his love of poetry so great) that he could be given any line from *Faust* and then "pick up the quotation and continue by memory, page by page." He could also recite long passages of Serbian epics.[33]

Tesla's only complaints during early schooling were being accident prone, sickly, and having (like Poincaré) extreme difficulty drawing. Yet, like the Pearsons, his visual imagination was so powerful, his descriptions so vivid, and his accomplishments so significant that he has been included here to underline the pattern and illustrate the rule with, apparently, one notable exception. One does not have to have verbal difficulties to have a powerful visual imagination, but looking at each type may help us to understand the other.

Tesla immigrated to America from what is now Yugoslavia in 1884, a time of great excitement over technical innovation. The son of a Serbian Orthodox priest, Tesla was relatively well educated in literature, science, and mathematics and had a strong inventive inclination. He worked for Thomas Edison when he first arrived in America, but had to leave in order to pursue his highly innovative but incompatible ideas.

Telsa is sometimes noted in the histories of science and creativity because of the way the crux of a major invention came to him suddenly when he was reciting poetry while walking with a friend.[34] But Tesla's most interesting quality was his powerful visual imagination, which appears to have been so highly developed that he could create complete models of real devices in his mind. It is significant that he seems to have experienced, initially, his powerful ability to visualize things not as a useful talent or wonderful gift but as a distinct problem.

> In my boyhood I suffered from a peculiar affliction due to the appearance of images, often accompanied by strong flashes of light, which marred the sight of real objects and interfered with my thought and action. They were pictures of things and scenes which I had really seen, never of those I had imagined. When a word was spoken to me the image of the object it designated would present itself vividly to my vision and sometimes I was quite unable to distinguish whether what I saw was tangible or not. This caused me great discomfort and anxiety. . . . These certainly were not hallucinations . . . for in other respects I was normal and composed.

In order to control these images, Tesla experimented with various mental exercises. In time, it became clear that the "affliction" was merely the negative side of what turned out to be a special and unusual talent. Tesla continued these exercises

> until I was about seventeen, when my thoughts turned seriously to invention. Then I observed to my delight that I could visualize with the greatest facility. I needed no models, drawings or experiments. I could picture them all as real in my mind. Thus I have been led unconsciously to evolve what I consider a new method of materializing inventive concepts and ideas, which is radically opposite to the purely experimental and is in my opinion ever so much more expeditious and efficient.[35]

Tesla explained that if an apparatus is constructed before it is fully developed and worked out in the mind, then the experimenter is often distracted by details. "The moment one constructs a device to carry into practice a crude idea he finds himself unavoidably engrost with the details and defects of the apparatus. As he goes on improving and reconstructing, his force of concentration diminishes and he loses sight of the great underlying principle."[36] Tesla's method was quite different and relied on his extraordinary ability to create a detailed and accurate model of reality in his mind.

> I do not rush into actual work. When I get an idea I start at once building it up in my imagination. I change the construction, make

improvements and operate the device in my mind. It is absolutely immaterial to me whether 1 run my turbine in thought or test it in my shop. I even note if it is out of balance. There is no difference whatever, the results were the same. In this way I am able to rapidly develop and perfect a conception without touching anything. When I have gone so far to embody in the invention every possible improvement I can think of and see no fault anywhere, I put into concrete form this final product of my brain. Invariably my device works as I conceived that it should, and the experiment comes out exactly as I planned it. In twenty years there has not been a single exception.

But how is this possible? How are we to believe this incredible ability? We know that Tesla was a great showman when demonstrating his tricks with electricity to the public, more like a magician than an engineer or scientist. Yet his tricks were often based on real scientific knowledge that was not understood by others until decades later. We also know that, like Edison and other inventors of the time, he was fond of telling extravagant stories to the press. But many of the extravagant tales, stories of laser beams, long-distance microwave power transmission, and ocean thermal electricity generation, are in fact now being realized scores of years after they were conceived in detail in Tesla's mind. Tesla had a ready explanation for his ability. "Why should it be otherwise? Engineering, electrical and mechanical, is positive in results. There is scarcely a subject that cannot be mathematically treated and the effects calculated or the results determined beforehand from the available theoretical and practical data. The carrying out into practice of a crude idea as is being generally done is, I hold, nothing but a waste of energy, money and time."[37]

Tesla argued that it was a waste of effort to build a model or prototype of anything until a number of variations have been tested in a powerful imagination such as his own. Virtually the same point is being made today by designers, engineers, and managers, but this time they are talking about the machine equivalent of Tesla's remarkable mind, what is now known as "three-dimensional computing," in which working models of aircraft, automobiles, golf clubs, or nuclear power plants can be constructed on a small but powerful computer and displayed on a screen, with images moving and changing quickly in what is known as "real time." These models can be operated and tested and modified much as Tesla was apparently able to do with his imagination alone. Proponents claim many advantages for the widespread use of three-dimensional computing, but two of the most important relate to increased creativity and reduced prototype building. In one study of the use of three-dimensional computing in five U.S. and Japanese companies,

> the speed and power of 3D Computing has all but eliminated the requirements to produce physical prototypes and models. This allows management and engineers to economically pursue more creative and sometimes high risk design options.
>
> NASA/Ames uses [3D] workstations to simulate a wide number of options for a Mach 25 aircraft that would have been cost prohibitive using the traditional wind tunnel practices.[38]

Tesla noted the speed and ease with which his mental modeling proceeded, free of the distractions of building an actual physical prototype. Creative designers often lament the time required to build a physical product of what could be built so quickly in the mind's eye. One important consequence of three-dimensional computing could be a marked decrease in frustration along with a marked increase in productivity.

> Users of 3D Computing reported increases in individuals' productivity of 20% to 50%. This higher productivity was used to expand the scope of individual job functions and to reduce the actual time to complete a project.
>
> The ability to "handle" the realistic electronic model led to improved interaction between the designer and the model resulting in a more intimate and accurate understanding of the model. This also resulted in more creativity, less frustration. We consistently observed that users had a positive work attitude and they preferred working in a 3D environment as compared to the manual or 2D environment in which they had previously worked.[39]

Such changes may make it possible for comparatively ordinary people to do with ease and speed what before only extraordinary people like Tesla could do in their heads. This development might very well favor those who are better at manipulating images than they are at manipulating codes, words, and mathematical symbols.

"A MAN WITHOUT LETTERS": LEONARDO DA VINCI

Although Leonardo da Vinci trained as a painter and sculptor, it is well known that he anticipated a large number of scientific and technological advances, often by hundreds of years. He is seen as a giant in the early development of many fields other than art—comparative anatomy and physiology, mechanical engineering, aeronautical engineering, philology, mathematics, astronomy, physics, music, architecture, optics, botany, geology, and geography. Indeed, such topics are often the subject of smaller books on Leonardo or of chapters for larger books. However, as one proceeds through a topic such as ours—the curious mixtures of great abilities and unexpected disabilities in a single person—one is often reminded of Leonardo's life and work.

Many of the people we have been discussing seemed to think visually about nearly everything. Sometimes they had trouble translating their powerful mental images into words, numbers, and formulas. Leonardo started with the image and seemed to go everywhere unfettered. He made the image central to his approach to observation and analysis; for him the picture came first, words were merely used to help to illuminate the picture.

Several of those we have been discussing were fascinated with mirror images and occasionally wrote "looking-glass" letters. The left-handed Leonardo nearly always wrote from right to left. As one scholar observed, Leonardo was "habitually left-handed in an eccentric manner even in the use of his sheets." "Like the Orientals," he "started from the last page."[40] Sometimes it is even clear that he drew and painted certain subjects, such as landscapes and village scenes, in mirror images.[41]

Many of the people we have profiled are known for the vast breadth of their interests. Leonardo's interests were so broad and varied that we can scarcely describe the range. As was clear from everything he did, he had the integrating perspective of the global thinker rather than that of the narrow and fragmented specialist. And partly as a result of this orientation, he had a habit of innovation, continually making connections among many diverse fields.

Education in Leonardo's time, as now, focused largely on words and numbers in various forms—reading, writing, counting, and memorizing texts. But Leonardo's interests were not verbal. He was trained and worked as an artist. In so many ways his was the opposite of the usual verbal educational orientation. Avoiding the Schoolmen philosophers of his time, he had a clear propensity to learn from direct experience and observation rather than from books and lectures.[42]

To gain a sense of how he worked, it is useful to look at just one of his many inventions. One of his lesser-known innovations provides an excellent example of the power of simple mental rotation and the application of similar structures to similar forces in a very different context. Leonardo used a concept that he took from the architecture of buildings—the simple, triangular arch. He rotated it in his mind and found that it was ideally suited to providing a self-sealing gate for a canal lock. In a building, the arch supports the weight of the roof and its own structure. The weight of the arch pushes the two parts of the central joint tightly together. Similar principles apply in a canal. In the lock gate, the water pressure comes from upstream rather than from above and keeps the gate tightly shut, in a perfectly analogous fashion.

Prior to Leonardo's innovation, a canal lock gate was more like a castle portcullis, a one-piece gate that was lowered into the canal from above. Leonardo had observed such gates in a canal being constructed near Milan and noted their disadvantages. Apparently Leonardo came to his solution because, about the same time (in the 1490s), he was studying the strength of architectural arches and had noted the similarities between the two kinds of engineering problems. Consequently, as science writer Richie Calder observed, he "laid the arch on its side" and the "mitred edges made a watertight joint." In fact, as Calder observed, Leonardo's design is "so elegantly simple" that it is "still the basic model for lock gates today."[43]

Leonardo shared with Einstein, Maxwell, and Yeats a high regard for geometry. He is credited with having devised a visually based proof of the Pythagorean theorem. His approach (a form of what is called the "dissection proof") relied heavily on mental rotation and the recognition of mirror-image similarities in triangles and polygons.[44]

While Leonardo's great talents are well known, very little is known of his weaknesses. Recently, an analysis of Leonardo's handwriting and spelling was performed by Giuseppe Sartori. Using modern neuropsychological techniques, the analysis of Leonardo's Renaissance Italian revealed that he made distinctive patterns of errors indicative of what is called "surface dysgraphia." According to

Sartori, surface dysgraphia is a "disorder of written spelling that can be observed either following brain damage to the left hemisphere or as a developmental disorder." One of the distinctive features of the condition is the frequent use of "incorrect spellings" that are "phonologically correct"—that is, "writing *there* for *their* or *rane* for *rain*."

Another important sign of surface dysgraphia is the more frequent accurate spelling of regular words (such as *ship*) than of irregular words (such as *yacht*). Accordingly, surface dysgraphia is said to arise from "disruption of the lexical-semantic route in writing." When there is such a disruption, the subject is "left with the nonlexical" or "phonological" route. This route "gives wrong results in writing irregular words" and words that have the same sound but different spellings.[45] Thus, according to this analysis, it is apparent that one of the two main routes used for word retrieval was not functioning properly. Leonardo used the phonological rather than lexical route to retrieve words.

Other verbal difficulties are evident. Although Italian is phonetic and highly regular, Leonardo's spelling has been described by various authors as being "by ear," "bizarre," "inconsistent." His errors are characterized by consonant doubling, letter substitutions, additions, blending, and word splitting. He made misspellings when copying from other texts, a rare form of error.[46]

Several authors have suggested that Leonardo's problems with learning Latin and his linguistic difficulties may have been the reason he studied art—and not law, as would have been expected in his family.[47] We will probably never know for certain. In any case, Leonardo was clearly aware of his own language problems, declaring in one instance, "They will say that, being without letters, I cannot say properly what I want to treat of." In another case he made an effort to justify his mixed talents to others. "You should prefer a good scientist without literary abilities than a literate without scientific skills."[48]

6

PROFILES, PART 3

Churchill, Patton, and Yeats

It is not pleasant to feel oneself so completely outclassed and left behind at the very beginning of the race.

Winston Churchill, *My Early Life*

"ONE ALL-EMBRACING REGARD": WINSTON S. CHURCHILL

Studies of creativity often focus primarily on writers, artists, composers, and scientists. Political leaders are not usually considered to be very creative. Indeed, it is sometimes argued that it is a good thing that leaders, like judges and accountants, are generally not very creative, since an excess of creativity in such rule-centered roles would lead to trouble. (In the massive financial troubles of 2008–2009 we may easily see the extent of trouble that can come from unchecked creative accounting.) A contrasting position can be argued, however—that some degree of creativity is desirable and recognizable in all walks of life, whether it is the research of a prize-winning scientist, a potter's formulation of a new glaze, or the discovery, in a more traditional society, of how three generations can live in the same house in relative harmony. Accordingly, creativity can be seen as the creation or discovery of any new idea, technique, form, or pattern that can be successfully applied to a particular need or used to solve a particular problem.[1]

Extraordinary leaders, especially those in power during extraordinary times, must display extraordinary abilities to see clearly what is needed in complex situations, among a profusion of conflicting advice and incomplete information. They must be quick to recognize mistakes and to reverse course to correct them. They must be able to communicate effectively and forcefully with the people at large. And, throughout, they must have a special capacity to focus on, and hold fast to, a vision of the larger whole and the longer term.

Winston Churchill, one of the most prominent and widely respected world leaders during a period of pivotal conflict, exhibited many of these qualities. Churchill is one of those rare political leaders who in time became a hero to large sections of the population. It is also perhaps significant that the paradoxical nature of mixed and uneven abilities holds a prominent position in the public mythology surrounding him. It is generally known, for example, that while Churchill became a masterful orator as an adult, he had a speech defect as a youth, a defect that never entirely disappeared.[2] Many people are also generally aware that he had a difficult time in his early schooling. And, from another perspective, while he has been seen as a leader with unusual energy and vision, he has also been seen as unpredictable and erratic, a figure who was at times frightening to more cautious and circumspect politicians. One reviewer of two 1988 biographies focused on this erratic quality, one that continues to puzzle professional and nonprofessional observers alike.

> What will historians say about Winston Churchill a hundred years from now? The question is pertinent—inescapable, in fact, because nearly a quarter-century after his death, we may remain too close to make an accurate judgment. Of all the larger-than-life figures of World War II . . . Churchill remains the hardest to assess. Rarely has a great leader been so often right. Or so often wrong. . . . As his early critics noted, Churchill was often "a genius without judgment," a man with "a zigzag streak of lightning in the brain."[3]

While Churchill's uneven talents and erratic nature are widely (although not universally) acknowledged, it is not generally appreciated to what extent he exhibited many of the distinctive talents and difficulties that are part of the larger pattern of traits we have been considering. As we might expect, many elements of this pattern of traits were most apparent during his early schooling. In the following description of Churchill, one biographer noted seemingly improbable combinations of strengths and weaknesses but assumed, in a way that has become familiar to us, that the weaknesses were the result of willful and obstinate behavior rather than part of the larger pattern we have been considering.

> Winston's own failure at public school was also a product of obstinacy [like his father's]. It was not that he was stupid or even lazy. He enjoyed the cadet corps, became a champion fencer, recited 1200 lines of Macaulay's *Lays of Ancient Rome* off by heart and learned how to write an English sentence—"a noble thing." But where it came to subjects like Latin and French he refused to invest an iota of his extraordinary powers of concentration. Indeed he wrote English essays for other boys in exchange for doing his Latin prose.[4]

While Churchill's school experience was indeed mixed in a number of ways, the above brief summary may give too great a weight to the positive aspects. The picture painted by Churchill himself in *My Early Life* is decidedly more bleak. Some might wish to construe the picture he provides as an exaggeration, provided largely for dramatic effect. How could such a great and clever man really have had such difficulties? It is hoped that readers of this book will see good reasons for taking Churchill and others like him at their word.

Churchill not only had difficulty in school, he was quite literally at the bottom of his class. What was worse, everyone knew it in a most public and humiliating way. While he was at Harrow School, his father was a very popular political figure and people would come to the small town on the outskirts of London to see the son marching to and from classes. But in those days, all the students at Harrow filed by in order of class rank. "Large numbers of visitors of both sexes used to wait on the school steps, in order to see me march by; and I frequently heard the irreverent comment, 'Why, he's last of all!'"

While it is acknowledged that Churchill had an unusually good memory, it is not often pointed out that Churchill's classmates and masters found his capacity for memorization to be surprising for a student who appeared so weak in nearly all other areas. "It was thought incongruous that while I apparently stagnated in the lowest form, I should gain a prize open to the whole school for reciting to the Headmaster twelve hundred lines of Macaulay's 'Lays of Ancient Rome' without making a single mistake. I also succeeded in passing the preliminary examination for the Army while still almost at the bottom of the school."[5]

Another indicator of the overall pattern as applied to Churchill is that his difficulties with languages continued throughout his life. Churchill's Latin in particular was terrible.

> When, as a young member of Asquith's cabinet, he larded his speech with occasional Latin tags, a look of surprise and pain would flit across the features of the scholarly Prime Minister. Nor did Winston's French progress much beyond the schoolboy stage. It remained an astounding mixture of high-flown Gallic words and English expressions pronounced with superb self-confidence in a John Bull accent. Only Frenchmen with a colloquial knowledge of English could understand it.[6]

Even Churchill's celebrated skill in the English language is associated with yet another string of defeats. With some ironic humor, Churchill explains, "By being so long in the lowest form I gained an immense advantage over the cleverer boys. They all went on to learn Latin and Greek and splendid things like that. But I was taught English. We were considered such dunces that we could learn only English. . . . As I remained in the Third Fourth (ß) three times as long as anyone else, I had three times as much of it. I learned it thoroughly. Thus I got into my bones the essential structure of the ordinary British sentence—which is a noble thing."[7]

As often happens with the late-blooming, learning-disabled actor or performer, when Churchill did finally develop skill in language, his interest and understanding and fluency were well beyond common capacity—he became "a connoisseur of language and enjoyed the sensation of rolling piquant phrases round his tongue."

It is often observed that children with dyslexia or learning disabilities hide their difficulties, if they can, or they lash out in rebellion and anger, showing at the same time their intense frustration at their own difficulties and their anger at others' inability to understand their predicament.

> Winston regarded Harrow as hell, a boring and irrelevant obstacle course impeding his entry into the great adventure of life. His behavior reflected this attitude. It was a standing affront to his headmaster, Dr. Welldon. Winston was unpunctual, careless, forgetful, spendthrift, opinionated and deliberately troublesome. Welldon acutely recognized that his refractory charge had "some great gifts" and obtusely sought to evoke them with a rod. He birched Winston more frequently than any other boy. Winston was unmoved and even had the impertinence to tell the headmaster how to carry out his duties. Winston invariably tried to teach his instructors and was always convinced that he knew better than the experts.[8]

Churchill was in constant trouble at Harrow and this bad behavior might be seen as an instance of the classic pattern of frustration. However, his rebellious behavior was distinctive in that it showed an exquisite arrogance, so that one is unsure of how much was genuine aristocratic pride (with some simple willfulness) and how much may have been the familiar defensive cloak for areas of perceived weakness and vulnerability.

Although well-born, Churchill had to deal with the same career diffaculties—often brought on by failure or near-failure in examinations—that is the almost universal experience of bright, learning-disabled adolescents.

> Winston's fate was determined by his toy soldiers. Inspecting them one day, and considering his son too stupid for any other profession (except perhaps the Church, which had been briefly considered and wisely rejected), Lord Randolph suggested a military career. Winston adopted the idea with alacrity. In 1893, he managed, at his third attempt, and with the help of a London crammer, to qualify for a cadetship at Sandhurst. But he only got into the cavalry, which required less intellectual ability and more private means from its recruits than the infantry. Lord Randolph was furious. He subjected Winston to a withering rebuke for his "slovenly, happy go lucky, harem scarum style of work" and his "idle, useless, unprofitable life." Unless he reformed, Lord Randolph continued, Winston

would degenerate into "a mere social wastrel," leading "a shabby, unhappy and futile existence." Winston dutifully apologized and promised to improve. But this setdown was a shattering conclusion to what had been the most miserable years of his life.[9]

Again like the classic late bloomer, Churchill did progressively better during his time at Sandhurst. Fortunately, this improvement was promoted by the course of instruction, which was more active and practical and attuned to his interests. But we might wonder whether a large part of the rapid improvement may have been the consequence of rapid changes within the young Winston himself. "I passed out with honors eighth in my batch of a hundred and fifty. . . . One could feel oneself growing up almost every week."[10]

Like Churchill, well-born dyslexics and other learning-disabled children may well have more educational opportunities than others, but often they are made to feel greater pressure to succeed in academic pursuits and they feel a greater sense of failure when, at crucial periods of their lives, their learning difficulties have their predictable consequences.

Not long ago, working class (and even some middle class) dyslexics could work around all of this by avoiding formal schooling and going directly into some trade without academic qualifications, as Faraday and Edison did. Going into a trade was the expected thing in any case, so there was no sense of failure. And for some, non-academic talents such as craftsmanship or business acumen could lead to very substantial success in time. Unfortunately, today, especially in developed economies, there are few alternatives for anyone in any class who would choose to avoid the academic route. Today, as even vocational schools are heavily oriented toward classroom work, written tests, and other staples of the academic approach, the alternatives have become very restricted and the adverse consequences of academic failure ever more pervasive.

For a high-born Englishman brought up in the late nineteenth century, Churchill shows a remarkable appreciation for alternatives to the conventional schooling that he so hated.

I would far rather have been apprenticed as a bricklayer's mate, or run errands as a messenger boy, or helped my father to dress the front windows of a grocer's shop. It would have been real; it would have been natural; it would have taught me more; and I should have done it much better. Also I should have got to know my father, which would have been a joy to me. . . .

Certainly the prolonged education indispensable to the progress of Society is not natural to mankind. It cuts against the grain. A boy would like to follow his father in pursuit of food or prey. He would like to be doing serviceable things so far as his utmost strength allowed. He would like to be earning wages however small to help to keep up the home. He would like to have some leisure of his own to use or misuse as he pleased. . . . And then perhaps in the evenings a real love of learning would come to those who were worthy—and why try to stuff it into those who are not?—and knowledge and thought would open the "magic casements" of the mind.[11]

Throughout his life, Churchill showed evidence of a number of traits relevant to the larger pattern we have been considering. Even as an adult Churchill was prone to rapid changes in emotion. He would be angry and then quickly repentant. Given the right circumstances, he could break into tears quite easily. "I'm a blubberer," he would explain to friends. Indeed, this tendency was so frequent and pronounced that biographer William Manchester suggested that Churchill's ample but controlled consumption of alcohol was in part a compensation to "furbish his macho image," needed because he cried "so often in public."[12]

Churchill's predisposition to weeping is referred to repeatedly in a number of places and contexts. It is given special significance in the biography by Henry Pelling, where it figures as the final image of the entire 644-page narrative as an indicator of Churchill's lack of remoteness and "evident humanity." Pelling quotes an incident of 1940 or 1941 that was recorded by one of Churchill's private secretaries: "Driving down to Chequers one Friday evening, when the bombing was at its worst, [Churchill] saw a very long queue of people lined up outside a shop in a poor quarter of London, and he stopped and sent his detective to see what the shortage was that had caused it. It was a queue for birdseed. Winston wept."[13]

When writing (actually, dictating) his speeches or his books, Churchill was easily distracted and needed absolute quiet. "Any noise, especially if high-pitched," was an abomination. "The jangling of cowbells will destroy his train of thought. But whistling [was] the worst."[14] This extreme sensitivity to noise and ease of distraction is likely a part of the reason for Churchill's unusual working hours, normally 11 P.M. until about 3 or 4 A.M., when everyone else was asleep—except his secretaries and research assistants.

Churchill had continual difficulty with time and was prone to being late for all kinds of occasions. He was often late for trains. His wife Clementine joked, "Winston's a sporting man; he always gives the train a chance to get away."[15] His difficulty with time was most apparent in his regular schedule at home in the 1930s. There was a "daily" lunch crisis. "The meal is to be served at 1:15 P.M.; often, eminent guests are arriving. And he is never there to greet them. He deplores tardiness in himself yet cannot break it, though everyone at Chartwell knows the explanation: he systematically underestimates, usually by about five minutes, the length of time he needs to do everything."[16] Churchill was also predisposed to inner dialogue. One observer wrote, "He is a poor listener, has little interest in what others have to say, and, if he is not the speaker, withdraws into silent communion with himself while his interior monologue, the flow of private rhetoric, soars on."[17]

With Churchill, visual or graphic presentations of numerical data were vastly preferable to numerical or statistical presentations. Such presentations were often prepared by his friend Frederick A. Lindemann (the "Prof"), a scientist who was valued for being able to explain all sorts of scientific information to Churchill in plain language. According to Manchester,

> Churchill loathes scientific terminology. He never even mastered public school arithmetic. The Prof provides him with the essential facts when he needs them without disturbing his concentration on other matters. . . . [using] clear, accurate charts which, by replacing statistics, present displays showing England's stockpiles of vital raw materials, the rate at which ships are being launched on the Clyde, . . . Britain's production of tanks, artillery, small arms, and warplanes in terms the prime minister can understand.[18]

Churchill "was first menaced with Education" while his family was living briefly in Ireland. By his own account he left Ireland and returned to England with his family "early in the year 1879," when he could not have been more than four and a half years old. During this time his nurse, Mrs. Everest, tried to teach him to read, before the arrival of "the Governess," who was to be his first real tutor. Churchill's description of his difficulties with reading, and then arithmetic, could be seen as a classic account of moderate dyslexia or even dyscalculia, were he not so very young and his reading difficulties so very brief.

> Mrs. Everest produced a book called *Reading Without Tears*. It certainly did not justify its title in my case. . . . Our preparations were by no means completed when the fateful hour struck and the Governess was due to arrive. I did what so many oppressed peoples have always done in similar circumstances: I took to the woods. . . . Hours passed before I was retrieved and handed over to "the Governess." We continued to toil every day, not only at letters but at words, and also at what was much worse, figures. Letters after all had only got to be known, and when they stood together in a certain way one recognised their formation and that it meant a certain sound or word which one uttered when pressed sufficiently. But the figures were tied into all sorts of tangles and did things to one another which it was extremely difficult to forecast with complete accuracy. . . . These complications cast a steadily gathering shadow over my daily life."[19]

Churchill continued to have difficulty with figures for the rest of his life (although, true to the usual paradoxical pattern, he became good at geometry).[20] He did finally learn to read, however, apparently without difficulty. During some of his earliest school years—when he was for two years in a new, fashionable, but rather brutal boarding school, from which he was later removed—his joy in reading was one of his few pleasures. "When I was nine and a half my father gave me *Treasure Island*, and I remember the delight with which I devoured it. My teachers saw me at once backward and precocious, reading books beyond my years and yet at the bottom of the Form. They were offended. They had large resources of compulsion at their disposal, but I was stubborn. Where my reason, imagination or interest were not engaged, I would not or could not learn."[21]

Here Churchill indicates his awareness of the puzzling nature of

his mixed performance and abilities—"at once backward and precocious" (a phrase which is as plainly descriptive, without clinical connotation, as "gifted and learning disabled" or "twice exceptional,"
for example). Furthermore, he seems in some doubt whether he
"would not" or "could not" learn.[22]

> In retrospect these years form not only the least agreeable, but the
> only barren and unhappy period of my life. I was happy as a child
> with my toys in my nursery. I have been happier every year since I
> became a man. But this interlude of school makes a sombre grey
> patch upon the chart of my journey. It was an unending spell of wor-
> ries that did not then seem petty, of toil uncheered by fruitation; a
> time of discomfort, restriction and purposeless monotony.
>
> This train of thought must not lead me to exaggerate the char-
> acter of my schooldays. Actually no doubt they were bouyed up by
> the high spirits of youth. Harrow was a very good school and a high
> standard of personal service prevailed among its masters. Most of
> the boys were very happy, and many found in its classrooms and
> upon its playing-fields the greatest distinction they have ever known
> in life. I can only record the fact that, no doubt through my own
> shortcomings, I was an exception. . . .
>
> I was on the whole considerably discouraged by my school days.
> Except in Fencing, in which I had won the Public school champi-
> onship, I had achieved no distinction. All my contemporaries and
> even younger boys seemed in every way better adapted to the con-
> ditions of our little world. They were far better both at the games
> and at the lessons. It is not pleasant to feel oneself so completely out-
> classed and left behind at the very beginning of the race.[23]

Churchill was clearly not dyslexic in the most restricted sense—
that is, of being unable to read or able to read only with extreme difficulty. However, those who would accept a broader definition of
dyslexia—difficulty with words—might use the term to describe
Churchill's problems. We have seen that he shared a pattern of
strengths and weaknesses consistent with the larger pattern of traits
we have been discussing. Many of these traits are evident in the earliest school days, although several of the most distinctive traits are
more evident in later life. And, as usual, some of these traits may
appear contradictory and paradoxical, at least on the surface.

As we have noted, Churchill was known as a master orator—

skillful at the surprise maneuver, the devastating attack, the memorable phrase, the brutal simplicity of plain speech. Yet his verbal abilities were more particular than general. In adulthood, he never entirely lost his slight speech defect. But, what is more important for our purposes, his public speeches did not come quickly or easily, however effortless and natural they might have appeared. They were never improvised. Churchill had to prepare, and he had to practice. Like Maxwell, Yeats, and others, he had to have time to formulate, compose, and revise.

This is a paradox that many find it difficult to understand or accept. Yet there it is—some of the best writers have a great deal of difficulty with words. Perhaps this difficulty is an essential element of their power. Perhaps these writers are drawing on something that is not directly rooted in words but rather in something that is other than words, beyond or underneath the words. Perhaps they are drawing on elements of thought that are more primitive and more powerful than words. Perhaps if they worked with greater facility on the level of words, alone, their words would be less moving and less powerful.

Churchill did not shine in the fast back-and-forth of debate. Apparently, the words did not come quickly enough, although when they did come they were powerful indeed. One observer summed up in a striking metaphor this combination of power without speed: "He had to wheel himself up to battle like an enormous gun."[24] Like Eileen Simpson and her grandnephew, it was possible for Churchill to lose his train of thought in the middle of a speech, as he once did, with devastating consequences. He never forgot the incident and took precautions ever afterward to avoid repetition of it.

All his speeches were carefully honed and polished in advance. Churchill was a superb orator but an indifferent debater. He expressed his ideas in vivid words but he could be nonplussed if the stream of his eloquence was interrupted. So in public speaking he relied on memory rather than on spontaneous inspiration. He could repeat a column of print accurately after having read it only four times and his practice was to write out his speeches in advance and learn them by heart. In 1904 he lost the thread of his argument while holding forth to the House of Commons and broke down. Members wondered whether this was an early sign that he would go the way of his father, but Churchill guarded against a recurrence of the disaster by always thereafter clutching full notes of his memorised speeches.

Rhetoric was the most powerful weapon in his armory and he took immense trouble with it. He thundered out his perorations in the bath. At his mother's country mansion he had an "aerial summerhouse" built in the branches of an old lime tree where he rehearsed his harangues.[25]

Other notable traits could reveal themselves when least expected. We have observed that often the people we are discussing retain some strikingly childlike qualities. In Churchill, the survival of the childlike imagination and playfulness could come out at the most unexpected times. His "fascination with martial manoeuvres was life-long. At the height of the Battle of Britain, in September 1940, Churchill spent an afternoon crawling round the library floor at Blenheim Palace re-enacting Marlborough's victory with tin soldiers, imitating the bangs of the cannons and providing the smoke with puffs from his cigar."[26] The love of model building among many of those we have been considering took on an imperious cast in Churchill. "He seemed to have no serious interests apart perhaps from military ones. He built an outdoor castle complete with moat and drawbridge and made a large catapult (chiefly used to shoot green apples at a cow)."[27]

Other distinctive but less obvious traits are evident here and there among Churchill's autobiographical essays. For example, dyslexics and others with varied learning disabilities commonly describe great problems looking up words in dictionaries, mainly because of sequencing difficulties (as well as problems with spelling and the distraction of seeing other interesting entries, among other factors). As part of his discussion of why he had so much difficulty with the study of Latin (despite his good memory for words and texts), Churchill complained, "I was always very slow at using a dictionary. It is easy to open it more or less at the right letter, but then you have to turn backwards and forwards and peer up and down the columns and very often find yourself three or four pages the wrong side of the word you want. In short I found it most laborious, while to other boys it seemed no trouble."[28]

At school, Churchill's performance left much to be desired in most games (except the special quickness that helped him in fencing). His physical awkwardness was even evident after he had left Harrow and started his military training at Sandhurst. "I did not much like the drill and indeed figured for several months in the 'Awkward Squad,' formed from those who required special smartening up."[29]

The theme of late-blooming reappears again and again with Churchill. He was not an early reader, but greatly loved reading once he became proficient. He had difficulty with speech as a youth, but developed, in time, an extraordinary sensitivity and skill with language. He seemed to be poor in nearly every aspect of school, until his late teens, when, at Sandhurst, he developed with great rapidity, feeling himself "growing up almost every week," and finishing well ahead of most of his peers. Even Churchill's great love of painting was developed quite late, when he was middle-aged. And, of course, his greatest achievements during World War II were reserved for the years in which most people would already have gone into retirement (and some time after he and others regarded his political career as essentially "finished"[30]).

What, then, can be said of Churchill's education as a writer and historian? His education during his years at Harrow (where, after all, he did poorly) would not seem sufficient to explain his great skill or depth of knowledge and understanding in later years. Nor would even his oft-repeated study of elementary English composition and grammar. His years at Sandhurst were designed for the active and practical military professional, not to provide a background in the literature of the military historian.

Where and when had he read the great authors, to provide a base for his native writing skills? Once again, late-blooming seems the answer and seems the dominant pattern. Like Faraday, Churchill started late but he never stopped. And he followed his own program, in his own time, for his own purposes.

After Sandhurst, and brief, exciting exploits in Cuba, Churchill was posted with his British Army unit to India. During this time he entered upon a program of reading to correct the deficiencies of his education at Harrow and Sandhurst. If we are correct in asserting that Churchill developed capabilities greater than others, but later than others (as some of those we have been considering), then it is not hard to imagine that his program of self-study had the right timing and conditions for the greatest benefit (perhaps much greater than one would usually obtain as part of a conventional university program of study).

In India, Churchill had apparently taken well to the easy routine of military duties and regimental competitions. But when his need for deeper and broader knowledge came it was abrupt and strong. "It was not until this winter of 1896, when I had almost completed my twenty-second year, that the desire for learning came upon me. I began to feel myself wanting in even the vaguest knowledge about many large spheres of thought." By this time, Churchill had developed a feeling for language and an appreciation for words "fitting and falling into their places like pennies in the slot." He had developed an extensive vocabulary, yet he was aware that he was not always sure of the meaning of certain words and was hesitant to use them "for fear of being absurd." He was aware that he knew something about a variety of topics, such as tactics, politics, and honorable behavior. But what of a topic such as ethics?

> In Bangalore there was no one to tell me about Ethics for love or money. . . . This was only typical of a dozen similar mental needs that now began to press insistently upon me. I knew of course that the youths at the universities were stuffed with all this patter at nineteen and twenty, and could pose you entrapping questions or give baffling answers. We never set much store by them or their affected superiority, remembering that they were only at their books, while we were commanding men and guarding the Empire. Nevertheless I had sometimes resented the apt and copious information which some of them seemed to possess, and I now wished I could find a competent teacher whom I could listen to and cross-examine for an hour or so every day.

So, without an instructor, Churchill taught himself. He asked his mother to send him books and started with Gibbon's *Decline and Fall of the Roman Empire.*

> I was immediately dominated both by the story and the style. All through the long glistening middle hours of the Indian day, from when we quited stables till the evening shadows proclaimed the hour of polo, I devoured Gibbon. I rode triumphantly through it from end to end and enjoyed it all. I scribbled all my opinions on the margins of the pages. . . . It was a curious education . . . because I approached it with an empty, hungry mind, and with fairly strong jaws; and what I got I bit.[31]

For a time during this period Churchill read history and philosophy four or five hours each day. He read Plato, Aristotle, Schopenhauer, Malthus, Darwin, and many others of "lesser standing." The education was "curious" but effective. As one biographer commented, "In fact, it was a very wide and remarkable one; Churchill's selection of books was eclectic and random, but the purpose was serious: what he read he remembered, and he challenged and questioned what he read. This self-education was the first real indication of his ability, his determination, and his independence. It may also be seen as the first clear sign of a personal ambition to succeed in life."[32]

This dedication to work and study continued through to Churchill's early years in the House of Commons and beyond. His dedication as a young M.P. was characterized by "living with Blue Books and sleeping with encyclopedias," according to one observer.[33] A friend during these years noted that when Churchill was "not busy with politics, he was reading or writing."[34] Considering the pace and timing and success of Churchill's program of self-study, it is perhaps not at all surprising that he thought it a "mistake to read too many good books when quite young." In characteristically plain but powerful language, he wrote,

A man once told me that he had read all the books that mattered. Cross questioned, he appeared to have read a great many, but they seemed to have made only a slight impression. How many had he understood? How many had entered into his mental composition? How many had been hammered on the anvils of his mind and afterwards ranged in an armoury of bright weapons ready to hand?

It is a great pity to read a book too soon in life. The first impression is the one that counts; and if it is a slight one, it may be all that can be hoped for. A later and second perusal may recoil from a surface already hardened by premature contact. Young people should be careful in their reading, as old people in eating their food. They should not eat too much. They should chew it well.[35]

The integration of diverse elements in Churchill's life has been seen by some as a characteristic of prime importance. One reviewer of Churchill biographies asserted that,

Churchill was not merely great as a man of affairs; he was the complete and rounded person—as poetic as rational; as visionary as practical; as imaginative as he was sturdy: *Integer vitae* might be the motto of his life. He combined artistry with hardheadedness and magnanimity with sturdiness. . . . In the years covered by these volumes he wrote his two-volume life of the first Duke of Marlborough, his famous ancestor; published six volumes of war memoirs, the first volume of which sold a quarter-million copies in one day and made him a fortune. He won a Nobel Prize for literature (few were so richly deserved) and exhibited his paintings at the Royal Academy and the Tate Gallery. All the while he fondly tended his goldfish, dogs, cats, pigs, swans, and racehorses and proved himself a gifted farmer and brick mason—and devoted friend.[36]

Churchill may have been a late bloomer with broad and integrated interests, but he was also a thinker with a definite propensity toward visual-spatial modes of thought. One might expect to find that one with such an orientation would greatly appreciate the skill of someone able to move with special grace and skill through three-dimensional space. In 1912, with some trepidation, Churchill started flying. He thought it part of his duties as First Lord of the Admiralty. In time, however, he came to develop a very special appreciation of this new world. Churchill's description of the experience is highly evocative and is very supportive of the point we are trying to make.

Once I had started flying from motives in which a sense of duty, as well as excitement and curiosity, played its part, I continued for sheer joy and pleasure. I went up in every kind of machine and at every air station under the Admiralty.

Then came the episode of Gustave Hamel in the spring of 1914. If ever there was a man born to fly, three parts a bird and the rest genius, it was Hamel. He belonged to the air rather than the earth, and handled the primitive machines of those days in what was then an unknown element, with a natural gift and confidence quite indescribable. . . .

Although I have flown hundreds of times, probably with a hundred pilots, I have never experienced that sense of the poetry of motion which Hamel imparted to those who were privileged to fly with him. It was like the most perfect skater on the rink, but the skating was through three dimensions, and all the curves and changes were faultless, and faultless not by rote and rule but by native instinct. He would bank his machine so steeply that there was nothing between us and the world far below, and would continue circling downwards so gently, so quietly, so smoothly, in such true harmony with the element in which he moved, that one would have believed that one wing tip was fastened to a pivot. As for the grim force of gravity—it was his slave. In all his flying there was no sense of struggle with difficulties, or effort at a complicated feat; everything happened as if it could never have happened in any other way. It seemed as easy as pouring water out of a jug.[37]

Churchill shows evidence of a special sensitivity for accomplishment in a visual-spatial realm. But is there, we might ask, evidence of a more purely visual mode of thought—the operation of the mind's eye? With Faraday, Maxwell, and Einstein, it seems clear that their deepest, most natural, most personal, and most productive modes of thought were intensely visual (both literally and by analogy with vision), even though this might not always be apparent in their more professional and public discussions. But what of Churchill and those like him? Can we expect to find evidence of similar hidden visual processes? Words and politics seem to lend themselves to the visual less than other things. Can we uncover evidence of an intensely visual approach lying hidden not far below the surface of verbal discourse, an underlying context of apt images and distant analogies that invisibly mold the discourse?

Small and large hints, here and there, provide some indication. We have already noted Churchill's preference for graphical presentation of numerical and statistical information. Another instance is the "magic lantern." Churchill took the trouble to make a point of explaining how much he liked (in comparison to books and ordinary lectures) a form of instruction involving an early type of slide projection, especially when used by an interesting and authoritative speaker. He said he could clearly recall material presented in this way for decades. Like the dyslexic pathologist Marcia (in a more extreme case) and many others, Churchill would seem to have a decided preference for combined visual and auditory methods of presentation. While he was at Harrow, Churchill wrote, "We used also to have lectures from eminent persons on scientific or historical subjects. These made a great impression on me. To have an exciting story told you by someone who is a great authority, especially if he has a magic lantern, is for me the best way of learning."[38]

In our search for indications of an underlying visual orientation, another shred of evidence that may be of importance is that Churchill was a great lover of political cartoons. Not only did he greatly appreciate them (an appreciation not always shared by his associates in politics), but he troubled himself to write a thirteen-page essay on them, displaying a clear understanding of their subtle and insidious power. We might wonder what he would have thought of the political cartoon's latter-day descendent—the use, in present-day politics, of highly orchestrated, emotionally evocative television images.

> I always loved cartoons. . . . The responsibility of . . . famous cartoonists must be very great. Many are the youthful eyes that have rested upon their designs, and many the lifelong impressions formed thereby. I got an entirely erroneous conception of Julius Caesar from this source. . . . Cartoons are the regular food on which the grown-up children of to-day are fed and nourished. On these very often they form their views of public men and public affairs; on these very often they vote.[39]

But these shreds of evidence are as nothing compared to the passionate love of painting described by Churchill in "Painting as a Pastime." The essay's title belies its content. We are not given, as the title would suggest, the idle musings of a hobbyist dabbler in semi-retirement. On the contrary, we are given, instead, the ardent passion of one who has discovered, before it is too late, a fresh new love in his middle years. This passion drew on such deep resources and reserves that one can only guess that these great engines of refined and skillful observation had previously had some other object in other facets of a rich and energetic life.

> One is quite astonished to find how many things there are in the landscape, and in every object in it, one never noticed before. And this is a tremendous new pleasure and interest which invests every walk or drive with an added object. So many colours on the hillside, each different in shadow and in sunlight; such brilliant reflections in the pool, each a key lower than what they repeat. . . . I found myself instinctively as I walked noting the tint and character of a leaf . . . the exquisite lacery of winter branches, the dim pale silhouettes of far horizons. And I had lived for over forty years without ever

noticing any of them except in a general way, as one might look at a crowd and say, "What a lot of people!" I think this heightened sense of observation of Nature is one of the chief delights that have come to me through trying to paint. . . .

Once you begin to study it, all Nature is equally interesting and equally charged with beauty. I was shown a picture by Cézanne of a blank wall of a house, which he had made distinct with the most delicate lights and colours. Now I often amuse myself when I am looking at a wall or a flat surface of any kind by trying to distinguish all the different colours and tints which can be discerned upon it, and considering whether these arise from reflections or from natural hue. You would be astonished the first time you tried this to see how many and what beautiful colours there are even in the most commonplace objects, and the more carefully and frequently you look the more variations do you perceive.[40]

Churchill's great love of painting seems to indicate a deep reservoir of native capacity which may have readily manifested itself in analogous ways in comparatively distant disciplines. Are not the fifteen hundred toy soldiers with which he spent so much time as a youth but a near analogy of real armies that must be managed with real tactics in real battles (and in primarily visual and spatial modes of thought and analysis)? Similarly, it is not hard to imagine that the architect of the grand Allied strategy of the world conflict of 1939–45 conceived and habitually considered this grand, overarching plan in primarily visual terms, using intellectual capacities that focused on the whole rather than the parts, the long view rather than the short, the simultaneous comprehension of vast and complex interrelationships.

But what justification have we for such an assertion? Are we not stretching the point? Granted, in some cases there may be real justification for drawing such a conclusion. It may be true of some scientists and some mathematicians and even some poets, perhaps. But painting and politics and military strategy (among other things)—can their close interconnection really be defended by a responsible observer?

Yes. One need go no further than Churchill's own thoughts and observations as laid out in his essay on painting. In seemingly an almost unwanted and unplanned digression, Churchill asserts that the great painters and the master artists were drawing on capacities useful in "any other high activity of the human intellect." He does not name "the great Italians," but we would expect that they include Michaelangelo and da Vinci—master artists known for their great skill in so many diverse areas of investigation, knowledge, and endeavor. Churchill does not elaborate on the point and he quickly returns to his main topic, almost as if he had momentarily forgotten himself, indulging in a distant digression in thought that had presented itself to him unbidden as he dictated his text.

> But it is in the use and withholding of their reserves that the great commanders have generally excelled. . . . In painting, the reserves consist in Proportion or Relation. And it is here that the art of the painter marches along the road which is traversed by all the greatest harmonies in thought. . . . It is wonderful—after one has tried and failed often—to see how easily and surely the true artist is able to produce every effect of light and shade, sunshine and shadow, of distance or nearness, simply by expressing justly the relations between the different planes and surfaces with which he is dealing. We think that this is founded upon a sense of proportion, trained no doubt by place, but which in its essence is a frigid manifestation of mental power and size. We think that the same mind's eye that can justly survey and appraise and prescribe beforehand the values of a truly great picture in one all-embracing regard, in one flash of simultaneous and homogeneous comprehension, would also with a certain acquaintance with the special technique be able to pronounce with sureness upon any other high activity of the human intellect. This was certainly true of the great Italians.[41]

Churchill's terminology alone shows the centrality of the passage to his thinking. It is almost unsettling in its unexpected aptness. Painting and military strategy and any other "high activity" of the human mind are seen in clearly visual-spatial, right-hemisphere terms, employing phrases now often used by professionals in this context: "proportion" and "mental power and size" together with "one all-embracing regard, in one flash of simultaneous and homogeneous comprehension."

Churchill never had an evident reading problem (except when very young), so it is clearly improper to speak of dyslexia, strictly defined, in his case. However, we can see that he does seem to have exhibited a pattern of positive and negative traits that is much like those experienced by those we have been discussing. He did poorly in school and worse in exams: he was disorganized, accident-prone, and sloppy; he had particular difficulty with modern and ancient languages; he loved model building; he retained childlike qualities in adult life; he was famous for his speeches but had to prepare them in advance, practice them thoroughly, and keep notes in case of memory lapses; he learned to be a great performer and was known for the power of his language, which came out of a strong preference for unusual simplicity and directness; he showed an extraordinary capacity to appreciate native grace in a highly visual-spatial skill such as flying, and he sensed the great, all-encompassing intellectual power hidden deep within the talent and methods of the great painters and sculptors.

The boy who spoke poorly, in time, came to deliver some of the most forceful and memorable speeches of his time. The boy who was disorganized, in time, became the man who was one of the foremost planners and leaders of an era. And the boy who was slow to develop in time advanced well beyond all his peers, by pressing energetically forward long after most others would have passed the baton.

GEORGE S. PATTON

George Patton is one of the most colorful and controversial military leaders in the history of American warfare. Many considered him to be among the most innovative military tacticians and talented communicators. Others thought him erratic and irresponsible, a posturing performer. When Patton's papers were published in 1972, the editor, Martin Blumenson, made no mention of dyslexia, but he did note one of its obvious indicators. He wrote, "Every attempt has been made to preserve the flavor of Patton's spelling and punctuation, but in some cases periods and capital letters have been added to help the reader."[42]

When he published a biography of Patton in 1985, however, Blumenson fully acknowledged the role of dyslexia in Patton's life. Indeed, he had come to view dyslexia and Patton's associated attention deficit disorder as major motivational forces.

In the evenings, [young George] and [his sister] Nita spent hours in Papa's lap or by his side, listening as he read aloud to them. This too [like the hunting and fishing trips] was mainly for Georgie's benefit. For although he was bright and intelligent and bursting with energy, he was unable to read and to write. To him, the letters on the printed page appeared upside down or reversed.

Half a century later, physicians and educators recognized this sort of abnormality and gave it the name "dyslexia"; still later they identified a similar neurological-chemical condition they called "attention deficit disorder." Symptoms of both include feelings of inadequacy, a frustration with books and studies, a limited span of concentration, an impairment of the learning process, and the need to compensate for the deficiency by accomplishment in other areas.

Georgie had all of these. His parents hardly comprehended his strange affliction, but they were extremely patient with him and enveloped him in affection. They kept him out of school, where the taunts of classmates and their cruel laughter at apparently stupid mistakes of pronunciation and penmanship might have seared his soul. They let him express his high spirits however he could and encouraged him to vent his frustrations in physical activity.

These two facts, his dyslexic flaw, which gave an enduring sense of insecurity, and the unbounded love of Mama and Papa, which provided him with self-assurance, were the basic elements of Patton's ambition and achievement. The clash of these tendencies shaped him. Without them, he would never have aspired with so much might, with so much determination to gain distinction, glory, and fame.[43]

One can admire the biographer's willingness to recognize the role of dyslexia and attention deficit disorder in Patton's life. However, it is possible that this analysis goes too far. Dyslexia can help motivate a person to accomplish formidable tasks and fight for recognition of compensatory achievements, but it is the central thesis of this book that, as Norman Geschwind has commented, "This explanation must convey at best a very fraction of the truth." The other side should be seen as well: the way the distinctive dyslexic mind can sometimes provide insights and intuitions and other unusual capacities that are, perhaps, more rare among those with "ordinary" brains.

In 1903 Patton entered the Virginia Military institute to prepare for West Point. The first letter Patton received from his father refers to Patton's difficulties with reading and spelling.

That must have been pretty embarrassing when you could not read the "no hazing pledge." How did you get out of it? I hope you managed some way to pass it off. I do not see how you are going to over-come this difficulty except by practicing reading all kinds of writing. Do not give it up, but when you start to read anything keep at it till you work it out. You misspelled hazing. The verb is "to haze" and you should remember the general rule—to drop the final "e" before "ing."[44]

Blumenson notes several characteristics of the adult Patton consistent with the impulsiveness often associated with dyslexia. "He was moody, temperamental, savagely profane, and easily moved to tears. . . . To enjoy group activities, he first had to school himself to overcome his fears, his uncertainties, his lack of confidence."[45]

Despite a certain degree of athletic ability, Patton, like many dyslexics, was accident-prone. "Patton . . . once informed his wife nonchalantly that he had just suffered his normal annual injury."[46] He showed evidence of the familiar slowness, late development, and school difficulties.

Far from brilliant in his early days, Patton was quite aware that many others were quicker in mind than he. But he considered this to be merely a handicap to overcome by will power, study, serious application, practice, and perseverance. Eventually he outdid and outshone his classmates. . . . He was a late bloomer, a man who developed the habit of study. . . . It took him five years to graduate from West Point.[47]

Patton's wife routinely helped him in his writing, a role commonly taken on by spouses of dyslexics. "She corrected his poor spelling, which had become second nature, his punctuation, his grammar. . . . She encouraged him to believe in his destiny and fate. She collected his aphorisms and nurtured his myth. She saved his papers, catalogued them, and, shortly after his death, published a book about him."[48]

In Patton's successes and accomplishments, we may see some evidence of the positive qualities sometimes associated with dyslexia. There are some indications of the familiar talent for performing and the high interest in mechanical and technical things. Even Patton's sense of history can be seen as consistent with a tendency to take on a more global view (although we probably would not want to make too much of this). His "showmanship . . . impressed the public with his toughness. . . . Constantly interested in technological advance, he strove to anticipate the effect of new weapons . . . on the methods of waging war. He had a wide range of interests . . . [and a] close rapport with history. . . . To discuss the development of mechanized forces, he started with the Trojan War in 1096 B.C."[49] Patton's sense of being a part of the vast sweep of history and his feeling of special rapport with certain other historical leaders was not unlike the special rapport seen among the visual-thinking scientists we have already considered. However, it is more notable that a special understanding of proper timing and a special feel for spatial relationships are seen as major sources for his acknowledged skill in command.

> A cavalryman at heart, Patton achieved fame as a tanker. The principles he utilized in armored warfare came from the cavalry. He constantly sought surprise, mobility, maneuver—that is, the outflanking movement, the envelopment, the encirclement—and the relentless pursuit. For these, as well as his understanding of space and time in warfare, he was indebted to Napoleon.[50]

Patton was a controversial leader. He showed many of the signs of classic dyslexia when young. Many residual traits were evident for the rest of his life. He was slow to read, but, in time, he read and wrote extensively. He was clumsy and accident-prone, but he lived for action. He was shy and insecure, but he became an unabashed performer when he felt the situation required it. He was a late bloomer who not only overcame his disabilities and surpassed his classmates, but also, in time, subdued formidable adversaries as well.

"A BALLOON IN A SHED": WILLIAM BUTLER YEATS

In an era that almost universally ignores serious poetry of any kind, William Butler Yeats has an enduring following. One is not surprised to hear a few lines quoted in a radio documentary or a stanza or two used by folk musicians. Nor is one surprised to see a photocopied Yeats poem on the office wall of a broadcast journalist or to hear a Yeats poem recited from memory (without school assignment) by an enthusiastic, rock-music-loving American teenager.

That Yeats was dyslexic, even in the most restricted sense of the term, is hardly subject to debate. Yet when one brings this up to people who love literature, one is immediately struck with a reaction of extreme incredulity. How is it possible that such an extraordinary master of expressive language could have had difficulty with reading, writing, and language in general? This is a paradox indeed.

As with most paradoxes, answering this question should help us to look deeper and see more clearly. It is a paradox only because we seem to assume that language competence is a generalized, unitary skill. What we don't ordinarily realize is that the most memorable language is fresh, apt, and unexpected language, sometimes, perhaps, language translated in an original way from ideas that may have been essentially non-verbal in origin. The truth of this paradox is easier to see when we contrast it with the extreme ease of expression of the articulate trial lawyer, news reporter, or television host who rarely hesitates or trips and is never at a loss for the right words to suit the occasion. However, these professionals often seem to be running the same words and phrases in the same furrows, never saying anything surprising or unexpected or memorable in any way. Verbal fluency can sometimes be the opposite of verbal felicity.

Yeats's pattern of strengths and weaknesses is not hard to discern but the connection is not always clear at first. Even Eileen Simpson, who is often so quick to identify hidden dyslexic traits in others, was surprised that she had missed the connection when she first read Yeats's own accounts of his reading and education problems. "What is curious is that when I first read *Autobiographies* . . . I did not have a shock of recognition. It was only recently, rereading it, that I was electrified: Yeats was clearly dyslexic."[51]

To document the disabilities among Yeats's special set of attributes, one does not need to go far. The editor of Yeats's *Memoirs* notes that his "handwriting is difficult. . . . As for spelling and punctuation, Yeats never mastered those skills. In the present volume errors of spelling and punctuation have been silently corrected."[52]

Other commentators are less generous. Referring to the newly published first volume of a series of Yeats's letters, one astonished and horrified reviewer, never once making reference to dyslexia or other learning disabilities, wrote in 1986,

The subtile and gorgious origonality of these vigerus Keltic letters shows such scholorship as to leave the reader fealing decidedly exausted. No. *The Economist* has not thrown orthography to the winds. That bogus sentence is composed of a sample of the astonishing misspellings that pepper the letters of W. B. Yeats.

They astonish because, as a poet, Yeats was fastidious, correcting and revising his work with consummate caution. In the letters spontaneity mattered more.[53]

One wonders how the reviewer could believe that spontaneity, alone, could be the cause of such varied and imaginative spellings.

The editor of the volume provides further evidence of these handwriting and spelling difficulties:

Yeats is constantly apologizing for his handwriting and has every reason to do so. . . . If Yeats' bad handwriting has one virtue it is that it disguises his even worse spelling. Indeed, in this respect legibility can sometimes let him down, and nowhere more notably than in a letter of 1911 sounding out the authorities at Trinity College, Dublin, about the possibility of his succeeding to Edward Dowden's professorship. Unhappily, the eager aspirant to a Chair of English contrives to spell the sought-after office "proffesrship."[54]

Besides the common difficulties with spelling and punctuation, Yeats clearly also had the most classic symptom, difficulty in reading. According to his father, writing of his wife's family, "The Pollexfen uncles and aunts, though fairly kind, were not very sympathetic; when they began to try to teach him to read—he did not know his alphabet at seven—they thought that he was mentally lacking. He seemed unsuccessful like his father, 'unsuccessful and therefore wicked.'"[55]

According to Yeats,

Because I had found it hard to attend to anything less interesting than my thoughts, I was difficult to teach. Several of my uncles and aunts had tried to teach me to read, and because they could not, and because I was much older than children who read easily, had come to think as I have learnt since, that I had not all my faculties. . . . My father [one Sunday] said if I would not go to church he would teach me to read. . . . He was an angry and impatient teacher and flung the reading-book at my head, and next Sunday I decided to go to church. My father had, however, got interested in teaching me, and only shifted the lesson to a week-day 'til he had conquered my wandering mind.[56]

It is worth particular note that in the same passage Yeats refers not once but twice to the high activity of his mind as a major difficulty in learning to read, indeed, as a major difficulty in any form of academic learning.

Fortunately, his father—the desultory lawyer turned passionate artist—supervised the homework and supplied the early literate education for the child who could not read. Yeats wrote, "In the evening [my father] heard me my lessons or read me some novel of Fenimore Cooper's."[57]

It is notable that in the next few pages of Yeats's autobiography, there are three more references to the father's role in educating the son.[58] It is sometimes the case that one parent, often the father, seems to be especially sympathetic to the dyslexic child, taking extra time to help him or her—seemingly because of a special understanding of the difficulties, achieved, perhaps, through some related personal experience. Patton's father seems to have played a similar role.

Miscellaneous evidence of certain dyslexic traits can be found in the most unlikely places. Many dyslexics are predisposed to disorganization, a difficulty that may improve in adolescence but persist in some form throughout adult life. When Yeats became a senator in the new Irish Parliament, one of his duties was to preside over the committee that selected the designs for the new national coinage, a task that made ample use of Yeats's broad historical and artistic knowledge and good sense. In reading the poet's remarks on the progress of the committee's assignment, one cannot help but be reminded of the awe with which some disorganized people hold those who are conspicuously well-organized. "Our work could not have been done so quickly nor so well had not the Department of Finance chosen Mr. McCauley for our Secretary. Courteous, able and patient he had a sense of order that fills me with wonder."[59]

There is evidence from several sources that Yeats's problems with language extended to curious difficulties with pronunciation as well as the meter and pacing of reading out loud—classic dyslexic traits, but strange ones for a famous poet, especially one known for the musicality of his verse. Here again, this apparent paradox may be an indication of our still-imperfect understanding of these talents and skills.

Eileen Simpson's husband, a poet and teacher, had attempted to comfort her by pointing out that she was in good company with her spelling and recitation difficulties. He had explained, "Yeats couldn't spell worth a pin, and probably couldn't read aloud either."[60] A recent biographer, A. Norman Jeffares, noted that Yeats "did not understand scansion."[61] And on one occasion when Yeats was reading a passage out loud, a family member made the following diary note: "His bad pronunciation had amused [one listener]. Willie had divided it up into any amount of full stops where there weren't any. . . . In truth it was rather like his natural way of reading."[62]

Like Faraday, Yeats was far more adept at learning by use of visual and oral means than by written ones. "I have remembered nothing that I read, but only those things that I heard or saw."[63]

In school, the classic (although by no means universal) athletic awkwardness is also quite evident in Yeats. "I was useless at games. I cannot remember that I ever kicked a goal or made a run, but I was a mine of knowledge when I and [three friends] . . . [would] look for butterflies and moths and beetles."[64] Yeats also shows some evidence of the high productivity into advanced age that we have seen in Faraday and Churchill. Just a few years before his death, Yeats wrote to a friend, "I have no consciousness of age, no sense of declining energy, no conscious need of rest. I am unbroken. I repent of nothing but sickness."[65]

According to Jeffares, he confided to another friend, "It was a curious experience . . . to have an infirm body and an intellect more alive than it had ever been, one poem leading to another as if he were smoking, lighting one cigarette from another."[66]

In the absence of basic knowledge of how to deal with dyslexia, several courses of action are possible. Both Faraday and Edison dropped out of school and were educated by their mothers, more or less, later taking on courses of extensive self-education. Einstein's relationship with the conventional school system alternated between grudging toleration and active resistance, until he too dropped out, but at a much later and more risky stage; fortunately, his experience at the unusually progressive school at Aarau allowed him to get back on track, to some extent, reviving his serious interest in his studies and allowing him to pass his university entrance examinations on his second attempt. Patton was tutored at home until he was ready to enter the conventional stream. Churchill limped through the conventional upper-class educational system, but his real education does not seem to have begun until he started his own self-study program as a young adult, while stationed with the British Army in India.

In the time of Yeats, Churchill, Patton, and Einstein, in contrast to the time of Faraday, school systems had become more pervasive and it had become increasingly difficult to skirt the conventional system without severe consequences. In the face of the squeeze of conventional and universal educational methods, Yeats seems to have accidentally found himself an acceptable alternate route: staying in less-demanding institutions until his special abilities began to mature. During the early years in London, Yeats may have been better off at a school that was less challenging, at least initially, in order to give him time to develop at his own pace and in his own way.

Parents and teachers may fault schools for not teaching certain skills at the expected ages. In most cases of learning difficulties, the best strategy seems clearly to be early identification and remediation. But in some cases, where delayed maturity in some specific area is a major factor, it may be best to take the pressure off and merely wait for a while. In these cases, it may be that too much pressure on remediation of certain skills, too early, is not only wasteful but destructive, especially when the pressure comes from a heavy-handed classroom teacher rather than a specially trained tutor.

Yeats's first school after the move from Ireland to London was run by a clergyman who was more concerned with gentility and athletics than scholarship. Regarding a student who did poorly in Greek but well in cricket, Yeats explains that the headmaster would comment, "Oh, leave him alone." As for Yeats himself,

I was unfitted for school work, and though I would often work well for weeks together, I had to give the whole evening to one lesson if I was to know it. My thoughts were a great excitement, but when I tried to do anything with them, it was like trying to pack a balloon in a shed in high wind. I was always near the bottom of my class, and always making excuses that but added to my timidity, but no master was rough with me. I was known to collect moths and butterflies and to get to no worse mischief than hiding now and again an old tailless white rat in my coat-pocket or my desk.[67]

One suspects that sometimes it may be better to let things slide, at least for a while (but always trying to make progress in certain areas of strength). If the neurologists are correct about the possible advantages of delayed maturation and the process of gradually learning to "guess" better based on greater life experience and other things, then it would appear that the dyslexic (and those more or less like them) can sometimes use to advantage plenty of extra time. That is, in the course of development of the gifted dyslexic (with or without identification and remediation), if maturation really is a major factor, then perhaps the best advice is to be patient and make educational arrangements that do the least damage to the child's self-conception while ensuring that high-quality content is provided in any way possible— until the late bloomer is suddenly ready to take off, racing past many of his peers.

Yeats's reference to his active mind in the above passage is accompanied by an apt and powerful metaphor, as one might expect—"it was like trying to pack a balloon in a shed in a high wind." It is also notable that Yeats described himself as near the bottom of his class, and that he chose to use a small animal for distraction in class, exactly as Susan Hampshire had done as a student.[68] Given the varied times and situations of their lives, the incidental similarities between the people we are considering can be quite striking.

The advantages of Yeats's earlier, less demanding schooling may be more apparent in comparison with his later school experience. At fifteen years old Yeats went to a new school at Harcourt Street in London. It was much more difficult and demanding than his previous London school had been.

I had not thought it possible that boys could work so hard. . . . Even had I never opened a book not in the school course, I could not have learned a quarter of my night's work. I had always done Euclid easily, making the problems out while the other boys were blundering at the blackboard, and it carried me from the bottom to the top of the class; but these boys had the same natural gift and instead of being in the fourth or fifth book were in the modern books at the end of the primer, and in place of a dozen lines of Virgil with a dictionary, I was expected to learn with the help of a crib a hundred and fifty lines. The other boys were able to learn the translation off, and to remember what words of Latin and English corresponded with one another, but I . . . made ridiculous mistakes; and what could I, who never worked when I was not interested, do with a history lesson that was but a column of seventy dates? I was worst of all at literature, for we read Shakespeare for his grammar exclusively.[69]

The irony is poignant. The work was unrelenting. Yeats learned his Latin lesson well once and then he was chided for not knowing it all the time. "No one knew that I had learnt it in the terror that alone could check my wandering mind." A curriculum more ill-designed for Yeats's kind of mind can scarcely be imagined. All of the subject matter seems to have been converted into cold data to be memorized (where those with skill only in memory could still shine), while Yeats's areas of interest and strength, whether literature or history, were transformed into further frigid and lifeless difficulties. Even his skill in geometry, the touchstone for so many of our visual thinkers with learning difficulties, was discounted for Yeats, not only by his school and peers, but also by his own, otherwise supportive father. "'Euclid,' he would say, 'is too easy. It comes naturally to the literary imagination.'"[70]

Despite this, Yeats's interest in geometric concepts persisted in curious ways in his subsequent creative work. This interest also provides a glimpse at his propensity for a curious form of visual thinking in this later work. For example, one of the dominant images he used in some of his most admired later poems was that of the "gyres." According to Yeats's description, these were two cones or vortices, one inverted inside the other, so that each vortex formed "from itself an opposing vortex, the apex of each vortex in the middle of the other's base."[71] This visual image was used to embody the basic concept of generalized inverse proportion or reciprocal action—that is, in various aspects of life and nature, as one thing increases, another diminishes.

Another of Yeats's important geometric images is of a conic sectioning through his two cones, perpendicular to the axis of rotation. Such sections give two circles, one increasing in area as the other decreases in area over time, as one circle shrinks to a point and the opposite point expands to a large circle. Thus, curiously, the poet drew on mathematical concepts to find patterns to shape his poetry.

So we have come full circuit. Earlier, we considered visual-thinking scientists, mathematicians, and inventors who thought in analogies and images like those of poets. In Yeats, we see a poet who repeatedly used major images of three-dimensional geometric models—images and patterns essentially mathematical in their conception.

Yeats, like many dyslexics, eventually had to make the best of his very limited academic and professional options. Also like many dyslexics, he chose to pretend to his parents that his decisions were more a matter of personal preference than bitter necessity. After all, the appearance of being in control can be quite important. Thus, when Yeats told his father that he would not go to Trinity College Dublin as three generations had before him, he preferred to have it seen as self-assertion or rebellion, but he confided, "I did not tell him that neither my classics nor my mathematics were good enough for any examination."[72] Yeats went on to arts college because he had few other options.

Yeats never did learn many of his "basics." He probably never would have done well on anyone's examinations of achievement. However, in time he became the leading poet in the Irish Literary Renaissance and the central playwright in the establishment of the Irish National Theater. Although he could never learn to speak Gaelic, he made extensive use of traditional high legends and tales. He had hated studying history as it was taught but became a major figure in the making of history and sat as a senator in the new Irish Parliament. He was slow to read, yet, in time, he learned to compose a distinctive and musical verse that is still among the most widely read English poetry of this century. Yeats never became anything like a scholar. Yet, in time, his work would be recognized by a Nobel Prize and hundreds of scholarly books would be written about his life and works. In time, Yeats learned to write. But he never learned to spell.

7

SPEECH AND NONVERBAL THOUGHT

But Moses said to the Lord, "Oh, my Lord, I am not eloquent, either heretofore or since thou has spoken to thy servant, but I am slow of speech and of tongue." Then the Lord said to him, "Who has made man's mouth? Who makes him dumb or deaf, or seeing, or blind? Is it not I, the Lord? Now therefore go, and I will be your mouth and teach you what you shall speak." But he said, "Oh my Lord, send, I pray, some other person." Then the anger of the Lord was kindled against Moses and he said, "Is there not Aaron, your brother, the Levite? I know that he can speak well; and behold, he is coming out to meet you, and when he sees you he will be glad in his heart. And you shall speak to him and put the words in his mouth; and I will be with your mouth and with his mouth, and will teach you what you should do. He shall speak for you to the people."

Exodus 4:10–17

Thoughtful writers on the nature of the brain have noted that its most obvious characteristic is that it is formed into two mirror-image parts.[1] They have wondered why something that seems to us so fundamentally unitary should be divided into two. How is it that the two constellations of functions assumed by these mirror parts are so different? Some have argued that the two halves of the brain are different because there are at least two dissimilar, antagonistic yet complementary modes of dealing with information about reality.

One of the earlier observations made as a result of split-brain research in the 1960s was that the left hemisphere seemed to "analyze" a stimulus, whereas the right hemisphere "immediately" seemed to apprehend a stimulus as an "integrated whole," or "Gestalt." Consequently, it was considered reasonable that "during evolution . . . Gestalt perception may have lateralized into the [largely] mute [right] hemisphere as a consequence of an antagonism between functions of language and perception."[2]

If these modes are inherently incompatible, then it should not be surprising if a good deal of effort and time were required to establish a common ground and a basis for translating information back and forth between one mode and the other.

VISUAL THOUGHT INTO WORDS

If in fact these modes are fundamentally incompatible, then perhaps it should not be surprising that individuals having a highly developed facility with one mode of information storage and processing would have great difficulty with performance in the complementary mode. If one is articulate with words, then one may be hopeless in drawing pictures. Or if one is unusually adroit in drawing or visualizing whole scenes, then it may not be surprising to find that one is less fluent in the verbal expression of these scenes, that one has difficulty in finding the right words for what is clearly seen in the mind. All this is, in fact, widely recognized to some extent in common experience. But what may not be fully realized is the possible magnitude of this split and the depth of its roots.

This perspective might also help us to understand better some of the most heated and intractable quarrels in the history of science and other disciplines—it may be that the opponents relied heavily, perhaps exclusively, on one or the other of these antagonistic and incompatible modes of thought. With language, basic ideas, and views of the world and life experience so fundamentally different, it is evident why these conflicts might be so difficult to resolve. There are many examples of these incompatibilities, and rarely can one person be expected to bridge the gap effectively. Indeed, one indicator of the dimensions of the split may be the rarity of individuals who can deal effectively with processing in both modes.

James Clerk Maxwell was such a person. He was capable of thinking in both modes, apparently with equal facility. He could see both sides as correct, within their respective frames of reference. He could see the points of view of both sides with the "conviction that the discrepancy did not arise from either party being wrong."[3] But such a man appears to be quite rare. What we usually have, it seems, is the strong culturally reinforced left shift.[4]

VISUAL IMAGINATION AND VERBAL DYSFLUENCY

The opposite tendency—to think in pictures instead of words—does occasionally manifest itself, however. In his *An Essay on the Psychology of Invention in the Mathematical Field*, French mathematician Jacques Hadamard discussed this tendency at some length. Hadamard noted that there are quite divergent views on whether words are required for clarity of thought. For example, Max Müller, the "celebrated philologist and orientalist," steadfastly maintained that ideas cannot be conceived except through language, indeed, that ideas exist only insofar as they are represented by words and, further, that human rationality depends upon language.[5] Hadamard, however, argues that different people should be expected to think in significantly different ways. He makes reference to Francis Galton, "the great geneticist," whose "habit of introspection" provides a basis for asserting that "whether he [was] playing billiards and calculating the course of his ball or investigating higher or more abstract questions, his thought is never accompanied by words."[6]

However, Galton's propensity for thinking in images rather than words was a source of no small inconvenience to him. Hadamard quotes Galton:

> It is . . . a serious drawback to me in writing, and still more in explaining myself, that I do not so easily think in words as otherwise. It often happens that after being hard at work, and having arrived at results that are perfectly clear and satisfactory to myself, when I try to express them in language I feel I must begin by putting myself on another intellectual plane. I have to translate my thoughts into a language that does not run very evenly with them. I therefore

waste a vast deal of time in seeking for appropriate words and phrases, and am conscious, when required to speak on a sudden, of being often very obscure through mere verbal maladroitness, and not through want of clearness of perception. That is one of the small annoyances of my life.

Hadamard himself found it useful "to reproduce at length that statement of Galton, because in his case I exactly recognize mine, including the rather regrettable consequence which I experience just as he does. . . . Just as for Galton, such a translation from thought to language always requires on my part a more or less difficult effort. . . . It is difficult for me to deliver a lecture on anything but mathematical subjects without having written down practically every part of it, the only means of avoiding constant and painful hesitation in the expression of thought which is very clear in my mind."[7]

Certain difficulties with speech, in some people, may be seen not as dysfunction per se, but rather as an indicator that information is being processed by a mode of thought wholly alien to speech. And the more dependent these people are on this mode of thought (that is, the more useful they find it), the more difficulty they are likely to have.

One is reminded of Einstein's comments on his two-stage thought processes. Galton noted that his own propensity to think in terms other than words slowed his writing and made his speaking hesitant and awkward, especially when he was startled or had insufficient time to think through a response. Like Einstein, he needed to prepare himself to words by putting himself on "another intellectual plane."[8] This observation is clearly consistent with our model of the two modes of thought. Galton was quite specific about his need to "translate" from the visual to the verbal mode. Furthermore, he is definite in indicating that the language of words "does not run very evenly" with the language of images, and so he has to "waste a vast deal of time" searching for suitable words. In both Galton and Hadamard we see clear evidence of the operation of the nonverbal mode and the difficulties that may be caused by reliance on it. It is less the matter of a defective instrument than a matter of an instrument designed for a different purpose.

CLEAR THOUGHTS AND OBSCURE DESCRIPTIONS

We find some surprising similarities and some major differences with Maxwell. He was a life-long stutterer and had a reputation for hesitant and obscure speech, which led to major career difficulties. Although he excelled as a university student and gradually gained recognition as one of the foremost scientists of his time, he fared poorly in his career, apparently because of his lack of verbal fluency.

> In 1860, Maxwell was unsuccessful in his application for the Chair of Natural Philosophy at Edinburgh University. . . . The curators of patronage preferred to appoint [his] friend and rival P. G. Tait, principally on account of his exceptional power of oral expression; likewise, it was Maxwell's well known deficiency in this power that caused him to be dismissed from his Chair at Aberdeen University when Marischal College and King's College were amalgamated that same year—despite the fact that he married the Principal's daughter.[9]

Maxwell's friend and biographer, Lewis Campbell, observed that Maxwell's "replies in ordinary conversation were indirect and enigmatical, often uttered with hesitation and in a monotonous key."[10] Campbell also reported that when Maxwell was ill at ease, he would make "chaotic statements."[11] Another biographer, Ivan Tolstoy, notes that Maxwell retained this impediment "until the end of his days."[12] Campbell, in an especially lucid passage containing a most apt metaphor, seems to strike to the heart of the matter, suggesting that Maxwell's inability to speak quickly and clearly may be the direct result of the great richness of his mind, not the result of some simple disability. "Another hindrance lay in the very richness of his imagination, and the swiftness of his wit. The ideas with which his mind was teeming were perpetually intersecting, and their interferences, like those of the waves of light, made 'dark bands' in the place of colour, to the unassisted eye."[13]

C. W. F. Everitt also noted Maxwell's difficulties with verbal communication. "The odd contrast between the clarity of his writing and the frequent obscurity of his speech was often remarked on."[14] And in *History of the Cavendish Laboratory* Arthur Schuster wrote,

Maxwell often showed a certain absent mindedness: A question put to him might remain unnoticed, or be answered by a remark which had no obvious connection with it. But it happened more than once that on the following day he would at once refer to the question in a manner which showed he had spent some time and thought on it. I never could make up my mind whether on these occasions the question had remained unconsciously dormant in his mind until something brought it back to him, or whether he had consciously put it aside for future consideration, but it was quite usual for him to begin a conversation with the remark: "You asked me a question the other day, and I have been thinking about it." Such an opening usually led to an interesting and original treatment of the subject.[15]

F. W. Farrar, who was dean of Canterbury Cathedral, had been a friend of Maxwell's at Cambridge and they were both members of a small society known as the Apostles. At the group's meetings Maxwell's comments

were often hardly intelligible to anyone who did not understand the characteristics of his mind, which were very marked in his conversation. If you said something to him, he would reply by a remark which seemed wide as poles from what you had mentioned. This often had the effect of diverting the conversation from the subject in hand, because the remark appeared wholly irrelevant. When this was the case, he usually dropped the discussion altogether, and, indeed, many of those who casually met him regarded him as incomprehensible for this reason. But if you gave him his bent, he would soon show you that his observation, so far from being *nihil ad rem,* really bore very closely on the heart of the question at issue. To this he would gradually approach, until the relevance of his first remark which seemed so distant from the topic under discussion, became abundantly manifest.[16]

Schuster observed that Maxwell sometimes lacked an understandable response, possibly because he was employing a mode of thought not directly related to verbal communication. Farrar observed that Maxwell's conversation could sometimes be difficult to follow because his mind had proceeded to points well beyond the usual limits of association for his listeners; that is, his mind seemed naturally and quickly to make apt associations between distant and apparently unrelated phenomena—just as would be expected in our classic creative mind. Many of us can do this from time to time, but some people do it so often and so extensively that it may be legitimately considered an affliction, especially at times when they would find it far more convenient to have their mind work in the conventional way.

This trait appears in some children who have learning difficulties in school. Of one nine-year-old a teacher wrote, "His power of abstraction is far beyond his years. In reading class, for example, or in talking about a story in writing class, what could begin as a rather meandering monologue of disassociated facts often turned into a hard-hitting, pertinent, imaginative contribution which left the teacher somewhat breathless. He could put on a similar display of erudition and thinking in science, for example."[17] One can imagine that if this child were not allowed to ramble on a bit, or if the teacher did not listen with real interest and respect, or if the teacher were insufficiently intelligent or well read to appreciate what the child was saying, then, of course, the child would be cut off and become frustrated and angry or withdrawn. The teacher would believe, mistakenly, that the child was inept, and would view the child as having an attitude or discipline problem.

SPONTANEOUS AND DEMAND LANGUAGE

Children with dyslexia or learning disabilities often have trouble speaking on demand—that is, when an immediate verbal response is required by the social situation. They are caught unawares "on another intellectual plane," to use Galton's words. However, these children may have little difficulty with what is called "spontaneous language," that is, language initiated by the speaker when the speaker is fully ready to speak. In *The Misunderstood Child*, Larry B. Silver provides a description of this anomaly that seems especially pertinent to our discussion.

> Children with a *specific language disability* usually have no difficulty with spontaneous language. They do, however, often have problems with demand language. The inconsistency can be quite striking. A

youngster may initiate all sorts of conversation, may never keep quiet, in fact, and may sound quite normal. But put into a situation that demands a response, the same child might answer "Huh?" or "What?" or "I don't know." Or the child may ask you to repeat the question to gain time, or not answer at all. If the child is forced to answer, the response may be so confusing or circumstantial that it is difficult to follow. She or he may sound totally unlike the child who was speaking so fluently just a minute ago. This inconsistency or confusion in language behavior often puzzles parents and teachers. A teacher might put a child down as lazy or negative because he or she does well when volunteering to speak or answer a question, but won't answer or says "I don't know" when called on. The explanation could be in the child's inability to handle demand language, but contradictory behavior like this makes sense only if you know about the disability.[18]

The applicability of Silver's description to Maxwell is clear. Once again we see a puzzling anomaly in some of the most creative thinkers that seems, incongruously, parallel to problems common among some of the poorest performers in the early grades of our conventional school systems.[19] In some cases it seems that the mode of thought best suited to comprehending the information is the one least well suited to communicating it.

This apparent need for some to remove one's thinking from the world of words is also evident in an anecdote about Einstein told by Banesh Hoffmann, one of Einstein's assistants in 1937. When Hoffmann and another assistant, Leopold Infeld, were stumped by an impassable obstacle in their work they would often go to Einstein for help. Once they had explained their problem,

> we would all pause and then Einstein would stand up quietly and say, in his quaint English, "I will a little think." So saying, he would pace up and down and walk around in circles, all the time twirling a lock of his long grey hair around his forefinger. At these moments of high drama, Infeld and I would remain completely still, not daring to move or make a sound, lest we interrupt his train of thought. [Suddenly,] Einstein would visibly relax and a smile would light up his face. . . . Then he would tell us the solution to the problem, and almost always the solution worked. . . . The solution was sometimes so simple we could have kicked ourselves for not having been able

to think of it by ourselves. But that magic was performed invisibly in the recesses of Einstein's mind, by a process that we could not fathom. From this point of view the whole thing was completely frustrating.[20]

There is no explicit reference to visual thinking in this passage, but we do have what seems to be a clear description of shifting into another mode of thought, "another intellectual plane," one that is different from a verbal approach to problem solving such as talking one's way through to a solution in a group setting for example. In any case, it does seem clear that Einstein found it useful to remove himself for a time from the world of words to find the solution in what he called "productive thought."

INTELLIGENCE WITHOUT VERBAL FLUENCY

A person's speech problems may take many forms, not all of which may ever come to the attention of speech pathologists or related professionals because of the subtlety of the difficulty. However, the case we are arguing here is that some problems of speech, however subtle and elusive, may be seen as indicators of differences in deep mental processes. The differences may be viewed as either positive or negative, depending upon the particular context. Put another way, a certain neurological organization may lead to a mode of thought that is ill-suited to task A (for example, rapid, responsive, articulate speech) but is ideally suited to task B (say, finding novel solutions to unusual problems). However, the professionals may be so concerned with correcting a problem that they miss special capabilities and advantages that go along with it.

In some cases, it seems that the greater the fluency with nonverbal thought, the greater the dysfluency of verbal communication. This tendency might create difficulties for those in universities and other institutions where verbal proficiency is seen as a major indicator of intellectual competence. Yet it seems that some of our greatest minds may fit this unexpected pattern. Once we are sensitive to this seeming paradox, we may see more evidence of it among the most talented in many groups.[21] Some instances are common knowledge: many artists, musicians, and architects are observed to be relatively inarticulate when compared with those who depend upon words in their professions, such as professors, psychiatrists, and diplomats.[22] Some radio reporters observe that cartoonists may be relatively inarticulate and may not provide good interview material.[23] But there may be some surprising variations. For example, it is now becoming clear that some actors have difficulty with "demand language" and find the predictability and assurance of a prepared script to be a great comfort.[24]

Perhaps if there were a greater awareness of this paradoxical tendency, we could begin to look past verbal dysfluency—or even fluency—to measure the true value of the ideas that lie behind. Perhaps more important still, we might also learn to see some of the real power of nonverbal modes of thought, however difficult they may be to communicate in words.

8
PATTERNS IN CREATIVITY

Scholars and artists thrown together are annoyed at the puzzle of where they differ. Both work from knowledge; but I suspect they differ most importantly in the way their knowledge is come by. Scholars get theirs with conscientious thoroughness along projected lines of logic; poets theirs cavalierly and as it happens in and out of books. They stick to nothing deliberately, but let what will stick to them like burrs where they walk in the fields. . . . The artist must value himself as he snatches a thing from some previous order with not so much as a ligature clinging to it of the old place where it was organic. . . . There must have been the greatest freedom of the material to move about in it and to establish relations in it regardless of time and space, previous relation, and everything but affinity.

Robert Frost, "The Figure a Poem Makes," *Complete Poems*

MISSED OPPORTUNITIES

Some years ago, a young researcher in biochemistry was performing a procedure devised to destroy DNA, the molecular blueprint for self-replication carried in all living cells. She was annoyed, however, at not being able to make the procedure work as intended. Each time she measured the results of her work, she came up with more DNA than she had started with rather than less.

The researcher tried again and again. But each time she was disappointed to discover that she had more DNA than she had originally introduced. Her co-workers were sympathetic and tried to help, but no solution to the problem could be found.

Some years later, another scientist in a different laboratory successfully developed a method to rapidly generate large quantities of DNA and he subsequently received a Nobel Prize for his discovery. The researcher and her former colleagues are still asking themselves how it is that they did not recognize what was really going on when her project repeatedly failed.[1]

Sometimes a gift is seen only as a problem, one that would be quickly wished away, had we the power. Sometimes the most important thing is to be able to recognize a gift for what it is, even though it was not requested or desired. For this to be possible, it is helpful (in spite of one's training) not to be wholly focused on the narrow interest of the moment, no matter how serious the task, no matter how large the grant, no matter how urgent the deadline. One has to be open to new possibilities, to looking at things in a different way, to being able to see what you have been given, even when it is not what you asked for. Burrs may prickle and itch, but they do stick—if we do not pull them off and thoughtlessly toss them away.

The role of chance and fortuitous accident is one of several themes that recur in the literature of creativity, especially creativity in the sciences. This chapter will discuss a number of such recurring patterns, focusing on those that appear to be associated with our consideration of visual thinking and various learning difficulties. We do not assume that all creativity is necessarily associated with some form of learning disability or learning difficulty. However, we do believe that a number of traits associated with dyslexia and other learning difficulties (especially high visual-spatial talents) may tend to predispose some individuals to greater creativity than might exist otherwise.

Being able to do what others want you to do, in the way they want you to do it, is seductive. If you can, you will. But if you cannot, you will have to find another way. It is a form of self-selection. If it is possible to do it the same way, successfully, often a new way will not be tried. Thus, if a truly original method is needed, the conventionally successful student or researcher may be the last one to find it. Sometimes only among those who have repeatedly failed is there a high likelihood of success.

DEEP PROBLEMS, DEEP CREATIVITY

Doubtless there is more creativity in ordinary life than we are led to believe. However, we must not assume that just because people are highly regarded by their professional associates or win major prizes that they have discovered something really revolutionary or really deep. Einstein received his Nobel Prize for his lesser work—his major achievements were still a matter of great debate.[2]

It is helpful to turn to the new science of "chaos" once again to see that there are several major levels of creativity, to see what is meant by really "deep," and to see that some of the most original work often comes from following up on things of little apparent consequence. James Gleick explained the meaning of the term "deep" as used among professional physicists by describing Mitchell Feigenbaum, one of the leading early researchers in this new science. When Feigenbaum joined the research section of the Los Alamos National Laboratory, he had a reputation for being extremely bright, but not very productive.

> "I understand you're real smart," [the director of the Los Alamos laboratory once] said to Feigenbaum. "If you're so smart, why don't you just solve laser fusion?"
>
> Even Feigenbaum's friends were wondering whether he was ever going to produce any work of his own. As willing as he was to do magic with their questions, he did not seem interested in devoting his own research to any problem that might pay off. He thought about turbulence in liquids and gases. . . . He thought about clouds, watching them from airplane windows (until, in 1975, his scientific travel privileges were officially suspended on the grounds of overuse) or from the hiking trails above the laboratory.

The study of clouds was something that had been largely ignored by the mainstream of physics researchers. It was not really considered an appropriate area of study.

> To a physicist, creating laser fusion was a legitimate problem; puzzling out the spin and color and flavor of small particles was a legitimate problem; dating the origin of the universe was a legitimate problem. Understanding clouds was a problem for a meteorologist.

Like other physicists, Feigenbaum used an understated, tough-guy vocabulary to rate such problems. *Such a thing is obvious*, he might say, meaning that a result could be understood by any skilled physicist after appropriate contemplation and calculation. *Not obvious* described work that commanded respect and Nobel prizes. For the hardest problems, the problems that would not give way without long looks into the universe's bowels, physicists reserved words like *deep*. In 1974, though few of his colleagues knew it, Feigenbaum was working on a problem that was deep: chaos.[3]

"REGARDLESS OF EVERYTHING BUT AFFINITY"

One of the patterns often observed in the most original discoveries is the need for great flexibility in basic concepts and assumptions. Faraday's idea of the "field" was wholly incompatible with the concepts used by scientists and mathematicians of his day. It was so original that it was not understood or accepted until it was described in mathematical terms and explained at length by Maxwell and subsequently confirmed experimentally by Helmholtz. Many would not give serious attention to Einstein's theories until his predictions were experimentally confirmed at the close of World War I by a group of astronomers from the enemy camp, that is, Britain, since Einstein was still in Germany.[4]

Major discoveries have sometimes been missed by the most capable scientists because they were unable or unwilling to reassess their basic assumptions and patterns of thought. All the necessary information lay in front of them, but they were unable to make the basic changes in their thinking that would permit them to see the pattern that would allow all the pieces to fit.

In a letter to a friend Faraday wrote of a colleague's researches on the magnetic condition of matter, "It is astonishing to think how he could have been so near the discovery of the great principle and fact, and yet so entirely miss them both, and fall back into old and preconceived notions."[5]

Reviewing his life's work as an old man, Einstein observed that one of the most difficult things he had to do in his own work was to unlearn old patterns of thought.

That the special theory of relativity is only the first step of a necessary development became completely clear to me only in my efforts
to represent gravitation in the framework of this theory. . . . This
happened in 1908. Why were another seven years required for the
construction of the general theory of relativity? The main reason lies
in the fact that it is not so easy to free oneself from the idea that
coordinates must have a direct metric significance.[6]

Einstein saw that he could not move from the special theory to the
general theory of relativity without first changing, in his own mind,
some extremely basic ideas and conceptions.

Einstein commented elsewhere on this problem—remarking that,
in time, some of his theories could be easily understood by young students, but that made them no easier to find in the beginning, when he
was wandering alone in the dark. The hard part, apparently, is seeing
for the first time things in a way that is different from the way they
have ever been seen before.

In the light of knowledge attained, the happy achievement seems
almost a matter of course, and any intelligent student can grasp it
without too much trouble. But the years of anxious searching in the
dark, with their intense longing, their alternations of confidence and
exhaustion, and the final emergence into the light—only those who
have experienced it can understand it.[7]

Presumably, many scientists are never able to do this deep exploration. They have neither the special ability nor the essential inclination. Basic concepts, once learned, are fixed for life.[8]

Thus we see that, sometimes, great quantities of knowledge are
not enough. Sometimes one has to be willing to change basic assumptions and thought processes in order to see clearly the unexpected
truths that would be evident—if only we could see them in the right
way. Sometimes knowing all the data is not nearly so important as
being able to view it from a different and truly original perspective.

It is often observed in the literature of creativity that unusually
creative persons appear to be able to provisionally affirm, at the same
time, several apparently incompatible assertions. We have observed
that the excess of connections and pathways seen in the brains of
dyslexics might be one of the factors that help them make associations

between distant and apparently unlike things.[9] To some, this hypothesis may appear naive and almost silly. Yet, as we slowly come to understand some of the more elusive capacities of the brain, this simple idea may not prove to be so far-fetched.

The observation that scientists sometimes miss discoveries because they cannot reassess their basic assumptions is almost true by definition. Scientists can be too successful in absorbing the knowledge and conventional beliefs of their professors and colleagues. One writer on creativity in the sciences, Horace Freeland Judson, has observed, "New Science must be surprising: if an idea follows from what's already known, though it may be a valuable corollary, it is redundant."[10] Judson quotes a leading contemporary British scientist, Sir Peter Medawar. "It is quite impossible to predict new ideas—the ideas that people are going to have in ten years' or in ten minutes' time—and we are caught in a logical paradox the moment we try to do so. . . . For to predict an idea is to have an idea, and if we have an idea it can no longer be the subject of prediction."[11]

This process may be aided by the unexpected in a particular form—sometimes those things that are truly original or unexpected are just those things that would have appeared previously to the well-trained professional as too incongruous or too absurd or too ridiculous to be so. Of course, not all ideas that seem initially to be silly or otherwise basically unacceptable prove to be right. We are just arguing that we must be alert to the possibility that such an initial appearance can prove to be a major barrier to acceptance of important and widely applicable ideas.

The idea that the world was made of solid rock sliding on massive, slowly moving plates was first seriously proposed in 1915 by a meteorologist, Alfred Wegener. The theory was greeted with amusement by the professional geologists of the time and for a long while after. It was not until the late 1960s that overwhelming physical evidence finally convinced an entire profession, virtually overnight, that they had been wrong all along and that the meteorologist had been right. Wegener's theory predicted the patterns of magnetic directionality of rock samples drilled from the deep Atlantic Ocean floor, whereas the conventional theories could make no sense of this puzzling but undeniable phenomenon. In recounting the story of this revolution, Nigel Calder describes Wegener as "a generalist, one of those rare men who do not fear to learn and use branches of knowledge in which they are not formally trained, in order to arrive at a greater synthesis: conversely, over-specialisation among Wegener's opponents blinkered their imagination."[12]

The apparently incongruous and absurd can take other forms. The most surprising and productive findings can sometimes be seen as funny—at first. Lewis Thomas has observed that one can easily tell when something of real consequence has been discovered in the laboratory because people start laughing—something has turned out in a way that no one expected and it is too unexpected to be believed.

> And I think one way to tell when something important is going on is by *laughter*. . . . It seems to me that whenever I have been around a laboratory at a time when something very interesting has happened, it has at first seemed to be quite funny. There's laughter connected with the surprise—it does look funny. And whenever you can hear laughter, and someone saying, "But that's *preposterous*!"—you can tell that things are going well and that something probably worth looking at has begun to happen in the lab.[13]

THE SUCCESS OF FAILURE, THE FAILURE OF SUCCESS

Well-trained and successful scientists are kept busy with many obligations—preparing lectures, advising students, consulting with coauthors, meeting journal deadlines, reviewing grant applications, making student recommendations, sitting on expert advisory groups and government commissions, and attending faculty parties and retirement dinners. Little wonder that Einstein recommended that a scientist should remain apart as much as possible from the politics of science ("the battle of the brains") and instead take work as a lighthouse keeper or shoemaker or some other undemanding employment in order to keep the mind free of interruptions.[14] Einstein's suggestions seem romantic to us now, but his basic approach has begun to appear increasingly sensible to experienced researchers who find their lives too full of career obligations to focus on really original work.

Strangely, adversity can be of benefit to the creative, giving them uninterrupted time to get the work done. One example is the paradoxical benefit of imprisonment—in the old days—in getting books written. (It was while he was in prison that Marco Polo set down the account of his extensive travels in China.[15]) At least one book has been written on the beneficial role of long illnesses in providing uninterrupted time for single-minded creative effort.[16] A not-too-successful career path may help. Maxwell wrote his two-volume *Treatise* during a period of semi-retirement in the middle of a career without much lustre.

If one wishes to be really creative, it seems that sometimes it is essential to have one's time less than fully committed, to be able to follow where one's thoughts lead rather than having to succeed in a series of tasks largely defined by one's career, one's competitors, or other outside forces. One wonders what might have happened to Einstein's early work without his period of independent study (following his own fancy) as a school dropout, his lecture-cutting and continued self-directed study during his university years, his two years of intermittent unemployment (ironically with mounting intellectual excitement) after graduation, and then his relatively undemanding patent office job once he did enter the world of conventional work. We might wonder what would have happened if Einstein had become immediately enmeshed in the teaching, administrative, and social demands of a conventionally successful career. As he observed, in such a path there is a strong tendency to do research that is comparatively superficial and predictable—little steps that do not risk serious failure or threaten existing beliefs, modest research programs that can be relied upon to produce publishable results and supportive, unthreatened mentors.[17]

Years of hard work and one's self-image as a competent professional may be closely bound up with a belief in what one has been taught, which, in time, one has often come to be teaching to others. Of course, little changes and corrections are needed here and there to keep up the momentum of gradual progress and to make one's reputation. But there is little incentive to question or overturn fundamental elements of the discipline, making obsolete both some of one's own career accomplishments as well as those of many others. Even worse is to blur the boundaries of the discipline, inviting territorial battles and the threat of lost professional status and credibility. This conservatism continues to be a powerful force in the emerging science of chaos.

The language of mathematics remained a serious barrier to communication. If only the academic world had room for hybrid mathematician/physicists—but it did not. . . . Mathematicians continued to speak one language, physicists another. As the physicist Murray Gell-Mann once remarked: Faculty members are familiar with a certain kind of person who looks to mathematicians like a good physicist and looks to physicists like a good mathematician. Very properly, they do not want that kind of person around." The standards of the two professions were different. Physicists had theorems, mathematicians had conjectures. The objects that made up their worlds were different. Their examples were different.[18]

It is much safer to clearly identify with one group or another. The risk of confusion or loss of credibility is often too great to be seriously considered by any prudent professional, especially those who have learned early and well the rewards of staying within the acceptable and desirable boundries. Balance a doubt against a certainty and stay within the conventions of normal science.

But in the end, there is a greater problem. The important thing is that truly original discoveries sometimes require unlearning and relearning not only what one has been taught, but also fundamental and basic elements in the way one thinks about things in general, some of the most fundamental concepts at the core of one's thought processes. We must not go too far down this road without pointing out that there are all kinds and levels of accomplishment and creative discovery. Each set of weekly and monthly science periodicals is a feast of enticing new developments. We are all too aware that the conventional system of university courses and grant programs and research laboratories is turning out vast quantities of wonderful, exciting and frightening things. Clearly, the conventional system does produce; it would be wrong to suggest otherwise. But it often produces pieces that make the whole less clear. The most general and comprehensive and integrating explanations are the most exciting, but they are also the most rare.

Of course, all of this is an administrative problem as well. An unconventional process is hard to manage and control. Perhaps all that can be done is to learn that the unorthodox approach is sometimes the correct one, to recognize such approaches as valuable when they are first contemplated.

In the end, probably the most effective deterrent to really original work is not so much the career distractions and disincentives as the fact that the professionals often have learned their lessons too well. If you have had great success in learning to think the way your teachers and associates think, then it is all the more difficult to think in some really original and unexpected way. In fairness, it should be noted that this problem clearly flows from the necessary double-bind of any accumulated knowledge. The vast majority of gains in knowledge are made through the further application of what is already known. However, occasionally this same factor is a major cause of error. This essential problem may explain why it is sometimes best—if one wants to make truly original contributions—to work in a field other than the one originally studied. In one's own field, one has already developed a strong internal editor, which may serve to criticize and demolish "silly" thoughts before they can take hold internally or get out to cause embarrassment. It is hard to unlearn what has been learned so well. Perhaps this is the reason it has been observed that the most original ideas often come not from those at the top of their fields, but from those who are at the fringes.

> Thus in subjects in which knowledge is still growing, or where the particular problem is a new one, or a new version of one already solved, all the advantage is with the expert, but where knowledge is no longer growing and the field has been worked out, a revolutionary new approach is required and this is more likely to come from the outsider. The scepticism with which the experts nearly always greet these revolutionary ideas confirms that the available knowledge has been a handicap.[19]

Of course, one has to be close enough to the conventional in order to obtain the needed information from conventional sources, to check one's findings, and to be able to explain one's new ideas in a way that is understandable and acceptable to conventional modes of thought.[20]

IMAGINARY DIFFICULTIES, IMMEDIATE RECOGNITION

The illusion of difficulty alone can be enough to deter progress, sometimes to a shocking extent. Some physicists and astronomers have recognized that the presumed difficulty of some of Einstein's ideas has long been greatly overstated and that the same attitude has significantly retarded advances in a number of related scientific areas—in this case, according to some, for a period of over forty years. Thus one prominent astronomer, who was closely acquainted with the scientists involved in the experimental proof of Einstein's general theory of relativity, observed in 1982, "I may parenthetically remark that this supposed difficulty in understanding the general theory of relativity was greatly exaggerated: it contributed to the stagnation of the subject for several decades. Many of the developments of the sixties and the seventies could easily have taken place during the twenties and the thirties."[21]

Another curious aspect of creative activity that we can learn from this source is the way some people can immediately recognize the validity of other people's work. No testing is required for their certainty, although objective verification is, of course, required for presentation to others. In 1918, British astronomer Sir Arthur Eddington (and his close friend, Astronomer Royal Sir Frank Dyson) mounted expeditions to Brazil and West Africa in order to make astronomical observations to verify Einstein's theories. One colleague, S. Chandrasekhar, had complimented Eddington for his courage in planning the expedition when the outcome seemed so uncertain. In Chandrasekhar's words, "To my surprise, Eddington disclaimed any credit on that account and told me that, had he been left to himself, he would not have planned the expeditions since he was fully convinced of the truth of the general theory of relativity!"[22]

Eddington never really had any doubt about the correctness of Einstein's theories. As soon as he had heard of Einstein's work, he knew Einstein had to be right. When Einstein formulated his fundamental field equations, he concluded his paper with the observation that "scarcely anyone who has fully understood this theory can escape from its magic."[23] Chandrasekhar comments that "Eddington must surely have been caught in its magic; for, within two years, he had written his Report on the Relativity of Gravitation for the Physical Society of London, a report that must have been written in white heat."[24]

"LET US LEARN TO DREAM, GENTLEMEN"

In the literature of creativity there are many references to instances of highly visual, dreamlike states as sources of major scientific discoveries. Some visions are literally the dreams of sleep. In one classic example, a professor of pharmacology was deeply involved in a problem and awoke one night from sleep with a brilliant idea. He made a few notes and returned to sleep. When he woke the next day, he was aware of having had an inspiration the previous night, but he could not make sense of the notes he had made. However, to his good fortune, he awoke again the next night with the same flash of insight. This time he carefully noted the idea in detail before returning to sleep. As it turned out, the consequences of this nighttime inspiration were wide ranging.

> The next day he went to his laboratory and in one of the neatest, simplest and most definite experiments in the history of biology brought proof of the chemical mediation of nerve impulses. He prepared two frogs' hearts which were kept beating by means of a salt solution. He stimulated the vagus nerve on one of the hearts, thus causing it to stop beating. He then removed the salt solution from this heart and applied it to the other one. To his great satisfaction the solution had the same effect on the second heart as the vagus stimulating had had on the first one: the pulsating muscle was brought to a standstill. This was the beginning of a host of investigations in many countries throughout the world on chemical intermediation, not only between nerves and the muscles and the glands they affect but also between nervous elements themselves.[25]

Other visions are daydreams or the dreams of a half sleep. One of the most famous and oft-quoted instances is related in the story of the German chemist Kekulé, who came upon the structure of the benzene ring, the solution to a basic problem that subsequently came to revolutionize organic chemistry. As Kekulé tells the story, he was working on his chemical textbook,

> but it did not go well; my spirit was with other things. I turned the chair to the fireplace and sank into a half sleep. The atoms flitted before my eyes. Long rows, variously, more closely, united; all in

movement wriggling and turning like snakes. And see, what was that? One of the snakes seized its own tail and the image whirled scornfully before my eyes. As though from a flash of lightning I awoke; I occupied the rest of the night in working out the consequences of the hypothesis. . . . Let us learn to dream, gentlemen.[26]

In this way, Kekulé somehow came to see that if the structure of benzene was six carbon atoms arranged in a ring then the pieces of the puzzle would fall into place and all the apparently contradictory evidence seemed finally to make sense.

Kekulé's vision is often recounted and is usually presented at face value, rarely commented on at length. But the imagery is rich with significant detail that should not be ignored. In the middle of his description Kekulé says, "And see, what was that?"—in the present tense, emphasizing the immediacy of the memory apparently still very clear in the speaker's mind. Then one of the snakes "seized" its own tail and "whirled scornfully" in front of his eyes. Why "scornfully"? As if to say, "understand me if you can"? This description of creative thought makes one wonder about the possibilities, as we become more accustomed to thinking of one part of the mind communicating with another. Perhaps a highly visual component of the mind, one with intuitive understanding but little verbal power—knowing the sought-for answer—deigns to communicate its perception to the conscious, verbal mind, but does so in a manner that underscores its own superiority.

We have not been trained to think of our own minds in this way. But as we become familiar with the recent research into neurology and artificial intelligence—books on it bear titles like *Multimind*, *The Social Brain*, and *The Society of Mind*—we may begin to understand that it is time to see the mind not as a single unit but as a collection of cooperating (or interfering) subunits.[27] We may increasingly come to see our old conception of a unified mind as just a useful illusion.

The productive dream vision described by Kekulé might be his rare vision of something familiar to some of those we have been considering—that fluid world of floating letters and whirling images common to dyslexics and others with similar learning difficulties. We can recall Faraday's need to be "saved by facts" because of his excessively vivid imagination. Could it be that the people we have been discussing, with their more symmetrical and more interconnected brains, could be more in touch with the various nonverbal components of their own brains? Could it be, on the other hand, that those who are more scholarly or technically proficient, presumably having more conventional asymmetric brains, might be generally relatively less in touch with the nonverbal parts of their brains?

We now know that the concept that people are "left brained" or "right brained" is misleading. However, the concept that people have "symmetric" or "asymmetrical" brains may help in making better sense of the diversity in thinking abilities that we see. Some analogies with political and economic processes may be helpful. As in a rigidly centralized and hierarchical system, such as a highly disciplined army, the asymmetrical system may be seen as more rapid and efficient in having decisions made and orders carried out. But such systems almost necessarily have complement weaknesses. The more symmetric neurological systems, in contrast, might be seen as more like a fractious representative democracy or decentralized management system that may work more slowly and may appear less responsive and less efficient—but it may operate more efficiently over the long run through the more effective use of a wide range of specialized agents, each with limited autonomy and limited power to respond to changes in a limited area, having very different abilities and points of view.

NOT ALWAYS "ON THE SHOULDERS OF GIANTS"

Toward the end of his life, Sir Isaac Newton said, with some modesty, that he was able to accomplish so much because he stood on the "shoulders of giants." In one way, this statement emphasizes the necessary cumulative nature of the scientific enterprise, each new discovery resting firmly on the work of others. It also reinforces the common belief that one can do little to advance a field until one has first mastered its literature. This has often been true, especially in recent times, but it is important to realize that this is not always true. Sometimes the most far-reaching and surprising advances come from people who have not followed the prescribed or usual route. Accordingly, really creative scientific work may not be as cumulative as it is often portrayed. Indeed, if one is to be really very original, it may be much easier if one goes a lot of the distance alone, in one's own way and one's own time. If one studies the work of others too closely, one might be drawn off in their direction. Einstein based his theories on the work of Faraday, Maxwell, and other earlier thinkers, but he made surprisingly little use of the relevant scientific literature of his contemporaries—as if to emphasize the extent to which he was largely alone in the development of his thought.

This pattern of independence is seen consistently in Einstein's early education. He followed his own program instead of the conventional educational curriculum, pursuing his own agenda whether through the classics of philosophy or through popular science books. Einstein explained that in his middle teens he learned the basics of mathematics and science through popular books. He read books on mathematics that were "not too particular regarding logical rigor, but that permitted the principal ideas to stand out clearly."[28] During his university years, Einstein infuriated professors because he would question everything they taught. But even after his uneasy bout with university education, it is clear that his earliest and most important work was accomplished largely on his own, and largely without consulting the published work of other scientists. According to physicist and novelist C. P. Snow,

> Albert Einstein, twenty-six years old, published in the *Annalen der Physik* in 1905 five papers on entirely different subjects. Three of them were among the greatest in the history of physics. . . . The third paper was the special theory of relativity, which quietly amalgamated space, time, and matter into one fundamental unity.
>
> This last paper contains no references and quotes no authority. All of them are written in a style unlike any other theoretical physicist's. They contain very little mathematics. There is a good deal of verbal commentary. The conclusions, the bizarre conclusions, emerge as though with the greatest of ease: the reasoning is unbreakable. It looks as though he had reached the conclusions by pure thought unaided, without listening to the opinions of others. To a surprisingly large extent, that is precisely what he had done.[29]

When asked in 1907 to prepare a review of other people's articles relating to his work on relativity, Einstein asked the journal editor for help finding references because of his difficulty in gaining access to much of the literature. "I should note that unfortunately I am not in a position to orient myself about *everything* that has been published on this subject, because the library is closed in my free time."[30] The biographer, Abraham Pais, acknowledges Einstein's practical problems at this time, but concluded that "Einstein's complaint about his difficulties in getting hold of books and journals, while no doubt genuine, is only a secondary factor in the understanding of his handling of existing literature. The truth of the matter is that he did not much care."[31]

As proof of this assertion, Pais quotes Einstein's introduction to a paper published in 1906.

> It seems to me to be in the nature of the subject, that what is to follow might already have been partially clarified by other authors. However, in view of the fact that the questions under consideration are treated here from a new point of view, I believed I could dispense with a literature search which would be very troublesome for me, especially since it is to be hoped that other authors will fill this gap, as was commendably done by Herr Plank and Herr Kaufmann on the occasion of my first paper on the principle of relativity.[32]

Pais sees this particular passage as not only clear evidence of the real independence of Einstein's way of working, but also an expression of Einstein's substantial lack of tact in expecting others (even those of considerable professional status) to do his literature searches for him. Pais comments, "To me these lines express ebullience, total self-assurance, and a notable lack of taste."[33] This attitude would be unthinkable for a true scholar in the conventional tradition, which implicitly assumes that all significant advances are the result of the cumulative efforts of a large number of researchers, all of whom are continuously aware of each other's work through the professional journals.

Einstein, by contrast, focused on the relevant literature largely after the basic creative work had already been completed. Here, the scientist is not gathering all the data or even seeing what all the specialists have said first—as we are taught to do, using conventional scientific or scholarly methods. Einstein's method was apparently the reverse of the conventionally accepted view of the "scientific method." One college physics teacher used to tell his students, in part for shock value, that Einstein's accomplishments were "black magic," because Einstein simply did not have enough data to develop his theories in the way prescribed by the conventional scientific method.[34] As Einstein himself often said, his laboratory was entirely in his own mind. The work of others could be consulted, after the fact, as a check on one's own work but it should not, in his view, be used to try to arrive at original work. Einstein explained, "A theory can be checked by experiment, but there is no path that leads from experiment to a theory that has not yet been established."[35]

WITHOUT "BIG SCIENCE"

Today it is pretty much a foregone conclusion that virtually all science of consequence is "big science." There seems to be a nearly universal belief that nothing of importance can be done without a large research staff, expensive equipment, and a massive budget. It may be true that much of modern science and technology requires such investment, but not, perhaps all of it. Consider the historical pantheon of American technological heroes. An illustration of what basic capabilities and determined effort may accomplish, where experts or gentlemen enthusiasts had failed repeatedly, is provided by the example of Wilbur and Orville Wright.

Periodically there seems to come a time when a full set of tools and techniques becomes available for relatively ordinary people to draw together what they need in some novel way. Once these circumstances converge, then the major needed ingredient is simply effort—determined, focused, passionate, and unrelenting—along with a willingness to risk many small failures in order to inch forward into unknown territory through a good deal of trial and error. The Wrights had only their bicycle business and such tools, skills, and income that it made available to them. Yet with these modest resources they took what was essentially an off-season hobby and turned it into a dramatically successful achievement, one that had previously eluded all professional efforts.

There seems to be an aspect of evolutionary selection here as well. It matters most of all, perhaps, that at a particular time and place all the resources to do a job are widely available. Many will fail. A few will succeed. But with widely distributed capabilities, the whole enterprise moves ahead at a much more rapid rate. During the late nineteenth century, we are told, the total number of inventions and patents increased dramatically. The number of foolish inventions also increased greatly. But what is more important is that the number of really good inventions increased greatly as well.[36]

Neither Wilbur nor Orville Wright ever finished high school, although other members of the family were college educated. (There is no evidence of learning disabilities in either brother.) Their father was an educated religious leader and administrator, a traveling bishop of the United Brethren in Christ. Their sister eventually attended Oberlin College to earn her teaching credentials. The brothers initially went into business as job printers and publishers of several small local newspapers, but they eventually stumbled into the suddenly popular and modestly profitable bicycle business that started to flourish in the early 1890s. The business involved bicycle sales (with weekly installment payments), rental and repair in the summer, and cottage-industry manufacturing in the winter. The manufacturing operation was easily run by the two brothers, who were observed to "combine mechanical ability with intelligence in about equal amounts." An old school friend who had originally joined their printing operation did the final bicycle assembly. Orville operated the enameling oven while Wilbur did the brazing using a brazier that they had designed themselves."[37]

There seemed to be a relatively aimless quality about the young adult years of the two brothers in Dayton. Their printing business was in part a continuation of Orville's summer job in high school years. Off and on Wilbur had considered going to college. But in high school a sporting injury and a "vaguely defined" heart ailment caused Wilbur to drop this plan and he stayed at home for several years, partly taking care of his semi-invalid mother until her death in 1889, while his father's work continued to require extensive travel and long absences from home.[38]

Wilbur's slow recovery and apparent lack of drive during these years exasperated his brother Reuchlin, who had married and moved to Kansas City. He could not understand how it was that Wilbur stayed at home for so long just reading and taking care of his ailing mother. Reuchlin wrote their sister Katharine, "What does Will do? ... He ought to do something. Is he still cook and chambermaid?"[39] This is not exactly the expected beginning for the senior member of the two originators of the dashing and daring field of aviation.[40]

Without formal training or special resources, the self-taught Wrights nonetheless seemed to have all they needed for their investigations. When they needed a windy site for their earliest glider experiments, they simply wrote to the U.S. Weather Service. Their early experiments were essentially large-scale kite experiments, but these yielded important information on lift, efficient wing shapes, and novel devices for control. Unlike many other early experimenters in aircraft design, the Wrights knew that they needed to teach themselves how to control the aircraft first. Consequently, well before employing an engine, they took many short gliding practice flights down a large sand dune to develop their own reflexes and the essential skills—to give themselves some time to learn by trial and error the "feel" of the machine and controls. They found that the tables on wing shape and lift published by a German engineer and professor were wrong, so they devised their own, partly from their own wind tunnel, itself made from simple parts. Indeed, in time, they came to distrust all data they had not tested themselves.

The brothers could find no automobile company willing to make the light and powerful engine they required, so they made the engine themselves to their own design, largely in their own shop, with the help of the machinist who worked in their bicycle business. At the time it was falsely believed that air propellers should be similar in design to water propellers. The brothers found otherwise and consequently had to devise their own theory of propeller design. And throughout their flying experiments, they took photographs of everything they did so they could access their progress and make a permanent record of their achievements.[41]

Those who are familiar with the way such a project would be staffed today, with teams of highly paid experts in dozens of fields, can easily see how rapidly budgets and development schedules for such an undertaking would expand. Of course, a very great deal more is known now in many fields than was known then. But at the edge of the new, the situation (now as then) may not be as different as it might appear at first. Small, determined groups with fresh ideas (although less well educated and less experienced) may still move more rapidly and effectively than large ones. For example, the first popular personal computer was developed not by a large, well-established computer company, but by two counter-culture adolescents in their now-famous California garage, largely using parts available to hobbyists.[42] Sometimes it is good not to be an expert, not to know too much. Sometimes it is far more important to have a vision and to be willing to learn by taking risks and making mistakes that experts would not make. Sometimes it is good not to know beforehand all the reasons why something will never work and why it will never sell.

In the time of the Wrights, the head of the Smithsonian Institution, Samuel Langley, a respected engineer and scientist, obtained a sizable grant of $50,000 from the War Department to develop a heavier-than-air aircraft, but his experiments sank in the Potomac, with "howls of derision from all quarters." Wilbur and Orville financed their experiments entirely out of their own modest personal resources and at a small fraction of the cost of the professional effort.[43]

But, we might ask, are not the efforts of the Wrights some eighty-five years ago really quite irrelevant to the realities of our times? In some ways, yes, but in other ways, no. Sometimes the most effective barrier to any given accomplishment is the simple belief that it cannot be done.

Perhaps we need now to consider if we might be at the beginning of a period comparable in some important ways to that of the Wrights.

In their own time, the Wrights had in their hands all the mechanical tools and skills needed for their novel task. Today, as more and more powerful electronic tools and skills become increasingly available in the hands of ordinary people, one wonders what determined individuals and small groups might be able to accomplish where the great companies and laboratories have so far failed.

In the time of the Wrights, sophisticated mechanical capabilities had become widely available at modest cost to comparatively ordinary people, people without special education or facilities. Today, highly sophisticated electronic capabilities are becoming widely available at modest cost to these same comparatively ordinary people. On reflection, perhaps it is only a matter of time before we should expect modern-day electronic Wrights to devise things as yet unimagined by the professionals. They may not have the expensive equipment or the big budgets, but if they are really original, they may find a totally new way of doing the job with far more modest resources.

NEW CREATIVE POSSIBILITIES

From what we have seen so far, it may be that we have identified an important and surprising paradox. Many of those who have the required knowledge in a scientific discipline may, because of the nature of their training and selection, be much less likely to make truly original contributions, while many of those most likely to make truly original contributions often do not have the required training, experience, and credentials. Thus, many of the really special discoveries might well come from the tiny space where two largely incompatible groups overlap—for argument's sake, say, perhaps 1 percent of each group. If this position is granted, at least for the sake of argument, then we can ask about the possibility of implementing educational and institutional change to effect an increase of this overlapping area, from our hypothetical 1 percent to, say, 2 percent or 5 percent or more. What then would be the rate of significant new discoveries and other substantial creative activity?

We are suggesting a structural change in the intellectual economy of creativity. Some measure of monopoly in science might be broken and some measure of healthy scientific entrepreneurship might be engendered. Healthy economies do not allow monopolies to take hold because, inevitably, costs rise as production efficiencies and innovation go down. In a healthy economy, entrepreneurs do not need an exclusive charter from the king to do business. They need only to be able to deliver higher-quality products and services at reduced cost. In business, advanced degrees may or may not be a help, but you do not need a doctorate to even be a player in the game. This is not true in science and technology, where one usually needs to have some form of advanced degree even to be in on the discussion. These degrees should be facilitators, as no doubt they often are. But they sometimes serve more as barriers instead. It would be a supreme irony if a demanding educational system served mainly to eliminate many of the most talented.

There is no question, of course, that a great deal of traditional specialist knowledge will always be required. However, this is not the hard part of what we are trying to get at. What we are after is useful and wise innovation, not just reliable sources of factual information. To be sure, in many areas, the growth of scientific information proceeds at a dizzying rate. Our organizations and institutions as they exist today are clearly being productive. Their output grows daily. But a lot of this growth is in descriptive information about new territories and new orders of magnitude just becoming available for the first time because of new techniques and instruments. This is the stuff of seeing and describing, like the mariner's tales of strange sights in the New World, or a biologist's first sight of unknown worlds in a drop of pond water under his primitive microscope. Observing, naming, identifying, and categorizing. These are essential steps, it's true, but these are not the stuff of real discovery of larger truths and larger patterns.

However, one wonders what would happen if the very different people we are discussing were brought together in a deliberate and organized fashion, not accidentally and in spite of all forces to the contrary, as so often in the past. What then would be the rate of growth and innovation of a university team or company or economy that deliberately adopted this policy and found effective ways to make it work? Nothing should be promised. But if many persistent social, economic, and environmental problems are essentially structural, as they now appear to be, there can be little doubt that some large magnitude of change might be expected as a result. We don't need just more facts. We do need more deep understanding.

One senior cancer researcher laments that he and his colleagues are so caught up in the grind of conventional scientific research that they do not have time to gain deeper understanding. While he is still cautious of open discussion of the problem, deep down he suspects that many answers are just sitting out there waiting to be plucked from the existing stores of knowledge. He acknowledges that he and his associates are compelled to churn out grant proposals, design studies, and hire promising post-doctoral researchers. That is the system. But he suspects that no more studies are really needed, at least for a while. He suspects that there is enough information available now to fit the pieces of the puzzle together if only there were time to sit in the library and quietly think it through. But there is no money for simply sitting in the library and thinking. So the grant applications are submitted and more numbers are produced for review by peers, leading to yet more studies and numbers. The machine grinds on with new numbers but little new understanding.[44]

THE CREAM DOES NOT ALWAYS RISE

It may be that certain special creative abilities are not really rare, just rarely recognized and developed. Could it be that some of those with the greatest potential for being truly great inventors, mathematicians, and scientists, as opposed to knowledgeable scholars and competent technicians, are to be found among those who are repairing cars, attending art school, driving trucks, managing small entrepreneurial companies, giving flying lessons, designing computerized animated graphic images, or buried unnoticed in mid-level positions deep inside some corporate or governmental bureaucracy?

Many will find this view difficult to credit. The belief in unified and stratified intelligence runs deep. The cream always rises, we are led to believe. Yet when we look fairly at the stories of Einstein and others we can see that this is not always so. We need to be able to see that some who are best at looking into the heart of nature may not be very good at the demands of the conventional educational system or of managing a successful career.

Let us not forget that Einstein did much of his most important early work while he was cutting lectures, intermittently unemployed, and working as an unknown junior bureaucrat—"patent clerk, third class." Indeed, when Einstein was sought out in those early days by one of the few who recognized the revolutionary nature of his initial work, he was amazed to find that Einstein was not a full professor at the university nor a high-ranking official with a big office; he was merely the "unimposing, shirt-sleeved employee whom [the visitor] at first gave scarcely a glance when he sought out Einstein at the Patent Office."[45]

Michael Faraday's Laboratory at the Royal Institution. From Jones, *Life and Letters*, 1870.

PROF. FARADAY.
(*From a photograph by Lewis Carroll.*)

Lewis Carroll built his own photographic studio at Christ Church College, Oxford, where he took many photographs of his friends and their children, as well as notables of the time. One of his earliest pictures was a likeness of "Prof. Faraday." Photograph, Lewis Carroll. From Collingwood, *Life and Letters*, 1898.

Lewis Carroll, from photograph facing title page of *The Life and Letters of Lewis Carroll (Rev. C. L. Dodgson)*, written by his nephew, Stuart Dodgson Collingwood, 1898.

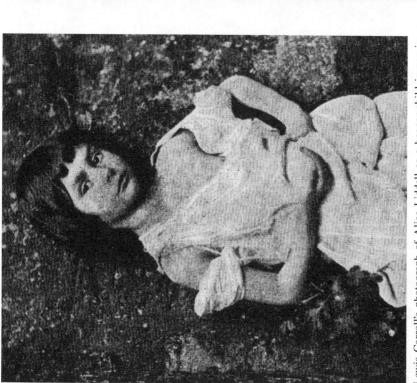

Lewis Carroll's photograph of Alice Liddell as a beggar-child is one in a series of costume photographs featuring children and adults. It was for Alice Liddell that *Alice in Wonderland* was composed and later prepared for publication at the suggestion of friends. Photograph, Lewis Carroll. From Collingwood, *Life and Letters*, 1898.

Sections of letter by dyslexic student with unintentional mirror writing. "First page shows standard orientation and left-right directionality. On the obverse side of paper, note that the entire one-half page shows right-left directionality and mirrored orientation, neither intended nor noticed." From Rawson, "Louise Baker and the Leonardo Syndrome," in *Annals of Dyslexia*, 1982. Courtesy of Margaret Rawson and the Orton Dyslexia Society.

Carroll's interest in mirror writing is evident in this facsimile "looking-glass" letter to Edith Ball, dated Nov. 6, 1893. From Collingwood, *Life and Letters*, 1898. When reversed, the text of the letter reads: "My dear Edith, I was very much pleased to get your nice little letter: and I hope you won't mind letting Maud have the Nursery Alice, now that you have got the real one. Some day I will send you the other book about Alice, called "Through the Looking-Glass" but you had better not have it just yet, for fear you should get them mixed in your mind. Which would you like best, do you think, a horse that draws you in a cab, or a lady that draws your picture, or a dentist, that draws your teeth, or a Mother, that draws you into her arms, to give you a kiss? And what order would you put the others in? Do you find Looking-Glass writing easy to read? I remain your loving, Lewis Carroll."

Left: In a section of a letter to his father dated 3 May 1843, Maxwell shows, at age twelve, his skill and delight in drawing as well as his fascination with mirror writing. From Campbell and Garnett, *Life*, 1882. It is a curious coincidence that the first lines of this extract refer to Maxwell's father's poor and ungrammatical writing in school (although he became an attorney in adulthood). It may also be noted in this extract that Maxwell never uses a period to end a sentence, that most "t"s are not crossed, and that most "i"s are not dotted. However, each sentence does begin with a capital letter. The reversed section of the letter reads: "Mrs Tis has finished my picture[.] She has been doing a picture of Hannah Gordon and some think the face too long, [error crossed out][.] I am one of them others think it too short[.] I am gaining up my places at the Academy and we have begun the Greek Extracts and Ovid[.] Monday was a fine day to look at but east wind[.] [Subject unclear] has been making woodcuts for a Constable[.]"

Below: James Clerk Maxwell, 1831–1879. From Campbell and Garnett, *Life*, 1882.

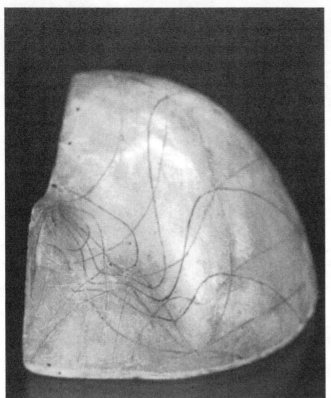

Maxwell's use of a plaster of Paris surface to render in three dimensions the data for the thermodynamic surface for water supplied by the American physicist J. Willard Gibbs. Yale University Collection. Photograph, Thomas G. West.

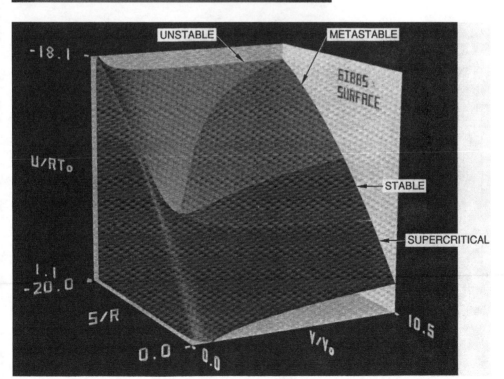

Modern computer graphics version of Gibbs's thermodynamic data similar to the one sculpted in clay and plaster by Maxwell more than a century earlier. Courtesy of K. R. Jolls and D. Coy.

(Jules-) Henri Poincaré, 1854–1912. Library of Congress Collection.

William Tomson (Baron Kelvin of Largs), 1824–1907. Library of Congress Collection.

Henri Poincaré, seated to the right of Madame Curie at the first Solvay Congress in 1911. The young Albert Einstein is standing behind him, at right, in this detail from a group photograph showing the cream of European physicists in the early years of the century. Courtesy of the American Institute of Physics.

Albert Einstein, 1879–1955. Library of Congress Collection.

COMMUNICATIONS PIONEERS—In 1921, David Sarnoff (front row, second from left) demonstrated RCA's experimental transoceanic communications station at New Brunswick, New Jersey, to a group of distinguished scientists. Later that year, RCA opened its "Radio Central"—the world's largest transmitting station—at Rocky Point, Long Island. The group, from left to right, included: first three men unidentified, David Sarnoff, Thomas J. Hayden, Dr. E. J. Berg, S. Benedict, Prof. Albert Einstein, Nikola Tesla, Dr. Charles P. Steinmetz, Dr. Alfred N. Goldsmith, A. Malsin, Dr. Irving Langmuir, Dr. Anthony W. Hull, E. B. Pillsbury, Dr. Saul Dushman, R. H. Ranger, Dr. G. A. Campbell, Ernst F. W. Alexanderson, last man unidentified. Courtesy of the David Sarnoff Research Center.

Thomas A. Edison, 1847–1931. *Upper left*: Edison at age of 14 years. *Upper right*: Edison in April 1878 when he demonstrated his phonograph to President Hayes and members of Congress in Washington, D.C. *Lower left*: Edison examining phonograph record with microscope in 1921. *Lower right*: Edison in his laboratory in 1906. Library of Congress Collection.

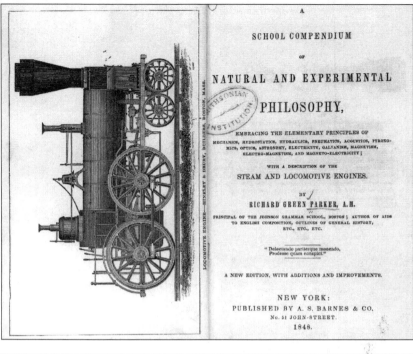

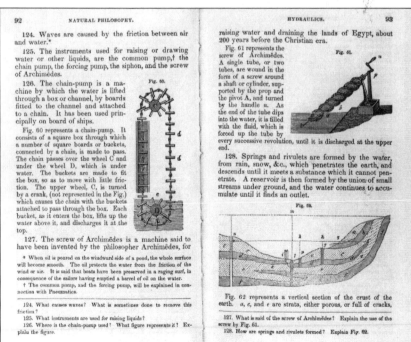

Top: Title page of the 1848 edition of Parker's *School Compendium*, the grammar-school science textbook given to Edison by his parents when he was nine years old. The boy had shown great interest in mechanical devices. In his inscription on the flyleaf of the copy he presented to Henry Ford for his museum, Edison wrote: "Parkers Philosophy was the first book in science that I had when a boy 9 years old. I picked [it] out as it was the first one I could understand." Inscription transcribed from facsimile, Fig. 1, Aaron, et al., "Famous Persons," in *J. Learning Disabilities*, 1988. *Bottom*: Sample pages from Parker's *School Compendium*, so much admired by Edison, show profuse illustration with brief text, notes, and questions. From Parker, *Compendium*, 1848.

Top left: Nikola Tesla, 1856–1943. Library of Congress Collection.

Top right: Statue of Nikola Tesla at Niagara Falls, New York, near the site of the hydroelectric power plant that first employed Tesla's alternating current system. Photograph, Thomas G. West.

Left: Tesla quietly reading at his Colorado Springs laboratory while several million volts discharge over his head. A time exposure exaggerates the effect. The sound could be heard ten miles away. Courtesy of the Burndy Library Collection.

The Deluge. Courtesy of the Windsor Castle Collection. Windsor Castle, Royal Library. ©1990. Her Majesty Queen Elizabeth II. The inventor of the term "fractals," mathematician Benoit B. Mandelbrot, explains that Leonardo da Vinci's close observation of nature in *The Deluge* brings the viewer to "the threshold of fractals." According to Mandelbrot: "This is one of many drawings in which Leonardo represented water flow as the superposition of eddies of many diverse sizes. Awareness of this eddy structure entered science belatedly, becoming partly formalized by Lewis F. Richardson in the 1920's into the 'scaling' view of the nature of turbulence. However, this view promptly drifted into a search for formulas, losing all geometric flavor, and also (this may not be a coincidence!) proving of limited effectiveness. The theory expounded in this book allows a return of geometry into the study of turbulence, and shows that many other fields of science are very analogous geometrically and can be handled by related techniques." From Mandelbrot, *Fractal Geometry*, 1977 (1983), pp. C2, C3. These same *Deluge* drawings have more recently been "put into motion" in a short film using computer "image-flow" techniques." From Whitney and Sims, "Excerpts," in *Conference Proceedings, SIGGRAPH 89*, 1989.

Mirror writing sample, with sketch, from the notebooks of Leonardo da Vinci. *Codex Atlanticus*, folio 332 recto-b. In Leonardo's notebooks and journals, nearly everything is in mirror image. As with books printed in Chinese, Japanese, or Arabic, his first page starts at what in the West is the end of the book. As in the drawings above, the images and course of discussion are mirrored as well. The beam ends are labeled, from right to left—a, b, c, d, e, f. Again from right to left, each beam is halved in length and is shown to be decreasingly deflected by a doubling of the weight—8, 16, 32. In translation, Leonardo's text is: "If *ab* bends 1/8 of its length for a weight of 8, *cd* if it is, as I believe, twice as strong as *ab*, will not bend 1/8 of its length for a lesser weight than 16, since it is half the length of *ab*, and likewise, *ef*, being half the length of *cd*, will be twice as strong and will sag 1/8 of its length for 32 weights. It should be kept in mind here that beam *cd*, being twice as strong as *ab*, will not bend 1/8 of its length under twice the load of *ab*, but will bend precisely 1/16." Uccelli, "Structures," in *Leonardo*, 1956.

The town of Amboise from a drawing by Leonardo da Vinci. One writer notes: "Those who have seen the place from across the Loire will only recognise this drawing if they look at it in a mirror; for it is done by the left-handed Leonardo, from right to left, just like his handwriting, so that what he saw on his left appears in his drawing on our right." Cook, *Curves of Life*, 1914.

Far left: Leonardo da Vinci was inclined to draw many views in his investigations, whether in science or art, apparently to record ("in several aspects") the full, three-dimensional form taking shape in his mind. In planning one piece of sculpture, Leonardo sketched it "from fully nineteen points of view." From Venturi, "Drawings," in *Leonardo,* 1956. In the sketches of the skeleton trunk and limbs, Leonardo provides five views on one page—back, right side, front, lower front, lower side left (with right leg brought forward for clarity). *Anat. Ms. A,* folio 13 r. In a similar fashion, modern physicians and scientists attempt to visualize structures or data with computer-generated slices from different points of view or with moving views of whole volumes.

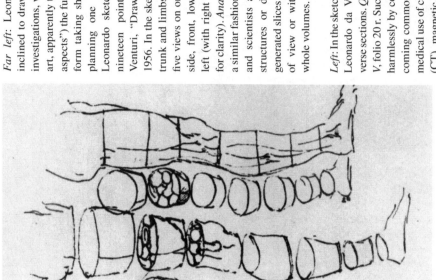

Left: In the sketches of the lower limb, Leonardo da Vinci provides transverse sections. *Quaderni di Anatomia V,* folio 20 r. Such sections, generated harmlessly by computer, are now becoming common with the increased medical use of computer tomography (CT) magnetic resonance imaging (MRI) of internal body parts.

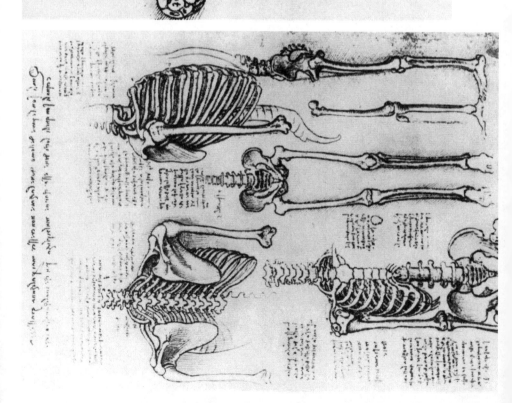

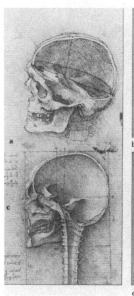

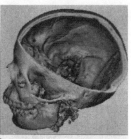

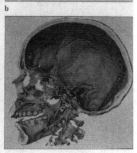

Modern researchers in scientific visualization techniques are very much aware that many of their problems and their solutions were anticipated some five hundred years ago by the investigations of Leonardo da Vinci. "A visualization by multiple surfaces and cuts is very well suited to locating and measuring objects. Transparent visualization lacks this property, which is critical for clinical practice. And shouldn't there be a reason Leonardo da Vinci, who was an expert on human anatomy and a genius in visualization, did not use transparency?" At left are "Leonardo da Vinci's famous drawings of a human head [a and c], together with analogous views of a 2,600-year-old mummy [b and d] generated from two hundred computer tomograms using gray-level gradient shading." From Tiede, Hoehne, et al., "Medical 3D-Rendering," in *IEEE Computer Graphics*, 1990, p. 51 and Fig. 12, p. 52. Courtesy Karl Heinz Hoehne, University of Hamburg, Germany.

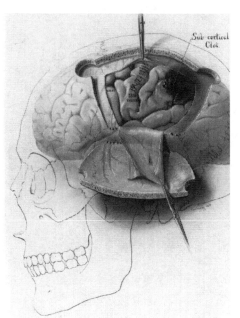

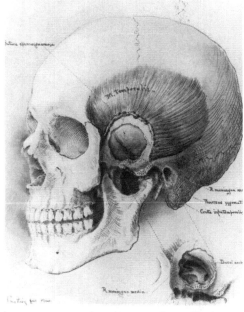

Left: Dr. Harvey Cushing, an extraordinarily skillful neurosurgeon and teacher, was also a gifted artist, but he had life-long difficulties with spelling. Shown here is "A Human Craniotomy." This is "one of Dr. Cushing's own drawings showing a brain clot and motor area (on which he has indicated the foci governing movement in certain parts of the body). The inner covering of the brain (dura mater) is held back by the two clamps." From Thompson, *Harvey Cushing: Surgeon, Author, Artist*, 1981. Photograph, courtesy of the Harvey Cushing/John Hay Whitney Medical Library, Yale University.

Right: Drawing by Harvey Cushing, signed and dated 1900, showing a skull with middle meningeal artery in two stages of a surgical procedure. Courtesy of the Harvey Cushing/John Hay Whitney Medical Library, Yale University.

Top left: Winston Churchill and Albert Einstein at Chartwell in the 1930s. Courtesy of Curtis Brown on behalf of Mary Soames. Copyright the Mary Soames Collection.

Bottom left: Churchill painting at the Villa Choisi in 1946. The Broadwater Collection, Churchill College Cambridge. Courtesy of Curtis Brown on behalf of Winston S. Churchill, MP. Peter Lofts Photography.

Center: Churchill at Portsmouth airfield, 1913. Press Association photo. Library of Congress Collection.

Above: Winston Spencer Churchill, 1874–1965. Photograph September 1941. Library of Congress Collection.

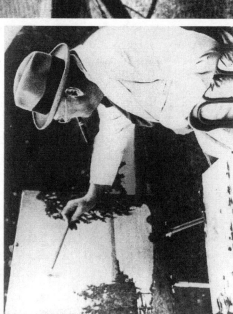

Top left: William Butler Yeats, 1865–1939. Photograph, Alice Boughton. Library of Congress Collection.

Top right: Patton, known as a brilliant and innovative commander, also cultivated a warrior mask with oversized stars of rank, impeccable dress, ivory-handled pistols, and his studied scowling face. Library of Congress Collection.

Left: General George S. Patton, 1885–1945. In battle helmet, reviewing troops of the II Army Corps south of El Guottar, Tunisia, March 1943. Library of Congress Collection.

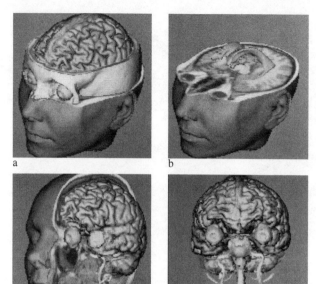

a b

c d

Computerized scientific visualization techniques are used with magnetic resonance data to "cut away" tissue in any desired manner, looking for a tumor inside the head of a living patient. "Different views of a head generated from 128 MR [magnetic resonance] images. The skin, bone, ventricle . . . and tumor . . . [behind the patient's left eye in c and d] are shaded using gray-level gradient shading." From Tiede, Hoehne, et al., "Medical 3D-Rendering," in *IEEE Computer Graphics*, 1990, Fig 11, p. 51. Courtesy Karl Heinz Hoehne, University of Hamburg, Germany.

Above: The graphical presentation of the mathematically generated "Mandelbrot set" may be seen as a "snowman" with a "skewer" running through its main rounded sections. Note that the "buds" on the sides of the "snowman" are emerging duplicates of itself, the continual self-duplication so characteristic of fractal images. The "snowman" is actually the empty space enclosed by the endlessly complex and irregular fractal curve. Although now known as the Mandelbrot set, the curve was called by Mandelbrot the "μ-map." From Mandelbrot, *Fractal Geometry of Nature*, 1977 (1983), bottom, plate 188, p. 188. Courtesy Benoit B. Mandelbrot.

III. TABLE OF CONTENTS

Left: Table of Contents from the *Guide* for *The Theorem of Pythagoras* videotape showing stills from the computer graphics used to describe a variety of proofs and related concepts. From Apostal, Gordon, and Blinn, *Project Mathematics!*, 1988.

9

IMAGES, COMPUTERS, AND MATHEMATICS

Mathematics is many things. It is measurement and counting. It is concepts, symbols, and rules learned in primary school—addition, subtraction, multiplication, division, fractions, decimals, and percents learned between the ages of six and twelve. Basic material. It is a few really profound, elementary concepts, although it may not seem so, but mostly it is repetition and rote memorization and practice.

In the beginning, it is learning a few simple rules and symbols and memorizing the results of many different combinations of these few rules and symbols—the "math facts": 7 and 9 are 16; 7 from 9 is 2; 7 times 9 is 63; 7 divided by 9 is less than 1 and is hard (unless you happen to have learned and can still remember that it is a decimal point followed by a string of 7s). Whether carpenter, clerk, shopkeeper, accountant, corporate rector, or Senate budget committee member, one needs very little more than this to perform well to the end of one's life. This is as true now as it was four hundred years ago.

Some may learn, in high school or college, some algebra, geometry, trigonometry, or calculus. But these are not often used. For those who study them, these are mainly rites of passage. For most, it is training the intellect rather than acquiring tools useful throughout life. Eventually, for others, the more advanced courses may be primarily obstacles, intended to weed out those who cannot do it or will not do it, a useful way of determining who is serious and really bright, or so it is thought. Most of the material is rarely used in business or accounting or law or medicine, except in certain small, specialized groups where the use of certain specific forms is common and routine. Of course, the advanced material is used a great deal by some physicists, statisticians, geneticists, and engineers, but these are relatively small groups. So far, anyway, the mathematics that most really need is generally quite uninteresting (in itself) and elementary in the extreme.

But there is an entirely different side to mathematics, one that we glimpse only faintly in the best books, articles, television programs, and films that attempt to explain mathematics to a general audience. In fact, although it may not be clear to us, at its base mathematics is mainly a study of patterns.

A MATHEMATICS OF PATTERNS

Mathematics is a way of looking at and talking about the way plants grow, the way a bridge is stressed, the way music flows. It involves some commonly agreed-upon ideas. It involves a chain of disciplined thought. It involves an orderly body of basic concepts with symbols, rules, and conventions for their use. It can be very difficult. It can be tedious, the way a strictly logical and careful argument can be tedious. But at its core there are just a few very simple ideas. All the vast complexity is like the complexity of nature, only the unfolding of the consequences and the interaction of a few simple ideas.

Surveying current developments, some observers point out that it is only fairly recently that the real nature of the discipline is coming to be fully appreciated. Fundamental developments during the last few decades have changed mathematics and mathematicians' views of themselves. According to one professional mathematician, Lynn Arthur Steen, writing in *Science*,

> Mathematics is often defined as the science of space and number, as the discipline rooted in geometry and arithmetic. Although the diversity of modern mathematics has always exceeded this definition, it was not until the recent resonance of computers and mathematics that a more apt definition became fully evident.

Mathematics is the science of patterns. The mathematician seeks patterns in number, in space, in science, in computers, and in imagination. Mathematical theories explain the relations among patterns. . . . Patterns suggest other patterns, often yielding patterns of patterns. . . .

To the extent that mathematics is the science of patterns, computers change not so much the nature of the discipline as its scale: computers are to mathematics what telescopes and microscopes are to science. They have increased by a millionfold the portfolio of patterns investigated by mathematical scientists. As this portfolio grows, so do applications of mathematics and the cross-linkages among subdisciplines of mathematics.

Because of computers, we see that mathematical discovery is like scientific discovery. It begins with the search for pattern in the data—perhaps in numbers, but often in geometric or algebraic structures. Generalization leads to abstraction, to patterns in the mind. Theories emerge as patterns of patterns, and significance is measured by the degree to which patterns in one area link to patterns in other areas.[1]

Some writers have observed the "uncanny" ability of mathematics to supply the needed tools and formulas whenever these are required by new discoveries and developments in science, as Riemann's non-Euclidean geometry was awaiting the needs of Einstein's revolutionary theories.[2] The basis of this ability, Steen has suggested, "may be that the patterns investigated by mathematicians are all the patterns that there are."[3]

Consequently, mathematics is more clearly seen today by some professional observers of the discipline as the study of patterns. No longer is it seen as mainly the domain of numbers and rigorous logical proof, with just a little geometry left over on the side for historical interest.[4] The long-term trend is reversing itself as geometry and related visual-spatial forms move to the center of interest once again.

Historically, geometry, the study of space, has been one of the major pillars of core mathematics. For various reasons, its role in the mathematical curriculum has declined over the past 20 years, so that even those with university degrees in mathematics often have little acquaintance with geometry beyond an archaic and typically rigid encounter with Euclidean proof in high school geometry. In sharp contrast to this curricular decline is the renaissance of geometry in research mathematics. In a very real sense, geometry is once again playing a central role on the stage of mathematics, much as it did in the Greek period.[5]

Steen points out that an indicator of this reversal of trend is that two out of the three 1986 Fields Medals (the Nobel Prizes of mathematics) went to researchers who made advances in mathematics related to geometry. It is also noteworthy that both medals were awarded for lines of research originally based on the work of people with whom we have become familiar—Henri Poincaré and James Clerk Maxwell, both of whom, as we have seen, had a strong visual and geometric orientation throughout their lives.[6]

REVERSAL OF A TREND: A MATHEMATICS OF IMAGES

Apparently, the trend is changing once again and the long drift away from visual-spatial approaches has begun to reverse itself. In time, these changes may affect not only the kinds of work that are done but also the kinds of people (with particular kinds of minds) who will find the discipline an attractive career, or even, perhaps, an enduring passion. As we saw earlier, in the case of the statistician Karl Pearson and his son, E. S. Pearson, some people are very good with symbols and rules and their manipulation, while other people are very good with mental images and their imaginative transformation. A few people are good with both. As the reversal proceeds, a new group of primarily visual thinkers may come to the fore once again—focusing on a mathematics of images—whether or not they have trouble with certain computational and other basic skills that are easy for others. As we have seen, in disciplines such as physics and mathematics, really original solutions to novel problems often (though not always) seem to come from those who work in the more fluid and malleable medium of images. This is apparent in the writings of the mathematician Jacques Hadamard.

> I insist that words are totally absent from my mind when I really think. . . . Even after reading or hearing a question, every word disappears at the very moment I am beginning to think it over; words

do not reappear in my consciousness before I have accomplished or given up the research . . . and I fully agree with Schopenhauer when he writes, "Thoughts die the moment they are embodied by words."

I think it is also essential to emphasize that I behave in this way not only about words, but even about algebraic signs. I use them when dealing with easy calculations; but whenever the matter looks more difficult, they become too heavy a baggage for me. I use concrete representations, but of a quite different nature.[7]

According to Hadamard, some teachers use pictures of circles (now commonly called "Venn" diagrams) to help show the properties of a logical argument such as a syllogism. Each circle shows a class, group, or category of things containing an unspecified number of elements. Sometimes the circles overlap; sometimes they are separate. Hadamard explains that he uses an analogous representation in his own mental images, but does not use the circles themselves. Rather, he uses something like a cloud of points. In his mind's eye he sees "spots of an undefined form, no precise shape being necessary for me to think of spots lying inside or outside of each other."

Images are being used here as representations of logical processes, not of spatial relationships. The spatial form, however, seems to function as a kind of analogy, converting the problem into a form that grants Hadamard greater latitude in processing and that is less prone to error:

> To consider a slightly less simple case, let us take an elementary and well-known proof in arithmetic, the theorem to be proved being: "The sequel of prime numbers is unlimited." I shall repeat the successive steps of the classic proof of the theorem, writing, opposite each of them, the corresponding mental picture in my mind. We have, for instance, to prove that there is a prime greater than 11.

STEPS IN THE PROOF	MY MENTAL PICTURES
I consider all primes from 2 to 11, say 2, 3, 5, 7, 11.	I see a confused mass.
I form their product, $2 \times 3 \times 5 \times 7 \times 11 = N$	N being a rather large number, I imagine a point rather remote from the confused mass.

I increase that product by 1, say N plus 1.	I see a second point a little beyond the first.
That number, if not a prime, must admit of a prime divisor, which is the required number.	I see a place somewhere between the confused mass and the first point.

It is not necessary to follow the precise steps of this proof. It is very important, however, to be aware of the distinctly different mental images that accompany Hadamard's mental processes. According to Hadamard, these images are vague, not really representing the precise concepts essential to the exercise—giving precision to such ideas would alter them and cause further confusion. The idea of undesirable consequences from an excess of precision is unexpected and may be especially noteworthy. What purpose, then, is served by such a mechanism? Hadamard explains: "I need it in order to have a simultaneous view of all elements of the argument, to hold them together, to make a whole of them—in short, to achieve that synthesis which we spoke of in the beginning of this section and give the problem its physiognomy."[8] The mechanism is not intended, then, to provide precision, but to provide a view of the whole, where, presumably, a view of less than the whole would lead to distortion and misunderstanding and false conclusions.

Hadamard's observation is especially instructive because of the terms used. He needs the mechanism to form a "simultaneous view," holding the parts of the problem "together" in order to form a "whole." The mechanism is needed to form the "synthesis" and provide for the problem its "physiognomy," that is, its face or countenance. All these terms refer to those aspects of visual modes of thought that appear to lie beyond the analogy of mere sight. They refer to the ability to see or consider all the parts and their relations to each other at the same time, in order to perceive something about the nature of the thing as a whole that is not otherwise apparent. The perfect analogy is the face, that most subtle assemblage of feature, proportional size, relative position, and subtle movement from which most of us can read so much. Here the talents of the actor and the sculptor and the mathematician might well overlap. We may speculate that all may be using similar, right-hemisphere mechanisms to achieve very different results in very different arenas. There is a similarity of function that seems immediately apparent. Indeed, perhaps an important part of the learning process is not one of absorbing information so much as it is of adapting a few basic processes to very different uses. Our minds are not computers. But computers give us a valuable set of models and metaphors with which to approach a new understanding of what may be going on in our own brains.

We can see a parallel in current research into face recognition. It is a common feature, we are told, of left-hemisphere processing of faces to focus on one aspect (as a moustache) and to assert an identification with great certainty, although it may often be wrong. In contrast, the typical right-hemisphere approach will often take longer and will be more tentative (considering many parts in relation to the whole) but is more frequently correct in its identifications.[9] If the recognition of solutions to problems is, in fact, similar to the recognition of faces (in at least some significant proportion of cases), then we can begin to see why Hadamard's reliance on a view of the whole, even if vague, is seen as so important. And we can also see how, possibly, some very poor judgments can be made by apparently very capable people, full of certainty and self confidence.

THE IMPORTANCE OF GEOMETRY; BRONOWSKI'S TRIANGLES, EINSTEIN'S PROOF

In the 1950s E. S. Pearson spoke of the increasing disinterest in the visual or "geometric" approach to statistics among his students and colleagues. It simply was not of much use to them. They all seemed to see things differently and to think in different ways. Writing of Maxwell, another modern observer noted the importance of geometry and lamented its eclipse in recent times. "Maxwell's starting point in mathematics was Euclidean geometry. Euclid is now so out of fashion that few people know the excitement of his intellectual rigor, but a discipline that could stir three young minds as powerful as those of Maxwell, Bertrand Russell, and Einstein deserves respect."[10]

In his *Autobiographical Notes*, Einstein gives us some idea of why he so loved geometry. As a child he was first deeply impressed with the mystery of a magnetic compass. Then,

at the age of twelve I experienced a second wonder of a totally different nature—in a little book dealing with Euclidean plane geometry, which came into my hands at the beginning of a school year.
Here were assertions . . . that—though by no means evident—could
nevertheless be proved with such certainty that any doubt appeared
to be out of the question. This lucidity and certainty made an indescribable impression upon me. That axioms had to be accepted
unproved did not disturb me. In any case it was quite sufficient for
me if I could base proofs on propositions whose validity appeared to
me beyond doubt. . . . For anyone who experiences it for the first
time, it is marvelous enough that man is capable at all of reaching
such a degree of certainty and purity in pure thinking as the Greeks
showed us for the first time to be possible in geometry."[11]

The famous theorem of Pythagoras (which was almost universally
known in the West, until comparatively recently, as proposition 47 in
Book I of Euclid's *Elements*) is usually taught in schools today by
using an algebraic equation, which, in words, is, "The square of the
hypotenuse of a right triangle is equivalent to the sum of the squares
of the two legs."[12]

According to the mathematician Jacob Bronowski, the theorem is
believed to have been demonstrated in an entirely different way in
ancient Greece, by similarity of triangles in a spatial, geometric formulation.[13] In this formulation, the theorem can be demonstrated by
positioning and repositioning flat, cut-out triangular pieces on a flat
surface, showing manually, by employing a kind of visual logic, that
the area of a square made with sides equal to the hypotenuse of a right
triangle is the same as the total area of two squares made from the
sides of the right triangle. The visual demonstration is intuitively
obvious and sufficient. No algebraic symbols or calculations are
required. In Bronowski's words, "We do not need any calculation. A
small game, such as children and mathematicians play, will reveal
more than calculation."[14]

When Einstein first encountered Euclidean geometry he immediately tried to prove the Pythagorean theorem on his own. "I
remember that an uncle told me about the Pythagorean theorem
before the holy geometry booklet had come into my hands. After
much effort I succeeded in 'proving' this theorem on the basis of the
similarity of triangles."[15]

Einstein's experience with geometry suggests two things. The first is that certain minds will respond in an immediate and powerful way to experiences that awaken faculties that may be virtually "wired in." Einstein's propensity to take a certain approach, even from the earliest days, may be another strong indicator of his powerful visual predisposition, apparently so similar to Faraday's and Maxwell's.

The second possibility is that, in many cases, there may be at least two entirely different ways of approaching certain problems (the logical-mathematical-algebraic and the visual-spatial—although there may be a number of variations within each basic approach).

The commonly used modern formulation of the Pythagorean theorem verifies its truth by converting it into an algebraic form. In contrast, the ancient method confirms the same spatial truth by spatial means. In the usual modern method we are trained to speak not of the area of the shape but of a line length squared. (On one level, of course, these statements are exactly equivalent; but on another level they could not be more different.) This instance may show, once again, how much the modern view is dominated by a one-sided approach. We cannot even properly discuss spatial things in spatial terms, but must convert them to algebraic terms.[16]

Since this other, more spatial approach has been so little used, we might suppose that the potential for new developments and new discoveries may be comparatively large. Or, putting it another way, we might suppose that those naturally more attuned to the spatial approach would have much to give if the conventional systems were modified to permit their contributions. Of course, the professional mathematician may point out, quite rightly, that at the higher levels of mathematics there are many branches and many of these always have had strongly spatial orientations. We might reply, however, that this variety at the top is of little consequence if most of those with a strong spatial orientation are eliminated by the educational system at the lower levels. It is one thing for educators and legislators to be concerned about students who cannot pass calculus. It is quite another thing to be concerned about a new calculus of space and time that has not yet been developed because the persons best suited to develop it never make it past Algebra I.

In the history of mathematics there are many examples of old, tedious methodologies crumbling in the face of fresh, elegant simplicity—sometimes when complex algebraic or arithmetic methods are abandoned for simpler and more direct diagrammatic methods.

One example is provided from the life of the French mathematician Gaspard Monge (1746–1818). He was known as a "born geometer" with "an unsurpassed gift for visualizing complicated space-relations." During his training as an army engineer, one of his tasks was to design fortifications so that no part of the works would be exposed to direct enemy fire. At the time, the conventional method for resolving the problem "demanded endless arithmetic." Consequently, when Monge completed his assignment in record time, his superior officer was incredulous. "'I can believe in a great facility in calculation, but not in miracles!'" But, as Monge explained, he had not done any calculation—because he had not used arithmetic. What he had used came, in time, to be called "descriptive geometry"—the basis of modern mechanical drawing and mechanical engineering. With his new method, fortification problems that had been "nightmares before—sometimes solved only by tearing down what had been built and beginning all over again—were now as simple as ABC." Indeed, the method was thought to be such an important innovation that it was kept a "jealously guarded military secret" for fifteen years.[17]

Another example is more recent—the story of Marjorie Rice, the housewife who revolutionized at least one field of mathematics by applying unconventional, visually oriented methods in place of the conventional, tedious, symbolic methods. Until recently, the study of "tiling the plane" (that is, the study of many-sided flat shapes that fit together like tiles on a bathroom floor) involved problems that traditionally "consisted merely of rows of symbols: numerals; English, Greek and Hebrew letters; compound characters made by stacking up bars and dots and tildes—enough symbols, all told, to give a typographer nightmares." Surprisingly, even in such a transparently visual area of study as tiling, diagrams were never used. These were forbidden by the "deductivist orthodoxy" that had insisted (since the nineteenth century) on symbols instead of pictures or diagrams. And so long as the deductivist orthodoxy held sway, "there was little room in mathematical discourse for diagrams or for arguments that appealed to common sense or intuition." But Rice, using her own methods ("a synthesis of pictures resembling hieroglyphics and an arcane code"), was able to break new ground in what was thought to be a closed and completed area of study. In 1978, her findings were reported in *Mathematics Magazine* by a professional mathematician. It is now clear that "Rice's methodology . . . mirrors a shift in the way mathematics is being done." Just at the time that Rice was "so vividly demonstrating the advantages of pictoral reasoning and argument, professional mathematicians were rediscovering them." The change has greatly influenced several areas of study. "This renaissance in the use of diagrams is seen throughout the mushrooming field known as combinatorics—not just in such inherently visual problems as tiling but even in problems that have no obvious connection to geometry."[18]

ALTERNATIVE APPROACHES TO MATHEMATICS, VISIONS OF THE WHOLE

Professors lament the sad state of mathematics education and legislators worry about the effects upon the nation's future technical and economic competitiveness. Yet, when one considers conventional modes of teaching a basic higher mathamatics course such as calculus, it would appear that many teachers have paid less attention to innovation in instruction than they have paid to their role as keepers of the gate to the technical professions. This problem is widely recognized. At a National Academy of Sciences meeting on the problem held in 1987, for example, "A strong mood of self-criticism prevailed . . . with both the calculus curriculum and the quality of teaching being questioned. There appeared to be a consensus that the teaching of calculus has been focused for too long on routine problem solving. New approaches are needed, for example, to come to terms with the use of sophisticated hand-held calculators and computers and, particularly, to give students a better conceptual understanding of the subject." One of the speakers noted that, "The 'national spotlight is on calculus' because of the 'linkage between mathematics and economic growth.' Calculus 'must become a pump rather than a filter in the pipeline.'"[19]

It appears that the field could be responsive to some fresh approaches, including the more visual approach we have been describing. But there is a further possible advantage to this approach. The more visual approach to mathematics may have the double advantage of being the common language of two important groups—

the many highly creative persons who may have extreme difficulty with the conventional approach, and the general public, which ordinarily would know virtually nothing of the subject. This new way might serve as a bridge, whereas traditional mathematical training seems often to have been more of a barrier. Of course, in many areas of mathematics the visual approach will probably not work or will work with indifferent success. We should not expect it to work well in those parts of mathematics where there is little visual content, directly or by analogy, or in those areas where visual intuition is likely to be misleading. It should not be expected to work well with students who have little natural visual intuition. It should not be expected to work well where the teachers have little facility with it. And it should not be expected to work well where the entire educational and career path is controlled by those who are strong in the traditional skills of symbol manipulation but weak in visual abilities and have little or no appreciation for a visual approach in any area.[20]

It may, however, be expected to work well in many areas where it has never been tried before, or where the approach was dropped long ago. It may be expected to work for those (such as Faraday) who would otherwise have given up all mathematics long before, some of whom may be able to make particularly valuable contributions if only because their contributions are so original and surprising. It may be expected to work well with those (such as Maxwell and Einstein) who can master the conventional approaches (with greater or lesser success) but whose native abilities seem to make them far more productive in the visual mode. Also, it may be expected to work in those institutional environments where truly innovative results are seen as far more important than the preservation of traditional approaches.

MAKING THE HARD EASY

Much of human progress is based on taking hard things and making them easy. Over and over again this process is opposed, sometimes for the best of reasons. Many strive with righteous resolve to avoid the erosion of high standards and traditional values. Others strive to avoid change primarily because their positions are based on keeping the old things hard so no one will be able to do the hard things without their help.

Before the adaptation of the "Hindu-Arabic" number system into Europe in the fifteenth century, we are told, even the simplest calculations had to be done by highly trained and highly paid specialists who knew all the tricks and special procedures required to make the old system work. But with the new system of numbers, the hard became easy, and every corner merchant could do what only the specialists had been able to do before. In *Capitalism and Arithmetic: The New Math of the 15th Century*, Frank Swetz shows how established interests succeeded in delaying change for hundreds of years.

> The new numerals had been known in Europe from about 1000 A.D. yet they had not been universally accepted for use. Computing and techniques of arithmetic still centered around the manipulation of counters and recording one's results with Roman numerals. There was a certain social status and prestige associated with the use of a counting table. . . . In a very true sense, the use of Roman numerals and counting boards had become an institution, one vested literally in the hands of the select few. Since the use of algorithms associated with the Hindu-Arabic numerals, if popularized, could be easily learned and performed without elaborate equipment, its knowledge presented a definite threat to the well-being and livelihood of established computers; therefore it was resisted. . . . Even in Italy, where a heightened sense of mathematical awareness existed, acceptance of the Hindu-Arabic system was slow in coming. . . . In 1299 . . . the City Council of Florence required that accounting book entries be in Roman numerals. In 1348, the University of Padua required that lists of its books have their prices affixed in Roman numerals—"non per cifras, sed per literas claras" (not by figures, but by clear letters). Ostensibly, such regulations were intended to reduce instances of fraud, as it was felt the new numerals were vulnerable to tampering [such as changing a zero into a 9 or a 6]. . . . Legal courts gave precedence to documents using Roman numerals over those bearing the new numerical symbols. In some instances, reckoning masters were simply forbidden to use Hindu-Arabic numerals. . . . But, despite the sanctions against their use, the Hindu-Arabic numbers gradually became accepted and admired for their recording and computational efficiency by the merchant houses of Italy and other countries.[21]

The issues vary, but the familiar pattern of resistance to change—to making the hard things easy—remains. This was the way of the medieval guild: you cannot work bronze or iron without our secret knowledge. This was the way of the priesthood: you cannot pray to God without our intercession. Until recently, this was also the way of the computer professional: you cannot instruct the machine to do your manifold and complex calculations without our hard-won programming skills.

Just as the guilds and priesthoods gave ground over time, so too modern technology is yielding access to its benefits. The capabilities that were a wonder only a few years ago—employing the largest, most expensive machines, the most highly trained programmers, and costly, custom-designed software, are now everywhere available with comparatively inexpensive machines and off-the-shelf software. We may wonder, then, if it is possible, in the not-too-distant future, that even some of the more obscure areas of mathematics might be opened up to an unprecedentedly large audience through a combination of visual approach and the widespread use of powerful, graphics-based personal computers. The personal computer could be used to teach and monitor largely individual courses of study, using a variety of visual and non-visual teaching approaches, each tailored and selected according to the learning style of the individual student. The teacher's role would change, but would probably greatly increase in quality and effectiveness. Such a system might be more like the classical or medieval tutor-student relationship, far different from the mass-production classroom or lecture theater of nineteenth-century origin. With the computer one could also work quite differently, focusing on new forms of visual analysis, detecting new patterns by creating moving images of data. The computer would also do all the tedious calculations and record keeping.

Some aspects of this approach to mathematics instruction are currently receiving serious attention. Several educational reform movements are trying to persuade traditional school systems to focus more on higher thinking skills and to incorporate calculators and computers into current programs. Two items from a recent set of proposals are of particular interest.

Only tests that measure higher order thinking skills should be used to assess mathematics. Teachers will teach whatever is required to enable their students to do well on assessment tests, and textbooks will be written to match the test objectives. Too often today's assessments dictate a curriculum filled with rote calculation and mimicry mathematics.

School mathematics should use computers and calculators. Computers now compute, so students should learn to think. More important, students need to learn at every grade level when to use their heads and when to use their machines.[22]

In the early Middle Ages it was common for only a tiny number of people to learn the skill of reading. Then, to be able to read without reading out loud or without moving one's lips was considered a wondrous achievement. In the midst of today's great problems in education, we might wonder whether what is now considered sophisticated mathematics would, over time, become quite commonly understood by virtually every educated person. While many creative dyslexics were on the wrong side of the long drive for universal literacy, they may be on the right side of a coming drive for widespread, visual-based sophistication in mathematics, a mathematics increasingly seen as more pattern recognition than symbol manipulation and rule memorization. It seems to fly in the face of common sense and hard-earned professional experience, but perhaps it is possible to leapfrog over part of the conventional curriculum and teach mathematics as, primarily, a language of patterns rather than a set of memorized facts, rigid rules, symbols, and logic. Of course, the rigorous part must come in sooner or later, but you do not have to start that way—full mastery of rote skills need not be the necessary prerequisite for learning all higher skills. Teachers need to be aware that some students who make the most errors at earlier stages will be capable, in time, of surpassing all their classmates and their teachers as well.[23]

Teachers often point out that the study of mathematics is sequential and cumulative. Doubtless they are right to a large extent, especially within the conventional curriculum. But there may be another way, one that comes to the same final destination by a different route.

As Faraday said of science study in a letter to a young student, one should start wherever one likes. If one keeps working, one will necessarily come around to the other parts in time. Perhaps we could as easily start with the study of space in Moorish building tiles as with Algebra I.

VISUAL MATHEMATICS AND CHAOS

It is encouraging that a complementary approach is apparent in at least one progressive movement in higher mathematics education. In the foreword to "The Visual Mathematics Library" editor Ralph Abraham declares,

> Our history shows the importance of the diffusion of mathematical ideas, and their effects upon the subsequent development of the sciences and technology. Today, there is a cultural resistance to mathematical ideas. Due to the widespread impression that mathematics is difficult to understand, or to a structural flaw in our educational system, or perhaps to other mechanisms, mathematics has become an esoteric subject. Intellectuals of all sorts now carry on their discourse in nearly total ignorance of mathematical ideas. We cannot help thinking that this is a critical situation, as we hold the view that mathematical ideas are essential for the future evolution of our society.
>
> The absence of visual representations in the curriculum may be part of the problem, contributing to mathematical illiteracy, and to the math-avoidance reflex. This series is based on the idea that mathematical concepts may be communicated easily in a format which combines visual, verbal, and symbolic representations in tight coordination. It aims to attack ignorance with an abundance of visual representations.
>
> In sum, the purpose of this series is to encourage the diffusion of mathematical ideas, by presenting them *visually*.[24]

One of the main focuses of this series is the new science of "chaos." This new approach to problems of extremely complex dynamic—systems the study of patterns that lie hidden under the apparent randomness of very large systems—involves an intense preoccupation with visual images of data that cannot be analyzed effectively unless they are so presented. According to James Gleick,

> Linking topology and dynamical systems is the possibility of using a shape to help visualize the whole range of behaviors of a system. For a simple system, the shape might be some kind of curved surface; for a complicated system, a manifold of many dimensions. A single point on such a surface represents the state of a system at an instant

frozen in time. As a system progresses through time, the point moves, tracing an orbit across this surface. Bending the shape a little corresponds to changing the system's parameters, making a fluid more viscous or driving a pendulum a little harder. Shapes that look roughly the same give roughly the same kinds of behavior. If you can visualize the shape, you can understand the system.[25]

This identification of a system's essence with a system's image or shape contributes in an important way to the argument we are trying to make. Thus, it seems that we have come a long way from the decline of the visual approach over the past fifty to a hundred years to the current resurgence of the visual approach to the center stage of research, in at least some areas. What is the reason for this change? In part the old ways—of simple, linear explanations and linear mathematics—for all their great success in certain areas work only to a certain extent and in certain circumstances. Ensuring that each part is functioning properly is not enough.

In many cases only the whole can provide the required information or indicate the important truths. To gain access to the whole it is necessary to give up reductionist ways of looking at things and find a new way of seeing. Sometimes the change is required by that which is studied. In one of Gleick's examples,

> One perplexing feature of fibrillation is that many of the heart's individual components can be working normally. Often the heart's pacemaking nodes continue to send out regular electrical ticks. Individual muscle cells respond properly. Each cell receives its stimulus, contracts, passes the stimulus on, and relaxes to wait for the next stimulus. In autopsy the muscle tissue may reveal no damage at all. That is one reason chaos experts believed that a new, global approach was necessary: the parts of a fibrillating heart seem to be working, yet the whole goes fatally awry. Fibrillation is a disorder of a complex system, just as mental disorders—whether or not they have chemical roots—are disorders of a complex system.[26]

Thus the need is seen for a broader scope, a global view, a new sense of the whole. As this need spreads into seemingly unrelated scientific fields, a long-term trend in science is being reversed—reductionism, the tendency to reduce every system to a sequence of elementary cause-and-effect relationships. "More and more [scientists] felt the compartmentalization of science as an impediment to their work. More and more felt the futility of studying parts in isolation from the whole. For them, chaos was the end of the reductionist program in science."[27]

POPULAR PRESENTATIONS AND ORDINARY LANGUAGE

For most people, mathematics is a most esoteric subject. Some mathematicians seem quite content to keep it esoteric. However, this was not the attitude of Maxwell or Faraday. Both men placed a great value on the ability to express mathematical ideas in ordinary language and to explain their results to ordinary people. A number of those we are dealing with were notably interested in popular explanations of their work: Einstein wrote several popular books explaining his theories; Poincaré was famous for his highly successful popular books on mathematics, philosophy of science, and creativity in the sciences; Karl Pearson gave regular popular lectures on statistics and other topics; and Faraday became famous for his annual Christmas lecture series designed for children and adults. According to Joseph Agassi, "In a letter to Maxwell [Faraday] expresses his admiration for the latter's ability to translate mathematical results into a language comprehensible to the experimenter. And Maxwell, the mathematical genius, always retained the feeling that there is an immense virtue in the ability to translate mathematical results into ordinary language."[28]

This view contrasts vividly with that of many specialists who could not imagine that anything they are doing would be of interest to or comprehensible to the general public. One modern lecturer on Faraday noted this attitude in a colleague. "An earlier professor of science in this University refused to give his inaugural lecture on the grounds that his subject, mathematics, could have no appeal to a general audience."[29]

This attitude is so very different from that of Faraday, Maxwell, Poincaré, Einstein, and others we are considering that one suspects that it is one major indicator of the contrasting mind-set of the limited, narrow specialist. Such a person may know his or her own small area quite well, but may be less likely to make an original contribution to the field, primarily because he or she can never see relationships with things outside the narrow specialty. Our more global thinkers—whatever their areas of real difficulty—rarely have this particular problem.

FARADAY'S ENDURING VISIONS WITHOUT MATHEMATICS

Maxwell was, in time, fully appreciated as a brilliant and original mathematician, even though he often took an approach that was out of the ordinary. He respected Faraday and the "mathematical" quality of his thought. Yet many professional scientists, even to this day, have tended to denigrate Faraday's accomplishments, primarily because of his "lack of mathematical culture," as one nineteenth-century scientist put it. However, Faraday's work was not totally devoid of mathematical content. According to Agassi,

> In his late memoirs Faraday presents his method of calculations. . . .
> He breaks his deductions into small simple tests; he shows that he has a simple technique of calculation. Yet he was not understood, and his results surprised people. Maxwell was the first who said that he found in Faraday's works a *mathematical* theory that he only translated into a symbolic language. . . .
> In his opening to his *Treatise* he said bluntly, "I perceived that his method of conceiving the phenomena was also a mathematical one, though not exhibited in the conventional form of mathematical symbols. . . . I translated what I considered to be Faraday's ideas into a mathematical form. . . ." Apart from the excessive humility, there is much truth in Maxwell's claim. I do not know why "2 × 2 = 4" impresses people more than "twice two equals four"; but so it is. . . . Faraday hated mathematical symbolism. His view was that you should calculate in your own way and give to the public an outline of your calculation in *ordinary* language to enable each person to repeat the calculation for himself and in his own way. I do not know how, with his deep aversion to symbolism, he succeeded in scrutinizing so many mathematical works of his time; but he made it clear in his writings that, once he got the idea, he translated it into his own language and proved the point to his own satisfaction.[30]

Faraday could deal with profound, fundamental mathematical concepts, but apparently he could not deal readily with the "basics." He had not acquired the habits of thought that would have been developed in a conventional mathematical education. However, according to Maxwell, this may have been a good thing.

> The method which Faraday employed in his researches consisted in a constant appeal to experiment as a means of testing the truth of his ideas, and a constant cultivation of ideas under the direct influence of experiment. In his published researches we find these ideas expressed in language which is all the better fitted for a nascent science, because it is somewhat alien from the style of physicists who have been accustomed to establish mathematical forms of thought. . . .
>
> It was perhaps for the advantage of science that Faraday, though thoroughly conscious of the fundamental forms of space, time and force, was not a professed mathematician. He was not tempted to enter into the many interesting researches in pure mathematics which his discoveries would have suggested if they had been exhibited in a mathematical form, and he did not feel called upon either to force his results into a shape acceptable to the mathematical taste of the time, or to express them in a form which mathematicians might attack. He was left at leisure to do his proper work, to coordinate his ideas with his facts, and to express them in natural untechnical language.
>
> It is mainly in the hope of making these ideas the basis of a mathematical method that I have undertaken this treatise.[31]

Even Maxwell, the master mathematician, could see that, sometimes, mathematics could stand in the way of understanding.

THE LIMITS OF NUMBERS: LORD KELVIN

Another case of mathematics standing in the way of understanding is that of William Thomson, Lord Kelvin, generally considered to be one of the great British physicists of the late nineteenth century. He was Maxwell's contemporary. Indeed, their families mingled in the same circles when they were growing up in Edinburgh. While Maxwell had been considered a bright student (after a slow start), he was nothing like the brilliant star that Kelvin had been as a child. Unlike Maxwell,

Kelvin had been an early achiever, "a true *Wunderkind*,"[32] a classic child prodigy—reading at two, attending and actively participating in his father's university mathematics lectures at ten, matriculating at university himself at twelve.[33] He is best known, and forever memorialized, by the temperature scale that uses his name, the scale that defines absolute zero (the temperature at which all molecular motion stops—273 degrees below zero Celsius) as its baseline.

Thomson rose to the apex of the scientific establishment of his time. He was given a life peerage by Queen Victoria in 1892, in his sixty-eighth year, hence "Lord Kelvin."[34] According to one biographer, "All over the world he came ultimately to be recognized as the greatest living scientific authority in almost all branches of physics. Every existing learned society sought to make him a Fellow."[35]

Kelvin's contemporaries thought his ability on a par with that of Sir Isaac Newton. He was buried at Westminster Abbey with full honors, near Newton's grave, in sharp contrast to Faraday, who insisted on the "simplest" burial possible, and to Maxwell, whose monumental achievements were not to be fully appreciated until many years after his untimely death at the age of forty-eight. "For William Thomson, who lived to the ripe old age of eighty-three, every honor that a scientist might hope for was showered on him, and the whole country seemed to mourn when he died on December 17, 1907."[36]

Despite his considerable scientific and professional achievements, however, Kelvin's reputation has continuously decreased since his death, in contrast to those of Faraday and Maxwell, whose reputations continue to grow in stature more than a century after their passing. Time has shown that Kelvin's work, while full of major achievements, is, in comparison with the greatest, still decidedly of lesser rank. He was "an extraordinarily influential figure in his time, and in some ways a paradigm of conventional, established scientific leadership."[37] However, today's historians of science observe that "despite the enormous range of his achievements, Kelvin did not quite attain the intellectual pinnacles that [Faraday and Maxwell] reached."[38]

In an oft-quoted statement Kelvin declared, "When you can measure what you are speaking about, and express it in numbers, you know something about it. But when you cannot—your knowledge is of a meagre and unsatisfactory kind."[39] Kelvin's position reflects the reverence of his time for quantification, still popularly regarded as the heart and soul of conventional contemporary science. Kelvin's early and continuing successes may have been, in time, one of his main sources of weakness. Perhaps, he was so certain about his many facts and little truths—what he had learned, accurately repeated, and then instilled in his students—that the larger truths sometimes escaped him completely.

Kelvin was a brilliant scientist, but he made serious errors. For example, he "proved" that man could not fly. "In 1900 Samuel Pierpont Langley delivered a lecture at the Royal Institution on the possibilities of flight by manned aircraft. At the end of the lecture Kelvin strode to the blackboard to demolish the arguments of Langley and demonstrate that manned flight by a vehicle heavier than air would be physically impossible."[40]

Relying on the limited knowledge of his day, he computed an age for the Earth so short that it was thought to disprove Darwin's theories. Of course, Kelvin knew nothing of the nuclear processes that drive the sun, and so, while his calculations, presumably, were exactly correct and his theories well established and widely believed, his conclusions could not have been more wrong. In Lewis Thomas's description,

> the problem at hand was the age of the earth and the solar system. Using what was then known about the sources of energy and the loss of energy from the physics of that day, he calculated that neither the earth nor the sun were older than several hundred million years. This caused a considerable stir in biological and geological circles, especially among the evolutionists.
>
> Darwin himself was distressed by the numbers; the time was much too short for the theory of evolution. Kelvin's figures were described by Darwin as one of his "sorest troubles."[41]

Kelvin complained that he could not comprehend Maxwell's revolutionary theories on electromagnetism, and so he was certain they were wrong. He "dismissed" Maxwell's theory because he could not reconcile it with his own, long-held views.

The narrowness of Kelvin's view seemed to carry over into other areas of his life. He well knew how to reap the benefits of his position as a successful electrical engineer. In contrast to many of those we are considering, he directed so much attention to these matters that he gives the impression of being comparatively small-minded. He was very interested in protecting his patent rights, and so he kept meticulous notes on the arrivals and departures of ships using his navigational equipment.

> [He] had become a prosperous electrical engineer by industry and hard work and by a careful eye to money matters. Although Kelvin published prodigiously on a wide variety of scientific topics, he was also very quick to patent and protect his rights on any practical inventions. Kelvin held the basic patent on the gyro-compass used on all of the modern ocean liners of his day, and he kept careful notes on the arrival and departure of every vessel to be sure his royalties were properly paid.[42]

In discussing Maxwell's use of Faraday's ideas, Everitt has pointed out, "Thomson had all the pieces in hand, but he never put them together. It is intriguing that Thomson, who in society appeared so self-confident, had for all his brilliance a streak of intellectual timidity, while Maxwell, who struck people on first meeting as shy and hesitant, met the scientific issues head on."[43]

Kelvin was especially proud of his early accomplishments, suggesting that serious students of science should be more like himself—show similar early knowledge of Greek, mathematics, and other subjects. He seemed too sure of himself and of what he knew to learn from conflicting evidence in nature. Kelvin loved numbers and rigor and precision. However, according to Lewis Thomas,

> Kelvin may have had things exactly the wrong way round. The task of converting words into numbers is the hardest of all, the last task rather than the first to be done, and it can be done only when you have learned, beforehand, a great deal about the observations themselves. You can, to be sure, achieve a very deep understanding of nature by quantitative measurement, but you must know what you are talking about before you can begin applying the numbers for making predictions.
>
> Kelvin's own strong conviction that science could not be genuine science without measuring things was catching. People in other fields of endeavor, hankering to turn their disciplines into exact sciences, beset by what has since been called "physics envy," set about converting whatever they knew into numbers and thence into equations with predictive pretensions. We have it with us still, in economics, sociology, psychology, history, even, I fear, in English-litera-

ture criticism and linguistics, and it frequently works, if it works at all, with indifferent success. The risks of untoward social consequences in work of this kind are considerable. It is as important—and as hard—to learn when to use mathematics as *how* to use it, and this matter should remain high on the agenda of consideration for education in the social and behavioral sciences. . . . There is no doubt about it: measurement works when the instruments work, and when you have a fairly clear idea of what it is that is being measured, and when you know what to do with the numbers when they tumble out. The system for gaining information and comprehension about nature works so well, indeed, that it carries another hazard: the risk of convincing yourself that you know everything.

Kelvin himself fell into this trap toward the end of the century. . . . He stated, in a summary of the achievements of nineteenth-century physics, that it was an almost completed science; virtually everything that needed knowing about the material universe had been learned; there were still a few loose ends to be tidied up, but this would be done within the next several years.[44]

Of course, Kelvin was wrong. The next few years brought not the final missing pieces but, instead, the first steps of a series of revolutions that were to reverberate throughout the twentieth century.

It is perhaps of some considerable value to learn early in one's life to be distrustful even of one's own perception of the world, of the slippery numbers or flowing letters that can bend and twist, change and transform themselves, confusing and misleading. Perhaps it is of some value to learn that sometimes, when most needed, the memory trace will not be there—to learn that one cannot always be sure that the right words will come out.

The fundamental tendency to doubt may come naturally to our visual thinking dyslexics (who sometimes possess too-powerful imaginations), but may be quite out of character for those who were fortunate enough to be able to learn—quickly, early, and with assurance—what is "known." The resulting self-assurance is unassailable so long as reality continues to confirm the knowledge that one was taught in one's youth, but when the old system begins to break down, when a whole new layer of truth is beginning to unfold, then perhaps fate favors those who have learned, at times painfully, more of doubt than of assurance. As Faraday noted, "All [are] *sure* in their days except the most wise. . . . He is the wisest philosopher who holds his theory with some doubt."[45]

MODELS IN MATHEMATICS, MODELS IN THE MIND

Mathematics is composed of abstractions made up of concepts, symbols, and rules. Models are simplifications of reality, often involving substantial reductions in size and complexity. Computerized models have become familiar as ways of understanding and anticipating future changes in phenomena as diverse as rocket flight and weather patterns. Some models are successful, others are not. Yet the core reality of modeling is the model of reality that is constructed inside the head, intuitively. We focus much energy on learning a mathematics of symbols, a representation of reality that is one or several steps removed from the source—that is, from the core reality. But we spend almost no time on developing the intuitive core of the understanding, on building up the ability to model reality in our minds.

Many of the greatest scientists build up such models in their minds, but scientists are not the only ones to do so. There is the athlete who seems to be able to carry the whole game and all the players in his head. He can speed up the action and seems to have the uncanny ability to anticipate the actions of teammates and opponents. There is the racing car driver who is able to time himself with his own stopwatch and vividly visualize an entire race in his head, complete with turns, road textures, skids, and inertial forces, and arrive at the imagined finish line within seconds of his actual time. There are the models of electrical devices that ran in the mind of Nikola Tesla.[46]

It is not hard to imagine that such intuitive models are built up in the minds of persons in many critical positions: army generals, captains of clipper ships and whaling ships, early Polynesian star navigators, political leaders—a vast variety of extraordinary people who must deal successfully with an immense volume of complex, incomplete, and sometimes contradictory information and must somehow intuit the nature of the whole without consequential error—for the consequences of error may be irreversible and disastrous for all.

In the long history of human survival, it seems probable that such abilities have played a major role. It seems probable that those groups that could neither produce, recognize, nor cultivate such talents did not long survive. Too often, we are led, reluctantly, to suppose that survival has something to do with audacity and brute power, selection by tooth and claw. This may be so in some cases. But, over long periods of time, there can be little doubt that it is the intelligence and wisdom of individuals and groups that prevail in the end. And an important part of this intelligence is, perhaps, the special ability to build accurate models of reality in one's mind.

But what does this mean for mathematical models? Perhaps intuitive models are uncertain and difficult to deal with. One never knows whether the intuitions are correct or not. Has the captain's ship and crew survived a dozen world voyages? Has the general's reputation survived a dozen battles? Experience can be an expensive way to learn. And it is hard to teach. If it can be reduced to mathematics, then anyone who understands the mathematics or any machine that is properly programmed can do it. It is reproducible and verifiable.

With any model reality must be reduced to a level of simplicity that can be manipulated with the tools available. To go beyond the most simple calculations, one needs either an extraordinary memory or some way of recording and processing masses of information. Few problems in the real world can tolerate such extreme simplification. (How the intuitive approach could internalize many levels of complexity, even if imperfectly and mostly unconsciously, will doubtless long remain a mystery.) If one wishes to go to another level of complexity, one needs more sophisticated mathematics and at least a primitive computer. It will work, but one has moved a number of important steps from the reality. The many layers of forced simplification will eventually exact their price. The model works only so long as you stay within the limits of its own crude picture of the truth. The layers of abstraction and distortion must always be kept in mind. The essential artificiality of conventional mathematical and computer models is described in straightforward language by Danny Hills, a young computer designer.

> Take a physical simulation problem. You're calculating the flow of air over an airplane wing. Now the way that's done on a serial computer is you first of all add a layer of abstraction on top of it. You say, "Let me try to write the differential equation for that." The dif-

ferential equation is of course only an approximation of what's really going on. You say, "Now my problem is to solve that differential equation. Well, I can't really do that, so what I'll do is make an approximation of that differential equation by breaking the area up into spaces and have the differential equation for each one of those chunks, and then I'll solve that simplified discrete version of the differential equation." Then you say, "I can't really exactly solve it, so I'll solve it using floating point approximation." By the time you've put all those layers of artificiality on top of it, you don't actually get a very good answer. It's a useful answer though. . . .

If you want to sell a machine to somebody who's doing that, their definition of the problem is, "I want to do so many floating point operations per second." What they really wanted to do in the first place is to figure out how the air flowed over the airplane wing.

There's a natural way to solve this. The air is a bunch of molecules bumping into each other, so you want to take hundreds of millions of molecules, bump them into each other, bump them into the airplane wing, and see how the air flows. It doesn't have anything to do with differential equations or floating point numbers or cutting up space.

On the . . . [parallel processing computer] that's a very natural way to do it. We use one processor to represent every air molecule, if you will. In fact we can probably answer the floating point question for them as well, and that's probably why they buy the machine.[47]

When really new and different tools become available, sometimes our whole conception of how to approach a problem has to change.

COMPUTERS TRANSFORMED

To operate a personal computer (or any larger computer) in the old days, which were not long ago, one had to be a walking dictionary of codes and contorted syntax, to be recalled quickly and accurately and typed in exactly the right order. This of course is the nightmare of the clumsy dyslexic with poor sequencing ability and an unreliable memory. But this has all changed recently. The dyslexic's nightmare has become the dyslexic's dream. And, as a consequence, the ability to give direction to a computer without having to use codes, words, or numbers is beginning to have profound consequences.

Many people hated the early machines and many still hate them—with good reason. But some of those who thought their problem was with the machine have found that the problem was not with the machine itself, but with the things one was forced to do to communicate with the machine. Dealing with the old machines was like driving a car with a typewriter. "Turn 2 degrees to the right. Slow down to 15 mph. Now turn 3.25 degrees to the left." All instructions had to be unnaturally mediated through words and numbers. Everything had to be letter perfect to make it work at all. One had to pay much more attention to the process of making the machine do the work than to using the machine to do the job. Worst of all, the older machines were just plain dumb (or, one might say, literal-minded). They did not know that we see only a little difference between "s b5" and "sb5." For the old machines these statements were entirely different. One was right and the other was incomprehensible. Consequently, all kinds of things could go wrong because of the smallest errors. The frustration levels could sometimes be quite high even for experienced users. It is not surprising that the early personal computers were often simply left unused.

Then, some years ago, a newer kind of personal computer became available, based on research that had been carried out some fifteen to twenty years before. The main idea was to make use of the machines as easy and natural as possible, largely avoiding special skills and special training. These new machines were made to handle pictures and graphics as easily as words and numbers. They were designed to allow people to work with graphic images on the screen, and with tools based on pictoral analogies with ordinary objects—stacks of paper, manila folders, wastebaskets, paint brushes, pencils, paint cans, rubber erasers. These machines were made to take directions by hand movement with an electronic pointing device, usually a "mouse." The machines were designed to accept instructions in varied forms. They had "menus" from which to choose appropriate commands. Consequently, subtle "syntax" or "sequence" or "illegal command" errors were rare. Errors caused by slips of the hand could be quickly fixed with an "Undo" command. With these developments, many of the problems people had had with computers began to disappear.[48]

It should comfort ordinary users to know that even eminent scientists have had great difficulty with the older kinds of personal computer systems. Donald Glaser of the University of California at

Berkeley is one such scientist. Apparently, one does not have to have any particular learning difficulty to have disliked the demands of the older machines.

> I have always had enough government money that I have . . . had programmers working for me. So I never learned to use the computer myself. And so it was only the students and the professional programmers who did it. . . . Then I tried to learn . . . and I have to admit I hated it because it was so fussy and I couldn't remember whether the asterisk came before or after the colon and I didn't use the thing for many hours a day. . . . Then when the [graphical interface computer] came, I decided this is the machine for me. So I have now learned to use it and I depend on the machine heavily.[49]

The superiority of the new machines derives from a simple change in approach: don't try to change people or train them to use a poorly designed system; rather, design the system to do things in the way people already work, using analogies with what they already know.[50] That is, allow people to focus on getting work done rather than learning how to use the system. Such a user-oriented system may require more effort to design, build, and program, but it is orders of magnitude easier for average people to use. The burden of the work is shifted to the designer, manufacturer, and programmer, and away from the user. The former make a greater effort in order to reduce the effort of the latter, as it should be.

As these machines become easier to use, further beneficial developments may be expected. With the widening use of computers that have sophisticated, two-dimensional and three-dimensional graphics capabilities, powerful interaction will be possible between people and machines at levels and in modes not possible before. In this environment, creative dyslexics and others who rely heavily on visual thinking might be able, in time, to work almost exclusively in a language of pictures and rely on the machine to translate these pictures into numbers, symbols, formulas, and other conventional structures when needed. Several years ago some of the programmers who were becoming accustomed to this new medium began to appreciate some of the dramatic long-term possibilities. One of these programmers, Scott Kim, saw a major milestone in the coming together of word and image after hundreds of years of technological separation.

Before Gutenberg, illustration and type were one and the same; they were inseparable. But afterward, the two disciplines became separate and diverged. Now that we've got the [graphic computer], I can see a medium where they come back together again. In [the new graphics software] there is no distinction between words and pictures.

The characters in our alphabet actually started out as pictures. They are a human-made object. . . . It is important to realize that all notations, whether music, or language, or computer languages, are just made up. They are symbols that can be changed. There is a choice.[51]

In the late 1980s, when most major companies were making computers and software that gradually incorporated user communication and control by the graphic interface, it became easier to see the beginning of this reintegration. These changes, of course, have not been confined to new ways of operating the machine. Gradually, they may come to be widely used for programming the machine as well. Whatever the programming language, most programming is still a process of working with hundreds of lines of obscure codes and contorted syntax. But this is changing. Increasingly, one can think of programming with images and pictures instead of words. According to Kim, "Everybody who's thinking about visual programming is actually thinking about a visual representation of programming. . . . I would like the computer to think visually, and the way for it to do that is to deal with exactly what the user is dealing with. . . . I would like people to be able to work with computers in something that looks more like pictures."[52]

This interest in various forms of visual programming has continued to grow and mature in the late 1980s. Indeed, it has extended to programming in ways that are in fact inherently visual, not merely visual representations of things that are verbal in origin. Two writers who have been observing the more recent evolution of this field explain:

With the availability of graphic workstations has come the increasing influence of visual technology on [computer] language environments. . . . The availability of visual technology is leading to the development of new approaches that are inherently visual. . . . In the nearly twenty years since the development of [the first visual programming experiments], the virtues of a visual, highly integrated language environment have become well accepted. . . . We have seen the transition from a strictly textual representation, through relatively straightforward visual representations of otherwise textual technology, and toward new investigations into more naturally visual uses of visual technology. . . . Perhaps most significantly, visual technology seems to be moving to a convergence between the language itself and the language environment, a convergence that goes beyond the visualization of existing textual approaches, a convergence that is naturally visual.[53]

The new visual technologies have had and are still having many varied effects on how computers are used, as well as how they are programmed. Increasingly, the ease of manipulating images suggests ways of doing things that could not have been imagined previously. Programmer Michael Hawley explains that powerful, graphics-oriented computers have "profound and far-reaching potential for applications in medical imagery, modeling of seismic data, and more. Just about any kind of graphic data that you can splat up on a screen, you can manipulate with this machine in dazzling ways."[54] The machines that Hawley is referring to are expensive, but it is just a matter of time before the small, modestly priced, personal machines will be able to perform similar feats. Exactly how all this will happen is still unclear. But as the tools change, becoming ever cheaper, smarter, and more powerful, and as these trends continue, it would appear that there will be only more and better opportunities for the kinds of people and the kinds of visually oriented minds we have been talking about.

VISUALIZATION: "HIGH TECH" COMES FULL CIRCLE

In the recent evolution of the most advanced supercomputers—the pinnacle products of the future-oriented "high tech" industries often referred to by our politicians and legislators—it is a curious and intriguing fact that the further along the scale of sophistication one proceeds, the more reliant many of these systems become on graphic and visually oriented modes of data presentation and analysis. The lay person might expect that the most sophisticated supercomputers would have ever more esoteric and incomprehensible machine output and data displays. But the strange fact is that in many cases the reverse is true. The more sophisticated these systems become, the more they employ visual displays that can be comparatively easy for ordinary people to understand, at least those ordinary people who are more or less accustomed to seeing things in a visual or graphic way.

In this process we may see another surprising reversal. Some computer professionals—those who have been in the business for two or three decades and are not very visually oriented, having long relied heavily on their ability to easily remember vast quantities of complex codes and programming tricks—may be, in time, increasingly threatened by a new era in computing. Indeed, in perfect contrast to the dyslexics and other visual thinkers we have been discussing, some of these computer professionals and other extremely verbally oriented people may have quite surprising difficulties with these heavily visual forms of presentation.

As elsewhere, in programming and operations we might expect much of the straightforward work to be increasingly taken over by the machines themselves, in a variety of machine-operated self-diagnostic routines. Of course, non-visual, detail-oriented people will always have important roles to play. But increasingly we might find that larger proportions of their work will be done by machines. In other areas, they will also probably gradually yield center stage as new modes of working increasingly require a new set of visual skills in which many of them do not happen to excel.

In many cases, the trends toward visualization have been a matter of necessity arising out of the nature of the data as well as hardware and software changes. In many circumstances visual presentation and analysis have come to be seen as the only option open to the scientists involved. Increasingly, there is simply too much data to handle in any other way. One observer experienced in the field explains that, "The deluge of data generated by supercomputers and other high-volume data sources (such as medical imaging systems and satellites) makes it impossible for users to quantitatively examine more than a tiny fraction of a given solution. That is, it is impossible to investigate the qualitative global nature of numerical solutions."[55]

However, the newly emerging sophistication of graphical computer technologies provides, ironically, a solution to the problems created by the prodigious production of other computer technologies.

With the advent of [computer] graphics, researchers can convert entire fields of variables (representing density, pressure, velocity . . . and so on) to color images. The information conveyed to the researcher undergoes a quantitative change because it brings the eye-brain system, with its great pattern recognition capabilities, into play in a way that is impossible with purely numeric data. . . . For example, an observer instantly sees the vortices, shock systems, and flow patterns in a visualization of a hydrodynamic calculation, while these same patterns are invisible in mere listings of several hundred thousand numbers, each representing field quantities at one moment in time. When computing a space-time solution to the laws of physics, the particular numeric quantities at each event . . . are not important; rather, what is important is understanding the global structure of the field variables that constitute the solution and the causal interconnections of the various components of that solution.[56]

Patterns in data are invisible until one can turn away from the individual data element, and focus instead on the "global structure of the field variables." In cases such as these, we can see a major shift from individual values and indicators and toward the consideration of complex things that make sense only when you can look at the whole of a system with each individual part seen in relation to all the other parts—in many respects an inherently visual frame of reference. These developments have come to be known as "scientific visualization," an approach to handling data that began to be used in many different fields in the late 1980s.[57]

Many fields of study are being changed dramatically by the shift toward more "global" perspectives. For example, marine scientists who were "once content to study a single estuary or reef" are now beginning to study the oceans as a "giant, integrated whole, a sort of grand circulatory system." Previously, the tools were just not available. But, as one researcher explains, "Only in the last few years have we finally had the tools and the expertise to adopt a world view of the oceans." The important tools are supercomputers to run the new models and satellites that can be used to study plankton growth. With these new global perspectives there is a greater sense of the interconnectedness of distant phenomena. As another researcher explained, "We realized that we needed to understand the currents in the Pacific to understand the weather in North America. . . . That got everybody's attention."[58]

One of the major attractions of these systems is that they sometimes provide new insights into old problems. In one example from the use of ultrasound in medical diagnosis, it was "found that much of the data from ultrasound images is usually discarded. But if a special iterative algorithm is applied to that data, it can reveal not only whether the tissue is healthy or diseased, but also differentiate among different diseases that might be present."[59]

The problem of data volume continues to be a major concern and promises to become increasingly severe in coming years. Business and political leaders as well as scientists have become concerned about ways to access, organize, and distribute the ever-increasing volumes of electronic information.[60] For example, in the late 1980s, with many projects just beginning, the volume of data received by NASA from previous projects was already more than scientists and analysts could cope with. "Some space scientists call it the black hole. Others refer to it as a tape landfill. By any name, the archives where NASA stores its space data is an embarrassment of riches. Over the past twenty-five years of space exploration NASA has accumulated some 125,000 data tapes."

According to one NASA computer official, "Less than 10 percent of that data has ever been looked at."[61] As many new NASA satellites and other projects are launched in the early 1990s, the glut of data is only expected to become much worse.[62] Part of the reason for these difficulties, some argue, is the resistance of program planners to include sufficient funds for data processing and analysis. The hardware projects are highly visible, the data analysis, less so. As difficult as it is to find money for the projects themselves, it is far more difficult to find sufficient funds for adequate information processing once the projects are launched.

Another, perhaps more important, part of the reason for these difficulties may be that available processing methods and equipment have been comparatively antiquated. It is often observed by computer professionals that many of the computer systems in routine use by government agencies involve major components that are based on technology and software that may be ten or twenty years old. Sometimes the backwardness of the technology is inherent to the specialized equipment. One astronomer observed with amusement that when he used a modern graphics-based personal computer, he could easily specify areas of star maps for analysis with a single pass of a mouse.

But when he went back to his vastly more expensive and powerful specialized computer equipment, he had to type several lines of programming code to get a similar result.

This sort of difficulty was recognized in a 1987 report on "scientific visualization" prepared for the National Science Foundation. "Secretaries who prepare manuscripts for scientists have better interactive control and visual feedback with their word processors than scientists have over large computing resources that cost several thousand times as much. . . . These difficulties were seen as especially wasteful because it was becoming clear that "the ability of scientists to visualize complex computations and simulations is absolutely essential to ensure the integrity of analyses, to provoke insights and to communicate those insights with others."[63]

One of the most interesting aspects of the visualization movement, scientific or otherwise, is that there is an intriguing convergence of the work of groups that would on the surface seem to be poles apart, whether they be mathematicians, astronomers, physicians, molecular biologists, or makers of children's cartoons, television advertising, and science fiction films. For example, a graphic computer system originally developed by the people who made the *Star Wars* science fiction film series has since come to be used for purposes as diverse as medical imaging and drilling for oil.

As a consequence, meetings, conferences, and product shows about computer graphics hardware and software have increasingly become improbable congregations of long-haired programmers and computer graphics artists together with short-haired electrical engineers and defense contractors. The same equipment and software that can simulate, in "real time," the flight of a military aircraft can also be used to animate the swimming of a group of sharks in a Disney-style cartoon.[64]

The need for very different skills and approaches as the field progresses is widely acknowledged. For example, at the National Center for Supercomputing Applications in Urbana-Champaign, Illinois, it has been necessary to develop the "Renaissance Team," a "closely knit group that includes scientists, a computer programmer and an artist tuned into the workings of computers, graphics and a field or fields of science." Each one of the team members has to to know something of each of the other team members' areas of knowledge and the conventional terminology of each area. Teams work through particular simulations, and members explain that, "There's a kind of synergy and you start coming up with ideas of how to communicate [these ideas] to a lot of different people."[65]

To provide a better sense of what is happening here, a few specific examples are likely to be helpful. The following summaries of several brief video presentations provide a sense of the range and extent of the work being done.

"The Lorenz Attractor" is a computer-generated animation that graphically portrays one of the central ideas in the new science of chaos—an idea known as "sensitivity to initial conditions." With points of light drawing lines in a three-dimensional graph (in the shape of butterfly wings), it is shown that several moving points may have very tiny differences in starting position on the graph but will, over time, greatly outdistance each other (like runners in a race) and will also switch back and forth between the two sides of the butterfly-wing pattern in an apparently random fashion. The viewer is left with a vivid visual image of what is in fact a powerful but highly abstract concept—that with certain kinds of phenomena, although the starting points may be virtually identical, the downstream consequences can be quite different and largely unpredictable. Consequently, in a classic example, if one were to run two models of a weather system on a computer, the weather patterns would soon begin to diverge even with extremely small initial differences in temperature or pressure. In such systems very tiny differences tend to be amplified and have greater and greater effects over time.[66]

"Displacement Animation of Intelligent Objects" shows brief clips of surrealistic animal and human forms walking, running, breathing, and moving their mouths as when speaking. It provides evidence of early sophistication in the manipulation of skin surfaces with the illusion of natural muscle and bone movement. A model of the three-dimensional body is built into the computer and moved around on the screen like a puppet or marionette. The animation is not that of a series of images, as with standard cartoons. Like using a material puppet, making the body takes a good deal of time, but manipulating the body is comparatively easy.[67] Recently, such a computer "puppet," "Dozo," is credited with helping the city of Atlanta, Georgia, win the right to be the site of the 1996 Olympic Games.[68]

"Mars Rover Sample Return Mission" is a NASA film that uses animation to show the rather complex steps required to send a robot mission to Mars and return with samples from the surface of the planet.[69]

"Mars: The Movie" and "Earth: The Movie" use massively compiled data to construct models of the surface of the two planets. These surfaces can then be "flown" over at will at various altitudes and speeds.[70]

"Numerical Simulation of a Thunderstorm Outflow" is a computer simulation of cool air moving along the ground away from a building thunderstorm, showing eddies and turbulance.[71]

"Simulated Treatment of an Ocular Tumor" shows how imaginary slices of a diseased eye are taken by means of tomography and converted into a three-dimensional model of an eyeball with a large tumor growing under the layer of the retina. Laser light is used to destroy tumor tissue without surgery or damage to surrounding healthy tissue.[72]

All of this may seem miles away from our main topic, but it is not. A visual approach to much of life and experience is fundamental to the mental life of many dyslexics and others more or less like them. In her autobiography Susan Hampshire indicates the basic importance of the visual approach, even in those areas that seem to have little visual structure or content. She discusses a number of misconceptions about dyslexia and dyslexics (such as the belief that dyslexia results primarily from emotional problems or low intelligence).

> But there is yet another prejudice that dyslexics, and those who try to help them, have to combat. This is the deep-rooted idea that all learning, all education, any expression of ideas, must be done through language, through words. The idea that it is possible to learn and communicate visually, through colour and shape, seems to be a heresy, though it is one that naturally occurs to dyslexics. It is, after all, the basis of the code I developed to cope with the problems of reading scripts. Much of the potential in dyslexic children is stamped out by the rigid appliance of the rules of literacy, simply because they work for the majority. Yet some very impressive intelligences have seen the value of visual learning and communications.
>
> Leonardo da Vinci wrote, in referring to his detailed anatomical drawings which he made for his own research, "No one could hope to convey so much true knowledge without an immense, tedious and

confused length of writing and time, except through this very short way of drawing from different aspects."[73]

WAITING PATTERNS, A "NOMAD BY CHOICE"

We have referred to the curious fact that sometimes scientists or engineers struggling with new phenomena are surprised to find already waiting for them, more or less completed, some key pattern that fits their problem worked out previously by mathematicians. As we saw, a great impression was made on Einstein when he found Riemann's non-Euclidean geometry of curved space waiting for him as he sought a way to describe his general theory of relativity.

Perhaps Steen is right. This should be expected to happen if, in fact, mathematics does study all the patterns that there are. In this regard the visual approach to mathematics may tend to expand the study of patterns, while the traditional rigorous approach might tend to limit the range of patterns studied. Of course, both are needed. We need energetic, risk-taking entrepreneurs as well as cautious auditors. We should just be careful that they are not allowed to switch jobs. Another story from the developing science of chaos will serve to illustrate our point and suggest the direction of the possibilities.

Benoit Mandelbrot has come to be recognized as one of the giants in the development of chaos theory. He invented the word "fractal" for fractional dimension, the concept that lies behind the mathematics and images associated with his name. James Gleick calls fractals a conceptual "high wire act."[74] We are accustomed to drawing in two dimensions and doing sculpture in three dimensions; but how can we conceive of doing anything in 2.5 dimensions, or worse, 0.63 dimensions? Mandelbrot's book, *The Fractal Geometry of Nature*, is acknowledged to be one of the major works in the field. Remarkably, it has also sold more copies over a few years (in its revised form) than any other book of higher mathematics, a surprisingly popular best seller of an unusual sort.[75] Mandelbrot's ability to anticipate future developments in this rapidly growing field were extraordinary. According to Gleick,

> Mandelbrot's book was wide-ranging and stuffed with the minutiae of mathematical history. Wherever chaos led, Mandelbrot had some

basis to claim that he had been there first. Little did it matter that most readers found his references obscure or even useless. They had to acknowledge his extraordinary intuition for the direction of advances in fields he had never actually studied, from seismology to physiology. It was sometimes uncanny, and sometimes irritating. Even an admirer would cry with exasperation, "Mandelbrot didn't have everybody's thoughts before they did."[76]

Yet, for a long time, Mandelbrot, like many other pioneers in this field, worked in comparative obscurity and largely alone, covertly following his interests in a variety of fields he had never studied (economics, engineering, medicine) as experts looked on with suspicion. "He was always an outsider, taking an unorthodox approach to an unfashionable corner of mathematics, exploring disciplines in which he was rarely welcomed, hiding his grandest ideas in efforts to get his papers published, surviving mainly on the confidence of his employers."[77]

Mandelbrot's way of working, we should not be surprised to discover, is described as intensely intuitive and visual. His early education was interrupted because he was hiding from the Nazis in the countryside of occupied France. When he had to take examinations to enter the university, Mandelbrot found that he could usually hide his lack of training by relying on his geometrical intuition.

> He had realized that, given an analytic problem, he could almost always think of it as some shape in his mind. Given a shape, he could always find a way of transforming it, altering its symmetries, making it more harmonious. Often his transformations led directly to a solution of an analogous problem. In physics and chemistry, where he could not apply geometry, he got poor grades. But in mathematics, questions he could never have answered using proper techniques melted away in the face of his manipulation of shapes.[78]

A self-avowed "nomad by choice" and "pioneer by necessity," Mandelbrot has worked under the shelter of IBM's Thomas J. Watson Research Center, journeying over some thirty years from "obscurity to eminence" but never really finding a true intellectual home. "Even mathematicians would say, without apparent malice, that whatever Mandelbrot was, he was not one of them."[79] Even so, there were practical problems to be solved, and in the discussion that follows we hope to show the practical power of the visual approach and the curious ability of mathematics to throw up patterns that often come to be seen, sooner or later, as critical solutions to previously unforeseen problems in unanticipated contexts.

Early in his stay at IBM, Mandelbrot came upon a practical difficulty that was of great interest to those around him. The company's engineers were puzzled by the sporadic static (called "noise") that affected transmission of information from computer to computer over telephone lines. The noise would occasionally knock out part of the signal and an error would be created. Try as they might, they could not get rid of the noise. It could be reduced but not eliminated by increasing the power of the electric current. The noise was random, but it tended to come in clusters. Working on the problem, "Mandelbrot soon learned that there was a piece of folklore about the errors that had never been written down, because it matched none of the standard ways of thinking: the more closely they looked at the clusters, the more complicated the pattern of errors seemed."[80]

This turned out to be the key. "Mandelbrot provided a way of describing the distribution of errors that predicted exactly the observed patterns. Yet it was exceedingly peculiar. . . . Engineers had no framework for understanding Mandelbrot's description, but mathematicians did."[81]

Mandelbrot saw that the pattern of the noise was the same as a mathematical pattern known as the "Cantor Set," developed by nineteenth century mathematician Georg Cantor.

Figure 11.1. Cantor Set

To make a Cantor set (Figure 11-1), one starts with a series of numbers that may be represented graphically by a horizontal bar.[82] In the first step, the bar may be represented as extending, say, across the entire width of the page. In the second step, one third of the bar is removed from the middle, leaving two bars (each of one third the previous length), one on either side of the page. In the third step, the operation is repeated on the two new bars. The operation can be continued any number of times, subdividing and subdividing, until the subdivisions of the bars can no longer be discerned. The numbers that correspond to the bars, of course, can be subdivided indefinitely. Mandelbrot saw that the noise in the computer signals going through the wires was of the same character. Within any period of clear signals, there was always some noise. But when one considered the noise carefully (enlarging its bars, as it were), one would find noise-free periods (the spaces between the bars). And so it would continue, no matter how finely the periods of time were divided.

Once one understands the pattern with some certainty, then it becomes clear what to do about it—and what not to do about it. The engineers saw that no matter how much they increased the power of the signal, there would always be some noise. So they could settle for modest power levels, since there was nothing to gain from extreme measures. They had to learn to live with the noise as an essential and unavoidable part of the system. But there was a fairly easy way to deal with the problem, once it was understood. They needed to send the information twice, so that the good signals could reinforce each other and the sporadic errors would fall out and be ignored by the system. According to Gleick, "Mandelbrot also changed the way IBM's engineers thought about the cause of noise. Bursts of errors had always sent the engineers looking for a man sticking a screwdriver somewhere. But Mandelbrot's scaling patterns suggested that the noise would never be explained on the basis of specific local events."[83] With his intensely visual approach, and "always abetted by an extravagant knowledge of the forgotten byways of scientific history," Mandelbrot was able not only to solve the practical problem but also to transform the engineers' views in a far more fundamental manner, forever altering the way they saw their world of information.

AGAIN, A MATHEMATICS OF IMAGES

Our discussion so far has indicated several things. First, and most important, some (but not all) of the most creative mathematicians and scientists show clear evidence of employing some form of visual thought to arrive at their most innovative results. They use conventional signs and symbols to communicate with others, but not as entities for their own productive thought. For some, then, "productive thought" is made up of images, not Greek letters and conventional mathematical symbols and concepts. A second major consideration is that some highly creative scientists (and even mathematicians) have been reported to show signs of curious difficulties with rather elementary parts of mathematics, while with the very "difficult" parts of mathematics (those frequently involving sophisticated mental imagery) they show great facility. Indeed, some scientists, such as Faraday, seem to have had severe difficulties handling even the simplest mathematical symbols in the conventional ways. Further, these inabilities have been regarded by some (such as Maxwell) as advantageous. In Faraday's case, the inabilities are presumed to have had a role in forcing (or allowing) Faraday to view electricity and magnetism in a manner very different from the ways they had been (and continued to be) viewed by conventional mathematicians.

If images are so important for these creative people and if the conventional mathematical symbols are so very difficult for some of them to handle, then one must ask the obvious question: would it be possible (or, to what extent would it be possible) to deal with mathematics in the language of images alone? Is it possible to pursue mathematics in a serious, conscientious, and productive fashion by using just the images and leaving the symbols and the logical rigor out of the process entirely (for a while), bringing these back into the process at some later stage, primarily for documentation, communication, and verification? Of course, some other logic of images, perhaps with some corresponding notation, might be expected to evolve in the process, if it is not already available. To what extent would this procedure be permitted for professional mathematicians and professional users of mathematics? For some, it seems that this sort of thing has always happened, but out of sight, as we observed with Hadamard and others. Once they had made their breakthroughs, however, they had to convert the results into conventional symbols and the conventional concepts they stood for. Einstein, as we saw, thought this final process of conversion difficult work.

Recent trends may have brought this alternative mode of dealing with mathematics out of the background and placed it solidly in the foreground. Professional mathematicians have traditionally progressed through the use of conventional symbols to develop rigorous, logical proofs. With the coming of the personal computer and the development of "chaos," "dynamics," and related studies, some mathematicians have shelved the conventional approach and logical rigor for a time and begun to treat mathematics as an experimental science in which the main object of study is the changes in the computer-generated images.

What, then, is the role of the conventional concepts and symbols and the process of rigorous proof? The answer is strikingly analogous to the changes we are addressing. The new mathematicians see a role for, first, following the images wherever they lead. They note that the conventional methods can be held for another stage, to provide the continuity and logical rigor that would ultimately be essential. One of these new mathematicians is Heinz-Otto Peitgen, who has struggled with the apparent conflict between conventional mathematical rigor and the promise of new discoveries by the use of the new methods and techniques involved in chaos.

> Peitgen shared little of the mathematicians' unease with the use of computers to conduct experiments. Granted, every result must eventually be made rigorous by the standard methods of proof, or it would not be mathematics. To see an image on a graphics screen does not guarantee its existence in the language of theorem and proof. But the very availability of that image was enough to change the evolution of mathematics. Computer exploration was giving mathematics the freedom to take a more natural path, Peitgen believed. Temporarily, for the moment, a mathematician could suspend the requirement of rigorous proof. He could go wherever experiments might lead him, just as a physicist could. The numerical power of computation and the visual cues to intuition would suggest promising avenues and spare the mathematician blind alleys. Then, new paths having been found and new objects isolated, a mathematician could return to standard proofs.[84]

TEACHING MATHEMATICS BACKWARDS

Mathematics is essentially sequential and cumulative. You cannot deal with concept or operation number 29 until you have mastered operations 1 through 28. That this is the most reasonable way to teach mathematics, there can be little debate, especially for those students who naturally take to learning first things first and last things last. But what should we do with students for whom the easy things are hard and the hard things are easy—those who naturally jump to the end and skip over the beginning, those who jump to the world of intuitive images without having mastered the basic elementary steps?

Perhaps, for these, one should consider teaching mathematics backwards, that is, teaching the images and patterns first and teaching the conventional symbol system, rules, and rigorous process later. This kind of fundamental change would surely be difficult, but may be worth the trouble, especially if it can be shown that some of those who could not do well with elementary mathematics may still do superlatively well with the most advanced forms. It may require entirely different ways of teaching, but it may, in the end, be more appropriate for a new era in mathematics and work, when all the easy things will be done by machines and the hard things will be the only things of value left for human beings to do.

10
PATTERNS, IMPLICATIONS, POSSIBILITIES

STUMBLING TOWARD THE TRUTH

Given what we have seen so far, it seems clear enough that there is some connection, at least in some people, between high visual talents and various forms of learning difficulties. The connection does not have to be the same in all cases. Indeed, the theories we have referred to would suggest that one should usually expect a wide variety of connections and interrelationships, a great many different combinations of traits and different degrees of severity. But where does such an observation lead us? And what, then, is the whole compass of the case that we have been making? We have noted, in the lives of a number of extraordinary people, several varied patterns of traits and we have considered a number of unexpected and intriguing possibilities. Although much is still uncertain, it seems that we have enough information to look at our world in a very different way and to see vast opportunities where, before, we would have seen barriers and difficulties. In the preceding chapters, we have seen:

- Some of the most original thinkers in the physical sciences, engineering, mathematics, politics, literature, and other areas relied heavily on visual modes of thought, employing images instead of words or numbers. Some of these same thinkers have shown evidence of a striking range of learning problems, including difficulties with reading, spelling, writing, calculation, speaking, and memory. We are led to expect that, conversely, when we look to the most original thinkers, whatever the field, we should not be surprised to find some similarly varied pattern of traits involving visual strengths and verbal weaknesses.

- According to recent research, there are good neurological reasons for the apparent association of visual talents with verbal difficulties. In some people, early changes in relative brain hemisphere size and in the "wiring" of the brain may tend to increase abilities in some areas at the expense of abilities in other areas.

- There is an enormous variety of identifiable traits within the larger pattern, perhaps a hundred or more (some even apparently contradicting or at opposite poles from others). But this great variety should be anticipated because the apparent causal mechanism appears to work as a kind of neurological random generator, producing great diversity in strengths as well as weaknesses, a diversity some believe may be important, over long periods of time, for the survival of a society or culture as a whole.

- Visual-spatial abilities can play a more important role in major creative accomplishments in many different fields—even when they are not commonly thought to be highly visual—than is commonly recognized.

- Visual and spatial modes of thought seem well-suited to dealing with certain complex problems and are often closely associated with major creative achievements in the sciences as well as the arts.

- After some four hundred to five hundred years of growth in a highly verbally oriented system of education and knowledge, we may be seeing the beginning of a new phase in which, in reverse fashion, certain kinds of complex information will be increasingly handled visually rather than verbally.

- Many of the problems of greatest importance in the modern world are ones of vast complexity, like understanding large-scale atmospheric or ecological systems. These problems could be practically considered in depth only recently because only recently have we gained the ability to acquire, store, and process enormous amounts of data at high speed and at comparatively modest cost.

- Some of these complex system problems may be most successfully addressed by certain gifted visual thinkers, using visually based analytic methods and employing increasingly sophisticated computer graphics technologies, similar to those now used in "scientific visualization."
- There may be fundamental changes in attitudes toward many of the skills that have long been the focus of conventional education—rapid reading, reliable recall of detailed factual information, rapid and accurate calculation, neat writing, correct spelling, and conventional verbal interpretation of routine numerical data. As skills such as these gradually come to be done better and faster and more cheaply by machines, they may come to be seen as increasingly less important and less valuable.
- Coming full cycle, we may soon begin to see that some of those who are best attuned to absorbing and fully understanding problems of vast complexity may be just the ones who sometimes have had the greatest difficulty at the lower levels of the conventional educational system—those for whom the "easy" is hard and the "hard" is easy.
- And finally, all this evidence suggests that the conventional educational system may be focusing on the wrong kinds of skills and on rewarding some of the wrong kinds of learning. Conventional educational practices may be systematically weeding out many of those who might have the most to give as many sectors of our economy and society continue to go through fundamental change, requiring deeper and more basic kinds of learning.

LEARNING ABOUT LEARNING

This book has dealt with visual thinkers and and the distinctive way they experience their world. But this book has also been about learning. Initially we were concerned with those who have unusual difficulties learning certain things, most obviously in their early schooling. We have also been concerned with creativity, which we have treated as basically a special form of learning. We started with those who have learning difficulties, but we came to see that we are often dealing with people who can be defined as being poor at mainly one form of learning, but possibly extraordinarily good at other forms. We have been forced to distinguish between different kinds of knowledge, between the clutter of facts and the power of elegant, overarching concepts. And we have come to understand that these other forms of learning can be critical. Knowledge in all forms must, of course, be passed from generation to generation. But in times of great change, it can be far more important to be able to learn things that were never known before—things that mostly must be learned directly from nature and experience, rather than from books and lectures—for when things really change, books and lectures may lead us down the wrong path.

So it is that we are led to our paradox: sometimes, or even many times, we find that those who may have had some of the greatest trouble in their early schooling may subsequently come to thrive when they are dealing with major creative problems at the edge of a developing area of knowledge—that these exceptional people are sometimes far better at creating new knowledge than in absorbing and retaining old knowledge, especially those forms of knowledge found in books and lectures rather than in experience and experiment. On the face of it, it still may be difficult to credit. We are so accustomed to thinking that really bright people usually get high grades, or at least that they always get high scores on tests of aptitude or intelligence, even if they don't work hard for high grades. It is still hard to see that some of the most extraordinary minds may be found at the bottom of the class. But this we have seen over and over and over again. The case is clear with Edison, Churchill, and Yeats, and only slightly more ambiguous with Patton, Einstein, and Faraday. Of course, these are very special cases in many ways. But it would seem that we are on to something here.

It would be silly to see all the students who are having trouble in today's schools as young Churchills, Edisons, or Faradays. But, given the evidence we have seen so far, there may be good reason to give them the benefit of the doubt and look for some similarities—to *not* write them off at the start. What we have seen should counsel more humility and circumspection on the part of teachers, parents, and psychologists, whatever the scores and grades say. There may be greater similarities than we ever would have imagined, especially when very different talents are becoming more important and the rules of the game are being changed in unpredictable ways.

Specialization is a cornerstone of our culture, as, indeed, it must be a part of any culture. We are all familiar with the reasons for specialization. Some people are good with words, some with numbers, some with images. After high school, we rarely ask the "number people" to draw or the "image people" to calculate. Instead, we might consider, within each group, experimentation with the basics of other specialties, not the endless details that clutter the mind but the major concepts and ideas that allow you to see clearly and not depend only upon the judgments of the experts. You will always need the experts to work out the details for you, but you should not let the experts make all decisions for you.

Suppose we insisted that each learn the essentials of the other's world, but using their own tools, not those of the world to be learned. Thus, artists might learn the essentials of mathematics and statistics through images, while mathematicians might learn the essentials of images through some special form of numerical analysis. In this way, each would have some common ground and a basis for mutual appreciation and respect, and neither would be as prone to being misled by the other. (Some believe it is an open question which is worse: what artists pay to have their taxes done, or what accountants pay for modern art.)

This new way should promote a healthier interdependence, where each has a clear idea of the fundamentals of what the other is doing, but knows when to pass the task to one who is more knowledgeable and proficient. In this way, we acknowledge the considerable differences, but use them as bridges rather than chasms between disciplines.

"DISPENSABLE ERUDITION"

This book has been filled with ironies and paradoxes. So many reversals of expectation may be disconcerting to those who like their world more straightforward and orderly. But often such is the way of life and nature. Everyone agrees that we have a problem. Our technological culture is drowning in its own success. Masses of data and information are accumulating everywhere. Up to now, the basic strategy for dealing with these growing masses of information has been long, mind-numbing education and reckless, blinkered specialization. That this strategy has been effective in a great many respects, so far, there can be little debate. The problems we are discussing are a tribute to its ample and abundant success, so far. However, after long success, it is becoming increasingly clear that this strategy may be entering a phase of diminishing return. It has long been recognized that this strategy has always had built-in problems. The more one knows in one's own, increasingly narrow area, the more one is ignorant in other areas, the more difficult is effective communication between unrelated areas, and the more unlikely it is that the larger whole will be properly perceived or understood. Like the student who reads too much small print, the specialist's habitual near focus often promotes the myopic perspective that precludes the comprehension of larger, more important patterns. The distant view of the whole is blurred and unclear. If you focus only on a small group of stars at the edge of the Milky Way, you will not perceive the larger structure of the whole galaxy of which the group is one tiny part.

The specialist strategy breeds its own limits. Pieces of the puzzle in separate areas remain far apart, or come together only after decades of specialist resistance, or success in one area leads to great problems in another. Material abundance produces waste-disposal problems; cars and aircraft produce wonderful mobility for many people, but also deplete resources, produce accidental fatalities, and increase pollution; success in vaccination, hygiene, and health care lead to all the problems of great concentrations of human population.

As the specialist strategy continues to be pursued, a sense of the whole is increasingly lost. Many know their areas; few see the whole. Many are expert; few are wise. But the visual thinkers, late bloomers, and creative dyslexics we have been dealing with have often been outsiders or reluctant participants in this specialist culture—especially those who are energetic, and globally minded, who seem always to be interested in everything, unable to settle down to a "serious" (that is, highly specialized) area of study. Even if they do settle into an acceptable specialty area, like Einstein or Maxwell, they become known for addressing the widest profusion of topics, from light particles to river courses, from cybernetic devices to the rings of Saturn. While many of the "best and brightest" have taken comfort in their own successes, digging into the warm, insulated, safe shelter of their chosen specialties, the global thinkers have often been left to blow around in the changing winds on the plain. The minds of these visual thinkers and creative dyslexics have been as restless and vibrantly alive as their transcripts and résumés have been varied and erratic.

The most successful of these creative visual thinkers do seem to learn how to still this restless curiosity to some extent—just enough, at least for them to focus their passion for a time and finish a few of the many projects they have started. More than others, such people probably need to know how to manage and discipline themselves—when to rein in and when to let go. But, in time, these same creative dyslexics and visual thinkers often have learned (if we are correct), by inclination and necessity, what their unaffected fellows cannot have learned—how to gain the most understanding with the least information, how to be savagely selective in their reading, how to guess what is unessential and focus only on the really important. The specialists may be able to work far more rapidly and retain more, but too often they are prone to wasting their time, often without even being aware of it. They do what the professor or the employer expects them to do, not what nature invites them to discover. They may focus too well on properly repeating someone else's DNA laboratory experiment, or on trying to solve the problem of laser fusion.

In any field or sub-field there is so much to do and so much to know that one can easily squander a lifetime without results of real consequences. There must be some sort of inner guide to help avoid the continuous acquisition of comparatively unessential information. This problem is more apparent today than it was many decades ago. Yet long ago, when he was trying to decide whether to go into physics or mathematics, Einstein recognized (as we saw before) the importance of this basic problem. "I saw mathematics was split up into numerous specialties, each of which could easily absorb the short lifetime granted to us. . . . My intuition was not strong enough in the field of mathematics to differentiate clearly the fundamentally important, that which is really basic, from the rest of the more or less dispensable erudition."[1]

The kinds of people we have been discussing in this book rarely have the option or the inclination or the temptation to stake a claim to one tiny hoard of knowledge, as many specialists do—holding off all comers with a barrage of facts, minefields of technical language, and bulwarks of prerequisites and qualifications. But the visual thinkers and creative dyslexics experience a different necessity. Whether their particular difficulty is with reading or memory or something else, from the outset many of them have had to learn how to judge what is worth knowing and what should be left aside. They have had to learn how to select, first for teachers, but then for life and the world. Because unconnected knowledge quickly slips away, they have had to integrate knowledge with what they already know in order to learn and retain it. They have had to learn basic concepts well enough to be able to generate and regenerate factual material that would not, alone, remain still, unchanging, and accessible in their minds. And, like Faraday, they have had to learn how to constantly check the validity of their imaginations and the accuracy of their conclusions against some really reliable standard—then check them again, remaining ever vigilant to ensure that yet another error does not creep in to spoil the result. When one is error-prone, one learns well the ways to avoid errors and how to recover from them once they are made.

The specialist has long been comforted by knowing 95 to 99 percent of what he or she needs to know. (No critic can challenge the completeness of the knowledge.) In contrast, many dyslexics have had to learn to survive despite being able to survey, absorb, and retain only, say, 20 or 30 percent of what they are expected to know. As information and knowledge grows by orders of magnitude and orders of magnitude again, in ever-decreasing periods of time, how long will it be before the specialist will have to be content with 85 percent, then 75 percent, then 65 percent or less of an ever more narrowly focused specialty, an awareness of the larger whole constantly receding? Which experience—seeking to know almost all, or making do by retaining only the most essential—is likely to be of the most use in the coming years and decades?

Of course, in the long run, we will always need both the specialist and the "global," visual thinker, and the rare individuals who somehow combine the strengths of each. The problem is not essentially with specialization itself, but with the way education and work are organized today, the way we are often led to believe that only the specialist knows anything, the way the specialist approach is believed to be adequate. "We are nearly there," they say. "We just need some more time and some more money." But sometimes a wholly different approach is needed before the answer can be found. Sometimes we need to back off a bit rather than burrow deeper.

In a book called *The Image*, Kenneth Boulding pointed out that professors have always wanted students to learn as much as possible. The students, on the other hand, have always been interested in learning as little as they could get away with. The irony of it all is that, in the end, the students, as Boulding points out, are clearly in the right, more so now than ever before.[2] And more so in the future than now.

NEW AND OLD IDEAS ON EDUCATION

Educational reform is an old story. Whatever the current situation, it never seems that we have got it right. Someone is always telling everyone else to do it a different way. It is probably inevitable that education should be a comparatively conservative and status-conscious enterprise. After all, for many, so much depends upon how demanding the system seems and how well one progresses through it. Whole lives rest in the balance. Around the world today, most other rationales for determining elite status have been swept away. Consequently, educational level and quality have become the primary criteria for many of the most desirable careers.

In the past, status was clearly a major consideration. If the aristocracy learned Latin, then all aspiring, middle-class parents wanted their children to learn Latin. Comparatively, usefulness was not important, emulation of those with high status was. Of course, Latin was (mostly) dropped from educational curricula some time ago. But even now everyone still seems to study the old, prestigious European languages like French and German (if they study a language at all), when, of course, they would find it far more useful to study Japanese, Chinese, Russian, Arabic, or Spanish. It is said that generals always fight the last war. It may be inevitable that schools will offer courses based on an old prestige that is increasingly irrelevant.

Sometimes selection among students seems to be education's main task. What is studied is less important than if it easily and credibly distinguishes between the very bright, the average, and the not so bright. It seems to matter little what is learned and what is tested as long as a small number rise to the top, and, preferably, the same small group in each case (otherwise things get confusing). Some wonder if education is really only a long and elaborate hazing process.

Scientific subjects, for example, have generally been taught in an authoritarian manner, although this is slowly beginning to change in some of the best schools. But in most schools the facts are more important than how the facts were come by. The truth is that the facts are not fixed and students should not be encouraged to believe that they are. As physician and essayist Lewis Thomas has observed,

> Over the past half century, we have been teaching the sciences . . . as though they would always be the same. The teaching of today's biology, for example, is pretty much the same kind of exercise as the teaching of Latin was when I was in high school long ago. First of all, the fundamentals, the underlying laws, the essential grammar, and then the reading of the texts. Once mastered, that is that: Latin is Latin. . . . And biology is precisely biology, a vast array of hard facts to be learned as fundamentals, followed by a reading of the texts. . . . We are teaching science as though its facts were somehow superior . . . more solid, . . . immutable. . . . And it is, of course, not like this at all. In real life, every field of science that I can think of is incomplete, and most of them . . . are still in the earliest stage of their starting point. . . . The next week's issue of any scientific journal can turn a whole field upside down, shaking out any number of immutable ideas and installing new bodies of dogma, and this is happening all the time. It is an almost everyday event in physics, in chemistry, in materials research, in neurobiology, in genetics, in immunology. The hard facts tend to soften overnight.[3]

A NEW REFORMATION

We may find it easier to make fundamental changes in our systems of education if we have some really new tools to work with. For decades, operating an old-fashioned mainframe computer required elite knowledge and skill. Now, the new personal computers can be operated in the language of the common people—those who are not particularly computer literate. This situation provides an important new source of power for original creation, for access to information and the communication of it, and increasingly, perhaps, for real self-reliance. Of course, the machine itself is not enough. Investors learned painfully some years ago: don't invest in "high technology" companies; invest in companies that have learned how to use high technology well. So it is, surely, with education. It is not a question of how many computers a school has, but what kind of computers it has and how they are used.

With the easy-to-use personal computer, as with Martin Luther long ago, the sacred texts are now translated into the common language and are now available to the masses. People can use the tool without bureaucratic intermediaries and without spending years learning a special language. If the analogy is apt, it is only a matter of time before the common people start acting on their own interpretation of these texts, independent of previously recognized authority. As with Dante Alighieri, who first wrote in Italian rather than Latin, the story of the universe, the guided journey through heaven and hell, is now being told in the vulgar language. Less and less will the common people have to wait for pearls dropped from the mouths of the fully qualified computer knowledge clergy.

But what is most important for our purposes is that, in time, the personal computer could make purposeful self-education—which was used so effectively by many of those we have been considering—more common and more efficient, gradually, perhaps, challenging even the authority of the conventional educational system. Many of our great visual thinkers and creative dyslexics relied almost exclusively on self-education, either leaving school at an early age like Edison and Faraday, or making an uneasy accommodation with the school system, like Einstein and Churchill. Long ago, when formal education was not widespread, it was mainly a process involving one tutor and one student, or just a handful of students. In the nineteenth century, education began to be mass produced, just as material goods were. There were economies of scale with school classrooms of thirty, forty, or fifty students and university lecture theaters with hundreds of students.

With the new personal computers becoming cheaper and more powerful with its software becoming every month more sophisticated and easy to use, it is only a matter of time before we will have come full cycle once again. This time the personal, one-on-one tutor can be the computer. Of course, there will need to be plenty of time for class interaction and discussion with a human teacher, but basic presentation of the material, using many senses and repeated exercises could be done on the computer. Many school systems still consider computers an expensive investment. The truth is otherwise. When properly designed and used, machines are always cheaper than human labor, especially human labor that is not being used effectively.

Just as personal computers promise to reverse education's mass-production orientation and begin a return to more individual learning, so there is a reversal taking place in the world of industry as well. At one time only mass production of identical products was profitable. Now, one of the most profitable enterprises is to find clever ways to make customized products for individual tastes.[4] This growing kind of industry requires a new kind of worker and the organization of workers into teams rather than as passive elements on an assembly line. These workers could benefit from the possible changes coming to education, from the broad unfolding of potential for interactive self-study that would, hopefully, continue through life, enriching the economy and the larger society as it enriches the individual. Then we might observe what is now only rarely seen—the auto mechanic who is interested in aeronautical engineering or fractal mathematics, the government worker interested in architecture or the new physics, the housewife interested in solving long-standing puzzles in the mathematics of tiles. Effective self-education requires easy access to information, and the personal computer is granting that access. With masses of information cheaply stored on laser disk (compact disc or CD-ROM), the World Wide Web or some other technology, it would seem that the personal computer is an ideal tool for such self-education.

It is not hard to imagine that in time all the resources of the Library of Congress or a major university library, text or visual, would be available in the home or at the local school or public library. The particular technology is less important than that the storage medium is durable, easy to access, and very cheap. The numbers are going the right way and are likely to continue in that direction for some time.

But self-education is nothing without performance, results, application, and (sometimes) official verification through some sort of credible examination. The inherent flexibility of the personal computer, however, as a primitive intelligence waiting to be formed like clay, would seem an ideal material for these tasks as well as all forms of creative pursuits—many not possible otherwise. It would seem likely that such developments would open up such pursuits to whole new sections of the population—especially those creative visual thinkers who could never pass the initial hurdles before.

MATURE ORGANIZATIONS

There may be little value in understanding the potential in those with mixed talents and disabilities and in designing appropriate educational systems for them if there is no way to ensure that companies, universities, government agencies, and other organizations allow these potentials to be realized. In the early days of companies and countries, there has always been, of course, a certain amount of disorganization, which usually has been a blessing to creative dyslexics and other people with "non-standard" qualifications. Edison had no qualifications for his life's work. Einstein's record and references were so undistinguished that for years he could find no regular work, until a friend's father helped him get a low-level job as a government clerk.

It is an old story. But as institutions become more organized and mature, and their personnel policies more rationalized, paper credentials become increasingly important. As institutions become more bureaucratized, and different groups and factions begin to compete more aggressively for a few positions providing high rewards, stability, remuneration, status, perquisites, and power, the infighting eventually backs everyone into a corner. The only apparently fair criteria for hiring and promotion come to be paper qualifications, education, and experience, not promise, or passion, or originality.

This situation is a disaster for the creative dyslexics and late bloomers because these qualifications depend so much upon just those qualities where they are the weakest, because so much relies on primarily academic skills such as rapid reading, ease of assimilation and recall, reliability, and organization (together with some degree of political savvy, perhaps). Those who do well in these areas are those who are good at doing what their teachers and supervisors want them to do. True, they are dependable. In many situations, these qualities could, of course, be most desirable, as in subordinate staff positions, for example. But in other situations and job positions, in those where vision is required, such abilities could lead to slow decline and eventual disaster for the entire organization.

Perhaps the biggest problem with "mature" companies is not their size or age, or their general bureaucratic sclerosis. Their main problem could be that their rational personnel policies, at long last, have been effectively implemented. They may have too many people perfectly qualified for their positions and perfectly trained for the tasks they must carry out. The original innovative, but, in contemporary terms, "unqualified," staff will have left or been fired or retired long before.

Thus, as soon as rational personnel policies finally are effectively implemented, then it may be time to start over, with a new company with fresh ideas, and a fresh, largely inexperienced and "unqualified" work force. Clearly, creative dyslexics and visual thinkers are more likely to play an important role in such revitalized companies than in mature and rationalized ones. C. Northcote Parkinson once observed, half in fun, that all really important things are done in garages and old warehouses. Once the proper building is "purpose built" for an organization, then the institution or industry is already well along the path to decline.[5]

MEDIEVAL CLERK TO RENAISSANCE MAN

If our view is correct, the extent of coming change may be very great. For some four hundred or five hundred years we have had our schools teaching basically the skills of the medieval clerk—reading, writing, counting, and memorizing texts. Now it seems that we might be on the verge of a new era, when we will wish to, and be required to, emphasize a very different set of skills—those of a Renaissance man such as Leonardo da Vinci. With such a change, traits that are considered desirable today might very well be obsolete and unwanted tomorrow. In place of the qualities desired in a well-trained clerk, we might, instead, find preferable a habit of innovation in many diverse fields, the perspective of the global generalist rather than the narrowly focused specialist, and an emphasis on visual content and analysis over parallel verbal modes.

If we continue to turn out people who primarily have the skills (and outlook) of the clerk, however well trained, we may increasingly be turning out people who will, like the unskilled laborer of the last century, have less and less to sell in the marketplace. Sometime in the not too distant future machines will be the best clerks. It will be left to humans to maximize what is most valued among human capabilities and what machines cannot do—and increasingly these are likely to involve the insightful and integrative capacities associated with visual modes of thought.

EPILOGUE

I knew I was different in the way that I thought, but I didn't realize why I was so dumb at spelling . . . and rote memory and arithmetic. . . . The first time I realized how different . . . brains could be . . . was when I bumped into Jim Olds at a dinner party back in the late sixties. Jim . . . was a professor here [at Caltech] . . . famous for his pleasure center work. . . . A speaker talked about the way we think and compared it to holography. Jim was across the table from me. I said, "Oh, yes. When I'm inventing an instrument or whatever, I see it in my head and I rotate it and try it out and move the gears. If it doesn't work, I rebuild it in my head." And he looked at me and said, "I don't see a thing in my head with my eyes closed." We spent the rest of the evening . . . trying to figure out how two professors—both obviously gifted people at Caltech in the Biology Division—could possibly think at all, because we were so different. So then I took this up with Roger Sperry [Nobel Laureate and near lab neighbor] and I realized that I had some amazing shortcomings as well as some amazing gifts.

The preceding passage is quoted from the oral history project at the California Institute of Technology in Pasadena.[1] The speaker is the late William J. Dreyer, Ph.D., who is increasingly recognized as one of the major innovators in the early days of the biotech revolution that is now washing over all of us. In September 2007, one of his inventions was placed in the National Museum of Health and Medicine in Washington, D.C.—the first gas-phase automated protein sequencer, which he patented in 1977. The sign over the machine on exhibit reads: "The Automated Gas-Phase Protein Sequencer: William J. Dreyer and the Creation of a New Technology."

A strong visual thinker and dyslexic, Dreyer developed new ways of thinking about molecular biology. With his powerful visual imagination, he could somehow see the molecules interacting with each other. Sometimes he was almost entirely alone. He (with his colleague J. Claude Bennett) advanced new ideas based on new data about how genes recombine themselves to create the immune system. These ideas turned out to be twelve years ahead of their time. Most did not like this new theory because it conflicted with the conventional beliefs held by most expects in the field at the time. "It was so counter to the dogma of the time that nobody believed it," his widow, Janet Dreyer, explained to me. Dreyer's approach also used a form of scientific investigation (peptide mapping) with which most immunologists were then unfamiliar. "Knowing what we know now pretty much any biologist would look at Bill's data and say that is what it has to mean. But few could understand it then," she noted. However, gradually, they all learned to think the way Dreyer thought. Then, it was obvious that Dreyer (and Bennett) had to be right.

TO SEE WHAT OTHERS CANNOT SEE

In his earlier school days, Dreyer had the usual difficulties experienced by dyslexics who are also very bright. But in college and graduate school he began to find roles that made use of his strengths while he learned to get help in his areas of weakness. He joined a study group. The others in the group all took careful notes in the lectures. He took no notes. He just sat there while he listened and observed carefully. Then after the lecture, they provided him with the detailed data, and he told them what it all meant. "He was giving the big picture and all the major concepts, " explained Janet Dreyer. Eventually, surviving a major life-threatening illness made him realize it was time to refocus his life—and then his fascination with the laboratory work began to draw him in.

Soon, the young Bill Dreyer became a star in the laboratory. While in graduate school in Seattle, and while working at the National Institutes of Health (NIH) in Bethesda, he could tell his professors and colleagues which were the best experiments to do. Somehow he knew how to proceed and where to go in this brand-new field of study that came to be known as protein chemistry. His professors and section heads would write the grants, get the funding, and write the papers for him based on his ideas and observations. "The money just came. Because he was doing good work, grants would just be there for him," observed Janet Dreyer. He was happy at the NIH but eventually (after a previous Caltech offer had been refused) in 1963 Caltech persuaded Dreyer to come to Pasadena as a full professor at the age of thirty-three. Clearly, the value of his pioneering work had been recognized.

However, later, because of the further development of his heretical ideas, William Dreyer could not get funding from academic or foundation sources for inventing his new instruments. His department head would get irate phone calls from professors from other institutions complaining about Dreyer's publications and talks. He gave many talks at the time, making some attendees angry, although some could see the importance of his innovative observations. "He was on the lecture circuit then and he [gave these talks] a lot." Of course, these were not really unproven theories, explained his widow Janet. She pointed out that Dreyer was sure of his ground because he had the data to prove the veracity of his ideas. "It was not merely a hypothesis in that paper, it was real data." However, it was data in a form so new and so alien that almost everyone in the field could not understand what he was talking about. In time, these professors, and all their students, came to see that William Dreyer had been right all along.[2]

Because he could not get funding from the usual sources, Dreyer went to private companies to manufacture his instruments—something quite unusual and discouraged at the time but now wildly popular among universities hoping for a share of large royalty payments. Seeing the potential for his inventions (and their scientific impact) but having a hatred of administration and corporate politics, Dreyer came to be, as he told me, the "idea man" for seven new biotech companies (including Applied Biosystems) and bought himself a high-altitude, pressurized, small airplane with some of the proceeds. Years later, when Susumu Tonegawa was awarded a Nobel Prize (Physiology or

Medicine, 1987) for work he had done in Switzerland, his innovative sequencing work proved (through experiments that were illegal in the United States at the time) that Dreyer and his colleague had been correct in their predictions many years earlier.[3]

LEARNING BY DOING

Later in his life, Dreyer taught molecular biology to his dyslexic grandson, who was clever with computers but was having a very hard time in high school. Employing the grandson as a kind of apprentice, Dreyer would start each workday (using a form of applied just-in-time learning) saying something like: "I want you to write this little search program for me today but first let me explain the biology you need to know to do this task." In time, working with Dreyer, the grandson skipped the latter part of high school, most of college, all of graduate school, and is now doing advanced "post-doc"-level work writing computer programs, doing advanced programming developing databases, graphic user interfaces (GUIs), and other tools. He also uses sophisticated scientific information visualization techniques to help link various human traits to sections of the genetic code. In doing this work, he notes that he uses his "visual thinking ability to design the architecture of the programs . . . visualizing the components in his head, trying it out and fixing what doesn't work, before I write the code—much like my grandfather." He is not only doing high-level work; some argue that the grandson is, in fact, working at the leading edge—in recent years coauthoring peer-reviewed journal articles.[4] Indeed, one of the grandson's work colleagues only got his own Ph.D. degree (and a required publication) because the grandson was able to write a tutorial and GUI that helped a member of the colleague's required publication review committee better understand the significance of the advanced work done by the colleague.[5]

Bill Dreyer, never one to read many books, did read *In the Mind's Eye* and telephoned me to explain: "Your book describes the way I think. This is my life. The next time you come to the LA area, let's talk. I want to tell you my story."[6] This contact led to many visits, many discussions, some recorded conversations, and a long-term friendship. Dreyer died of cancer in the spring of 2004. One of the enduring passions of his later work had been to try to understand the relationship among dyslexia, visual thinking, and the high levels of creativity he had experienced in his own life and work. He had participated in a small conference on visualization technologies and dyslexia held at the National Library of Medicine in Bethesda, Maryland, flying east with Janet in his own plane.[7] Years afterward, as his health declined, Janet eventually sent out news to friends that he had stopped eating and was nearing the end. I read the e-mail at an Internet cafe in Dublin, Ireland, where I had been giving talks for the Irish Dyslexia Association. I immediately phoned Bill from our hotel and to my surprise we had a long conversation, our last. Shortly afterward, I traveled back home to D.C. and then on to Pasadena, arriving the day before he died. He was then unable to talk, but I assured him that I would continue the work that he thought so important. My second book, *Thinking Like Einstein*, is dedicated to: "William J. Dreyer, 1928–2004, molecular biologist, strong visual thinker, prescient inventor, instrument maker, who loved to fly high to see what others could not see, frequently alone."

MAGNIFICENTLY ILL-ADAPTED ENGINES OF DISCOVERY

The story of the life of William Dreyer and his grandson, Brandon King, brings into sharp focus the considerable advantages, in the right setting, of the dyslexic kind of brain—at least of certain variations within the great diversity of dyslexic brains. (Of course, this story also strongly suggests what sometimes might be possible employing non-traditional educational approaches such as apprenticeship or home schooling.) We can see that this kind of brain—seemingly so magnificently ill adapted to conventional education—can be a powerful engine of insight, innovation, and discovery.

This kind of brain may cause many problems in early schooling, but it may also, sometimes, raise some individuals rapidly to the top of a new field of knowledge, pushing forward way beyond the many who are conventionally successful students but who find it hard to conceive of anything really new or really important. Perhaps they cannot see through to the novel, unexpected solution because they have learned too well exactly what the teacher wanted them to learn, what was expected on the conventional test. They cannot easily unlearn what they have been taught. (One high-achieving researcher at the NIH, with three professional degrees, in law, medicine, and pharmacology, once admitted to me—to my amazement—that he was aware of his own limitations, constrained beneath a kind of glass ceiling. He was aware that in spite of all his academic accomplishments, he "was not dyslexic enough" to do really original, creative, and important work—as he had seen in his dyslexic colleagues.)[8]

With stories such as these, we can begin to understand that these visual-thinking dyslexics do indeed see the world differently. They think differently. They are not like non-dyslexics. They are not like each other. Often, they seem to "see things that others do not see." (I have been surprised at how this same phrase—with almost exactly the same words—reoccurs in many different and unconnected settings.) Yet these same individuals have great difficulty with things that are easy for almost everyone else—especially at the lower levels of education. In schools, they are constantly tested on what they are not good at—almost by definition.

Why are they never tested, we should ask, in the areas where they have enormous talent and can make major contributions in their later life and work? Can teachers and school psychologists believe that this is possible? I hope that some of the stories offered here have created and will continue to create a new vision of what is possible. But this new vision may also require the development of new tests and measures—ones quite different from conventional academic measures, but perhaps ones that are better suited to the new realities of life and work, suited for the visual-thinking dyslexics but also suited for many non-dyslexics as well.

At a recent conference, I met a child and adolescent psychiatrist who said he had been using *In the Mind's Eye* as a diagnostic tool for years. He explained that he had given his clients something like forty or fifty copies so far. He asked them to highlight in yellow all those traits that were like themselves and cross out all those that were unlike themselves. I said, "Oh you mean the list at the end of the book." He said, "Oh no, I use the whole book—it is much more useful than the usual tests and measures. They are all devised by linear thinkers for linear thinkers." Afterward, it occurred to me that the whole book indeed could readily serve as a rambling catalogue of traits, but that it also would not hurt that these clients would be forced to see in themselves traits shared by important persons who accomplished a great deal, sometimes in spite of their difficulties but more often because of their difficulties and their very different ways of thinking.[9]

To succeed with such extremely mixed abilities, as these individuals often do, one needs to have a deep reservoir of confidence and fortitude to carry on in spite of the judgments of others that you are, in fact, really slow and lazy and stupid. To maintain the required drive, determination, and sense of mission in the face of almost constant early failure and humiliation is often nothing short of miraculous. It would appear that only a comparatively small number survive these early days with enough confidence and drive to press on, against all odds, to find success in some area of special knowledge, deep understanding, and passionate interest. As we have seen, much of *In the Mind's Eye* has been an attempt to understand the nature of this kind of success and the remarkable individuals who seem able to find their way around so many obstacles, seeking an area where they are at home with their work, often performing at very high levels of proficiency and productivity.

I have come to believe that those of us who are trying to understand and to help dyslexics (along with others more or less like them) must come to see that conventional academic remediation is only part of the job—and not the most interesting or important part. We need to seek ways to help dyslexics find and develop their own talents, large or small, so that they cannot be beaten down—hiding their talents along with their disabilities. I, for one, believe that one of the best ways—perhaps the only really effective way—to do this is to study the lives and work of highly successful dyslexics (in some detail and in all their great diversity)—to allow other dyslexics to see what can be done as well as showing how it can be done.

AMAZING SHORTCOMINGS, AMAZING GIFTS

I wanted to begin this epilogue with Bill Dreyer and his grandson because their story shows so clearly the mixed problems and great potential of dyslexic individuals and dyslexic families in a most modern, scientifically sophisticated, and technologically advanced context. However, as noted previously, I also want to use this epilogue to give briefly a sense of the broad range of developments and accomplishments since *In the Mind's Eye* was first published years ago. There are very good books that deal with understanding weaknesses and ways to remediate various difficulties—and many of these are listed in my bibliography. But this is not my purpose.

I want, rather, to show how the talents that many dyslexics exhibit are powerful and valuable assets (frequently hidden and misunderstood) in a rapidly changing world. These individuals may appear to be slow and backward, but in many cases they are way ahead of nearly everyone around them, those who are mostly blind to what visual thinking dyslexics can do and what they can contribute. Accordingly, I have put together here a selection of brief snapshots to suggest what we have been learning from individual stories as well as from a few more systematic studies—what has been going right and what has been going wrong. I want to convey the impression that much has been learned but there is much work still to be done.

Over the years, more and more dyslexic individuals have become aware of their own special talents as they confront their long-hidden weaknesses and humiliations. Many are finally coming to understand the positive aspects of their own mixed abilities well enough to give themselves permission to talk about and think about things they no longer need to see as only failures and weaknesses to be hidden and denied. They have discovered that it does not go away just because you pretend it is not there.

Fathers are realizing that they cannot drive it out of their sons by ever-more-rigid discipline. Rather, they are learning that it is best to confront it, face on, with the new realization that there are hidden talents to be acknowledged (and used) as well as fears that will increasingly fade away in the clear light of day. (To my surprise, I have often found that only one hour of talking about talented dyslexics and new visual technologies can free these fathers, and others like them, to see themselves and their families in very different ways, allowing themselves to think and say things never possible before. They come up to me after a talk and say, "I'm not really dyslexic but let me tell you . . . I've never told this to anyone before. . . .")

Learning to see the positive side can be powerful indeed. Of course, there is still a great deal of work to be done, but it is focused on increasing strengths rather than decreasing weaknesses. Consequently, I think it is urgent at this time to outline the kinds of things that need to be done—to take seriously, at long last, the varied talents and considerable strengths of dyslexics. The time is right. The time is late. The time is long overdue. Those on the front lines—the teachers, tutors, parents, advocates, and school psychologists—those who have cared the most, those who have been able to understand when no one else did—unfortunately, they have often done less than they could have done because they have attended to only half of the job. This should change, and I hope that it will change soon.

TWENTY YEARS AHEAD

Some eighteen years have passed since *In the Mind's Eye* was first published in the spring of 1991. Shortly afterward, two reviewers asserted that the book was some twenty years "ahead of current educational thinking." As a first-time author, I was, of course, greatly pleased to read this. But I did not take it very seriously at the time. However, over the years since, I have come to wonder more and more why so many efforts in school reform have so often ended in failure or inconsequence and how the perspectives outlined here have been so uniformly ignored by the professionals—although not ignored by creative, visual-thinking dyslexics, their families, and a handful of insightful teachers and educational institutions.

I am beginning to think that perhaps we might get some different results if we were to learn to see education through truly different eyes. Perhaps this might help us understand how we can find the islands of hidden talent in many students, creating motivation and a sense of hope that never existed before—and so find ways to do less damage during all those years of education.

It is perhaps worth our looking at one of these reviews with some care to see what might be helpful. The following remarks were made by the late Professor T. R. Miles, Ph.D., who, among many other accomplishments, was founder of the Dyslexia Unit at the University of Wales, Bangor, and was founding editor of the peer-reviewed professional journal *Dyslexia*. Professor Miles wrote: "I entirely agree with [Dr. Doris Kelly] when she says that [*In the Mind's Eye*] is 'about 20 years ahead of current educational thinking.' Many of us have spent long hours considering all the things that dyslexics are supposed to be weak at. What Tom West reminds us of is that we need also to consider dyslexics' strengths. . . . At present, so he implies, education is in the hands of those who possess all the traditional skills; and since, not surprisingly, they assume that others are like themselves, the needs of some very gifted thinkers whose brain organization is different are not being adequately met. I very much hope that both teachers and educational planners will read this book and take its message seriously."[10]

Professor Miles touches on an aspect that is almost never addressed but may be a major point in our considerations—that is, that most of the people involved in the study and remediation of dyslexia are not dyslexic themselves and were, in many cases, excellent pupils in their own school days. Accordingly, it may be very difficult for them to see the emerging great strengths and creative powers possessed by the students sitting before them, who seem such helpless fools in doing even the most elementary academic work. Over the years, I have become more and more impressed with the extreme difficulty many have in separating the concept of intelligence from academic performance and test taking. Dr. Orton did not have this problem. With his first dyslexic patient, Orton made a point of identifying high intelligence that did not correspond to conventional academic skills.

However, since his time, many seem to be like Dr. Starr—referred to in chapter 1, by Eileen Simpson. Dr. Starr was full of good intentions in helping the struggling children but, apparently, was completely unable to believe that the children in her center could be highly intelligent. She thought Simpson was bright and capable—indeed, sufficiently able to follow her as head of the center. Simpson was smart; consequently, Simpson could not possibly be dyslexic herself. It is simply unthinkable. ("What nonsense! . . . Dyslexic? Impossible"). We all may wonder how many in this field hold, deep, deep down, the same beliefs as Dr. Starr, in spite of the best intentions and in spite of all protestations to the contrary. We may also wonder how many children pick up on these beliefs, buying into a life of low expectation and unrealized potential.

I am not arguing, of course, that all dyslexics have great talents, nor that all non-dyslexics are blind to the talents of dyslexics. But I believe we do need to consider that the kinds of talents they do have, great or small, may be just the kinds of talents that are invisible to conventional teachers and conventional tests and conventional measures of academic ability. This is why I feel that developing a whole new family of tests and measurement instruments is so critical.

In the ways of the world, it is a simple truth that one cannot be considered to be really bright unless there exists some test on which you can get a top score. And, as we have been trying to show throughout this book, there are many talents and abilities that are important in life and work that are never measured by conventional psychological and academic tests. This needs to change.

To do this properly, we will probably have to get highly successful dyslexics involved in the process because many conventional educators and test designers may be quite unable to see what needs to be measured, how it can be measured, and why it is important to measure it. Old habits of thought are hard to break—especially when you have always gotten top grades on your papers and examinations. But perhaps, once again, we will need to rely on dyslexics to "see what others do not see or cannot see."

Clearly, it is time to develop new ways of assessing the strengths and weaknesses of students as early as possible. Sometimes great abilities can be hidden beneath striking difficulties. Sometimes, we are beginning to see, the kid who is having a lot of trouble with reading or spelling or arithmetic may turn out to do very well indeed with astrophysics or advanced mathematics or molecular biology or computer information visualization—areas where visual thinking and image manipulation are more highly valued than rapid recall of memorized names or math facts or large quantities of data. Sometimes, when the conceptual context and the technologies change in dramatic ways, the high talents that were once marginalized or considered of low value in the old era may suddenly move to center stage, providing the exact set of skills required in the new era.

Somehow, we need to be able to observe these changes with an open mind—alert to seeing potential and opportunity rather than only failure and restriction. Sometimes, we might discover, the kids who are having the most trouble should not be held back. Rather, perhaps, sometimes, they should be pushed a long way forward—if the right area can be identified by some new and innovative screening device or testing method. As we have seen, those who are most gifted in higher mathematics can have persistent problems with arithmetic;

some great writers can never learn to spell. Sometimes, our conventional ideas about tests of grade-level basic skills make no sense at all.

However, identifying the right area of strength for specific students can be quite important. It would help to hold their attention. But more important, perhaps it will allow them to use talents never recognized before. Perhaps it will allow them to learn in ways that are quite different from conventional schooling (and out of conventional educational sequence). Perhaps it will allow them to gain respect from others (and for themselves) for being able to do things that are challenging for other students—or even challenging for their teachers. Of course, not all will be able to move ahead quickly, but even the most limited student may have islands of strength that no one knew existed. We must make it our business to help them find these islands. Sometimes, almost anything will do to start. But in the end, it is really important for them to be able to say, "I have a lot of trouble with this but I am the best in my class (or my school) at doing that." Sometimes, a whole life hangs in the balance.

In many cases, of course, such an approach could be an administrative nightmare. How can the system cope with such extremes of diversity, with so many different measurement scales? Life is so much easier when there is one scale—conveniently showing those who are the top in everything and those who are at the bottom of everything. With some new system, with so many scoring high on at least one or two subtests, how do you know which ones are really bright and which ones are really not so bright? However, it is clearly not beyond our capacity to make it work if we are convinced that it must be made to work—if we are convinced of the real value of diversity in brains and abilities.

We now have many new and sophisticated tools at hand. And the need is great. It is high time to give up the illusion of uniformity and begin to take advantage—for the sake of these individuals as well as for the needs of society at large—of vast differences in abilities in many diverse fields. When we all are having to compete with many millions of others globally (in an increasingly uncertain and changing economy; with fast transportation and cheap light-speed communication), it is suddenly essential that all of us quickly find whatever special talents we have and develop these to a very high level, whether or not it is part of the conventional academic curriculum.

True, it is not yet perfectly clear how this can be done. But it is clear enough that it will need to be done—and in ways that are very different from traditional educational pathways—and most likely there will be extensive use of the newest information visualization technologies. Sometimes, just listening to the improbable life stories of highly successful dyslexics is enough to give us a few really new ideas about how to move forward in this direction.

BABY DINOSAURS AND ANCIENT RED BLOOD CELLS

A case in point is the story of John R. (Jack) Horner, an example of a highly successful dyslexic with minimal traditional academic skills but maximum productivity in his field of research. Horner flunked out of the University of Montana seven times. However, after he had established himself, "his brilliant synthesis of evidence . . . forced paleontologists to revise their ideas about dinosaur behavior, physiology, and evolution." Horner never earned an undergraduate degree or a graduate degree. But now he is a professor with many graduate students, an honorary degree, and many, many honors. He failed "just about all his science courses, and never [completed] his undergraduate work." Although he had great difficulty with his course work, it is clear that at a deeper level he was continuously learning—absorbing the knowledge needed to understand and then revolutionize a field of knowledge.

As Horner tells the story, his difficult beginnings helped him to be a risk taker. "'Back in the days when I was growing up, nobody knew what dyslexia was. . . . So everybody thought you were lazy or stupid or both. And I didn't think I was, but I wasn't sure. I had a lot of drive, and if somebody told me I was stupid, that usually helped—it really helped me take a lot more risks. For someone that everybody thinks is going to grow up to pump gas, you can take all the risks you want. Because if you fail, it doesn't matter.'"[11]

But the risks paid off. According to the curator of the museum of vertebrate paleontology at the University of California at Berkeley: "A lot of people have tended to underestimate Jack because he hasn't come through the traditional academic route. But he is, without question, one of the two or three most important people in the world today studying dinosaurs." Horner is able to see things differently and he observes things others do not see. For example, he believes that it is really of little interest to find the fossil bones of a large adult dinosaur. What he is interested in finding are fossils of many dinosaurs of many sizes, in their environment, in order to understand the life of the animals and the way they interacted with other animals and plants in that environment. Horner is known not only for his markedly different way of looking at things but also for his unusual ability to see, in the field, the tiny fossil bones of baby dinosaurs that other experts cannot find. According to another researcher, "He has a gift. . . . He can see things the rest of us don't see."[12]

Horner is especially worth noting because, in spite of his persistent academic failures, he came eventually to be acknowledged as one who has transformed some of the fundamental thinking in his field. His story forces us to reconsider in a deep fashion what is really important in one's work and what is not. Horner proved to have extraordinary difficulties with things that are largely peripheral to his discipline (reading, composition, and test taking), but he also proved to be unusually gifted in those things that lie at the heart of his discipline (being unusually observant while searching for fossil bones in the field, being able to interpret the surprising patterns that emerge, being able to visualize easily changes to terrain over very long periods of time, thinking his way beyond and around his associates, seeing ways of using new technologies, and developing innovative and persuasive arguments based on looking at the fossil evidence in a very different way).

Horner says he tries to teach his students "to think like a dyslexic" because that is where the "good stuff" comes from—learning to read the book of nature with careful personal observations and fresh insight without being distracted by the theories of others. He says the rest is "just memorization." One of Horner's students, dyslexic herself, recently made discoveries thought "impossible"—finding red blood cells and flexible blood vessels inside a sixty-five-million-year-old fossil bone. Horner points out that this discovery was never made before because "all the books in the world" would say that it could not be done. He notes that it is easy for dyslexics "to think outside the box" because "they have never been in the box."[13] We need to see the truth of Horner's observation that dyslexia is "certainly not something that needs to be fixed, or cured, or suppressed!"

Indeed, we need to see that, as Jack says (in a recent article), "maybe it's time for a revolution"—or at least (from a separate interview) "it may be time to start something."[14]

MOST REWARDING AND MOST PAINFUL

Jack Horner's story is in some ways parallel to the experience of Dr. Marc I. Rowe—whose story came to my attention via e-mail recently. A continuing interest of mine has been the way the mixed abilities experienced by dyslexics and strong visual thinkers intersect with substantial accomplishment and real-life experience in various occupations. I have done no systematic questionnaires or large-scale surveys. But since *In the Mind's Eye* has been around so long, a number of stories have found their way to me. And I am persuaded that these case studies are often more valuable and revealing than many conventional surveys. They often reveal, or begin to reveal, the complex patterns apparent during a long and successful life—with many ups and downs, crashes and recoveries, changes in the economy or career or technological context—but follow the growth of significant accomplishment through it all. Without such observations, I sometimes wonder, how can a researcher know what survey questions to ask, what to count, or what testing instruments to administer (or what new instruments need to be designed)?

One example of the stories that have come to me, from time to time, is, of course, Dr. William J. Dreyer from Caltech (as described above). Another wonderful example is Dr. Rowe's story, which came to me unexpectedly last fall. A retired pediatric surgeon who had won a major honor in his field, Dr. Rowe had been the subject of a series of interviews about his life, and he decided to try to understand how his substantial career successes were somehow linked to his early school failures. It is best to allow him to speak for himself—in the clarity and elegance of his own words—in the e-mail of November 12, 2008, sent to me via the Web master of the Krasnow Institute for Advanced Study:

> Dear Mr. West, Reading your book, *In the Minds Eye,* has been one of the most rewarding but also one of the most painful experiences of my 78 years of life.

I am a retired pediatric surgeon living in . . . Florida. My last position was Surgeon in Chief of Pittsburgh Children's Hospital, Benjamin Fischer Professor of Pediatric Surgery and Chief of the Division of Pediatric Surgery, the University of Pittsburgh School of Medicine. I have immodestly attached a brief summary of my CV because I think the information concerning my external accomplishments may be of interest to you.

Although I was never tested, I was always aware that I had severe learning problems, particularly related to spelling, punctuation, pronunciation, foreign languages, remembering numbers, dates, multiplication tables and concepts that require using formulas in chemistry and physics. My major failing is and was arithmetic. . . . My reading skills are good but I still cannot pronounce new words that I encounter. My wife checks my spelling and pronunciation and the computer spell check has been a Godsend.

Although I was considered backward during my pre-college years, I confused people because often I would grasp a complex concept before anyone else. I used visual images and film and cartoon strips [in my head] to think and could do this rapidly. Often I was considered impolite because, once I "got the pictures" I could manipulate them rapidly and "I get it" quickly. I then turned my attention elsewhere.

I could understand and explain complex systems such as physiologic and pathologic systems by reducing them to a cartoon sequence. My memory, although faulty in many regards, astonished people by its exactness when it came to surgical operative sequences and detailed anatomy and physiology. When asked about a certain step in a surgical procedure, I would play that part of the operation in my mind and actually see that part of the procedure unfold.

Three things happened recently that encouraged me to write to you: (1) I began studying Tai Chi Quan. The Tai Chi was significant because my instructor, a famous martial artist and teacher, took me aside and told me I do not think like other people. This got me [wondering]. (2) I had been awarded the Ladd Medal by the American Academy of Pediatrics some years ago. Since this is the most respected award in the field and is only given periodically and sparingly the Academy decided to record the life histories of the living recipients. (3) When surfing the web, I discovered your book and immediately bought and read it.

Being interviewed for hours as a Ladd Medal recipient and having my life story recorded brought back all sorts of memories of painful experiences: periods of self-doubt and disgust, embarrassing incidents and failures and triumphs. The biographies in your book had me actually breaking out in a sweat sometimes.

Here is a brief overview of some episodes in my life: Elementary school—segregated into the Dumb Class. Considered by my father as lazy, sloppy and an under-achiever who lacked discipline and perhaps was stupid. Parents where advised by high school guidance teacher that I was below normal in intelligence and should not consider college—it would be a tragedy. I should learn a trade. Was enrolled in welding school to begin after high school graduation.

In my senior year of high school I entered the New England Wrestling Championship Tournament. Made it to the finals where I wrestled the captain of the Brown University wrestling team. I got the silver medal; he got the gold. The coach of the Brown team refused to believe I was stupid and brought me to Brown University for testing. I was then admitted to Brown without submitting an application. I got by in physics and chemistry by blind memory. I passed a French proficiency test by memorizing almost the entire French vocabulary with flash cards without knowing grammar or pronunciation.

In medical school I was rooming with two other medical students during my first year. We studied together and I mimicked their method of learning. Within three months I was flunking out of Medical School. I moved out and lived alone and developed my own way of studying medicine . . . using case studies from the *New England Journal of Medicine*. At that time the *Journal* provided descriptions of cases and then provided a commentary that worked toward a diagnosis. I researched various body systems based on these cases and what I learned using this method seemed to stay with me.

Once I began the clinical years, everything became easy.

I discovered surgery in medical school and it was like coming home.

I became well known for my diagnostic skill. I would review all the data then I would sit quietly by myself and listen to [what I call figuratively] the "Little Men." They do not read the journals or go to conferences but they always know. However, they only speak in whispers so you have to listen with the third ear. My lectures using self-drawn cartoons to describe concepts, systems and processes became well known. I was fortunate to lecture in Korea, Japan, Australia, Canada, Mexico, South America, Central America, South Africa, Greece, Turkey, Italy, Spain, Ireland and England. . . . My summary CV traces much of my medical career [provided here in an endnote]. Sorry if this letter is rambling but I thought perhaps my story may be of interest to you. Signed, Marc I. Rowe, MD[15]

Similar in some ways to the experience of Jack Horner, the life story provided by Dr. Rowe forces us to reconsider and think more deeply about what we assume we know about talent, intelligence, and capability. Two of his statements hold our attention as central elements: "Once I began the clinical years, *everything became easy.*" "I discovered surgery in Medical School and *it was like coming home.*" This story compels us to wonder how it can be so. How can one be so powerfully adept in the hands-on, three-dimensional world of surgery and physiology (with tissues and structures rapidly growing and changing in each patient) yet have so much trouble with basic school subjects that are comparatively easy for almost everyone else. I suspect that individuals such as Dr. Rowe can help provide a window into aspects of human capability and talent that are now poorly understood.

DOING MATH INSTEAD OF WATCHING MATH

The changes in work and education that we envision involve not only new ways of seeing people such as Horner and Rowe but also new ways of using advanced technology. Not surprisingly, visually oriented people seem able to quickly adapt to visually oriented technologies. In the past, as we have been saying, visualization was rare in many fields. This has been changing. As we saw in chapter 9, the world of the professional mathematician has been undergoing fundamental change in recent years—reversing, in many respects, more than a hundred years of development in the opposite direction. In more recent years, some professional mathematicians have been rethinking the way they view their whole discipline—as well as the way they think their discipline should be taught. In the old days (not very long ago), logic and rigorous proof were seen as the most important aspects of serious high-level mathematics. In recent years, however, this has changed. Currently, many leading professional mathematicians now see that visualization, experimentation, and original discovery are of prime importance—a position unthinkable by most respectable mathematicians only a short time ago.[16]

An emerging consensus point of view has been described by one mathematics professor who is familiar with years of debate within the profession. As we saw in chapter 9, he observed: "Mathematics is often defined as the science of space and number, as the discipline rooted in geometry and arithmetic. Although the diversity of modern mathematics has always exceeded this definition, it was not until the recent resonance of computers and mathematics that a more apt definition became fully evident. Mathematics is the science of patterns. The mathematician seeks patterns in number, in space, in science, in computers, and in imagination. . . . To the extent that mathematics is the science of patterns, computers change not so much the nature of the discipline as its scale: computers are to mathematics what telescopes and microscopes are to science. . . . Because of computers, we see that mathematical discovery is like scientific discovery. . . . Theories emerge as patterns of patterns, and significance is measured by the degree to which patterns in one area link to patterns in other areas."[17]

The far-reaching consequences of this change in perspective can be partly seen in the concurrent major reevaluation of certain university-level mathematics courses in recent years. Although this reevaluation has been widespread—with many alternative proposals for improvements and extensive debate among professional mathematicians—in most instances real change has been slow to take place. And in many cases those changes actually implemented have been relatively modest in scope.

In some cases, on the other hand, the changes have been quite extensive, with dramatic results. For example, some time ago, three professors developed innovative courseware for teaching calculus as an interactive laboratory course using a graphics computer together with a high-level mathematics program—one designed to do mathematics in all of its three major forms: numerical, symbolic, and graphical.

Unlike many other course innovations, such changes are not just additions to the regular class lectures, but rather, they have had an enormous impact in transforming all aspects of the teaching and learning process. (Indeed, this courseware may be seen as a preferred model for the transformation of many other disciplines and learning environments.) Instead of spending lots of time learning by hand routines that can be quickly done by the computer, the students are pressed to move rapidly on to high-level conceptual matters and a variety of practical problems, focusing mainly on examples from medicine, biology, and the life sciences. This is in marked contrast to the traditional calculus problem sets that are now seen by professional mathematicians in Europe as well as in America as being highly contrived and artificial, with little relevance to real mathematics in either research or application.

An unpublished evaluation summarized some of the radical curricular innovations and the increased effectiveness of this new type of laboratory calculus course: "The [new] course changed the delivery of calculus from lectures and texts to a laboratory course through an electronic interactive text. . . . One of the most remarkable characteristics was [the students'] exploration through calculation and plottings. In the traditional calculus courses, the instructor announces the mathematical theory and then reinforces it with examples and exercises, and students recite the theory and solve problems illustrating the theory. [In the new course], however, the learning pattern of students . . . was dramatically different. The experimentation by redoing, reformatting, rethinking, adapting, and making changes led students to discover the basic concepts and principles [for themselves]. . . . The students . . . indicated that they had a feel for 'doing' mathematics instead of 'watching' mathematics."[18]

As we try to identify the causes of success in this approach, it may be no small matter that the students are encouraged to think and learn visually first (and describe what they see in ordinary language)—before attending traditional lectures with conventional terminology and notation. A major shift in learning technique (along with a delightful informality and irreverence) is apparent in the authors' explanation to their students: "One of the beauties of learning the CALCULUS&Mathematica way is your opportunity to learn through graphics you can interact with. *In this course, your eyes will send ideas directly to your brain.* And this will happen without the distraction of translating what your eyes see into words. Take advantage of this opportunity to learn visually with pure thought uncorrupted by strange words. The words go onto an idea only after the idea has already settled in your mind. This aspect of CALCULUS&Mathematica distinguishes it from other math courses."[19]

It is perhaps also of no small importance that students who learn in this new way have shown that, in comparison with the traditional courses, they understand the basic concepts better, can remember the information longer, and can apply the concepts to practical uses more effectively. It is increasingly apparent that many of the consequences seen in this new teaching approach—using interactive graphical computer systems with advanced software and courseware—may indicate possibilities for effective innovation in many other disciplines. Thus, these new teaching approaches may be merely one manifestation of a much larger trend—as professors in many disciplines come to see the great value of visual thinking and visual interactive learning for all kinds of subject matter and all kinds of students.

THE SMARTEST LAD

The links between dyslexia and talent have a long history. In the first description of developmental reading disability in the English language medical literature, in 1896 (as we have seen), it was noted that one student could not learn to read in spite of "laborious and persistent training." However, his headmaster observed that this student "would be the smartest lad in the school if the instruction were entirely oral."[20]

From the time of the earliest researchers (in the 1890s) until Samuel Torrey Orton (in the 1920s) and Norman Geschwind (in the 1980s), the central puzzle of dyslexia has always been the linkage of high ability in some areas with remarkable and unexpected difficulties and disabilities in other areas. For more than a century we have recognized this pattern, but we have generally focused on only one aspect. With the best of intentions, we have learned much about how to fix the problems that dyslexics experience, but we have done almost nothing to develop a deeper understanding of the varied and hard-to-measure talents that many dyslexics clearly do possess.

Highly successful dyslexics nearly always say that their accomplishments and special ways of seeing come directly from their dyslexia—not in spite of their dyslexia, as is sometimes argued. We should take them at their word and give credence to what they say. Most professionals in the field agree that talents are important, but eventually they almost always come to focus exclusively on the serious business of reading and academic remediation alone. We need to change this.

THE OTHER HALF OF THE JOB

I believe the time has come to be serious about trying to understand the talents of dyslexics—to do the other half of the job—and trying to understand the puzzle that so fascinated William Dreyer at Caltech until the end of his life. Accordingly, I believe that it is time to think about building a bold and ambitious plan of action (within research institutes, private foundations, universities, creative technology companies, and appropriate government agencies) that will focus primarily on talent. The major intent of these initiatives would be:

> To build a program with its primary focus on understanding and developing the strengths and talents that dyslexics have—rather than mainly focusing on areas of remarkable weakness. As dyslexic real estate entrepreneur Barbara Corcoran says, "use what you've got." We would be supplying the missing half of what dyslexics need for life and work—about aspects of their lives that are not yet well understood but should be.

> To build a bold program that would, in time, be as large as all current academic remediation programs in effort, resources, and impact on the lives of dyslexic children and adults—including funding, research, training, and development of best practices. It took over a hundred years for us to arrive at our current position. Now that we know the importance of what we are doing and what is still urgently needed, we should plan to deliver substantial results in, say, about one tenth of that time, that is, ten or perhaps fifteen years.

As a dyslexic myself, I feel a growing sense of personal responsibility to dyslexics as a group. I feel the need to substantially change the course of what we are trying to do within the field. I feel we need to seriously embrace a radical change now or there will be no change at all—allowing additional generations of dyslexics to suffer needlessly, wasting distinctive talents that are greatly needed by the society and the economy at large as we enter an age of great uncertainty on many fronts. We should recognize that we badly need the big picture thinking and original insights that seem to be the signature contributions of the most successful dyslexics. (It is a paradox, but it may be that those who would appear, initially, to need the most help are, in time, those most likely to be able to help the most.)

Much good has been done over the years, but we have been doing only half the job. A small group of researchers and practitioners have been talking about talents for years. But almost nothing has happened. Indeed, on the whole, in most aspects, it has gotten worse. In the late 1980s, talents and strengths were often discussed at national and international dyslexia conferences—especially by the old-timers who had been in the field for decades. But in recent times, almost everyone has been focusing almost exclusively on reading and related academic skills—without any attention to other skills of real value that are not taught or tested in conventional schools.

LOOKING AGAIN AT OLD IDEAS

As we have seen throughout this book, talent is fundamental to the perspectives provided by Samuel Torrey Orton and Norman Geschwind. But most researchers and practitioners have focused on remediation—on fixing problems—not on developing new understandings of special and hard-to-measure talents. This is especially true of talents that seem (on the surface) to have nothing to do with school and conventional academics but, in fact, may have everything to do with success in life and, sometimes, very high-level work. While all agree that talents are important, usually almost nothing has been done. And of course, there has been virtually no funding for research of this kind. We need to find a way to change this.

In my view, we need to reassess what we are doing in the dyslexia field so that at each step of the way we are helping dyslexic children and adults see themselves as capable and valuable—rather than as wounded, broken, or needing to be fixed. As we have learned, sometimes the best intentions can lead to obvious problems—along with missed opportunities. In my talks and writings since *In the Mind's Eye* was first published, I have always advocated a focus on the special talents seen among dyslexics. Through examination of several individual cases, I have tried to understand and communicate how these special talents are linked to dyslexia—and how we can help dyslexic children and adults to lead better lives by learning from the lives of highly successful dyslexics.

The areas of weakness are now well understood. But when we look at high success in entrepreneurial business, artistic creation, technological design, or scientific discovery, we see that we need to find ways to focus on what it is that the dyslexic brain is doing much better than those around them. I do not think we know this yet. How do we identify it? How do we measure it? How do we develop it once identified? One thing seems clear, it is quite different from reading books, listening to lectures, and memorizing long lists of names, numbers, and facts.

We do not yet understand it, but I suspect it has something to do with, as we have seen, having a global view, seeing the big picture, having strikingly unusual or unexpected insights, being able to build complex mental models, being able to look over the horizon to see things that others do not see because of an ability to think in ways that others do not think, observing patterns in nature and human institutions that others do not see or cannot see. These are not easy things to measure or understand. But we have whole families of new tools and technologies to help us do the job—many of them visual and graphical in orientation and therefore well suited to the kinds of strengths we are seeking to understand. We just have to be convinced that it is an important job to do. To date, apparently, almost no one has believed this.

As Albert Galaburda pointed out years ago, the brain research done in the 1980s could have been done some forty or fifty years earlier—if only it had been thought important to look at the wiring and microscopic structure of the brain. Orton had lamented, in his day, the same lack of interest in the structure of the brain. The psychoanalytic and then behavioral approaches that dominated for decades cared nothing for the brain's structure.

TIME TO GET SERIOUS ABOUT THE TALENTS OF DYSLEXICS

I think that we (advocates and professionals, adult dyslexics and family members) need to start dyslexic-centered programs—as if the talents of dyslexics really did matter. We must not be mainly school centered, or tradition centered, as we are now. Many professionals continue to believe that traditional academics will always dominate and drive all other sources of knowledge and understanding. But many things are changing in fundamental ways. It is time for all of us to completely rethink what we should be doing in schools and colleges to prepare students for today's global economy. Often our thinking is imprisoned by our deeply held but outdated assumptions about what is essential for success in education and work and life.

Last year, at a meeting of high-level educators talking about the future of US education, a colleague observed with dismay that it was like listening to General Motors and the rest of Detroit talking about the future of the US auto industry. Sometimes the conventional experts, for all their education, experience, and high positions, have no idea what is needed and how to proceed in a time of major change. The best of the old will remain, but much is to be discovered or rediscovered anew. But sometimes, the alternative path may be more clear to those who have been forced to deal, in one way or another, with unusual forms of high intelligence and unusual forms of high academic disability—in a rapidly and deeply changing technological and economic context.[21]

Careful investigation of the life and work and accomplishments of highly successful dyslexics—where insight and innovation are more important than book knowledge—may show us how wrong we can be using conventional perspectives. Technological change is redefining the kinds of things that need to be learned—trends often completely ignored by conventional educational debates (or are dealt with in the most superficial manner).

Many dyslexics excel at high-market-value creative and entrepreneurial skills while they often fail in low-market-value school-based clerical and memorization skills. To the amazement and consternation of conventional teachers and school psychologists, some dyslexics excel at very high-level mathematics when they still have not mastered "basic" mathematics. Some brains seem designed to do the high-level work while the elementary is stubbornly problematic. For some, breaking through conventional expectations is routine.

It is growing increasingly apparent that we need a serious and systematic study of highly varied but distinctive talents among dyslexics.

Probably, we will need whole new families of tests and measures based on new assumptions and employing advanced and sophisticated technologies. These tests and measures should be helpful to all students—but it seems that the consideration of highly successful dyslexics may serve us best by forcing us to think differently about what is really important.

In the early days of neurology, scientists thought the left hemisphere of the brain was the important one (the "major hemisphere"). It was believed to be the seat of reason and it could talk. The right hemisphere (the "minor hemisphere") was seen as merely a low-level vestige of our early evolution. It did not seem to be very rational and it (mostly) could not talk. Now we know that if the right hemisphere is not functioning well, it is far more disabling than if the left were not functioning well. Sometimes, our conventional assumptions overwhelm our powers of observation so that important distinctions are completely misunderstood from the outset.

AN ENGINE OF ECONOMIC DEVELOPMENT—
CREATIVE DYSLEXICS

Doing this new work, we will have to deeply reconsider what we think we know about intelligence, talent, ability, and creativity. We will also need to note relevant trends in other fields. For example, we need to look to the growing awareness in business and economic development literature of the high value of innovative and entrepreneurial skills—the same skills that many dyslexics exhibit. As, for example, we have noted with Richard Florida's *The Rise of the Creative Class* and *The Flight of the Creative Class*, we can see how insights from city planning and the making of the three *Lord of the Rings* films can reshape our ideas about who is really generating new wealth and where.

Florida's book *The Flight of the Creative Class* begins with his description of his visit with Peter Jackson—who was describing his efforts, working with Richard Taylor of Weta Workshop and others, to build through the three *Lord of the Rings* films a core group of highly creative people in Wellington, New Zealand. This is just the sort of effort that Florida had come to endorse, noting that city planners and others concerned with economic development have come to learn that to build up local and regional economies, it is not enough to build shopping malls and sports stadiums. Rather, one needs to provide the conditions to attract highly creative people and, in turn, these will attract other creative people and build new companies and businesses.[22] Consequently, since many of these highly creative people are likely to be dyslexic, it may not be a stretch to speak of "creative dyslexics as an engine of economic development."

A recent experience is instructive. This past August I attended the computer graphics conference (ACM-SIGGRAPH) in Los Angeles, as I have done for many years. Among the companies and products I have been interested in lately is Massive Software from Auckland, New Zealand. Massive is a computer program that allows filmmakers to animate, more or less independently (with simple menus and sliders), individual behavior among thousands and thousands of figures on the screen—as in the *Lord of the Rings* battle scenes or in certain beer commercials. I visited the Massive hotel suite (they were not on the exhibits floor this time), having just heard a technical panel discussion about how Massive Software had been used by Pixar, Digital Domain, and other major computer graphics companies in their own recent projects (such as *Wall-E*). Also, I had long been interested in the history of Massive and its association with the *Lord of the Rings* films—with a view to possibly using some of this material in a future book. On entering the hotel suite, I briefly described who I was and what my books are about. At the outset, I was surprised and delighted to discover a very high level of interest in my research by virtually all the Massive staff I had contact with that afternoon. Eventually, we had dinner together and exchanged many stories of extremely talented dyslexics working in the computer graphics field in many different parts of the world.

This experience underscored for me what I had long known—that some (or many) of those who are creating the new technologies and valued products around the world are just the ones who are often suffering the most in current conventional educational systems. It is becoming more and more clear to me that we need to rethink what we are trying to do in education and what our unspoken and unexamined assumptions are. We need to use the newest technologies to prepare our students for the realities of modern markets—and in so doing tap into talents that have rarely been noticed or developed before. Accordingly, we need to understand the ways creative dyslexics are creating high-value products and services in a new world economy that often has little to do with conventional academic skills.

DISCOVERING WHERE DYSLEXICS THRIVE

We need to move beyond fixing problems. Rather, we need to discover where dyslexics thrive. To do this, we need to push forward in several directions. As we develop new assessment tools beyond conventional measures, doubtless we will need to use new technologies, new insights, and new perspectives to measure capabilities not possible to measure before. It is possible, even likely, that we will come to measure things we thought unimportant previously. Hopefully, we will come to understand surprising results, such as the great relative speed with which dyslexics could accurately recognize certain patterns before non-dyslexics—especially when they are often much slower at many other tasks. We need to develop mentor programs targeted to dyslexics of several different types. We need to find funding or enthusiastic outlets for documentary films, graphic novels, dramas, children's books, and other informal and visual media that will communicate these insights and perceptions to a larger audience—always moving past the usual concern with problems and remediation—to reveal the reality of high-level talent and unexpected potential.

I believe we need to develop a range of scholarships designed for talented dyslexics—not to compensate for low performance but to take advantage of idiosyncratic high performance, that is, to bring out high levels of hidden talent. We need to establish special grants for highly gifted individuals who exhibit great talent but also have areas of weakness or disability that would normally result in their exclusion from conventional forms of higher education and career development. We need to assess the institutional changes required so that dyslexics with markedly mixed talents (and others more or less like them) can still work well within established larger institutional structures. We need systematic studies of how this works and does not work.

We should begin to recruit to our investigations creative workers who understand nonconventional areas of technology and talent and use them in their own work every day. We need to design research, education, and conference programs that will be of interest to those working in these fields—those working in fields where dyslexics often thrive, such as designers, filmmakers, engineers, architects, artists, craftsmen, technicians, scientists, computer graphic artists, and specialists in scientific information visualization, those who process and communicate information visually and graphically (using the most advanced technologies) rather than the printed words and numbers that are central to traditional education. We will need to do outreach to occupational groups that include many dyslexics, groups that have learned to fully appreciate the kinds of special talents that many dyslexics have—talents that are seen as especially useful within these groups. (Some have estimated that more than 50 percent of computer graphics artists are dyslexic, while the top groups may near 100 percent dyslexic.) Talks and workshops need to be provided for these groups at their own professional conferences and meetings (as well as at selected dyslexia meetings).

An example of recent developments in links between dyslexia and certain occupations is a study now being conducted (with National Science Foundation support) by the Harvard-Smithsonian Center for Astrophysics. As the center has noted on its Web site:

> Could people with dyslexia be predisposed to science? The Laboratory for Visual Learning [at the Center for Astrophysics] is investigating a hypothesis that people with dyslexia, because of differences in neurology, may be predisposed to certain forms of visual processing that are useful in science. We are currently carrying out research to test this hypothesis, specifically looking at how dyslexia affects abilities of astronomers to analyze image-processed data.[23]

The Harvard-Smithsonian research program could be just the beginning of a whole series of unexpected downstream consequences based on the continuously unfolding computer and Internet revolution. Some of these consequences may have no overt connection with dyslexia but could, in backwards fashion, play to the visual-thinking strengths that many dyslexics exhibit. A program called "Galaxy Zoo" is now providing an Internet platform for nonprofessionals to use their visual talents and capabilities to survey thousands of newly discovered galaxies and categorize them for later investigation by professional astronomers.[24]

An even more exciting new Internet program called Foldit involves understanding and predicting the patterns of folding in proteins—the enormously large and complex molecules that are essential for all life. The interaction of each particular type of protein with its environment is largely determined by the way it rolls itself up or folds itself to take up less space, exposing only part of itself as an outside surface to interact with the outside world (and making pockets within its folds to allow certain chemical reactions to proceed without contact with water, which has been squeezed out of the pocket). These days, it is not hard to know the exact elements and atoms that make up each protein molecule. But it can be very difficult to figure out how a certain type of protein will fold itself according to certain known physical rules—different parts of the molecule attracting and repelling parts of itself as if it were covered with tiny magnets.

The scientists involved in this research realized that computers could not do the job of modeling the folding because it is too complex and would take hundreds of years even with modern super-fast computers. Accordingly, they have devised an online game so that hundreds or thousands of nonprofessional players might use their human intuition and three-dimensional thinking skills to figure out how best to fold the protein according to the given physical rules. The designers hope that the game will help to solve certain scientific puzzles and perhaps lead to new drugs to cure certain diseases. The players are given scores for their achievements. It is intended that their names will be listed in the scientific papers that are produced—and even share in scientific awards such as the Nobel Prize, they say.

Of course, the game designers are mainly interested in making discoveries—figuring out how different proteins are most likely to fold themselves. (They also plan to study how people solve the folding problems.) However, when I first heard of the game, I immediately thought that this could be a wonderful test to measure extremely high three-dimensional visualization talents of the kinds we have observed in many dyslexics (and perhaps measure it on a global basis, broadly and very cheaply!). The game designers and program managers suggest that the field is wide open. One says: "I imagine there's a 12-year-old in Indonesia who can see all this in their head." They say nothing about visually talented dyslexics, but they are clearly on a similar path. They say that they hope to find "protein-folding prodigies" and they expect to find a different kind of person who will thrive in this new scientific environment.[25]

I would not be surprised if the designers were to discover, in time, that many of their top players could be found to be among the three-dimensional visualizing dyslexics that we have been discussing. Perhaps, in time, their game could be modified in such a way as to provide an excellent test for these high-level three-dimensional visualization skills. This approach may also be especially valuable because there may be no upper limit as in conventional human-designed tests and measures. In contrast, these tests, based on endlessly complex patterns in nature, rather than puzzles devised by psychologists, could permit the identification of high levels of talent and capability impossible to measure before.[26]

The astronomical surveys and the protein folding game may be just the beginning. There might be a long series of new tasks and areas of research where highly visual dyslexics (and others more or less like them) will thrive and prosper. As we have observed before, brains that seem ill adapted to one technological context can be superlatively well adapted to a very different technological context. Of course, this is what deep neurological diversity is all about. The child who has struggled the most with conventional academic skills may be perfectly adapted to lead the way with these new and powerful computer visualization technologies. We just need an educational establishment capable of recognizing and adjusting to such major shifts in what is wanted and what is needed.

DYSLEXIC ENTREPRENEURS—"PERFECT FOR BUSINESS"

Clearly, there is much to gain by looking at dyslexia from the other side. For many non-dyslexics, this can be very hard to do; but for dyslexics it is as natural as breathing. For entrepreneur Barbara Corcoran, her own dyslexia is a considerable plus. Corcoran, a former New York City real estate developer and author, explains that she has long seen her dyslexia as a major advantage in the world of business. Her story underscores the importance of special skill in pattern recognition and communication as well as big-picture thinking:

I think a dyslexic personality is perfect for business. . . . If it doesn't take [a lot of book] study, if you can get [going] using your mouth or your feet, right from the beginning, my God, you are going to do well in business—you have a leg up. . . . I was always surprised when I was put into a room with a bunch of Harvard MBAs, well-educated attorneys, all the A students, [who] would be working on some conceptual problem, some new direction—somewhere new we wanted to take the business or industry—and there were a lot of ideas in the room. But, to be honest with you, there were a lot of little ideas in the room. I had the ability to sit there like a sponge, kind of zone out on it, kind of get the little pieces—and come up with the big idea, each and every time. And more important than that, I could see how each person in the room was going to fit in a specific role in making it happen. . . . When I said it, "Whoah, I've got it," people learned to listen to me because I always got it. And most importantly, I could paint that big, bright picture, and everyone could see it. . . . Nothing is better than giving a bunch of people running in different directions a road map that they all [could see] in living color and it would motivate them and get them running off the page in the same direction. So, visualization and an ability to communicate are really the only two things that you need to [deal with] a bunch of disparate parts and make them a team. . . . If there is one thing that dyslexic people can very often do [it] is make a bunch of people go left, right and in between—a big team buying into a big picture. But you have to be able to convey that picture. [27]

In this passage, Corcoran sums up in a wonderfully colorful way a perceptive insight into what may be one of the most important and distinctive characteristics shared by many dyslexics (within great diversity). When it comes to details, they may falter. They are not so good at remembering exactly what the teacher said or the exact argument used by this author or that. They may be a bit vague about the numbers cited or the lists of names given. However, sometimes, perhaps often, they can be very good at listening carefully and drinking in the whole situation in all its complexity—and slowly, quietly, working toward seeing a much larger integration of many diverse elements.

I cannot help but compare Corcoran's observations to Bill Dreyer's role in graduate school, noted above, of sitting quietly in biology lectures, taking no notes, taking it all in as a whole, and then explaining the "big picture" to his classmates in the study group, making sense of the notes they had dutifully and skillfully transcribed but did not really understand. Sometimes, it is not so much what the talents are as whether the talents can be recognized and brought to use in the task at hand—among team members with very different but complementary talents and skills.

The "big picture" is an extraordinarily apt metaphor here. We see the phase used so often. Corcoran can paint the "big, bright picture" "in living color" to convey the vision that all can understand and be guided by. She makes it clear that those dyslexics who have this remarkable set of abilities, and there do seem to be a good number, should be seen as perfectly well suited for the entrepreneurial side of business, that is, the most creative side of business, often involving high levels of risk. Of course, they may need to rely on non-dyslexics to do the reading, research, and detailed analysis that they find difficult or impossible to do. But, otherwise, they would appear to be supremely well suited for positions where it is important to see the larger patterns, to see what others do not see, to anticipate what will happen, to see the world differently so that where others may see only barriers and difficulties, they can find openings and opportunities.

Corcoran's observations are especially revealing with respect to the highly educated, the consistent A students. Members of this group have always been very good at doing pretty much exactly what the teacher wanted, exactly what the teacher expected. They are very good at the expected. It would seem, however, that they are not very good at the unexpected. They make great staff members—but, perhaps often, poor entrepreneurs or poor visionary leaders.

We need to develop a better understanding of what is happening when someone like Corcoran "zones out" and then develops an integrated vision of what is to be done along with each person's role in working to that vision. (Is this somehow connected to Dr. Rowe's "Little Men"?) We also need to think through the origins of the social mythology that the Harvard MBA or the lawyer with high grades has the right kind of intelligence and talent to grow the business or manage well in a time of opportunity or in a time of crisis. We need to remind ourselves that there is really no obvious connection between conventional academic achievement and the talents we really need and should be seeking. We are surrounded by people who believe this mythology, in spite of much evidence to the contrary. So we come to believe it as well. Often, it simply is not so. Perhaps it is time for a change.

(The recent financial crisis is ample testament to how a great many very smart and well-educated people can do very dumb things for a very long time—and seem surprised when the system reaches a point of collapse. One would hope we will find a way to behave differently with respect to the climate changes that are not yet fully upon us but are clearly on the horizon for those who are willing to use their eyes.)[28]

The world of entrepreneurial business, with so many opportunities, is also full of risk and uncertainty—requiring people who are able to learn from mistakes, those who are able to fall and fail and pick themselves up again, wiser but with renewed conviction and energy. According to Corcoran, it would seem that dyslexics (at least some of them, perhaps lots of them) are also remarkably well suited to the downside of entrepreneurial business as well:

> It really is easy to run and get the [winning] cup. The hard part is losing. . . . What I think has been so helpful to me is that I spent all my early years losing. So, my God, how sweet the winning feels. . . . How easy it is to win. But a lot of people who have everything come easily—particularly the As and Bs in school—they don't know really what it feels like to lose. So it is pretty shocking when they get thrown out into the real world. For me, the more hits I took and the more failures I had, the more I felt at home.[29]

DYSLEXIC ENTREPRENEURS—
"SECRET OF THE SUPER SUCCESSFUL . . . THEY'RE DYSLEXIC"

Interest in dyslexic entrepreneurs has continued to surface from time to time over the years, sometimes when it is not expected or particularly sought after. It is one thing to look at a group of entrepreneurs and ask how many are dyslexic or how many more are dyslexic in one place compared to another place; it is quite another to look at a small subgroup of the most highly successful entrepreneurs (in terms of money earned) and to find that the most common trait (among many possible traits) shared among all of them is dyslexia. An amazing discovery indeed. Several years ago the headline "The Secret of the Super Successful . . . They're Dyslexic" appeared on the front page of the *Sunday Times* (London), peaking just above the fold.[30] In breezy journalistic style, the *Times* article described the findings of a study linked to a BBC2 television series:

> You don't have to be dyslexic, but it helps. A study has revealed that millionaires are significantly more likely to suffer from the condition than the rest of the population. Psychologists who analyzed the mental makeup of business winners found learning difficulties are one of the most important precursors of financial success. About 40 percent of the 300 studied had been diagnosed with the condition— four times the rate in the general population. Experts believe one reason may be that dyslexics, who tend not to be good at details, learn to excel by grasping the bigger picture and producing original ideas. They might also be more motivated because of the social exclusion many feel.

It is striking that such views are considered front-page news in the popular press in Britain at a time when most dyslexia research (and the professional literature) around the world is devoted almost exclusively to a deficit model—that is, with research and practice almost wholly devoted (as we have noted) to reading problems and ways they might be corrected. With few exceptions, researchers and other professionals in the field seem to be uninterested in special talents or ways to promote the development of these talents. Although some researchers such as Dr. Norman Geschwind, as we have seen in earlier chapters, have argued that dyslexia is likely to be tightly associated with certain special talents, many researchers appear to believe that talents are either nonexistent or are unrelated to the dyslexia. Often it seems consideration of talents is seen as an unwelcome distraction from the main business of fixing reading problems.[31]

However, it should be emphasized that it is of no small significance to find—within a study targeting traits among highly successful individuals in business—that the most common trait is, in fact, dyslexia. On reflection, these findings may be seen as quite startling—that among many traits that might be shared among members of this group, dyslexia should be the most common. Consequently, in view of the study results, it would appear that teachers, researchers, and educational planners should find ways to balance their efforts in reading and spelling and help their dyslexic students to develop, as early as possible, high-level business and entrepreneurial skills (not to be confused with the clerical or accounting skills that would be needed by the staff working for these entrepreneurs but not by the entrepreneurs themselves).

For most educators, these would be shocking recommendations. But if one is serious about learning something from such studies (instead of merely reinforcing conventional beliefs), then it would appear that such recommendations should receive serious consideration. Indeed, it would seem clear enough that the teachers should be helping non-dyslexics to think like dyslexics (as Jack Horner has advised) in order to help them to be better equipped themselves to deal with a rapidly changing and highly competitive world economy. Such a reversal of the usual educational program could also serve to generate respect for the dyslexics from the non-dyslexics—and could promote a context where both could work together at high levels of creativity and productivity, through complementary talents and genuine mutual respect. Not a bad combination—although very different from conventional educational methods and outcomes.

SCHOOL FAILURE, WORK SUCCESS

We see that the view from the world of work can sometimes be quite different from the view from within the world of education. We have seen this in Corcoran's observations and in many other places. For some time it has not been surprising to see references to successful dyslexics in the conventional business media—as well as in media relating to technology, politics, and other fields.[32] Indeed, several years ago, *Fortune*, a major American business magazine targeted to corporate heads, did a long cover article on dyslexic chief executive officers (CEOs) that included Charles Schwab (founder of an innovative stock brokerage company), John Chambers (Cisco Systems), Paul Orfalea (founder of Kinko's copy shops, sold to FedEx several years ago), Richard Branson (founder of some 250 companies, including Virgin Atlantic Airways), David Boies (high-profile trial lawyer), Gaston Caperton (former governor of West Virginia, head of the College Board), William Dreyer (molecular biologist, biotech entrepreneur), Craig McCaw (entrepreneur, mobile phones), Don Winkler (Ford Financial among other companies), John Reed (Citibank, NYSE), and others.[33]

A later issue of *Fortune* deals with Richard Branson (yet again)—

focusing on the high success of the innovative businessman, mentioning his dyslexia only briefly in passing. On the cover of this special issue of *Fortune* we see a photo of a broadly grinning Richard Branson (seated on a wall at home on his personal island, Necker, in the British Virgin Islands) with the text: "The Man Who Has Everything. The Money. The Family. The Island. (Damn Him.)" And on the inside: "The outlines of the story are familiar: He was a middle-class British kid with dyslexia who nearly flunked out of one school, was expelled from another and finally dropped out altogether at age 16 to start a youth-culture magazine called *Student* that he hoped one day would be Britain's *Rolling Stone*."[34]

So, we might ask, why does the popular press, especially the business press in the United States and the United Kingdom, seem to be so fascinated by highly successful dyslexics? Indeed, why do they seem to be so far ahead of professional researchers, educators, and practitioners in this field—as well as research institutions and funding agencies? Are they just going for a sensational story, or are they tapping into something that merits close attention? Do the writers and editors and readers simply not understand the deeper nature of dyslexia, or are they seeing something more clearly because of their work-oriented rather than education-oriented focus? Are they dealing with highly successful dyslexic individuals who are wholly unlike most other dyslexics, or are they looking at a group that could teach us much about the potential of all dyslexics have (if and when they learn to build their lives around their talents rather than only focusing on correcting their deficiencies)? Is their perspective naive or wrongheaded, or rather, are they helping us to refocus on the larger realities of life and work?

Years ago, as we have seen before, Dr. Norman Geschwind proposed that dyslexics should be expected to show evidence of certain forms of talent, especially with respect to visual, spatial, mechanical, and mental model building.[35] Geschwind argued that the dyslexic trait would not be so common unless it conferred advantages to the human race over long periods of time. He also suggested that the same mechanism that produced the varied difficulties could produce the advantages as well. Clearly, from the earliest days, there were strong arguments for considering talents along with disabilities. However, something has been lost along the way—as most professionals have long focused on problems rather than potential.

TALENT MEETING

For several years a small group of researchers has been interested in trying to establish an empirical basis for the hypothesis that dyslexics are more talented in certain areas than non-dyslexics. In recent years, some of these researchers have worked with the Dyslexia Foundation (formerly the National Dyslexia Research Foundation) to move this research agenda forward.

Accordingly, a small meeting was convened at the MIT Conference Center near Boston, Massachusetts. The conference was built around Geschwind's hypothesis "that the same brain organization that led to language disabilities for dyslexics might also lead to certain high-level abilities." The goal of the conference acknowledged "that Geschwind's theory—dyslexics may have special talents or unusual abilities as compared to their non-dyslexic peers—while compelling, needs to be examined with increased scientific rigor."[36] The meeting participants and planners totaled twenty-two individuals—including dyslexia researchers, a facilitator, and a number of successful dyslexics (a scientist, a photographer, an actor, an accountant, an economist, a TV producer, an educator, a computer graphics artist and inventor). The basic idea was that researchers should listen to the dyslexics as they discuss their successes and strengths in order to begin to develop new ways of investigating these talents within a scientific context.

According to the meeting report, all the participating dyslexics "agreed that dyslexia is not just reading but a different way of thinking, of processing information; they 'see' things differently from non-dyslexic individuals. This could be an ability to make inferences more quickly than non-dyslexics, a visual-spatial approach to problem solving that may be unique to dyslexics, or some sort of unique perception or processing ability."[37] The general agreement that dyslexia is more than reading is noteworthy. It is even more noteworthy that the capacity to "see" differently comes up in such discussions with truly remarkable frequency—whether the field is radiology, magnetic resonance imaging, ultrasound, dermatology, or art fraud detection and authentication.

ADVANTAGES TO BE STUDIED

Similar observations came from Dr. Baruj Benacerraf, who is dyslexic, a former head of New York's Dana Farber Cancer Institute, and a Nobel Prize winner in immunology. He was invited to the MIT conference center meeting but was unable to attend. However, he expressed great interest in the dyslexia and talent project and said he would be happy to work with the group sometime in the future. Indeed, he made several statements during a telephone conversation that he said he would be happy to have included in the meeting report.

He said (in paraphrase): "Yes, there is definitely a positive side to dyslexia and this should be studied. One can deal with the problems with special techniques and lots of hard work." However, he asserted that there are definite advantages—seemingly often having to do with distinctive ways of perceiving space and visual material. But these advantages have not been studied. They seem to be little understood and are rarely developed explicitly. As an example, he spoke of his daughter, who is a specialist in ultrasound imaging. He said, "She can see things that others cannot or do not see."[38]

Dr. Benacerraf originally learned of his own dyslexia through the traits diagnosed in his daughter and his grandson—not an uncommon pattern. Of course, he was aware all along of his own reading, spelling, handwriting, and other difficulties. In part, he attributes his success in science to his dyslexia—since he believes the dyslexia allows him to have a better sense of time and three-dimensional space than others in his field.

IMPOSSIBLE FIGURES, POSSIBLE MEASURES

Many valuable insights came out of the MIT Conference Center meeting. However, perhaps the most important development was the general agreement that the thin edge of the wedge in talent research had already been recognized and replicated. Several researchers at the meeting indicated that they had hoped, years ago, to uncover hidden talents among dyslexic children and adults they were studying. They were then greatly disappointed not to be able to document these expectations using conventional testing instruments and measures.

However, based on the results of two studies discussed at the meeting, it seems evident that finding talents among dyslexics may require different forms of measurement. In other words, real talents are evident in life and work, but the usual methods of assessing talent do not appear to be appropriate for the task.

Several years ago, one group of researchers hoped to better understand aspects of these talents by comparing visual abilities among dyslexic and non-dyslexic school children. To their surprise and consternation, the first set of tests indicated the dyslexics were mostly slower and less accurate than the non-dyslexic students. There was one exception, however. In one part, the test of what is called "impossible figures" (line drawings of objects not possible to construct in three-dimensional space), the dyslexic children were faster but no less accurate.[39]

Some thought that this was an unimpressive finding. Others felt that this finding might be very important indeed—that it may be all that is needed to make a break into a deeper understanding of the dyslexic kind of brain and its distinctive (and hard to measure) special capacities. This task, unlike others, seemed to tap into apparently distinctive dyslexic abilities, seeing things as wholes rather than as parts and an ability to perform better on novel tasks.

Briefly, it appeared that the other, more conventional visual-spatial tests included a number of merely mechanical "traps" that tended to slow the dyslexics and make their answers less accurate—such as filling in the right circle on the wrong line of the answer sheet. On the other hand, the "impossible figure" tasks seemed well suited to the distinctive abilities of the dyslexics—as well as being relatively free of mechanical "traps."

With this in mind, a second study was carried out—with substantially similar results, largely replicating the previous study. The results of the two studies were reported in *Brain and Language* in an article titled "Dyslexia Linked to Talent: Global Visual-Spatial Ability."[40] In the discussion, these authors observe:

> Given that individuals with dyslexia typically read slowly, . . . the finding that individuals with dyslexia are faster than controls on any task is surprising. The compelling implication of this finding is that dyslexia should not be characterized only by deficit, but also by

talent. Global visual-spatial processing (what we refer to as "holistic inspection") may underlie important real-world activities such as mechanical skill, carpentry, invention, visual artistry, surgery, and interpreting x-rays or magnetic resonance images (MRI). Linking dyslexia to talent casts this condition in far more optimistic light than linking it to a deficit only. . . . The discovery of talent associated with dyslexia may eventually lead to more effective educational strategies and help guide individuals with dyslexia to professions in which they can excel.[41]

Thus, perhaps we might conclude, in spite of initial appearances to the contrary, that the authors of this study and their associates are indeed way out in front by looking at the talents of dyslexics: not only out in front of most other researchers, but perhaps even out in front of the popular and business press as well.

DIVERSITY IN TIME OF NEED—
CHURCHILL IN FROM THE WILDERNESS

Throughout *In the Mind's Eye* we have been dealing with diversity and mixed talents in many different forms. However, there are some deep questions that seem to lie under all of our considerations. We want superiority. Why then do we need diversity? It is a very old question. Perhaps the best reply is that we are now coming to understand that we need many kinds of superiority and that we cannot have all kinds of superiority at once.

There are many implications. Thus, it seems that we should encourage diversity not only to be civil, not only to be respectful, not only to be humane, not only to be just, but also because we have a particular stake in diversity that is rarely, if ever, fully articulated. We want there to be people who have abilities we do not yet know that we need, abilities that we have not ever tried to measure because we did not know that we needed them, abilities that may be in no way associated with the abilities and talents that we now measure by formal or informal means.

As we have seen, adapting to change has been a major feature in human survival, as with all of life. We have made the point several times that as technology and other factors in the environment change, they sometimes substantially redefine the kinds of talents and abilities (and passions) that are wanted. The theory of multiple intelligences is very important in this context. If there is only one kind of intelligence (as many have been taught to believe), then you have only more of it or less of it. But if there are in fact many forms of intelligence, then the whole discussion is transformed. Accordingly, in this context, the main idea is that changes in the environment often occur too quickly for either evolutionary or cultural adaptation to respond. We are capable of learning and adapting in many ways and at many levels, but it takes time.

What we want, therefore, is to find the means to tolerate and cultivate the talents in a wide diversity of individuals—with supportive institutions and organizations so that when we need a certain set of talents and abilities, it is already out there ready to be brought into service, sometimes, perhaps often, at the last moment, when finally it is realized that the old leaders or the old ideas are no longer working. Time is short and a radical, perhaps even frightening change must be made, whatever the risks.

In this connection, it is instructive to revisit one of the extraordinary people we have already profiled (one who has continued to hold my attention to a surprising degree over the years). With historical distance, it is now hard to imagine, but it was in many ways a frightening and risky act of desperation to make Winston Churchill prime minister of Great Britain in May of 1940—as all of Europe was about to collapse before the Nazi onslaught.

The situation at the time is worth some elaboration: The Parliamentary leaders did not really want Churchill. He was too unpredictable. "Only a month earlier [Anthony] Eden's followers in Parliament had outnumbered Churchill's, and some of Churchill's closest friends preferred Lloyd George as an alternative to Chamberlain."[42] The king did not want him either. He was not his sort. As Churchill's biographer William Manchester noted, "The King . . . liked Tories to be orthodox, conventional, loyal party men, and Churchill was none of these."[43] What is even more worthy of note, perhaps, is the fact that the professionals in the British Civil Service (many of whom, unlike Churchill, had been to university) expected that Churchill would fail and Chamberlain would be asked eventually to come back to lead the war effort. As impossible as it is now to believe, one insider noted in his diary: "There seems to be some indication in Whitehall to believe that Winston will be a complete failure and that Neville will return." Much later, this same insider was to observe: "Seldom can a Prime Minister have taken office with the Establishment . . . so dubious of the choice and so prepared to have its doubts justified." Fortunately, "among the general public it was different" and Churchill was well respected and quite popular.[44]

There is a special irony in Churchill being called back into action —an irony that might apply to many outsiders as they are called to serve, where, strangely, distance and even failure can be seen as considerable advantages. As we noted before, Churchill's past failures and former lack of power came to be seen as major advantages in the task that lay before him. As Churchill wrote: "Thus at the outset of this mightly battle, I acquired the chief power in the State. . . . As I went to bed at about 3 A.M., I was conscious of a profound sense of relief. At last I had the authority to give directions over the whole scene." He wrote that he felt "as if I were walking with Destiny, and all my past life had been but a preparation for this hour and for this trial." He saw that many "years in the political wilderness had freed me from ordinary party antagonisms. My warnings over the past six years had been so numerous, so detailed, and were now so terribly vindicated, that no one could gainsay me. I could not be reproached either for making war or with want of preparation for it. . . . Therefore, although impatient for the morning, I slept soundly and had no need for cheering dreams."[45]

However, for those charged with selecting a leader in a time of crisis, the decision sometimes can be quite difficult. After all, the risks can be very great. And in an atmosphere of high risk it is striking how observations about apparent differences in ways of thinking can influence the debate. Referring to Churchill, another government insider noted in his diary: "I have seldom met anybody with stranger gaps of knowledge or whose mind worked in greater jerks. Will it be possible to make it work in orderly fashion? On this much depends?"[46]

Sometimes, nonetheless, the high risk cannot be avoided. Sometimes the only thing that is clear is the inevitability of disaster if a major change is not made, if a major risk is not taken. Those who had led Britain during the 1930s had "seen a strong Germany as a buffer against bolshevism" but seemed to have no idea of the longer-term consequences of seeking "accommodation with a criminal regime." Eventually, however, members of Parliament saw what had to be done. The end of the old group of leaders "came when the House of Commons, in a revolt of conscience, wrenched power from them and summoned . . . the one man who had foretold all that had passed, who had tried, year after year, alone and mocked, to prevent the war by urging the only policy which could have done the job. And now, in the desperate spring of 1940, with the reins of power at last firm in his grasp, he resolved to lead Britain and her fading empire in one last great struggle worthy of all they had been and meant."[47]

You may ask whether Churchill's leadership at the beginning of World War II is really relevant to our interests. Surely our concerns are more modest in scope. The patterns do not apply. However, I would reply that many of us are charged with some responsibility for an institution, a family, an organization or business—however large or small—all of which must respond to changes and reversals. And with these changes, the one certain thing is that a major crisis will come sooner or later. And when the crisis comes, we want to have people like Churchill around to jump in and do what is needed.

Peter Drucker, discussing the management of organizations, refers to Churchill and notes that "the most successful leader of this century was Winston Churchill. But for twelve years, from 1928 until Dunkirk in 1940, he was totally on the sidelines, almost discredited—because there was no need for a Churchill. Things were routine or, at any rate, looked routine. When the catastrophe came, thank goodness, he was available. Fortunately or unfortunately, the one predictable thing in any organization is the crisis. That always comes. That's when you *do* need the leader."[48]

This is one big reason, perhaps, why we do not want everyone to be the same. Diversity can be seen as a deep survival strategy. We do not know when our "best and brightest" (our most certified and homogenized) are going to be very wrong. Sometimes the best and the brightest—for all their smartness, quickness, vast knowledge, and long history of success—really have no idea of what is going wrong and what to do about it.

Thus, we need to keep in mind the possibility that the solution to our problem lies with turning to someone who may a bit unusual, a bit of an outsider, a bit unpredictable, someone who may not fit the traditional patterns of academic and career success. Sometimes the visual thinkers and "dyslexic visionaries" may see things that others do not see. They may be ready to take actions that others, in their pride and arrogance, are not ready to take. As individuals and as institutions, we need to be open to the idea that sometimes, to find our way in a time of crisis, we will have to turn to someone who had been at the bottom of the class.

Thomas G. West
July 2009

Appendix A
SYMPTOMATOLOGY

SYMPTOMATOLOGY
U.S. DEPARTMENT OF HEALTH, EDUCATION, AND WELFARE (1966)

Despite the fact that it is over forty years old, the following listing of ninety-nine traits is still one of the most comprehensive available. The introductory paragraphs indicate a concern with complexity of terminology and definition that has persisted to the present time. The section has been excerpted in full, using exact quotations. However, the original numbering system for each category has been changed to one that is cumulative. Asterisks have been added to indicate those characteristics considered most pertinent to the individuals profiled in the present study—forty-two of the ninety-nine traits listed. In some cases, definitions of medical terms have been added in brackets. This listing may include some symptoms that would not now be considered appropriate for a consideration of "dyslexia," "specific language disability," or "learning disabilities." However, some factors may be related, although they might initially appear to be unrelated. As we have seen, the genetic and environmental factors that affect the very early development of the brain may also affect the development of apparently unrelated body systems. (Clements, *Brain*, 1966, pp. 11–13.)

VI. SYMPTOMATOLOGY—IDENTIFICATION OF THE CHILD

In a search for symptoms attributed to children with minimal brain dysfunctioning, over 100 recent publications were reviewed.

Many different terms were used to describe the same symptoms, e.g., excessive motor activity for age might be referred to as any one of the following: hyperactivity, hyperkinesis, organic drivenness, restlessness, motor obsessiveness, fidgitiness, motor disinhibition, or nervousness.

A large number of terms were too broad for other than limited value, e.g., "poor academic achievement"; others were more specific, e.g., "reading ability two grade levels below grade placement." A few are mentioned one time only, e.g., "inclined to have fainting spells." Others are too general (or judgmental) to classify, e.g., "often good looking." Opposite characteristics are common: "physically immature for age"—"physically advanced for age"; "fearless"—"phobic"; "outgoing"—"shy"; "hyperactive"—"hypoactive."

These examples represent some of the difficulties encountered in developing a scheme for classification of the symptoms, and indicate the variety of syndromes contained within the primary diagnosis of minimal brain dysfunctioning. The following represents an attempt to classify some of the descriptive elements culled from the literature.

PRELIMINARY CATEGORIES OF SIGNS AND SYMPTOMS

A. *Test Performance Indicators*:

*(1) Spotty or patchy intellectual deficits. Achievement low in some areas; high in others.

(2) Below mental age level on drawing tests (man, house, etc.).

(3) Geometric figure drawings poor for age and measured intelligence.

(4) Poor performance on block design and marble board tests.

(5) Poor showing on group tests (intelligence and achievement) and daily classroom examinations which require reading.

*(6) Characteristic subtest patterns on the Wechler Intelligence Scale for Children, including "scatter" within both Verbal and Performance Scales; high Verbal-low Performance; low Verbal-high Performance.

B. *Impairments of Perception and Concept-formation*:

(7)   Impaired discrimination of size.
*(8) Impaired discrimination of right-left and up-down.
(9)   Impaired tactile discrimination.
(10) Poor spatial orientation.
*(11) Impaired orientation in time.
(12) Distorted concept of body image.
(13) Impaired judgment of distance.
(14) Impaired discrimination of figure-ground.
(15) Impaired discrimination of part-whole.
*(16) Frequent perceptual reversals in reading and in writing letters and numbers
(17) Poor perceptual integration. Child cannot fuse sensory impressions into meaningful entities.

C. *Specific Neurologic Indicators*:

(18) Few, if any, apparent gross abnormalities.
(19) Many "soft," equivocal, or borderline findings.
(20) Reflex asymmetry frequent.
(21) Frequency of mild visual or hearing impairments.
(22) Strabismus [inability to attain binocular vision].
(23) Nystagmus [rapid involuntary oscillation of the eyes].
*(24) High incidence of left and mixed laterality and confused perception of laterality.
*(25) Hyperkinesis [abnormally increased motor function or activity].
(26) Hypokinesis [abnormally decreased motor function or activity].
*(27) General awkwardness.
*(28) Poor fine visual-motor coordination.

D. *Disorders of Speech and Communication*:

   (29) Impaired discrimination of auditory stimuli.
   (30) Various categories of aphasia [loss of power to use or understand speech].
*(31) Slow language development.
   (32) Frequent mild hearing loss.
*(33) Frequent mild speech irregularities.

E. *Disorders of Motor Function*:

   (34) Frequent athetoid, choreiform, tremulous, or rigid movements of hands.
*(35) Frequent delayed motor milestones.
*(36) General clumsiness or awkwardness.
   (37) Frequent tics or grimaces.
*(38) Poor fine or gross visual-motor coordination.
*(39) Hyperactivity [abnormally increased motor function or activity].
   (40) Hypoactivity [abnormally decreased motor function or activity].

F. *Academic Achievement and Adjustment (chief complaints about the child by his parents and teachers)*:

*(41) Reading disabilities.
*(42) Arithmetic disabilities.
*(43) Spelling disabilities.
*(44) Poor printing, writing, or drawing ability.
   (45) Variability in performance from day to day and even hour to hour.
*(46) Poor ability to organize work.
*(47) Slowness in finishing work.
   (48) Frequent confusion about instructions, yet success with verbal tasks.

G. *Disorders of Thinking Processes*:

   (49) Poor ability for abstract reasoning.
*(50) Thinking generally concrete.
   (51) Difficulties in concept formation.
*(52) Thinking frequently disorganized.
*(53) Poor short-term and long-term memory.
*(54) Thinking sometimes autistic [preoccupation with inner thoughts, daydreams, fantasies].
   (55) Frequent thought perseveration.

H. *Physical Characteristics*:

   (56) Excessive drooling in the young child.
   (57) Thumb-sucking, nail-biting, head-banging, and teeth-grinding in the young child.
   (58) Food habits often peculiar.
   (59) Slow to toilet train.
   (60) Easy fatigabiity.
   (61) High frequency of enuresis [incontinence of urine].
   (62) Encopresis [incontinence of feces].

I. *Emotional Characteristics*:

*(63) Impulsive.
   (64) Explosive.
*(65) Poor emotional and impulse control.
*(66) Low tolerance for frustration.
*(67) Reckless and uninhibited; impulsive then remorseful.

J. *Sleep Characteristics*:

   (68) Body or head rocking before falling into sleep.
*(69) Irregular sleep patterns in the young child.
   (70) Excessive movement during sleep.
*(71) Sleep abnormally light or deep.
*(72) Resistance to naps and early bedtime, e.g., seems to require less sleep than average child.

K. *Relationship Capacities*:

(73) Peer group relationships generally poor.
(74) Overexcitable in normal play with other children.
(75) Better adjustment when playmates are limited to one or two.
*(76) Frequently poor judgment in social and interpersonal situations.
*(77) Socially bold and aggressive.
(78) Inappropriate, unselective, and often excessive displays of affection.
(79) Easy acceptance of others alternating with withdrawal and shyness.
(80) Excessive need to touch, cling, and hold on to others.

L. *Variations of Physical Development*:

*(81) Frequent lags in development milestones, e.g., motor, language, etc.
*(82) Generalized maturational lag during early school years.
*(83) Physically immature; or
(84) Physical development normal or advanced for age.

M. *Characteristics of Social Behavior*:

*(85) Social competence frequently below average for age and measured intelligence.
*(86) Behavior often inappropriate for situation, and consequences apparently not foreseen.
(87) Possibly negative and aggressive to authority.
(88) Possibly antisocial behavior.

N. *Variations of Personality*:

(89) Overly gullible and easily led by peers and older youngsters.
(90) Frequent rage reactions and tantrums when crossed.
(91) Very sensitive to others.

(92) Excessive variation in mood and responsiveness from day to day and even hour to hour.

(93) Poor adjustment to environmental changes.

(94) Sweet and even tempered, cooperative and friendly (most commonly the so-called hypokinetic child).

O. *Disorders of Attention and Concentration:*

*(95) Short attention span for age.

*(96) Overly distractible for age.

*(97) Impaired concentration ability.

(98) Motor or verbal perseveration.

(99) Impaired ability to make decisions, particularly from many choices.

Several authors note that many of the characteristics tend to improve with the normal maturation of the central nervous system. As the child matures, various complex motor acts and differences appear or are more easily acquired.

Variability beyond that expected for age and measured intelligence appears throughout most of the signs and symptoms. This, of course, limits predictability and expands misunderstanding of the child by his parents, peers, teachers, and often the clinicians who work with him.

Ten characteristics most often cited by the various authors, in order of frequency:

1. Hyperactivity.
2. Perceptual-motor impairments.
3. Emotional lability [emotions prone to change].
4. General coordination deficits.
5. Disorders of attention (short attention span, distractibility, perseveration)
6. Impulsivity.
7. Disorders of memory and thinking.
8. Specific learning disabilities:
   a. Reading.
   b. Arithmetic.
   c. Writing.
   d. Spelling.

9. Disorders of speech and hearing.
10. Equivocal neurological signs and electro-encephalographic irregularities.

The "sign" approach can serve only as a guideline for the purpose of identification and diagnosis.

The protean [exceedingly variable] nature of the disability is the obvious conclusion from the approach to symptomatology and identification taken above.

The situation, however, is not as irremediable as it might appear. Order is somewhat salvaged by the fact that certain symptoms do tend to cluster to form recognizable clinical entities. This is particularly true of the "hyperkinetic syndrome," within the broader context of minimal brain dysfunctioning. The "hypokinetic syndrome," primary reading retardation, and to some extent the aphasias [loss of the power to use or understand speech], are other such examples.

Recognition and acceptance of these specific symptom complexes as subcategories, within the general category of minimal brain dysfunctioning, would facilitate classification and the development of appropriate management and education procedures.

Appendix B
SOURCES OF INFORMATION

Provided below is a sampling of names and web addresses for a range of organizations, websites and blogs which relate to the topics dealt with in *In the Mind's Eye*—from computer graphics and scientific information visualization to dyslexia, giftedness, creativity and neuroscience. Most sites will lead to many other organizations and sources of information. With the advent of Google and Wikipedia together with other search engines and ready sources of information on the Internet, web searches have become extraordinarily easy and rapid. However, with this ease and speed, the enduring problem of determining the reliability of information sources has become greater that ever. The organizations listed below should serve as helpful and reliable points of departure. (The usual Internet address prefix "http://" has been dropped from the list below unless the secondary prefix "www" is not used.)

ORGANIZATIONS, WEBSITES AND BLOGS WITHIN THE UNITED STATES

ACM-SIGCHI
(Special Interest Group for Human-Computer Interaction)
www.sigchi.org

ACM-SIGGRAPH
(Special Interest Group on Computer Graphics of the Assn. for
   Computing Machinery)
www.siggraph.org

American Speech-Language-Hearing Association (ASHA)
www.asha.org

Americans with Disabilities Act (ADA)
www.ada.gov

Association on Higher Education and Disability (AHEAD)
www.ahead.org

Council for Exceptional Children (CEC)
www.cec.org

Children and Adults with Attention Deficit Disorder (CHADD)
www.chadd.org

Council for Learning Disabilities (CLD)
www.cldinternational.org

Dana Alliance for Brain Initiatives
www.dana.org/dana alliances

Disability Rights Advocates
www.dralegal.org/

Dyslexic Advantage
(Dedicated to fostering the gifts and talents of all people with
   dyslexia)
http://dyslexicadvantage.ning.com/

Educational Resources Information Center (ERIC)
www.eric.ed.gov

Edutopia
(Educational magazine of the George Lucas Foundation)
www.edutopia.org

Eide Neurolearning Blog
(Drs. Fernette and Brock Eide, authors, *The Mislabeled Child*)
http://eideneurolearningblog.blogspot.com/

Ewing Marion Kauffman Foundation
(Foundation of Entrepreneurship)
www.kauffman.org

Free Appropriate Public Education under Section 504
www.ed.gov/about/offices/list/ocr/docs/edlite-FAPE504.html

IEEE Computer Society
www.ieee.org

International Dyslexia Association
(Formerly, The Orton Dyslexia Society)
www.interdys.org

In the Mind's Eye, Dyslexic Renaissance Blog
(Thomas G. West, author, *In the Mind's Eye* and *Thinking Like
    Einstein*)
http://inthemindseyedyslexicrenaissance.blogspot.com/

Krasnow Institute for Advanced Study, George Mason University
http://krasnow.gmu.edu/

Learning Disability Association of America (LDA)
www.ldanatl.org

Santa Fe Institute
www.santafe.edu

Southwest Branch of the International Dyslexia Association
www.southwestida.com

What Works Clearing House
http://ies.ed.gov/ncee/wwc/

Wrightslaw Special Education Law and Advocacy
www.wrightslaw.com

Yale Center for Dyslexia & Creativity
http://dyslexia.yale.edu/

ORGANIZATIONS, WEBSITES OUTSIDE THE UNITED STATES

Adult Dyslexia Organisation
www.adult-dyslexia.org/

Arts Dyslexia Trust
http://artsdyslexiatrust.org/

Barrington Stoke Ltd
(Books for reluctant readers)
www.barringtonstoke.co.uk

Brazilian Dyslexia Association
www.dislexia.org.br

British Dyslexia Association
www.bdadyslexia.org.uk/

Berufsverband akademischer LRS—Therapeutinnen (Austria)
(Professional Association of Academic Dyslexia—Therapists)
www.lrs-therapeuten.org/

Bundesverband Legasthenie & Dyskalkulie e.V. (Germany)
(Dyslexia & Dyscalculia)
www.bvl-legasthenie.de

Center for Child Evaluation & Teaching (Kuwait)
www.ccetkuwait.org/

Dyslexia Association of Ireland
www.dyslexia.ie

Dyslexia Association of Singapore
www.das.org.sg/

Maharashtra Dyslexia Association (India)
www.mdamumbai.com

Pro Futuro (Latvia)
www.disleksija.lv

NOTES

CHAPTER 1. SLOW WORDS, QUICK IMAGES: AN OVERVIEW

1. Faraday, quoted in Tyndall, *Discoverer*, 1868, pp. 77–78. The preceding paragraph relies heavily on Tyndall's description. It is perhaps a foreshadowing of the core idea of our current narrative that Faraday continues this passage, "How often are the things we fear and esteem as troubles made to become blessings to those who are led to receive them with humility and patience" (Jones, *Life and Letters*, 1870, p. 152).

2. A few examples of studies drawn from the literature of creativity are Hadamard, *Psychology of Invention*, 1945; Beveridge, *Scientific Investigation*, 1957; Koestler, *Act of Creation*, 1964; Braithwaite, *Scientific Explanation*, 1968; Storr, *Dynamics of Creation*, 1972; Arieti, *Magic Synthesis*, 1976; and Judson, *Search for Solutions*, 1980. A sampling of professional and popular surveys dealing with different forms of creativity and including specific consideration of the two hemispheres of the brain are Bogen and Bogen, "The Other Side . . . Creativity," 1969; Blakeslee, *The Right Brain*, 1980; Springer, *Left Brain, Right Brain*, 1981; Ehrenwald, *Anatomy of Genius*, 1984; and Edwards, *Artist Within*, 1986. A series of articles by the Bogens and others reviewing recent research concerning the two hemispheres and creativity can be found in the September 1988 issue of *Psychiatric Clinics of North America*, pp. 287–491. It is noteworthy that the Roger Sperry or R. W. Sperry mentioned in this section is the same Roger Sperry at Caltech who figures in the story of William Dreyer that is told at the very beginning of the epilogue of this edition.

3. Geschwind and Galaburda, *Cerebral Lateralization*, 1987, pp. 1–4. Some of the associations proposed by Geschwind and his colleagues are being confirmed by some recent studies, while other evidence is more mixed. In a recent review of the evidence, Galaburda focused on what is known as the "testosterone hypotheses," the intrauterine action of the male hormone testosterone during gestation and its relationship to non-righthandedness, immune disorders, and learning disabilities, including dyslexia. To date, several studies (although not fully representative) have provided evidence that there are links between learning disorders and non-righthandedness as well as between learning disorders and immune disease—while links between immune disorders and non-righthandedness are less well supported. (Galaburda, "The Testosterone Hypothesis: Assessment since Geschwind and Behan, 1982" in *Annals*, 1990, pp. 18–38.) Another recent study assessed the association between handedness and a variety of disorders, talents, and skills in subjects, parents, and siblings. It was found that mathematical, artistic, and musical talents did vary as a function of handedness. The study found that verbal skills, stuttering, and asthma were also significant discriminators. Certain disorders in parents were also found to be related to handedness in offspring (Smith, Meyers, and Kline, "For Better Or for Worse: Left-Handedness, Pathology and Talent," *J. Clin. & Exp. Neuropsych*, vol. 11, no. 6, 1989, pp. 944–58).

Other studies have addressed the possible connections between non-righthandedness, asthma, and other allergies, the action of testosterone, enhanced right-hemisphere development, and extremely high mathematical and verbal reasoning abilities. The outcomes of these studies are complex, but they do tend to reflect that in the very highly gifted certain patterns that are also found in those with learning difficulties. There do appear to be physiologically based (rather than environmentally based) associations between high levels of giftedness and left-handedness, allergies, and other traits such as myopia. Furthermore, there seems to be a connection between intellectual precocity and a high degree of right-hemisphere involvement during higher-level reasoning, whether mathematical or verbal, a pattern that differs from that in average persons (Benbow, "Physiological Correlates of Extreme Intellectual Precocity," in *Neuropsychologia*, 1986, pp. 719–25; Benbow and Benbow, "Extreme Mathematical Talent: A Hormonally Induced Ability?" *Duality and Unity of the Brain*, 1987, pp. 147–57; Benbow, "Sex Differences in Mathematical Reasoning Ability in Intellectually Talented Preadolescents," *Behavioral and Brain Sciences*, 1988, pp. 169–232; and O'Boyle and Benbow, "Enhanced Right Hemisphere Involvement During Cognitive Processing May Relate to Intellectual Precocity," in *Neuropsychologia*, 1990, pp. 211–16).

4. While many see face and pattern recognition as a right-hemisphere function, some argue that this function is more complex, involving both hemispheres (Springer and Deutsch, *Left Brain, Right Brain*, 1981, pp. 190–93). Others argue since different forms of recognition are damaged with lesions to either the left or right hemisphere—that the hemispheres may use different strategies for different forms of recognition. Thus, one hemisphere may recognize (or falsely recognize, with great certainty) a face based on one isolated detail (such as a hair parted in the middle or a discolored tooth), whereas the other hemisphere will recognise through the slower and less certain consideration of many different elements in a "global frame" (Damasio, "Reflections on Visual Recognition," *Reading to Neurons*, 1989, pp. 361–71).

5. Springer and Deutsch, *Left Brain, Right Brain*, 1981, pp. 17, 37–43, 165.

6. Brownell et al., "Connotation," *Brain and Lang.*, 1984, vol. 22, pp. 253–65.

7. Thus, in this passage, we see here how a more sophisticated understanding of these functions forces us to subdivide the various components of language into various groups, rather than continuing to think that all of the aspects of language can be seen as one thing.

8. We also need to be cognizant of the need for some measure of circumspection with regard to this discussion, for, as Roger Sperry observed in his Nobel Prize speech, "The left-right dichotomy in cognitive mode is an idea with which it is very easy to run wild" (Sperry, "Effects of Disconnecting the Cerebral Hemispheres," *Science*, 1982, p. 1225). Some argue that the idea of hemispheric specialization has not held up well under close examination (see articles by Denenberg, Bradshaw, and Nettleton, and Puccetti in the March 1981 issue of *Behavioral and Brain Sciences*). Nonetheless, it may be argued that while the ideas associated with hemispheric specialization may require substantial refinement, profoundly important insights have already been gained, and that, while the first waves of professional and popular interest in these ideas have already passed, it may be that the long-term effect of these ideas is just beginning to be felt.

9. Among the specialized functions identified for the right hemisphere are many that are highly related to basic survival: the analysis of external space, the orientation of the body in space, the experience and expression of emotion, the appreciation of emotion in others, the regulation of attention, and certain autonomic activities. "The right hemisphere thus has a special role in a group of activities essential for survival. It is not surprising that right hemisphere dominance might have appeared early both in the course of evolution and in individual development" (Geschwind and Galaburda, *Cerebral Lateralization*, 1987, pp. 44–45).

10. Olson, "Hemispheric Information Processing," *Gifted Child Quarterly*, 1977, p. 9; also, more recently, O'Boyle and Benbow, "Enhanced Right Hemisphere Involvement During Cognitive Processing May Relate to Intellectual Precocity," *Neuropsychologia*, 1990, pp. 211–16.

11. The Orton Dyslexia Society, for example, uses this term rather broadly. "The Orton Dyslexia Society is a non-profit, scientific and educational association committed to the study, prevention and treatment of Specific Language Disability or Developmental Dyslexia. It is specifically concerned with the many children and adults with average or superior intelligence who experience difficulty in the learning of certain skills such as speaking, reading, writing, spelling and math" (Statement from society announcements, January 1987).

12. Denckla, "Resolving a Paradox: How a Gifted Brain Can Also Be Learning Disabled," audiotape of a presentation to Parents of Gifted/Learning Disabled Children, November 20, 1989.

13. The National Joint Committee on Learning Disabilities (NJCLD), quoted in Hammill, "On Defining Learning Disabilities: An Emerging Consensus," *Journal of Learning Disabilities*, 1990, p. 77.

14. Ministry of Education, Province of Quebec, *Document EI*, 1983, p. 229; quoted in Nichols et al., "Cross-Validation Study," *Journal of Learning Disabilities*, 1988, p. 506.

15. There is an extensive and growing literature on dyslexia and learning disabilities. For example, one annotated bibliography on dyslexia published in 1982 runs to over six hundred pages and briefly summarizes some 2,400 books and articles (*Dyslexia*, by Martha M. Evans). The level of continuing national interest is indicated by a government report that describes current programs, issues, and research priorities (Interagency Committee, *Learning Disabilities: A Report to the U.S. Congress*, 1987). A significant part of this literature addresses parents, teachers, and tutors and deals with learning problems and therapeutic approaches. Three basic guides designed for the lay reader are *No Easy Answers*, by Sally L. Smith, 1979 (1981); *Learning Disabilities: A Family Affair*, by Betty B. Osman, 1979; and *The Misunderstood Child*, by Larry B. Silver, 1984.

Three book-length autobiographical accounts by dyslexics are *Reversals*, by Eileen Simpson, 1979; *Susan's Story*, by Susan Hampshire, 1981; and *An Uncommon Gift*, by James S. Evans, 1983. These books and others document, often in painful detail, the considerable life problems experienced by dyslexics and those with either severe or moderate learning disabilities or learning difficulties. The author does not intend to diminish these considerable difficulties by emphasizing the special talents that may exist along with these difficulties in many (but not all) cases. Some of the many varied and distinctive life problems are taken up in chapter 2.

16. References are principally from Thompson, "Men of Eminence," in *Bulletin*, 1969, pp. 114–19. Additional references can be found in Simpson, *Reversals*, 1979, pp. 184–85 and 237–39; Smith, *Answers*, 1979, pp. 6–7; Silver, *Misunderstood*, 1984, p. 192, and others. It should be noted that some authors (Adelman and Adelman, "Rodin, Patton . . ." in *Journal of Learning Disabilities*, 1987, pp. 270–79; Coles, *Learning Mystique*, 1987, pp. 106–30) have questioned these identifications or criticized Thompson and others for lack of rigor in definition and methodology. Many of these authors use narrow definitions and thus dismiss an identification of dyslexia or learning disability because the person in question can be seen to have read widely and deeply. However, these dismissals often rest on a restrictive understanding of the problem—focusing on reading problems alone rather than a more generalized pattern of language difficulties, often accompanied by exceptional visual-spatial talents. As we shall see, dyslexics may read broadly or to great depth, although slowly and with great difficulty.

While it is agreed that care should be taken in identifying historical persons with learning disabilities, it is nonetheless important to investigate these possibilities, wherever relevant, in an effort to gain a deeper understanding of the nature of exceptional abilities. If we are correct in emphasizing the wide range of human potential, it would seem a great missed opportunity to avoid investigation of such individuals just because they are not available for standardized testing and other empirical measuring. Furthermore, some experienced clinicians would argue that a great deal can be learned from a patient history, by itself, without standardized testing.

It is important to note that as the study of these persons proceeds with greater methodological rigor and to greater depth in source materials, it appears that many of the earliest observations may well be shown to be largely correct. For example, a comparatively rigorous recent article (Aaron, et al., "Reading Disability in . . . Famous Persons" in *Journal of Learning Disabilities*, 1988, pp. 523–38), prepared partly as a response to the earlier article by Adelman and Adelman, provides extensive evidence that Thomas Edison, Woodrow Wilson, Hans Christian Andersen, and Leonardo da Vinci had "a number of characteristics that are associated with developmental reading disability." Similarly, recently released letters and other primary source materials concerning Einstein and others seem to demonstrate that they had a stronger pattern of traits than previously apparent.

Additional note to the second edition: The controversies concerning historical persons and dyslexia outlined here persist to this day. However, I have seen no reason to change the arguments and rationale provided here. It seems that most organizations dealing with dyslexia today provide a list of names of some sort. I always ask for the evidence from primary sources because some names would appear to be doubtful. However, the major point is that some vetry capable people may have had some substantial difficulties with verbal material in their early school days. Too many biographers, knowing little about the neurology, would just think—this person was very smart—so he could not be dyslexic. They are wrong and this is the main point, as is argued throught this volume. As a case in point, there have been a several articles published in New Zealand in early 2009 that argued whether Einstein and Churchill were or were not dyslexic. (The government of New Zealand was going through a change of policy regarding dyslexia at the time.) The simple answer is that if one uses a very narrow definition that focuses on reading only, Einstein and Churchill are clearly not dyslexic; they do not fit the narrow definition given. However, if one uses the broader definition of substantial difficulties with words in various forms (often balanced by substantial visual-spacial talents) then it is appropriate to use the term dyslexia—as it is used by many neurologists and neuroscientists. The profiles on Einstein and Churchill provided in this volume argue exactly this point with abundant details indicating both the areas of weakness and the areas of strength. It is mainly a matter of definition. Some groups want to look at reading alone. Other groups think it is a great mistake to focus on one aspect alone when the whole brain is affected—with complex benefits and difficulties—and while lives hang in the balance.

17. In recent years several organizations have made a point of recognizing the accomplishments of prominent living dyslexics: The Foundation for Learning Disabilities (New York, N.Y.), The Kingsbury Center (Washington, D.C.), The National Institute of Dyslexia (Chevy Chase, Md.), The Lab School (Washington, D.C.), The Orton Dyslexia Society (Baltimore, Md.), The Landmark School (Beverly, Mass.), and others. Some of those who have received awards or other recognition are Nobel laureate immunologist Baruj Benacerraf, experimental psychologist William F. Brewer, adventurer and North Pole explorer Ann Bancroft, inventor John F. Adams, Grand Prix racing car driver Jackie Stewart, Olympic gold medal winner Bruce Jenner, Olympic gold medal diver Gregory E. Louganis, actor and comedian Harry Anderson, film actor Tom Cruise, actor and director Henry Winkler, singer and actress Cher, modern artist Robert Rauschenberg, U.S. Fish and Wildlife Service Director Frank H. Dunkle, businesswoman Stephanie Clark, senior corporate executive Michael A. Tita, investment banker G. Chris Andersen, real estate developer Richard C. Strauss, and architect Hugh Newell Jacobsen (Sources: "The Honor Roll: Outstanding Learning Disabled Achiever Awards Recipients," 1985, 1986, and 1990 brochures, The Lab School, Washington, D.C.; Landmark School graduation ceremony, reported by Leighton, "Jackie Stewart and Son Both Overcome Dyslexia," in the *Beverly*

Times, June 21, 1986; "Dyslexic and Distinguished: Recipients of the 1988 Margaret Byrd Rawson Awards," brochure, and "Dyslexic Inventor Honored," press release, March 15, 1989, The National Institute of Dyslexia, Chevy Chase, Md.).

18. Various observations have been made by different writers. For example, "Dyslexics often have important talents in the visual arts, athletics, music, and mathematics" (Galaburda, "A Review," in *Annals*, 1985, p. 21). In some cases, the connection is not surprising. For example, one neurologist specializing in dyslexia did an informal study of her own patient records over a five-year period and found that among the dyslexic children who had a parent trained as a physician, the most frequent medical specialty was radiology—a specialty that relies heavily on highly developed visual and spatial talents (Denckla, "Resolving a Paradox: How a Gifted Brain Can Also Be Learning Disabled," audiotape of a presentation to Parents of Gifted/Learning Disabled Children, November 20, 1989).

In other cases, the connection is not immediately apparent. For example, some engineers may be more intuitive and visually oriented, relying heavily on mental models, while other engineers may rely far more on memorized formulas and conventional training. Alternatively, some lawyers may rely heavily on their personal communication skills and their ability to perform like an actor to persuade a jury, while others may be quite the opposite and rely heavily on their extensive knowledge of legal precedent and their skill with procedure. As for scientists, a sizable portion of this book will help to illustrate the ways such traits may be more evident in more creative scientists.

19. A similar perspective is arising out of the study of child prodigies. Researcher David Henry Feldman has said, "What happens with a prodigy, you see, is that a child, and a field, and a point in time, and a moment in history, come together. If the child is off in some remote part of the world where chess isn't played or music isn't taught, no matter what the child's abilities are, the opportunity to express them won't be made available." "Nova," no. 1209, 1985. With Lynn T. Goldsmith, David H. Feldman is the author of *Nature's Gambit: Child Prodigies and the Development of Human Potential*. New York: Basic Books, 1986.

20. This and subsequent quotations from Geschwind, "Orton Was Right," 1982, pp. 13–30—emphasis in original. Geschwind had been affiliated with the Harvard Medical School, the Massachusetts Institute of Technology, the Beth Israel Hospital, Boston, and had been working in cooperation with the Orton Dyslexia Society for several years before his untimely death in the fall of 1984. A book review in *Science* described Geschwind's career: "For the past twenty years Geschwind and his colleagues have led the field of clinical behavioral neurology. Geschwind himself was almost single-

handedly responsible for making behavioral neurology a field of study in the United States. His classic set of papers on disconnection syndromes, published in 1965, set neurology, anatomy, and psychology spinning. . . . In the ensuing years he made countless contributions to the study of aphasia, apraxia, and human anatomy. . . . In the present volume he and Albert Galaburda offer up another set of intriguing ideas on the biological foundations of cerebral dominance. . . . It will remain for future research to determine whether Norman Geschwind left us with another major contribution." The review is of *Cerebral Dominance*, Norman Geschwind and Albert M. Galaburda, eds., Harvard University Press, Cambridge, Mass., 1984. The reviewer is Michael S. Gazzaniga of Cornell University Medical School, who previously worked with Roger Sperry on split brain research. *Science*, vol. 227, March 15, 1985, pp. 1331–32.

The work of Geschwind and Galaburda concerning cerebral lateralization was summarized in a series of three special articles in *Archives of Neurology*, vol. 42, May, June, and July issues, 1985. This material has been published in book form by the MIT Press as *Cerebral Lateralization*.

21. For example, it has been observed about one important and highly productive mathematician (Leonard Euler, 1707–1783), "Even total blindness during the last seventeen years of his life did not retard his unparalleled productivity; indeed, if anything, the loss of his eyesight sharpened Euler's perceptions in the inner world of his imagination" (Bell, *Men of Mathematics*, 1937 [1986], p. 139).

22. Geschwind and Galaburda, "Lateralization," in *Arch. Neuro.*, 1985, p. 652.

23. Although one of the main purposes of this book is to investigate apparent fundamental links between dyslexia and certain special talents, it should be noted that there are many cases where these links do not exist. Howard Gardner points out, "Dyslexics can be totally ungifted and non-dyslexics may have all the gifts which some dyslexics exhibit" (Personal communication, March 25, 1986).

24. A. Galaburda, 1984, Orion Dyslexia Society Tape No. 30. It should be noted that this quotation came from informal remarks made during a question period after a formal paper had been presented. Cases examined since this time largely confirm the main points stated here (Galaburda, "Neuroscience Issues in Dyslexia: Research Update," Orton Dyslexia Society Conference, Nov. 2, 1990).

25. Remarks made by A. Galaburda, 1984, Orion Dyslexia Society Tape No. 30. In this instance, Galaburda is referring to work carried out by Netley (1982), Money (1972), D. C. Taylor (1969), Waber (1977), and others.

26. Einstein to James Frank, quoted in Clark, *Life and Times*, 1971, p. 10.

27. This passage is, in fact, part of a response to a questionnaire sent to a large number of scientists and mathematicians. It appeared originally in Hadamard, *Invention*, 1945 (1954), pp. 142–43.

28. In Hadamard, *Invention*, 1945, p. 143, the author points out in a note that the mental images referred to by Einstein "are substantially analogous" to those mentioned elsewhere in his book.

29. Bogan and Bogan, "The Other Side . . . Creativity," in *Bull. L.A. Neuro. Soc.*, 1969, pp. 191–220.

30. Sperry, "Effects of Disconnecting," in *Science*, 1982, vol. 217, p. 43; J. E. Bogen, "The Other Side . . . Commissurotomy," in *Bull L.A. Neuro. Soc.*, 1969, p. 105.

31. Simpson, *Reversals*, 1979, pp. 59–60.

32. Graves and Goodglass, "Paralexia," 1983, p. 359. The authors define "semantic paralexias" as "incorrect but meaningfully related errors, daisy—'rose,' father—'brother,' etc." Errors such as these are discussed in a series of articles collected in Colheart (ed.), *Deep Dyslexia*, 1980 and 1987.

33. It is notable that the memory sorting and storage mode suggested here finds support in recent work in neuroscience. In *Brain and Psyche*, Jonathan Winson of Rockefeller University investigates physical evidence for the theories of Sigmund Freud, especially those concerning dreams and the unconscious. While Winson finds much that supports Freud, he also challenges Freud in a number of areas. One that is relevant here is Winson's argument that dream images should not be seen primarily as an attempt of the mind to camouflage unpleasant thoughts with symbols. Rather, he argues that these images may merely provide clues to the way the brain works. Winson observes that, "Chances are, anything that looks like a tall stick is filed near anything else that looks like one." Thus, what is called phallic imagery may be little more than evidence of the filing system, used by the brain. Clearly, Winson's view of memory storage (by similarity of image) is compatible with the second mode of memory storage described here.

34. It may be significant that one of the most innovative and forward looking of nineteenth-century neurologists expressed a view comparable to the duality of function described here. In 1874, John Hughlings Jackson observed, "That the nervous system is double physically is evident enough. This is a very striking fact, but one so well known that we are in danger of ceasing to think of its significance—of ceasing to wonder at it. A truth becomes a truism. The chief significance of the duality lies, I think, in its bearing on what is most fundamental in mental operations—the double process of tracing reactions of likeness and unlikeness" (Jackson, "Duality," in *Writings*, 1874 [1932], p. 129).

35. Some researchers term these two modes as "sequential processing"

and "parallel processing" arguing that the important issue is manner of retrieval rather than manner of storage (P. G. Aaron, personal communication, November 1989).

36. Gardner, *Frames*, 1983, p. 176.

37. Koestler, *Creation*, 1969, p. 439.

38. Asimov, *History*, 1966, pp. 476 and 478.

39. Tolstoy, *Maxwell*, 1981, p. 127. Emphasis in original.

40. Feynman, *Lectures*, 1963, pp. 1–11.

41. Maxwell, *Treatise*, 1891 (1954), pp. viii and ix.

42. Maxwell, *Treatise*, 1891 (1954), pp. ix and x.

43. Tricker, *Contributions*, 1966, p. 97.

44. Maxwell "was awarded the Royal Society's Rumford Medal for his opus 'On the Theory of Color Vision' (1860) which, though less original than his other writings, was more comprehensible to his contemporaries" (Forbes, "Maxwell," 1982, p. 6). A similar reference includes Maxwell's closest associates. "The Campbell and Garnett book contains a summary of Maxwell's work by Garnett—his assistant at the Cavendish illustrating, albeit unintentionally, how little the profound significance of his great work on electromagnetism was understood by his contemporaries. Neither Garnett, nor indeed most of Maxwell's more distinguished colleagues, ever grasped its revolutionary nature. In the 1931 commemorative volume, of course, with its homages by Einstein, Plank, Jeans and others, one sees his work universally and fully admired" (Tolstoy, *Maxwell*, 1981, p. viii).

45. It is also worth noting that the research for this book focused attention on Faraday and Maxwell primarily because of Einstein's high regard for their work and their ways of thinking. The verbal difficulties and visual propensities were subsequently discovered and taken as unexpected, further, strong evidence for the provisional hypotheses proposed here.

46. Koestler, *Creation*, 1969, p. 439.

47. Einstein, "Electrodynamics," 1905 (1979), *Centenary*, p. 281.

48. Hoffmann, *Rebel*, 1972, pp. 30, 34, 47.

49. Dukas and Hoffmann, *Human*, 1979, p. 99.

50. Einstein, *Notes*, 1949, p. 31.

51. Gardner, *Frames*, 1983, pp. 176–77.

52. Karl Pearson, quoted in E. S. Pearson, "Statistics," 1956 (1966), *Papers*, p. 252.

53. E. S. Pearson, "Statistics," 1956 (1966), *Papers*, p. 252. It is expected that this situation continues to the present.

54. E. S. Pearson, "Statistics," 1956 (1966), *Papers*, pp. 253–54.

55. Kolata, "Computer Graphics," *Science*, 1982, vol. 217, pp. 919–20. Such visual modes of analysis have proven to be so powerful that a new

cross-disciplinary field, "scientific visualization," has evolved in recent years. Indeed, this mode has proven so fruitful in many diverse areas that by 1989 "scientific visualization" had become a major focus of various computer periodicals, shows, and conferences, often linked to the most advanced applications of large and small supercomputers. Some of the fields receiving primary attention are molecular modeling, medical imaging, brain structure and function, mathematics, the earth sciences and meteorology, space exploration, astrophysics, materials stress analysis, and fluid flow modeling. An overview by major figures in this rapidly evolving field is provided in DeFanti, Brown, and McCormick, "Visualization: Expanding Scientific and Engineering Research Opportunities," *Computer*, August 1989, pp. 12–25.

56. Following from Gleick, *Chaos*, 1987, pp. 4–5, 11–16, 83–107, 280–92.

57. Gleick, *Chaos*, 1987, pp. 38–39.

58. Gardner, *Frames*, 1983, p. 177. Although this book deals mainly with just two modes of thought, verbal and visual-spatial, it is apparent from the work of Gardner and others that additional and very different major modes of thought might be expected in some people. For some, patterns in music or the movement of muscles or even varieties of smells may be as important as words or images to those discussed here. Of course, it should be noted that even Einstein—in the passage quoted earlier—refers to the importance of muscular movement, in addition to visual images, in his personal pattern of creative and productive thought. One experienced researcher, Margaret Rawson, has proposed another study that focuses on the "mind's ear" as we have focused here on the "mind's eye" (Margaret Rawson, personal communication, June 1989).

59. Gardner, *Frames*, 1983, p. 204.

60. Tolstoy, *Maxwell*, 1981, p. vii.

61. Hoffmann, *Rebel*, 1972, pp. 113–27.

62. The opposite one-sided tendency may be just as pernicious, however. Artistic creativity may be uniformly sterile without the discipline imposed by imitation of nature and some form of testing from experience.

63. Holton, "Genius," *Scholar*, 1972, vol. 41, p. 102.

64. For example, studies of gifted learning disabled children find "wide fluctuation in subtest profiles" on such assessment instruments as the Weschler Intelligence Scale for Children, Revised (WISC-R) (Barton and Starnes, "Identifying Distinguishing Characteristics of Gifted and Talented/Learning Disabled Students," *Roeper Review*, 1989, p. 26).

65. Hall, *Culture*, 1981, pp. 183–84.

66. There is a growing literature on the benefits and problems of simulators as well as the sometimes puzzling short- and long-term effects of simulators

on the human nervous system. See, for example, Hamilton and Kantor, "Simulator Sickness," *Aviation . . . Medicine*, 1989, pp. 246–51; Lyons and Simpson, "Giant Hand Phenomenon," in *Aviation . . . Medicine*, 1989, pp. 64–66.

67. This observation is supported by a recent opinion article in *IEEE Spectrum*, the professional journal for electrical and electronic engineers. The author, Walter W. Frey, argues that in his experience many of the best engineers are "compensated dyslexics" or "strongly right-brained" persons who use their strong mental visualization abilities to produce innovative and superior designs. He points out that increasingly demanding educational and employment standards (emphasizing "left brain" academic skills) are gradually eliminating some of the most gifted design engineers (Frey, "Schools Miss Out on Dyslexic Engineers," *IEEE Spectrum*, December 1990, p. 6).

68. Kay, "Trends," 1987. The power and speed required to do three-dimensional computer graphics and modeling in "real time" has been long awaited by Kay and other researchers, but this capability only began to become widely available in about 1989.

With costs for such high performance capabilities being reduced by 50 percent each year or two, there is little doubt that such equipment will be widely available at comparatively modest costs before very long and that the stage for intensive, broad-based experimentation will have been set. As one industry observer has noted: "Over the past three decades, [computer graphics] has moved from being a cure for no known disease to being a cure for every known disease" (Machover, "Computer Graphics Market," *Computer Pictures*, 1990, p. 44).

69. One commentator on the gifted and the creative has observed, "Heretofore we have harvested creativity wild. We have used as creative only those persons who stubbornly remain creative despite all efforts of the family, religion, education, and politics to grind it out of them. . . . As a result of these misguided efforts, our society produces only a small percentage of its potential of creative individuals, and they are the ones with the most uncooperative dispositions. If we learn to domesticate creativity—that is, to enhance rather than deny it in our culture—we can increase the number of creative persons in our midst several fold. That would put the number and percent of such individuals over the "critical mass" point. When this level is reached in a culture, as it was in Periclean Athens, the Renaissance . . . Elizabethan England, and our own Federalist Fathers, an escalation of results and civilization makes a great leap forward. We can have a golden age of this type, such as the world has never seen; I am convinced that it will occur early in the twenty-first century. But we must make preparations now. . . . The alternatives are too dreadful for even a Huxley or an Orwell to contemplate" (Gowan, "Gifted-Child," *Creative*, 1977, pp. 22–23).

CHAPTER 2. DYSLEXIA AND LEARNING DIFFICULTIES FROM THE INSIDE

1. Simpson, *Reversals*, 1979, pp. viii–ix.
2. Hinshelwood, *Word Blindness*, 1917, pp. 3–6.
3. Smith, *Dilemma*, 1968, p. 5. Material from *The Dilemma of a Dyslexic Man* by Bert Kruger Smith © 1968 Hogg Foundation for Mental Health, The University of Texas at Austin. Reprinted by permission.
4. J. Johns, personal communication, March 1984. Here it should be noted that while estimates of the relative incidence of dyslexia vary, the ratio of four to one is commonly cited. However, when extensive study is made of the families of dyslexics, diagnostic tests indicate a greater incidence among girls than had been thought to be the case. In fact, the most recent findings (when whole groups are tested rather than just those who were referred) suggest the true ratio is close to one to one, indicating that girls are extensively under identified. See further discussion in chapter 3 (Shaywitz and Shaywitz, et al., "Prevalence," *JAMA*, 1990, pp. 998ff).
5. Simpson, *Reversals*, 1979, p. vii.
6. Smith, *Dilemma*, 1968, p. 7. The use of memorization to conceal an inability to read has been observed frequently from the earliest accounts of word blindness and dyslexia. Four of the five initial cases presented by Hinshelwood were observed to have been able to use this device because of a superior auditory memory. For example, one boy "concealed his defect for a time by learning his lesson by heart, so that when it came to his turn and he got a few words at the beginning, he could repeat the lesson by heart" (Hinshelwood, *Congenital Word Blindness*, 1917, pp. 45–51).
7. J. Johns, personal communications, March 1984 and July 1988.
8. Rome, "Aspects," 1971, pp. 68–69.
9. Smith, *Dilemma*, 1968, p. 9.
10. Smith, *Dilemma*, 1968, pp. 7–8.
11. Hampshire, *Susan's Story*, 1981, pp. 11, 108–14.
12. Aaron, et al., "Famous Persons," in *Journal of Learning Disabilities*, 1988, pp. 529ff.
13. "In his adult notebooks he not only used . . . 'mirror-writing' but also grammalogues, as stenographers do, amalgamating words or using phrase symbols" (Ritchie-Calder, *Leonardo and the Age of the Eye*, 1970, p. 36).
14. A systematic study of symbol systems devised by dyslexics may yield significant patterns in their personal forms of notation and perhaps some notable variations on conventional concepts of language development. This approach may be especially helpful with written languages directly related to images, such as Chinese ideographs and ancient Egyptian hieroglyphs.

15. Smith, *Dilemma*, 1968, p. 9. Similar tactics were used by a middle-aged dyslexic steel worker in the 1987 television film "Bluffing It." The character portrayed would claim that he could not fill out the application because he had left his reading glasses at home.

16. Smith, *Dilemma*, 1968, p. 10.

17. Wanderman, "Remedial," *Review*, 1984, pp. 40–41.

18. Simpson, *Reversals*, 1979, p. 174.

19. Simpson, *Reversals*, 1979, p. 181.

20. Smith, *Dilemma*, 1968, p. 12.

21. Simpson, *Reversals*, 1979, pp. 59–60.

22. Simpson, *Reversals*, 1979, p. 59.

23. Hampshire, *Story*, 1981, pp. 54–56.

24. Simpson, *Reversals*, 1979, pp. 208–209.

25. Adelman and Adelman, "Rodin, Patton . . ." 1987, p. 273.

26. Nice, "The Gift of Dyslexia: Another Point of View," presentation, Orton Dyslexia Society Conference, November 6, 1987.

27. Simpson, *Reversals*, 1979, pp. 223–26.

28. Hampshire, *Story*, 1981, pp. 117–19.

29. Quoted in Whitmore and Maker, "Marcia," in *Giftedness*, 1985, p. 175.

30. A case similar to Marcia's has been reported in an article on programs for learning disabled students on "highly selective" college campuses. According to program coordinators, "One dyslexic student at the Dartmouth Medical School confesses that summaries and subtitles are about all she reads other than her own class or lecture notes" (Pompian and Thum, Dyslexic . . . Students at Dartmouth," in *Annals*, 1988, p. 279).

31. Whitmore and Maker, "Marcia," *Giftedness*, 1985, p. 183.

32. Whitmore and Maker, "Marcia," *Giftedness*, 1985, pp. 181–82.

33. Whitmore and Maker, "Marcia," *Giftedness*, 1985, p. 184.

34. Hampshire, *Story*, 1981, p. 26.

35. This quotation and related material are from the National Institute of Dyslexia, "Dyslexic and Distinguished: Recipients of the 1988 Margaret Byrd Rawson Award," 1988.

36. Evans, *Gift*, 1983, pp. 17–18.

37. "The incidence of learning disabilities is four times more common with adopted children than with natural children" (Silver, *Misunderstood Child*, 1984, p. 14).

38. Ritchie-Calder, *Leonardo and the Age of the Eye*, 1970, p. 36, and Carusi, "Leonardo's Manuscripts," in *Leonardo da Vinci*, 1956, p. 157.

39. Rawson, "Leonardo Syndrome," in *Annals*, 1982, p. 289. Laterality and left-right considerations are important not only for neurological systems

but in many areas of science, from the polarization of light to subatomic particles to the growth of plants. Many scientists are cautious about drawing possible connections between these various manifestations. However, Geschwind and Galaburda have found these concerns to be a special interest. "Recent studies have suggested to us . . . that there may in fact be a continuous sequence from asymmetry in the spin of the neutrino all the way to human cerebral dominance" (*Cerebral Lateralization*, 1987, p. 223). The preoccupation with laterality, mirror reversals, and related matters has been a productive orientation in a wide variety of scientific studies. In *The Ambidextrous Universe: Left, Right, and the Fall of Parity* (1964), science writer Martin Gardner follows these themes in mirrors, music, poetry, stars and planets, plants and animals, the human body, crystals, molecules, and neutrinos. A strong interest in laterality and mirror images or mirror writing is evident in several of those people we will be discussing in the profiles that follow.

40. Rawson, "Leonardo Syndrome," in *Annals*, 1982, p. 282.

41. Louise Baker, quoted in Rawson, "Leonardo Syndrome," in *Annals*, 1982, p. 293.

42. Rawson, "Leonardo Syndrome," in *Annals*, 1982, p. 293.

43. Louise Baker, quoted in Rawson, "Leonardo Syndrome," in *Annals*, 1982, p. 303. The original letter is presented in Rawson's article in facsimile; in this transcription, several misspellings and letter reversals have been silently corrected to avoid needless distraction from the content of the text.

44. Louise Baker, in Rawson, "Leonardo Syndrome," in *Annals*, 1982, Fig. 6, p. 303.

45. Louise Baker, in Rawson, "Leonardo Syndrome," in *Annals*, 1982, Fig. 6, p. 303. Given Baker's description, it becomes easier to imagine that each of two different hemispheres may have some power of language, each competing for a period of expression, each recognizable partly by the hand that is used in writing and partly by whether the affected person uses conventional left-to-right writing or lapses into mirror writing.

Some researchers hypothesize that mirror writing (and reading) may derive from what appears to be a natural mirrored presentation of visual and motor information in each hemisphere. Thus, left-handed writing would have a certain natural tendency to be mirrored, if it is not reversed by some mechanism within the brain. These researchers argue that this mirror tendency is usually "transformed" or "suppressed" neurologically, unless the natural reversing mechanism is damaged. This hypothesis is partly supported by experience with stroke victims and animal studies. (Chan and Ross, "Left-Handed Mirror Writing Following Right Anterior Cerebral Artery Infarction: Evidence for Nonmirror Transformation of Motor Programs by Right

Supplementary Motor Area," *Neurology*, 1988, pp. 59–63). These consider-ations are similar to some of Orton's 1925 speculations on mirror writing.

46. Pollack and Branden, "Odyssey," *Annals*, 1982, pp. 275–87.

47. Pollack and Branden, "Odyssey," *Annals*, 1982, pp. 277–78.

48. D. Smith, interview quoted in Pollack and Branden, "Odyssey," in *Annals*, 1982, p. 282. It may be noted that Mozart was also fond of rever-sals in music (as well as word games).

49. Pollack and Branden, "Odyssey," *Annals*, 1982, p. 283.

50. Pollack and Branden, "Odyssey," *Annals*, 1982, pp. 283 and 281. Since this study was written, another pattern of note has become apparent in Smith's life. He has long been an economist in New York, but in recent years he has become a frequent commentator on cable television and public radio, providing analysis of economic and financial events that may have occurred only minutes before his broadcast. He explains he has found that, unlike many of his professional associates, he feels much more at home in the fast-paced world of the electronic media. His associates, on the other hand, often feel much more at home with the pace of printed media and feel uncomfort-able with radio and television (D. Smith, personal communication, December 1989).

51. Simpson, *Reversals*, 1979, p. 226.

52. Simpson, *Reversals*, 1979, p. 153. In fairness to Simpson, it should be noted that she is leading up to making a different point here—that is, that she found it very difficult to train herself to learn in the long-term, cumula-tive, methodical way that one must if one is to have control of the vast amounts of information required in certain professions.

53. Creativity Workshop, Smithsonian Institution, April 1988.

54. Simpson, *Reversals*, 1979, pp. 217–18.

55. Simpson, *Reversals*, 1979, pp. 218–20.

CHAPTER 3. CONSTELLATIONS OF TRAITS, SOME NEUROLOGICAL PERSPECTIVES

1. Hinshelwood, *Word-Blindness*, 1917, p. 3.

2. Hinshelwood, *Word-Blindness*, 1917, pp. 3–4 and 6.

3. Hinshelwood, *Word-Blindness*. 1917, p. 4.

4. Hinshelwood, "Word-Blindness and Visual Memory," *The Lancet*, December 21, 1895, p. 1564. Hinshelwood credits the first identification of pure word blindness, without additional complicating speech or memory problems, to Kussmaul, "Disturbances of Speech," in *Ziemssen's Cyclopdia*, 1877, vol. 14.

5. Morgan, "A Case of Congenital Word-Blindness," *British Medical J.*, November 7, 1896, p. 1378.

6. Morgan, "A Case of Congenital Word-Blindness," *British Medical J.*, November 7, 1896, p. 1378.

7. Morgan, "A Case of Congenital Word-Blindness," *British Medical J.*, November 7, 1896, p. 1378.

8. Hinshelwood, *Word-Blindness*, 1917.

9. Orton, "Word-blindness," in *Papers*, 1925 (1966), p. 18.

10. June L. Orton, "A Biographical Sketch," in *Papers*, 1966, p. 4.

11. Orton, "Word-blindness," in *Papers*, 1925 (1966), p. 20.

12. Orton, "Word-blindness," in *Papers*, 1925 (1966), p. 20.

13. When Orton started college, he was uncertain whether to study medicine or mechanical engineering. His wife reported that although Orton chose medicine, "his mechanical bent perhaps accounted for his persistent search to discover how things worked, most of all, the human brain. His recreation was in designing and building—boats, tennis courts, gardens, garages, laboratories, hospitals—and in inventing better methods and techniques, from ways of pouring slabs of cement to staining and cutting brain sections for the microscope. . . . His insatiable interest in things about him carried over to people. He added to his store of information wherever he went through easy conversations with a plumber or a president, a small boy or a senior scientist. He admired all forms of good workmanship but he was intolerant of careless techniques" (June L. Orton, "A Biographical Sketch," in *Papers*, 1966, p. 2).

14. The limits of such verbally oriented tests are now commonly recognized. However, such factors may continue to influence professional judgement in subtle ways that are still not fully appreciated. One neurologist who works with dyslexic children and adults has noted that she has become increasingly aware of one variant of this problem. Through her clinical experience working with dyslexics, she has become much more sensitive to the sophistication of the cognitive abilities (as well as visual-spatial and motor skills) required to excel in many sports, much more sensitive than her own medical training or own cultural milieu—a milieu that focused more on books than on athletics—would have made her (Denckla, "Paradox," taped presentation, Parents of Gifted/Learning Disabled Children, November 1989). This observation is, of course, just one case of a larger trend—a gradually developing acceptance of the idea of a number of different forms of intelligence, as described by Howard Gardner and others (Gardner, *Frames of Mind*, 1983).

15. Orton, "Word-blindness," in *Papers*, 1925 (1966), p. 21.

16. Orton, "Word-blindness," in *Papers*, 1925 (1966), p. 21. The ability

to read mirror-reversed material continues to generate interest and debate. Three recent studies have addressed this ability among those who are primarily left handed and those who are primarily right handed. One study found that left handers were superior in reading mirror-reversed material, while two subsequent studies came to the opposite conclusion (Bradshaw and Bradshaw, "Reading Mirror-Reversed Text: Sinistrals Really Are Inferior," in *Brain Lang.*, 1988, pp. 189–92).

17. Indeed, Orton pointed out that some emotional problems themselves could be caused directly by neurological factors as well as indirectly by the learning problems.

18. Orton, "Remarks," in *Papers*, 1942 (1966), p. 11.

19. An example of a recent book that emphasizes the primacy of psychological and interpersonal factors and criticizes what is seen as an excessive concern with neurological factors is Coles, *Learning Mystique*, 1987 (1989).

20. Continuing professional concern about the role of viruses in generating new diseases through their own high rates of genetic mutation is discussed in Weiss, "Viral Advantage," *Science News*, 1989, pp. 200–203.

21. MIT artificial intelligence researcher Marvin Minsky suspects that in time we will discover that the mind is actually composed of some two hundred to three hundred special-purpose brains all adapted to work together to accomplish a variety of tasks (Minsky, "Artificial Intelligence," in *Frontiers in Science*, Smithsonian Institution, 1987).

22. Geschwind, "Individual," *Annals*, 1984, p. 320.

23. Some think that "learning disabilities" is more a legal than a medical or educational term (Aaron, personal communication, December 1989).

24. Geschwind and Galaburda, *Lateralization*, 1985, pp. 10–15.

25. One of the terms commonly used in this field some time ago was "minimal brain damage." In one sense, this term might be seen as applicable but inherently misleading. Once again, it would appear to focus on only one half of a condition, ignoring the special talents that often (but not always) may also be present. For further discussion of this approach, see Gilger and Kaplan, "Atypical Brain Development: A Conceptual Framework for Understanding Developmental Learning Disabilities," *Developmental Neuropsychology*, vol. 20, issue 2, January 2001, pp. 465–81.

26. Geschwind, "Individual," *Annals*, 1984, p. 325.

27. An instructive listing of the many terms that have been used in referring to learning disabled children is provided by Sally Smith in *No Easy Answers*, 1979 (1981), pp. 22–23:

"Association deficit pathology, Attention disorders, Brain-injured child, Central nervous system disorder, Conceptually handicapped, Congenital alexia, Congenital strephosymbolia, Diffuse brain damage, Dysgraphia, Dyscalculia, Dyslexia, Educationally handicapped, Hidden handicap, Hyperactivity, Hyperkinetic behavior syndrome, Hypoactivity, Hypokinetic behavior syndrome, Language disability, Language disordered child, Maturational lag, Minimal brain damage, Minimal brain disfunction (MBD), Minimal brain injury, Minimal cerebral dysfunction, Minimal cerebral palsy, Minimal chronic brain syndrome, Multisensory disorders, Neurological immaturity, Neurologically handicapped, Neurophrenia, Neurophysiological dysynchrony, Organic brain dysfunction, Organicity, Perceptually handicapped, Primary reading retardation, Psycholinguistic disabilities, Psychoneurological disorders, Reading disability, Specific dyslexia, Specific learning disabilities, Strephosymbolia, Strauss syndrome, The child with multisensory difficulties, The interjacent child, The invisibly handicapped child, The other child, Waysider, Word blindness."

Some researchers in the field have long objected to the use of terminology that focuses on brain damage. Addressing a conference some years ago, one professional experienced in the field said, "Usually we are not dealing with brain damage but with developmental lag. I think we should avoid all terminology that implies or suggests brain damage. I could explain in detail how findings in psychological tests, EEG tracings, and the 'soft neurological signs' are often interpreted as evidence of brain damage, whereas they usually stem from developmental lags. Expressions such as 'neurologically handicapped' and 'minimal brain dysfunction' are apt to connote to the parents, the teachers, the physicians, and even to the child himself that his brain has been damaged. True, dyslexia is a dysfunction in the brain and sometimes not so minimal, but there are many such dysfunctions stemming from developmental lags and not from damage to the brain. Personally I find little to quarrel with in the term 'dyslexia.' In the word the 'dys' means hard or difficult and 'lexia' from the Greek word 'lexikos,' means pertaining to words; so, difficulty with words—words *seen*, words *heard*, words *spoken*, words *felt* as in writing and the inner elaboration of words is what 'dyslexia' means. Of course, to be precise, the qualifying term 'developmental' should be prefixed but let us stay away from this 'brain damage' stuff! (Applause)" (L. Thompson, "Remarks," *Bulletin*, 1971, p. 8).

28. Orton, in *"Word-blindness" . . . and Other Papers*, 1966, p. 46 (reprinted from the *Archives of Neurology and Psychiatry*, November 1925, vol. 14, pp. 581–615). In proposing this term, Orton was specific about what he intended it to mean, using distinctive metaphors. "The prefix 'strepho' has been chosen to indicate the turning or reversals as it does in the word 'bustrophedon,' [meaning 'ox turns,' as in a man and ox ploughing a field back and forth; after an ancient form of written language that Orton describes as

'. . . writing one line toward the right and then reversing and writing the next toward the left' (p.33)]. 'Symbolon' is used in its original meaning of 'word,' 'sign' or 'token,' and not as in Finkelnburg's usage in 'asymbolia,' in which it included recognition of the meaning of objects as well as of symbols, nor as in the very restricted sense of Oppenheim as a synonym for apraxia [difficulty with physical movements]. Strephosymbolia thus seems nicely suited to our cases in which our analysis points to confusion, because of reversals, in the memory images of symbols resulting in a failure of association between the visually presented stimulus and its concept."

29. Although the term "strephosymbolia" is rarely, if ever, used in professional circles, the term is listed in *Webster's Third . . . Unabridged*, 1981, p. 2259.

30. It should be noted that this focus on reversals in reading and writing has lately come to be seen as being out of date. However, it is this same perception that is the basis of Eileen Simpson's extraordinarily apt title for her autobiography, *Reversals*. Currently, some clinicians and researchers are finding, contrary to recent fashion, that reversals are in fact an important part of understanding what some dyslexics are dealing with. For example, Drs. Brock and Fernette Eide have provided the following observations: "Regarding . . . reversals, this seems to us to be one of the most misunderstood issues of all relating to dyslexic children. It has become [increasingly common] in recent years to deny that there is any relationship between the tendency to reverse words and letters and dyslexia. . . . There is a general attitude currently in the [reading remediation] community that doubts that . . . dyslexic children have any visual perceptual issues related to reversals. But in our work with dyslexic children, it is clear that there is a subgroup (probably about 15 percent) that is very prone to making reversals or spatial rotations not only with words and letters but with visual materials of all types—because we test them with all sorts of visual materials, not just words and letters. And what is really interesting about this group is that they include many of the most clearly spatially talented of all the children we see, as manifested in their 'outside work' involving construction, art, fashion design, etc. I think your speculations on why it might be that spatially talented people might have difficulty 'fixing' their letters and words in a particular direction are right on target. Almost always these children will show clear signs of mixed hemispheric dominance (like left eye-right hand dominance, ambidexterity or late handedness, or left handedness)" (Personal communication, December 9, 2008. Brock Eide, MD, MA, and Fernette Eide, MD, are authors of the *Mislabelled Child*, Hyperion, 2006).

31. Minsky, *Society of Mind*, 1987. However, newer types of computers are currently being developed to work more like the human brain and less

like logic machines. Called "neural networks" or "connectionist machines," these computers are designed on entirely different principles from those used with conventional machines. Compared to conventional computers, these newer machines promise to be relatively good at recognition tasks and relatively poor at tasks involving strict logical reasoning. As one researcher explains, "What makes our brains bad at doing logic tasks is actually the essence of our higher-level cognitive functions. . . .

With a connectionist type of machine, it's easy to recognize your mother and hard to do logic. With a conventional computer, it's hard to recognize your mother and easy to do logic. So what does it mean to be really intelligent?" (Jay McClelland, quoted in Allinan, *Apprentices of Wonder*, 1989, p. 33).

32. Neurosurgeon Harvey Cushing is sometimes included on lists of dyslexics, although he may not fully qualify in the most strict usage of the term. There is no evidence of difficulty with reading or even speaking. His chief distinguishing trait is the puzzling life-long difficulty he had with spelling. His biographer noted that as a youth Cushing had the reputation for being the worst speller in the school; words seemingly learned were soon forgotten and "there were certain words he misspelled all his life." Some of the examples given are: "exhonourate, fortolled, neybour, swoolen, hammard, Sweed, church quire, characature, moskito, Turkish bizarre, sacaraligious, exchecour, malitia, and mediocher." However, as noted below, Cushing was recognized as an extraordinarily skillful neurosurgeon (he pioneered dramatically improved success rates) and as a great innovator and teacher in his field (a medical society was formed in his name). Indeed, his work was so superior that, in time, his teaching is credited with reversing a long-standing tradition in medical education. Before Cushing, American medical students had always gone to Europe for advanced study; but in Cushing's time European medical students began to come to America to study with him. His extraordinary artistic ability was also widely recognized, and he showed this great skill by illustrating many of his own medical journal articles (Thompson, *Harvey Cushing: Surgeon, Author, Artist*, 1981, pp. 13ff). With this distinctive combination of traits, it is hard not to imagine that some of Cushing's extraordinary skill as a neurosurgeon might be attributed to an ability to reconstruct in his own mind's eye an accurate view of microscopic brain structures, so as to be able to isolate and remove a tiny, deeply hidden tumor (for example) without damage to the surrounding tissues.

33. Molecular modeling is one of the many areas benefiting from recent developments in hardware and software for scientific visualization. One recent survey is Zoll and Rosenberg, "Of Pixels and Polymers: Molecular Modeling Software Enables Chemists to Test Compounds On-Screen," *Computer Graphics World*, 1990, p. 103–104 and 106.

34. This point of view is discussed by Margaret Rawson in "A Diversity Model for Dyslexia," in *The Many Faces of Dyslexia*, 1988, pp. 204–220.

35. Often social and economic discussions consider whether a given nation or group grants promotions to individuals based on merit or privilege. From our new perspective, however, we should also consider what the definition of "merit" has come to be. In our culture this may mean only an ability to take a number of courses, absorb some information and get a certain set of grades—nearly all verbal and organizational skills. No deep understanding of the work is needed. Of course, much depends upon the exact type of work, but many times, perhaps, the verbal abilities may have little to do with the real requirements of the position, to which someone has been promoted through "merit."

36. Minsky, "Intelligence," *New Frontiers in Science*, Smithsonian Institution, December 3, 1988.

37. One example of such an expert system that has performed well is the medical consulting system "AI/Rheum." This system is "designed to offer assistance in the diagnosis and management of rheumatologic cases to physicians without specialty training in rheumatology." Involving the work of three teams over eight years, the preliminary evaluations of the system provided scores of 92 to 96 percent agreement with the consensus diagnoses of a panel of rheumatology specialists (Kingsland, et al., "Anatomy of a Knowledge-Based Consultant System: AI/Rheum," *M.D. Computing*, 1986, pp. 18–26).

38. LaPlante, "Expert Systems," *InfoWorld*, 1990, pp. 55 and 60. Also, Winner, Mythinformation in the High-tech Era," in Forester, ed., *Computers in the Human Context*, 1989, p. 82–96.

39. One early indicator of the seriousness with which some companies are approaching this prospect is a joint effort by five U.S. companies to pool their accumulated corporate knowledge in a uniformly constructed computer system. According to a recent report, "The alliance, called the Initiative for Managing Knowledge Assets, is aimed at developing a next-generation software that will capture the skills and knowledge of a company's employees and make it available to others through a computer system." The project is seen by the companies as a way of managing knowledge assets in the same way that they manage capital or financial assets. Knowledge and skills of special interest are "design experience, engineering skills, financial analysis, marketplace knowledge and knowledge of a company's policies, practices and goals." The joint effort was started in 1988, but not announced until the spring of 1990. The five companies are Digital Equipment Corp., Ford Motor Co., Texas Instruments, Inc., US West Inc. (the Colorado-based regional telephone company), and Carnegie Group, Inc. (a Pittsburgh-based

software company) (Ziegler, "Computer Group," *Washington Post*, 1990, p. G1).

40. Many observers in this field have long denied that workers will lose jobs because of these machines. "One very common fear on the part of corporate end-users is whether their jobs will be at stake when their companies complete their expert system projects. All industry observers, however, completely debunk that theory." They argue that the new systems will be able to take care of the routine tasks, freeing workers to "spend more quality time on the tougher situations where you really need human judgment" (LaPlante, "Expert," *Infoworld*, 1990, p. 55). This much may be true. However, a more insidious effect is likely. The machines, if properly designed and used (that is, to create a competitive advantage in the marketplace), would almost certainly result in the hiring of fewer new workers in the future—if the enterprise expands, for example. After all, by definition, in order to have increased productivity it matters little whether the same people do more work or fewer people do the same work.

41. Minsky, "The Future of Intelligence: Can Computers Think?" *New Frontiers in Science*, Smithsonian Institution, December 3, 1988.

42. Minsky, as paraphrased in Allman, *Apprentices of Wonder*, 1989, p. 29.

43. However, it should be acknowledged once again that the opposite is sometimes true—that some others in this large and necessarily heterogeneous group are known to be relatively blind to various subtle cues in social interaction.

44. Weiner, *Cybernetics*, (1948) 1961, pp. 27–28.

45. Some advocates of interactive computer learning systems refer to "*just in time* learning and understanding, borrowing the phrase from the modern manufacturing method of planning and controlling parts and materials inventories to arrive at the factory at the moment they are needed." They argue that "the vast and ever-growing quantity of information available today makes it imperative that we develop easy ways to access exactly what we need to know, when we need to know it" (Floyd, "J.I.T. Learning," in *Human Capital*, 1989, p. 48). The information revolution created by Google and other sophisticated search engines over recent years has substantially contributed to the realization of the changes envisioned here.

46. "The concept of *dyslexia as diversity* can be both liberating and productive" (Rawson, "A Diversity Model," in *Many Faces*, 1988, p. 220).

47. Adapted from several sources: Houck, *Concepts*, 1984, pp. 27ff; Smith, *No Easy Answers*, 1979 (1987), pp. 28ff; Silver, *Misunderstood*, 1984, pp. 19ff; Clements, "Symptomatology," in *Minimal Brain Dysfunction in Children*, 1966, pp. 11ff (provided in full as Appendix A); and others.

Coexistence of traits and symptoms does not imply causal relationships; for a discussion of this problem, see Marshall, "Description and Interpretation," in *Reading to Neurons*, 1989, pp. 78–80.

48. Geschwind, "Why Orton Was Right," *Annals*, 1982, p. 19.

49. Geschwind, "Why Orton Was Right," *Annals*, 1982, pp. 15–19. The item referring to possible areas of brain damage was anticipated by W. Pringle Morgan and others.

50. Orton's continuing influence in connection with speech difficulties is noted by various authors. One recent paper provides a summary. "Contemporary research on the neurological and cognitive underpinnings of stuttering has been very much influenced by a neuropsychological theory of stuttering proposed more than fifty years ago by Orton (1928) and Travis (1931). This theory attributed stuttering to 'aberrant interhemispheric relations' (Travis, 1978, p. 278), specifically to a lack of normal hemispheric lateralization of speech mechanisms and a consequent 'mistiming of neural impulses to the bilateral speech musculature' (Travis, 1978, p. 278). In very broad terms, the theory has found some support in current research, although the precise nature of the aberrant interhemispheric relations still remains unclear" (Webster, "Neural Mechanisms Underlying Stuttering," in *Brain and Language*, 1988, p. 226).

51. Orton also believed that there is a preponderance of dyslexia among males. More recent evidence indicates that the true ratio of boys to girls may be closer to one to one. It was long known that boys would "act out" more often in the classroom and were therefore more readily identified as having reading difficulties and other related problems. Consequently, boys were long thought to be somewhat overrepresented, but not to the extent that has recently been found. However, when a consistent definition is applied to tests available on a total school population, boys and girls are identified in about equal numbers. In the words of the recent report, "Our data indicate that school-identified samples are almost unavoidably subject to referral bias and that reports of an increased prevalence of reading disability in boys may reflect this bias in ascertainment. These findings caution against relying solely on schools for identification of reading-disabled children (Shaywitz and Shaywitz, et al., "Prevalence of Reading Disability in Boys and Girls: Results of the Connecticut Longitudinal Study," *JAMA*, August 22/29, 1990, pp. 998ff).

52. Disorganization and poor time management are problems especially common among those children identified as both gifted and learning disabled. In these children, apparently, the "executive" functions of the frontal sections of the brain are slower to complete their formation than in other children. Difficulties may persist until the individual is twenty or thirty years

old, because certain changes in brain development may continue through these ages. In some individuals, such conditions may persist, to some extent, throughout a lifetime. In such cases, the individual may need the continuing support of a spouse or coworker to allow considerable talents to yield tangible finished products (Denckla, "Paradox of Giftedness," 1989).

53. Smith, *No Easy Answers*, 1979 (1981), pp. 26–28; and others.

54. It is noteworthy that this trait has been noticed by some authors, but rejected by others as too difficult to describe in a scientific manner. "A large number of terms were too broad for other than limited value. Others are too general (or judgmental) to classify, e.g., 'often good looking'" (Clements, "Symptomatology," in *Dysfunction*, 1966, p. 11, and provided as Appendix A).

55. One neurologist points out that there are several kinds of right-hemisphere skills and that these may vary greatly in any given individual. For example, some people (often women) may have extreme difficulty with certain right-hemisphere spatial skills, such as how to make a piece of furniture fit through a doorway, but may be extremely proficient in other right-hemisphere capabilities, such as social skills involving tone of voice, to which many men are less sensitive (Denckla, "Paradox of Giftedness," 1989).

56. Adelman and Taylor, "Problems of Definition," *J. Learn. Disabilities*, 1986, pp. 514–20, and Adelman and Adelman, "Rodin, Patton . . ." *JLD*, 1987, pp. 270–79.

57. De Hirsch, "Hyperlexics," in *J. Spec. Educ.*, 1971, pp. 243–45, and Evans, *Dyslexia*, 1982, p. 32.

58. Hartlage, "Comparison," *Neurology*, 1973, pp. 436–37, and Evans, *Dyslexia*, 1982, p. 73.

59. These subjects averaged better than those in two other test groups; they received "better scores than the nondyslexic, otherwise learning-disabled and the normal groups" (Denckla, "Motor Coordination," in Duffy and Geschwind, *Dyslexia*, 1985, p. 190).

60. Denckla, "Motor Coordination," in Duffy and Geschwind, *Dyslexia*, 1985, p. 194.

61. In *The Dynamics of Creation*, Anthony Storr points out that, "The human infant . . . is born in a particularly dependent and helpless condition, and remains in this state for a relatively longer time than the young of many other species." Anatomically, "it has long been recognized that human beings continue to display, in adult life, characteristics which in other species of primates belong to the foetus, and which generally disappear or are superseded in the mature animal." Finally, many parents, "reflecting ruefully upon the emotional and financial commitments involved [in normal human delayed maturity], might be glad to see their offspring mature and become independent at a very much earlier age. But if they did so, they would bypass much

of what makes them human and civilized; for the price of culture is delayed maturity" (Storr, *Dynamics*, 1972 [1983], pp. 205–206).

62. Walker, "Early Humans," *New Frontiers in Science*, Smithsonian Institution, Oct. 29, 1988.

63. Thompson, "The Structure of Bone," in *On Growth and Form*, vol. 2, 1917 (1972), pp. 976–77.

64. This and subsequent quotations from Galaburda, "Research Report," Orton Dyslexia Society Conference, November 4–7, 1987; also, Galaburda, personal communication, Nov. 26, 1990. Other researchers currently investigating neurological aspects of creativity continue to see a special role for these connections between hemispheres (Bogen and Bogen, "Creativity and the Corpus Callosum," *Psych. Clinics of North Am.*, 1988, pp. 293–301, and Hoppe, 'Hemispheric Specialization and Creativity," in *Psych. Clinics of North Am.*, 1988, pp. 303–15).

CHAPTER 4. PROFILES, PART 1

1. Williams, *Faraday*, 1965, p. 102.

2. Agassi, *Faraday*, 1971, p. x.

3. Berkson, *Fields*, 1974, p. xi.

4. In Britain, the term "nonconformist" means, even today, any Protestant church other than the Church of England. The Sandemanian sect is described at some length in Jones's *Life and Letters*, vol. 1, 1870, pp. 4–6. Selected passages follow: "Several of these congregations were formed in different parts of England by the writings and preaching of Robert Sandeman, the son-in-law of the Reverend John Glas, a Presbyterian clergyman in Scotland. Thus the Church in London was formed in 1760. In 1763 the congregation at Kirkby Stephen numbered between twenty and thirty persons. Sandeman ultimately went to America to make his views known, and he died there in 1771. In 1728 Glas was deposed by the Presbyterian Church Courts, because he taught that the Church should be subject to no league nor covenant, but be governed only by the doctrines of Christ and His Apostles. He held that Christianity never was, nor could be, the established religion of any nation without becoming the reverse of what it was when first instituted . . . that the Bible, and that alone . . . was the sole and sufficient guide for each individual, at all times and circumstances."

5. Ludwig, *Faraday*, 1978, p. xiii.

6. J. P. Gassiot, letter of Nov. 28, 1867, quoted in Tyndall, *Discoverer*, 1870, p. 5.

7. Forgan, "Servant to Savant," in *Rediscovered*, 1985, pp. 51 ff.

8. Gooding and James, eds., "Introduction," in *Rediscovered*, 1985, pp. 12–13.

9. Faraday, letter of Sept. 2, 1858, quoted in Tyndall, *Discoverer*, 1870, pp. 7–8.

10. Agassi, *Faraday*, 1971, pp. 7–8.

11. Agassi, *Faraday*, 1971, p. 144.

12. Citadel student, Successful Dyslexic Panel, Orton Dyslexia Society Annual Conference, Winston-Salem, N.C., November 1984.

13. Letter from Michael Faraday to Dr. J. Tyndall, April 19, 1851. Jones, *Life and Letters*, 1870, vol. 2, pp. 294–95.

14. Kahlbaum and Darbishire, eds., "Preface," *Letters*, 1899, p. vii.

15. Williams, in Faraday, *Correspondence*, 1971, p. vii.

16. Faraday, *Correspondence*, 1971, p. 506.

17. Agassi, *Faraday*, 1971, p. 144.

18. From Jones, *Life and Letters*, vol. 2, p. 440, quoted in Agassi, *Faraday*, 1971, p. 23.

19. A modern example is noted by computer industry executive Jean-Louis Gassée, who finds certain personal computer software especially helpful in giving order to his own "scattered thoughts" (Gassée, *Third Apple*, 1987, p. 58).

20. Crawford, "Learning from Experience," in *Rediscovered*, 1985, p. 220.

21. Emphasis in original.

21. Agassi, *Faraday*, 1971, p. 126.

22. From *Faraday Lectures*, p. 118, quoted in Agassi, *Faraday*, 1971, pp. 126–27.

23. Forgan, "Servant to Savant," in *Rediscovered*, 1985, pp. 62–63.

24. From Tyndall, *Discoverer*, 1870, p. 55, quoted in Agassi, *Faraday*, 1971, pp. 128–29.

25. Forgan, "Servant to Savant," in *Rediscovered*, 1985, pp. 62–63.

26. Everitt, "Maxwell's Scientific Creativity," in *Springs*, 1983, pp. 71–74.

27. Adapted from Everitt, "Maxwell's Scientific Creativity," in *Springs*, 1983, p. 74.

28. Everitt, "Maxwell's Scientific Creativity," in *Springs*, 1983, p. 74.

29. Campbell and Garnett, *Life*, 1882, p. 28.

30. Everitt, "Maxwell's Scientific Creativity," in *Springs*, 1983, p. 90.

31. Campbell and Garnett, *Life*, 1882, pp. 105–106.

32. Everitt, "Maxwell's Scientific Creativity," in *Spring*, 1983, p. 121.

33. Jolls and Coy, "Art of Thermodynamics," *IRIS Universe*, 1990, p. 35.

34. J. C. Maxwell to Thomas Andrews (November 1874), in Tait and Brown, "Memoir of Dr. Thomas Andrews," *Scientific Papers of the Late Thomas Andrews*, P. G. Tait and A. C. Brown, eds., 1889, pp. ix–xii, quoted in Jolls and Coy, "Art of Thermodynamics," *IRIS Universe*, 1990, p. 35.

35. Jolls and Coy, "Art of Thermodynamics," *IRIS Universe*, 1990, pp. 31–35.

36. Everitt, "Maxwell's Scientific Creativity," in *Springs*, 1983, p. 79.

37. Everitt, "Maxwell's Scientific Creativity," in *Springs*, 1983, p. 120.

38. Hoffmann, *Rebel*, 1972, p. 14.

39. Pais, *Subtle*, 1982, p. 38. When the young Albert was just seven years old (he had apparently just finished second grade at the Catholic primary school he attended), his mother described him as being at the top of his class. "Yesterday Albert got his grades, once again he was ranked first, he got a splendid report card" (Letter from Pauline Einstein to Fanny Einstein, August 1, 1886, Einstein, *Papers*, vol. 1, 1987, p. 3). Some see this statement as sufficient reason to drop Einstein from the list of those we are considering. Others feel we should not be surprised at such occasional peak performances, which may be seen as just part of the overall pattern of uneven talents and achievements. This pattern of mixed performance is clearly described in the letter (cited below) from his father to his teacher in Aarau, when Albert was sixteen years old (Letter from Hermann Einstein to Jost Winteler, October 29, 1895. Einstein, *Papers*, vol. 1, 1987, p. 10). (P G. Aaron, personal communication, November 1989.)

40. In her 1979 book, *Reversals*, Eileen Simpson was persuaded that Einstein should be dropped from the list of dyslexics. She cited two reasons. She had noted that Ronald W. Clark, in his 1971 biography of Einstein, had considered the dyslexia claim as "understandable special pleading." She also noted that Einstein authority Gerald Holton wrote, in answer to her inquiry, "While Einstein was slow to speak as a child, he was not slow to read. He sometimes made spelling errors in English, but not in his native language" (Quoted in Simpson, *Reversals*, 1979, p. 238). It is not known whether Simpson or her sources may have modified their views in more recent years. However, it is argued here that their conclusions are probably largely based on a more restrictive definition of the term and that Einstein's experience would generally fit the broader definition used by neurologists and some educators in the 1980s. As we shall see below, there is some difference of opinion as to Einstein's difficulties with certain specific skills such as spelling. According to the translator of his letters, Einstein did apparently have difficulty spelling the names of persons and places when writing in his own language, although a number of these names were probably foreign in origin.

41. Hoffmann, *Rebel*, 1972, pp. 19–20.

42. Hoffmann, *Rebel*, 1972, p. 20.

43. Maja Winteler-Einstein, "Biographical Sketch," in Einstein, *Papers*, vol. 1, 1987. While parts of this material have been quoted from the original manuscript (currently in the possession of Dr. Marc Besso of Basel) in some earlier biographies, the excerpted sketch was not widely available until the publication of Volume I of the *Collected Papers* in 1987.

44. Winteler-Einstein, "Sketch," in *Papers*, vol. 1, 1987, p. xviii.

45. Winteler-Einstein, "Sketch," in *Papers*, vol. 1, 1987, p. xix.

46. Winteler-Einstein, "Sketch," in *Papers*, vol. 1, 1987, p. xxi.

47. Letter from A. Einstein to Mileva Maric [December 17, 1901]. Einstein, *Papers*, vol. 1, 1987, p. 187. Today, in an age of greater affluence and material abundance, some adolescent dyslexics, after years of clutter and confusion in their youth, find themselves compelled to clear out their rooms and live in monkish simplicity. Extreme orderliness can sometimes be an effective compensation.

48. Winteler-Einstein, "Sketch," in *Papers*, vol, 1, 1987, p. xix.

49. Hoffmann, *Rebel*, 1972, pp. 121–23 and 127–28.

50. "As computers increase in power, some parts of mathematics become less important while other parts become more important. While arithmetic proficiency may have been 'good enough' for many in the middle of the century, anyone whose mathematical skills are limited to computation has little to offer today's society that is not done better by an inexpensive machine" (National Research Council, *Everybody Counts*, 1989, p. 45 ff).

51. Letter from A. Einstein to Mileva Maric, December 17, 1901, *Papers*, vol. 1, 1987, p. 187.

52. From Constance Reid's biography of Hilbert, 1970, quoted in French, "Story of General Relativity," in *Centenary*, 1979, p. 111. Einstein's relationship with the mathematicians as described by Hilbert is similar to Faraday's relationship with them as described by Maxwell. It seems that the more visually oriented Einstein was able to accomplish the truly original work that the better-trained and more logically and formally oriented mathematicians seemed unable to. The background and approach of some highly trained mathematicians may make them ill-adapted for certain forms of highly original work.

53. Pais, *Subtle*, 1982, p. 172.

54. Quoted in Hoffmann, *Rebel*, 1972, p. 25. Hoffmann notes, "This was the teacher of Greek who had prophesied that Einstein would never amount to anything."

55. Biographer Ronald Clark argues that Einstein's problems in school had more to do with his hatred of Prussian discipline than with language difficulties. Although Clark notes that "nothing in Einstein's early history sug-

gests dormant genius," and although he does not dispute the lateness of his speech, Clark does dispute the claim that Einstein was dyslexic. He considers "far more plausible" the explanation that Einstein was "withdrawn from the world even as a boy—a pupil for whom teachers held out only poor prospects" (Clark, *Einstein*, 1971, pp. 9–10). In his own book, psychologist Gerald Coles reiterates Clark's explanation. While Coles does admit that Einstein "did have some learning difficulties" (presumably in the more general sense of the term), he argues that "categorizing Einstein as learning disabled and identifying his language difficulties as seminal to his school problems is another instance of LD mistaken identity" (Coles, *Learning Mystique*, 1987 [1989], pp. 124–25). It is argued here, however, that while Einstein's hatred for mindless discipline and his social distance may have been significant, they were not the only factors in his learning difficulties and probably not the most important ones. We should pay close attention to Einstein's own words. It seems clear enough from Einstein's phrasing in this passage that his school problems were mainly the result of his poor memory for words in a school system where memorization of facts and texts was highly prized and where it was assumed that able students could memorize well enough if properly motivated, through repeated punishment if necessary.

56. Hoffmann, *Rebel*, 1972, p. 27. Gerald Coles argues that Einstein failed this examination because of the "plain fact that he did not study for it" mainly because of his opposition to his father's wish that he pursue a practical profession (Coles, *Learning Mystique*, 1987 [1989], p. 125). That Einstein did not study as thoroughly as he might have during his Italian "idyll" and needed another year of school for proper preparation is not really subject to debate. That he was mainly opposing his father is another matter. This consideration may or may not have been significant, but it should not be allowed to obscure the major importance of non-psychological factors— that is, the overarching pattern in strengths and weaknesses outlined here. Rather, we should look at the specific material Einstein had trouble with, foreign languages and botany, and those he loved, theoretical science and philosophy, to get some idea of his abilities and how his mind worked. There can be little doubt that various psychological considerations are always important, to a greater or lesser extent, but in many cases it may be a great mistake to allow psychological considerations to obscure a growing understanding of important neurological factors.

57. Letter from Hermann Einstein to Jost Winteler, October 29, 1985, *Papers*, vol. 1, 1987, p. 10.

58. Frederick Kirsh, diary, quoted in Clark, *Life and Times*, 1971, p. 393.

59. Letter from Hermann Einstein to Jost Winteler, December 30, 1985, *Papers*, vol. 1, 1987, p. 11.

60. Hoffmann, *Rebel*, 1972, pp. 28–30.

61. Carl Seelig, *Albert Einstein*, 1960, p. 176, quoted in Pais, *Subtle*, 1982, p. 44. There is some evidence, however, that although Einstein was "disappointed by the neglect of contemporary topics, such as Maxwell's theory," he had been, at least initially, enthusiastic about Weber's lectures (Stachel, ed., *Papers*, vol. I [German volume], 1987, p. 60).

62. Beck (trans.), *Papers*, 1987, p. xiv. Einstein's difficulties with spelling became more apparent after he moved to the United States and had to deal with the many non-phonetic irregularities of English spelling. "Almost all of the correspondence between Einstein and [Max] Wertheimer (the chief founder of Gestalt psychology) was in German. They were more comfortable writing in German, even when they had been in the United States for ten years and could speak and read English fluently, 'But I cannot write in English,' Einstein explained to Born, in a letter of September 7, 1944, 'because of the treacherous spelling. When I am reading, I only hear it and am unable to remember what the written word looks like'" (Luchins and Luchins, "Einstein-Wertheimer Correspondence," *Intelligencer*, 1990, p. 37. Einstein quotations from Born, *Born-Einstein Letters*, 1971, p. 148).

63. Esther Salaman, "A Talk with Einstein," *The Listener*, September 8, 1955, quoted in Clark, *Life and Times*, 1984, p. 19.

64. Vallentin, *Drama*, 1954, p. 31.

65. From E. H. Hutten, in G. J. Whitrow, *Einstein: The Man and His Achievement*, quoted in French, ed., *Centenary*, 1979, p. 176.

66. Einstein, *Notes*, 1979, p. 15.

67. Hoffmann, *Rebel*, 1972, pp. 31–32; Stachel, ed., *Papers*, vol. I (German volume), 1987, p. xxxvii.

68. Vallentin, *Drama*, 1954, pp. 33–34.

69. Letter from A. Einstein to Maja Einstein, Zurich, 1898, *Papers*, vol. 1, 1987, p. 123. In the German volume, the editorial note to the first sentence of this letter indicates, "After the failure of [the Einstein company] in 1896, Einstein attempted to dissuade his father from starting a new electrical firm in Milan. The new firm was liquidated about the time of this letter" (p. 211).

70. Quoted in Hoffmann, *Rebel*, 1972, pp. 33–34.

71. Hoffmann, *Rebel*, 1972, pp. 34–35.

72. Stachel, ed., *Papers*, vol. I (German volume), 1987, p. xxxvii. Little is known of the daughter. Stachel's comments are brief. "Their child, a girl called 'Lieserl' in their letters, was born early in 1902. Einstein was appointed to the Patent Office in June of that year, and he and Maric were married in Bern early in 1903. In a letter to Maric written before Lieserl's birth, Einstein took for granted that the child would join them after he began work at the Patent Office. But in fact Lieserl did not join them. A letter indi-

cates that she survived an attack of scarlet fever in 1903. Beyond that, no further information about her fate has yet been found, in spite of our efforts to locate records in Yugoslavia." (pp. xxxvii–xxxviii)

73. Quoted in Hoffmann, *Rebel*, 1972, p. 36.

74. Quoted in Loewenberg, "Einstein in His Youth," *Science*, 1988, p. 510.

75. Letter from A. Einstein to Mileva Maric, December 12, 1901. *Papers*, vol. 1, 1987, p. 186.

76. Calder, *Einstein's Universe*, 1979, pp. 2 and 3.

CHAPTER 5. PROFILES, PART 2

1. See, for example, the listing of traits designed for the general reader by T. R. Miles, provided as Appendix I, "Recognizing the Dyslexic Child," in the paperback edition of *Susan's Story* by Susan Hampshire, 1981, pp. 172–75.

2. From Dodgson's description dated June 1888, quoted in Collingwood, *Lewis Carroll*, 1898 (1967), pp. 268–69.

3. Collingwood, *Lewis Carroll*, 1898 (1967), p. 267. "Defects in the recognition of face identity, generally known as prosopagnosia, can appear in relative isolation (pure prosopagnosia) or as part of an amnesic syndrome" (Damasio, "Reflections," in Galaburda, ed., *Reading to Neurons*, 1989, p. 361). It is remarkable that difficulty with recognizing faces is not that unusual. Drs. Brock and Fernette Eide have noted: "Human face recognition is handled by a discrete region of the cortex that so far as anyone can tell does nothing else. Prosopagnosia, or difficulty with face recognition, is surprisingly common. The gene for this condition was recently found, and it's prevalence in the U.S. population is 1.7 percent. We have seen one family who combined relatively extensive dyslexic challenges with prosopagnosia, but we have seen many more non-dyslexic prosopagnosics, and because this particular aspect of visual processing seems both largely functionally and genetically discrete from other aspects of visual processing, I would tend to see Dodgson's issues in this area an important and interesting feature that is unrelated to his spatial talents. Interestingly, though, we have heard from some prosopagnosics that they believe their condition can give them advantages in certain areas. For example, one psychologist whose milder form of prosopagnosia allows him to see facial features as isolated fragments but is unable to form a single gestalt image of a human face. (More severe cases of prosopagnosia also exist where the entire face and all features are essentially a vacant blur.) This psychologist tells us that he thinks his need to examine

each feature independently makes it easier for him to tell when people are trying to bluff him (e.g., eyes, mouth, and nasal folds not agreeing) . . ." (Personal communication, December 9, 2008).

4. A facsimile "looking-glass letter" is provided in Collingwood, *Lewis Carroll*, 1898 (1967), pp, 414–15. It is noteworthy that this letter is not unlike one written by Maxwell when he was a boy of twelve—to be read by his father "backwards through the paper" (Campbell and Garnett, *Life*, 1884 [1969], p. 57).

5. Collingwood, *Lewis Carroll*, 1898 (1967), pp. 74 and 76.

6. Corballis and Beale, *Ambivalent Mind*, 1983, p. 227, and Wood, *The Snark*, 1966.

7. Bell, *Men of Mathematics*, 1937 (1965), p. 527.

8. Bell, *Men of Mathematics*, 1937 (1965), p. 538.

9. Pais, *Subtle*, 1982, pp. 169–70.

10. Poincaré, quoted in Hoffmann, *Rebel*, 1972, p. 99.

11. "This study, like everything which could be written on mathematical invention, was first inspired by Henri Poincaré's famous lecture before the Société de Psychologie in Paris" (Hadamard, *Invention*, 1945 [1954], p. vii).

12. Bell, *Men of Mathematics*, 1937 (1965), p. 532.

13. Handwriting and doodlings by Poincaré are reproduced in Figures 6.1 (a), 6.1 (b), and 6.2 in Miller, *Imagery*, 1986, pp. 236–38.

14. Bell, *Men of Mathematics*, 1937 (1965), p. 532.

15. Bell, *Men of Mathematics*, 1937 (1965), p. 532–33. Euler was an eighteenth-century Swiss mathematician who began, among other things, the study of surfaces called topology.

16. Bell, *Men of Mathematics*, 1937 (1965), pp. 534–35.

17. Compare Adelman and Adelman, "Rodin, Patton . . ." 1987, pp. 274–76, and Aaron et al., ". . . Famous Persons," in *Journal of Learning Disabilities*, 1988, pp. 523–45.

18. From Edison obituary, New York *Herald Tribune*, October 19, 1931, quoted in Josephson, *Edison*, 1959, p. 14.

19. Conot, *Luck*, 1979, p. 6.

20. Edison, *Diary*, 1971, p. 56. In this passage the punctuation and capitalization shown follow exactly Edison's handwriting as reproduced in this facsimile edition.

21. Thompson, "Eminence," 1969, pp. 114–19, and Josephson, *Edison*, 1969, pp. 19–20.

22. In *Streak of Luck*, Conot describes the young Edison as absorbing knowledge at a rapid rate, but more from practical experience in the lively industrial city of Detroit than through books or the classroom. In a footnote,

Conot points out, "When he was fifteen [Edison] joined the Young Men's Society of Detroit and decided he would read his way through the association's library shelf by shelf. After scanning ten rather dry volumes, however, he changed his mind and gave up the encyclopedic enterprise" (Conot, *Streak*, 1979, p. 10, footnote).

23. Edison, *Diary*, 1948, pp. 44, 46, 48–54.

24. Edison, *Diary*, 1948, p. 45.

25. Edison, *Diary*, 1971, entries of July 12 and 20, 1885, pp. 12ff.

26. Edison, *Diary*, 1948, p. 45.

27. Adelman and Adelman, "Rodin, Patton . . ." 1987, p. 275. The article cites Edison's reading of advanced, adult-level books as further evidence of his early reading skill. "It was also noted [in Josephson's biography] that at the age of nine, his mother had him reading Gibson's [sic] *Decline and Fall of the Roman Empire*, Hume's *History of England* and literary classics ranging from Shakespeare to Dickens" (p. 275). However, this particular argument hangs on what appears to be an incorrect reading of Josephson's words. Josephson remarked that mothers of the 1850s preferred ladies' magazines for themselves and preferred for their children certain popular children's books of the era. "But Nancy Edison had superior taste. Believing that her son, far from being dull-witted, had unusual reasoning powers, she read to him from such books as Gibbon's *Decline and Fall of the Roman Empire*," etc. (Josephson, *Edison*, 1959, p. 21). With the proper reading of Josephson, Edison's experience is seen as more in keeping with the pattern we have been describing—well within the tradition of Yeats and Patton, who also had advanced books read out loud to them by a father or mother. However, an important additional problem is cited by Adelman and Adelman. Josephson asserts, "While immature and ill-disciplined in some respects, [Edison] was advanced in others and soon became a very rapid reader" (p. 21). Another biographer, Conot, makes a simliar assertion. During a later brief return to regular school, "two or three children had to share each book, and Alva, a rapid reader, had no patience with his classmates" (Conot, *Streak*, 1979, p. 7). No further evidence is given by either writer. However, as we have seen, the pattern described by Orton and others does not require late or slow reading. These are just parts of the pattern that may or may not be present along with other relevant traits.

28. Because it was his favorite book as a child, Edison presented the gift of Parker's *Compendium* to Henry Ford—a great admirer of Edison—for the Ford museum of technology at Dearborn, Michigan, where Edison's Menlo Park, N.J. laboratory was moved and rebuilt.

29. Isaac Newton particularly loved a very similar book when he was a young boy, although he showed no signs of dyslexia or other learning diffi-

culties: John Bate's *Mysteries of Nature*, 1635 (1654). Other books like Bate's *Mysteries* were published at about the same time for example, William Oughtred's 1653 *Mathematicall Recreations*. Like Edison's, Newton's favorite book is filled with illustrations of primitive pumps, steam engines, Chinese rockets, and other exciting devices. It has been acknowledged by some historians of science that the influence of the early books and toys of great scientists, mathematicians, and inventors has not been adequately studied. In his essay on Einstein, Gerald Holton refers to the role of such books and toys in the lives of Newton, Edison, the Wright brothers, and others (Holton, "Genius," *American Scholar*, 1972, p. 109, note 8).

30. Broad, "Subtle Analogies . . . Edison's Genius," *New York Times*, 1985, p. 15. For Edison's use of analogy in invention, see also Friedel, Israel, and Finn, *Electric Light*, 1986; Israel, "Telegraphy," *Working*, 1989; Jenkins and Nier, "Record," *Transactions*, 1984, pp. 191–96.

31. Broad, "Subtle Analogies . . . Edison's Genius," *New York Times*, 1985, p. 16.

32. Hunt and Draper, *Lightning*, 1964, pp. 91–95.

33. Hunt and Draper, "Tesla's Friendship with Robert Underwood Johnson," in *Lightning in His Hand*, 1964, p. 201. It now appears to be very clear that Tesla's unusual mix of remarkable talents and difficulties fits the profile associated with Asperger syndrome (see Thomas G. West, "With Tesla, from Visualization to Asperger," *Thinking Like Einstein*, 2004, pp. 181–186).

34. Miller, *Imagery*, 1986, p. 262.

35. Tesla, *Inventions*, 1919 (1982), pp. 31–32.

36. Tesla, *Inventions*, 1919 (1982), p. 33. Note Tesla's idiosyncratic phonetic misspellings ("engrost"), which were deliberately not changed in the current reprinting, as they were not corrected, presumably unintentionally, in the original 1919 series of magazine articles. Not too much is to be made of this, since Tesla immigrated and started using English regularly only as a young adult. Evidence, pro or con, from his native language would be more indicative.

37. Tesla, *Inventions*, 1919 (1982), p. 33.

38. KPMG Peat Marwick, *Competitive Benefits from 3D Computing*, 1989, p. 10. The companies included in the study were Hitachi Power Group, Hitachi City, Japan, a producer of nuclear power plants for the electrical utility industry; Douglas Aircraft Company, Long Beach, California, a major manufacturer of military and commercial aircraft; Karsten Manufacturing, Phoenix, Arizona, a producer of customized golf clubs; NASA/Ames, Mountain View, California, an internationally recognized center for aerodynamic research; and Chrysler Motors Corporation, Detroit, Michigan, a producer of passenger cars, vans, and light trucks (p. 2).

39. KPMG Peat Marwick, *Competitive Benefits*, 1989, p. 12.

40. Carusi, "Leonardo's Manuscripts," in *Leonardo*, 1956, p. 158.

41. Cook, *Curves of Life*, 1914 (1949), p. 370.

42. Carusi et al., *Leonardo da Vinci*, 1956, and R. Calder, *Leonardo*, 1970.

43. R. Calder, *Leonardo*, 1970, pp. 128–30.

44. Apostal, *Mathematics! Project Workbook . . . Pythagoras*, 1988, p. 27.

45. Sartori, "Leonardo," *Cognitive Neuropsychology*, 1987, pp. 1–2.

46. Sartori, "Leonardo," *Cognitive Neuropsychology*, 1987, pp. 3–7.

47. Aaron et al., "Famous Persons," *Journal of Learning Disabilities*, 1988, p. 534.

48. Sartori, "Leonardo," *Cognitive Neuropsychology*, 1987, pp. 9–10.

CHAPTER 6. PROFILES, PART 3

1. This view is quite different from the contemporary view, wherein almost anything that is different from the conventional is considered creative. Instead, the view set forth here emphasizes the need for some form of internal editing function as well as some way of selecting the best solution or design in a particular case from among a wide range of possibilities.

2. One reference to Churchill's speech difficulties includes a description of preparatory whispering that is reminiscent of the very young Einstein, although Churchill's whispering may have been for very different reasons. When Churchill was visiting New York in December 1931, he was hit by car and injured. As he was recovering, he hired a new secretary, "Miss Moir, to whom he dictated a constant stream of notes and observations—she had yet to master his lisp, and was disconcerted by 'his curious habit of whispering each phrase to himself before he said it aloud.'" Quoted in Manchester, *Last Lion: Visions of Glory*, 1983, p. 881.

3. Clarke, "Lightning in His Brain," *Time*, October 31, 1988, p. 87.

4. Brendon, *Churchill*, 1984, p. 12. The differences of interpretation given in reference to Brendon's account should not be construed as criticism. Brendon's brief biography of Churchill is a masterpiece of readable compression, without a word wasted.

5. Churchill, *My Early Life*, 1930, pp. 16–18.

6. Brendon, *Churchill*, 1984, pp. 12–13. Churchill had some early success with languages while in school in Brighton, before entering Harrow. "He was first in his classics class and near the top in English [and] French" (Manchester, *Last Lion: Visions of Glory*, 1983, p. 127). These early successes may

have come from his special ability to memorize texts. Different abilities would have been required to attain greater language fluency later.

7. Churchill, *My Early Life*, 1930, pp. 16–17.

8. Brendon, *Churchill*, 1984, pp. 13–14. There are differing views among biographers about the extent of Churchill's bad behavior and the frequency of his punishments while at school. Henry Pelling attributes Churchill's difficulties less to willful troublesomeness than to being "forgetful, careless and unpunctual." Pelling claims that Churchill was caned only once (Pelling, *Churchill*, 1974, p. 33). Whichever version is more accurate, it would appear that the overall pattern remains substantially the same.

9. Brendon, *Churchill*, 1984, p. 15, and R. S. Churchill, *Churchill*, 1966, pp. 196–200. In a similar fashion, Charles Darwin's father briefly suggested that he take up a career in the church because the boy seemed so remarkably devoid of intellectual talent and academic ability (Gruber, *Darwin on Man: A Psychological Study of Scientific Creativity*, 1974 [1981]).

10. Churchill, *My Early Life*, 1930, p. 59.

11. Churchill, *My Early Life*, 1930, pp. 38–39.

12. Manchester, *Last Lion: Alone*, 1988, p. 10.

13. Peck, *Atlantic Monthly*, 1965, p. 70, quoted in Pelling, *Churchill*, 1974, p. 644.

14. Manchester, *Last Lion: Alone*, 1988, p. 5.

15. Manchester, *Last Lion: Alone*, 1988, pp. 11–12.

16. Manchester, *Last Lion: Alone*, 1988, p. 5.

17. Manchester, *Last Lion: Alone*, 1988, p. 17.

18. Manchester, *Last Lion: Alone*, 1988, p. 16.

19. Churchill, *My Early Life*, 1930, pp. 1–4.

20. While in school at Brighton, before Harrow, Churchill wrote that he was "getting on capitally in Euclid. I and another boy are top of the school in it we have got up to the XXX Proposition" (quoted, exactly as written, in Manchester, *Last Lion: Visions of Glory*, 1983, p. 128).

21. Churchill, *My Early Life*, 1930, pp. 12–13.

22. Some biographers view Churchill's poor school performance mainly from a psychological perspective, as primarily a rebellion against authority because of resentment toward the parents who showed him little attention and affection as a child. "At the same time—and this would cripple his schooling—the deprivation of parental attachment bred resentment of authority" (Manchester, *Last Lion: Visions of Glory*, 1983, p. 118). As indicated previously, there is no inherent contradiction between this psychological perspective and the neurological perspective we have been discussing. While many agree that these two perspectives are closely related, it is argued

here that excessive emphasis on psychological considerations should not be allowed to obscure the importance of traits that are probably largely neurological in origin. Both perspectives would appear to be needed to gain an understanding of the complex motivations, strengths, and weaknesses we are considering,

23. Churchill, *My Early Life*, 1930, pp. 38–39. The term "public schools" refers to the oldest and most prestigious private schools in Britain.

24. Aneurin Bevan, quoted in Pelling, *Churchill*, 1974, p. 642.

25. Brendon, *Churchill*, 1984, p. 36. The full extent to which Churchill's speeches were contrived as a thorough performance is indicated by another biographer. "When Churchill rises to speak in the House, he holds in his band not notes on the issues he means to address, but the entire text of what he has to say. . . . Because his delivery gives an illusion of spontaneity and the notes include stage directions ('pause; grope for word' and 'stammer; correct self'), each of his speeches is a dramatic, vibrant occasion" (Manchester, *Last Lion: Alone*, 1988, p. 34).

26. Brendon, *Churchill*, 1984, p. 15. There are other stories. Even as a middle-aged man he liked to play in the bath. "When on impulse he turned a somersault, 'exactly like a porpoise,' a spectator recalls, the tub overflowed, damaging the ceiling below and, worse, drenching the frock coat of an eminent Frenchman there who called to pay his respects" (Manchester, *Last Lion: Alone*, 1988, p. 8).

27. Brendon, *Churchill*, 1984, pp. 14–15.

28. Churchill, *My Early Life*, 1930, p. 20. Descriptions of similar difficulties with dictionaries are provided in Hampshire, *Story*, 1983, pp. 28–29, and in Simpson, *Reversals*, 1979, p. 105.

29. Churchill, *My Early Life*, 1930, p. 43.

30. Cowles, *Churchill*, 1953, p. 285, quoted in Manchester, *Last Lion: Visions of Glory*, 1983, p. 883 (also see pp. 676–77). The general pattern would seem to hold although it may not be uncommon for heads of state to assume high office in their later years.

31. Churchill, *My Early Life*, 1930, pp. 109–12.

32. James, *Study in Failure*, 1970, p. 6.

33. High Massingham, quoted in James, *Study in Failure*, 1970, p. 16.

34. J. B. Atkins, quoted in James, *Study in Failure*, 1970, p. 6.

35. Churchill, *Thoughts and Adventures*, 1932, pp. 300–301. Churchill's interest in actually being changed by reading and learning, instead of just absorbing information, is remarkably similar to the perceptions of some of those who are studying the nature of Faraday's creativity. "In creative learning, the kind of learning which is celebrated when Faraday is studied, there is a change in the personal internal world of mind. . . . There

is a distinction between this kind of learning, in which the learner has changed or grown in the process of getting to know something, and the kind of learning which is simply acquiring knowledge about a topic, but which does not involve changes in the individual's states of mind" (Crawford, "Learning from Experience," in *Faraday Rediscovered*, 1985, p. 14).

36. Yoder, "Statesman for All Seasons" *Book World*, 1988, p. 14.

37. Churchill, *Thoughts and Adventures*, 1932, pp. 183–86.

38. Churchill, *My Early Life*, 1930, p. 41. A description of the "magic lantern" mentioned by Churchill is found in Parker's *Compendium* (1848, pp. 182–83), the school textbook so loved and admired by Edison. "The Magic Lantern is an instrument constructed on the principle of the solar microscope, but the light is supplied by a lamp instead of the sun. 1. The objects to be viewed by the magic lantern are generally painted with transparent colors, on glass slides, which are received into an opening in front of the lantern. The light from the lamp in the lantern passes through them, and carries the pictures, painted on the slides, through the lenses, by means of which a magnified image is thrown upon the wall, on a white surface prepared to receive it."

39. Churchill, *Thoughts and Adventures*, 1932, pp. 23 and 26.

40. Churchill, *Thoughts and Adventures*, 1932, pp. 310 and 316.

41. Churchill, *Thoughts and Adventures*, 1932, pp. 311–12.

42. Blumenson, ed., Patton, *Letters*, 1972, p. xiii.

43. Blumenson, ed., *Patton*, 1985, pp. 16–17.

44. Quoted in Patton, *Letters*, 1972, p. 61.

45. Blumenson, ed., "Prologue," in Patton, *Letters*, 1972, pp. 6–7.

46. Blumenson, ed., *Patton*, 1985, p. 8. Here the biographer suggests injuries may have produced a "subdural haematoma" that may have contributed to "changes in personality."

47. Blumenson, ed., *Patton*, 1985, p. 13.

48. Blumenson, ed., *Patton*, 1985, p. 63.

49. Blumenson, ed., *Patton*, 1985, p. 15. Some writers have taken Patton's extensive reading and interest in history and biography as evidence that he was not, in fact, dyslexic at all. As noted previously, this apparent contradiction is seen here as one of the many paradoxes of dyslexia. Intelligent dyslexics with a passionate interest in some subject can be expected to read a great deal, even though they may read slowly, awkwardly, and with great difficulty (Adelman and Adelman, "Rodin, Patton . . ." 1987, p. 273).

50. Blumenson, ed., Patton, *Letters*, 1972, p. 16. If the influence of Napoleon is sufficient cause, then why were other well-read generals not more like Patton? Or is it more likely that Napoleon shared some more fundamental traits with Patton? Unfortunately, this line of inquiry must remain outside the scope of the present study.

51. Simpson, *Reversals*, 1979, pp. 184–85.

52. Donoghue, ed., "Introduction," in Yeats, *Memoirs*, 1972, p. 15.

53. "Poet Off Parade," *The Economist*, 1986, p. 90. When Yeats is viewed as dyslexic, the great care he took in "correcting and revising his work" can be seen partly as his persistent struggle to obtain precisely what he wanted in his poetic work, but also partly as his persistent struggle with his unusual difficulties in the basic mechanics of writing and spelling.

54. Kelly, "Introduction," in Yeats, *Collected Letters*, vol. 1, 1986, pp. xli.

55. Letter from John Butler Yeats to Lily Yeats, September 15, 1916, quoted in Murphy, *Prodigal Father*, 1978, p. 94, and in Jeffares, *Yeats*, 1988, p. 6. It is worth noting that the most recent biography of Yeats (Jeffares, *Yeats*, 1988), makes many references (pp. 6, 8, 9, and 19) to Yeats's educational difficulties—his inability to read, his father's impatient teaching, his poor spelling, his not attending Trinity College, Dublin, etc. However, Jeffares makes no comment on these difficulties except to note Yeats's own observations about the distraction of the great excitement of his thoughts. As to the possible reasons for Yeats not attending Trinity College, Jeffares speculates that Yeats may have been unable to pass the entrance examination (although Jeffares indicates that it was known to be quite easy), that Yeats wanted to delay academic study, and that a shortage of family money made attendance impossible.

56. Yeats, *Autobiography*, 1936, pp. 23–24. Gerald Coles acknowledges that Yeats says that learning to read was difficult because it was so much less interesting than his own thoughts. However, Coles argues that Yeats could not have really been dyslexic or learning disabled since the reading difficulties described occurred at the rather young age of eight years and because Yeats was later interested in a "multi-volumed encyclopedia" and a "prose retelling of the *Iliad*," as well as, by the age fifteen years, "Darwin and Wallace, Huxley and Haeckel" (Coles, *Learning Mystique*, 1987, p. 129, note 94). However, as we have noted previously, bright and gifted dyslexics can often be expected to read widely and deeply, in time, even if slowly and with great difficulty.

57. Yeats, *Autobiography*, 1936, p. 27.

58. Yeats, *Autobiography*, 1936, pp. 42–44.

59. Yeats, "What We Did or Tried to Do," in *W. B. Yeats and the Designing of Ireland's Coinage*, 1972, p. 20. Selected by the committee from entries in a competition in 1926, the designs of the coins, based on those of ancient Greek and Carthaginian coins, are distinctive in their portrayal of animals associated with Ireland instead of famous persons such as heads of state. From the half crown to the farthing, the designs included the harp of

Ireland on the reverse of all the coins. On the obverse were the Irish hunting horse, salmon, bull, wolf-hound, hare, hen, pig, and woodcock.

60. Simpson, *Reversals*, 1979, p. 184.

61. Jeffares, *Yeats*, 1988, p. 18.

62. Lollie Yeats, diary entry, January 18, 1888, quoted in Jeffares, *Yeats*, 1988, p. 42.

63. Yeats, letter to Olivia Shakespear, April 10, 1936, quoted in Jeffares, *Yeats*, 1988, p. 331. Edison also made a number of references to his preference for seeing a thing rather than merely hearing or reading about it (Edison, *Diary*, 1948, pp. 112–13).

64. Jeffares, *Yeats*, 1988, p. 332.

65. Yeats, *Autobiography*, 1936, p. 44.

66. Yeats, *Autobiography*, 1936, p. 43, as paraphrased in Jeffares.

67. Yeats, *Autobiography*, 1936, p. 38.

68. Hampshire, *Story*, 1983, pp. 32–33.

69. Yeats, *Autobiography*, 1936, p. 51.

70. Yeats, *Autobiography*, 1936, p. 52.

71. Yeats, *A Vision*, 1937 (1971), pp. 68–69 and 74–75.

72. Yeats, *Autobiography*, 1936, p.71.

CHAPTER 7. SPEECH AND NONVERBAL THOUGHT

1. Bogen and Bogen, "Other Side . . . Creativity," *Bulletin L. A. Neurological Societies*, 1969, p. 105, and Jackson, "Duality," in *Writings*, 1874 (1932), p. 129.

2. Levy, "Possible Basis . . ." *Nature*, 1969, pp. 614–15. After these early observations had been published, it became evident that, rather than being entirely mute, the right hemisphere had limited use of language. The author has taken the liberty of slightly altering this quotation to avoid any misunderstanding in this regard.

3. Maxwell, *Treatise*, 1891 (1954), p. vii.

4. One might speculate that many in the middle of the normal distribution may be inherently more malleable—that is, they could be seen as more responsive to being molded in whatever way the culture of the moment forms them. This is strangely consistent with the concept of a faster learner, one who quickly adapts to the local situation whatever the long-term consequences. In contrast those at the tail of the distribution having greater talents might be seen as both less willing and less able to respond to the pressures of the immediate society or culture.

5. Hadamard, *Invention*, 1945 (1954), pp. 66–67.

6. Hadamard, *Invention*, 1945 (1954), p. 69. On the other hand, Hadamard points out that Galton sometimes found his thought accompanied by "*nonsense* words, just 'as the notes of a song might accompany thought.'"

7. Hadamard, *Invention*, 1945 (1954), pp. 69–70.

8. One will sometimes find references to this difficulty among other scientists and mathematicians: they often make reference to the inadequacy of words to communicate their ideas. In a rarely quoted section of the letter that provides the description of his visual thought referred to in chapter 1, Einstein says, "In the following I am trying to answer in brief your questions as well as I am able. I am not satisfied myself with those answers and I am willing to answer more questions if you believe this could be of any advantage for the very interesting and difficult work you have undertaken" (Hadamard, *Invention*, 1945 [1954], p. 144).

9. Forbes, *Maxwell*, 1982, p. 30.

10. Campbell and Garnett, *Life*, 1882, p. 106.

11. Campbell and Garnett, *Life*, 1882, p. 259.

12. Tolstoy, *Biography*, 1981, p. 5.

13. Campbell and Garnett, *Life*, 1882, p. 259.

14. Everitt, "Maxwell's," *Springs*, 1983, p. 132.

15. Schuster, *Cavendish*, 1910, p. 31. Maxwell established and headed the Cavendish laboratory from 1871 until his death in 1879.

16. Farrar, *Men*, 1897, pp. 136–37. A further description of this group is provided in Campbell and Garnett (*Life*, 1882, p. 165): "In the course of the winter [1851–52] he was elected a member of the Select Essay Club, the *crème* of Cambridge intellects, familiarly known (because limited to the number twelve) as 'the Apostles.'"

17. P. Baker, personal communication, June, 1983.

18. Silver, *Misunderstood*, 1984, pp. 26–27.

19. It may be noted here that although these students seem to perform poorly in the early years, some of them may begin to "take off' in junior high school or high school. These students may sometimes completely displace former "A" students, to the amazement of teachers, parents, and classmates (and to the delight of tutors and professionals who are often mistakenly presumed to be exclusively responsible for the change). The change is often a combination of delayed development, remedial instruction, and changes in subject matter studied—the more advanced curriculum gives greater emphasis to sophisticated concepts where these students often excel rather than on rote memory, repetition of sequential tasks, and organizational skills, areas in which these students often have remarkably limited abilities.

20. Holton, "Einstein's Answer," in *Centenary*, 1979, p. 153.

21. When one is attentive to this paradox, suggestive clues may appear

in the least likely places. For example, in his *Autobiography*, Benjamin Franklin noted that many of his associates viewed him as a skillful speaker. But he viewed himself as a hesitant and awkward speaker. The appearance of false modesty (although not typical of Franklin) may divert us from this promising clue. It may be important that this creative, highly visual, mechanically inclined, innovative scientist and statesman saw himself as having difficulty finding the right words—but was known for the power, simplicity, and effectiveness of his language once they were found. It may also be important that Franklin—who was thought to be more like his mother's family, the many-talented Folgers of Nantucket Island, than the more "ordinary" Franklins—had a relative, Walter Folger, who was known as a mechanical genius (with little formal education, he built a highly complex clock when he was twenty-one) and who was also known to have difficulty with hesistant speech. One needs to be careful of assertions based on such small clues, but, on the other hand, such clues may be helpful in leading us to significant and verifiable insights.

22. Hall, *Culture*, 1981, p. 175.
23. A. van Oss, personal communication, February 20, 1987.
24. L. Silver, personal communication, April 8, 1987.

CHAPTER 8. PATTERNS IN CREATIVITY

1. Personal communication, July 25, 1984. Kary B. Mullis, Ph.D., shared the 1993 Nobel Prize in Chemistry with Michael Smith. Mullis received the prize for his development of the Polymerase Chain Reaction (PCR) that makes it possible to rapidly make thousands or millions of copies of specific DNA sequences. The improvements provided by Mullis have made PCR a technique of central importance in molecular biology and biochemistry. According to the Nobel Prize presentation speech given by Professor Carl-Ivor Branden of the Royal Swedish Academy of Sciences: "the isolation and amplification of a specific gene was one of the outstanding problems in DNA technology, including site-directed mutagenesis, until 1985 when Kary Mullis presented the Polymerase Chain Reaction, now commonly known as PCR. Using this method it is possible to amplify and isolate in a test tube a specific DNA segment within a background of a complex gene pool. In this repetitive process the number of copies of the specific DNA segment doubles during each cycle. In a few hours it is possible to achieve more than 20 cycles, which produces over a million copies." (Source, Nobelprize.org.)

2. The enormous prestige of the Nobel Prize makes it difficult to see that this award, like any other, is partly a reflection of the limited knowledge

in a particular discipline at a particular time. See Hoffmann, *Creator*, 1972, p. 150.

3. Gleick, *Chaos*, 1987, pp. 2–3.

4. At the close of the war, while Einstein was still living and working in Germany, British astronomer Sir Arthur Eddington mounted expeditions to Africa and South America to prove or disprove Einstein's theory. The expeditions were intended to produce photographs of star positions near the eclipsed sun to show whether gravity would bend light rays slightly (in the way Einstein had predicted) as these rays passed close to a massive body such as the sun (Chandrasekhar, *Eddington*, 1983, p. 30).

5. Quoted in Jones, *Life and Letters*, 1870, vol. II, p. 214.

6. Einstein, *Autobiographical Notes*, 1949 (1979), pp. 59–63.

7. Einstein, quoted in Judson, *Solutions*, 1980, p. 5.

8. Once again, paradoxically, this lack of change should be recognized as the chief advantage of one particular kind of mind—one opposite from that we are focusing on.

9. This hypothesis is given greater credibility by the recent finding that this excess of connections includes a large number of "long-distance" connections—that is, those that connect distant parts of the brain (Galaburda, "Research Findings," Orton Dyslexia Society Annual Conference, November 1989).

10. Judson, *Search for Solutions*, 1980, p. 68.

11. Quoted in Judson, *Search for Solutions*, 1980, p. 68.

12. Calder, *Restless Earth*, 1972, pp. 42–45. It is a curious fact that just as Wegener revolutionized geology, so too mathematics and a great many sciences are being revolutionized by "chaos," a fresh way of looking at things partly pioneered by another meteorologist Edward Lorenz (Gleick, *Chaos*, 1987, pp. 11 ff). One wonders whether there could be something about the kind of mind attracted by meteorology that favors truly original work in large, fluid, and complex systems or, alternatively, whether the discipline of constantly dealing with large and complex fluid systems might also be a major contributing factor to a certain highly productive perspective.

13. Lewis Thomas, quoted in Judson, *Search for Solutions*, 1980, p. 69.

14. Dukas and Hoffmann, eds., *Human Side*, 1979, pp. 54–57.

15. A number of other cases of writing and other creative work done in the enforced solitude of incarceration are referred to in Anthony Storr, *Solitude*, 1988, pp. 42–61.

16. Pickering, *Creative Malady: Illness in the Lives and Minds of Charles Darwin, Florence Nightingale, Mary Baker Eddy, Sigmund Freud, Marcel Proust, Elizabeth Barrett Browning*, 1974, pp. 7–8.

17. Dukas and Hoffmann, eds., *Human Side*, p. 57.

18. Gleick, *Chaos*, 1987, p. 66.

19. Beveridge, *Art of Scientific Investigation*, 1950, p. 6. See also Kuhn, *Structure of Scientific Revolutions*, 1970.

20. A recurring theme in the history of science is that some new ideas are unacceptable to conventional modes of thought. Sometimes the problem is that the ideas are not really perceived as being new. It is assumed that what is important is already known and well understood. A current example of this sort of problem is the theory of atmospheric chemistry known as the "Gala Hypothesis." The theory has been advanced since the late 1960s by British scientist and instrument designer James E. Lovelock and others. The basic idea is that the kinds and amounts of gases in the earth's atmosphere are regulated mainly by microbial life. If certain gases, like oxygen and methane, were not being constantly produced, they would be expected to combine with each other, making the proportions of these gases in the uncombined state much less prevalent. Consequently, according to the theory, life can be detected on any planet through atmospheric measurements. One Lovelock coworker, Lynn Margulis, indicated that it was some time before even she was able to understand the full significance of Lovelock's still-controversial ideas. Lovelock "couldn't get anyone to understand what he was saying. I know, because I worked with him for two years before I could understand it. . . . It's not his fault. It's not my fault. It was just that he was coming up with something very new. What we tended to hear was what we had heard before. Oh, we would say, we know all about that already—which is just the response you are getting today from today's academics. [But] it's a genuinely original idea." There are further possible reasons for the continuing resistance to Lovelock's approach, ones that touch on the familiar problems of specialization and definition of professional domain. According to Margulis, "If this kind of analysis is correct, then atmospheric chemists will have to know something about microbiology. And even worse, microbiologists will have to know something about atmospheric chemistry, etc." Many specialists are not enthusiastic, in part, perhaps, because "they are going to have to re-educate" themselves, which many do not wish to do (Lynn Margulis, "Rethinking Evolution," Smithsonian Institution, April 23, 1990).

21. Chandrasekhar, *Eddington*, 1983, p. 30.

22. Chandrasekhar, *Eddington*, 1983, p. 25.

23. Einstein, quoted in Chandrasekhar, *Eddington*, 1983, p. 24.

24. Chandrasekhar, *Eddington*, 1983, p. 24.

25. Cannon, *Investigator*, 1945, quoted in Beveridge, *The Art of Scientific Investigation*, 1957, p. 71.

26. Kekulé, quoted in Beveridge, *Scientific Investigation*, 1957, p. 56.

27. Ornstein, *Multimind*, 1986, Gazzaniga, *The Social Brain*, 1985, and Minsky, *The Society of Mind*, 1986.

28. In the German version, "Bernsteins naturwissenschaftliche Volks-bucher." Einstein, *Notes*, 1979, pp. 13 and 15.

29. Snow, "Albert Einstein, 1879–1955," in *Centenary*, 1979, p. 3.

30. Quoted in Pais, *Subtle*, 1986, p. 164. (The emphasis is Einstein's.)

31. Pais, *Subtle*, 1986, p. 165.

32. Pais, *Subtle*, 1986, p. 165.

33. Pais, *Subtle*, 1986, p. 165. Pais is more explicit in his footnote to this passage. "Einstein was evidently able to get the literature if he set his mind to it. A number of journals are quoted in his 1907 paper . . . including even the *American Journal of Science* of 1887, in which the Michelson-Morley experiment was reported. I would not be surprised if Einstein had copied that reference from one of Lorentz's papers."

34. R. Marra, personal communication, circa 1963.

35. Quoted in Vallentin, *Drama*, 1954, p. 31.

36. Kay, "Emerging Trends," Apple, 1987. (Kay is referring to com-ments made by Alfred North Whitehead and Marshall McLuhan.)

37. Howard, *Wilbur and Orville*, 1987, pp. 8–9 and 11–13.

38. Howard, *Wilbur and Orville*, 1987, pp. 7–8.

39. Howard, *Wilbur and Orville*, 1987, p. 7.

40. It is not unusual, however, for highly creative people to have "fallow" periods for thought, research, and reflection—to allow their ideas to take shape. These periods, or alternating cycles of productivity and com-parative inactivity, have often been noted. For example, the third chapter of L. Pearce Williams's biography, *Michael Faraday*, is titled "The Fallow Years." An almost identical chapter title, "Fallow Years, 1844–1849," is used in Karl Pearson's 1914 *Life, Letters and Labours of Francis Galton*.

41. "The company began, in true American-dream fashion, in a garage in 1977. In six short years Apple had made the *Fortune* 500 roster, becoming the youngest firm to be on that exalted list" (Slater, "Steven Jobs: Cofounder of Apple," *Portraits in Silicon*, 1987 [1989], p. 309–21. Also Levering et al., "Steve Jobs: Apple Computer," *Computer Entrepreneurs*, 1984, pp. 55–56).

42. Howard, *Wilbur and Orville*, 1987, pp. 125–32.

43. "For years the Wrights had been strict with their money. Their total out-of-pocket expenditures, right up to the point where they made their flights on December 17, 1903, had not quite reached one thousand dollars" (Combs, *Kill Devil Hill*, 1979 [1986], pp. 320–21). Of course, the Langley and Wright expenditures are not strictly comparable, since there is presum-ably no allowance for Wilbur and Orville's own time, nor for their bicycle shop machinist, nor for the assistance they received from Kitty Hawk-area

locals. Nonetheless, the difference is a dramatic indication of possible ill effects when fully qualified people embark on a project with ample resources. One Wright biographer pointed out, "As administrator of the country's most prestigious scientific institution, Langley was in an enviable position when it came to producing such an aircraft, but in some ways the wealth of manpower and resources at his disposal was a hindrance" (Howard, *Wilbur and Orville*, 1987, p. 125).

44. Personal communication, June 1984.

45. Hoffmann, *Rebel*, 1972, p. 84.

CHAPTER 9. IMAGES, COMPUTERS, AND MATHEMATICS

1. Steen, "Science of Patterns," *Science*, 1988, p. 616. Lynn Arthur Steen is professor of mathematics at St. Olaf College in Northfield, Minn., and has served as chairman of the Conference Board of the Mathematical Sciences.

2. Hoffmann, *Rebel*, 1972, pp. 126–27.

3. Steen, "Science of Patterns," *Science*, 1988, p. 616.

4. The strong position of rigorous proof in traditional mathematics continues to function for some as a severe impediment to major advances in new areas of mathematics. For some, without the rigorous proof, it is just not real mathematics. See Gleick, *Chaos*, 1987, pp. 88–89 and 183–84.

5. Steen, "Science of Patterns," *Science*, 1988, p. 614.

6. Steen, "Science of Patterns," *Science*, 1988, p. 614.

7. Hadamard, *Invention*, 1945 (1954), pp. 75–76.

8. Hadamard, *Invention*, 1945 (1954), p. 77.

9. Damasio, "Visual Recognition," 1987, ODS Tape G3, Damasio, "Reflections on Visual Recognition," in Galaburda, ed., *Reading to Neurons*, 1989, pp. 361–74, and Palca, "Insights from Broken Brains," *Science*, 1990, pp. 812–14.

10. Everitt, *Springs*, 1983, p. 121. Both Bertrand Russell and Thomas Hobbes were reported to have had extraordinary reactions to their first contact with geometry, especially the theorem of Pythagoras.

11. Einstein, *Notes*, 1949 (1979), pp. 9–11. Of course, here Einstein is fascinated by the deductive logic involved, but this logic is concerned with the spatial relationships that remain the main focus.

12. Shute, *Geometry*, 1957, p. 265.

13. Other approaches to the proof have been used in other cultures and times, but many of these were spatial rather than symbolic or algebraic. For example, a new series of videotapes from Project Mathematics! (which uses

computer graphics to teach mathematical concepts to high school students) lists seven different approaches and variants to proving the Pythagorean theorem, all spatial in approach: the Pythagorean triples; the Chinese proof (a variant of this proof was discovered by James A. Garfield, just a few years before he became the twentieth president of the United States); a proof by a Hindu mathematician of A.D. 1150 similar to the Chinese proof; Euclid's classic proof; a dissection proof; and a variant of the dissection proof credited to Leonardo da Vinci (Apostol, Gordon, and Blinn, *Theorem of Pythagoras . . . Workbook*, 1988, pp. 17–27).

14. Bronowski, *Ascent of Man*, 1973, pp. 158–60. Here Bronowski is taken to be making a double joke: that one can do powerful things without calculation (in contrast to modern general belief); and that professional mathematicians and children can accomplish much through what would appear to be games of little consequence.

15. Einstein, *Notes*, 1949 (1979), pp. 9–11.

16. Although these two statements are mathematically equivalent, it is significant which form one prefers to use.

17. Bell, *Men of Mathematics*, 1937 (1986), pp. 183–85.

18. Rival, "Picture Puzzling," *The Sciences*, 1987, pp. 40–46.

19. Walsh, "Calculus . . . Hurdle," *Science*, 1987, p. 749. See also Halmos, "Turmoil," *Focus*, 1990, pp. 1–3.

20. Mathematics would appear to be such a pure and abstract discipline that it would be relatively immune to the whims of fashion and the pressures of power politics. However, outsiders will be interested to know that in at least one case a secret society was formed to purify and reform mathematics by doing away with all visual and diagrammatic content. Founded in France, this group of mathematicians, the Séminaire Bourbaki, was enormously influential in the early and middle parts of the twentieth century, forming an orthodoxy inhospitable to visually oriented mathematicians such as Henri Poincaré and Benoit Mandelbrot (Gleick, *Chaos*, 1987). In more recent years, the Bourbaki group itself seems to have softened, recently inviting, for example, a talk by a visually oriented mathematician whose work was inspired by children's Lego blocks (Rival, "Picture Puzzling," *The Sciences*, 1988, p. 46). However, it seems that elsewhere opposition to the visual approach is breaking out once again among mainstream mathematicians annoyed by the great success of Mandelbrot's "fractals" in recent years. One critic argues that, "Fractal geometry . . . has not solved any problems. It is not even clear that it has created any new ones" (S. Krantz, quoted in Pool, "Fractal Fracas: The Math Community Is in a Flap Over the Question of Whether Fractals Are Just Pretty Pictures—Or More Substantial Tools," in *Science*, July 27, 1990, pp. 363–64).

21. Swetz, *New Math of the 15th Century*, 1987, pp. 181–83. Several of Swetz's footnote references have been dropped from the quoted text.

22. Steen, "Mathematics Education," *Science*, 1987, p. 302.

23. Steven Wolfram, a professor of mathematics, winner of a MacArthur Prize, and creator of the innovative, visually oriented mathematics software program "Mathematics," explained, "When I started off doing mathematics, I wasn't very good at it. I never learned my multiplication tables and it was certainly the conclusion of my teachers at that time that there was no way I would ever go on and do anything . . . mathematically oriented. As it turned out, I found out about computers and found out that you could make computers do these kinds of things." Quoted in "Macintosh + Mathematics = Infinity" (13 min.), "Apple User Group Connection Videotape," Apple Computer, April 1989. The approach to mathematics instruction presented in chapter 9 seems to be gaining wider recognition in some quarters. Dr. Brock and Fernette Eide have noted: ". . . Your comments about math instruction are absolutely spot on, and desperately important. We cannot tell you how many potentially brilliant mathematicians we see who are perpetually kept from moving on to higher math until they can 'master arithmetic.' There are few things we see more tragic than the brilliant young natural mathematician whose love of math is suffocated under a crushing mountain of worksheets. Perhaps the saddest example of this was a brilliant young boy with a tremendous natural mathematical aptitude. When we saw him at age 5 he spent most of his exam period constantly pestering us to give him 'x problems,' which was his term for algebraic story problems. He was unable to write, so he did them in his head: 'If two trains were one hundred miles apart and one was traveling twenty miles an hour toward the other which was traveling at ten miles an hour, how long would it take until they met?' I can still see his little eyes roll up toward his furrowing brow while his little lips worked with the calculation. . . . He never made a mistake. Within two years his school's insistence that he write out all his problem sets—which was extremely difficult for him given his dyslexia and dysgraphia—had so extinguished his love of math that he was refusing to do math work of any kind" (Personal communication, December 9, 2008).

24. Abraham, "Series Foreword," *Dynamics*, 1984, p. iii. Such innovative visual approaches to mathematics are featured in some recently developed basic geometry textbooks. One example that incorporates a variety of visual material not normally found in geometry textbooks is Serra, *Discovering Geometry: An Inductive Approach*, 1989.

25. Gleick, *Chaos*, 1987, p. 47.

26. Gleick, *Chaos*, 1987, pp. 283–84.

27. Gleick, *Chaos*, 1987, p. 304.

28. Agassi, *Philosopher*, 1971, p. 306.

29. Hills, *Inheritance*, 1964, p. 3. This same speaker makes reference to a similar attitude among Faraday's contemporaries. At Faraday's public and children's lectures, "the packed audiences . . . the kindly interest of Mr. Punch and the keen interest of high society all helped to promote an atmosphere congenial to science and education which the Prince Consort did much to foster but which the Universities of that time steadfastly resisted and to their everlasting shame almost stamped out" (p. 5).

30. Agassi, *Philosopher*, 1971, p. 306.

31. Maxwell, *Treatise*, 1891 (1954), vol. 2, pp. 175–76.

32. Tolstoy, *Maxwell*, 1981, p. 22.

33. MacDonald, *Faraday*, 1964, pp. 105–106.

34. A concise summary of Lord Kelvin's contributions to science is provided in the *New Encyclopaedia Britannica* (vol. 22, fifteenth ed., pp. 503 ff). "William Thompson, who was knighted in 1866 and was raised to the peerage in 1892 (as Baron Kelvin of Largs) in recognition of his work in engineering and physics, was foremost among the small group of British scientists who helped to lay the foundations of modern physics. His contributions to science included a major role in the development of the second law of thermodynamics; the absolute temperature scale (measured in kelvins); the dynamical theory of heat; the mathematical analysis of electricity and magnetism, including the basic ideas for the electromagnetic theory of light; the geophysical determination of the age of the Earth; and fundamental work in hydrodynamics. His theoretical work on submarine telegraphy and his inventions for use on submarine cables aided Britain in capturing a preeminent place in world communications."

35. Gray, *Kelvin*, 1908 (1973), p. 299.

36. MacDonald, *Faraday*, 1964, p. 103.

37. Thomas, "Humanities," *Thoughts*, 1984, p. 143.

38. MacDonald, *Faraday, Maxwell and Kelvin*, 1964, p. 104.

39. Kelvin, quoted in Thomas, "Humanities," *Thoughts*, 1984, pp. 143–44.

40. Howard, "Rayleigh," in *Springs*, 1983, p. 184.

41. Thomas, *Thoughts*, 1984, p. 144.

42. Howard, "Rayleigh," in *Springs*, 1983, p. 184.

43. Everitt, "Maxwell's," in *Springs*, 1983, p. 127.

44. Thomas, *Thoughts*, 1984, pp. 144–46.

45. Faraday, *Life and Letters*, 1870, p. 179.

46. T. Cline, personal communication, December 1987; D. Rosenblum, personal communication, January 28, 1989.

47. Hillis, quoted in Brand, "New Machine," *Whole Earth Review*, 1987, p. 110. See also, Hillis, *Connection Machine*, 1985, pp. 137–44.

48. Many of the innovative features mentioned here were originally developed at the Xerox Palo Alto Research Laboratory and in the Xerox Systems Development Department. These features received initial commercial exposure with the introduction of the Xerox 8010 "Star" computer in April 1981. A discussion of the evolution of these features is provided, by some of those directly involved, in Johnson et al., "The Xerox Star: A Retrospective," *Computer*, September 1989, pp. 11–26 and 28–29. Similar features first became available on personal computers with the introduction of the Apple Lisa in 1983. However, they did not begin to gain wide exposure until the introduction of the Apple Macintosh in January 1984. During 1987, 1988, and 1989, many of these features gradually became available on new machines and software produced by IBM, Hewlett Packard, NEXT Computer, Microsoft Corporation, and others. Although some traditional users still preferred to remain with the older interface systems with which they had become accustomed, by mid-1989 it was generally conceded within the industry that the "graphic user interface" was the interface of choice for most new personal computing systems—and some much more powerful computer "workstations" and other larger computer systems as well (See Howard Reingold, "The Interface of Tomorrow, Today," *Infoworld*, July 10, 1989, pp. 42–48). While the original work in graphic interfaces was pioneered by certain professional computer researchers, other, more traditional computer programmers and system analysts treated the early graphics-oriented computers with condescension, considering the graphical icons just "cute pictures" and the hardware requirements of the interface an unnecessary waste of computer power. Gradually, however, it became apparent that the special advantages of the graphical interface were widely useful. For example, some designers of database systems were reporting that "graphical interfaces are becoming increasingly important because they simplify access to computers for both technical and nontechnical users. . . . The main advantage of graphical schema representations is that they provide a high level of abstraction that people can easily understand." Also, the use of direct manipulation of diagram elements tends to work better than forcing a user to "write a symbolic expression in a disciplined style using a formal query language" (Czejdo et al., "A Graphical Data Manipulation Language for an Extended Entity-Relationship Model," in *Computer*, 1990, pp. 26–27).

49. Glaser, "Mathematics," in "User Group Connection Videotape," 1989. Donald A. Glaser is a Nobel laureate and professor of physics, molecular biology, and neuroscience at the University of California, Berkeley. Glaser also indicates that creativity in his field is likely to be related to the quality of the visual imagination. The personal computer simply allows more time for this creative, visual side because the more tedious aspects of research

work are done by the machine. Manufacturers' names have been deleted. Such observations as are provided in this passage may be seen as an evaluation of personal preference for the graphical user interface rather than as an endorsement of one manufacturer in particular. Early machines made by Apple Computer and other manufacturers had non-graphic interfaces similar to the one that subsequently became best known on the personal computers manufactured by IBM and its imitators. However, most of the advanced machines made by IBM and other manufacturers after 1988 have been redesigned to employ graphic interfaces quite similar to the one first used in the Xerox "Star" and first widely popularized on the Apple Macintosh. It should be noted, on the other hand, that some users have a great distaste for the graphic interface, with its menus, mouse, and other innovations. For such users, who apparently have no trouble remembering all the routines and command codes, these innovations are considered distractions that slow down the operator. In contrast to many non-professionals, they love the codes and passionately hate the mouse. Such practical considerations as these underscore the deep reality of individual differences and the folly of trying to impose one system or another on everyone. Fortunately, there is general acceptance of the continued coexistence of several quite different but compatible user interface standards, making the whole field of personal computing much more available to different kinds of working styles while recognizing important differences in personal preferences (A. Cline, personal communication, October 1989).

50. To be fair to the earlier designs and designers, it should be pointed out that the early machines simply did not have enough memory capacity to make them easy to use. It was only with the coming of inexpensive memory in large quantifies in the mid-1980s that inexpensive machines could be designed to be truly easy to use.

51. Kim, in Lammers, *Programmers*, 1986, p. 285.

52. Kim, in Lammers, *Programmers*, 1986, pp. 283–84.

53. Ambler and Burnett, "Visual Technology," in *Computer*, 1989, pp. 9 and 21.

54. Hawley, in Lammers, *Programmers*, 1986, p. 307.

55. DeFanti, Brown, and McCormick, "Visualization," in *Computer*, 1989, p. 12.

56. DeFanti, Brown, and McCormick, "Visualization," in *Computer*, 1989, p. 12. This book emphasizes the way the new computer-graphic capabilities allow those without unusual gifts for visualization to benefit: "The computer democratizes visual thinking" (Friedhoff and Benzon, *Visualization*, 1989, p. 16).

57. Allen, "Visualization," in *Supercomputing*, 1989, p. 28. By late

1990, it was reported that "visualization, making raw numbers into pictures, is probably the most important trend in supercomputing" (Malamud, "Beyond the PC," in *Infoworld*, December 3, 1990, p. 50).

58. Booth, "Global Scale . . . Oceans," in the *Washington Post*, 1990, pp. A9–A10.

59. McGraw, New Insights," in *Supercomputing*, 1989, p. 34.

60. Richards, "Data Deluge," in the *Washington Post*, 1989, pp. H1 ff.

61. Wolkomir, "Data Deluge," in *Air & Space*, 1989, p. 79.

62. Scheduled for deployment in the early 1990s are the Cosmic Background Explorer, the Galileo mission to Jupiter, the Gamma Ray Observer, the Ulysses mission to the sun's poles, the Mars Observer, and the TOPEX/Poseiden ocean-sensing satellite (Wolkomir, "Data Deluge," in *Air & Space*, 1989, p. 79). The flawed Hubble Space Telescope was launched in 1990.

63. McCormick et al., "Visualization in Scientific Computing," 1987, quoted in Allen, "Visualization," *Supercomputing*, 1989, p. 30.

64. The making of such a cartoon with an Evans and Sutherland flight simulator is described by Alan Kay in "Emerging Trends," Apple Computer, videotape, 1987.

65. Allen, "Visualization," in *Supercomputing*, 1989, p. 29.

66. Hobill et al., "Lorenz," NCSA, *SIGGRAPH Video Review*, issue 49, 1989.

67. Elson et al., "Displacement," Symbolics, *Finalists*, 1989.

68. Hughes, "Dozo Goes for the Gold in Atlanta . . . and Wins," in *Supercomputing Review*, 1990, p. 77.

69. Sabionski et al., "Mars Rover, NASA, in *Finalists*, NCGA, 1989.

70. Hall et al., "Mars: The Movie," Jet Propulsion Laboratory, in *SIGGRAPH Video Review*, issue 49, 1989; Hall et al., "Earth: The Movie," JPL, in *SIGGRAPH Video Review*, issue 49, 1989.

71. Wilhemson et al., "Thunderstorm Outflow," National Center for Supercomputing Applications, in *SIGGRAPH Video Review*, issue 28, 1987.

72. Lytle et al., "Ocular Tumor," Cornell National Supercomputing Facility, in *SIGGRAPH Video Review*, issue 49, 1989.

73. Hampshire, *Story*, 1983, pp. 157–58.

74. Gleick, *Chaos*, 1987, p. 98. This section relies heavily on Gleick's work.

75. Gleick, *Chaos*, 1987, p. 104.

76. Gleick, *Chaos*, 1987, p. 112.

77. Gleick, *Chaos*, 1987, pp. 86–87.

78. Gleick, *Chaos*, 1987, p. 88.

79. Gleick, *Chaos*, 1987, p. 90.

80. Gleick, *Chaos*, 1987, p. 91.

81. Gleick, *Chaos*, 1987, pp. 91–92.

82. The Cantor set shown here was generated using software ("The Cantor Set/Random Walk"—created Oct. 28, 1988, modified Nov. 1, 1988, version WA01) produced by a group of chaos researchers based in Santa Cruz, Calif. (Ariel Press, Dynamics, vol. 1 & 2, 1989).

83. Gleick, *Chaos*, 1987, p. 92.

84. Gleick, *Chaos*, 1987, pp. 230–31.

CHAPTER 10. PATTERNS, IMPLICATIONS, POSSIBILITIES

1. Einstein, *Autobiographical Notes*, 1949 (1979), p. 15.

2. Boulding, *The Image*, 1956, pp. 162–63.

3. Thomas, *Night Thoughts*, 1984, pp. 147–49.

4. Hiatt; "Japan Creating Mass-Production Customization," *Washington Post*, 1990, p. A29.

5. Parkinson, *Parkinson's Law*, 1957, pp. 79–90.

EPILOGUE

1. California Institute of Technology, Oral History Project, session one, tape 1, side 1, interview of February 18, 1999, with Shirley K. Cohen, published by Caltech Archives 2005 (available as PDF at http://oralhistories .library.caltech.edu/108/). Dreyer's high interest in his own visual thinking is evident in his first introductory remarks at the beginning of the five days of interviews: "I was just at UCLA two days ago with people studying brain imaging. . . . They tended to want a uniform brain, with everyone having the same anatomy and thinking the same way. That isn't at all true; it's amazing how different people can be. And in particular the book that I loaned to you—*In the Mind's Eye* by Thomas G. West—is about the only one I've ever seen that deals with the subject of people who have extreme visual imagery in the way they think. I wanted to preface all of this [set of interviews] with this little story, because . . . it has a profound implication." The story that is quoted at the beginning of this epilogue immediately follows Dreyer's introductory statement. (It happens that the Jim Olds mentioned here is the father of another Jim Olds who happens to be the current director of the Krasnow Institute for Advanced Study, George Mason University, Fairfax, Virginia. Roger Sperry, also mentioned in this quotation, was Caltech Hixon Professor

of Psychobiology 1954–1984. Sperry was awarded the Nobel Prize in Physiology or Medicine in 1981.)

2. Janet Roman Dreyer, Ph.D., molecular biologist, second wife and widow of William J. Dreyer. Based on interview with Thomas G. West, June 28, 2005.

3. Tauber and Podolsky, *Generation of Diversity*, 1997, p. 207. In the words of Tauber and Podolsky: "This experiment marked the point of no return for the domination of the antibody diversity question by nucleotide studies: it was Susumu Tonegawa's final proof of the Dreyer-Bennett V-C translocation hypothesis through the use of restriction enzymes."

4. J. C. Roden, B. W. King, D. Trout, A. Mortazavi, B. J. Wold, and C. E. Hart, "Mining Gene Expression Data by Interpreting Principal Components," *BMC Bioinformatics* 7 (April 7, 2006): 194; C. E. Hart, L. Sharenbroich, B. J. Bornstein, D. Trout, B. King, E. Mjolsness, and B. J. Wold, "A Mathematical and Computational Framework for Quantitative Comparison and Integration of Large-Scale Gene Expression Data," *Nucleic Acids Research* 33, no. 8 (May 10, 2005): 2580–94.

5. Multiple conversations with William Dreyer, Janet Dreyer, and Brandon King, 2001–2004. Additional clarifications and further details were provided by Brandon King via e-mail, March 23, 2009. This additional material, supporting the summary descriptions provided in the main text, is provided here in full, with some light editing of the informal e-mail text: "Hi Tom, Thank you for forwarding to this to me. I did get a chance to review part of it and wanted to mention a few clarifications. One minor one is that while I have done visualization software, it is less than 20 percent, maybe even 10 percent of the work that I do and have done. I am [mostly] doing advanced programming developing databases/GUIs/tools [for] solving leading edge problems ([in] all of which I use my visual thinking ability to design the architecture of the programs), but many programs do not involve advanced visualization techniques. Handling the massive amount of data and tracking information about the data (meta data), requires a lot of software infrastructure that does not yet exist. Building the visualization tools that I would like to see requires this software infrastructure to be built in order to be able to pull all the right pieces together. While advanced visualization is one of my goals, like my grandfather, I've discovered the need to develop new infrastructure (tools/software) before building more advanced visualization techniques. So to summarize: I'm working on leading edge stuff, much of which has been the non-visual software infrastructure (which I build by visualizing the components in my head, trying it out and fixing what doesn't work, before I write the code—much like my grandfather), but instead of turning gears in my head to build a new physical machine, I am designing, building and tweaking software infrastructure in my

head. Also, when it comes to the story of the Ph.D. student, I feel it's important to correct this one. . . . What happened is that each Ph.D. student needs to [have a] publication in a scientific journal in order to receive their Ph.D. When he submitted his paper to the journal for review it was rejected because the reviewers couldn't understand the significance of the software (visualization + infrastructure) and how it was leading to some pretty amazing conclusions. What I did next was [that] I wrote a GUI (Graphical User Interface) that combined the infrastructure and visualization—which previously required that: (1) you know how to program in the Python programming language and (2) could understand and use the clustering and visualization tools [provided] within Python—into a simple tool. This tool allows the user to load the data, do the clustering of the data, and visualize and compare the data using the advanced visualization tools the Ph.D. student had written (all from an easy to use interface with no programming experience needed). I then took the data from the Ph.D. student's paper and wrote a tutorial showing how to use the GUI to load and analyze the data much like the Ph.D. student had done. The paper was submitted for a second review—this time with my name on it as well—which mentioned the GUI and tutorial in the paper. Upon [the second] review, one of the reviewers . . . changed their mind and said yes. [The reviewer] mentioned . . . [that] using the GUI and the tutorial gave [them] a better understanding of what the Ph.D. student had accomplished. [It] . . . was hard to understand the significance without being able to use the tools. Since I was able to bridge that gap for the reviewers, the paper was accepted and published. I got my first publication, and the Ph.D. student (who did amazingly advanced work, by the way, which is why the reviewers had trouble with it) got the publication he needed in order to meet the publication requirement for getting his Ph.D. That's pretty much it for clarification. Thanks again, Tom, for sending this along."

6. Personal communication, William J. Dreyer, August 1995. Quotation given is actually a paraphrase of the initial contact.

7. "Visualization Research Agenda Meeting" held February 15–16, 2000. This meeting, organized by the National Library of Medicine, was intended to develop a research agenda on the impact of visualization technologies and possible implications for visual thinkers and dyslexics. New computer graphic and information visualization technologies are seen as an emerging force in redefining the abilities required to do high-level work in many fields—and as a unifying force across the traditional boundaries between science, medicine, art, history, geography, and culture. Participants included: Donald Lindberg, director of the National Library of Medicine; Alvy Ray Smith, Pixar and Microsoft; Jock Mackinlay, Xerox PARC; Gordon Sherman, Harvard Medical School; Guinevere Eden, Georgetown University, James Olds, Krasnow Institute for Advanced Study, George

Mason University; and William J. Dreyer, California Institute of Technology; among others from the NIH as well as commercial and academic institutions.

8. Personal communication, R.S., March 2000.

9. Personal communication, S. M., Santa Barbara DARC conference, January 31, 2009. (Quotations are in paraphase.)

10. T. R. Miles, Ph.D., in *Dyslexia Contact*, June 1993, pp. 14–15. The late Dr. Miles was professor emeritus and founder of the Dyslexia Unit at the University College of North Wales. He was also founding editor of the journal *Dyslexia* and vice president of the British Dyslexia Association.

11. "The Iconoclastic Fossil Hunter," cover article, *Chronicle of Higher Education*, November 16, 1994.

12. McDonald 1994.

13. Horner and Gorman, *How to Build a Dinosaur*, 2009.

14. West, "Time to Get Serious," IDA *Perspectives*, 2008. (Parts of this commentary appear in different form in this epilogue.)

15. Based on e-mail of November 12, 2008, and personal telephone conversation of December 5, 2008. Summary CV provided by Marc I. Rowe, M.D., follows. *Education*: Brown University BA, Phi Beta Kappa, High Honors, 1952; Tufts University School of Medicine—M.D, 1956; Master of Science Tufts (Surgery), 1963. General Surgical Residency—Boston City Hospital, 1956 to 1963; Pediatric Surgery Residency— Columbus Children's Hospital, 1964 to1966; Research Fellow—Tufts, 1960 to 1961; Captain U.S. Army Medical Corps.,1958 to 1960. *Positions:* Wyler Children's Hospital, U. of Chicago, assistant professor of pediatric surgery—1966 to 1968; University of Miami School of Medicine, professor of pediatric surgery and pediatrics and chief of the Division of Surgery—1968 to 1981; Benjamin R. Fischer Professor of Surgery and chief, Division of Pediatric Surgery University of Pittsburgh School of Medicine; surgeon in chief, Children's Hospital of Pittsburgh, 1981–1999. *Certification, Offices Held, Honors*: Certified by the American Board of Surgery—general surgery, pediatric surgery (certificate number 4), surgical critical care (certificate number 10); director and examiner, the American Board of Surgery—sixteen years; Member of the Residency Review Committee—six years. Associate editor of the *Journal of Pediatric Surgery*. Chairman of Surgical Section of American Academy of Pediatrics—1979. Founding member of the American Pediatric Surgery Association. President of the American Pediatric Surgery Association—1999. First recipient of the Endowed Chair in Pediatric Surgery, University of Pittsburgh. Ladd Medal, for Pediatric Surgical Excellence—American Academy of Pediatrics. Distinguished Service Award, American Pediatric Surgery Association. Phi Beta Kappa and AOA. *Publications:* Refereed journals—186; book chapters—98; book editor—5. *Present:* Visiting professor, University of

Miami Department of Surgery; emeritus professor of surgery, University of Pittsburgh School of Medicine. (It should be noted here that a profile of another dyslexic individual who trained to be a surgeon is provided in, Guyer, *The Pretenders*, 1997, chapter 5, pp. 67–82.)

16. See Zimmerman and Cunningham, *Visualization in . . . Mathematics*, 1991.

17. Steen, "Patterns," *Science*, 1988, p. 616.

18. Park, *Study*, 1993, p. 162. Some italics have been deleted from the quoted text.

19. Davis, Porta, and Uhl, *Welcome to* CALCULUS&*Mathematica*, 1994, p. 11.

20. Morgan, "Word Blindness," 1896, p. 1378.

21. National Academy of Education conference, "Education Policy in Transition: Public Forum," November 18. 2008. Observation by C. O.

22. See Richard Florida Web site, "Creative Class" (http://creative class.com/).

23. Harvard dyslexia study. See http://www.cfa.harvard.edu/dyslexia/

24. Galaxy Zoo. See http://zoo1.galaxyzoo.org/.

25. Hannah Hickey, "Game's High Score Could Win the Nobel Prize," press release, University of Washington, May 8, 2008, p. 2. See http://uwnews.washington.edu/ni/article.asp?articleID=41558.

26. See http://fold.it/portal/info/science.

27. Corcoran, *Creative Brains*, SWIDA DVD, 2005, no page number.

28. See Phillips, *Bad Money*, 2008.

29. Corcoran, *Creative Brains*, SWIDA DVD, 2005, no page number.

30. Dowell, October 5, 2003. Four years after the BBC2 study, another UK study compared dyslexic entrepreneurs in the United States and those in the United Kingdom. See Cass Business School, "Failures in Educational System . . ." (November 2007).

31. Geschwind, 1982, 1987.

32. See related articles and documentaries listed in full in the bibliography: Agence France Press, Bass, Channel Four TV, *Financial News*, Frey, Hussin, Kupfer, McDonald, Negroponte, Robins, Petzinger, West, 1997, 1998, 1999, 2001, and Yeo, among others.

33. Morris, *Fortune*, May 20, 2002.

34. Morris, *Fortune*, October 6, 2003.

35. Geschwind, 1982, 1984.

36. Dyslexia Foundation, "Talent & Dyslexia," 2003; West, "Secret," *Thalamus*, 2003. (Parts of the Thalamus article appear in different form in this epilogue.)

37. Dyslexia Foundation, "Talent & Dyslexia," 2003.

38. Personal conversation, via telephone with T. G. West, March 2003.

39. Von Károlyi 2001; von Károlyi et al. 2003a; von Károlyi et al. 2003b; Winner et al. 2000; Winner et al. 2001.

40. Von Károlyi, Winner, Gray, and Sherman, 2003.

41. Von Károlyi et al. 2003.

42. Manchester, *Alone*, 1998, p. 677.

43. Manchester, *Alone*, 1998, p. 677.

44. Sir John Colville, personal diary and personal interviews by William Manchester; quoted in Manchester, *Alone*, 1988, p. 677.

45. Winston Churchill (*Storm*, pp. 666-67); quoted in Manchester, *Alone*, 1988, p. 676.

46. Sir John Reith, quoted in Manchester, *Alone*, 1988, p. 673.

47. Manchester, *Alone*, 1998, pp. 683–84.

48. Drucker, *Non-Profit*, 1990, 1992, p. 9.

BIBLIOGRAPHY

Aaron, P. G., Scott Phillips, and Steen Larsen, 1988. "Specific Learning Disability in Historically Famous Persons," *Journal of Learning Disabilities*, vol. 21, no. 9, pp. 523–45.

Abraham, Ralph H., and Christopher D. Shaw, 1984. *Dynamics—The Geometry of Behavior, Part 1: Periodic Behavior.* The Visual Mathematics Library. Santa Cruz, Calif.: Aerial.

———, 1988. *Dynamics—The Geometry of Behavior, Part 4: Bifurcation Behavior.* The Visual Mathematics Library. Santa Cruz, Calif.: Aerial

Adelman, Howard S., Bennett A. Lauber, Perry Nelson, and Douglas C. Smith, 1989. "Toward a Procedure for Minimizing and Detecting False Positive Diagnosis of Learning Disability," *Journal of Learning Disabilities*, vol. 22, no. 4, pp. 234–44.

Adelman, Howard S., and Linda Taylor, 1986. "The Problems of Definition and Differentiation and the Need for a Classification Schema," *Journal of Learning Disabilities*, vol. 19, no. 9, pp. 514–20.

Adelman, Kimberly A., and Howard S. Adelman, 1987. "Rodin, Patton, Edison, Wilson, Einstein. Were They Really Learning Disabled?" *Journal of Learning Disabilities*, vol. 20, pp. 270–79.

Aeppel, Timothy, 1997. "The Favorite—Picked by Her Father, Tough Daughter Runs Building-Supply Chain—Joe Hardy Passed over Sons for 84 Lumber Co. Job; A Chip Off the Old Block," *Wall Street Journal*, April 24, pp. 1, 12.

Agassi, Joseph, 1971. *Faraday as a Natural Philosopher.* Chicago: University of Chicago Press.

Agence France Presse, 1996. "Why Lee Kuan Yew Was Lost for Words," *South China Morning Post*, Hong Kong, January 18.

Allen, William, 1989. "Scientific Visualization: Where Science and Art Merge," *Supercomputing Review*, vol. 2, no. 8, pp. 28–30 and 32–33.

Allman, William F., 1989. *Apprentices of Wonder: Inside the Neural Network Revolution*. New York: Bantam.

Ambler, Allen L, and Margaret M. Burnett, 1989. "Influence of Visual Technology on the Evolution of Language Environments," *Computer*, vol. 22, no. 10, pp. 9–22.

American Association for the Advancement of Science, 1990. *The Liberal Art of Science: Agenda for Action*. The Report of the Project on Liberal Education and the Sciences. Washington, D.C.: American Association for the Advancement of Science.

American Psychiatric Association, 1983. *Diagnostic and Statistical Manual of Mental Disorders*. Third ed. Washington, D.C.: American Psychiatric Association.

Apostol, Tom M., James F. Blinn, et al., 1989. *Project Mathematics! Program Guide and Workbook to Accompany the Videotape on the Story of Pi*. Animated computer graphics by James F. Blinn et al. Pasadena, Calif.: California Institute of Technology.

Apostol, Tom M., Basil Gordon, James F. Blinn et al., 1988. *Project Mathematics! Program Guide and Workbook to Accompany the Videotape on the Theorem of Pythagoras*. Animated computer graphics by James F. Blinn et al. Pasadena, Calif.: California Institute of Technology.

———, 1990. *Project Mathematics! Program Guide and Workbook to Accompany the Videotape on Similarity*. Animated computer graphics by James F. Blinn et al., Pasadena, Calif.: California Institute of Technology.

Apple Computer, Inc., 1989. "Macintosh + Mathematica = Infinity," in The Apple User Group Connection Videotape Series (13 minutes, seventh of seven items). Cupertino, Calif.: Apple Computer, Inc.

Appleyard, Diana, 1997. "The Art of Being Dyslexic," *Independent* (London), February 27, 1997, p. 4.

Argiro, Vincent, 1990. "Seeing in Volume," *Pixel*, July/August, pp. 35–39.

Arieti, Silvano, 1976. *Creativity: The Magic Synthesis*. New York: Basic Books.

Arnheim, Rudolf, 1969. *Visual Thinking*. Berkeley: University of California Press.

———, 1986. *New Essays on the Psychology of Art*. Berkeley: University of California Press.

Arrott, Matthew, 1990. "Communication as It Pertains to Scientific Visualization," in *State of the Art in Data Visualization*, Course Notes No. 27 (Advanced Courses, SIGGRAPH '90, 17th International Conference on

Computer Graphics and Interactive Techniques, August 6–10, Dallas, Texas), pp. IV–1 to IV–12.

Asimov, Isaac, 1966. *The History of Physics*. New York: Walker.

Barinaga, Marcia, 1990. "Bottom-Up Revolution in Science Teaching: A California Program Relies on Soviet Principles—And Teachers' Creativity—To Put Some New Zip in Science Education," *Science*, vol. 249, no. 4972, pp. 978–79.

Barton, Jean M., and Waveline T. Starnes, 1989. "Identifying Distinguishing Characteristics of Gifted and Talented/Learning Disabled Students," *Roeper Review*, vol. 12, no. 1, pp. 23–29.

Bass, T. A., 1995. "Being Nicholas: The Media Lab's Visionary Founder Nicholas Negroponte Is the Most Wired Man We Know (And That Is Saying Something)," *Wired*, vol. 3 no. 11, November 1995, pp. 146 ff., 204. Cover interview.

Bate, John, 1635 (1654). *The Mysteries of Nature and Art in Foure Severall Parts*. [London]: Printed for Ralph Mabb.

Baum, Susan, 1990. "Gifted but Learning Disabled: A Puzzling Paradox," *ERIC Digest*, no. E479.

Beaton, Alan, 1985. *Left Side, Right Side: A Review of Laterality Research*. New Haven: Yale University Press.

Beck, Anna, 1987. "Preface," in *The Collected Papers of Albert Einstein, Volume 1, The Early Years: 1879–1902*. Princeton, N.J.: Princeton University Press.

Bell, E. T., 1937 (1986). *Men of Mathematics: The Lives and Achievements of the Great Mathematicians from Zeno to Poincaré*. New York: Simon & Schuster.

Belluck, Pam, 1996. "Using a Ruling for Education of [the] Disabled: Private Schools Offer More Special Help," *New York Times*, October 27, pp. 35, 40.

Benbow, C. P., and J. C. Stanley, 1980. "Sex Differences in Mathematical Ability: Fact or Artifact?" *Science*, vol. 210, pp. 1262–64.

———, 1983. "Sex Differences in Mathematical Ability: More Facts," *Science*, vol. 222, pp. 1029–31.

Benbow, C. P., and R. M. Benbow, 1987. "Extreme Mathematical Talent: Hormonal Induced Ability?" In *Duality and Unity of the Brain*, D. Ottoson, ed., pp. 147–57. New York: Macmillan.

Benbow, Camilla Perrson, 1986. "Physiological Correlates of Extreme Intellectual Precocity," *Neuropsychologia*, vol. 24, no. 2, pp. 719–25.

———, 1986. "Sex Differences in Mathematical Reading Ability in Intellectually Talented Preadolescents: Their Nature, Effects, and Possible Causes," *Behavioral Brain Sciences*, vol. 11, pp. 169–232.

Berger, John, 1977. *Ways of Seeing*. London: British Broadcasting Corporation and Penguin Books.

Bergeron, R. Daniel, and Arie E. Kaufman, eds., 1994. *Proceedings of Visualization '94, Washington, D.C., October 17–21, 1994*. Los Alamitos, CA: IEEE Computer Society Press.

Berkson, William, 1974. *Fields of Force: The Development of a World View from Faraday to Einstein*. London: Routledge & Kegan Paul.

———, 1984. *Learning from Error*. La Salle, Ill.: Open Court.

Betancur, Catalina, Adolfo Vélez, Guy Caranieu, Michel LeMoal, and Pierre J. Neveu, 1990. "Association between Left-Handedness and Allergy: A Reappraisal," *Neuropsychologia*, vol. 28, no. 2, pp. 223–27.

Beveridge, William Ian Beardmore, 1957. *The Art of Scientific Investigation*. New York: W. W. Norton. (Republished by Vintage, Random House, New York, 1990.)

Blakeslee, Thomas R., 1980. *The Right Brain: A New Understanding of the Unconscious Mind and Its Creative Powers*. New York: Anchor/Doubleday.

Blumenson, Martin, 1985. *Patton: The Man behind the Legend 1885–1945*. New York: William Morrow.

Boder, Elena, 1972. "Developmental Dyslexia: A Review of Prevailing Diagnostic Criteria." In *Claremont Reading Conference, Thirty-Sixth Yearbook*. Malcolm P. Douglass, ed. Claremont, Calif.: Claremont Reading Conference.

Bogen, G. M., 1986. "On the Relationship of Cerebral Duality to Creativity," *Bulletin of Clinical Neurosciences*, vol. 51, pp. 30–32.

Bogen, Joseph E., 1969. "The Other Side of the Brain I: Dysgraphia and Dyscopia following Cerebral Commissurotomy," *Bulletin of the Los Angeles Neurological Societies*, vol. 34, no. 2, pp. 73–105.

———, 1986. "Mental Duality in the Intact Brain," *Bulletin of Clinical Neurosciences*, vol. 51, pp. 3–29.

Bogen, Joseph E., and Glenda M. Bogen, 1969. "The Other Side of the Brain III: The Corpus Callosum and Creativity," *Bulletin of the Los Angeles Neurological Societies*, vol. 34, no. 4, pp. 191–220.

———, 1988. "Creativity and the Corpus Callosum," *Psychiatric Clinics of North America*, vol. 11, no. 3, pp. 293–301.

Boies, David, 2004. *Courting Justice*. New York: Hyperion.

Bolger, Andrew, 1995. "Employers Urged to Use Dyslexics' Full Potential," *Financial Times* (London), Wednesday, March 1, 1995.

Bond, Matthew, 1995. "Letters Don't Always Make a Lot of Sense," *Times*, July 26, 1995.

Booth, William, 1990. "On Global Scale, Scientists Seek to Weigh How Oceans Tide over Life," *Washington Post*, November 23, pp. A9–10.

Born, Max, 1971. *The Born-Einstein Letters: The Correspondence between Albert Einstein and Max and Hedwig Born, 1916–1955*. Irene Born, trans. New York: Walker.

Bouchard, Thomas J., Jr., David T. Lykken, Matthew McGue, Nancy L. Segal, and Auke Tellegen, 1990. "Sources of Human Psychological Differences: The Minnesota Study of Twins Reared Apart," *Science*, vol. 250, no. 4978, pp. 223–28.

Boulding, Kenneth E., 1956 (1959). *The Image: Knowledge in Life and Society*. Ann Arbor: University of Michigan Press.

Bower, Bruce, 1988. "Chaotic Connections: Do Learning and Memory Spring from Chaos Generated by Brain Cells?" *Science News*, vol. 133, no. 4, pp. 58–59.

Bradshaw, J. L., and N. C. Nettleton, 1981. "The Nature of Hemispheric Specialization" in *Man, Behavioral and Brain Sciences*, vol. 4, March, pp. 51–91.

Bradshaw, J. L., and J. A. Bradshaw, 1988. "Reading Mirror-Reversed Text: Sinistrals Really Are Inferior," *Brain and Language*, vol. 33, no. 1, pp. 189–92.

Brady, Dan, Brent Tutly, and Michelle Mercer, 1988. "Large-Scale Structure in the Universe," National Center for Supercomputing Applications (NCSA), Champaign, Ill. In *ACM SIGGRAPH Video Review*, issue 50, Special Issue on Visualization in Scientific Computing, July 1989. Videotape.

Braithwaite, Richard Bevan, 1968. *Scientific Explanation: A Study of the Function of Theory, Probability and Law in Science*. Cambridge: Cambridge University Press.

Brand, Stewart, 1987. "Implications of a Truly New Machine: A Conversation with Danny Hillis," *Whole Earth Review*, issue no. 54, pp. 108–15.

———, 1987. *The Media Lab: Inventing the Future at MIT*. New York: Viking Penguin.

Branson, Richard, 2008. *Business Stripped Bare: Adventures of a Global Entrepreneur*. London: Virgin Books.

Brendon, Piers, 1984. *Winston Churchill: A Biography*. New York: Harper & Row.

Briggs, John, and F. David Peat, 1989. *Turbulent Mirror: An Illustrated Guide to Chaos Theory and the Science of Wholeness*. Illustrations by Cindy Tavernise. New York: Harper & Row.

British Broadcasting Corporation, 1985. "Mystery of the Left Hand." BBC-TV, Horizon Series.

———, 1995. "Lost for Words," BBC Television science documentary series, *QED*, first broadcast July 25.

Broad, William J., 1985. "Subtle Analogies Found at the Core of Edison's Genius: Papers Reveal Reliance on Analogous Reasoning Not Instant Insight," *New York Times*, March 12, "Science Times" section, pp. 15–16.

Bronowski, Jacob, 1973. *The Ascent of Man*. Boston: Little, Brown.

———, 1978. *The Visionary Eye: Essays in the Arts, Literature, and Science*. Selected and edited by Piero E. Ariotti in collaboration with Rita Bronowski. Cambridge, Mass.: MIT Press.

Brooks, Frederick P., Jr., 1995. *The Mythical Man-Month: Essays on Software Engineering*. Reading, Mass.: Addison-Wesley.

Brown, Judith R., Rae Earnshaw, Mikael Jern, and John Vince, 1995. *Visualization Using Computer Graphics to Explore Data and Present Information*. New York. John Wiley & Sons.

Brown, Maxine D., and Thomas A. DeFanti, 1989. "The Role of Visualization in Scientific Discovery, Comprehension and Communication," in *NCGA '89 Conference Proceedings*, National Computer Graphics Association, 10th Annual Conference and Exposition Dedicated to Computer Graphics, Philadelphia, vol. 3, April 17–20, pp. 282–89.

Brownell, H. H., H. H. Potter, D. Michelow, and H. Gardner, 1984. "Sensitivity to Lexical Denotation and Connotation in Brain-Damaged Patients: A Double Dissociation?" *Brain and Language*, vol. 22, pp. 253–65.

Brush, Stephen G., 1990. "Kelvin in His Times," a review of Crosbie Smith and M. Norton Wise, 1989, *Energy and Empire: A Biographical Study of Lord Kelvin*, *Science*, vol. 284, pp. 875–77.

Buckner, Noel, Janet Mendelsohn, and Rob Whittlesey, 1985. "Child's Play: Prodigies and Possibilities," *Nova*, no. 1209, Boston: WGBH Educational Foundation.

Burdett, Richard, ed., 1995. *Richard Rogers Partnership: Works and Projects*. New York: Monacelli Press.

Burns, Matthew, 1991. "Scientific Visualization Wars." *Supercomputing Review*, October 1991, pp. 31–35.

Cahan, David, 1990. "Einstein Getting Established," a review of *The Collected Papers of Albert Einstein, Vol. 2, The Swiss Years: Writings, 1900–1909*, John Stachel, ed., *Science*, vol. 284, pp. 878–79.

Calder, Nigel, 1979. *Einstein's Universe*. New York: Viking.

———, 1972. *The Restless Earth: A Report on the New Geology*. New York: Viking.

Calder, Nigel, 1983. *Timescale: An Atlas of the Fourth Dimension*. New York: Viking.

Calfee, Robert, 1983. "The Mind of the Dyslexic," *Annals of Dyslexia*, vol. 33, pp. 9–27.

California Institute of Technology, Oral History Project, session one, tape 1, side 1, interview of February 18, 1999, with Shirley K. Cohen, published by Caltech Archives 2005. (Available as PDF at http://oralhistories .library.caltech.edu/108/.)

Calvin, William H., 1983. *The Throwing Madonna: Essays on the Brain.* New York: McGraw-Hill.

Campbell, Alfred W., 1905. *Histological Studies on the Localisation of Cerebral Function.* Cambridge: Cambridge University Press.

Campbell, Lewis, and William Garnett, 1882 (1969). *The Life of James Clerk Maxwell.* London: Macmillan, New York: Johnson Reprint Corporation.

Campione, Joseph C., 1989. "Assisted Assessment: A Taxonomy of Approaches and an Outline of Strengths and Weaknesses," *Journal of Learning Disabilities*, vol. 22, no. 3, pp. 151–65.

Caplan, Lincoln, 1988. "Profiles: An Architecture of Possibilities," *New Yorker*, November 14, 1988, pp. 47–96. (Profile of British architect Sir Richard Rogers.)

Caroe, G. M., 1978. *William Henry Bragg, 1862–1942: Man and Scientist.* Cambridge: Cambridge University Press.

Carretta, Thomas R., 1989. "USAF Pilot Selection and Classification Systems," *Aviation, Space, and Environmental Medicine*, vol. 60, no. 1, pp. 46–49.

Carter, Violet Bonham, 1965. *Winston Churchill. An Intimate Portrait.* New York: Harcourt Brace & World.

Carusi, Enrico, 1956. "Leonardo's Manuscripts." In *Leonardo da Vinci.* New York: Reynal.

Casey, M. Beth, and Mary M. Brabeck, 1989. "Exceptions to the Male Advantage on a Spatial Task: Family Handedness and College Major as Factors Identifying Women Who Excel," *Neuropsychologia*, vol. 27, no. 5, pp. 689–96.

Cass Business School, 2007. "Failures in Education System Cause UK to Produce Less Dyslexic Entrereneurs Than the US." Press release summarizing findings of study by Julie Logan, Professor of Entrepreneurship at Cass, November 15, 2007. (Available at http://www.cass.city.ac.uk.)

Caudill, Maureen, and Charles Butler, 1990. *Naturally Intelligent Systems.* Cambridge, Mass.: MIT Press.

Chan, Jin-Lieh, and Elliot D. Ross, 1988. "Left-Handed Mirror Writing Following Right Anterior Cerebral Artery Infarction: Evidence for Non-mirror Transformation of Motor Programs by Right Supplementary Motor Area," *Neurology*, vol. 38, no. 1, pp. 59–63.

Chandrasekhar, S., 1983. *Eddington: The Most Distinguished Astrophysicist of His Time.* Cambridge: Cambridge University Press.

Channel Four Television, 1999. "Dyslexia." Three 30-minute television programs produced by *20/20* for Channel Four Television; broadcast in the United Kingdom, May 1999. Persons interviewed include Richard Branson, Sally Shaywitz, Paula Tallal, and Thomas West.

Chase, C., and A. Jenner, 1993. "Magnocellular Visual Deficits Affect Temporal Processing of Dyslexics." In P. Tallal, A. M. Galaburda, R. Llinas, and C. von Euler, eds., *Temporal Information Processing in the Nervous System, with Special Reference to Dyslexia and Dysphasia*. New York: New York Academy of Sciences.

Chen, Andrew C. N., and Kathleen C. Buckley, 1988. "Neural Perspectives of Cerebral Correlates of Giftedness," *International Journal of Neuroscience*, vol. 41, pp. 115–25.

Cheney, Margaret, 1981. *Tesla: Man Out of Time*. New York: Dell.

Churchill, Randolph S., 1966. *Winston S. Churchill, Volume I: Youth, 1874–1900*. London: Heinemann.

Churchill, Winston Leonard S., 1973. *The Collected Works of Sir Winston Churchill*. London: Library of Imperial History.

Churchill, Winston S., 1930. *A Roving Commission; My Early Life*. New York: Scribner's.

———, 1932. *Amid These Storms; Thoughts and Adventures*. London: Butterworth.

———, 1950. *Painting as a Pastime*. New York: Whittlesey.

———, 1976. *The Collected Essays of Sir Winston Churchill*. Michael Wolff, ed. London: Library of Imperial History.

Cipra, Barry A., 1988. "Calculus: Crisis Looms in Mathematics' Future—Researchers and Educators Are Debating How Calculus Should Be Taught to Increasingly Recalcitrant Students," *Science*, vol. 239, pp. 1491–92.

Clark, Ronald W., 1971. *Einstein: The Life and Times*. New York: World.

———, 1977. *Edison: The Man Who Made the Future*. New York: G. P. Putnam's Sons.

Clarke, Gerald, 1988. "Lightning in His Brain," a review of William Manchester, *The Last Lion: Winston Spencer Churchill; Alone: 1932–1940*, and Martin Gilbert, *Winston S. Churchill, Vol. VIII: Never Despair 1945–1965. Time*, October 31, pp. 87–88.

Clements, Sam D., 1966. *Minimal Brain Dysfunction in Children: Terminology and Identification*. National Institute of Neurological Diseases and Blindness, monograph, no. 3, PHS pub. no. 1415. Washington, D.C.: Public Health Service.

Cleveland, William S., 1993. *Visualizing Data*. Summit, N.J.: Hobart Press.

Cohen, Morton N., and Roger Lancelyn Green, eds., 1979. *The Letters of Lewis Carroll*. New York: Oxford University Press.

Coles, Gerald, 1987 (1989). *The Learning Mystique: A Critical Look at "Learning Disabilities."* New York: Fawcett Columbine.

Collingwood, Stuart Dodgson, 1898 (1967). *The Life and Letters of Lewis Carroll (Rev. C. L. Dodgson).* New York: Century Co.; Detroit: Gale Research.

Coltheart, M., 1981. "Disorders of Reading and Their Implications for Models of Normal Reading," *Visible Language*, vol. 15, pp. 245–86.

———, 1982. "The Psycholinguistic Analysis of Acquired Dyslexias," *Philosophical Transactions of the Royal Society*, vol. B298, pp. 151–64.

Coltheart, M., J. Masterson, S. Bung, M. Prior, and M. J. Riddoch, 1983. "Surface Dyslexia," *Quarterly Journal of Experimental Psychology*, vol. 35A, pp. 469–95.

Coltheart, M., Karalyn Patterson, and John C. Marshall, eds., 1980, 1987. *Deep Dyslexia*. First and second editions. London: Routledge & Kegan Paul.

Combs, Harry, with Martin Caidin, 1979 (1986). *Kill Devil Hill: Discovering the Secret of the Wright Brothers*. Englewood, Colo.: TernStyle.

Connolly, Thomas J., Bishop B. Blackwell, and Lewis F. Lester, 1989. "A Simulation-Based Approach to Training in Aeronautical Decision Making," *Aviation, Space, and Environmental Medicine*, vol. 60, no. 1, pp. 50–52.

Conot, Robert E., 1979. *A Streak of Luck*. New York: Seaview.

Cook, Theodore Andrea, 1914 (1979). *The Curves of Life*. New York: Dover.

Coombs, David, 1967. *Churchill: His Paintings*. London: Hamish Hamilton.

Corballis, M., 1980. "Laterality and Myth," *American Psychologist*, vol. 35, no. 3, pp. 284–95.

Corballis, Michael C., 1983. *Human Laterality*. New York: Academic.

Corballis, Michael C., and Ivan L. Beale, 1983. *The Ambivalent Mind: The Neuropsychology of Right and Left*. Chicago: Nelson-Hall.

Corcoran, Barbara, with Bruce Littlefield, 2003. *Use What You've Got and Other Business Lessons I Learned from My Mom*. New York: Portfolio, Penguin Putnam, Inc.

Corcoran, John, 1994. *The Teacher Who Couldn't Read*. Colorado Springs: Focus on the Family Publishing.

Cornell Theory Center, 1993. *Cornell Theory Center: Scientific Visualizations, vol. 1*. Ithaca, N.Y.: Cornell University Press, 1993.

Courtemanche, Marc, and Arthur T. Winfree, 1990. "A Two-Dimensional Model of Electrical Waves in the Heart: Supercomputer Experiments Based on Observational Studies of Cardiac Electrophysiology May Provide Clues to the Lethal Mechanism of Fibrillation," *Pixel*, vol. 1, no. 2, pp. 24–31.

Cox, Donna, 1989. "Tao of Visualization." In *Computer Art in Context: SIGGRAPH '89 Art Show Catalog*, pp. 21–24. New York: Pergamon.

Coyle, Pamela, 1996. "What Dyslexic Lawyers Confront When They Read or Write," *American Bar Association Journal*, vol. 82, September 1996, pp. 64–67.

Cratty, Bryant J., and Richard L Goldman, eds., 1996. *Learning Disabilities: Contemporary Viewpoints*. Amsterdam: Harwood Academic Publishers.

Crawford, Elspeth, 1985. "Learning from Experience." In *Faraday Rediscovered: Essays on the Life and Work of Michael Faraday, 1791–1867*. New York: Stockton.

Crick, Michael, 1997. *Michael Heseltine: A Biography*. London: Hamish Hamilton.

Critchley, Julian, 1987, 1994. *Heseltine*. Rev. ed. London: Hodder and Stoughton.

Critchley, M., 1970. *The Dyslexic Child*. London: Heinemann.

Croall, Jonathan, 1995. "A Man of His Word . . . Thomas West's Relentless Fight for the Extraordinary Skills of Dyslexic People to Be Recognised." *Times* (London) *Educational Supplement*, London, England, Features, April 7, 1995, p. 4.

Crouch, Tom D., 1989. *The Bishop's Boys: A Life of Wilbur and Orville Wright*. New York: W. W. Norton.

Crovitz, Herbert F., 1970. *Galton's Walk: Methods for the Analysis of Thinking, Intelligence and Creativity*. London: Harper & Row.

Crustfield, Julia, and Ian Smythe, 1993. *The Dyslexia Handbook 1993/4*. Reading, U.K.: British Dyslexia Association.

Cruz-Neira, Carolina, Daniel J. Sandin, and Thomas A. DeFanti, 1993. "Surround-Screen Projection-Based Virtual Reality: The Design and Implementation," *Computer Graphics*, Proceedings, SIGGRAPH Annual Conference, August 1–6, p. 135.

Culross, Rita R., 1992. "Book Review of *In the Mind's Eye*," *Roeper Review on Gifted Children*, vol. 15, no. 1.

Czejdo, Bogdan, Ramez Elmasri, Marek Rusinkiewicz, and David W. Embley, 1990. "A Graphical Data Manipulation Language for an Extended Entity-Relationship Model," *Computer*, vol. 23, no. 3, pp. 26–36.

Damasio, A. R., 1987. "Disturbances of Visual Recognition." Norman Geschwind Memorial Lecture, Orton Dyslexia Society Annual Conference, session tape no. G3.

———, 1989. "Reflections on Visual Recognition." In *From Reading to Neurons*, pp. 361–76. A. M. Galaburda, ed. Cambridge, Mass.: MIT Press.

Damasio, A. R., and H. Damasio, 1986. "Hemianopia, Hemiachromatopsia and the Mechanisms of Alexia," *Cortex*, vol. 22, no. 1, pp. 161–69.

Damasio, A. R., H. Damasio, and G. W. Van Hoesen, 1982. "Prosopagnosia: Anatomic Basis and Behavioral Mechanisms," *Neurology*, vol. 32, no. 4, pp. 331–41.

Damasio, A. R., and A. M. Galaburda, 1985. "Norman Geschwind," *Archives of Neurology*, vol. 42, no. 5, pp. 500–504.

Damasio, Antonio D., 1994. *Descartes' Error: Emotion, Reason, and the Human Brain.* New York: G.P. Putnam's Sons.

Daniels, Paul R., 1983. *Teaching the Gifted/Learning Disabled Child.* Rockville, Md.: Aspen Systems.

Dantzig, Tobias, 1954 (1968). *Henri Poincaré: Critic of Crisis, Reflections on His Universe of Discourse.* New York: Greenwood.

Dartmouth-Hitchcock Medical Center, 1996. "Attention Deficit Disorder: Children," in the television documentary series *The Doctor Is In*, produced by the Dartmouth-Hitchcock Medical Center, Lebanon, N.H.

———, 1997. "Dyslexia," in the television documentary series *The Doctor Is In.* Videotape interview, December 10, 1996, for 30-minute television documentary produced by the Dartmouth-Hitchcock Medical Center. Released in 1997 to 90 PBS television stations.

Darwin, Charles, 1887, 1958. *The Autobiography of Charles Darwin, 1809–1882.* Complete edition with original omissions restored, edited by Nora Barlow. New York: W. W. Norton and Company.

Davis, Bill, Horacio Porta, and Jerry Uhl, 1994. "Welcome to Calculus&*Mathematica*," in Calculus&*Mathematica*, courseware (Version 1.0) with four texts ("Approximations," "Derivatives," "Integrals," and "Vector Calculus"). Reading, Mass.: Addison-Wesley, p. 84.

Dawkins, Richard, 1976, 1989. *The Selfish Gene.* New York: Oxford University Press.

———, 1996. *Climbing Mount Improbable.* New York: Viking.

De Hirsch, 1971. "Are Hyperlexics Dyslexics?" *Journal of Special Education*, vol. 5, no. 3, pp. 243–45.

DeFanti, Thomas A., Maxine D. Brown, and Bruce H. McCormick, 1989. "Visualization: Expanding Scientific and Engineering Research Opportunities," *Computer*, vol. 22, no. 8, pp. 12–16 and 22–25.

DeFries, J. C., and Sadie N. Decker, 1982. "Genetic Aspects of Reading Disability: A Family Study." In *Reading Disorders: Varieties and Treatments*. R. N. Malatesha and P. G. Aaron, eds. New York: Academic.

DeFries, J. C., and Laura A. Baker, 1983. "Colorado Family Reading Study: Longitudinal Analyses," *Annals of Dyslexia*, vol. 33, pp. 153–62.

DeMent, Gloria, and Stoney Dement, n.d. *Shining a Light: Celebrating*

Dyslexic Artists. Newport Beach, Calif.: National Dyslexia Research Foundation (now The Dyslexia Foundation).

Denckla, M. B., and R. G. Rudel, 1976. "Rapid Automatized Naming: Dyslexia Differentiated from Other Learning Disabilities," *Neuropsychologia*, vol. 14, pp. 471–79.

Denckla, M. B., R. P. Rudel, and M. Broman, 1978. A review of *The Neuropsychology of Learning Disorders: Theoretical Approaches*, Robert M. Knights and Dirk J. Bakker, eds., *Harvard Education Review*, vol. 48, no, 1, pp. 99–103.

———, 1980. "The Development of Spatial Orientation Skill in Normal, Learning-Disabled, and Neurologically Impaired Children." In *Biological Studies of Mental Processes.* D. Caplan, ed. Cambridge, Mass.: MIT Press.

———, 1985. "Motor Coordination in Dyslexic Children: The Theoretical and Clinical Implications." In *Dyslexia: A Neuroscientific Approach to Clinical Evaluation.* Frank H. Duffy and Norman Geschwind, eds. Boston: Little, Brown.

———, 1987. "Applications of Disconnection Concepts to Developmental Dyslexia," *Annals of Dyslexia*, vol. 37, pp. 51–61.

Denckla, Martha B., 1985. "Revised Physical and Neurological Examination for Subtle Signs," *Psychopharmacology Bulletin*, vol. 21, pp. 778–800.

———, 1988. "Gifts and Talents Coexist with Learning Disabilities: Two Sides of the Constitutional Coin?" address presented at "The Many Faces of Intelligence," the Fiftieth Anniversary Symposium of the Kingsbury Center, Washington, D.C., September 24, 1988.

———, 1989. "The Paradox of Giftedness and Learning Disabilities," presented at the November 20 meeting of Parents of Gifted/Learning Disabled Children, Montgomery County, Maryland.

———, 1989. "Subtypes of Dyslexia: The Quest for the Holy Grail." *The Spectrum of Developmental Disabilities XI: Dyslexia—Clinical and Research Issues*, March 13–15. Baltimore: Johns Hopkins Medical Institutions, Office of Continuing Education.

Denenberg, Victor H., 1981. "Hemispheric Laterality in Animals and the Effects of Early Experience," *Behavioral and Brain Sciences*, vol. 4, pp. 1–49.

DeYoung, H. Garret, 1989. "Graphics as Guinea Pig: Imaging and Simulation Can Reduce the Number of Live Specimens Needed in Lab Tests," *Computer Graphics World*, vol. 12, no. 12, pp. 85–89.

Diehl, Charles F., 1958. *A Compendium of Research and Theory on Stuttering.* Springfield, Ill.: Charles C. Thomas.

Dimond, Stewart J., 1976. "Drugs to Improve Learning in Man: Implications and Neuropsychologjcal Analysis." In *The Neuropsychology of Learning Disorders: Theoretical Approaches*, pp. 367–79. Robert M. Knights and Dirk J. Bakker, eds. Baltimore: University Park.

Dimond, Stewart J., and J. Graham Beumont, eds., 1974. *Hemisphere Function in the Human Brain*. New York: John Wiley & Sons.

The Dissectable Human, 1996. Hybred CD-ROM. Mosby Year Book, Inc., and Engineering Animation, Inc.; http:www.eai.com.

Dowell, Ben, 2003. "Secret of the Super Successful . . . They're Dyslexic." *Sunday Times*. October 5, 2003, p. 1.

Draffan, E. A., 1996. *Multimedia Assessment and Training for Literacy Skill*. Report of a Winston Churchill Travelling Fellowship to the USA in 1995. London: Winston Churchill Memorial Trust.

Dreyer, William J., and J. C. Bennett, 1965. "The Molecular Basis of Antibody Formation: A Paradox," *Proceedings of the National Academy of Sciences (USA)*, vol. 54, pp. 864–69.

Dreyer, William J., W. R. Gray, and L. Hood, 1967. "The Genetic, Molecular, and Cellular Basis of Antibody Formation: Some Facts and a Unifying Hypothesis," *Cold Spring Harbor Symposium on Quantitative Biology*, vol. 32, pp. 353–67.

Dronkers, Nina F., and Robert T. Knight, 1989. "Right-Sided Neglect in a Left-Hander: Evidence for Reversed Hemispheric Specialization of Attention Capacity," *Neuropsychologia*, vol. 27, no. 5, pp. 729–35.

Drucker, Peter F., 1990, 1992. *Managing the Non-Profit Organization: Practices and Principles*. New York: Harper Business.

Druckman, Daniel, and Robert A. Bjork, eds., 1991. *In the Mind's Eye: Enhancing Human Performance*. Committee on Techniques for the Enhancement of Human Performance, Commission on Behavioral and Social Sciences and Education, National Research Council. Washington, D.C.: National Academy Press.

Duane, Drake D., 1984. "Underachievement in Written Language: Auditory Aspects." In *Progress in Learning Disabilities*, vol. 5. Helmer R. Myklebust, ed. New York: Grune & Stratton.

———, 1989. "Commentary on Dyslexia and Neurodevelopmental Pathology," *Journal of Learning Disabilities*, vol. 22, no. 4, pp. 219–20.

Duane, Drake D., and David B. Gray, eds., 1991. *The Reading Brain: The Biological Basis of Dyslexia*. Parkton, Md.: York Press.

Duffy, Frank H., and Norman Geschwind, 1985. *Dyslexia: A Neuroscientific Approach to Clinical Evaluation*. Boston: Little, Brown.

Dukes, Helen, and Banesh Hoffman, 1979. *Albert Einstein: The Human Side*. Princeton, N.J.: Princeton University Press.

The Dynamic Human: The 3-D Guide to Anatomy and Physiology, 1996.

Windows or Macintosh CD-ROM. Mosby Year Book, Inc., and Engineering Animation, Inc.; http://www.eai.com.

Dyslexia Foundation, 2003. "Talent & Dyslexia: Report of a 'Think Tank' Meeting, MIT Endicott House, April 26–27, 2003." Unpublished, undated draft report. Meeting planners and participants included: Will Baker, Joyce Bulifant, Drake Duane, Jeff Gilger, Jerome Kagan, Peggy McArdle, Renee Merow, Phil Pasho, William F. Patterson, Charlotte Raymond, Glenn Rosen, Trey Roski, Daniel J. Sandin, Steve Schecter, Gordon F. Sherman, Delos R. Smith, Nicolas Smit, Catya von Károlyi, Thomas G. West, Ellen Winner, Maryanne Wolf, and Frank Wood.

Economist, 1986. "Poet Off Parade," a review of *The Collected Letters of W B. Yeats: Volume 1(1865–1895)*, John Kelly and Eric Domville, eds., March 15, p. 90.

———, 1992. "Coming Top: A Survey of Education," November 21, pp. 3–18.

———, 1994. "Oriental Renaissance: A Survey of Japan," July 9, pp. 3–18.

———, 1994. "The Third Age: A Survey of The Computer Industry," September 17, 1994, pp. 3–22.

———, 1995. "Seeing Is Believing," August 19, 1995, p. 71

———, 1995. "Technology, the Future of Your Job and Other Misplaced Panics." February 11–17, p. 13.

———, 1995. "A World without Jobs?" February 11–17, pp. 21–23.

Edison, Thomas A., 1971. *The Diary of Thomas A. Edison*, a facsimile edition of Edison's July 1885 diary. Old Greenwich, Conn.: Chatham.

Edwards, Betty, 1986. *Drawing on the Artist Within*. New York: Simon & Schuster.

Ehrenwald, Jan, 1984. *Anatomy of Genius: Split Brains and Global Minds*. New York. Human Sciences.

Eide, Brock and Fernette, 2006. *The Mislabeled Child*. New York: Hyperion.

Einstein, Albert, 1916 (1961). *Relativity: The Special and the General Theory*. Robert W. Lawson, trans. New York: Crown.

———, 1949 (1979). *Autobiographical Notes*. Paul Arthur Schilpp, ed., trans. (German and English on opposing pages). La Salle and Chicago, Ill.: Open Court. Originally vol. 7 of *The Library of Living Philosophers*, Evanston, Illinois.

———, 1979. *Albert Einstein, The Human Side: New Glimpses from His Archives*. Helen Dukas and Banesh Hoffmann, eds. Princeton, N.J.: Princeton University Press.

———, 1979. *Einstein: A Centenary Volume*. A. P. French, ed. Cambridge, Mass.: Harvard University Press.

———, 1987. *The Collected Papers of Albert Einstein, Volume 1: The Early*

Years: 1879–1902 and *Volume 2: The Swiss Years: Writings, 1900–1909.* John Stachel, ed. Documents in German and other original languages, with parallel translation into English. Princeton, N.J.: Princeton University Press.

Elmer-Dewitt, Philip, 1989. "Through the 3-D Looking Glass: With New Power and an Oscar, Computer Graphics Comes of Age," *Time*, May 1, pp. 65–66.

Elson, M., et.al., 1989. "Displacement Animation of Intelligent Objects," Symbolics Corporation, in *Finalists, Animation Competition, National Computer Graphics*, 1989. (Videotape).

Epstein, Herman T., 1982. "Developmental Biology and Disorders of Reading." In *Reading Disorders: Varieties and Treatments.* R. N. Malatesha and P. G. Aaron, eds. New York: Academic.

Esham, Barbara, 2008. *Last to Finish: A Story about the Smartest Boy in Math Class.* Illustrated by Mike and Carl Gordon. Ocean City, Md.: Mainstream Connections.

Evans, James S., 1983. *An Uncommon Gift.* Philadelphia: Westminster.

Evans, Martha M., 1982. *Dyslexia: An Annotated Bibliography.* Westport, Conn.: Greenwood.

Everitt, C. W. F., 1983. "Maxwell's Scientific Creativity." In *Springs of Scientific Creativity: Essays on Founders of Modern Science.* Rutherford Aris, H. Ted Davis, and Roger H. Stuewer, eds. Minneapolis: University of Minnesota Press.

Faraday, Michael, 1842. *Chemical Manipulation: Being Instructions to Students in Chemistry.* London: John Murray.

——, 1855 (1965). *Experimental Researches in Electricity.* New York: Dover. Original publication by Taylor and Francis.

——, 1903. *The Chemical History of a Candle.* New York: Harper.

——, 1932–36. *Faraday's Diary: Being the Various Philosophical Notes of Experimental Investigation.* Vol. 1. London: G. Bell and Sons.

——, 1971. *The Selected Correspondence of Michael Faraday. Volume I, 1812–1848.* L Pearce Williams, ed. Cambridge: Cambridge University Press.

Faraday, Michael, and Christian Friedrich Schoenbein, 1899. *The Letters of Faraday and Schoenbein, 1836–1862.* Georg W. A. Kahlbaum and Francis V. Darbishire, eds. London: Williams & Norgate.

Farago, Ladislas, 1963. *Patton: Ordeal and Triumph.* New York: Dell.

Faffar, Frederick, W., 1897. *Men I Have Known.* New York: Thomas Y. Crowell.

Favaro, Giuseppe, 1956. "Anatomy and the Biological Sciences." In *Leonardo da Vinci.* New York: Reynal.

444 BIBLIOGRAPHY

Feiner, Steven, and Clifford Beshers, 1990. "Visualizing *n*-Dimensional Virtual Worlds with *n*-Vision." In *Proceedings: 1990 Symposium on Interactive 3D Graphics, Snowbird Utah, 25th–28th March 1990, Computer Graphics SIGGRAPH)*, vol. 24, no. 2, pp. 37–38.

Feldman, David Henry, with Lynn T. Goldsmith, 1986. *Nature's Gambit: Child Prodigies and the Development of Human Potential.* New York: Basic Books.

Feldman, Laurence A., 1990. "The Right Tools for the Task," *IRIS Universe*, no. 11, pp. 17–21 and 24–27.

Ferguson, Eugene S., 1992. *Engineering and the Mind's Eye.* Cambridge, Mass.: MIT Press.

Feynman, Richard P., Robert B. Leighton, and Matthew Sands, 1963. *The Feynman Lectures on Physics.* Reading, Mass.: Addison-Wesley.

Financial News, 2000. "Bringing the Gift of Sight to the Word Blind—Ben Thomson Is Chief Executive of the Noble Group, the Investment Banking Firm Based in Edinburgh. His Ruling Passion Is Dyslexia." September 18.

Finke, Ronald A., 1989. *Principles of Mental Imagery.* Cambridge, Mass.: MIT Press.

Finucci, J. M., 1978. "Genetic Consideration in Dyslexia." In *Progress in Learning Disabilities*, vol. 4, pp. 41–64. H. R. Myklebust, ed. New York: Grune & Stratton.

Fisher, R. A., 1914. "Frequency Distribution of the Values of the Correlation Coefficient in Samples from an Indefinitely Large Population," *Biometrika: A Journal for the Statistical Study of Biological Problems*, vol. 10, pp. 507–21.

Flanagan, Dennis, 1990. "Viewpoint: Words and Pictures," *Pixel*, vol. 1, no. 2, pp. 42–44.

Fleming, Elizabeth, 1984. *Believe the Heart: Our Dyslexic Days.* Falls Church, Va.: LF.

Florida, Richard, 2002. *The Rise of the Creative Class.* New York: Basic Books.

———, 2005. *The Flight of the Creative Class: The New Global Competition for Talent.* New York: Harper Business.

Floyd, Steve, 1989. "J.I.T. Learning Fulfills Technology's Promise," *Human Capital*, vol. 1, no. 1, November/December, pp. 45–48.

Foley, James D., Andries van Dam, Steven K. Feiner, and John F. Hughes, 1990. *Computer Graphics: Principles and Practice.* Second ed. New York: Addison-Wesley.

Foley, Vernard, and Werner Soedel, 1986. "Leonardo's Contributions to Theoretical Mechanics: A Close Look at His Visual Mode of Thinking, Particularly in His Studies of the Crossbow, Reveals That His Ideas Had a

Bearing on the Evolution of Four Aspects of Mechanics," *Scientific American*, pp. 108–13.

Forbes, Eric G., 1982. "James Clerk Maxwell, F.R.S.E., F.R.S. (1831–1879)." In *Scottish Men of Science* (series). Edinburgh: History of Medicine and Science Unit, University of Edinburgh.

Forester, Tom, ed., 1989. *Computers in the Human Context: Information Technology, Productivity, and People.* Cambridge, Mass.: MIT Press.

Forgan, Sophie, 1985. "Faraday—From Servant to Savant: The Institutional Text." In *Faraday Rediscovered: Essays on the Life and Work of Michael Faraday, 1791–1867.* David Gooding and Frank A. J. L. James, eds. New York: Stockton.

Foster, R. F., 1997. *W. B. Yeats: A Life. The Apprentice Mage, 1865–1914.* Oxford: Oxford University Press.

Fox, Edward A., 1989. "The Coming Revolution in Interactive Digital Video," in *Communications of the ACM*, vol. 32, no. 7, pp. 794–801.

Fox, Lynn H., Linda Brody, and Dianne Tobin, 1983. *Learning-Disabled/Gifted Children: Identification and Programming.* Baltimore: University Park.

Francis, Joyce, and Ross Toedte, 1990. "Scientific Visualization: New Insights by Computer," *Oak Ridge National Laboratory Review*, vol. 23, no. 2, pp. 29–35.

French, A. P., 1979. "The Story of General Relativity." In *Einstein: A Centenary Volume* Cambridge, Mass.: Harvard University Press.

Frankel, Karen A., 1989. "Volume Rendering," *Communications of the Association for Computing Machinery*, vol. 32, no. 4, pp. 426–35.

Frey, Walter, 1990. "Schools Miss Out on Dyslexic Engineers." *IEEE Spectrum*. December 1990, p. 6.

Friedel, Robert D., and Paul Israel with Bernard S. Finn, 1986. *Edison's Electric Light: Biography of an Invention.* New Brunswick, N.J.: Rutgers University Press.

Friedhoff, Richard Mark, and William Benzon, 1989. *Visualization: The Second Computer Revolution.* New York: Harry N. Abrams.

Friedman, R. B., and M. B. Perlman, 1982. "On the Underlying Causes of Semantic Paralexias in a Patient with Deep Dyslexia," *Neuropsychologia*, vol. 20, pp. 559–68.

Frith, Chris, and Uta Frith, 1996. "A Biological Marker for Dyslexia," *Nature*, vol. 382, July 4, pp. 19–20.

Frith, U., 1985. "Beneath the Surface of Developmental Dyslexia." In *Surface Dyslexia: Neuropsychological and Cognitive Studies of Phonological Reading.* K. E. Patterson, J. C. Marshall, and M. Coltheart, eds. London: Lawrence Erlbaum.

Frost, Robert, 1951 (1967). *Complete Poems.* London: Jonathan Cape.

Futurist, 1992. "Book Review of *In the Mind's Eye*," May–June 1992, p. 46.

Galaburda, A. M., 1983. "Developmental Dyslexia: Current Anatomical Research," *Annals of Dyslexia*, vol. 33, pp. 41–53.

——, 1984. "Neuroanatomical Studies: Five Consecutive Cases," lecture tape no. 30, November 17, Orton Dyslexia Society Annual Conference.

——, 1985. "Developmental Dyslexia: A Review of Biological Interactions," *Annals of Dyslexia*, vol. 35, pp. 21–33.

——, 1986. "Animal Studies and the Neurology of Developmental Dyslexia." In *Dyslexia: Its Neuropsychology and Treatment*, pp. 39–50. G. T. Pavlidis and D. F. Fisher, eds. New York: Wiley.

——, 1986. "Human Studies in the Anatomy of Dyslexia," paper delivered at the Thirty-Sixth Annual Conference of the Orton Dyslexia Society, Chicago, Ill.

——, 1986. "Response to 'The Many Faces of Dyslexia.'" *Annals of Dyslexia*, vol. 36, pp. 192–95.

——, 1987. "Neurobiology of Dyslexia: Recent Advances," lecture no. F31, November 6, 1987, Thirty-Eighth Orton Dyslexia Society Annual Conference.

——, 1989. "Ordinary and Extraordinary Brain Development, Anatomical Variation in Developmental Dyslexia," *Annals of Dyslexia*, vol. 39, pp. 67–80.

——, 1989. "Recent Research: Anatomy of Dyslexia," personal tape of March 14 presentation at "The Spectrum of Developmental Disabilities XI: Dyslexia—Clinical and Research Issues," March 13–15. Baltimore: Johns Hopkins Medical Institutions, Office of Continuing Education.

——, 1990. "Neuroscience Issues in Dyslexia: Research Update," presentation F46, November 2, Orton Dyslexia Society Annual Conference.

——, 1990. "The Testosterone Hypothesis: Assessment since Geschwind and Behan, 1982," *Annals of Dyslexia*, vol. 40, pp. 18–38.

Galaburda, A. M., ed., 1993. *Dyslexia and Development: Neurobiological Aspects of Extra-Ordinary Brains*. Cambridge, Mass.: Harvard University Press.

Galaburda, A. M., F. Aboitiz, G. D. Rosen, and G. F. Sherman, 1986. "Histological Asymmetry in the Primary Visual Cortex of the Rat: Implications for Mechanisms of Cerebral Asymmetry," in *Cortex*, vol. 22, no. 1, pp. 151–60.

Galaburda, A. M., M. LeMay, T. L Kemper, and N. Geschwind, 1978. "Right-Left Asymmetries in the Brain," *Science*, vol. 199, pp. 852 ff.

Galaburda, A. M., and T. L. Kemper, 1979. "Cytoarchitectonic Abnormalities in Developmental Dyslexia: A Case Study," *Annals of Neurology*, vol. 6, pp. 94–100.

Galaburda, A. M., G. F. Sherman, G. D. Rosen, et al., 1985. "Developmental Dyslexia: Four Consecutive Cases with Cortical Anomalies," *Annals of Neurology*, vol. 18, pp. 222–33.

Galaburda, Albert M., and Gordon F. Sherman, 1996. "Anatomic Bases of Perceptual and Cognitive Deficits in Developmental Dyslexia," *47th Annual Conference Booklet*, Orton Dyslexia Society, November 6–9, Boston, Mass., pp. 17–19.

Galton, Francis, 1908 (1974). *Memories of My Life*. London: Methuen.

Ganschow, Leonore, Jenafer Lloyd-Jones, and T. R. Miles, 1994. "Dyslexia and Musical Notation,"*Annals of Dyslexia*, vol. 44, pp. 185–202.

Gantz, John, 1990. "CD-ROM Starts Muscling Microfilm, On-Line Searches Aside," *Infoworld*, vol. 12, no. 8, p. 46.

Gardner, Ann Marie, 2007. "Digging for Dinos in the Land of Genghis Khan," *Discover*, September 2007, pp. 34–40.

Gardner, Howard, 1982. *Art, Mind and Brain*. New York: Basic Books.

———, 1983. *Frames of Mind: The Theory of Multiple Intelligences*. New York: Basic Books.

———, 1985. *The Mind's New Science: A History of the Cognitive Revolution*. New York: Basic Books.

———, 1987. "The Theory of Multiple Intelligences," *Annals of Dyslexia*, vol. 37, pp. 19–35.

———, 1988. "The Many Faces of Intelligence," keynote address at the Fiftieth Anniversary Symposium of the Kingsbury Center.

———, 1989. *To Open Minds: Chinese Clues to the Dilemma of Contemporary Education*. New York: Basic Books.

———, 1993. *Creating Minds: An Anatomy of Creativity Seen through the Lives of Freud, Einstein, Picasso, Stravinsky, Eliot, Graham, and Gandhi*. New York: Basic Books.

———, 1993. *Multiple Intelligences: The Theory in Practice*. New York: Basic Books.

———, 1995. *Leading Minds: An Anatomy of Leadership*. New York: Basic Books. (In collaboration with Emma Laskin.)

Gardner, Howard, 1999. *Intelligence Reframed—Multiple Intelligences for the 21st Century*. New York: Basic Books/Perseus Books.

Gardner, Martin, 1964. *The Ambidextrous Universe: Left Right and the Fall of Parity*. New York: New American Library.

———, 1990. *The New Ambidextrous Universe: Symmetry and Asymmetry from Mirror Reflections to Superstrings*. Third rev. ed. New York: W. H. Freeman.

Gaskins, I., 1982. "Let's End the Reading Disabilities/Learning Disabilities Debate," *Journal of Learning Disabilities*, vol. 15, no. 2, pp. 81–83.

Gassée, Jean-Louis, 1987. *The Third Apple: Personal Computers & the Cultural Revolution*. New York: Harcourt Brace Jovanovich.

Gather, Paul J., Rick Ginsberg, and Henry B. Reiff, 1992. "Identifying Alterable Patterns in Employment Success for Highly Successful Adults with Learning Disabilities," *Journal of Learning Disabilities*, vol. 25, no. 8, pp. 475–87.

Gazzaniga, M., 1983. "Right Hemisphere Language Following Brain Bisection: A 20-Year Perspective," *American Psychologist*, vol. 38, pp. 525–37.

———, 1985. *The Social Brain*. New York: Basic Books.

Gerber, Paul J., and Dale Brown, eds., 1997. *Learning Disabilities and Employment*. Austin, Tex.: ProEd.

Gerber, Paul J., Rick Ginsberg, and Henry B. Reiff, 1992. "Identifying Alterable Patterns in Employment Success for Highly Successful Adults with Learning Disabilities," *Journal of Learning Disabilities*, vol. 25, no. 8, pp. 475–87.

Gernsheim, Heimut, 1969. *Lewis Carroll: Photographer*. New York: Dover.

Geschwind. N., 1977. "Psychiatric Complications in the Epilepsies," *Maclean Hospital Journal*, June, pp. 6–8.

Geschwind. N., and P. Behan, 1982. "Left-Handedness: Association with Immune Disease, Migraine, and Developmental Learning Disorder," *Proceedings of the National Academy of Sciences*, vol. 79, pp. 5097–5100.

Geschwind, Norman, 1962. "The Anatomy of Acquired Disorders of Reading." In *Reading Disability, Progress and Research Needs in Dyslexia*. J. Money, ed. Baltimore: Johns Hopkins University Press.

———, 1970. "The Organization of Language and the Brain," *Science*, vol. 170, pp. 940–44.

———, 1972. "Anatomical Evolution and the Human Brain," *Bulletin of the Orion Society*, vol. 22, pp. 7–13.

———, 1982. "Why Orton Was Right," *Annals of Dyslexia*, vol. 32, Orton Dyslexia Society reprint no. 98.

———, 1983. "Biological Associations of Left-Handedness," *Annals of Dyslexia*, vol. 33, pp. 29–40.

———, 1984. "The Brain of a Learning-Disabled Individual," *Annals of Dyslexia*, vol. 34, pp. 319–27.

———, 1984. Personal communication to Margaret Byrd Rawson, quoted in Rawson, "Faces of Dyslexia," *Annals of Dyslexia*, 1986, p. 184.

———, 1985. "Biological Foundations of Reading." In *Dyslexia: A Neuroscientific Approach to Clinical Evaluation*. Boston: Little, Brown.

Geschwind, Norman, and A. M. Galaburda, 1985. "Cerebral Lateralization,

Biogical Mechanisms, Associations, and Pathology: A Hypothesis and a Program for Research, Parts I–Ill," *Archives of Neurology*, vol. 42, May, pp. 428–59, June, pp. 521–52, and July, pp. 634–54.

———, 1987. *Cerebral Lateralization: Biological Mechanisms, Associations; and Pathology.* Cambridge, Mass.: MIT Press.

———, eds., 1984. *Cerebral Dominance: The Biological Foundations.* Cambridge, Mass.: Harvard University Press.

Geschwind, Norman, and W. Levitsky, 1968. "Human Brain: Left-Right Brain Asymmetries in Temporal Speech Region," *Science*, vol. 161, pp. 186–87.

Gibbs, Josiah Willard, 1906 (1961). *The Scientific Papers of J. Willard Gibbs. Volume 1, Thermodynamics.* London: Longmans, Green; republished New York: Dover.

Giedymin, Jerzy, 1982. *Science and Convention: Essays on Henri Poincaré's Philosophy of Science and the Conventionalist Tradition.* Oxford: Pergamin.

Gilbert, Martin, 1974. *Churchill. A Photographic Portrait.* Boston: Houghton Mifflin.

Gilger, Jeffrey W., and Bonnie J. Kaplin, 2001. "Atypical Brain Development: A Conceptual Framework for Understanding Developmental Learning Disabilities," *Developmental Neuropsychology*, vol. 20, issue 2, January 2001, pp. 465–81.

Gleick, James, 1987. *Chaos: Making a New Science.* New York: Viking.

Glusker, Anne, 1997. "Deficit Selling," *Washington Post Magazine*, March 30, pp. 13–27.

Goertzel, Mildred George, Victor Goertzel, and Ted George Goertzel, 1978. *Three Hundred Eminent Personalities.* San Francisco: Jossey-Bass.

Goertzel, Victor, and Mildred George Goertzel, 1962. *Cradles of Eminence.* Boston: Little, Brown.

Goldman, Martin, 1983. *The Demon in the Aether: The Story of James Clerk Maxwell*, Edinburgh: Paul Harris.

Goldman, Patricia S., 1978. "Neurological Plasticity in Primate Telencephalon: Anomalous Projections Induced by Prenatal Removal of Frontal Cortex," *Science*, vol. 202, pp. 768–70.

Goodglass, H., 1986. "Norman Geschwind (1926–1984)," *Cortex* (Milan), vol. 22, no. 1, pp. 7–10.

Goodglass, H., and N. Geschwind, 1976. "Language Disorders (Aphasia)." In *Handbook of Perception*, volume 7. E. C. Carterette and P. Friedman, eds. New York: Academic.

Gooding, David, and Frank A. J. L. James, eds., 1985. *Faraday Rediscovered: Essays on the Life and Work of Michael Faraday, 1791–1857.* New York: Stockton.

Goodstein, Judith R., 1991. *Millikan's School: A History of the California Institute of Technology.* New York: W.W. Norton.

Gordon, Harold W., 1983. "Learning Disabled Are Cognitively Right," *Topics in Learning and Learning Disabilities,* vol. 3, no. 1, pp. 29–39.

Goth, Nikki C. "Rule No. 1: Less Is More. Rather Than Piling on the Bells and Whistles, Web Designers Look to Classic Graphics Principles," *Hits,* vol. 1, p. 72.

Gould, Stephen Jay, 1981. *The Mismeasure of Man.* New York: W. W. Norton.

——, 1993. *Eight Little Piggies: Reflections in Natural History.* New York: W.W. Norton.

——, 1996. *Full House: The Spread of Excellence from Plato to Darwin.* New York: Harmony Books.

Gowan, John Curtis, 1977. "Background and History of the Gifted-Child Movement." In *The Gifted and the Creative: A Fifty-Year Perspective,* Julian C. Stanley, William C. George, and Cecilia H. Solano, eds. Baltimore and London: Johns Hopkins University Press.

Grandin, Temple, 1995. *Thinking in Pictures: And Other Reports from My Life with Autism.* With foreword by Oliver Sacks. New York: Doubleday.

Graves, Roger, and Harold Goodglass, 1983. "Semantic Paralexia: A Release of Right Hemispheric Function from Left Hemispheric Control?" *Neuropsychologia,* vol. 22, no. 4, pp. 359–64.

Gray, Andrew, 1908 (1973). *Lord Kelvin: An Account of His Scientific Life and Work.* London: English Men of Science Series, republished New York: Chelsea.

Grebogi, Celso, Edward Ott, and James A. Yorke, 1987. "Chaos, Strange Attractors, and Fractal Basin Boundaries in Nonlinear Dynamics," *Science,* vol. 238, no. 4827, pp. 632–38.

Green, Roger Lancelyn, 1960. *Lewis Carroll.* London: Bodley Head.

Grimes, Sally, 1995. "Dyslexia: Reputation, Recognition, Remediation," *Learning Disabilities Journal,* vol. 5, no. 3, pp. 1–14.

Grossman, Paul David, 1993. *Employment Discrimination for the Learning Disabled Community.* Northridge: California State University Press.

Grzanka, Leonard, 1990. "An Animated Discussion: Visualizing the Future," *Supercomputing Review,* vol. 3, no. 9, pp. 9–10.

Gumerman, George J. and Murray Gell-Mann, eds., 1994. *Understanding Complexity in the Prehistoric Southwest, Proceedings, vol. 16, Santa Fe Institute, Studies in the Science of Complexity.* Reading, Mass.: Addison-Wesley.

Gunn, Charlie, and Delle Maxwell, 1991. *Not Knot.* Geometry Center, University of Minnesota. Videotape distributed by Jones and Bartlett Publishers, Boston, Mass.

Guyer, Barbara P., 1997. *The Pretenders: Gifted People Who Have Difficulty Learning*. Howewood, Ill.: High Tide Press.

Hadamard, Jacques, 1945 (1954). *The Psychology of Invention in the Mathematical Field*. New York: Dover.

Haiman, P. M., ed., 1985. *Wranglers and Physicists: Studies on Cambridge Physics in the Nineteenth Century*. Manchester: Manchester University Press.

Halberstam, David, 1969, 1992. *The Best and the Brightest*. New York: Ballantine Books.

Hall, Betsy A., Moustafa Chahine, Kevin Hussey, et al., 1989. "Earth: The Movie," Jet Propulsion Laboratory, NASA, Pasadena, Calif., *ACM SIGGRAPH Video Review*, issue 49, July. Videotape.

Hall, Betsy A., Kevin Hussey, Robert A. Mortensen, et al., 1989. "Mars: The Movie," Jet Propulsion Laboratory, NASA, Pasadena, Calif., *ACM SIGGRAPH Video Review*, issue 49, July. Videotape.

Hall, Edward T., 1981. *Beyond Culture*. Garden City, N.Y.: Anchor/ Doubleday.

Hallowell, Edward, 1996. *When You Worry about the Child You Love: Emotional and Learning Problems in Children*. New York: Simon & Schuster.

Hallowell, Edward M., and John J. Ratey, 1994, 1995. *Driven to Distraction: Recognizing and Coping with Attention Deficit Disorder from Childhood through Adulthood*. New York: Simon & Schuster.

Halmos, Paul R., 1990. "The Calculus Turmoil," *Focus* (the newsletter of the Mathematical Association of America), vol. 10, no. 6, November–December, pp. 1–3.

Hamilton, Kevin M., Lida Kantor, and Lochian E. Magee, 1989. "Limitations of Postural Equilibrium Tests for Examining Simulator Sickness," *Aviation, Space, and Environmental Medicine*, vol. 60, no. 3, pp. 246–51.

Hammill, Donald D., 1990. "On Defining Learning Disabilities: An Emerging Consensus," *Journal of Learning Disabilities*, vol. 23, no. 2, pp. 74–84.

Hampshire, Susan, 1983. *Susan's Story: An Autobiographical Account of My Struggle with Words*. London: Sphere.

Hanington, David, 1995. "Lost for Words," a program in the BBC Television prime-time science documentary series, *QED*, first broadcast July 25, 1995. Produced and Directed by David Hanington.

Hart, C. E., L. Sharenbroich, B. J. Bornstein, D. Trout, B. King, E. Mjolsness, and B. J. Wold, 2005. "A Mathematical and Computational Framework for Quantitative Comparison and Integration of Large-Scale Gene Expression Data," *Nucleic Acids Research*, vol. 33, no. 8, May 10, pp. 2580–94.

Hartevelt, John, 2009. "Reading Performance—Remedial Methods 'Outdated.'"*A4 News*, January 13.

Hartford, Maggie, 1996. "Bid to Improve the Lot of Word-Blind Workers: Don't Just Write Us Off Please." *Oxford Mail*, Oxford, England, Tuesday, May 28.

Hartlage, Lawrence C., and Cathy F. Telzrow, 1984. "Neuropsychological Basis of Educational Assessment and Programming." In *Clinical Neuropsychology: A Multidisciplinary Approach*. Patrick E. Logue and James M. Schear, eds. Springfield, Ill.: Charles C. Thomas.

Hasuike, R., O. Tzeng, and D. Hung, 1986. "Script Effects and Cerebral Lateralization: The Case of Chinese Characters." In *Language Processing in Bilinguals: Psycholinguistic and Neurolinguistic Perspectives*. J. Vaid, ed. Hillsdale, N.J.: Erlbaum.

Hayashi, M. N., H. K. Ulatowska, and S. Sasanuma, 1985. "Subcortical Aphasia and Deep Dyslexia: A Case Study of a Japanese Patient," *Brain and Language*, vol. 25, pp. 293–313.

Hayes, Brian, 1990. "Thoughts on Mathematics," *Pixel*, vol. 1, no. 1, pp. 28–35.

Healey, Jane M., and Dorothy M. Aram, 1986. "Hyperlexia and Dyslexia: A Family Study," *Annals of Dyslexia*, vol. 36, pp. 237–52.

Healey, J. M., J. Liederman, and N. Geschwind, 1986. "Handedness Is Not a Unidimensional Trait," *Cortex*, vol. 22, no. 1, pp. 33–53.

Heer, Jeffrey, Fernanda B. Viégas, and Martin Wattenberg, 2009. "Voyagers and Voyeurs: Supportive Asynchronous Colloboartive Visualization," *Communications of the ACM*, vol. 52. no. 1, January, pp. 87–97.

Heilman, H. M., G. Howell, E. Valenstein, and L Rothi, 1980. "Mirror Reading and Writing in Association with Right-Left Spatial Disorientation," *Journal of Neurology, Neurosurgery, and Psychiatry*, vol. 43, pp. 774–80.

Heller, Wendy, 1990. "Of One Mind: Second Thoughts about the Brain's Dual Nature," *Sciences*, May/June, pp. 38–44.

Hellion, Richard P., ed., 1978. *The Wright Brothers: Heirs of Prometheus*. Washington, D.C.: Smithsonian Institution.

Hempel, Carl Gustav, 1966. *Philosophy of Natural Science*. Englewood Cliffs, N.J.: Prentice-Hall.

Henry, John, 1986. *James Clerk Maxwell and the Theory of the Electromagnetic Field*. Bristol, UK: Adam Hilger, Ltd.

Herr, Laurin, et al., 1989. "Volume Visualization: State of the Art," *ACM SIGGRAPH Video Review*, issue 44. Pacific Interface/Dupont.

Hiatt, Fred, 1990. "Japan Creating Mass-Produced Customization: New Industrial Revolution Seen Having Huge Impact," *Washington Post*, March 25, pp. A29–30.

Hibbard, William, and David Santek, 1989. "Visualizing Large Data Sets in the Earth Sciences," *Computer*, vol. 22, no. 8, pp. 53–57.

Hickey, Hannah, 2008. "Game's High Score Could Earn Nobel Prize in Medicine." Press release, University of Washington, May 8, p.2. http://uwnews.washington.edu/ni/article.asp?articleID=41558.

Hier, D. B., M. LeMay, P. B. Rosenberger, et al., 1978. "Developmental Dyslexia: Evidence for a Subgroup with a Reversal of Cerebral Asymmetry," *Archives of Neurology*, vol. 35, pp. 90–92.

Hilbert, D., and S. Cohn-Vossen, 1952. *Geometry and the Imagination*. P. Nomenyi, trans. New York: Chelsea.

Hillis, W. Daniel, 1985. *The Connection Machine*. Cambridge, Mass.: MIT Press.

Hills, G. J., 1964. *The Inheritance of Michael Faraday. An Inaugural Lecture Delivered at the University on 25th February, 1964*. Southampton: University of Southampton Press.

Hines, Pamela J., Barbara R. Jasny, and Jeffrey Mervis, 2009. "Adding a T to the Three R's—Introduction to a Special Section on Education & Technology." *Science*, vol. 323, issue 5910, January 2, pp. 53–93.

Hinshelwood, J., 1929. "Four Cases of Congenital Word Blindness Occuring in the Same Family," *British Medical Journal*, vol. 2, pp. 1229–99.

Hinshelwood, James, 1917. *Congenital Word-Blindness*. London: H. K. Lewis.

Hiscock, Merrill, and Marcel Kinsbourne, 1982. "Laterality and Dyslexia: A Critical View," *Annals of Dyslexia*, vol. 32, pp. 177–228.

Hobill, David, David Berstein, Larry Smarr, Donna Cox, et al., 1989. "Numerical Relativity: Black Hole Spacetimes," National Center for Supercomputing Applications, *ACM SIGGRAPH Video Review*, issue 49, July. Videotape.

Hobill, David, Daniel Simkins, et al., 1989. "The Lorenz Attractor," National Center for Supercomputing Applications, *ACM SIGGRAPH Video Review*, issue 49, July. Videotape.

Hoffmann, Banesh, with Helen Dukas, 1972. *Albert Einstein: Creator and Rebel*. New York: New American Library.

Holcomb, William R., Russell A. Hardesty, Nicholas A. Adams, and Howard M. Ponder, 1987. "WISC-R Types of Learning Disabilities: A Profile Analysis with Cross-Validation," *Journal of Learning Disabilities*, vol. 20, no. 6, pp. 369–73.

Holton, Gerald, 1972. "On Trying to Understand Scientific Genius," *American Scholar*, vol. 41, no. 1, pp. 95–110.

——, 1978. *The Scientific Imagination: Case Studies.* Cambridge: Cambridge University Press.

——, 1979. "What, Precisely, Is 'Thinking?' Einstein's Answer." In *Einstein: A Centenary Volume*, A. P. French, ed. Cambridge, Mass.: Harvard University Press.

Hoppe, Klaus D., 1988. "Hemispheric Specialization and Creativity," *Psychiatric Clinics of North America*, vol. 11, no. 3, September, pp. 303–15.

Horner, Jack, and James Gorman, 2009. *How to Build a Dinosaur: Extinction Doesn't Have to Be Forever.* New York: Dutton.

Houck, C. K., 1984. *Learning Disabilities: Understanding Concepts, Characteristics, and Issues.* Englewood Cliffs, N.J.: Prentice-Hall.

Howard, D., 1987. "Reading without Letters." In *The Cognitive Neuropsychology of Language.* M. Coltheart, R. Job, and G. Sartori, eds. London: Lawrence Erlbaum.

Howard, Fred, 1987. *Wilbur and Orville: A Biography of the Wright Brothers.* New York: Ballantine.

Howard Rheingold, ed., 1992. "Book review of *In the Mind's Eye*," *Whole Earth Review*, Summer 1992, p. 37.

Huang, C. Y., 1983. "Varieties of Deep Dyslexia in Chinese Orthography," *Excerpta Medica*, Asia Pacific Congress Series, no. 22, vol. 36.

Hudson, Derek, 1976. *Lewis Carroll.* Rev. ed. Folcroft, Pa.: Folcroft Library.

Hughes, Richard, 1990. "Dozo Goes for the Gold in Atlanta . . . and Wins!" *Supercomputing Review*, vol. 3, no. 11, p. 77.

Hunt, Inez, and Wanetta W. Draper, 1964. *Lightning in His Hand: The Life Story of Nikola Tesla.* Denver: Sage.

Hussin, Aziz, 1996. "S[enior] M[inister] Donates Royalties to Dyslexia Body," *Straits Times* (Singapore), January 18, p. 3.

Interagency Committee on Learning Disabilities, 1987. *Learning Disabilities: A Report to the U.S. Congress.* Washington, D.C.: Department of Health and Human Services.

Isaacson, Walter, 2007. *Einstein: His Life and Universe.* New York: Simon & Schuster.

Israel, Paul, 1989. "Telegraphy and Edison's Invention Factory." In *Working at Inventing: Thomas A. Edison and the Menlo Park Experience.* William S. Pretzer, ed. Dearborn, Mich.: Henry Ford Museum & Greenfield Village.

J. S., 1995. Personal electronic mail communication from the United Kingdom.

Jackson, John Hughlings, 1874 (1932). "On the Nature of the Duality of the

Brain." In *Selected Writings, Volume Two*, James Taylor, ed. London: Hodder and Stoughton. Originally published in *Medical Press and Circular*, vol. 1, pp. 19, 41, and 63.

Jackson, Sally, 1992. "Author Urges Shift from Verbal to Visual Learning— Schools Wasting Talents of Dyslexics," Education Review section, edited by Helen Trinca, *Weekend Australian*, November 14–15, p. 51.

Jackson, Tim, 1994, 1995. *Virgin King: Inside Richard Branson's Business Empire*. London: HarperCollins.

James, A. J. L., 1985. "'The Optical Mode of Investigation': Light and Matter in Faraday's Natural Philosophy." In *Faraday Rediscovered: Essays on the Life and Work of Michael Faraday, 1791–1867*. New York: Stockton.

James, Robert Rhodes, 1970. *Churchill: A Study in Failures, 1900–1939*. New York: World.

Jeffares, A. Norman, 1971. *W. B. Yeats*. London: Routledge & Kegan Paul.

———, 1975. *A Commentary on the Collected Poems of W. B. Yeats*. London: Macmillan.

———, 1984. *A New Commentary on the Collected Poems of W. B. Yeats*. London: Macmillan.

Jenkins, Reese V., and Keith A. Nier, 1984. "A Record for Invention: Thomas Edison and His Papers," *IEEE Transactions on Education*, vol. E–27, no. 4, November 1984, pp. 191–96.

Jenkins, Reese V., et al., eds., 1989. *The Papers of Thomas A. Edison: Volume 1, The Making of an Inventor, February 1847–June 1873*. Baltimore: Johns Hopkins University Press.

Jerome, Marty, 1989. "The Electric Cadaver: Doctors and Medical Students Await Benefits of Computerized Anatomy Lessons and Digital Dissection," *PC/Computing*, vol. 2, no. 2, pp. 257–59.

Johnson, Jeff, Teresa L. Roberts, William Verplank, David C. Smith, Charles H. Irby, Marian Beard, and Kevin Mackey, 1989. "The Xerox Star: A Retrospective," *Computer*, vol. 22, no. 9, pp. 11–26 and 28–29.

Jolls, Kenneth R., 1989. "Understanding Thermodynamics through Interactive Computer Graphics," *Chemical Engineering Progress*, February, pp. 64–69.

———, 1990. "The Art of Thermodynamics," B. F. Ruth Chemical Engineering Research Symposium VI. Preprint 89130, Iowa State University, College of Engineering.

———, 1990. "Drawings and Conclusions: The Art of Doing Science," IFIP Conference on Computer Graphics and Education. Preprint 91106, Iowa State University, College of Engineering.

Jolls, Kenneth R., and Daniel C. Coy, 1990. The Art of Thermodynamics," *IRIS Universe*, no. 12, pp. 31–36.

Jones, B. H., 1986. "The Gifted Dyslexic," *Annals of Dyslexia*, vol. 36, pp. 301–17.

Jones, Bence, 1870. *The Life and Letters of Faraday. Volumes I & II.* Philadelphia: J. B. Lippincott.

Jones, G. V., and M. Martin, 1985. "Deep Dyslexia and the Right Hemisphere Hypothesis for Semantic Paralexia: A Reply to Marshall and Patterson," *Neuropsychologia*, vol. 23, pp. 685–88.

Josephson, M., 1959. *Edison: A Biography*. New York: McGraw-Hill.

———, 1969. *Edison*. New York: McGraw-Hill.

Judson, Horace Freeland, 1980. *The Search for Solutions*. New York: Holt, Reinhart and Winston.

Juggins, Mike, 2006. *Dyslexia—Focus on Ability*. A DVD compilation of six shirt films: "Going to War with the 3Rs," "Changing Perceptions," "Dyspel," "The Lexics," "Dyslexia Experiences," "Dyslexia, Visual Jazz." http://www.mikejuggins.com.

K. M., 1995, 1996. Personal electronic mail communication, October 12, 1995, and October 14, 1996.

Kahlbaum, Georg W. A., and Francis V. Darbishire, eds., 1899. *The Letters of Faraday and Schoenbein, 1836–1862*. London: Williams & Norgate.

Kandel, Gillray L., and Yao-Chung Tsao, 1981. "Implications of Neuropsychological Findings for the Reading Instruction of Boys and Girls." In *Sex Differences in Dyslexia*. A. Ansara, N. Geschwind, A. Galaburda, et al., eds. Towson, Md.: Orton Dyslexia Society.

Katz, Irvin R., Robert Mack, and Linn Marks, eds., 1995. *Human Factors in Computing Systems: CHI '95 Conference Proceedings, Denver, CO, May 7–11, 1995*. Reading, Mass.: Addison-Wesley.

Kaufman, Alan S., 1981. "The WISC-R and Learning Disabilities Assessment: State of the Art," *Journal of Learning Disabilities*, vol. 14, no. 9, pp. 520–26.

Kaufmann, W. J., III, and L. L. Smarr, 1993. *Supercomputing and the Transformation of Science*. New York: Scientific American Library, a division of HPHLP.

Kavanagh, James F., and Tom J. Truss Jr., eds. 1988. *Learning Disabilities: Proceedings of the National Conference*. Parkton, Md.: York.

Kay, Alan, 1987. "Emerging Trends," VCR Tape Program No. 1. Cupertino, Calif.: User Group University, Apple User Group Connection, Apple Computer, Inc.

Kelly, Doris, 1992. Book Review *In the Mind's Eye. Dyslexia Contact* (United Kingdom), vol. 11, no. 1, June, p. 17.

Kennedy, R. S., M. G. Lillienthal, K. S. Berbaum, D. R. Baltzley, and M. E. McCauley, 1989. "Simulator Sickness in U.S. Navy Flight Simulators," *Aviation, Space, and Environmental Medicine*, vol. 60, no. 1, pp. 10–16.

Khan, Aamir, 2007. *Taare Zameen Par Every Child Is Special*. An Aamir Kahn Production presented by pvr pictures. Produced and directed by Aamir Kahn.

Kim, Scott, 1981. *Inversions*. New York: W. H. Freeman.

King, Clarence, 1972. *The Half-Share Man: Peter Folger of Nantucket; Grandfather of Benjamin Franklin*. Nantucket, Mass.: Poets Corner.

Kingsland, Lawrence C., Donald A. B. Indberg, and Gordon C. Sharp, 1986. "Anatomy of a Knowledge-Based Consultant System: AI/Rheum," *M.D. Computing*, vol. 3, no. 5, pp. 18–26.

Kinsbourne, Marcel, 1983. "Models of Learning Disability," *Topics in Learning and Learning Disabilities*, vol. 3, no. 1, pp. 1–13.

Kleymeyer, C., 1985. Personal communication.

Kneller, George F., 1965. *The Art and Science of Creativity*. New York: Holt, Reinhart and Winston.

Koestler, Arthur, 1969. *The Act of Creation*. London: Macmillan.

Kolata, Gina, 1982. "Computer Graphics Comes to Statistics," *Science*, vol. 217, pp. 919–20.

KPMG Peat Marwick, 1989. "Report Summary. The Competitive Benefits from 3D Computing: A Study of Silicon Graphics' Customers." Mountain View, Calif.: Silicon Graphics, Inc.

Kress, Gunther, and Theo van Leeuwen, 1996. *Reading Images: The Grammar of Visual Design*. London: Routledge.

Krystal, Henry, 1988. "On Some Roots of Creativity," *Psychiatric Clinics of North America*, vol. 11, no. 3, pp. 475–91.

Kuhn, Thomas S., 1970. *The Structure of Scientific Revolutions*. Second ed. Chicago: University of Chicago Press.

Kupfer, Andrew, 1996. "Craig McCaw Sees an Internet in the Sky," *Fortune*, May 27, pp. 62–72.

———, 1996. "Craig McCaw Sees an Internet in the Sky," *Fortune*, May 27, p. 64ff.

Kussmaul, Adolph, 1877. ". . . Word-Blindness . . ." In *Cyclopedia of the Practice of Medicine*, H. von Ziemssen, ed. Vol. 14, chap. 27, pp. 770–78. New York: William Wood.

Lammers, Susan, ed., 1986. *Programmers at Work: Interviews, First Series*. Redmond, Wash.: Microsoft.

Landis, T., M. Regard, R. Graves, and H. Goodglass, 1983. "Semantic Paralexia: A Release of Right Hemisphere Function from Left Hemisphere Inhibition," *Neuropsychologia*, vol. 21, pp. 359–64.

Landis, T., R. Graves, and H. Goodglass, 1982. "Aphasic Reading and Writing: Possible Evidence for Right Hemisphere Participation," *Cortex*, vol. 18, pp. 105–12.

Langton, Christopher G., Charles Taylor, J. Doyne Farmer, and Steven Rasmussen, eds., 1992. *Artificial Life: The Proceedings of the Workshop on Artificial Life, Held February 1990 in Santa Fe, New Mexico.* Menlo Park, CA: Addison-Wesley.

LaPlante, Alice, 1990. "Bring in the Expert: Expert Systems Can't Solve All Problems, but They're Learning," *Infoworld*, vol. 12, no. 40, pp. 55 and 60.

Lassek, Arthur M., 1970. *The Unique Legacy of Doctor Hughlings Jackson.* Springfield, Ill.: Charles C. Thomas.

Lasseter, John, William Reeves, Eben Ostby, et al., 1986, 1987, 1988. "Luxo Jr.," "Red's Dream," and "'Tin Toy" (with videocassette jacket notes), from Pixar, San Rafael, and Los Angeles, Calif.: Direct Cinema. Videotapes.

Lee, Alfred T., and Steven R. Bussolari, 1989. "Flight Simulator Platform Motion and Air Transport Pilot Training," *Aviation, Space, and Environmental Medicine*, vol. 60, no. 2, pp. 136–40.

Lee, Jenny, 1996. "Views Differ on Changing the Face of Education in the Computer Age," *Vancouver Sun*, April 15.

Leigh, Jim 1987. "The Council for Learning Disabilities Position Statements: Development and Purpose," *Journal of Learning Disabilities*, vol. 20, no. 6, pp. 347–50.

Leighton, Paul, 1986. "Jackie Stewart and Son Both Overcome Dyslexia," *Beverly Times* (Beverly, Mass.), vol. 96, no. 146.

Lemann, Nicholas, 1999. *The Big Test: The Secret History of the American Meritocracy.* New York: Farrar, Straus and Giroux.

Lennon, Florence Becker, 1962 (1972). *The Life of Lewis Carroll.* New York: Dover.

Leong, Che Kan, 1986. "What Does Accessing a Morphemic Script Tell Us about Reading and Reading Disorders in an Alphabetic Script?" *Annals of Dyslexia*, vol. 36, pp. 82–102.

Levering, Robert, Michael Katz, and Milton Moskowitz, 1984. *The Computer Entrepreneurs.* New York: New American Library.

Levine, Mel, 1990. *Keeping a Head in School: A Student's Book about Learning Abilities and Learning Disorders.* Cambridge, Mass.: Educators Publishing Service.

———, 1993. *All Kinds of Minds: A Young Student's Book about Learning Abilities and Learning Disorders.* Cambridge, Mass.: Educators Publishing Service.

Levoy, Marc, 1988. "Volume Rendering: Display of Surfaces from Volume Data," *IEEE Computer Graphics & Applications*, May.

Levy, G. C., 1969. "Possible Basis for the Evolution of Lateral Specialization of the Human Brain," *Nature*, vol. 224, pp. 614–15.

————, 1988. "How Changes in Computer Technology Are Revolutionizing the Practice of Chemistry," *Journal of Chemical Information and Computer Sciences*, vol. 28, no. 4, pp. 167–74.

Levy, J., 1983. "Language, Cognition and the Right Hemisphere: A Response to Gazzaniga," *American Psychologist*, vol. 38, pp. 538–41.

Lindberg, Donald, 1993. "High Performance Libraries," British Library Dainton Lecture on Scientific and Technical Information, March 29.

Lisankie, Kevin, 1989. "Soon Students Will Study the 'Unseen,'" *NCGA Computer Graphics Today*, vol. 6, no. 4, pp. 1, 29, and 31.

Loewenberg, Peter, 1988. "Einstein in His Youth." A book review of *The Collected Papers of Albert Einstein, Volume I, The Early Years, 1879–1902*, John Stachel, ed. *Science*, vol. 239, pp. 510–12.

Loye, David, 1988. "Hemisphericity and Creativity: Group Process and the Dream Factory," *Psychiatric Clinics of North America*, vol. 11, no. 3, pp. 415–26.

Luchins, Abraham S., and Edith H. Luchins, 1990. "The Einstein-Wertheimer Correspondence on Geometric Proofs and Mathematical Puzzles," *Mathematical Intelligencer*, vol. 12, no. 2, pp. 35–43.

Ludwig, Charles, 1978. *Michael Faraday: Father of Electronics*. Scottdale, Penn.: Herald.

Lufi, Dubi, and Arie Cohen, 1988. "Differential Diagnosis of Learning Disability versus Emotional Disturbance Using the WISC-R," *Journal of Learning Disabilities*, vol. 21, no. 8, pp. 515–16.

Lyon, G. Reid, 1983. "Learning-Disabled Readers: Identification of Subgroups." In *Progress in Learning Disabilities, Volume V*, Helmer R. Myklebust, ed., pp. 103–33. New York: Grune & Stratton.

————, 1995. "Toward a Definition of Dyslexia," *Annals of Dyslexia*, vol. 45, pp. 3–27.

Lyon, G. Reid, and Judith M. Rumsey, eds., 1996. *Neuroimaging: A Window to the Neurological Foundations of Learning and Behavior in Children*. Baltimore: Brookes.

Lyons, Terence J., and Carl G. Simpson, 1989. "The Giant Hand Phenomenon," *Aviation, Space, and Environmental Medicine*, vol. 60, no. 1, pp. 64–66.

Lytle, Wayne, Mark Rondeau, and Anne Dumke, 1989. "Simulated Treatment of an Ocular Tumor," Cornell National Supercomputer Facility, *SIGGRAPH Video Review*, issue 49, July. Videotape.

Lytton, W. W., and J. C. M. Brust, 1989. "Direct Dyslexia: Preserved Oral Reading of Real Words in Wernicke's Aphasia," *Brain*, vol. 112, part 3, June, pp. 583–94.

M., R., 1993. Personal communication. (ACM SIGGRAPH conference with additional meetings and discussions. Electronic mail confirmation with specific permission, 1996.)

MacDonald, D. K. C., 1964. *Faraday, Maxwell and Kelvin.* New York: Anchor/Doubleday.

Machover, Carl, 1990. "A Vision of the American Computer Graphics Market," *Computer Graphics,* vol. 8, no. 2, pp. 44–45.

Maddox, Brenda, 2002. *Rosalind Franklin: The Dark Lady of DNA.* New York: HarperCollins.

Makita, K., 1968. "The Rarity of Reading Disability in Japanese Children," *American Journal of Orthopsychiatry,* vol. 38, pp. 599–614.

Malamud, Carl, 1990. "Beyond the PC," *Infoworld,* vol. 12, no. 49, December 3, pp. 46–52.

Manchester, William, 1983. *The Last Lion. Winston Spencer Churchill, Visions of Glory, 1874–1932.* New York: Bantam Doubleday Dell.

———, 1988. *The Last Lion: Winston Spencer Churchill, Alone 1932–1940.* New York: Bantam Doubleday Dell.

Mandelbrot, Benoit B., 1977 (1983). *The Fractal Geometry of Nature.* Updated ed. New York: W. H. Freeman.

———, 1989. "Fractals and an Art for the Sake of Science." In *Computer Art in Context: SIGGRAPH '89 Art Show Catalog,* pp. 21–24. New York: Pergamon.

Margulis, Lynn, 1990. "Rethinking Evolution," *Smithsonian Institution,* April 23.

Markel, Geraldine, and Judith Greenbaum, 1996. *Performance Breakthroughs for Adolescents with Learning Disabilities or ADD.* Champaign, Ill.: Research Press.

Marshall, Eliot, 1990. "Science beyond the Pale: Researchers with Maverick Ideas—Particularly in Space Physics—Find Themselves Fighting an Uphill Battle for Acceptance; Should the System Be More Tolerant of Unorthodoxy?" *Science,* vol. 249, July 9, 1990, pp. 14–16.

Marshall, J. C., 1989. "The Description and Interpretation of Acquired and Developmental Reading Disorders." In *From Reading to Neurons,* A. M. Galaburda, ed., pp. 68–86. Cambridge, Mass.: MIT Press.

Marshall, J. C., and K. E. Patterson, 1983. "Semantic Paralexias and the Wrong Hemisphere: A Note on Landis, Regard, Graves, and Goodglass (1983)," *Neuropsychologia,* vol. 4, pp. 425–27.

———, 1985. "Left Is Still Left for Semantic Paralexia: A Reply to Jones and Martin," *Neuropsycholgia,* vol. 23, pp. 689–90.

Martin, Lawrence, 1995. *Chrétien (Volume 1): The Will to Win.* Toronto: Lester.

Matthews, Anne, 1997. *Bright College Years: Inside the American Campus Today.* New York: Simon & Schuster.

Maxwell, James Clerk, 1876. *Matter and Motion.* New York: D. Van Nostrand.

———, 1889. Letter of November 1874, J. C. Maxwell to Thomas Andrews, in P. G. Tait and A. C. Brown, "Memoir of Dr. Thomas Andrews," in *Scientific Papers of the Late Thomas Andrews,* P. G. Tait and A. C. Brown, eds., pp ix–xii. London: Macmillan.

———, 1891 (1954). *A Treatise on Electricity and Magnetism,* vol. 1, unabridged. Republished New York: Dover.

McCombs, Phil, 1996. "The Golden Age of Guggenheim: The Local Documentary Filmmaker, Keeping Focused—and Up for a Fifth Oscar," *Washington Post,* March 17, pp. G1–G6.

McDonald, K. A., 1994. "The Iconoclastic Fossil Hunter," *Chronicle of Higher Education,* November 16, pp. A9–A17. (Cover Interview.)

McEntire, Elizabeth, 1983. "Learning Disabilities and Mathematics," *Topics in Learning and Learning Disabilities,* vol. 3, no. 3, pp. 1–18.

McGraw, Tim, 1989. "Computer Imaging Offers New Insights Into Old Problems," *Supercomputing Review,* vol. 2, no. 8, pp. 34–36 and 38.

McLeod, T. M., and W. D. Crump, 1978. "The Relationship of Visuospatial Skills and Verbal Ability to Learning Disabilities in Mathematics," *Journal of Learning Disabilities,* vol. 11, pp. 237–41.

McLoughlin, David, Gary Fitzgibbon, and Vivienne Young, 1994. *Adult Dyslexia: Assessment, Counselling and Training.* London: Whurr.

Meighan, Roland, 1988. *Flexi-Schooling: Education for Tomorrow, Starting Yesterday.* Ticknall, U.K.: Education Now Publishing Cooperative, Limited.

———, 1994. *The Freethinkers' Guide to the Educational Universe: A Selection of Quotations on Education.* Bramcote Hills, U.K.: Educational Heretics Press.

———, 1995. *John Holt: Personalised Education and the Reconstruction of Schooling.* Bramcote Hills, U.K.: Educational Heretics Press.

Meighan, Roland, and Philip Toogood, 1992. *Anatomy of Choice in Education.* Ticknall, U.K.: Education Now Publishing Cooperative.

Michelmore, Peter, 1962. *Einstein: Profile of the Man.* New York: Dodd, Mead.

Miles, T. R., 1993. *Dyslexia: The Pattern of Difficulties.* Second Edition. London: Whurr.

——— 1993. *Dyslexia Contact,* June, pp. 14–15.

Miles, T. R., and Mary N. Haslum, 1986. "Dyslexia: Anomaly or Normal Variation?" *Annals of Dyslexia,* vol. 36, pp. 103–17.

Miles, T.R., and Elaine Miles, 1991. *Dyslexia: A Hundred Years On.* Milton Keynes, U.K.: Open University Press.

Miller, Arthur I., 1986. *Imagery in Scientific Thought: Creating 20th-Century Physics*. Cambridge, Mass.: MIT Press.

Miller, John Laurence, 1990. "Apocalypse or Renaissance or Something in Between? Toward a Realistic Appraisal of *The Learning Mystique*," *Journal of Learning Disabilities*, vol. 23, no. 2, pp. 86–91.

Ministry of Education, Province of Quebec, 1983. *Document EI; Provisions Constituting Collective Agreements*. Quebec City: Government Printing Office.

Minsky, Margaret, Ouh-Young Ming, Oliver Steele, Frederick P. Brooks Jr., and Max Behensky, 1990. "Feeling and Seeing: Issues in Force Display," in *Proceedings: 1990 Symposium on Interactive 3D Graphics, Snowbird, Utah, 25th–28th March 1990, Computer Graphics (ACM SIGGRAPH)*, vol. 24, no. 2, pp. 235–43.

Minsky, Marvin, 1986. *The Society of Mind*. New York: Simon & Schuster.

———, 1987. "The Future of Intelligence: Can Computers Think?" "New Frontiers of Science," December 3, transcript of one in a course of lectures sponsored by the Smithsonian Institution in collaboration with the American Association for the Advancement of Science.

Minsky, Marvin, and Seymour Papert, 1974. *Artificial Intelligence*. Eugene: Oregon State System of Higher Education.

Mitchell, R., et al., 1995. "The Schwab Revolution," *Business Week*, December 19.

Mochizuki, Hiroshi, and Ruriko Ohtomo, 1988. "Pure Alexia in Japanese and Agraphia without Alexia in Kanji: The Ability Dissociation between Reading and Writing in Kanji vs. Kana," *Archives of Neurology*, vol. 45, pp. 1157–59.

Money, J., 1972. "Studies in the Function of Sighting Dominance," *Journal of Experimental Psychology*, vol. 24, pp. 454–64.

Monroe, Paul, 1908. *A Brief Course in the History of Education*. New York: MacMillan.

Montelione, John, 1989. "Workstations: The Third-Generation Imaging Workhorse," *Computer Graphics Review*, vol. 4, no. 4, pp. 52–58.

Moravec, Hans, 1988. *Mind Children: The Future of Robot and Human Intelligence*. Cambridge, Mass.: Harvard University Press.

———, 1989. "Human Culture: A Genetic Takeover Underway." In *Artificial Life: Proceedings of an Interdisciplinary Workshop on the Synthesis and Simulation of Living Systems*. Christopher G. Langton, ed. Center for Nonlinear Studies, Los Alamos National Laboratory. Vol. 6, *Studies in the Sciences of Complexity*, Santa Fe Institute. Redwood City, Calif.: Addison-Wesley.

Morgan, W. Pringle, 1896. "A Case of Congentital Word Blindness," *British Medical Journal*, November 7, p. 1378.

Morris, Betsy, 2002. "The Dyslexic CEO: Charles Schwab, Richard Branson, Craig McCaw & John Chambers Triumphed Over America's No.1 Learning Disorder. Your Kid Can Too," *Fortune*, May 20. 2002.

————, 2003. "What a Life." *Fortune* Special: The Business Life Issue, October 6. pp. 50–60.

Morton, J., and S. Sasanuma, 1984. "Lexical Access in Japanese." In *Orthographies and Reading*, L. Henderson, ed. London: Lawrence Erlbaum.

Mosle, Sara, 1996. "The Answer Is Standards: Education Is a Campaign Issue without a Focus." *New York Times Magazine*, October 27, pp. 45–68.

Murphy, William M., 1978. *Prodigal Father*. Ithaca, N.Y.: Cornell University Press.

Myklebust, Helmer R., ed., 1983. *Progress in Learning Disabilties, Volume V*. New York: Grime & Stratton.

Nakamae, Eihachiro, Takao Ishizaki, Tomoyuki Nishita, and Shinichi Takital, 1989. "Compositing 3D Images with Antialiasing and Various Shading Effects," *IEEE Computer Graphics and Applications*, vol. 9, no. 2, pp. 21–29.

Nash, J. Madeleine, 1997. "Special Report: How A Child's Brain Develops, and What It Means for Child Care and Welfare Reform." *Time*, February 3, pp. 48–63.

National Board of Medical Examiners, 1988. "The Computer-Based Test," pp. 1–4. Philadelphia: National Board of Medical Examiners.

National Research Council, 1989. *Everybody Counts: A Report to the Nation on the Future of Mathematics Education*. Washington, D.C.: National Academy.

Negroponte, Nicholas, 1995. *Being Digital*. New York: Alfred A. Knopf.

Nekkei, 1994. "Review of *Geniuses Who Hated School*," July 2. (*Nikkei* is known as the *Wall Street Journal* of Japan. Review translated by Yoshiko G. Doherty.)

Netley, C., and J. Rovet, 1982. "Handedness in 47 XXY Males," *Lancet*, no. 2, p. 264.

Newcombe, F., and J. C. Marshall, 1984. "On the Psycholinguistic Classifications of the Acquired Dyslexias," *Bulletin of the Orton Society*, vol. 31, pp. 29–46.

Nice, Jake, 1987. "The Gift of Dyslexia: Another Point of View." Presentation, November 6, 1987. Orton Dyslexia Society Annual Conference.

Nichols, Lane, 2009. "Guidelines to Help Pupils' Literacy Rate."

Nicholes, E. G., James Inglis, J. S. Lawson, and Ian MacKay, 1988. "A Cross-Validation Study of Patterns of Cognitive Ability in Children with

Learning Difficulties, as Described by Factorially Defined WISC-R Verbal and Performance IQs," *Journal of Learning Disabilities*, vol. 21, no. 8, pp. 504–508.

Nielson, Gregory M., 1989. "Guest Editor's Introduction: Visualization in Scientific Computing," *Computer*, vol. 22, no. 8, pp. 10–11.

Norman, Donald A., 1993. *Things That Make Us Smart: Defending Human Attributes in an Age of the Machine*. New York: Addison-Wesley.

O'Boyle, Michael W., and Camilla Perrson Benbow, 1990. "Enhanced Right Hemisphere Involvement during Cognitive Processing May Relate to Intellectual Precocity," *Neuropsychologia*, vol. 28, no. 2, pp. 211–16.

Ohmae, Kenichi, 1991. *The Borderless World: Power and Strategy in the Interlinked Economy*. New York: Harper Perennial.

Olivier, Carolyn, and Rosemary F. Bowler, 1996. *Learning to Learn*. New York: Simon & Schuster.

Olson, Lynne, 2007. *Troublesome Young Men: The Rebels Who Brought Churchill to Power and Helped to Save England*. New York: Farrar, Straus and Giroux.

Olson, Meredith B., 1977. "Visual Field Usage as an Indicator of Right or Left Hemispheric Information Processing in Mathematically Precocious Students." Presented at the Annual Northwest Mathematics Conference, October 13.

Olson, Richard K., 2006. "Genes, Environment, and Dyslexia: The 2005 Norman Geschwind Memorial Lecture," *Annals of Dyslexia*, vol. 56, no. 2, pp. 205–38.

Omstein, Robert E., 1977. *The Psychology of Consciousness*. Second ed. New York: Harcourt Brace Jovanovich.

O'Neill, Helen, 2003. *Life without Limits: The Remarkable Story of David Pescud and His Fight for Survival in a Sea of Words*. Sydney, Australia: Bantam Books.

Orfalea, Paul, and Anne Marsh, 2005. *Copy This! Lessons from a Hyperactive Dyslexic Who Turned a Bright Idea into One of America's Best Companies*. New York: Workman.

Ornstein, Robert, 1986. *Multimind*. New York: Doubleday.

Orr, Joel N., 1990. "Fascinating Rhythm—We Can Reap More from Computers That Respond to Our Rhythmical Nature," *Computer Graphics World*, vol. 13, no. 8, pp. 117–20.

Orton, Samuel Torrey, 1937. *Reading, Writing and Speech Problems in Children: Certain Types of Disorders in the Development of Language Faculty*. New York: W. W. Norton.

———, 1966. "Word Blindness." In *School Children and Other Papers on Strephosymbolia (Specific Language Disabilty—Dyslexia), 1925–1946*.

Monograph no. 2, June Lynday Orton, ed. Pomfret, Conn.: Orton Society.

Osborn, Alex F., 1957. *Applied Imagination: Principles and Procedures of Creative Thinking.* Rev. ed. New York: Scribner's.

Osman, Betty B., 1979. *Learning Disabilities: A Family Affair.* New York: Random House.

Osmond, John, 1993. *The Reality of Dyslexia.* A Channel Four Book. London: Cassell Educational Limited.

Oughtred, William, 1653. *Mathematical Recreations: A Collection of . . . Experiments in Arithmetick, Geometry . . . Navigation, Music, Opticks . . . Mechanicks, Chemistry, Water-works, Fire-works, &c.* London: Printed for William Leake.

Padgett, Ian, and Beverly Steffert, 1999. *Visual Spatial Ability and Dyslexia.* London: Central Saint Martins College of Art and Design.

Pais, Abraham, 1982. *"Subtle Is the Lord . . .": The Science and the Life of Albert Einstein.* Oxford: Oxford University Press.

Palca, Joseph, 1990. "Insights from Broken Brains," *Science,* vol. 248, pp. 812–14.

Paradis, M., H. Hagiwara, and N. Hildebrandt, 1985. *Neurolinguistic Aspects of the Japanese Writing System.* New York: Academic.

Park, Kyungmee, 1993. *A Comparative Study of the Traditional Calculus Course vs. the Calculus & Mathematica Course.* Unpublished doctoral dissertation, Graduate School of Education, University of Illinois at Urbana-Champaign.

Parker, Richard Green, 1848. *A School Compendium of Natural and Experimental Philosophy, Embracing the Elementary Principles of Mechanics, Hydrostatics, Hydraulics, Pneumatics, Acoustics, Pyronomics, Optics, Electricity, Galvanism, Magnetism, Electromagnetism, Magneto- electricity, and Astronomy.* New York: A. S. Barnes.

Parkinson, C. Northcote, 1957. *Parkinson's Law.* New York: Ballantine.

Parkinson, Susan, ed., 1992. *Newsletter of The Arts Dyslexia Trust* (United Kingdom), November 1992.

Patterson, K., and D. Besner, 1984. "Is the Right Hemisphere Literate?" *Cognitive Neuropsychology,* vol. 1, pp. 315–42.

Patton, George, S., 1972. *The Patton Papers: 1885–1940.* Martin Blumenson, ed., Boston: Houghton Mifflin.

Pearson, E. S. 1938. *Karl Pearson: An Appreciation of Some Aspects of His Life and Work.* Cambridge: Cambridge University Press.

———, 1956 (1966). "Some Aspects of the Geometry of Statistics: The Use of Visual Presentation in Understanding the Theory and Application of Mathematical Statistics." In *The Selected Papers of E. S. Pearson.* Inaugural address of the president to the Royal Statistical Society. Republished Los Angeles: University of California Press.

Pearson, Karl, 1914. *The Life, Letters and Labours of Francis Galton. Volume I: Birth 1822 to Marriage 1853*. Cambridge: Cambridge University Press.

Pelling, Henry, 1974 (1977). *Winston Churchill*. London: Macmillan.

Pennington, Bruce F., 1991. *Diagnosing Learning Disorders: A Neuropsychological Framework*. New York: Guilford Press.

Pentland, Alex, Irfan Essa, Martin Friedman, Bradley Horowitz, and Stanley E. Sclaroff, 1990. "The Thing World Modeling System: Virtual Sculpting by Modal Forces," in *Proceedings: 1990 Symposium on Interactive 3D Graphics, Snowbirrd, Utah, 25th–28th March 1990, Computer Graphics (ACM SIGGRAPH)*, vol. 24, no. 2, pp. 143–44.

PERC, 1993. *Newsletter of the Parents' Educational Resource Center*, San Mateo, Calif., Spring 1993.

Perino, Sheila C., and Joseph Perino, 1981. *Parenting the Gifted: Developing the Promise*. New York: R. R. Bowker.

Pestalozzi, Johann Heinrich, 1801. *Leonard and Gertrude: A Popular Story, Written Originally in German; Translated into French, and Now Attempted in English; With the Hope of Its Being Useful to All Classes of Society*. Philadelphia: Printed for Joseph Groff.

———, 1894 (1973). *How Gertrude Teaches Her Children*, Lucy E. Holland and Francis C. Turner, trans. New York: Garden. Reprint of the 1894 English translation from the 1801 German original.

Petersen, Anne C., 1981. "Sex Differences in Performance on Spatial Tasks: Biopsychosocial Influences." In *Sex Differences in Dyslexia*, A. Ansara, N. Geschwind, A. Galaburda, et al., eds. Towson, Md.: Orton Dyslexia Society.

Petersen, Anne C., and Michele Andrisin Wittig, 1979. "Overview." In *Sex-Related Differences in Cognitive Functioning*, Michele Andrisin Wittig and Anne C. Petersen, eds. New York: Academic.

Petersen, Ivars, 1984. "Escape into Chaos: Even Simple Mathematical Expressions Can Behave in Unexpected Ways and Display Patterns of Startling Beauty," *Science News*, vol. 125, pp. 328–29.

———, 1987. "Twists of Space: An Artist, a Computer Programmer and a Mathematician Work Together to Visualize Exotic Geometric Forms," *Science News*, vol. 132, pp. 264–66.

———, 1988. "Computing the Way a Liquid Drips," *Science News*, vol. 134, p. 21.

———, 1988. "Tiling to Infinity," *Science News*, vol. 134, p. 42.

———, 1990. "Equations in Stone: A Mathematician [Helaman Ferguson]

Turns to Sculpture to Convey the Beauty of Mathematics," *Science News*, vol. 138, no. 10, pp. 152–54.

Petty, Thomas L., 2003. *History of the University of Colorado Division of Pulmonary Science and Critical Care Medicine: A Personal Perspective Over Half a Century.* Denver, Colo.: Snowdrift Pulmonary Foundation.

Petzinger, Thomas, 1998. "A Banc One Executive Credits His Success to Mastering Dyslexia," *Wall Street Journal*, April 24, p. B1.

Phillips, Kevin, 2008. *Bad Money: Reckless Finance, Failed Politics, and the Global Crisis of American Capitalism.* New York: Viking.

Pickering, George, 1974. *Creative Malady: Illness in the Lives and Minds of Charles Darwin, Florence Nightingale, Mary Baker Eddy, Sigmund Freud, Marcel Proust, Elizabeth Barrett Browning.* New York: Oxford University Press.

Pickover, Clifford A., 1989. "A Short Recipe for Seashell Synthesis," *IEEE Computer Graphics and Applications*, vol. 9, no. 6, pp. 8–11.

Piermme, Thomas E., and Robert I. Keimowitz, 1989. "Results of CBT Research to Date." In *The NBME's Computer-Based Testing (CBT) Software: Summary Reports from Twenty-three CBT Phase I Schools*, pp. 17–19. National Board of Medical Examiners.

Plato, 1961. *Plato: Collected Dialogues.* Princeton, N.J.: Princeton University Press.

Poincaré, Henri, 1913 (1921). *The Foundations of Science*, George Bruce Halsted, trans. New York: Sciences.

Pollack, Cecelia, and Ann Branden, 1982. "Odyssey of a 'Mirrored' Personality," *Annals of Dyslexia*, vol. 32, pp. 275–87.

Polzella, Donald J., and Gary B. Reid, 1989. "Multidimensional Scaling Analysis of Simulated Air Combat Maneuvering Performance Data," *Aviation, Space, and Environmental Medicine*, vol. 60, no. 2, pp. 141–44.

Pompiom, Nancy W, and Carl P. Thum, 1988, "Dyslexic/Learning Disabled Students at Dartmouth College," *Annals of Dyslexia*, vol. 38, pp. 276–84.

Ponting, Bob, 1989. "Developers See Gaps in Windows, PM," *Infoworld*, vol. 11, no. 33, p. 22.

Pool, Robert, 1990. "Fractal Fracas," *Science*, vol. 249, pp. 363–64.

Pope, Loren, 2006. *Colleges That Change Lives: 40 Schools That Will Change the Way You Think about Colleges.* New York: Penguin Books.

Poplin, Mary S., 1992. "Looking through Other Lenses and Listening to Other Voices." In *Alternative Views of Learning Disabilities: Issues for the 21st Century*, edited by Mary Poplin and Patricia Tefft Cousin, p. 4. Austin: Pro-Ed.

Popper, Karl R., 1959. *The Logic of Scientific Discovery.* New York: Basic Books.

Potts, Marjory, and Robert Potts, 1997. *LD/LA—Learning Disabilities/Learning Abilities.* Martha's Vineyard Island, Mass. Vineyard Video Productions. Videotape.

Price, Elunid, 1996. "The Skill That Dares Not Spell Its Name," *Evening Standard,* (London), June 4.

Price, Lucian, 1954 (1964). *Dialogues of Alfred North Whitehead.* New York: New American Library, Mentor.

Prigogine, Ilya, 1971. *Interpretations of Life and Mind: Essays around the Problem of Reduction.* London: Routledge & Kegan Paul.

———, 1984. *Order Out of Chaos.* New York: Bantam.

Province, Charles M., 1983. *The Unknown Patton.* New York: Bonanza.

Puccetti, Roland, 1981. "The Case for Mental Duality: Evidence from Split-Brain Data and Other Considerations," *Behavioral and Brain Sciences,* vol. 4, March, pp. 93–123.

R. M., 1993. Personal electronic mail communication.

Rawson, M. B., 1968. *Developmental Language Disability: Adult Accomplishments of Dyslexic Boys.* Baltimore: Johns Hopkins University Press.

———, 1981. "A Diversity Model for Dyslexia." In *Dyslexia Research and Its Applications to Education,* pp. 13–34. London and New York: John Wiley & Sons.

———, 1982. "Louise Baker and the Leonardo Syndrome," *Annals of Dyslexia,* 32, pp. 289–304.

———, 1986. "The Many Faces of Dyslexia," *Annals of Dyslexia,* vol. 36, pp. 179–91.

Rawson, Margaret Byrd, 1995. *Dyslexia over the Lifespan: A Fifty-five-Year Longitudinal Study.* Cambridge, Mass.: Educators Publishing Service.

Red Herring, 1996. "Beyond the Browser Wars. Netscape's Marc Andressen and Microsoft's John Ludwig Debate the Future of the Internet," October, pp. 38–41.

Reeves, Frank, 1993. *Community Need and Further Education: The Practice of Community-Centred Education at Bilston Community College.* Ticknall, U.K.: Education Now Publishing Co-operative.

Regard, M., and T. Landis, 1984. "Experimentally Induced Semantic Paralexias in Normals: A Property of the Right Hemisphere," *Cortex,* vol. 20, pp. 263–70.

Reich, Cary, 1996. *The Life of Nelson Rockefeller: Worlds to Conquer, 1908–1958.* New York: Doubleday.

Reid, Gavin, 1994. *Specific Learning Difficulties (Dyslexia): A Handbook for Study and Practice.* Edinburgh: Moray House.

———, 1996. "The 'Other Side' of Dyslexia," *Dimensions of Dyslexia*, vol. 2, pp. 489–90.

———, ed., 1994. *Specific Learning Difficulties (Dyslexia): Perspectives on Practice*. Edinburgh: Moray House.

Rheingold, Howard, 1989. "The Interface of Tomorrow," *Infoworld*, vol. 11, no. 128, pp. 42–48.

Rhodes, Robert, 1970. *Churchill: A Study in Failure, 1900–1939*. London: Weiderfeld & Nicolson.

Richard, Paul, 1996. "Towering Words of Art: 34-Volume Dictionary Paints a Stunning Visual History," *Washington Post*, October 16, pp. B1 ff.

Richards, Evelyn, 1989. "The Data Deluge: Exotic Electronic Systems May Hold Key to Future Access," *Washington Post*, September 24, pp. H1 ff.

Richardson, M., 1958. *Fundamentals of Mathematics*. Rev. ed. New York: Macmillan.

Riddick, Barbara, 1996. *Living with Dyslexia: The Social and Emotional Consequences of Specific Learning Difficulties*. London: Routledge.

Ritchie-Calder, Peter R., 1970. *Leonardo & the Age of the Eye*. New York: Simon & Schuster.

Rival, Ivan, 1987. "Picture Puzzling: Mathematicians Are Rediscovering the Power of Pictorial Reasoning," *Sciences*, January/February, pp. 40–46.

Rivers, Diane, and Tom E. C. Smith, 1988. "Traditional Eligibility Criteria for Identifying Students as Specific Learning Disabled," *Journal of Learning Disabilities*, vol. 21, no. 10, pp. 642–44.

Robins, C., 1992. "One Man's Battle against Dyslexia—How Financier Charles Schwab Is Helping Others Whose Kids Have Learning Disabilities," *San Francisco Examiner*, March 8, pp. D-3, D-10.

Roden, J.C., B. W. King, D. Trout, A. Mortazavi, B. J. Wold, and C. E. Hart, 2006. "Mining Gene Expression Data by Interpreting Principal Components," *BMC Bioinformatics*, vol. 7, April 7, p. 194.

Romney, Jonathan, 1995. "Bound to Put a Spell on You," *Guardian*, July 26.

Root-Bernstein, Robert S., 1988. "Setting the Stage for Discovery: Breakthroughs Depend on More Than Luck," *Sciences*, May/June, pp. 26–34.

———, 1990. "Sensual Education," *Sciences*, September/October, pp. 12–14.

Rose, David H., Anne Meyer, and Chuck Hitchcock, 2005. *The Universally Designed Classroom: Accessible Curriculum and Digital Technologies*. Cambridge, Mass.: Harvard Education Press.

Rose, Steven, 1992. *The Making of Memory: From Molecules to Mind*. New York: Bantam Books.

Rosenblum, Lawrence J., 1989. "Scientific Visualization at Research Laboratories," *Computer*, vol. 22, no. 8, pp. 68–70.

Rosenthal, M. L, 1962. "The Poetry of Yeats." In *Selected Poems and the Plays of William Butler Yeats*, pp. xv–xxxix. New York: Macmillan.

Rothenberg, Albert, 1988. "Creativity and the Homospatial Process: Experimental Studies," *Psychiatric Clinics of North America*, vol. 11, no. 3, pp. 443–59.

Rothenberg, Albert, and Carl R. Hausman, 1976. *The Creativity Question*. Durham, N.C.: Duke University Press.

Rowe, Marc I., 2008. *Oral History Project: Marc I. Rowe, MD*. Interview by Jay L. Grosfeld, MD, Pediatric History Center, American Academy of Pediatrics, February 3, Sanibel, Florida. (Unpublished manuscript.)

Rozin, Paul, Susan Poritsky, and Raina Sotsky, 1971. "American Children with Reading Problems Can Easily Learn to Read English Represented by Chinese Characters," *Science*, vol. 171, pp. 1264–67.

Rumsey, Judith M., R. Dorwart, M. Vermess, M. B. Denckla, M. J. P. Kruesi, and J. L Rapoport, 1986. "Magnetic Resonance Imaging of Brain Anatomy in Severe Developmental Dyslexia," *Archives of Neurology*, vol. 43, pp. 1045–46.

SIGGRAPH, 1994. *SIGGRAPH Video Review, Issue 101: SIGGRAPH 94 Electronic Theater*. (Supplement to the ACM SIGGRAPH publication *Computer Graphics*.) http:/Iwww.siggraph.org/library/SVR/SVR.html.

Sabionski, Gunter, Ed Kramer, Tom Robinson, et al., 1989. "Mars Rover Sample Return Mission," Johnson Space Center, NASA, Houston, Texas, in *1989 International Computer Animation Competition Finalists*. National Computer Graphics Association. Videotape.

Sacks, Oliver, 1987. *The Man Who Mistook His Wife for a Hat and Other Clinical Tales*. New York: Harper & Row.

Salzman, David, and Jack Grimes, 1989. "Guest Editors' Introduction: Graphic Superworkstations and the Last Hurrah," *IEEE Computer Graphics and Applications*, July, pp. 27–29.

Santillana, G. D., 1966. "Man without Letters." In *Leonardo da Vinci: Aspects of the Renaissance Genius*, M. Philipson, ed., pp. 77–109. New York: George Braziller.

Sapwater, E., 1996. "Adventure Knows No Path," *Photo-Electric Imaging*, vol. 39, no. 8, pp. 6–12.

Sartori, Giuseppe, 1987. "Leonardo Da Vinci, Omo Sanza Lettere: A Case of Surface Dysgraphia." *Cognitive Neuropsychology*, vol. 4, no. 1, pp. 1–10.

Schilpp, Paul A., ed., 1970. *Albert Einstein: Philosopher-Scientist*. La Salle, Ill.: Open Court.

Schultz, Brad, 1988. "Scientific Visualization: Transforming Numbers into Computer Pictures," *Computer Pictures*, vol. 6, no. 1, pp. 11–16.

Schuster, A., 1910. *History of the Cavendish Laboratory*. London: Macmillan.

Schweber, Silvan S., 2008. *Einstein & Oppenheimer: The Meaning of Genius*. Cambridge, Mass.: Harvard University Press.

Scurfield, Matthew, 2008. *I Could Be Anyone*. Gharb, Gozo, Malta: Monticello Publishing.

Seddon, G. M., and R. G. Moore, 1986. "The Structure of Abilities in Visualising the Rotation of Three-Dimensional Structures Presented as Models and Diagrams," *British Journal of Educational Psychology*, vol. 56, pp. 138–49.

Serra, Michael, 1989. *Discovering Geometry: An Inductive Approach*. Berkeley, Calif.: Key Curriculum.

Seymour Philip H. K., 1986. *Cognitive Analysis of Dyslexia*. London: Routledge & Kegan Paul.

Sharrer, Terry, 2007. "Foundations: The Dreyer Peptide and Protein Sequencer." *Scientist*, July, p. 96.

Shaywitz, Sally E., Bennett A. Shaywitz, et al., 1990. "Prevalence of Reading Disability in Boys and Girls: Results of the Connecticut Longitudinal Study," *Journal of the American Medical Association*, vol. 264, no. 8, pp. 998–1002.

Shneiderman, Ben, 2002. *Leonardo's Laptop: Human Needs and the New Computing Technologies*. Cambridge, Mass.: MIT Press.

Shute, William G., William W. Shirk, and George F. Porter, 1957. *Plane Geometry*. New York: American Book.

Siegel, L. S., 1985. "Deep Dyslexia and Developmental Dyslexia: A Parallel," *Language Sciences*, vol. 7, pp. 53–71.

Sifneos, P. E., 1988. "Alexiththymia and Its Relationship to Hemispheric Specialization, Affect, and Creativity," *Psychiatric Clinics of North America*, vol. 11, no.3, pp. 287–92.

Silber, Kate, 1973. *Pestalozzi: The Man and His Work*. London: Routledge & Kegan Paul.

Silver, Larry, 1992. *The Misunderstood Child: A Guide for Parents of Children with Learning Disabilities*. Second ed. New York: TAB Books.

Silver, Larry B., 1987. "The 'Magic Cure': A Review of the Current Controversial Approaches for Treating Learning Disabilities," *Journal of Learning Disabilities*, vol. 20, no. 8, pp. 498–504.

———, 1990. "Attention Deficit-Hyperactivity Disorder: Is It a Learning Disability or a Related Disorder?" *Journal of Learning Disabilities*, vol. 23, no. 7, pp. 394–97.

Simpson, Eileen B., 1991. *Reversals: A Personal Account of Victory over Dyslexia*. Revised edition. New York: Noonday Press.

Sims, Karl, 1990. "Particle Animation and Rendering Using Data Parallel Computation," *Computer Graphics*, vol. 24, no. 4, pp. 405–13.

Sims, Karl, 1994. "Evolving Virtual Creatures," *Computer Graphics Proceedings*, SIGGRAPH 94, pp. 15–22.

Slater, Robert. 1987 (1989). *Portraits in Silicon*. Cambridge, Mass.: MIT Press.

Slosson, Edwin E., 1914. "Henri Poincaré." In *Major Prophets of Today*. Boston: Little, Brown.

Smarr, L. L., 1994. Personal communication.

Smith, Barry D., Marilyn B. Meyers, and Robert Kline, 1989. "For Better or for Worse: Left-Handedness, Pathology, and Talent," *Journal of Clinical and Experimental Neuropsychology*, vol. 11, no. 6, pp. 944–58.

Smith, Bert Kruger, 1968. *The Dilemma of a Dyslexic Man*. Austin, Tex.: Hogg Foundation for Mental Health and University of Texas.

Smith, Douglas K., Mark E. St. Martin, and Mark A. Lyon, 1989. "A Validity Study of the Stanford-Binet: Fourth Edition with Students with Learning Disabilities," *Journal of Learning Disabilities*, vol. 22, no. 4, pp. 260–61.

Smith, Sally L., 1979. *No Easy Answers: Teaching the Learning Disabled Child*. Cambridge, Mass.: Winthrop.

Snow, C. P., 1979. "Albert Einstein, 1879–1955." In *Einstein: A Centenary Volume*, A. P. French, ed. Cambridge, Mass.: Harvard University Press.

Snowling, Margaret, and Michael Thompson, eds., 1992. *Dyslexia: Integrating Theory and Practice: Selected Papers from the Second International Conference of the British Dyslexia Association, Oxford, 1991*. London: Whurr Publishers.

Soames, Mary, 1990. *Winston Churchill: His Life as a Painter*. Boston: Houghton Mifflin.

Soma, Y., M. Sugishita, K. Kitamura, S. Maruyama, and H. lmanaga, 1989. "Lexical Agraphia in the Japanese Language: Pure Agraphia for Kanji Due to Left Posteroinferior Temporal Lesions," *Brain*, vol. 112, part 6, pp. 1549–61.

Solden, Sari, 1995. *Women with Attention Deficit Disorder: Embracing Disorganization at Home and in the Workplace*. Grass Valley, Calif.: Underwood Books.

South China Morning Post, 1996. "Why Lee Kuan Yew Was Lost for Words." Agence France Presse in *South China Morning Post*, Hong Kong, February.

Sperry, R. W., 1982. "Some Effects of Disconnecting the Cerebral Hemispheres," *Science*, vol. 217, pp. 1223–26.

———, 1983. *Science and Moral Priority: Merging Mind, Brain and Human Values*. New York: Columbia University Press.

Springer, Sally, and Georg Deutsch, 1981. *Left Brain, Right Brain.* New York: W. H. Freeman.

Stapleton, Lisa, 1990. "Visualizing Math: Computer Graphics Transforms the Face of Traditional Math Education," *Computer Graphics World,* vol. 13, no. 6, pp. 59–64.

Steen, Lynn Arthur, 1987. "Mathematics Education: A Predictor of Scientific Competitiveness," *Science,* vol. 237, pp. 251–52 and 302.

———, 1988. "The Science of Patterns," *Science,* vol. 240, pp. 611–16.

Steen, Lynn Arthur, Jerome A. Goldstein, Eleanor Green Jones, et al., 1990. "Challenges for College Mathematics: An Agenda for the Next Decade," bound between pages 8 and 9 in *Focus,* vol. 10, no. 6, pp. 1–28.

Steeves, K. Joyce, 1983. "Memory as a Factor in the Computational Efficiency of Dyslexic Children with High Abstract Reasoning Ability," *Annals of Dyslexia,* vol. 33, pp. 141–52.

Stewart, Ian, 1990. "The Symplectic Revolution: A New, Suppler Geometry Is Transforming Physics and Mathematics," *Sciences,* May/June, pp. 29–36.

Storr, Anthony, 1972. *The Dynamics of Creation.* Harmondsworth, U.K.: Penguin.

———, 1988. *Solitude.* New York: Free Press.

Sugimoto, Kenji, 1989. *Albert Einstein: A Photographic Biography.* Barbara Harshav, trans. New York: Schoken.

Sullivan, Karen, and Thomas G. West, 1997. "Is the World Ready for Visual Literacy?" A proposed panel session for SIGGRAPH '97, the 24th International Conference on Computer Graphics and Interactive Techniques, Los Angeles, August 3–8, 1997. (Unpublished.)

Summers, Edward G., 1986. "The Information Flood in Learning Disabilities: A Bibliometric Analysis of the Journal Literature," *Remedial and Special Education,* vol. 7, no. 1, pp. 49–60.

Swetz, Frank J., 1987. *Capitalism and Arithmetic. The New Math of the 15th Century, Including the Full Text of the Treviso Arithmetic of 1478.* David Eugene Smith, trans. Peru, Ill.: Open Court.

SWIDA, Togi Associates, 2005. *Creative Brains, Gifted, Talented and Dyslexic. The Other Side of Dyslexia, the Creative Side.* Southwest Branch of the International Dyslexia Association. http://www.south westida.com.

Sylwester, Robert, 1995. *A Celebration of Neurons: An Educator's Guide to the Human Brain.* Alexandria, Va.: Association for Supervision and Curriculum Development.

Tallal, Paula, 1996. "Language Learning Impairment: Integrating Research and Remediation," *47th Annual Conference Booklet,* Orton Dyslexia Society Conference, November 6–9, Boston, Mass., pp. 22–24.

Tallal, Paula, S. L. Miller, G. Bedi, G. Byma, X. Q. Wang, S. S. Nagarajan, C. Schreiner, W. M. Jenkins, and M. M. Merzenich, 1996. "Language Comprehension in Language-Learning Impaired Children Improved with Acoustically Modified Speech," *Science*, vol. 271, pp. 81–84.

Tammet, Daniel, 2009. *Embracing the Wide Sky: A Tour across the Horizons of the Human Brain.* New York: Free Press.

Tauber, Alfred I., and Scott H. Podolsky, 1997. *The Generation of Diversity: Clonal Selection Theory and the Rise of Molecular Immunology.* Cambridge, Mass.: Harvard University Press.

Taylor, D. C, 1969. "Differential Rates of Cerebral Maturation between Sexes and between Hemispheres," *Lancet*, no. 2, pp. 140–42.

Teoh, Eliza, 1996. "S[enior] M[inister] Lee Has Mild Dyslexia, Says Daughter Who's Dyslexic." *Straits Times* (Singapore), January 18, p. 1.

Tesla, Nikola, 1904. *Experiments with Alternate Currents of High Potential and High Frequency . . . [and] Transmission of Electric Energy without Wires.* New York: McGraw.

———, 1919 (1982). *My Inventions: The Autobiography of Nikola Tesla.* Ben Johnson, ed. Williston, Vt.: Hart Brothers.

Thomas, John M., and Sir David Phillips, eds., 1990. *Selections and Reflections: The Legacy of Sir Lawrence Bragg.* Northwood, UK: Royal Institution of Great Britain.

Thomas, Lewis, 1979. *The Medusa and the Snail.* New York: Viking.

———, 1983. *The Youngest Science: Notes of a Medicine-Watcher.* New York: Bantam.

———, 1984. *Late Night Thoughts on Listening to Mahler's Ninth Symphony.* New York: Bantam.

Thompson, D'Arcy Wentworth, 1917 (1972). *On Growth and Form.* Vols. 1 and 2, second ed., 1942. Cambridge: Cambridge University Press. Reprinted in the Netherlands by Ysel Press, Deventer.

Thompson, Elizabeth H., 1950 (1981). *Harvey Cushing: Surgeon, Author, Artist.* New York: Neale Watson Academic.

Thompson, Lloyd J., 1969. "Language Disabilities in Men of Eminence," *Bulletin of the Orton Society*, vol. 19, pp. 113–20, reprint no. 27.

———, 1971. "Remarks on Receiving Orton Award," *Bulletin of the Orton Society*, vol. 21, p. 8.

Thompson, Silvanus P., 1910 (1976). *The Life of Lord Kelvin.* Reprinted New York: Chelsea.

Thomson, Michael E., 1991. *Developmental Dyslexia.* Third Edition. London: Whurr.

Thomson, Patience, 2009. *101 Ways to Get Your Child to Read.* Edinburgh: Barrington Stoke Ltd.

Tiede, Ulf, Karl Heinz Hoehne, Michael Bomans, Andreas Pommert, Martin Riemer, and Gunnar Wiebecke, 1990. "Surface Rendering: Investigation of Medical 3D-Rendering Algorithms," *IEEE Computer Graphics and Applications*, vol. 10, no. 2, pp. 41–52.

Tolstoy, Ivan, 1981. *James Clerk Maxwell: A Biography*. Chicago: University of Chicago Press.

Torgesen, Joseph K., 1977. "Memorization Processes in Reading-Disabled Children," *Journal of Educational Psychology*, vol. 69, pp. 571–78.

———, 1988. "The Cognitive and Behavioral Characteristics of Children with Disabilities: An Overview," *Journal of Learning Disabilities*, vol. 21, pp. 587–89.

———, 1988. "Studies of Children with Learning Disabilities Who Perform Poorly on Memory Span Tasks," *Journal of Learning Disabilities*, vol. 21, no. 10, pp. 605–12.

Tranel, D., and A. R. Damasio, 1985. "Knowledge without Awareness: An Autonomic Index of Facial Recognition by Prosopagnosics," *Science*, vol. 228 (4706), pp.1453–54.

Tranel, D., A. R. Damasio, and H. Damasio, 1988. "Intact Recognition of Facial Expression, Gender, and Age in Patients with Impaired Recognition of Face Identity," *Neurology*, vol. 38, no. 5, pp. 690–96.

Travis, L. E., 1931. *Speech Pathology*. New York: Appleton.

———, 1978. "The Cerebral Dominance Theory of Stuttering: 1931–1978," *Journal of Speech and Hearing Disorders*, vol. 43, pp. 278–81.

Treffert, Donald A., 1989. *Extraordinary People: Understanding "Idiot Savants."* New York: Harper & Row.

Treinish, Lloyd A., James D. Foley, William J. Campbell, Robert B. Haber, and Robert F. Gurwitz, 1989. "Effective Software Systems for Scientific Data Visualization," *Computer Graphics: Panel Proceedings, ACM SIGGR4PH '89*, vol. 23, no. 5, pp. 111–36.

Tricker, R. A. R., 1966. *The Contributions of Faraday and Maxwell to Electrical Science*. Oxford: Pergamon.

Tufte, Edward R., 1997. *Visual Explanations: Images and Quantities, Evidence and Narrative*. Cheshire, Conn.: Graphics Press.

Tweney, Ryan D., M. E. Doherty, and C. Mynatt, 1981. *On Scientific Thinking*. New York: Columbia University Press.

Tyndall, John, 1868. *Faraday as a Discoverer*. London: Longmans, Green.

Uccelli, Arturo, 1956. "The Science of Structures." In *Leonardo da Vinci*. New York: Reynal.

Ullmer, Eldon J., 1989. *Videodisk Technology*. Bethesda, Md.: U.S. Dept. of Health and Human Services, National Institutes of Health, National Library of Medicine.

Ungs, Timothy J., 1989. "Simulator Induced Syndrome: Evidence for Long-Term Aftereffects," *Aviation, Space, and Environmental Medicine*, vol. 60, no. 3, pp. 252–55.

Upson, Craig, ed., 1989. *Chapel Hill Workshop on Volume Visualization: Conference Proceedings, May 18–19, 1989*, Chapel Hill: Department of Computer Science, University of North Carolina, Chapel Hill.

Vail, Priscilla L., 1990. "Gifts, Talents, and the Dyslexias: Wellsprings, Springboards, and Finding Foley's Rocks," *Annals of Dyslexia*, vol. 40, pp. 3–17.

——, 1996. *Words Fail Me: How Language Works and What Happens When It Doesn't*. Rosemont, N.J.: Modern Learning Press.

Vallentin, Antonina, 1954. *The Drama of Albert Einstein*. Moura Budberg, trans. Garden City, N.Y.: Doubleday.

Van der Wissel, A., 1988. "Hampered Production of Words as a Characteristic of School Failure," *Journal of Learning Disabilities*, vol. 21, no. 8, pp. 517–18.

Vellutino, F., and D. Scanlon, 1982. "Verbal Memory in Poor and Normal Readers." In *Verbal Processes in Children: Progress in Cognitive Development Research*. New York: Springer-Verlag.

Venturi, Adolfo, 1956. "The Drawings of Leonardo." In *Leonardo da Vinci*. New York: Reynal.

von Károlyi, Catya, 2001. "Visual-Spatial Strength in Dyslexia: Rapid Discrimination of Impossible Figures," *Journal of Learning Disabilities*, vol. 34, no. 4, July/August, pp. 380–91.

von Károlyi, Catya, and Ellen Winner, 2003. "Dyslexia and Visual Spatial Talents: Are They Connected?" In *Students with Both Gifts and Learning Disabilities*. R. J. Sternberg and T. Newman, eds.

von Károlyi, Catya, Ellen Winner, Wendy Gray, and Gordon Sherman, 2003. "Dyslexia Linked to Talent: Global Visual-Spatial Ability," *Brain and Language*, 2003.

Waber, D. P., 1977. "Sex Differences in Mental Abilities, Hemispheric Lateralization, and Rate of Physical Growth in Adolescence," *Developmental Psychology*, vol. 13, pp. 29–38.

——, 1979. "Cognitive Abilities and Sex-Related Variations in the Maturation of Cortical Functions." In *Sex-Related Differences in Cognitive Functioning*. M. A. Wittig and A. C. Petersen, eds. New York: Academic.

——, 1981. "Environmental Influences on Brain and Behavior." In *Sex Differences in Dyslexia*, pp. 73–79. A. Ansara, N. Geschwind, A. Galaburda, et al., eds. Towson, Md.: Orton Dyslexia Society.

Wachhorst, Wyn, 1981. *Thomas Alva Edison: An American Myth*. Cambridge, Mass.: MIT Press.

Wada, J. A., R. Clark, and A. Hamm, 1975. "Cerebral Hemisphere Asymmetry in Humans: Cortical Speech Zones in 100 Adult and 100 Infant Brains," *Archives of Neurology*, vol. 32, pp. 239–46.

Wada, J. A., and J. E. Davies, 1977. "Fundamental Nature of Infants' Brain Asymmetry," *Canadian Journal of Neurological Science*, vol. 4, pp. 303 ff.

Wahl, Bernt, 1988, "Cantor Set/Random Walk." In *Chaos: Mathematics for the 21st Century Dynamics Disks I & II*. Santa Cruz, Calif.: Aerial.

Waldron, Karen A., Diane G. Saphire, and Sue Ann Rosenblum, 1987. "Learning Disabilities and Giftedness: Identification Based on Self-Concept, Behavior, and Academic Patterns," *Journal of Learning Disabilities*, vol. 20, no. 6, pp. 422–27.

Waldrop, M. Mitchell, 1992. *Complexity: The Emerging Science at the Edge of Order and Chaos*. New York: Simon & Schuster.

Walker, Alan, 1987. "Early Humans: Evolution or Revolution," *New Frontiers of Science*, October 29. One in a course of lectures sponsored by the Smithsonian Institution in collaboration with the American Association for the Advancement of Science.

Walsh, John, 1987. "Why Is Calculus Such a Hurdle?" *Science*, vol. 238, p. 749.

Wanderman, Richard, 1984. "Word Processing Computers as Remedial Writing Tools," *Whole Earth Software Review*, Spring.

Ward, Geofrey C., 1996. "A Charmed Life—Almost: From Boyhood On, Nelson Rockefeller Got Everything He Ever Wanted. Except the Presidency." *New York Times Book Review*, November 3, pp. 10–11. (Review of *The Life of Nelson Rockefeller: Worlds to Conquer, 1908–1958*, by Cary Reich. New York: Doubleday.)

Watson, James D., 1968. *The Double Helix: A Personal Account of the Discovery of the Structure of DNA*. New York: Atheneum.

———, 1980. *The Double Helix: A Personal Account of the Discovery of the Structure of DNA*. With text, commentary, reviews and original papers. Edited by Gunther S. Strent. New York: W.W. Norton.

Weatherford, Jack, 1988. *Indian Givers: How the Indians of the Americas Transformed the World*. New York: Fawcett Columbine.

Webster, William G., 1988. "Neural Mechanisms Underlying Stuttering: Evidence from Bimanual Handwriting Performance," *Brain and Language*, vol. 33, no. 2, pp. 226–44.

Weger, Ronald E., 1989. *A Layman's Look at Dyslexia: The Social Costs and the Personal Trauma and Frustration of Dyslexics and their Families*. Lansing: Michigan Dyslexia Institute.

Weiner, Norbert, 1948 (1961). *Cybernetics: Control and Communication in the Animal and the Machine*. Cambridge, Mass.: MIT Press.

Weintraub, Sandra, and M. Marsel Mesulam, 1983. "Developmental Learning Disabilities of the Right Hemisphere: Emotional, Interpersonal, and Cognitive Components," *Archives of Neurology*, vol. 40, pp. 463–68.

Wescott, Lynanne, and Paula Degen, 1981. *Wind and Sand: The Story of the Wright Brothers at Kitty Hawk, Told through Their Own Words and Photographs*. New York: Harry N. Abrams.

West, Thomas G., 1990. "Visualization in the Mind's Eye," *IRIS Universe: The Magazine of Visual Processing*, no. 14, November.

———, 1991. *In the Mind's Eye: Visual Thinkers, Gifted People with Learning Difficulties, Computer Images, and the Ironies of Creativity.* Amherst, N.Y.: Prometheus Books. (Updated edition, 1997.)

———, 1992. "A Return to Visual Thinking—In Education and in the Workplace, We'll See a Higher Regard for Visualization Skills and Talents," *Computer Graphics World*, November, pp. 115–16.

———, 1992. "Visual Thinkers, Mental Models and Computer Visualization." In *Interactive Learning through Visualization: The Impact of Computer Graphics in Education*, pp. 91–102. Steve Cunningham and R. J. Hubbold, eds. Heidelberg, Germany: Springer-Verlag.

———, 1992. "A Future of Reversals: Dyslexic Talents in a World of Computer Visualization," *Annals of Dyslexia*, vol. 42, November, pp. 124–39.

———, 1993. "Visual Thinkers in an Age of Computer Visualization: Problems and Possibilities." A Panel summarized in *Computer Graphics*, Proceedings, SIGGRAPH Annual Conference, August 1–6, 1993, pp. 379–80.

———, 1994. "Abstract from the 'Doors of Perception' conference presentation: 'Medieval Clerk to Renaissance Thinker: Design, Visualization and Technological Change' and 'Summary of *In the Mind's Eye*.'" Text in digital form for the "Laboratorium Voor Architectuur," Eindhoven University of Technology, Netherlands, Faculty of Architecture, Building and Planning. Text published: Eindhoven Internet server February 9, 1994. E-mail: lava@urc.tue.nl. Gopher: gopher.tue.nl.

———, 1994. "Advanced Interaction: A Return to Mental Models and Learning by Doing," *Computers & Graphics*, Special Issue on Advanced Interaction, vol. 18, no. 5, September/October, pp. 685–89.

———, 1994. "Medieval Clerk to Renaissance Thinker: Design, Visualization and Technological Change." Presentation published on CD-ROM, multimedia with integrated text, images and QuickTime (TM) segments, documenting the proceedings of the first "Doors of Perception" Conference, Stedelijk Museum, Amsterdam, Holland, October 30–31, 1993, the first project of the newly formed Netherlands Design Institute. Published September 1994 as part of *Mediamatic Magazine*, summer 1994, vol. 8, no. 1.

———, 1994. "A Return to Visual Thinking." In *Proceedings, Science and Scientific Computing: Visions of a Creative Symbiosis. Symposium of Computer Users in the Max Planck Gesellschaft*. P. Wittenburg and T Plesser, eds.Göttingen, Germany, November.

———, 1994. *Geniuses Who Hated School*. Japanese translation of *In the Mind's Eye*. Translated by Katsumi Kushimoto. Tokyo, Japan: Kodansha Scientific.

———, 1995. "Awakening to Dyslexic Talents in the 'New Economy,'" *Innovations and Insights, Dyslexia—An International Journal of Research and Practice*, the journal of the British Dyslexia Association, vol. 1, no. 1.

———, 1995. "Forward into the Past: A Revival of Old Visual Talents with Computer Visualization," *Computer Graphics*, vol. 29, no. 4, November, pp. 14–19.

———, 1996. "'Strephs,' Tumbling Symbols and Technological Change—the Implications of Dyslexia Research in a World Turned Upside Down." Audio tape.

———, 1996. "Consequences: Unintended, Unexpected," *Computer Graphics*, November.

———, 1996. "Playing with Images: A Return to Thinking in Pictures," *Computers in Physics*, vol. 10, no. 5, September/October 1996, p. 413.

———, 1996. "Special Talents in a Not-So-New Population." In *Hidden Abilities in Higher Education: New College Students with Disabilities*. Linda Lucas Walling, ed., Monograph Series, no. 21, October, pp. 7–12. Columbia: University of South Carolina Press.

———, 1996. "Talking Less, Drawing More," *Computer Graphics*, August, pp. 81–82.

———, 1996. "Unintended, Unexpected Consequences—SIGGRAPH'96," *Computer Graphics*, November.

———, 1996. "Upside Down: Visual-Spatial Talents and Technological Change," *Understanding Our Gifted*, January–February.

———, 1997. "Dyslexics Leading the Way: The Technological Transformation of Higher Education." Proceedings, brief summary of keynote address at the Second International Conference on Dyslexia in Higher Education at Dartington Hall, Totnes, Devon, England, in cooperation with the University of Plymouth, November 11–13.

———, 1997. "Slow Words, Quick Images: Dyslexia as an Advantage in Tomorrow's Workplace." In *Learning Disabilities and Employment*.

Paul J. Gerber and Dale Brown, eds. Austin, TX: ProEd; New York: Dutton.

———, 1997. "Word Bound, the Power of Seeing," *Computer Graphics,* 1997.

———, 1997. *In the Mind's Eye: Visual Thinkers, Gifted People with Dyslexia and Other Learning Difficulties, Computer Images, and the Ironies of Creativity.* Updated edition with new preface, epilogue and notes. Amherst, N.Y.: Prometheus Books.

———, 1998. "Brain Drain, Reconsidering Spatial Ability," *Computer Graphics,* August, pp. 15.

———, 1999. "One All-Embracing Regard." In *Art Works: Arts Dyslexia Trust.* Bristol, U.K. Wild Conversations.

———, 1999. "The Abilities of Those with Reading Disabilities: Focusing on the Talents of People with Dyslexia." In *Reading and Attention Disorders: Neurobiological Correlates,* Drake D. Duane, ed. Baltimore, Md.: York Press.

———, 2001. "Visual Thinkers and Nobel Prizes," *Computer Graphics,* February.

———, 2003. "Secret of the Super Successful . . . They're Dyslexic," *Thalamus,* the Journal of the International Academy for Research in Learning Disabilities, vol. 21, no. 1, 48–52.

———, 2004. *In the Mind's Eye.* Chinese translation by Wei-Pai Lu. Taipei, Taiwan: Hung Yeh.

———, 2004. *Thinking Like Einstein: Returning to Our Visual Roots with the Emerging Revolution in Computer Information Visualization.* Amherst, N.Y.: Prometheus Books.

———, 2005. "The Gifts of Dyslexia: Talents among Dyslexics and Their Families," *Hong Kong Journal of Paediatrics,* vol. 10, pp. 153–58.

———, 2008. "It Is Time to Get Serious about the Talents of Dyslexics," *Perspectives,* a publication of the International Dyslexia Association, Summer.

Whitmore, Joanne Rand, 1980. *Giftedness, Conflict, and Underachievement* Boston: Allyn and Bacon.

Whitmore, Joanne Rand, and C. June Maker, 1985. "Intellectually Gifted Persons with Specific Learning Disabilities—A Case Study: Marcia." In *Intellectual Giftedness in Disabled Persons.* Rockville, Md.: Aspen Systems.

Whitney, Mark, and Carlo Pedretti, 1990. "Leonardo's Deluge." In *Art on Film,* videotape produced by the Metropolitan Museum of Art and the J. Paul Getty Trust.

Whitney, Mark, and Karl Sims, 1989. "Excerpts from 'Leonardo's Deluge.'" Hollywood, Calif.: Optomystic. Videotape.

Wilhelmson et al., 1987. "Numerical Simulation of a Thunderstorm Out-flow," *SIGGRAPH Video Review*, issue 28, *Computer Graphics*, vol. 21, no. 6. Videotape.

Williams, L Pearce, n.d. *Michael Faraday: A Biography*. New York: Da Capo.

———, ed., 1971. *The Selected Correspondence of Michael Faraday. Volume I, 1812–1848*. Cambridge: Cambridge University Press.

Winner, Ellen, 1996. *Gifted Children: Myths and Realities*. New York; Basic Books.

Winner, Ellen, Catya von Károlyi, and Daphna Malinsky, 2000. "Dyslexia and Visual-Spatial Talents: No Clear Link," *Perspectives*, Spring, pp. 27–30.

Winner, Ellen, Catya von Károlyi, Daphna Malinsky, Lisa French, Colleen Seliger, Erin Ross, and Christina Weber, 2001. "Dyslexia and Visual-Spatial Talents: Compensation vs. Deficit Model," *Brain and Language*, vol. 76, pp. 81–110.

Winson, Jonathan, 1985. *Brain and Psyche: The Biology of the Unconscious*. New York: Anchor/Doubleday.

Witelson, S., 1977. "Developmental Dyslexia: Two Right Hemispheres and None Left?" *Science*, pp. 309–11.

Wolkomir, Richard, 1989. "NASA's Data Deluge," *Air & Space*, vol. 4, no. 4, pp. 78–82.

Wood, J. P., 1966. *The Snark Was a Boojam: A Life of Lewis Carroll*. New York: Pantheon.

Wood, Prudence Anne Tallman, 2006. *Where the Birds Warble Sweet*. Unpublished manuscript.

Wright, John Dutton, 1915. *What the Mother of a Deaf Child Ought to Know*. New York: Frederick A. Stokes Company.

Yamada, Jun, and Adam Banks, 1994. "Evidence for and Characteristics of Dyslexia among Japanese Children," *Annals of Dyslexia*, vol. 44, pp. 105–19.

Yeats, W. B., 1937 (1971). *A Vision*. New York: Collier.

———, 1938. *The Autobiography of William Butler Yeats*. New York: Macmillan.

———, 1972. "What We Did or Tried to Do." In *W. B. Yeats and the Designing of Ireland's Coinage*. Brian Cleeve, ed. Dublin: Dolmen.

———, 1973. *Memoirs: Autobiography—First Draft, Journal*. Denis Donoghue, ed. New York: MacMillan.

———, 1986. *The Letters of W. B. Yeats*. Oxford: Clarendon.

Yeo, Geraldine, 1996. "Dyslexia: S[enior] M[inister]'s Case Gives Parents Hope—They Are Motivated, Encouraged by His Example," *Straits Times* (Singapore), January 19, p. 25.

Yoder, Edwin M., Jr., 1988. "Churchill: A Statesman for All Seasons." Review of William Manchester, *The Last Lion Alone: Winston Spencer Churchill 1932–40*, Martin Gilbert, *Winston Churchill, Vol. 8: Never Despair, 1945–1965*, and Martin Gilbert, *Churchill: A Photographic Portrait*, *Washington Post Book World*, vol. 18, no. 42, pp. 1 and 14.

Young, Lois, and Francesca Benson, n.d. *Visions of Hope: In Celebration of Dyslexic Artists*. Princeton, N.J.: Newgrange School and Educational Outreach Center.

Zaidel, E., 1983. "A Response to Gazzaniga: Language in the Right Hemisphere, Convergent Perspectives," *American Psychologist*, vol. 38, pp. 542–46.

Zaidel, E, and A. Schweiger, 1984. "On Wrong Hypotheses about the Right Hemisphere: Commentary on K. Patterson and D. Besner, 'Is the Right Hemisphere Literate?'" *Cognitive Neuropsychology*, vol. 1, pp. 351–64.

Ziegler, Bart, 1990. "Five U.S. Companies Form Computer Group: Goal Is 'Knowledge Processing' Software," *Washington Post*, April 25, p. G1.

Zoll, Mary, and Debra Rosenberg, 1990. "Of Pixels and Polymers: Molecular Modeling Software Enables Chemists to Test Compounds On-Screen," *Computer Graphics World*, vol. 13, no. 3, pp. 103–104, and 106.

ACKNOWLEDGMENTS

I wish to thank the many individuals who have encouraged and supported this research through their enthusiasm, comments, suggestions, and constructive criticism. I have very much appreciated the oral and written comments on various draft chapters. I have found especially helpful the stories from personal experience and other suggestions that many have provided. A few of these illustrated some important point very well and eventually came to be used in the text.

I am especially grateful to those professionals and specialists, whether physician, speech therapist, computer scientist, physicist, psychologist, neurologist, or mathematician, who took the time to read sections of the manuscript, helping me to avoid the many errors that the nonspecialist writer risks by dipping into so much unfamiliar territory. Of course, I alone am responsible for any errors that remain. I would further like to thank those specialists in the new field of computer graphics who were so generous with their time in interviews, telephone conversations, and background discussions.

I want to express my deep appreciation to those dyslexics—Eileen Simpson, Susan Hampshire, and others—who have had the courage to reveal to the public their personal experiences so that others may begin to understand.

I would especially like to express my gratitude for the work of the late Norman Geschwind and his students, who have done so much to bring a fresh perspective to the study of the neurological factors that underlie dyslexia and related difficulties and talents.

Where appropriate, specific personal communications have been credited in the reference notes. Other contributions have been more general, but no less influential. Many have contributed in ways of which they would hardly be aware.

It is customary for an author to write that space does not allow the listing of all the persons who assisted with a research project such as this. I will take a different approach and try to list as many as I can recall of those who have helped in one way or another during the long gestation and development of this project, knowing that some may inadvertently be omitted.

Accordingly, I would like to express my gratitude to the following individuals: Albert Galaburda, Ann Wooldridge, Barbara Seeber, Barry Reichert, Bob Basil, Bruce Martin, Chuck Kleymeyer, Cindy Brandt, Dan Coy, Daniel Gage, David Prescott, David Taggart, Denis Goulet, Dick Rubinstein, Dick Warner, Donna Hawkins, Elise Boulding, Ginny Frank, Harlan Bertram, Howard Gardner, Jeannie Johns, Jim Sample, Jim Turley, Joel Orr, John Farina, Karl Sims, Ken Jolls, Larry Silver, Laura Rubinoff, Lennice Zekefoose, Lewis Thomas, Lucy Warner, Maggie Vancik, Margaret Rawson, Marie Anderson, Matt Elson, Mia Sample, Michael Panich, Nancy Waller, Ned Gaylin, Norman Holly, P. G. Aaron, Pat Baker, Patty Anderson, Patty Eisen, Reg Gilbert, Richey Sharrett, Ronal Larson, Sandy Wade, Sharon Biegalski, Stan Ovshinsky, Susan Boulding, Tim Cline, Tom Pauls, and Vincent Argiro.

For staff assistance and facility use, I would like to express my gratitude to two institutions without which this project would not have been possible: The National Library of Medicine, Bethesda, Maryland, and The Library of Congress, Washington, D.C. Rarely is tax money so well spent as in the support of these institutions.

I want to thank Anne W. West for teaching me that a handicap can be comparatively unimportant when you build your life around your talents rather than your disabilities. I want to thank Benjamin and Jonathan for helping me to see, for a second time, what growing up is all about. And, lastly, I would like to thank Margaret for the title and much, much more.

For this second edition of *In the Mind's Eye*, I want to express my gratitude to a number friends and colleagues (and members of several organizations) for their encouragement and counsel over the years— and to some for their special help with the new edition, for reading sections or the whole, for indicating what needed to be changed, for going to the trouble of seeing what did not have to be changed and for providing new support for past observations. I am also grateful for the many things these friends and colleagues have done over the years to advance the cause of better understanding the talents of dyslexics and creative visual thinkers. Their support of conferences and exhibitions, starting new centers and websites, their talks, papers, interviews, documentaries and commentaries have moved the field a long way forward, sometimes against formidable odds. Although much still remains to be done, we all would be the poorer without their substantial efforts.

Malcolm Alexander, Chrissy Aull, Patricia McGlannan and staff of the Wye River Upper School, Will Baker and The Dyslexia Foundation, Baruj Benacerraf, Moira Buchanan and the Learning and Behavior Charitable Trust of New Zealand, the Oral History Project of the California Institute of Technology, Tony and Gigi Carlson, Pat Carson, Barbara Corcoran, Donna Cox, Emerson and Georgette Dickman, Bill and Janet Dreyer, Drake Duane, Guinevere Eden, Brock and Fernette Eide, Emma Elliot, Joan and Les Esposito, Angela and David Fawcett, Roy Follendore, Jeff Gilger, Barbara Given, Jack Horner, Harvey Hubbell and Captured Time Productions, Gary Huber, Mike Juggins, Catya von Karolyi, Brandon King, Jane Kirk, CK Leong, Wei-Pai Lu, Hung Yeh and the Learning Disability Association of Taiwan, Don and Mary Lindberg, James Martinez and the Education Committee of ACM SIGGRAPH, Hideyuki Masumoto and the NHK documentary film crew (Tomoyuki Shirakawa, producer, Fujio Takatsu, sound, Hiroyuki Kozako, camera), Mike McGrath, Tim Miles, Carol Mills, Harold Morowitz and Vijayasarathy Srinivasan, Betsy Morris and *Fortune* magazine, Adrianne Noe and the National Museum of Health and Medicine, Jim Olds and the Krasnow Institute for Advanced Study, George Mason University, Carolyn Olivier, Sue Parkinson and the Arts Dyslexia Trust, Bill Paterson, Mary Peterson and the Museum of the Rockies, Thomas Petty, Loren Pope, Guy Pope-Mayell and the Dyslexia Foundation of

New Zealand, Charlotte Raymond, Lennox Reed and the Neuhaus Educational Foundation, Gavin Reid, Lois Rothschild, Mary Gilroy and The Southwest Branch of the International Dyslexia Association, Marc Rowe, Terence Ryan, Dan Sandin, Nira Scherz-Busch, Sally and Bennett Shaywitz and the Yale Center for Dyslexia and Creativity, Gordon Sherman, Chris Smart and the *Unwrapped Gift* team, Alvy Ray Smith, Delos Smith and Renee Merow, John Stein, Richard Taylor and the Weta Workshop, Fran Thompson, Patience and David Thomson, Jo and Richard Todd, Jerry Uhl, Oliver West, Ellen Winner, Maryanne Wolf and Lois Young. I want to express my special thanks to Oliver Sacks (and Kate Edgar) for the kind words in the blurb and Foreword that they generously provided.

COPYRIGHT
ACKNOWLEDGMENTS

INDEX

WHAT THE CRITICS ARE SAYING ABOUT *IN THE MIND'S EYE*:

"I read [*In the Mind's Eye*] with considerable interest. I wasn't aware, and I am enormously proud, that I share my learning problems with such distinguished characters as Albert Einstein, Michael Faraday, James Clerk Maxwell, Sir Winston Churchill, Gen. George Patton, and William Butler Yeats. I found [West's] detailed analysis of the various deficiencies very informative and I think [his] book is a real contribution to the field."

Baruj Benacerraf, M.D.
Nobel Laureate, Fabyan Professor of Comparative Pathology, emeritus, Harvard Medical School, and past president of the Dana-Farber Cancer Institute, Boston

"Since he first published *In the Mind's Eye* eighteen years ago, Thomas G. West has been at the forefront of a growing number of experts who recognize that the 'dys' in dyslexia is often far less important to those who have it than the often remarkable abilities in reasoning, visualization, and pattern recognition that frequently accompany this condition. The impact of this now classic work upon the dyslexic families and individuals that we have the privilege to work with—the encouragement and insight it has provided—is incalculable. . . . Everyone who is dyslexic, has a child with dyslexia, or works with such individuals will be encouraged and enlightened by this marvelous book. For those tired of an educational system that too often treats dyslexic children like ugly ducklings, it is a field guide to the glories of the swan. We cannot possibly recommend it highly enough."

Brock Eide, M.D., M.A., and Fernette Eide, M.D.
Founders of the Eide Neurolearning Clinic in Edmonds, Washington, and authors of *The Mislabeled Child*

"Perhaps no one has championed the association between dyslexia and talent more than Thomas G. West. . . . West's research focuses on the correlation of very high success with the prevalence of dyslexia, a relationship that will likely be the focus of more research in the years ahead."

Jim Romeo
New York Academy of Sciences

"In the Mind's Eye . . . [is] scholarly, encyclopedic, and endlessly fascinating. . . . [It] is a great public service and one long overdue. Every family concerned about a learning problem—or even the usual problems of dealing with a teenage student—should have it in the house. . . . If I were dictator, every teacher everywhere would have to pass a test on it."

Loren Pope
Author of *Colleges That Change Lives:*
40 Schools That Will Change the Way You Think about Colleges

"Tom West argues that the legitimacy of visualization as a first-order attack on problem solving is . . . being established after generations of quiet use by only some creators—and some of the best at that. He claims that visualization is not only a legitimate way to solve problems, it is a superior way: the best minds have used it. West urges us to join the dyslexics of the world and use pictures instead of words. In the process we get fascinating glimpses of how other minds have worked—minds that have changed the world."

Alvy Ray Smith
Cofounder of Pixar Animation Studios,
former director of computer graphics at Lucasfilm, Ltd., and
Graphics Fellow, Advanced Technology, Microsoft Corporation

"We rewrote much of our material based on insights gained from [*In the Mind's Eye*]. Previously, we had not realized fully how central the role of visualization was to what we were trying to do. . . . In our project *CALCULUS& Mathematica*, we have learned the effectiveness of teaching the concepts visually using graphic software prior to verbal explanations. Our students have gained a deeper understanding of the subject and they can recall and apply the material long afterward, which is rare for students taught with conventional methods."

Dr. J. Jerry Uhl
Department of Mathematics, University of Illinois at
Urbana-Champaign, and author of (with W. Davis and H. Porta)
the interactive courseware *CALCULUS&Mathematica*

"There is a lot of overlap in points we have both been making for years. I have often argued in my public talks that the graduate education process that produces physicists is totally skewed to selecting those with analytic skills and rejecting those with visual or holistic skills. I have claimed that with the rise of scientific visualization as a new mode of scientific discovery, a new class of minds will arise as scientists."

Larry L. Smarr
Director of the National Center for Supercomputing Applications,
professor of physics and astronomy at the University of Illinois,
and author (with W. J. Kaufmann) of
Supercomputing and the Transformation of Science

"West's weaving of case studies and ideas to promote his arguments is intriguing and convincing. If what he says is true, then the waste of high ability is very much worse than we might have thought. But using his reasoning, if we were to change our educational outlook to a more positive and humane one, then millions more children would be enabled to develop into creative, productive, and fulfilled adults."

European Journal for High Ability

"Tom West argues convincingly that brains which learn differently may contribute a unique set of talents to the world. Although these brains may present a variety of educational challenges, this book stresses the importance of individual differences and biological variation for adaptation to future environmental challenges. We should consider the design of educational environments within this context."

Gordon F. Sherman, Ph.D.
Former director, Dyslexia Research Laboratory,
Department of Neurology, Beth Israel Hospital,
Harvard Medical School,
and past president of the International Dyslexia Association

"At last, here is a book that can be whole-heartedly and enthusiastically recommended to all our readers. Thoroughly researched, clearly, and delightfully written, it says many of the important things about visual thinking that we have long been waiting to hear. . . . Arguably, it represents the most significant turning point in educational thought this century. Everyone with concern for the future of education in this country, and particularly those involved with the education of dyslexics, should read it—*now*."

Susan Parkinson
Editor of the newsletter of the Arts Dyslexia Trust
(United Kingdom)

"If you accept [Thomas West's] arguments, then the period of the domination of Western scientific thought by printed papers and mathematical formulae may be just another transitory period, perhaps akin to that of the introverted and argumentative world of medieval scholasticism before the new vision of the Renaissance and the practical empiricism of the Enlightenment."

Lord Renwick
Chairman, European Informatics Market (EURIM),
and vice president and past chairman of the
British Dyslexia Association

"[West] raises . . . an important question, asking us to look again at what are fundamental abilities in a time when computers can do the simple work in place of humans and to reconsider the educational system while keeping in mind the variety of human brains that exist."

Review in *Kagaku Asahi*,
the monthly Japanese science magazine

"I recommend *In the Mind's Eye* to parents of dyslexics many times every week. They find in it an extraordinary emancipation when they learn that their children have, along with their disability, a super ability—the extraordinary power of imagination and three-dimensional thought that will allow them to become the leaders of the twenty-first century. After reading this book, you will treasure your child's abilities as I have, discovering that they have the greatest intelligence of all—the ability to imagine."

Bob Arnot, M.D.
Senior Medical Correspondent, CBS News

"West . . . presents a valuable insight into this 'other side of dyslexia.'"

Gavin Reid
Editor of *Dimensions of Dyslexia*

"[This book] will shed light on the term 'learning disabled.'"

Parent's Educational Resource Center Newsletter

". . . informative and exciting."

Larry Silver, M.D.
Author of *The Misunderstood Child:*
A Guide for Parents of Learning Disabled Children